Essays on Opera, 1750–1800

The Ashgate Library of Essays in Opera Studies
Series Editor: Roberta Montemorra Marvin

Titles in the Series:

Studies in Seventeenth-Century Opera
Beth L. Glixon

Opera Remade, 1700–1750
Charles Dill

Essays on Opera, 1750–1800
John A. Rice

**National Traditions in Nineteenth-Century Opera,
Volume I
Italy, France, England and the Americas**
Steven Huebner

**National Traditions in Nineteenth-Century Opera,
Volume II
Central and Eastern Europe**
Michael C. Tusa

Opera After 1900
Margaret Notley

Essays on Opera, 1750–1800

Edited by
John A. Rice

ASHGATE

© John A. Rice 2010. For copyright of individual articles please refer to the Acknowledgements.

All rights reserved. No part of this publication may be reproduced, stored in a retrieval system or transmitted in any form or by any means, electronic, mechanical, photocopying, recording or otherwise without the prior permission of the publisher.

Wherever possible, these reprints are made from a copy of the original printing, but these can themselves be of very variable quality. Whilst the publisher has made every effort to ensure the quality of the reprint, some variability may inevitably remain.

Published by
Ashgate Publishing Limited
Wey Court East
Union Road
Farnham
Surrey GU9 7PT
England

Ashgate Publishing Company
Suite 420
101 Cherry Street
Burlington
VT 05401-4405
USA

www.ashgate.com

British Library Cataloguing in Publication Data
Essays on opera, 1750-1800. -- (The Ashgate library of
  essays in opera studies)
  1. Opera--18th century.
  I. Series II. Rice, John A.
  782.1'09033-dc22

Library of Congress Control Number: 2010925876

ISBN 9780754629047

Printed and bound in Great Britain by
TJ International Ltd, Padstow, Cornwall

Contents

Acknowledgements ix
Series Preface xi
Introduction xiii

PART I   AESTHETICS AND DRAMATURGY

1   Julian Rushton (1972), 'The Theory and Practice of Piccinnisme', *Proceedings of the Royal Musical Association*, **98**, pp. 31–46.   3
2   Raymond Monelle (1978), 'Recitative and Dramaturgy in the *Dramma per Musica*', *Music & Letters*, **59**, pp. 245–67.   19
3   Thomas Bauman (1977), 'Opera versus Drama: *Romeo and Juliet* in Eighteenth-Century Germany', *Eighteenth-Century Studies*, **11**, pp. 186–203.   43
4   James Webster (1990), 'Mozart's Operas and the Myth of Musical Unity', *Cambridge Opera Journal*, **2**, pp. 197–218.   61

PART II   SINGERS

5   Daniel Heartz (1974), 'Raaff's Last Aria: A Mozartian Idyll in the Spirit of Hasse', *The Musical Quarterly*, **60**, pp. 517–43.   85
6   Dale E. Monson (1986), 'Galuppi, Tenducci, and *Motezuma*: A Commentary on the History and Musical Style of *Opera Seria* after 1750', in Maria Teresa Muraro and Franco Rossi (eds), *Galuppiana 1985: Studi e ricerche: Atti del convegno internazionale (Venezia, 28–30 ottobre 1985)*, Florence: Olschki, pp. 279–300.   113
7   Patricia Lewy Gidwitz (1991), '"Ich bin die erste Sängerin": Vocal Profiles of Two Mozart Sopranos', *Early Music*, **19**, pp. 565–79.   135
8   Paul Corneilson (2001), 'Mozart's Ilia and Elettra: New Perspectives on *Idomeneo*', in Theodor Göllner and Stephan Hörner (eds), *Mozarts Idomeneo und die Musik in München zur Zeit Karl Theodors*, Munich: Verlag der Bayerischen Akademie der Wissenschaften, pp. 97–113.   149

PART III   SENSIBILITY, SENTIMENT AND THE PASTORAL

9   Mary Hunter (1985), '"Pamela": The Offspring of Richardson's Heroine in Eighteenth-Century Opera', *Mosaic: A Journal for the Interdisciplinary Study of Literature*, **18**, pp. 61–76.   169
10   Wye J. Allanbrook (1991), 'Human Nature in the Unnatural Garden: *Figaro* as Pastoral', *Current Musicology*, **51**, pp. 82–93.   185

11 Stefano Castelvecchi (1996), 'From *Nina* to *Nina*: Psychodrama, Absorption and Sentiment in the 1780s', *Cambridge Opera Journal*, **8**, pp. 91–112. 197
12 Dorothea Link (1996), '*L'arbore di Diana*: A Model for *Così fan tutte*', in Stanley Sadie (ed.), *Wolfgang Amadè Mozart: Essays on his Life and his Music*, Oxford: Clarendon Press, pp. 362–73. 219
13 Edmund J. Goehring (1997), 'The Sentimental Muse of *Opera Buffa*', in Mary Hunter and James Webster (eds), *Opera Buffa in Mozart's Vienna*, Cambridge: Cambridge University Press, pp. 115–45. 231

PART IV ORIENTALISM AND EXOTICISM

14 Benjamin Perl (2000), 'Mozart in Turkey', *Cambridge Opera Journal*, **12**, pp. 219–35. 265
15 Pierpaolo Polzonetti (2007), 'Oriental Tyranny in the Extreme West: Reflections on *Amiti e Ontario* and *Le gare generose*', *Eighteenth-Century Music*, **4**, pp. 27–53. 283

PART V OPERA AND POLITICS

16 Elizabeth C. Bartlet (1992), 'On the Freedom of the Theatre and Censorship: The *Adrien* Controversy (1792)', in Antoine Hennion (ed.), *1789–1989: Musique, Histoire, Démocratie*, 1, Paris: Maison des Sciences de l'Homme, pp. 15–30. 313
17 Estelle Joubert (2006), 'Songs to Shape a German Nation: Hiller's Comic Operas and the Public Sphere', *Eighteenth-Century Music*, **3**, pp. 213–30. 329

PART VI MOZART AND HIS VIENNESE CONTEMPORARIES

18 Dexter Edge (1991), 'Mozart's Fee for *Così fan tutte*', *Journal of the Royal Musical Association*, **116**, pp. 211–35. 349
19 John Platoff (1992), 'How Original was Mozart? Evidence from *Opera Buffa*', *Early Music*, **20**, pp. 105–17. 375
20 Bruce Alan Brown and John A. Rice (1996), 'Salieri's *Così fan tutte*', *Cambridge Opera Journal*, **8**, pp. 17–43. 389
21 David J. Buch (2004), '*Die Zauberflöte*, Masonic Opera, and Other Fairy Tales', *Acta Musicologica*, **76**, pp. 193–219. 417

PART VII *OPERA SERIA*

22 Marita P. McClymonds (1989), 'The Venetian Role in the Transformation of Italian *Opera Seria* during the 1790s', in Maria Teresa Muraro and David Bryant (eds), *I vicini di Mozart*, 1, Florence: Olschki, pp. 221–40. 447
23 Scott L. Balthazar (1989), 'Mayr, Rossini, and the Development of the *Opera Seria* Duet: Some Preliminary Conclusions', in Maria Teresa Muraro and David Bryant (eds), *I vicini di Mozart*, 1, Florence: Olschki, pp. 377–98. 465

24 Sergio Durante (1991), '*La clemenza di Tito* and Other Two-Act Reductions of
    the Late 18th Century', *Mozart-Jahrbuch*, pp. 733–41.   487
25 Martha Feldman (2000), 'The Absent Mother in *Opera Seria*', in Mary Ann Smart
    (ed.), *Siren Songs: Representations of Gender and Sexuality in Opera*, Princeton,
    NJ: Princeton University Press, pp. 29–46, 254–59.   497
26 Margaret R. Butler (2006), 'Producing the Operatic Chorus at Parma's Teatro
    Ducale, 1759–1769', *Eighteenth-Century Music*, **3**, pp. 231–51.   521

Name Index   *543*

Acknowledgements

The editor and publishers wish to thank the following for permission to use copyright material.

Acta Musicologica for the essay: David J. Buch (2004), '*Die Zauberflöte*, Masonic Opera, and Other Fairy Tales', *Acta Musicologica*, **76**, pp. 193–219.

Cambridge University Press for the essays: James Webster (1990), 'Mozart's Operas and the Myth of Musical Unity', *Cambridge Opera Journal*, **2**, pp. 197–218. Copyright © 1990 Cambridge University Press; Stefano Castelvecchi (1996), 'From *Nina* to *Nina*: Psychodrama, Absorption and Sentiment in the 1780s', *Cambridge Opera Journal*, **8**, pp. 91–112. Copyright © 1996 Cambridge University Press; Edmund J. Goehring (1997), 'The Sentimental Muse of *Opera Buffa*', in Mary Hunter and James Webster (eds), *Opera Buffa in Mozart's Vienna*, Cambridge: Cambridge University Press, pp. 115–45; Copyright © 1997 Cambridge University Press; Benjamin Perl (2000), 'Mozart in Turkey', *Cambridge Opera Journal*, **12**, pp. 219–35. Copyright © 2000 Cambridge University Press; Pierpaolo Polzonetti (2007), 'Oriental Tyranny in the Extreme West: Reflections on *Amiti e Ontario* and *Le gare generose*', *Eighteenth-Century Music*, **4**, pp. 27–53. Copyright © 2007 Cambridge University Press; Estelle Joubert (2006), 'Songs to Shape a German Nation: Hiller's Comic Operas and the Public Sphere', *Eighteenth-Century Music*, **3**, pp. 213–30. Copyright © 2006 Cambridge University Press; Bruce Alan Brown and John A. Rice (1996), 'Salieri's *Così fan tutte*', *Cambridge Opera Journal*, **8**, pp. 17–43. Copyright © 1996 Cambridge University Press; Margaret R. Butler (2006), 'Producing the Operatic Chorus at Parma's Teatro Ducale, 1759–1769', *Eighteenth-Century Music*, **3**, pp. 231–51. Copyright © 2006 Cambridge University Press.

Current Musicology for the essay: Wye J. Allanbrook (1991), 'Human Nature in the Unnatural Garden: *Figaro* as Pastoral', *Current Musicology*, **51**, pp. 82–93. Copyright © 1993 Columbia University.

Editions de la MSH for the essay: Elizabeth C. Bartlet (1992), 'On the Freedom of the Theatre and Censorship: The *Adrien* Controversy (1792)', in Antoine Hennion (ed.), *1789–1989: Musique, Histoire, Démocratie*, 1, Paris: Maison des Sciences de l'Homme, pp. 15–30.

Internationale Stiftung Mozarteum for the essays: Sergio Durante (1991), '*La clemenza di Tito* and Other Two-Act Reductions of the Late 18th Century', *Mozart-Jahrbuch*, pp. 733–41.

Johns Hopkins University Press for the essay: Thomas Bauman (1977), 'Opera versus Drama: *Romeo and Juliet* in Eighteenth-Century Germany', *Eighteenth-Century Studies*, **11**, pp. 186–203. Copyright © 1977 The American Society for Eighteenth-Century Studies.

Leo S. Olschki for the essays: Dale E. Monson (1986), 'Galuppi, Tenducci, and *Motezuma*: A Commentary on the History and Musical Style of *Opera Seria* after 1750', in Maria Teresa Muraro and Franco Rossi (eds), *Galuppiana 1985: Studi e ricerche: Atti del convegno internazionale (Venezia, 28–30 ottobre 1985)*, Florence: Olschki, pp. 279–300; Marita P. McClymonds (1989), 'The Venetian Role in the Transformation of Italian *Opera Seria* during the 1790s', in Maria Teresa Muraro and David Bryant (eds), *I vicini di Mozart*, 1, Florence: Olschki, pp. 221–40; Scott L. Balthazar (1989), 'Mayr, Rossini, and the Development of the *Opera Seria* Duet: Some Preliminary Conclusions', in Maria Teresa Muraro and David Bryant (eds), *I vicini di Mozart*, 1, Florence: Olschki, pp. 377–98.

Mosaic for the essay: Mary Hunter (1985), '"Pamela": The Offspring of Richardson's Heroine in Eighteenth-Century Opera', *Mosaic: A Journal for the Interdisciplinary Study of Literature*, **18**, pp. 61–76. Copyright © 1985 Mosaic.

Oxford University Press for the essays: Raymond Monelle (1978), 'Recitative and Dramaturgy in the *Dramma per Musica*', *Music & Letters*, **59**, pp. 245–67. Copyright © 1978 Music & Letters Ltd and Contributors; Daniel Heartz (1974), 'Raaff's Last Aria: A Mozartian Idyll in the Spirit of Hasse', *The Musical Quarterly*, **60**, pp. 517–43. Copyright © 1974 by G. Schirmer, Inc.; Patricia Lewy Gidwitz (1991), '"Ich bin die erste Sängerin": Vocal Profiles of Two Mozart Sopranos', *Early Music*, **19**, pp. 565–79; Dorothea Link (1996), '*L'arbore di Diana*: A Model for *Così fan tutte*', in Stanley Sadie (ed.), *Wolfgang Amadè Mozart: Essays on his Life and his Music*, Oxford: Clarendon Press, pp. 362–73. John Platoff (1992), 'How Original was Mozart? Evidence from *Opera Buffa*', *Early Music*, **20**, pp. 105–17.

Paul Corneilson for the essay: Paul Corneilson (2001), 'Mozart's Ilia and Elettra: New Perspectives on *Idomeneo*', in Theodor Göllner and Stephan Hörner (eds), *Mozarts Idomeneo und die Musik in München zur Zeit Karl Theodors*, Munich: Verlag der Bayerischen Akademie der Wissenschaften, pp. 97–113.

Princeton University Press for the essay: Martha Feldman (2000), 'The Absent Mother in *Opera Seria*', in Mary Ann Smart (ed.), *Siren Songs: Representations of Gender and Sexuality in Opera*, Princeton, NJ: Princeton University Press, pp. 29–46, 254–59. Copyright © 2000 Princeton University Press.

Taylor & Francis Ltd for the essays: Julian Rushton (1972), 'The Theory and Practice of Piccinnisme', *Proceedings of the Royal Musical Association*, **98**, pp. 31–46. Copyright © 1972 The Royal Musical Association and the Authors; Dexter Edge (1991), 'Mozart's Fee for *Così fan tutte*', *Journal of the Royal Musical Association*, **116**, pp. 211–35.

Every effort has been made to trace all the copyright holders, but if any have been inadvertently overlooked the publishers will be pleased to make the necessary arrangement at the first opportunity.

Series Preface

The Ashgate Library of Essays in Opera Studies draws together articles and essays from a disparate group of scholarly journals and collected volumes, some now difficult to locate. This reprint series comprises an authoritative set of six volumes: one devoted to the seventeenth century, two to the eighteenth century, two to the nineteenth century, and one to the twentieth/twenty-first centuries. Each volume has been edited by a recognized authority in the area and offers a selection of the most important and influential English-language scholarship in opera studies.

Each volume editor provides a substantial, detailed introduction surveying the current state of the field, giving an overview of important issues and new discoveries, and explaining the significance of the texts in the collection. There is also a select bibliography of the sources cited in each introduction. Because of the nature of the scholarship and the operatic repertory for different times and places, volumes are organized in differing ways designed to serve readers' needs and to embrace various topics and approaches as appropriate to the repertory of diverse eras.

Recent years have witnessed an acute awareness of the nature of scholarship about opera; those who have reflected on the issues surrounding the genre's study have changed the course of scholarship in significant ways. The new perspectives on opera scholarship that writers (from various disciplines) have contributed bring together the best of both musical and non-musical criticism. The rich and varied selection of approaches represented in the collection – addressing sources, works, audiences, performers, creators, culture, and theory – deal with operatic works as historical and contemporary entities with aesthetic, theoretical, and ideological complexities.

No particular method or approach is favoured or excluded in these volumes; the series thus provides researchers, scholars, and graduate students throughout the world with fairly comprehensive coverage of currently important topics and approaches. Presented in a compact, easy-to-access format, this series is especially useful for scholars new to the area as well as for experienced scholars who may have overlooked an important essay published in a journal with limited circulation.

ROBERTA MONTEMORRA MARVIN
Series Editor

Introduction

The study of opera in the second half of the eighteenth century has flourished during the last several decades, and our knowledge of the operas written during that period and of their aesthetic, social and political contexts has vastly increased. Much of what we have learned in these and other areas of scholarship has been recorded in the form of articles published in scholarly journals and in collections of essays. This volume will explore opera and operatic life in the years 1750–1800 through several English-language essays, in a selection intended to represent the last few decades of scholarship in all its excitement and variety.

This introduction provides some context for the essays that follow. It briefly discusses some of the institutional developments and intellectual trends that have informed scholarship in eighteenth-century opera and mentions some of the criteria that have guided my choice of the essays reprinted here.

National Traditions, Academic Institutions

Although scholars in all the English-speaking countries have been actively involved in research in opera of the second half of the eighteenth century, some countries seem to have developed particular specializations and strengths, thanks in part to the presence of especially productive and influential scholars. In England, for example, Julian Rushton's work on *tragédie lyrique* and David Charlton's on *opéra-comique* have helped the study of French opera thrive. In the United States, in contrast, research on Italian opera, both comic and serious, has prospered under the leadership of scholars such as Daniel Heartz and James Webster. Americans who have specialized in French opera, such as Elizabeth C. Bartlet and Karin Pendle, and Britons who have specialized in Italian opera, such as Michael Robinson, have led productive careers, but mostly on their own.

Certain graduate programmes have produced particularly large numbers of successful students of eighteenth-century opera. Cornell University, in Ithaca, New York, is remarkable in this respect. Although no member of its faculty claims eighteenth-century opera as his or her primary field of study, several Cornell students, including Caryl Clark, Paul Horsley, Mary Hunter, Pierpaolo Polzonetti, Ronald J. Rabin and Jessica Waldoff, have written dissertations in the field. Just as productive has been the University of California, Berkeley, where Heartz has directed the dissertations of several students who have gone on to make important contributions to the study of eighteenth-century opera, including Thomas Bauman, Bruce Alan Brown, Kathleen Hansell, Marita P. McClymonds and John A. Rice.

Cornell students have tended to devote their dissertations to the relatively familiar genre of *opera buffa* and to the works of Mozart (Waldoff, 1995; Rabin, 1996) and Haydn (Hunter, 1982; Clark, 1991). Horsley's dissertation on Dittersdorf's German operas (1988) and Polzonetti's on *opera buffa* and the American Revolution (2003) are exceptional in directing readers' attention away from Mozart and Haydn. Berkeley students, in contrast, have tended to look farther afield: to composers such as Gluck (Brown, 1986) or Jommelli (McClymonds, 1978), to operatic centres such as Milan (Hansell, 1979) or Florence (Rice, 1987), and to genres such as *Singspiel* (Bauman, 1977), *opera seria* (McClymonds, 1978; Hansell, 1979; Rice, 1987) and *opéra-comique* (Brown, 1986). The intellectual ferment generated in 1994 by a conference at Cornell on *opera buffa* in Mozart's Vienna was partly a result of its having brought together the Berkeley and Cornell 'schools' in friendly collaboration (see Hunter and Webster, 1997).

Another important development over the last few decades has been the arrival of young Italian scholars in American graduate schools. Having taken advantage of both Italy's excellent system of elementary and secondary education and the professional training in which a few American graduate programmes still excel, scholars such as Polzonetti, Alessandra Campana, Stefano Castelvecchi and Sergio Durante have contributed a great deal to our understanding of eighteenth-century opera.

Aesthetics and Dramaturgy

Most opera lovers are familiar with only a few operas written during the second half of the eighteenth century. Even some of those who know and love the late operas of Mozart may not be thoroughly familiar with the aesthetic and dramaturgical systems that underlie these and other operas. Most if not all essays about opera in this period deal, at least implicitly, with problems of aesthetics and dramaturgy. But some confront those problems more openly than others, and this book opens with a sample of such essays.

In Chapter 1 Rushton elegantly and perceptively brings the abstractions of a Parisian pamphlet war of the 1770s into contact with the works by Niccolò Piccinni that were the subject of debate. Raymond Monelle, in Chapter 2, furthers our understanding of the function of recitative and the relationship between recitative and aria in *opera seria*. The happy ending so prevalent in eighteenth-century dramaturgy is one of the subjects explored by Bauman in Chapter 3, a stimulating study of German operatic treatments of the story of Romeo and Juliet. Chapter 4, Webster's typically thought-provoking essay on the problem of musical unity in Mozart's operas, calls attention to the difference between the way an opera is perceived when studied in a score and when heard and seen in performance.

Singers

One of the fields of research that has been cultivated with particular energy and originality (especially in the United States) is the study of singers and their role in operatic production. With the help of Claudio Sartori's catalogue of Italian librettos published before 1800 (1990–94), a new and immensely valuable research tool that appeared in seven volumes, scholars have reconstructed, with more detail and accuracy than previously possible, the careers of many of the period's greatest singers. From the music written for these singers historians have extracted vocal profiles that allow us to interpret the music they sang as the product of interaction between a composer's imagination and a singer's vocal abilities and artistic personality.

Here again Heartz has led the way, with his early essay on Anton Raaff, the tenor who created the title role in *Idomeneo* (Chapter 5). His student Patricia Lewy Gidwitz wrote an important dissertation (1991) and published some of her most valuable insights in two essays, one on Caterina Cavalieri and Aloysia Lange, reprinted here as Chapter 7, the other on Adriana Ferrarese del Bene (1996). Other historians have focused more attention on *opera seria* singers. Dennis Libby (1989) asserted the primacy of vocal improvisation in the production of serious opera in Naples and Venice. In Chapter 6 Dale Monson shows how the male soprano Ferdinando Tenducci contributed to the shaping of the music written for him. Paul Corneilson and Rice have followed the careers and analysed the vocal profiles of some of the women who created roles in Mozart's *Idomeneo* (Corneilson, Chapter 8, this volume) and *La clemenza di Tito* (Rice, 1995). Bauman (1991) has shown how a single singer, Valentin Adamberger, brought a distinct vocal profile to his work in a wide variety of vocal genres, from *Singspiel* to Italian oratorio. Dorothea Link has directed much of her interest in singers who created roles in Mozart's *opere buffe* into the production of editions of arias written for those singers by composers other than Mozart (beginning with Link, 2002 and Link, 2004; others are forthcoming). Among her essays on singers active in Vienna during the 1780s is a study of Anna Morichelli, who created roles in several operas by Vicente Martín y Soler (Link, 2010).

Arias and Ensembles

Another fruitful field of study has been the close analysis of arias both as musical form and as dramatic expression. Aria types such as the *buffo* aria, the two-tempo *rondò* and the *cavatina* are all more clearly understood now than they were thirty years ago, in terms not only of their musical and poetic structure but also of the way they contribute to characterization and the unfolding drama. Webster's encyclopedic survey of the types and forms of arias in Mozart's operas (1991) built on Hunter's work on Haydn's arias (1982, 1989) and John Platoff's on Mozart and his compositional contemporaries in 1780s Vienna (1990). Heartz's study of Mozart's *La clemenza di Tito* as a product of a musical culture that Mozart shared with leading Italian composers of the 1780s and 1790s (1978–79) focused attention on the two-tempo *rondò* as an aria of particular importance to singers and audiences alike. The *rondò* was subsequently the object of a great deal of scholarly attention. Rice (1986) analysed an influential early example of the aria type, Giuseppe Sarti's 'Mia speranza io pur vorrei'. John Platoff (1991b) examined a poem that Lorenzo Da Ponte intended for Mozart to set as a two-tempo *rondò* for Susanna in *Le nozze di Figaro* ('Non tardar amato bene') but that ended up being composed not by Mozart but by Vincenzo Righini. Don Neville (1994) surveyed the two-tempo *rondò* in Mozart's late operas.

Equally productive has been the study of ensembles, from duets to finales. In Chapter 23 Scott Balthazar follows the development of the *opera seria* duet from the mid-eighteenth century to the early nineteenth century in one of several essays on ensembles in serious opera that also include Heartz (1980) on the quartet 'Andrò ramingo e solo' in Mozart's *Idomeneo* and McClymonds (1996) on the *Idomeneo* quartet viewed within the tradition of quartets in *opera seria*. Platoff (1989, 1991a, 1997) has increased our understanding of the ensembles in Mozart's comic operas in a rich series of essays. Elisabeth Cook (1992), a student of Charlton at the University of East Anglia, has shown that research on eighteenth-century operatic ensembles is by no means limited to Italian opera in her study of ensembles in *opéra-comique*.

Sensibility, Sentiment and the Pastoral

A cult of sensibility spread through Europe during the second third of the eighteenth century, partly in reaction to the Enlightenment's emphasis on reason, partly in response to the Enlightenment's confidence in the innate goodness of human nature. Like so many eighteenth-century fashions, the cult of sensibility owed a great deal to England. Richardson's novels made sensibility – defined by Diderot's *Encyclopédie* as 'disposition tendre et delicate de l'âme, qui la rend facile à être émue, à être touchée' ('a tender, delicate disposition of the soul that makes it susceptible to being moved, to being touched') – an emotional state that was cultivated by sophisticated people all over Europe. Several historians have investigated the effect of the cult of sensibility on the creation and perception of opera. Rice (1986) called attention to the way in which the cult of sensibility shaped the reception of a great singer's performance in a serious opera in Milan, but another essay published the previous year, dealing with the role of sensibility in *opera buffa*, excited much more interest: Hunter's essay (Chapter 9) on Richardson's *Pamela* and how it and in particular the sensibility of his heroine influenced eighteenth-century opera initiated a remarkable series of studies during the following two decades, including Castelvecchi (Chapter 11) on Nina as sentimental heroine in operas by Dalayrac and Paisiello, Edmund Goehring (Chapter 13) on sensibility in Viennese *opera buffa* of the 1780s, Waldoff (1998) on Haydn's *La vera costanza* and Castelvecchi (2000) on Mozart's *Figaro*.

Closely related to eighteenth-century opera's adoption of the cult of sensibility was its exploitation of pastoral themes. An idealized natural world in which people live in harmony with nature and with each other – the mythical Arcadia of pastoral poets – served as the setting of many eighteenth-century operas and provided important thematic elements to others. Bartlet (1984–85) called attention to the importance of the pastoral in an opera written to celebrate the marriage of Marie Antoinette to the dauphin of France, Grétry's *La rosière de Salency*. Among Mozart's operas, pastoral elements of two in particular – *Le nozze di Figaro* and *Così fan tutte* – have attracted the attention of scholars, including Wye Jamison Allanbrook (Chapter 10), Goehring (1995) and Link (Chapter 12). Bauman (1995), in a more widely ranging exploration of the pastoral in eighteenth-century music, starts, unexpectedly, with a famous painting by the seventeenth-century artist Poussin.

Orientalism and Exoticism

In yet another productive area of study, historians have analysed the depiction of non-Western cultures in opera, exploring themes of orientalism and exoticism in works such as Haydn's *Lo speziale*, Gluck's *Iphigénie en Tauride*, Mozart's *Die Entführung aus dem Serail* and Salieri's *Axur re d'Ormus*. Interest in the way non-European culture is depicted in these and other operas is part of a wider scholarly interest in musical exoticism that has produced a collection of essays on the exotic in Western music (Bellman, 1998). Included in that book is an essay by Hunter (1998) (devoted only partly to opera), which concerns a kind of musical exoticism – the attempt to convey some of the sonic qualities of Turkish janissary music – that was particularly characteristic of the second half of the eighteenth century. Other English-language analyses of exoticism in opera include Thomas Betzwieser (1994) on changes that Beaumarchais and Salieri made to their *Tarare* during the French Revolution, Margaret R. Butler (2006) on De Maio's *Motezuma* in Turin and two essays reprinted here – Chapter 14 by Benjamin Perl, on Mozart's Turkish style, and Chapter 15 by Polzonetti, on operas set in the New World.

Genre Studies

The differences between the operatic genres that flourished in the eighteenth century – *opera buffa, opera seria, Singspiel, opéra-comique, tragédie lyrique* – and the relations between these genres have inspired many important essays. Bertil van Boer (1988) analysed the influence of English ballad opera on the development of *Singspiel* in Germany in the middle of the century; Alfred R. Neumann (1963) followed the subsequent evolution of the genre. Robinson (1978–81) and Rice (2000) discussed a subgenre of Italian comic opera, the Roman *intermezzo*, that had not received much attention from scholars. Although most of Robinson's work has involved Italian opera, he has by no means limited his research to Italy; in an essay published in 1992 he showed how Italian comic opera contributed to the development of French opera. Stephen C. Willis's study of Luigi Cherubini's transition from *opera seria* to *opéra-comique* (1982) is yet another study of generic influence and transformation in Paris during the second half of the eighteenth century.

But perhaps the generic interaction that has proved most stimulating to writers on opera has been the interaction between *opera seria* and *opera buffa*, and especially *opera buffa*'s incorporation of elements of *opera seria*. To what extent does that incorporation involve parody? And what does the parody signify? Hunter (1986, 1991) has been particularly active in exploring relations between serious and comic in Italian opera. The interaction between serious and comic in Haydn's operas has been the subject of studies by Brown (1987), on *Orlando Paladino*, and Clark (1993), on *La fedeltà premiata*.

Opera and Politics

As with any theatrical performance involving an audience, no matter how small or select, the performance of an opera is a political act, with the potential for communicating political messages of many kinds and in many directions. Rarely are such messages completely clear and unambiguous, but that has not kept scholars from trying to elucidate the political implications of eighteenth-century opera.

One of the ways rulers manipulated opera's ability to communicate political meaning was through censorship. This is the subject of Chapter 16 by Bartlet, which examines the controversy surrounding an opera by Méhul that during the French Revolution was suspected of encouraging Royalist sympathies. Betzwieser (1994) also looked at an opera through the lens of French Revolutionary politics. Bauman (1986) showed how the early repertory of the Teatro la Fenice reflected the political situation in late eighteenth-century Venice, and this essay strongly influenced a later discussion of Venetian opera in the same period by Martha

Feldman (2007). Opera was no less powerful a conveyer of political meaning in the German-speaking part of Europe, as Estelle Joubert demonstrates in Chapter 17 on the political implications of Hiller's *Singspiele*.

Manuscript Studies

Another important development in the study of eighteenth-century opera – largely independent of the Cornell and Berkeley 'schools', neither of which has encouraged this kind of research – has been the study of music manuscripts. Alan Tyson, in a stimulating series of essays written during the 1970s and 1980s, shed new light on Mozart's autographs and the paper on which they are written. His catalogue of the watermarks in the paper that Mozart used constituted another monumental contribution to our knowledge of the autograph scores (Tyson, 1992). Dexter Edge's doctoral dissertation (2001) on Mozart's Viennese copyists did for manuscript copies (that is, the work of professional copyists) what Tyson had done for the autographs: it made available vast amounts of new information and important methodological insights whose influence will undoubtedly be felt for a long time – and not only by Mozart scholars. Corneilson and Eugene K. Wolf (1994) brought similar methodological rigour to their study of operatic sources from Mannheim, one of eighteenth-century Germany's most important courts. David J. Buch (1997) has subjected the manuscripts associated with the Theater auf der Wieden (the theatre for which Mozart wrote *Die Zauberflöte*) to intensive investigation, while Daniel Melamed (2003–2004) has extended Tyson's analytical techniques to Mozart's *Singspiel, Die Entführung aus dem Serail*.

Staging, Scenery, Orchestras, Theatres

In an age in which opera houses have largely abdicated the staging of opera to directors who seem neither to know nor to care how librettists and composers intended their works to be staged, historians have had little practical reason to elucidate the principles and practices of eighteenth-century stage design. Yet many of them have done so, perhaps with the hope of offering historically-informed alternatives to the often trashy *Regietheater* that predominates in so many prestigious theatres today, in grotesque contrast to the faithfulness to the score with which singers and orchestras are expected to perform the music.

Thanks to the work of several scholars we know more than ever about the theatres in which eighteenth-century operas were performed. Heartz (1982) has elucidated the construction and remodelling of Vienna's Burgtheater; Corneilson (1997) has done the same for a theatre that Charles Burney called 'one of the largest and most splendid theatres in Europe', the Mannheim Court Theatre. While Corneilson's reconstruction took place in his scholarly imagination, Curtis Price *et al.* (1991) examined the actual design and construction of the King's Theatre, Haymarket, in the period 1789–91.

Several essays have explored the size and composition of the orchestras and choruses that performed in these and other theatres: examples include Butler (Chapter 26) on the chorus at Parma that took part in the important series of French-inspired Italian serious operas during the 1760s, Charlton (1985) on the orchestra and chorus of one of Paris's leading theatres in the second half of the eighteenth century, and Edge (1992) on the orchestras that accompanied Mozart's Viennese operas.

How operas were staged in the eighteenth century has been the subject of numerous studies. Sven Hansell (1974), Roger Savage (1998) and Nicholas Solomon (1989) have contributed to our knowledge of the positions, movements and gestures of the singers on the eighteenth-century stage. Betzwieser (2000) has shown how music and action corresponded in French opera, with each enhancing the effect of the other. Clark (2003) has identified a set of eighteenth-century costume designs as possibly intended for a production of Salieri's early opera, *Armida*. Such studies, valuable now, will be even more valuable when opera houses and audiences, having tired of the antics of *Regietheater*, discover that eighteenth-century operas can best be appreciated when presented in settings that respect the visual as well as the musical conventions within which they were conceived.

Archival Studies

Archival research has greatly enhanced our understanding of eighteenth-century opera's institutional history, allowing scholars to shed new light on the role of rulers, courts and impresarios in the production of opera. Among several historians who have profitably worked in Italian archives are Butler (2002, for Turin; Chapter 26, this volume, for Parma), Robinson (1990, for Naples) and Anthony DelDonna (2002, also for Naples). Edge has made many important discoveries in the archives of Vienna, including those presented and analysed in Chapter 18, his study of the fees that Mozart and other composers received for composing operas for the court theatres in the 1780s and early 1790s. Historians of opera in England have been just as willing to get their hands dirty, producing a large number of essays based largely on hitherto unknown archival documents (see, for example, Gibson, 1990; Milhous and Hume, 1997). Several historians have intensively studied the origins of particular operas, and these studies have generally depended, in part, on archival research. Brown (1983, 2000) explored the origins of important Viennese operas of the 1760s; Durante (1999) clarified our understanding of how one of Mozart's last operas, *La clemenza di Tito*, came into being.

Mozart and his Viennese Contemporaries

It will be obvious to anyone who has read up to this point that Mozart's operas have been a focus of attention for many – probably most – of the historians who have studied opera of the second half of the eighteenth century.

One way of illustrating the wealth of scholarship on Mozart's operas published during the last quarter of a century is to mention some of the English-language essays about a single opera, *Le nozze di Figaro*. Some of these essays discuss the origins of *Figaro* (Tyson, 1981; Heartz, 1986b); some are concerned with its large-scale structure (Heartz, 1987; Waldoff and Webster, 1996); some focus our attention on sentiment and sensibility (Allanbrook, Chapter 10, this volume; Castelvecchi, 2000); some examine individual arias and ensembles (Heartz, 1991; Platoff, 1991a; Leeson, 2004; see also two pieces written in response to Leeson's essay: Woodfield, 2006 and Rumph, 2006); some direct attention to particular characters, such as Susanna (Tishkoff, 1990), the Countess (Hunter, 1997) or Figaro (Rabin, 1997). One could easily draw up equally long lists, full of equally intriguing titles, of essays on *Don Giovanni*, *Così fan tutte* and *Die Zauberflöte*.

Mozart's operas have also played an important role in studies that compare them with the works of his contemporaries, or that study those works in order to understand the context of Mozart's operatic achievement. Most of the essays on Mozart's singers mentioned earlier in this introduction involve the analysis of music written for those singers by composers other than Mozart. Link (Chapter 12) examines Martín y Soler's *L'arbore di Diana* and proposes it as a possible model for *Così fan tutte*; in Chapter 19 and elsewhere Platoff has produced valuable studies of the musical techniques of *opera buffa* in Vienna during the 1780s (see also Platoff, 1989, 1990, 1991a, 1991b). Buch, in Chapter 21, shows how *Die Zauberflöte* took shape within and reflects the dramatic and musical values of Emanuel Schikaneder's troupe at the Theater auf der Wieden (see also Buch, 1997). In Chapter 20 Brown and Rice discuss Salieri's aborted attempt to set to music the libretto that later became known, in Mozart's setting, as *Così fan tutte*.

Opera Seria

No operatic genre has enjoyed a more dramatic increase in the amount of scholarly attention it has received during the last thirty years than Italian serious opera, and this attention has produced not only valuable dissertations and books but also essays. As in so many other areas of research into eighteenth-century opera, Heartz (1970) set an example with a path-breaking publication that put *opera seria* at the forefront of musical life and stylistic change; he continued with a series of classic essays, including Chapter 5 in this volume, that followed the evolution of the genre from Hasse to Mozart and elucidated some of its most characteristic elements (Heartz, 1978–79, 1978–81, 1980, 1986a). Many of Heartz's students have contributed to our knowledge of *opera seria* and related genres – for example, Bauman (1986) on the building and the early repertory of the Teatro la Fenice in late eighteenth-century Venice, Brown (2000) on Hasse's *Alcide al Bivio* and Hansell (2000) on the operas that Mozart wrote for Milan in the early 1770s.

But easily the most prolific of Heartz's students in the area of *opera seria* has been McClymonds, whose essays if reprinted together would constitute an outstanding history of the genre. Chapter 22 is her 1989 essay on new trends in Venetian *opera seria* at the end of the eighteenth century. Among the finest of those that have not already been cited are her essays on Jommelli's late operas (McClymonds, 1980), on the increasing popularity of tragic endings in Venetian opera of the 1790s (McClymonds, 1990), on operas based on the story of Armida (McClymonds, 1993), comparing the musical styles of *opera seria* and *opera buffa* (McClymonds, 1997) and on the reform of *opera seria* in Italy (McClymonds, 2003).

The research on *opera seria* by Heartz and his students has inspired further work by many scholars on both sides of the Atlantic. But while members of the Berkeley 'school' have generally shown equal interest in the music of Mozart and his contemporaries, most others have focused on one or the other. Feldman's research on serious opera in Italy has resulted not only in a magisterial book (2007) but also in several important essays, including that reprinted here as Chapter 25 (see also Feldman, 1995). Other essays devoted mostly or entirely to opera in Italy include Butler's studies of repertory and production in Turin and Parma (in particular Chapter 26; see also Butler, 2002, 2006) and Balthazar's study of the evolution of the *opera seria* duet (Chapter 23). Chapter 24 by Durante is among the essays that mainly concern Mozart's *opere serie* (see also Rushton, 1991, 1998, 2003; Durante, 1999). (Rushton is unusual in moving freely between *opera buffa*, *opera seria* and *tragédie lyrique*, and in demonstrating the same level of expertise in writing about all three genres.) Corneilson, though not a student of Heartz, has followed the Berkeley historian in studying the *opere serie* of Mozart (see Chapter 8) and others, such as J.C. Bach (Corneilson, 1994), with equal success.

Essay Selection

It will be obvious that I have not been able to include in this book all the essays mentioned in this introduction. Both to maximize the number of items in this volume and because I believe that brevity is a quality to be valued in essays, I have limited my selection to essays of thirty pages or less. This has meant omitting many of the important essays that I have mentioned already, such as those by Buch (1997), Durante (1999), Feldman (1995), Waldoff (1998), Waldoff and Webster (1996) and Webster (1991). A particularly influential and widely admired essay that I have not included because of its length is that by Libby (1989) on opera in Naples and Venice. I have chosen essays that have not already been republished, either in anthologies or in collections of papers by a single author. This has kept out some of the best essays by the field's busiest cultivators. Many of Heartz's essays on Mozart's opera have been collected in one volume (Heartz,1990); many others can be conveniently read together (Heartz, 2004). Most of Charlton's numerous essays on *opéra-comique* have been reprinted (Charlton, 2000) and most of Tyson's manuscript studies have been brought together (Tyson, 1987).

Finally, to maximize the variety of voices to be heard in this volume, each scholar is represented here by a single essay. This is, of course, grossly unfair to the several scholars who have written many essays that, if I were judging by quality and importance alone, should be included here. Limiting myself, for illustrative purposes, to just three prolific and original students of eighteenth-century opera, and citing only essays that I have not already mentioned in this introduction, it is with regret that I have omitted Bauman's essay on the conditions in Vienna in the mid-1780s that led to exceptional achievements in *opera buffa* (1993), Hunter's study of 'Gothic' settings in *opera buffa* of the 1770s (1993) and Platoff's analysis of tonal planning in Mozart's operas (1996). An anthology of essays by Bauman, Hunter and Platoff alone would make a fine, large book.

Selected Bibliography

Bartlet, Elizabeth C. (1984–85), 'Grétry, Marie Antoinette and *La rosière de Salency*', *Proceedings of the Royal Musical Association*, **111**, pp. 92–120.

Bauman, Thomas (1977), 'Music and Drama in Germany: The Repertory of a Traveling Company, 1767–1781', PhD diss., University of California, Berkeley.

Bauman, Thomas (1981), 'Benda, the Germans, and Simple Recitative', *Journal of the American Musicological Society*, **34**, pp. 119–31.

Bauman, Thomas (1986), 'The Society of La Fenice and its First Impresarios', *Journal of the American Musicological Society*, **39**, pp. 332–54.

Bauman, Thomas (1991), 'Mozart's Belmonte', *Early Music*, **19**, pp. 557–63.

Bauman, Thomas (1993), 'Salieri, Da Ponte and Mozart: The Renewal of Viennese *Opera Buffa* in the 1780s', in Ingrid Fuchs (ed.), *Internationaler Musikwissenschaftlicher Kongreß zum Mozartjahr 1991, Baden-Wien: Bericht*, Tutzing: Schneider, pp. 65–70.

Bauman, Thomas (1995), 'Moralizing at the Tomb: Poussin's Arcadian Shepherds in Eighteenth-Century England and Germany', in Thomas Bauman and Marita P. McClymonds (eds), *Opera and the Enlightenment*, Cambridge: Cambridge University Press, pp. 23–42.

Bellman, Jonathan (ed.) (1998), *The Exotic in Western Music*, Boston: Northeastern University Press.

Betzwieser, Thomas (1994), 'Exoticism and Politics: Beaumarchais' and Salieri's *Le couronnement de Tarare*, 1790', *Cambridge Opera Journal*, **6**, pp. 91–112.

Betzwieser, Thomas (2000), 'Musical Setting and Scenic Movement: Chorus and *Choeur dancé* in Eighteenth-Century Parisian Opera', *Cambridge Opera Journal*, **12**, pp. 1–28.

Boer, Bertil van (1988), 'Coffey's *The Devil to Pay*, the Comic War, and the Emergence of the German Singspiel', *Journal of Musicological Research*, **8**, pp. 119–39.

Brown, Bruce Alan (1983), 'Gluck's *La Rencontre imprevue* and its Revisions', *Journal of the American Musicological Society*, **36**, pp. 498–515.

Brown, Bruce Alan (1986), 'Christoph Willibald Gluck and *Opéra comique* in Vienna, 1754–1764', PhD diss., University of California, Berkeley.

Brown, Bruce Alan (1987), '*Le pazzie d'Orlando, Orlando Paladino*, and the Uses of Parody', *Italica*, **64**, pp. 583–605.

Brown, Bruce Alan (2000), '"Mon opéra italien": Giacomo Durazzo and the Genesis of *Alcide al Bivio*', in Andrea Sommer-Mathis and Elisabeth Theresia Hilscher (eds), *Pietro Metastasio: Uomo universale (1698–1782)*, Vienna: Österreichische Akademie der Wissenschaften, pp. 115–42.

Buch, David J. (1997), 'Mozart and the Theater auf der Wieden: New Attributions and Perspectives', *Cambridge Opera Journal*, **9**, pp. 195–232.

Butler, Margaret (2002), 'Administration and Innovation at Turin's Teatro Regio: Producing *Sofonisba* (1764) and *Oreste* (1766)', *Cambridge Opera Journal*, **14**, pp. 243–62.

Butler, Margaret (2006), 'Exoticism in Eighteenth-Century Turinese Opera: *Motezuma* in context', in Mara E. Parker (ed.), *Music in Eighteenth-Century Cities, Courts, Churches*, Ann Arbor, MI: Steglein, pp. 105–124.

Castelvecchi, Stefano (2000), 'Sentimental and Anti-Sentimental in *Le nozze di Figaro*', *Journal of the American Musicological Society*, **53**, pp. 1–24.

Charlton, David (1985), 'Orchestra and Chorus at the Comédie Italienne, 1755–99', in Malcolm Brown and Roland Wiley (eds), *Slavonic and Western Music: Essays for Gerald Abraham*, Oxford: Oxford University Press, pp. 87–108.

Charlton, David (2000), *French Opera, 1730–1830: Meaning and Media*, Aldershot: Ashgate.

Clark, Caryl (1991), 'The *Opera Buffa* Finales of Joseph Haydn', PhD diss., Cornell University.

Clark, Caryl (1993), 'Intertextual Play and Haydn's *La fedeltà premiata*', *Current Musicology*, **51**, pp. 59–81.

Clark, Caryl (2003), 'Fabricating Magic: Costuming Salieri's *Armida*', *Early Music*, **31**, pp. 451–62.

Cook, Elisabeth (1992), 'Developments in Vocal Ensemble Compositon in *Opéra-comique*', in Philippe Vendrix (ed.), *Grétry et l'Europe de l'opéra-comique*, Liège: Pierre Mardaga, pp. 113–92.

Corneilson, Paul (1994), 'The Case of J.C. Bach's *Lucio Silla*', *Journal of Musicology*, **12**, pp. 206–18.

Corneilson, Paul (1997), 'Reconstructing the Mannheim Court Theater', *Early Music*, **35**, pp. 63–68, 70–76, 79–81.

Corneilson, Paul and Wolf, Eugene K. (1994), 'Newly Identified Manuscripts of Operas and Related Works from Mannheim', *Journal of the American Musicological Society*, **47**, pp. 244–74.

DelDonna, Anthony (2002), 'Behind the Scenes: The Musical Life and Organizational Structure of the San Carlo Opera Orchestra in Late Eighteenth-Century Naples', in Paologiovanni Maione (ed.),

Le fonti d'archivio per la storia della musica a Napoli dal XVI al XVIII secolo, Naples: Editoriale Scientifica, pp. 427–48.

Durante, Sergio (1999), 'The Chronology of Mozart's *La clemenza di Tito* Reconsidered', *Music & Letters*, **80**, pp. 560–94.

Edge, Dexter (1992), 'Mozart's Viennese Orchestras', *Early Music*, **20**, pp. 64–65, 67–69, 71–88.

Edge, Dexter (2001), 'Mozart's Viennese Copyists', PhD diss., University of Southern California.

Feldman, Martha (1995), 'Magic Mirrors and the *Seria* Stage: Thoughts Toward a Ritual View', *Journal of the American Musicological Society*, **48**, pp. 423–84.

Feldman, Martha (2007), *Opera and Sovereignty: Transforming Myths in Eighteenth-Century Italy*, Chicago, IL: University of Chicago Press.

Gibson, Elizabeth (1990), 'Italian Opera in London, 1750–75: Management and Finances', *Early Music*, **18**, pp. 47–59.

Gidwitz, Patricia Lewy (1991), 'Vocal Profiles of Four Mozart's Sopranos', PhD diss., University of California, Berkeley.

Gidwitz, Patricia Lewy (1996), 'Mozart's Fiordiligi: Adriana Ferrarese del Bene', *Cambridge Opera Journal*, **8**, pp. 199–214.

Goehring, Edmund (1995), 'Despina, Cupid, and the Pastoral Mode of *Così fan tutte*', *Cambridge Opera Journal*, **7**, pp. 107–33.

Hansell, Kathleen (1979), 'Opera and Ballet at the Regio Ducal Teatro of Milan, 1771–1776: A Musical and Social History', PhD diss., University of California, Berkeley.

Hansell, Kathleen (2000), 'Mozart's Milanese Theatrical Works', in Susan Parisi (ed.), *Music in the Theater, Church, and Villa: Essays in Honor of Robert Lamar Weaver and Norma Wright Weaver*, Warren, MI: Harmonie Park Press, pp. 195–212.

Hansell, Sven (1974), 'Stage Deportment and Scenographic Design in the Italian *Opera Seria* of the Settecento', in Henrik Glahn, Søren Sørensen and Peter Ryom (eds), *Report of the 11th Congress of the International Musicological Society, Copenhagen 1972*, Copenhagen: Hansen, I, pp. 415–24.

Heartz, Daniel (1970), 'Opera and the Periodization of Eighteenth-Century Music', in Dragotin Cvetko (ed.), *Report of the 10th Congress of the International Musicological Society, Ljubljana, 1967*, Kassel: Bärenreiter, pp. 160–68.

Heartz, Daniel (1978–79), 'Mozart and his Italian Contemporaries: *La clemenza di Tito*', *Mozart-Jahrbuch*, pp. 275–93. Rpt in Daniel Heartz (1990), *Mozart's Operas*, Berkeley: University of California Press, pp. 298–317.

Heartz, Daniel (1978–81), 'Hasse, Galuppi, and Metastasio', in Maria Teresa Muraro (ed.), *Venezia e il melodramma nel Settecento*, Florence: Olschki, I, pp. 309–40.

Heartz, Daniel (1980), 'The Great Quartet in *Idomeneo*', *Music Forum*, **5**, pp. 233–56.

Heartz, Daniel (1982), 'Nicolas Jadot and the Building of the Burgtheater', *The Musical Quarterly*, **68**, pp. 1–31.

Heartz, Daniel (1986a), 'Metastasio, "Maestro dei maestri di cappella dramatici"', in Maria Teresa Muraro (ed.), *Metastasio e il mondo musicale*, Florence: Olschki, pp. 315–38. Rpt in Daniel Heartz (2004), *From Garrick to Gluck: Essays on Opera in the Age of Enlightenment*, ed. John A. Rice, Hillsdale, NY: Pendragon, pp. 69–83.

Heartz, Daniel (1986b) 'Setting the Stage for *Figaro*', *Musical Times*, **127**, pp. 256–60. Rpt in Daniel Heartz (1990), *Mozart's Operas*, Berkeley: University of California Press, pp. 122–31.

Heartz, Daniel (1987), 'Constructing *Le nozze di Figaro*', *Journal of the Royal Musical Association*, **112**, pp. 77–98. Rpt in Daniel Heartz (1990), *Mozart's Operas*, Berkeley: University of California Press, pp. 132–55.

Heartz, Daniel (1990), *Mozart's Operas*, ed., with contributing essays, ed. Thomas Bauman, Berkeley: University of California Press.

Heartz, Daniel (1991), 'Susanna's Hat', *Early Music*, **19**, pp. 585–89.

Heartz, Daniel (2004), *From Garrick to Gluck: Essays on Opera in the Age of Enlightenment*, ed. John A. Rice, Hillsdale, NY: Pendragon.

Horsley, Paul (1988), 'Dittersdorf and the Finale in Late-Eighteenth-Century German Comic Opera', PhD diss., Cornell University

Hunter, Mary (1982), 'Haydn's Aria Forms: A Study of the Arias in the Italian Operas Written at Eszterháza, 1766–1783', PhD diss., Cornell University.

Hunter, Mary (1986), 'The Fusion and Juxtaposition of Genres in *Opera Buffa*, 1770–1800: Anelli and Piccinni's *Griselda*', *Music & Letters*, **67**, pp. 363–80.

Hunter, Mary (1989), 'Text, Music, and Drama in Haydn's Italian Opera Arias: Four Case Studies', *Journal of Musicology*, **7**, pp. 29–57.

Hunter, Mary (1991), 'Some Representations of *Opera Seria* in *Opera Buffa*', *Cambridge Opera Journal*, **3**, pp. 89–108.

Hunter, Mary (1993), 'Landscapes, Gardens and Gothic Settings in the *Opere Buffe* of Mozart and his Italian Contemporaries', *Current Musicology*, **51**, pp. 94–104.

Hunter, Mary (1997), 'Rousseau, the Countess, and the Female Domain', in Cliff Eisen (ed.), *Mozart Studies 2*, New York: Oxford University Press, pp. 1–26.

Hunter, Mary (1998), 'The *Alla Turca* Style in the Late Eighteenth Century: Race and Gender in the Symphony and the Seraglio', in Jonathan Bellman (ed.), *The Exotic in Western Music*, Boston: Northeastern University Press, pp. 43–73.

Hunter, Mary and Webster, James (eds) (1997), *Opera Buffa in Mozart's Vienna*, Cambridge: Cambridge University Press.

Leeson, Daniel (2004), 'Mozart's *Le nozze di Figaro*: A Hidden Dramatic Detail', *Eighteenth-Century Music*, **1**, pp. 301–304.

Libby, Dennis (1989), 'Italy: Two Opera Centres', in Neal Zaslaw (ed.), *The Classical Era: From the 1740s to the End of the 18th Century*, Englewood Cliffs, NJ: Prentice Hall, pp. 15–60.

Link, Dorothea (2002), *Arias for Nancy Storace*, Middleton, WI: A-R Editions

Link, Dorothea (2004), *Arias for Francesco Benucci*, Middleton, WI: A-R Editions

Link, Dorothea (2010), 'La cantante Anna Morichelli, paladín de Vicente Martín y Soler', in Dorothea Link and Leonardo J. Waisman (eds.), *Los siete mundos de Vicente Martín y Soler*, Valencia: Institut Valencia de la Musica, pp. 328-62.

McClymonds, Marita P. (1978), 'Niccolò Jommelli: The Last Years', PhD diss., University of California, Berkeley.

McClymonds, Marita P. (1980), 'The Evolution of Jommelli's Operatic Style', *Journal of the American Musicological Society*, **33**, pp. 326–55.

McClymonds, Marita P. (1990), '*La morte di Semiramide, ossia La vendetta di Nino* and the Restoration of Death and Tragedy to the Italian Operatic Stage in the 1780s and '90s'', in Angelo Pompilio et al. (eds), *Atti del XIV congresso della Società Internazionale di Musicologia, Bologna, 1987: Trasmissione e recezione delle forme di cultura musicale*, Turin: EDT, Part 3, pp. 285–92.

McClymonds, Marita P. (1993), 'Haydn and the *Opera Seria* Tradition: *Armida*', in Bianca Maria Antolini and Wolfgang Witzenmann (eds), *Napoli e il teatro musicale in Europa tra Sette e Ottocento: Studi in onore di Friedrich Lippmann*, Florence: Olschki, pp. 191–206.

McClymonds, Marita P. (1996), 'The Great Quartet in *Idomeneo* and the Italian *Opera Seria* Tradition', in Stanley Sadie (ed.), *Wolfgang Amadè Mozart: Essays on his Life and his Music*, Oxford: Clarendon, pp. 449–76.

McClymonds, Marita P. (1997), '*Opera seria*? *Opera buffa*? Genre and Style as Sign', in Mary Hunter and James Webster (eds), *Opera Buffa in Mozart's Vienna*, Cambridge: Cambridge University Press, pp. 197–231.

McClymonds, Marita P. (2003), 'Opera Reform in Italy, 1750–80', in Bianca Maria Antolini, Teresa M. Gialdroni and Annunziato Pugliese (eds), *'Et facciam dolci canti': Studi in onore di Agostino Ziino in occasione del suo 65° compleanno*, Lucca: Libreria Musicale Italiana, II, pp. 895–912.

Melamed, Daniel (2003–2004), 'Evidence on the Genesis of *Die Entführung aus dem Serail* from Mozart's Autograph Score', *Mozart-Jahrbuch*, pp. 25–42.

Milhous, Judith and Hume, Robert D. (1997), 'Librettist versus Composer: The Property Rights to Arne's *Henry and Emma* and *Don Saverio*', *Journal of the Royal Musical Association*, **122**, pp. 52–67.

Neumann, Alfred R. (1963), 'The Changing Concept of the Singspiel in the Eighteenth Century', in Carl Hammer (ed.), *Studies in German Literature*, Baton Rouge: Louisiana State University Press, pp. 63–71.

Neville, Don (1994), 'The "Rondò" in Mozart's Late Operas', *Mozart-Jahrbuch*, pp. 141–55.

Platoff, John (1989), 'Musical and Dramatic Structure in the *Opera Buffa* Finale', *Journal of Musicology*, **7**, pp. 191–230.

Platoff, John (1990), 'The *Buffa* Aria in Mozart's Vienna', *Cambridge Opera Journal*, **2**, pp. 99–120.

Platoff, John (1991a), 'Tonal Organization in *Buffo* Finales and the Act II Finale of *Le nozze di Figaro*', *Music & Letters*, **72**, pp. 387–403.

Platoff, John (1991b), '"Non tardar amato bene" Completed – but not by Mozart', *Musical Times*, **132**, pp. 557–60.

Platoff, John (1996), 'Myths and Realities about Tonal Planning in Mozart's Operas', *Cambridge Opera Journal*, **8**, pp. 3–15.

Platoff, John (1997), 'Operatic Ensembles and the Problem of the *Don Giovanni* Sextet', in Mary Hunter and James Webster (eds), *Opera Buffa in Mozart's Vienna*, Cambridge: Cambridge University Press, pp. 378–405.

Polzonetti, Pierpaolo (2003), '*Opera Buffa* and the American Revolution', Ph.D. diss., Cornell University.

Price, Curtis, Milhous, Judith and Hume, Robert D. (1991), 'The Rebuilding of the King's Theatre, Haymarket, 1789–1791', *Theatre Journal*, **43**, pp. 421–44.

Rabin, Ronald J. (1996), 'Mozart and the Dramaturgy of *Opera Buffa*: Italian Comic Opera in Vienna, 1783–1791', PhD diss., Cornell University.

Rabin, Ronald J. (1997), 'Figaro as Misogynist: On Aria Types and Aria Rhetoric', in Mary Hunter and James Webster (eds), *Opera Buffa in Mozart's Vienna*, Cambridge: Cambridge University Press, pp. 232–60.

Rice, John A. (1986), 'Sense, Sensibility, and *Opera Seria*: An Epistolary Debate', *Studi musicali*, **15**, pp. 101–38.

Rice, John A. (1987), 'Emperor and Impresario: Leopold II and the Transformation of Viennese Musical Theater, 1790–1792', PhD diss., University of California, Berkeley.

Rice, John A. (1995), 'Mozart and his Singers: The Case of Maria Marchetti Fantozzi, the First Vitellia', *The Opera Quarterly*, **11**, pp. 31–52.

Rice, John A. (2000), 'The Roman *intermezzo* and Sacchini's *La contadina in corte*', *Cambridge Opera Journal*, **12**, pp. 91–107.

Robinson, Michael (1978–81), 'Three Versions of Goldoni's *Il filosofo di campagna*', in Maria Teresa Muraro (ed.) *Venezia e il melodramma nel Settecento*, Florence: Olschki, I, pp. 75–85.

Robinson, Michael (1990), 'A Late Eighteenth-Century Account Book of the San Carlo Theatre, Naples', *Early Music*, **18**, pp. 73–81.

Robinson, Michael (1992), '*Opera Buffa* into *Opéra Comique*', in Malcolm Boyd (ed.), *Music and the French Revolution*, Cambridge: Cambridge University Press, pp. 37–56.

Rumph, Stephen (2006), 'Unveiling Cherubino', *Eighteenth-Century Music*, **3**, pp. 131–40.

Rushton, Julian (1991), '"La vittima è Idamante": Did Mozart Have a Motive?', *Cambridge Opera Journal*, **3**, pp. 1–21.
Rushton, Julian (1998), 'Mozart's Art of Rhetoric: Understanding an *Opera Seria* Aria', *Contemporary Music Review*, **17**, pp. 15–29.
Rushton, Julian (2003), 'Mozart and *Opera Seria*', in Simon Keefe (ed.), *The Cambridge Companion to Mozart*, Cambridge: Cambridge University Press, pp. 147–55.
Sartori, Claudio (1990–94), *I libretti italiani a stampa dalle origini al 1800*, 7 vols, Cuneo: Bertola & Locatelli.
Savage, Roger (1998), 'Staging an Opera: Letters from the Cesarian Poet', *Early Music*, **26**, pp. 583–95.
Solomon, Nicholas (1989), 'Signs of the Times: A Look at Late 18th-Century Gesturing', *Early Music*, **17**, pp. 551–64.
Tishkoff, Doris P. (1990), 'The Call to Revolution in the Boudoir: A New Look at Mozart's Susanna in *The Marriage of Figaro*', in Kinley Brauer and William E. Wright (eds), *Austria in the Age of the French Revolution, 1789–1815*, Minneapolis: Center for Austrian Studies, pp. 91–106.
Tyson, Alan (1981), '*Le nozze di Figaro*: Lessons from the Autograph Score', *Musical Times*, **122**, pp. 456–61. Rpt in Alan Tyson (1987), *Mozart: Studies of the Autograph Scores*, Cambridge, MA: Harvard University Press, pp. 114–24.
Tyson, Alan (1987), *Mozart: Studies of the Autograph Scores*, Cambridge, MA: Harvard University Press.
Tyson, Alan (1992), *Wasserzeichen-Katalog*, Neue Mozart Ausgabe, X/33/Abteilung 2, Kassel: Bärenreiter.
Waldoff, Jessica (1995), 'The Music of Recognition on Mozart's Operas', PhD diss., Cornell University.
Waldoff, Jessica (1998), 'Sentiment and Sensibility in *La vera costanza*', in W. Dean Sutcliffe (ed.), *Haydn Studies*, Cambridge: Cambridge University Press, pp. 70–119.
Waldoff, Jessica and Webster, James (1996), 'Operatic Plotting in *Le nozze di Figaro*', in Stanley Sadie (ed.), *Wolfgang Amadé Mozart: Essays in his Life and his Music*, Oxford: Oxford University Press, pp. 250–95.
Webster, James (1991), 'The Analysis of Mozart's Arias', in Cliff Eisen (ed.), *Mozart Studies*, Oxford: Oxford University Press, pp. 101–99.
Willis, Stephen C. (1982), 'Cherubini: From *Opera Seria* to *Opéra-Comique*', *Studies in Music from the University of Western Ontario*, **7**, pp. 155–82.
Woodfield, Ian (2006), 'Reflections on Mozart's 'Non so più cosa son, cosa faccio', *Eighteenth-Century Music*, **3**, pp. 133–39.

Part I
Aesthetics and Dramaturgy

[1]
The Theory and Practice of Piccinnisme

JULIAN RUSHTON

THE OPERATIC reforms of Gluck and his subsequent conquest of Paris have received much critical attention, but discussion of his rival Piccinni tends to be anecdotal rather than analytical.[1] The term 'Piccinnisme' is also liable to misunderstanding. Terry, for example, setting the scene for J. C. Bach's French opera, refers to Gluck's 'heresies' against Lully and Rameau, and states that his opponents summoned Piccinni as a champion of orthodoxy.[2] Although the previous alternatives to Gluck, in the critics' eyes, were those representatives of a style since decayed, Piccinni was certainly not their champion and his supporters must be numbered among those who would gladly have buried the traditional French opera once for all.

To us it may seem that Gluck had buried it, despite the occasional revival of Lully and Rameau (much mutilated) at least until 1781, two years after Gluck had left Paris in disgust at the failure of *Echo et Narcisse*. But it probably did not escape the attention of those who disliked his music that Gluck's work was, as Alfred Einstein said, 'at once a blow to French opera and a renewal of it'.[3] Unfortunately we cannot simply reverse Terry's formulation to speak of Piccinni's heresies and the orthodoxy of Gluck; nor is it relevant of Einstein to suggest that the controversy would only have been resolved if Piccinni could have shown that '*opera seria* had not been dethroned by Gluck's reforms'.[4] The theatre of their rivalry was not Vienna or Italy but Paris, where *opera seria* had never reigned and where Gluck himself, particularly in the use of long arias often adapted from Italian texts (in *Alceste* and *Iphigénie en Tauride*) had in fact done much

---

[1] Eric Blom (*Stepchildren of Music*, London, 1925) is an honourable exception. A detailed discussion of Piccinni's French operas, from which this paper contains generalizations, is included in my unpublished thesis, *Music and Drama at the Académie Royale de Musique (Paris) 1774–1789*, Oxford University, 1969.
[2] C. S. Terry, *J. C. Bach*, London, 1929, p. 132.
[3] *Gluck*, London, 1936, p. 138.
[4] Ibid., p. 152.

to establish some elements of *opera seria*. Indeed a crucial aspect of Gluck's Paris career is his successful implementation of the policy of Philidor and Gossec: the Italianization of music at the Académie Royale, or Opéra, that bastion of conservatism upon which the controversies centred while the Opéra Comique went its own way. Thus while Gluck certainly seemed at first to be the executioner of traditional French opera, he came to it as a reformer, not a revolutionary, and in many respects was quite conservative (French opera had of course influenced his Italian 'reform'). Gluck's work and Piccinni's should be contrasted in the light of a general Italianization of French music, for Gluck's music is Italian in the way Mozart's is, and what his detractors chiefly objected to was the musical consequence of his rugged personality.

Piccinni had not the reforming mentality, and he left no manifesto to compare with the *Alceste* dedication, a French translation of which had preceded performance of Gluck's first French operas in 1774. It is possible, however, to deduce some sort of reasonably coherent aesthetic from the writings of the 'Piccinnistes', and the relation of that aesthetic to the relevant operas is not without problems. It might at least show if the term 'Piccinnisme' has any useful application. Piccinni's arrival was prepared by a broadside from his principal collaborator, Jean François Marmontel, the adaptor of Quinault for modern use, whose somewhat brutal surgical methods on the work of Lully's librettist suggested to Grimm the adjective 'marmontelisé'. His *Essai sur les révolutions de la musique en France*[5] appeared in 1777, the year of Gluck's *Armide*, and thus provided Piccinniste opera with a theoretical base some months before the performance of Piccinni's first French opera, *Roland*, in January 1778.

Marmontel's *Essai* is an attempt at brilliant polemic, which fails partly because its negative aspect, the abuse of Gluck, is so unpersuasive. Marmontel outlines the history of French and Italian music, to conclude that real music began with the early eighteenth-century Neapolitans and that France, the last citadel to resist this all-conquering style, would do better to yield at once than be side-tracked by a German who tries to disguise his lack of melodic invention by mere noise. He represents Gluckism as a conspiracy to keep true melody out of the Opéra:

---

[5] Reprinted in G. M. le Blond, *Mémoires pour servir à l'histoire de la révolution opérée dans la musique par M. le Chevalier Gluck*, Naples, 1781, pp. 153–90.

THE THEORY AND PRACTICE OF PICCINNISME

> All would be lost if the melodious singing which delights us in our concerts should by some mischance be accepted in our theatre; if our ears should grow accustomed to simple and natural modulations, to harmony as clear in its power as in its sweetness, to vocal music which is not a cry of physical anguish but the voice of the soul itself, to those pure and elegant curves of the musical period whose secret belongs to the Italians.[6]

Before discussing this 'musical period' ('la Période Musicale') it might be as well to clarify the area of conflict. Both sides are agreed in discontinuing the attempt to perpetuate the old French style, and on keeping nevertheless certain elements from French opera, particularly its relative freedom of structure; but both sides want Italianate music. Yet it is too simple to reduce the conflict to one of personalities—the clash between Piccinni and Gluck which Einstein compared to the collision of a sponge with an agate. Nor is the opposition one between a 'singers' opera' and 'dramatic opera'. Piccinni's French operas are just as dramatic in intention as Gluck's: *Atys*, *Didon*, *Iphigénie* and *Pénélope* in no way mitigate the seriousness of the subject-matter. Marmontel contended that Gluck was too crudely emotional; drama should move the spectator from a distance, so that tragedy gives a certain kind of pleasure:

> If one only wanted to be moved, one would go among the people to hear a mother who has lost her son, children who have lost their mother ... there undoubtedly the expression of grief is artless, and there also it is very energetic. But what pleasure would one get from these heart-rending emotions? The pangs of sorrow should be accompanied by salve for the wound ... The salve is the pleasure of the mind, or of the senses ... and it is caused by the art of the musician ...[7]

This consistent aesthetic, coupled with misunderstanding of Gluck, is inevitably reminiscent of Hanslick and Wagner.

The positive side of Marmontel's case is his plea for Italian melody. Like Burney, he says that Italian music in the days of Lully was as bad as French, but the Italians had sought true melody and

> ... their real moment of glory was when *Vinci* for the first time plotted the curve of periodic song, that song which with its pure, elegant, and logical design, presents to the ear ... the development of a fully matured thought. It was then that the great mystery of melody was revealed.[8]

---

[6] Le Blond, *Mémoires*, p. 163.
[7] Ibid., p. 167. Compare the effect of Voltaire's 'sensibilité': 'Audiences wept for Zaïre and for the impassioned Mérope ... not to purge their emotions so much as to enjoy them' (Daniel Heartz, 'From Garrick to Gluck', *Proceedings of the Royal Musical Association*, xciv (1967/68), 114).
[8] Le Blond, *Mémoires*, p. 169.

A periodic phrase-structure based generally on two- and four-bar units is admittedly an important musical phenomenon, but this description seems unnecessarily grandiose. 'La Période', however, became the war-cry of Piccinnisme. It is found, still in 1777, in La Harpe's review of *Armide*;[9] and above all in the *Discours* of Framery on music and declamation which appeared after the heat of the controversy had died down, in 1802. For Framery—which is strange in a biographer of Haydn—musical periodicity, symmetry, regularity, were canon law, to be insisted upon in instrumental music as in dance music and setting of lyric verse:

> how should they not also be required in arias [*airs de scène*] ... when the passions of the characters, heated by degrees, explode with a force which the poet and composer have produced by all the resources of their art? Would one seriously pretend that this symmetry is incompatible with disordered passions?[10]

His justification is by a parallel with verse drama:

> What could be more symmetrical or regular [*compassé*] than the Alexandrine verses with which RACINE, VOLTAIRE and others have so naturally depicted these tumults of passion? Would one want a host of sublime pieces ... in order to be even truer, rewritten in prose?[11]

Marmontel had hurled the epithet 'prosateur' at Gluck, and suggested that Gluck was to Piccinni as Shakespeare to Racine[12]—which, in eighteenth-century France, was no compliment to Gluck. It is important to remember that Framery is speaking of measured music, of the aria; not of recitative, in which free tempo is normal. He seems to forget a crucial difference between verse and music. Verse when declaimed still allows a constant fluctuation of tempo not possible in musical polyphony. Racine is not to be declaimed rigidly, but with the metre stretched, emphasis being thereby placed on important words, just as Gluck picks out particular words for emphasis in recitative. The aria requires other means, and the expressive nuance given to verse by irregularity needs to be composed. Racine remains poetry partly by virtue of the rhyme; this acts like the tonal organisation of an articulated phrase-structure which does not have to be in four-bar phrases to achieve coherence. Foreground irregularity against

---

[9] Ibid., pp. 259-70.
[10] N. E. Framery, *Discours qui a remporté le prix de musique et déclamation proposé par l'Institut National de France* ..., Paris, an X [1802], p. 20.
[11] Ibid.
[12] Le Blond, *Mémoires*, p. 180.

a background of implied regularity such as Haydn and Gluck often used is suggested by Framery's next remark: 'What the words gain in being versified, music also gains in periodic pieces, when the composer has the talent to dissimulate their regularity'.[13] Mozart was quite prepared to use regular phrases in the expression of emotional disorder, as is shown by Electra's 'Tutte nel cor vi sento' in *Idomeneo*; but he achieves it by an orchestral mastery and a harmonic daring beyond the resources of the Piccinnistes. It is not easy to see what Framery meant by dissimulation; regularity is generally quite apparent in Piccinni, and in Framery's collaborator Sacchini it is unashamedly, albeit elegantly, obvious.

Parallel to this insistence on the 'période' is the decided view the Piccinnistes take on 'dessin' (or 'dessein'), which became a Piccinniste watchword and the title of an article by Piccinni's biographer Ginguené in the *Encyclopédie méthodique*.[14] An aria should have one tempo, one metre, one basic affection, whatever contrasts are implied by the words. Piccinni reportedly

> ... criticised the tendency to change the metre and motifs suddenly in the course of an aria ... The composer who did not know how to bend the motif he had taken to the variety of expression demanded by the words ... was in his eyes nothing but a botcher [*croque-notes*].[15]

Framery's expression of this is characteristically dogmatic:

> A periodic aria contains, or should contain, only one affection ... if it contains several, they are in opposition, which forms a *rapport* between them, and still constitutes a single idea. The poetry will present it in several ways, the music repeats it in the same way.[16]

In effect, this invites the composer to set contradictory feelings to the same music. Gluck had developed a type of aria in different tempi, and had been criticised by Rousseau for this before he even reached Paris: 'Where is the unity of design? ... what we have here is no aria, but a suite of several arias'.[17] Framery made the same criticism of 'Non, ce n'est point un sacrifice' from the French *Alceste*, in an article called 'Décousu' (unstitched).[18] This aria has a rondo

---

[13] *Discours*, p. 20.
[14] *Encylopédie méthodique: Musique*, 2 vols., Paris, 1791, and Liège, 1818.
[15] P. L. Ginguené, *Notice sur la vie et les oeuvres de N. Piccinni*, Paris, an IX [1801], p. 111.
[16] *Discours*, p. 50.
[17] J. J. Rousseau, 'Fragmens d'observations sur l'Alceste italien de M. le Chevalier Gluck', *Traités sur la musique*, Geneva, 1781, p. 420.
[18] *Encyclopédie méthodique: Musique*, i. 411. See also the *Discours*, p. 17.

design, with modifications of tempo in the episodes; the main section expresses Alceste's willingness to die for her husband, the episodes her regret at being torn from him and from their children. The sectional form presents the situation from different angles; the total form expresses the resolution which overcomes her regrets. Thus, far from being disordered, as Framery asserted, it is an ordered expression of complex feelings.

Piccinniste aria was to display Italian music in its beautiful simplicity, without what Marmontel called its irrationalities, the long ritornelli and the coloratura; and contrasting affections were to be governed by one musical idea. Given an unambiguous text, a Piccinniste 'unité de dessin' is necessarily right and there are several Gluck arias to which no Piccinniste could take exception; but with complex feelings it is otherwise. Although Framery and Marmontel would have repudiated this interpretation, their method of dealing with complex feelings encourages emotional generalization; by allowing musical unity to ride roughshod over dramatic meaning, it can lead either to the reduction of emotional nuances to bland uniformity, or to complete neglect of the dramatic situation In one of Piccinni's best French operas, *Pénélope* (1785), Ulysse's return to Ithaca is the weakest part. His joy at homecoming is soured by the suitors in his palace, and he sings an aria (the text is by Marmontel):

> Quel malheur m'est prédit encore?
> N'ai-je donc pas assez souffert?
> Je te revois, isle chérie,
> Et ne puis te voir sans effroi.
> (II. 9)

Piccinni expresses only the peace for which Ulysse is longing, but which still eludes him; a placid 'andantino sostenuto' in C major which never leaves the tonic. When he sings 'J'échappe la mer en furie,/Le calme renaît pour moi,' the music, rooted to a pedal G, suggests only that calm; but the sense of the text is ironic and should have called forth some contradiction of the words, as in Gluck's 'Le calme rentre dans mon coeur'. According to Ginguené, Piccinni had firm ideas on key-change:

> Modulation . . . is not difficult in itself . . . What is difficult is to make a change of key, like all the other procedures of music, a means of just expression and proper variety.[19]

---

[19] Ginguené, *Notice*, p. 111.

THE THEORY AND PRACTICE OF PICCINNISME

Perhaps because he lacked verbal justification, Piccinni often does not change key in an aria, which is unusual in a period when stylistic expectations and formal principles alike are allied to key-change. The resultant monotony, one feels, can hardly have been the composer's intention. This criticism is applicable both to *cantabile* arias such as Atys' 'Brulé d'une flamme qui fait mon malheur' (*Atys*, I.1) and to vehement, blustering ones such as Oreste's 'Faites éclater la foudre' (*Iphigénie*, II.1), both in Piccinni's favourite key of E♭ major.

A good example of the latter type of aria, one very common with Piccinni despite his reputation for melodic sweetness, was singled out by Grimm from *Diane et Endymion* (1784) as 'the finest aria M. Piccinni has written in France'.[20] Gluck also used such ejaculatory voice parts with continuity provided by the orchestra, for example, Oreste's 'Dieux qui me poursuivez'; but he gives the orchestra material of some significance, whereas Piccinni confines it to a supporting role without building the vocal line into anything of comparable musical interest. Ginguené considered this aria to be a triumph, against difficult poetic odds, of good 'dessin':

> Almost every line contains a different affection, and would seem to require a new motif ... I am not concerned with the right or wrong of the poet's provision of so many opposed ideas in the same aria. I merely say that this aria, as it stands, would seem absolutely to exclude unity of *design*.[21]

The offending verse, by De Liroux, reads:

> Diane: Cesse d'agiter mon âme,
> Vengeance, amour sans espoir.
> Faut-il éteindre ma flamme,
> Ou céder à ton pouvoir?
> Fuis, cruelle jalousie,
> Amour, rends-moi mon amant.
> (II. 2)

Gluck's habitual method in an extended aria is to start from a low level of emotional tension and build to a climax. Even in his most Piccinnian aria, 'Alceste, au nom des Dieux', this can be seen: the short phrases based on a steady ascent of pitch, and the normal, relatively relaxing, movement from C minor to E♭ quickly countered by a return to the tonic and a powerful and unusual move to D minor. Piccinni accepts

---

[20] F. M. von Grimm, *Correspondance littéraire, philosophique, et critique*, Paris, 1813, Part III, iii. 37.
[21] *Encyclopédie méthodique: Musique*, i. 417 (art. 'Dessin').

38 THE THEORY AND PRACTICE OF PICCINNISME

the normal move from C minor to E♭. He splits up his vocal line into short phrases, and uses in his first few bars the whole vocal range, so that the intensity at the beginning is not exceeded later on (Ex. 1). The phrasing is not absolutely regular, but the expression is mainly in the harmony and dynamics—the opposition of 'vengeance', *f*, to 'amour', *p*. 'Amour' is then repeated *f* and in the drive to the first (C minor) cadence both words are absorbed into a generalized complaint; the dilemma, Diane's love for Endymion and her urge to annihilate him for loving Isménie, is barely suggested.

The couplets are neatly compartmentalized by the cadences, of a decisiveness Gluck would probably have avoided so early in an aria. The second couplet brings the modulation,

Ex. 1

which seems more easy to justify musically than by the words. If uncertainty of key reflects the uncertainty of the question ('faut-il'), it is quickly overridden by repeating the second line to establish E♭. The third couplet employs a new contrast, between major ('jalousie') and minor ('amour'); but the resumption of *tremolo*, *f*, quickly erases the contrast. The very regularity of the opposition and the continual rhythmic emphasis tend to generalize the feeling. The verse perhaps allowed little else, and Framery would have applauded; the opposed ideas are in 'rapport', constituting a single idea. But 'dessin' is achieved at the price, which Gluck would have refused to pay, of dramatic insight.

A far better aria, one of Piccinni's most successful, is Roland's 'Je me reconnais' (II.3; text by Marmontel). The hero deludes himself that he has overcome the fatal love for Angélique which has distracted him from his true *métier*, 'la gloire'. His aria is held together by its bold sweep—'dessin'—of continuous quavers, broken only for a few decisive cadences. Although much of the material is conventional, a real contrast is made between the ejaculatory opening idea and the *cantabile* 'Je crois sortir d'un long délire', which takes the place of a 'second group' in a sort of sonata form.ª Unfortunately the very length and firm structure of the aria militate against dramatic sense. Roland relapses at once: 'Malheureux, je me flatte, et ma colère est vaine'. He is in love as much as ever, but the admission is set to flimsy recitative, which cannot efface the powerful affirmation of freedom in the aria: the illusory self-control is given decisive musical form, while the moment of truth is barely noticed.

Other elements of Piccinniste opera are scarcely touched on by theorists, and there is no space to discuss them here. Of the overture, it must suffice to say that Piccinnisme takes little account of the precepts of Gluck's *Alceste* preface. The chorus is used freely, both in involvement with the action and in situations derived from traditional *divertissement*. The excellent choral lament near the end of *Atys*—the original version ended in E♭ minor in such Stygian gloom that it had to be changed—partakes of both functions, and is directly derived from Lully's practice (this was of course another Quinault libretto 'marmontelisé'). There is nothing to approach the vast choral tableaux of *Alceste*, but these were watered down for Paris.[22]

Recitative demands more consideration, since its importance matches that of the aria. It is all orchestrated, but a clear distinction is made between orchestral *secco* recitative, with short or sustained chords, and the true *accompagnato* type which was always orchestrated in Italian opera, and which Marmontel placed first among elements to be imitated therefrom.[23] The normal practice in such recitative is to interpolate orchestral material between vocal phrases, usually unaccompanied. Gluck had used it already in France, on a large scale (*Iphigénie en Aulide*, II. 7), and in this he had been anticipated by Philidor, Dauvergne (*Enée et Lavinie*, 1757), and Rameau himself, although the French tended to make both voice and orchestra more continuous (*Hippolyte et Aricie*, Act IV) and preserved the declamatory manner called by the Piccinnistes 'psalmodie'. In later French works, Gluck modified

---

[22] See F. W. Sternfeld, 'Expression and Revision in Gluck's "Orfeo" and "Alceste"', *Essays for Egon Wellesz*, ed. J. A. Westrup, London, 1966, pp. 114–29.
[23] Le Blond, *Mémoires*, p. 185: 'obbligato recitatives, where without the assistance of a clamorous orchestra, a voice, even a weak voice, upheld by a few chords, conveys to the soul all the feelings it expresses'.

his practice away from the somewhat mechanical alternation of voice and orchestra, achieving admirable effects from expressive harmonic change without interrupting the flow of words. Grétry is said to have accused Gluck of putting the statue in the orchestra, the pedestal on the stage; but Gluck took great care to make his declamation not merely correct but expressive, and in his last operas threw more weight than before on to the vocal part, at the expense of the orchestra.

Apart from passages of arioso somewhat in the French tradition, Piccinniste recitative is modelled on Italian practice. In general, however, it scarcely fulfils Marmontel's prescription. Probably difficulties with the language account for the disappointing quality of the recitative in *Roland*. Peculiarly unsuccessful is the Oresteian frenzy in *Iphigénie en Tauride* (II.1), in which the massive chords, jerky dotted rhythms and rapid scales used to depict the Furies are rendered impotent by lack of harmonic interest, and are placed between unaccompanied vocal phrases of complete blankness.[24] Piccinni certainly tried to improve his recitative, but the improvement generally takes the form of more interesting orchestral music. In *Diane et Endymion*, with no discernible dramatic significance, he uses fragments of the overture in the second scene, and in parts of *Atys* he achieves a delicate effect by confiding the accompaniment to the lower strings, with divided violas. At moments of excitement he is inclined to be hysterical. He is not without imagination, but he is without control. It might be argued that some of his characters, like Orestes, are under stress and not in control of themselves, and thus should have uncontrolled music. Apart from the fact that this argument goes clean against the views of Framery and Marmontel expressed above, the continual exaggeration, the orchestral clamour and cries as of physical anguish which Marmontel complained of in Gluck and could have heard in Piccinni, lead only to monotony. Even in Piccinni's most affecting recitative the interest of the orchestral part far outweighs the vocal, a stark contradiction of Piccinniste theory (Ex. 2).

One aspect of Gluck's reforms is generally said to have been that he made opera more continuous. This reform was scarcely necessary in France, where short arias and arioso were normal. The Italian composers who followed Gluck

[24] See Julian Rushton, 'Iphigénie en Tauride: the Operas of Gluck and Piccinni', *Music & Letters*, liii (1972), 424–7.

THE THEORY AND PRACTICE OF PICCINNISME

adapted themselves readily to this aspect of French practice, and some of Piccinni's most dramatically effective music takes the form of arioso and short aria. The arioso is used most, and to excellent effect, in the title-role of *Roland*, and the scene in which he vainly awaits Angélique in the forest

(III. 2) rivals in eloquence Lully's setting of the same scene (IV. 2). Thereafter Piccinni used less arioso, so that *Roland* is, paradoxically, at once his most Italianate French opera (because of the recitative and the nature of the arias) and his closest approach to French tradition.

The Piccinnistes also cultivated open-ended and interrupted arias. The traditional French short air, like the short aria of Gluck, is self-contained and complete; the Piccinniste short aria is usually like a long one truncated, sometimes ending in a subsidiary key. The phrasing has the feel of a full-length aria, not the terseness of Gluck. Thus while Marmontel complained 'why not finish a song once it is begun?' it was his party which adopted this technique, and only occasionally for the benefit of the drama. Sacchini, a specialist in melting arioso, was particularly addicted to the interrupted aria, and to link the final cadence of an aria to the next recitative became almost a mannerism with him. This is a form of continuity for which Gluck was not responsible and which may be termed Piccinniste. The method was adopted by Méhul, to lead not into recitative but into spoken dialogue.[25]

It is inevitable that operas of the fifteen years preceding the French Revolution should be measured against those of Gluck. Nevertheless, their style and dramatic approach are nearly always closer to Piccinni's. This is partly because Piccinni and Sacchini were members of the next generation, and they were followed by contemporaries of Mozart, whose idiom could not be expected to resemble that of a man born in 1714. Even Gluck's accredited successors, Salieri and J. C. Vogel, apart from a few echoes of Gluck, are closer to Piccinni; and most of these echoes are in *Les Danaïdes*, which passed muster for several performances as partly the work of Gluck himself.

The influence of Gluck was a general one, in that he confirmed a taste for vigorously dramatic opera with the basically Italianate musical idiom for which Marmontel pleaded. Marmontel almost admits this, but resorts to calling Gluck German and spreading the *canard* that he was despised in Italy. Piccinni could never have established such an operatic manner unaided where stronger talents than his had already failed. Even before Gluck, Philidor and Gossec, whose good qualities Gluck was happy to acknowledge, had tried unsuccessfully to establish the new musical idiom at the Opéra. Gossec's *Sabinus* (1774) was hampered by a ponderous libretto in five acts, but Philidor's *Ernelinde* (1767) is more streamlined and contains two arias that combine conflicting sentiments with impeccable 'unité de dessin'. This work has been said to anticipate Gluck, to whom it is certainly indebted, but really it is a Piccinniste opera *avant la lettre*, whose importance was acknowledged by Marmontel and

[25] See Winton Dean, 'Opera under the French Revolution', *Proceedings of the Royal Musical Association*, cxiv (1967/68), 93–95.

Ginguené.[26] Significantly it met with substantial success only in a revised version in 1777. It was Gluck, too, who restricted the use of ballet, although in his first French operas (*Iphigénie en Aulide* and *Orphée*) he was as much hampered by it as Gossec had been, or Piccinni was to be. *Iphigénie en Tauride*, however, points the way to its virtual exclusion, or its transmutation into part of the action in Salieri's *Les Horaces* (1786).

In these respects (as Tovey observed) Piccinni was himself something of a Gluckiste, and Grimm, who affected neutrality, noted that 'les zélateurs de Gluck . . . sont les plus grands partisans de Didon'.[27] It would probably be more true to say that whatever the Piccinnistes learnt from Gluck they misunderstood, and they never learnt the most important lesson, Gluck's iron control, the secret of his power: control in recitative, in placement of arias, and economy of orchestration. For one example, Gluck's use of trombones is invariably conscious of their particular tonal quality. In *Iphigénie en Tauride* (II. 3–4), when repeating essentially the same music, he uses them not as well as, but instead of, the horns; they are confined to the music of the supernatural (Furies) and mourning. Piccinnistes tend to apply trombones for the sake of volume, and in crude chordal daubs. What Gluck did for the Piccinnistes was to break down a barrier of conventions at the Opéra; in this respect he had an enormous heritage, but it remains true that he formed no school.

There were French Piccinnistes: Lemoyne (*Phèdre*, *Nephté*), Gossec (*Thésée*), Méreaux, even Philidor in parts of *Persée*. There were Italians: Salieri, Cherubini, Zingarelli, although the first two were closer to Gluck than most. There were even Germans, for J. C. Bach's one French opera (*Amadis*, 1779) is essentially a Piccinniste work by a superior composer,[28] with an interesting experiment in integration of the leitmotiv type.[29] Only Sacchini, who is still occasionally and quite falsely termed Gluck's successor, stands apart. He was so successful as to diminish Piccinni's popularity, and the Opéra in the late 1780s was divided between his highly successful

---

[26] Guingené calls it 'cet ouvrage, qui fait époque...' (*Encylopédie méthodique: Musique*, i. 620). See also Le Blond, *Mémoires*, p. 159.

[27] *Correspondance littéraire*, Part III, ii. 324.

[28] Thus I cannot accept the description of *Amadis* by Ernest Warburton ('J. C. Bach's Operas', *Proceedings of the Royal Musical Association*, xcii (1965/66), 104) as 'along outmoded lines'; the remnants of French tradition (more Quinault 'marmontelisé') are over-shadowed by Italianate music.

[29] Julian Rushton, 'An Early Essay in Leitmotiv: J. B. Lemoyne's *Electre*', *Music & Letters*, lii (1971), 398–400.

formula, which may be summarised as the evasion of dramatic responsibilities in the interests of abundant musical charm, and a tendency to cultivate the sensational and the exotic (Candeille, *Pizarre*; Salieri, *Tarare*); these last types are perhaps the true fathers of opera under the Empire and Restoration.

In practice, then, 'Piccinnisme' means opera of serious dramatic pretensions, giving free play to symmetrical musical development in arias. It differs from its Italian forbears by its freer structure, the simpler (usually mythological) plot, and the use of chorus; and from its French forbears by the musical style, the reduction of *divertissement*, and the use of long arias in contexts other than soliloquy, to which Gluck and French Baroque opera had confined them. The idea of continuity, but not the methods used, came from the French tradition and from Gluck. One can no more call such operas Gluckiste than one could term Gluck a Piccinniste. Piccinnisme is indebted to Gluck, among other influences; and within this general definition falls a wide variety of talent. In short Piccinnisme is the normal operatic practice in France (excluding opera with spoken dialogue) from about 1777 onwards; it produced no drama like *Alceste*—perhaps Gluck's most influential opera—but many like Piccinni's greatest success, *Didon*. Piccinnisme is a trend, an atmosphere; it is not a school, and to give it Piccinni's name is perhaps a convenient falsification, since at least two operas before Gluck, and Gluck himself, were aiming at the same sort of synthesis of French and Italian elements. But the failure of Philidor and Gossec, the uniqueness of Gluck, and the symbolical role of Piccinni as his rival, may justify the term.

Piccinnisme outlived the Académie Royale; as it became Nationale and Impériale, many of the pre-revolutionary operas were still played, and it contributed much to the *opéra comique* of the Revolution although by definition that was not Piccinniste. It may also be relevant, in assessing its influence, to recall Eric Blom's comment that '*Idomeneo* comes nearer in spirit to Piccinni than to Gluck'. Mozart saw *Roland* in Paris in 1778.[30] Had he been invited to write French operas, he would unquestionably have been 'Piccinniste'—influenced by Gluck and French opera, as is *Idomeneo* in places, but inclined to assert the supremacy of music over the

---

[30] The resemblance between the great quartet in *Idomeneo* and the quartet in *Atys* (performed 1780) is probably coincidental.

word and revelling in richly scored recitatives and expansive arias.

Piccinnisme was a perfectly satisfactory formula for musical drama, and it needed only a composer of substance at the Académie to exploit its possibilities. Circumstances which favoured *opéra comique* at other theatres prevented Cherubini or Méhul from being that composer, although in *Démophoön* (1788) the former showed his mastery of the idiom and a welcome excellence of orchestration. The composer who is the greatest Piccinniste is generally known by another title; Einstein[31] called him 'last of the Gluckians', Gerald Abraham[32] favours 'last of the Gluckists'. Of course, like all Piccinnistes but no more than most, Spontini was influenced by Gluck. But not only is he conspicuously Italian; his expansive, occasionally voluptuous musical manner is entirely free from Gluck's parsimony, while the continuous richness of his orchestration and the 'dessin' of his arias are Piccinniste. The Italian quality is obvious in *cantabile* writing, but his Piccinnisme is most striking in moments of great dramatic intensity. It has been well said that 'Gluck's highest pathos is in the major mode'.[33] Piccinnisme prefers to rely on the intrinsic expressiveness of the minor. Where Gluck's finest arias proceed by a steady growth in intensity to a climax ('O malheureuse Iphigénie' is perhaps the *locus classicus*), Piccinniste expression is concentrated into the main motif, and is at or near its maximum intensity from the start. Piccinniste phrasing tends to regularity, and if it has not Gluck's angular *ostinati*, it is frequently governed by an urgent rhythmic drive. Although the recitative before it is clearly indebted to *Alceste*, the Piccinniste aria *par excellence* is Julie's 'Impitoyables Dieux' from the second act of *La Vestale*.[b]

Piccinnisme appears in unexpected places, even in Gluck's most percipient nineteenth-century admirer, Berlioz. Much of the recitative in *Les Troyens* has a frenetic quality as unlike Gluck as it is unlike Wagner; it is of Piccinni that the recitatives in Cassandre's first monologue and the dialogue with Chorèbe (Act I) and Didon's monologue (Act V) may remind us, immeasurably superior in voice and orchestra though they are to any of his own. In both scenes, however, the placing and effect of the arias, especially 'Adieu, fière cité,' are Gluckian.

---

[31] *Gluck*, p. 42.
[32] 'The Best of Spontini', *Music & Letters*, xxiii (1942), 163–71.
[33] D. F. Tovey, 'Christopher Willibald Gluck', *The Heritage of Music*, ed. H. Foss, 2 vols., London, 1927 and 1934, ii. 110.

46 THE THEORY AND PRACTICE OF PICCINNISME

Thus although T. de Lajarte[34] called the period 1774–1807 'L'Epoque de Gluck' (followed by that of Spontini), the dominant style and method of the period are better exemplified by Piccinni, and it could be argued that *La Vestale* was not so much the inauguration of a new period as the culmination of the era of Piccinnisme.

The following musical illustrations were heard during the course of the lecture:

[a] Part of the aria 'Je me reconnais' from Piccinni's *Roland*, Act II, played by the author on the piano.
[b] A gramophone recording (HLP 20) of the aria 'Impitoyables Dieux', with some of the preceding recitative, from Spontini's *La Vestale*, Act II: Rita Gorr and the Philharmonia Orchestra, conducted by Lawrence Collingwood.

[34] *Bibliothèque musicale du théâtre de l'Opéra*, Paris, 1878.

[2]

RECITATIVE AND DRAMATURGY IN THE DRAMMA PER MUSICA

By Raymond Monelle

It is assumed today that Neapolitan opera was inherently undramatic, a mere singing concert. This view is linked with an assessment of *recitativo semplice* that dismisses as empty and cynical a form highly esteemed by its contemporaries. Our modern writers tell of the 'barren wastes of *secco*' that separated the arias of eighteenth-century opera; it had 'descended to an unemotional, hasty, matter-of-fact *parlando* with a few routine chords on the harpsichord'. Now, if *recitativo semplice* were proved to be an expressive and dramatic medium, these operas might be reinstated as works of dramatic as well as musical interest.

There are several reasons for our insensitivity to Neapolitan recitative. First, we have inherited the tradition of the later eighteenth century, when accompanied recitative was favoured at the expense of *recitativo semplice* and the term 'dry'—*secco*—became current for the latter kind; according to Friedrich-Heinrich Neumann, Cramer introduced the term into Germany as late as 1785.[1] Secondly, it has not been thought necessary to take the texts of these operas seriously; the poetry of Metastasio, which has always enjoyed a good reputation with at least a section of Italian literary opinion, has been consistently misunderstood by

---

[1] *Die Ästhetik des Rezitativs*, Strasbourg & Baden-Baden, 1962, p. 37 and p. 97 n. 393.

non-Italians.² Thus the medium in which most of the text was delivered is considered as perfunctory as the text is ridiculous. Another reason for our insensitivity is the extreme subtlety of musical effect in *recitativo semplice*, which makes it seem conventional and plain to all but the most attentive ears. Furthermore scholars have not had easy access to any of the highest achievements in this form: Pergolesi remained an immature composer; Vinci and Porpora are still locked in manuscript; Hasse has been represented by an oratorio, a rather unsatisfactory *dramma* and some cantatas, the recent addition of *Larinda e Vanesio* (1726) and *Ruggiero* (1771) doing little to improve the coverage of Hasse's best periods.³ The simple recitative of Gluck, Haydn and Mozart is decadent.

The proper approach would be to take a significant opera from the greatest period and apply to it criteria drawn from contemporary writers. The *dramma per musica* probably reached its high point in the 1730s, before the taste for accompanied recitative began to distort the aesthetic emphasis of the form. Quite clearly, it is to those operas which have been most ignored that we must turn if we wish to understand simple recitative; for these are the works with the minimum of purely musical effects. Not only has our preoccupation with arias, ensembles, choruses, sinfonias focussed our attention on the period after 1750; it has also tended to draw us to works written for non-Italian stages, since the emphasis on simple recitative continued much later in Italy. Hermann Abert, for example, gave more attention to Jommelli's Stuttgart operas than to his *Creso* and *Temistocle*, written in 1757 for Italian theatres.⁴

Contemporary writing on *recitativo semplice* is summarized by Neumann and Downes.⁵ The most extensive account is Friedrich Wilhelm Marpurg's series of articles in the *Kritische Briefe*.⁶ The greater part of this treatise is concerned with punctuation and its musical treatment; there is some consideration of key and modulation, but only with regard to what is possible and correct. That is to say, there is very little regard for the expressive qualities of recitative. Perhaps this is to be expected of a German in the 1760s: Marpurg's distrust of his readers' Italian is shown by the German translations that he furnishes for samples of Italian recitative, and by his taking a German sacred text for his own composed illustrations. Often he seems to state the obvious (for instance, when he warns against placing a full close on a final weak syllable),⁷ so this essay must have

---

² See my article 'The Rehabilitation of Metastasio', *Music & Letters*. lvii (1976), 268–91.
³ *La conversione di Sant' Agostino*, ed. A. Schering ('Denkmäler deutscher Tonkunst', xx), Leipzig, 1905; *Arminio*, ed. R. Gerber ('Das Erbe deutscher Musik', xxvii–xxviii), Mainz, 1957 & 1966; four solo cantatas, ed. S. H. Hansell, in the series 'Le Pupitre', Paris, 1968; *Larinda e Vanesio*, ed. L. Bettarini, Milan, n.d.; *Ruggiero*, ed. K. Hortschansky ('Concentus musicus', i), Cologne, 1973.
⁴ *Niccolo Jommelli als Opernkomponist*, Halle, 1908, pp. 346 ff.
⁵ Neumann, op. cit.; E. O. Downes, 'Secco Recitative in Early Classical Opera', *Journal of the American Musicological Society*, xiv (1961), 50–69.
⁶ *Kritische Briefe über die Tonkunst*, ii (Berlin 1762–3), 253–416.
⁷ p. 350.

been intended for the German amateur or apprentice, rather than the professional opera composer. It has, however, certain large virtues. It shows beyond doubt that recitative was scrupulously matched to the punctuation and sense of the text; the examples, taken from Hasse and Graun, are conclusive evidence of this. But Marpurg's principles can mostly be applied to any recitative by a major composer. He introduces terms for the types of musical punctuation, like 'schwebender' and 'periodischer Absatz', and shows how they fit textual punctuation, the real and unreal full-stop, colon, semi-colon, full and half comma, and the interrogatory and parenthetical marks. There are excellent words of general advice: modern taste, says Marpurg, does not favour realism in recitative, like the setting of 'Himmel' to a rising figure and 'Erde' to a falling one.[8] Harmonic freedoms and enharmony must not be multiplied, as operatic recitative has to be learnt by heart. Plenty of rests should be written; they deter the inexperienced singer from rushing senselessly onward.[9]

Nevertheless, when Marpurg comes to analyse his example, his chief concern is clearly the close following of the rhetorical details of the text, without regard for general expressiveness. Such a discussion is insufficient to counter the attacks of later opponents of the Italian tradition like Gluck and Wagner. However impresssive was the fidelity of an Italian composer to his text, it must also be shown that he had a regard for dramaturgy: dramatic rhythm, characterization, variety of diction and expression within an overall plan—these things must be discussed if the *dramma per musica* is to be compared with other great manifestations of operatic art. Here Marpurg is found wanting. For instance, he does not tell us that his example from Hasse's *Ezio* (beginning 'Signor, vincemmo') is the opening of Ezio's majestic speech in scene 2 of Act I, which follows a short and characteristically problematic first scene in which Massimo is revealed to be the secret enemy of the emperor. Scene 1 is a foil for the bellicose sinfonia that begins scene 2, and the flourish with which the victorious general Ezio enters the action. His heroic speech, describing the flight of the defeated Huns, is naturally full of varied emphasis and an ideal specimen for Marpurg to dissect.

In some degree, then, our desire to follow contemporary criticism in our examination of recitative is frustrated. The German writer is too concerned with the minutiae and rudiments of recitative composition; the Italians are silent on the matter. As Neumann found, they concern themselves with general issues—whether recitative is a 'singing speech' or a 'speaking song'—and they discuss practical problems, like the anticlimax after an aria and how it might be avoided, but they help very little with the question of

[8] p. 281.
[9] p. 267.

expressiveness.

If our investigation is to be empirical we may take two comments of Marpurg as starting-points. First, he assumes a distinction between 'historisches' and 'pathetisches Recitativ', saying for example that change of key depends in historic recitative on punctuation, in pathetic recitative on the rise and fall of *Affekt*.[10] Unfortunnately he does not explain how the types are distinguished, though it is clear that they are not synonyms for *semplice* and *stromentato*, or theatrical and chamber recitative, as these distinctions have already been made in the previous chapter.

Secondly Marpurg speaks of 'rhetorical accent', of which he gives several examples.[11] The stressing of a word is always accomplished with a high note, either higher than all its neighbours or higher than the following note. The difference in pitch need not be more than a semitone. His example is a setting of the text 'Ist das der Trost? sind das die Freuden?'. Although the word 'das' falls on a weak beat in both cases, it is each time sung to the highest note of the phrase. However, the note before the accent may be at the same pitch as the note bearing the accent, provided the following note is perceptibly lower. Sometimes the highest note comes on the syllable before that to be emphasized, giving a kind of reflected accent: in a setting of 'Sein Schicksal ist nicht grausam' the word 'nicht' is in fact sung to the highest note, but an accent on the appoggiatura of 'grausam' is intended, this word falling on a strong beat.

A style of word-setting which can be both historic and pathetic, which can exploit various kinds of accent or can be unaccented, this is already taking the shape of a true dramatic style. But what is meant by 'historic' and 'pathetic'? Much careful reading of recitative reveals that there are two basic styles which are usually, but by no means always, associated with certain kinds of action and feeling. The first of these is predominantly major and diatonic, venturing no further into dissonance than the dominant seventh, and often containing triadic figures. It is used for ordinary dialogue and narrative, and for the expression of noble and joyful sentiments. The other kind is typified by the diminished seventh both melodic and harmonic, both implicit and explicit. It is largely in minor keys, makes use of dissonant intervals including the diminished and augmented fourth both in melody and bass, and is often chromatic—though here one must be cautious, for there are certain chromatic effects which are normal in the first kind, like the rising chromatic bass for increasing excitement. This second style is associated with amorous sentiments and with paternal and filial tenderness. Both kinds can be accented or unaccented. Sometimes, of course, one or other of these types of setting is selected with no apparent justification in the

[10] p. 263.
[11] pp. 279–81.

text. But there are points where the swing from one style to the other is so obviously connected with the feeling of the text that one can justifiably adopt Marpurg's terminology and call the first style of setting 'historic', the second 'pathetic'.

Often a single scene contains a mixture of historic and pathetic recitative according to the content and rhythm of the text. Such a scene is selected here as an example. Hasse's *Il re pastore* was almost contemporary with his *Ezio*. In the first scene Aminta and Elisa, who are ostensibly a shepherd and a shepherdess, and are in love, are speaking of the occupation of Sidon, their homeland, by the army of Alessandro. Although Aminta fears for Elisa's safety under war conditions, Elisa insists that Alessandro is a hero and therefore honourable. The two expository themes of this section—the lovers' feelings and Alessandro's power and honour—cause an alternation of styles in the recitative. 'Why do you expose yourself all alone', asks Aminta, 'to the insolent licence of the military?' 'My only fear', replies Elisa, 'is that I may not see you'. Into this tender and demure reply Metastasio writes a rhyme, and it causes an immediate shift into pathetic recitative (Ex. 1). Here every feature is pathetic. The two keys are minor. The initial move of the bass is an augmented second, and the resultant dominant chord becomes a diminished seventh almost at once. The last phrase, in leaping an augmented fourth, gives an implied diminished seventh, outlined by the g' and the $a'\sharp$.

Ex. 1

In the following lines Elisa expresses her 'felici speranze', which she wishes to share. But Aminta anxiously suggests that they find somewhere safer for their conversation, to which Elisa protests that his anxiety is a slight to Alessandro's virtue. These practical considerations and especially the mention of the heroic Alessandro, cause a return to historic style (Ex. 2). The shift from A minor to D major is adroitly managed.[12] But Aminta's common-sense interrup-

Ex. 2

[12] The figuring is from the manuscript (in the Reid Library, University of Edinburgh), which is unusually rich in figures.

tion is already diatonic and triadic. Elisa's protest is a little fanfare on a major triad, aptly evoking the hero; it is also syncopated, beginning a quaver early—Elisa is 'of the noble line of Cadmus' and cannot bear an insult to a man of honour. The rest of her protest is quieter, more poised, a nice sequel to her impulsive burst. The whole passage is major-mode, diatonic, triadic, and ends with a typical cadence using a dominant seventh.

Two more examples may be given from the same scene. Metastasio's characters are often close to comic opera, and Elisa in this scene is a lightly-drawn character, young, impulsive, sentimental, typically Metastasian. When, in the middle of a narrative she mentions her mother, she cannot resist a little puerile rapture and Hasse switches at once to a pathetic effect which is almost ludicrous (Ex. 3).

Historic recitative is not merely neutral and suitable only for perfunctory narratives and expository dialogue. It can be strongly accented and it can express joyful or loyal feelings. The end of this scene is an instance. Elisa is happy in their apparently fortunate love and anticipates marriage. 'Soon', she cries, 'I need never leave you again: the sun shall see us always together' (Ex. 4). 'Oh dolce vita' receives here a stronger accent than any we have seen and is syncopated like many of Elisa's exclamations. The tritone within the dominant seventh chord is regarded as diatonic and is freely used, even as a melodic interval, in passages that are not pathetic.

Hasse's *Il re pastore*, a late work like *Ezio*, is less interesting to the student of *recitativo semplice* than many earlier operas. The 1730 version of *Artaserse* is of special interest for a number of reasons. It was Hasse's first Metastasio setting, and he set it simultaneously with Vinci, Vinci writing for Rome and Hasse for Venice. Certain parts of the text were specially altered for Hasse, by Metastasio himself according to Charles de Brosses.[13] Hasse often revived his *Artaserse*, never wholly abandoning the music of the first version. In 1734 he turned it into a pasticcio for the London stage; in 1740 and 1760 he adapted it radically for Dresden, scores of both these adaptations having survived. Sonneck in his article on the three versions pointed out that the score in the British Library (Add. MS 32582) represents the original 1730 opera, not the London pasticcio.[14] Only after 1760 did Hasse become Metastasio's regular collaborator, so this apparent early collaboration is of outstanding interest.

The text alone is considered important by sympathetic students of Metastasio. Walter Binni considers *Demofoonte* and *L'Olimpiade* the dual climax of Metastasio's career and *Artaserse* 'the most notable result of the phase of trials and experiments' before 1733.[15] In structure it is a remarkable example of Metastasio's dramatic rhythm. Binni comments: 'Already the external plot assumes its function as bearer of the internal plot of sentiments and their poetic expression'.[16] The purpose of action is to generate perplexity, elegiac sadness, dilemmas of the heart, and the dramatist begins each part of his structure with some action or peripeteia, usually expressed in recitative, then allows characters to react in different ways, naturally flowing into arias with different *Affekte*. In *Artaserse* this is as true of the whole opera as it is of the sections and acts; there is very little action in Act III except for the mechanical denouement of the final scene.

A synopsis of the plot is necessary to any further discussion. The acts are divided into sections according to the changes of scene.

ACT I SECTION i (scenes 1–7)
Arbace, the bosom friend of Prince Artaserse, is in love with Artaserse's sister Mandane. Their father King Serse has forbidden the lovers to meet as Arbace is a commoner. The opera begins with their last farewells in the palace garden.

But Arbace's father, Artabano, ambitious for his son, has assassinated the king (offstage) in the hope of getting the princes, Artaserse and his brother Dario, to destroy each other so that Arbace can usurp the throne. He changes swords with Arbace and urges him to flee with the bloody weapon. Artaserse, distracted, is easily persuaded that his brother was the murderer and hastily orders his execution.

Artaserse rushes away, leaving Semira, Arbace's sister, desolate,

---

[13] *Lettres historiques et critiques sur l'Italie*, Paris, [1799], iii. 278.
[14] O. G. Sonneck, 'Die drei Fassungen der Hasse'schen "Artaserse"', *Sammelbände der internationalen Musikgesellschaft*, xiv (1912–13), 226–42.
[15] *L'Arcadia e il Metastasio*, Florence, 1963, p. 350.
[16] Ibid.

for she loves Artaserse. A conspirator called Megabise tries to make love to Semira. She spurns him, and left alone, she foresees that she must lose her beloved whether he wins or loses: for Artaserse, becoming king, must reject her commoner's hand.

SECTION ii (scenes 8–15)
Dario has been duly killed by Artabano, but Artaserse is horrified when the news arrives that Dario was not guilty as the real culprit has been caught. The malefactor is brought to him: it is his friend Arbace, who was taken while fleeing with the sword.

Each of the major characters reacts in an aria, Artaserse, Artabano, Semira. Mandane, refusing to credit her lover's innocence, is left to close the act.[17]

ACT II SECTION i (scenes 1–7)
Artabano speaks in private to his son: by a new plot the means of flight is offered to Arbace. Arbace rejects this and reproaches his father.

Artabano and Megabise decide to attack Artaserse at once; but Semira is promised to Megabise to secure his fidelity. She is told of this peremptorily. If Megabise really loves her, she says, he may prove it by refusing this marriage. Not likely! replies Megabise, somewhat coarsely.

Semira and Mandane express their conflicting feelings.

SECTION ii (scenes 8–15)
Mandane, before the assembled peers, demands her lover's death; Semira implores mercy, in an effective scene copied from Corneille's *Le Cid*. Artaserse cannot bear to judge his best friend, so in a typical *coup de théâtre* he consigns the judgement to Arbace's own father Artabano. Artabano condemns his son to conceal his own guilt. With feminine inconsistency Mandane turns on him angrily, and Semira reproaches Artaserse. Artaserse and Artabano compare their predicaments.

Artabano, left alone, is maddened with remorse, singing a very effective *recitativo stromentato* and aria.[18]

ACT III SECTION i (scenes 1–4)
Artaserse visits his friend in prison. He wishes Arbace to escape, and will put it out that he has been killed. Arbace refuses, so Artaserse makes it a royal command.

Artabano cannot find his son. Megabise, insolent and confident, tells him to pull himself together. Artaserse will be poisoned by the sacred cup with which he swears the royal oath.

SECTION ii (scenes 5–7)
Semira brings to Mandane false news of Arbace's death: mad with grief, she accuses Mandane of having caused it.

Arbace comes in time to prevent Mandane from killing herself. They sing a duet full of perplexity.

SECTION iii (scenes 8–10)
Artaserse delivers his coronation speech. As he goes to drink from the sacred cup, a rebellion is reported; then comes news that it has been quashed by Arbace, who is alive after all, and Megabise has been

---

[17] In Metastasio's original plan as set by Vinci and published in the Metastasio editions (Venice, 1733–58, and Paris, 1755–7) Mandane departs, leaving Arbace to finish the act. Hasse omits this closing scene of Arbace.

[18] De Brosses specifically mentions this scene as having been specially written for Hasse (see above, note 13).

killed.

Artaserse asks Arbace, who now enters, to swear innocence of his previous crimes by drinking of the sacred cup. Artabano cannot bear to see his son die and blurts out that the cup is poisoned.

Artabano shall die, orders Artaserse. Arbace will not allow this, asking to die with his father. Artaserse, impressed with the son's fidelity, changes the sentence to exile. At last Artaserse can marry Semira and Arbace Mandane.

Each of the first two acts begins with an expository passage in which certain offstage developments, plots or murders, are reported, and ends with a passage of sentimental drama, the situations being strikingly reversed: Artabano, source of all the action, is successful in Act I, full or remorse in Act II. Almost the whole of Act III is sentimental interreaction. The feelings of the friends, of the father, of the sister, of the lovers, are portrayed in turn. This is the technique called *sfaccettamento* (cutting into facets) by Claudio Varese in the definitive study of Metastasio's dramaturgy.[19] Only in the pantomimic *dénouement* of the *scena ultima* does any action occur.

Binni in fact finds the 'logical schematism' of this opera too clear for its artistic health.[20] Not only is the layout of the plot schematic; the characters also are parallelled and contrasted. For example Mandane and Smira are chiastically sister and beloved of Artaserse and Arbace, and their reactions can be matched nicely, as they are in the scene copied from Corneille. Artabano is balanced between his son's loyalty and Megabise's opportunism, being fatally susceptible to both. In Artabano Binni finds a really interesting malefactor; his remorse is caused not by abstract scruples as in other operas, but by his paternal feelings. Binni discerns an especially pure relation of recitative and aria in this piece. He gives as an example the conventional aria of Megabise in Act I, 'Sogna il guerrier le schiere', which would normally be a picturesque irrelevance, a trace of the opera's kinship with pastoral occasional works. Here, Megabise has just assailed Semira with his impudent offer of love, she being already deeply troubled. This aria is pure insolence. 'I can't help dreaming of you—it has become second nature'. Thus the aria echoes the close of the recitative.

> Quando il costume
> Si converta in natura,
> L'alma quel che non ha sogna e figura.

> Sogna il guerrier le schiere,
> Le selve il cacciator,
> E sogna il pescator
> Le reti e l'amo.

---

[19] *Saggio sul Metastasio*, Florence, 1950. Unfortunately Varese does not discuss *Artaserse* at any length.

[20] Binni speaks of an 'eccesso di schematismo che è pure corrispettivo della tensione a sintetizzare l'analisi della situazione e del sentimento' (op. cit., p. 350 n. 1).

Sopito in dolce oblio,
Sogno pur io così
Colei, che tutto il dì
Sospiro e chiamo.

When its habits become its very nature, the soul pictures and dreams of that which it has not.

The warrior dreams of armies,
The hunter of woods,
The fisherman dreams
Of nets and hooks.
   Thus soothed in sweet oblivion,
   Even I dream
Of her whom all the day I sigh and call for.

Similar examples may be found in the arias which close Act I. Artabano's refusal of pity to his son is expressed in an aria:

ARBACE	Senta pietà del figlio il padre almeno.
ARTABANO	Non ti son padre, Non mi sei figlio . . .

ARBACE	At least my father must feel pity for his son.
ARTABANO	I am not your father, You are not my son . . .

And so is Semira's rejection of her brother:

ARBACE	M'ascolti, mi compianga almen Semira.
SEMIRA	Torna innocente, e poi T'ascolterò, se vuoi . . .

ARBACE	At least Semira will listen to me and sympathize.
SEMIRA	Be innocent again, and then I will listen, if you wish . . .

In reviewing the music of this opera, certain features are apparent. First, the close integration of every theme and phrase, especially where this adds to coherence. In recitative a phrase may be echoed where the text discusses the same matter on two occasions. In the first scene Mandane and Arbace are discussing her father, Serse. Arbace hates Serse for prohibiting their meetings, of course. Contradicting Mandane neatly, he takes up her original phrase at the same pitch, but changing the harmony, leads it into another key (Ex. 5).

Ex. 5

MANDANE	No, I have no hopes that your heart, hating my father, can love his daughter.
ARBACE	But this hatred, Mandane, is a proof of my love.

A more extensive example is to be found in scene 6 of the same act, where Megabise tries to win Semira over, and she demands that he forget her. He insolently advises: 'Choose a lover who is your social equal. You should know that love thrives on equality' (Ex. 6).

Ex. 6

Semira's reply matches this: 'But I wish to give you different advice in return, and it seems to me more apposite than yours: cease to love me' (Ex. 7). The second figure, Megabise's 'uguale al grado tuo', is clearly copied, and his following two figures are conflated in Semira's 'e parmi più opportuno del tuo', the falling fourth, originally a setting of 'l'amore', now being underlined by its ironic crotchets; when the fourth of the close comes on the same notes as a setting of 'lascia d'amarmi', the antithesis is plain.

Ex. 7

As for Binni's point about the unity of recitative and aria, there is some evidence that the composer aimed at a similar unity. For example, in Act III scene 5 Semira taunts the already distressed Mandane with having caused the death of Arbace, calling her 'crudel, inumana'. The momentum does not cease as recitative runs out into aria.

255

MANDANE	Taci, parti da me.
SEMIRA	Ch'io parta e taccia?
	Fin che vita ti resta,
	Sempre intorno m'avrai; sempre importuna
	Rendere i giorni tuoi voglio infelici.
MANDANE	E quando io meritai tanti nemici?
	Mi credi spietata?
	Mi chiami crudele?
	Non tanto furore,
	Non tante querele,
	Ché basta il dolore
	Per farmi morir.

MANDANE	Be silent, leave me.
SEMIRA	You ask me to go away and be silent? As long as you live I shall always be near you; I wish by constant nagging to make your life unpleasant.
MANDANE	And when did I come to deserve so many enemies? You think me pitiless? You call me cruel? Grief scarcely needs So much fury, So many complaints, To kill me.

The last line of recitative (Ex. 8a) with its uncommon falling triad may be compared with the aria theme in its orchestral and vocal versions (Exx. 8b and 8c). The end of the recitative, a normal question formula, would be sung as an appoggiatura, and this reappears in the aria theme.

Ex. 8
(a) MANDANE

(b) (Allegro)

(c)

The first act of this opera, with its neat pattern, merits a closer examination. The perfectly contrived rhythm of its two sections can be tabulated (Table I). The second section is perhaps a model of the Metastasian plan, all recitative at the start but with many arias later, the characters having been gradually massed on the stage so that each can depart with an aria. The earlier scenes in each

TABLE I

SECTION i			SECTION ii		
Scene	Characters on stage	Whether aria	Scene	Characters on stage	Whether aria
1	2	aria	8	2	
2	2	aria	9	3	
3	3	Metastasio's aria omitted	10	4	
4	2		11	6	Metastasio's aria omitted
5	3	aria	12	5	aria
6	2	aria	13	4	aria
7	1	aria	14	3	aria
			15	1	aria

section are much longer than the later: scene 1 is extremely long, scene 7 has only eight lines. The last scene, Mandane's soliloquy, is mostly *stromentato*.

How does the musical setting enhance this rhythm? Section i exemplifies the process. It clearly has a dramatic accelerando in its midst, heightened by Hasse's omission of the aria in scene 3. Binni sees the whole process as flowing out of the tender but ominous first scene.

> The whole of the first act is already exemplary for the true Metastasian tone and the poetic possibilities of its language; the pathetic opening, with a long farewell for the two lovers Arbace and Mandane ... leads aptly, in harmony with the dolorous atmosphere which suggests a night of horror and trouble, evoked by a dense and sober air ... to a series of scenes, well conceived and convincing, which present all the characters in pathetic action and reaction.[21]

This opening is predictably a fine instance of 'pathetic recitative'. It is night; the lovers are meeting secretly in a moonlit garden. There is already an undertone of danger ('Questo real soggiorno periglioso è per te'), but Arbace and Mandane are shown as sincere and dignified. The slowish pace of the dialogue is betrayed by the variety of rhythmic values, especially the crotchets, and the frequent rests and strong accents. At the point where Mandane bursts into tears may be seen the musical counterpart of what Binni calls 'the sentimental exploration [*scavo*] that would fascinate Leopardi: "Perhaps I shall never see you again; maybe this is our last time together" ' (Ex. 9). As Mandane's head falls on to Arbace's shoulder

Ex. 9

[21] *L'Arcadia e il Metastasio*, pp. 351–2.

Maybe this is our last time together... oh God... you are weeping! Ah! do not weep, my love. I am weak enough, without your tears.

there is an interruption in the rising chromatic bass, and when this is resumed the next step, $f\sharp$, is an augmented second away, a very tart movement. In spite of this the upward sequence is retained, so that the setting of 'I am weak enough, without your tears' echoes, poignantly, the moment when her tears began to flow. Mandane's tears were provoked by the slow crotchets, strong accent and diminished seventh that began this passage, the heart-rending climax of Arbace's speech. The following accents are progressively stronger, the word 'pianger' on its second occurrence being sung to a descending tritone, the harmony being presumably a diminished seventh.

Mandane's lovely exit aria 'Conservati fedele' is one of those limpid, lyrical pieces which are the essence of Hassian opera and match Metastasio's 'vibrazione patetica'. Its theme, as presented in the ritornello (Ex. 10), contains not only a delicate, tremulous setting of the first line, but a reflection of two ideas later in the text.

> Conservati fedele;
> Pensa ch'io resto e peno,
> E qualche volta almeno
> Ricordati di me:
>   Ch'io per virtù d'amore,
> Parlando col mio core,
> Ragionerò con te.
>
> > Remain faithful:
> > Think of me, staying behind and grieving,
> > And at least occasionally
> > Remember me.
> >   Think of me, conversing with you
> > By talking to my own heart,
> > Through the power of love.

The word 'peno' suggests a change to the tonic minor—later 'io peno' is repeated by the singer in that key—and the charming notion of the silent communion of hearts is represented by soft echoes of

258

Ex. 10 Moderato

short phrases: the last figure of the ritornello occurs in this manner after the second stanza, ending 'ragionerò con te', has been sung. The effect of a tremulous heart is reinforced by a gentle *Trommelbass*.

The second scene brings an instant change of tone both in text and music. This is a rapid, urgent exchange (Ex. 11): Artabano

Ex. 11

ARTABANO	Arbace, my son.
ARBACE	Sir.
ARTABANO	Give me your sword.
ARBACE	Here it is.
ARTABANO	Take mine, fly, hide this blood from every gaze.
ARBACE	Ye gods!

must get rid of the sword as soon as he can. The equal values, both of notes and rests, the stationary basses, in spite of alternation of speakers, the simple harmonies, the absence of rests on two occasions, the rapped 'Eccolo', all betray haste, the singers almost toppling over each other. Nevertheless this is more than a mere action scene, for Arbace, not yet knowing who his father's victim was, is full of dark forebodings and continually arrests the flow with a strong accent or a pathetic effect. His aria which closes the scene is more than the expected *presto-cum-tremolando* affair that its text might seem to require.[22]

---

[22] Its text resembles 'Fra mille furori' (*Ciro riconosciuto*, Act I scene 10), which John Brown quotes as an *aria infuriata* ('Mr. John Brown, painter', *Letters upon the Poetry and Music of the Italian Opera*, Edinburgh, 1789, p. 108).

259

> Fra cento affanni e cento
> Palpito, tremo e sento
> Che freddo dalle vene
> Fugge il mio sangue al cor.
>> Amidst hundred upon hundred of troubles
>> I palpitate, I tremble, and I feel
>> My blood rushing cold
>> From my veins to my heart.

Instead of this it is a piece in moderate tempo with a shuddering accompaniment on violas and second violins; it is in such a piece that the tradition of picturesque or realistic orchestration (the illustration of blood rushing to the heart) is passing over into direct emotional expression, for this is a very dramatic aria, and fills out Arbace as a character: loyal to his beloved and to his father, he is capable of emotions deeper than conventional amorousness or terror.

The core of this section follows, two scenes in historic recitative and without arias, in which the death of Serse becomes known to Artaserse and the murder of Dario is prepared. Nevertheless the characterization goes forward in the recitative. In scene 4 the contrast of Megabise and Artaserse is apt (Ex. 12). Megabise happens to have a high soprano voice, suiting his resolute insolence, while Artaserse is a tenor, a voice associated with comic opera. Megabise's bass and most of his vocal figures have an upward tendency; a single diminished seventh—Artaserse's 'private offences' —is quickly gone, and he ends with a bright major cadence. Artaserse droops; he has cold feet over the forthcoming murder and his two harmonic movements are typical, each an inversion of the dominant seventh with voice and bass falling—in fact most of his basses and vocal figures fall in this scene.

Ex. 12

This section is not the close of an act. It must lead smoothly to a scene change and a further section before the resort to sentimental reaction and, in this case, *recitativo stromentato* and an *aria di bravura*. Nevertheless the tempo slows a little from scene 5 on. Artaserse—never a wholly satisfactory character—offends Semira by having to rush away, and stung with remorse he bursts out before he leaves with an aria imploring pity: 'Have I not troubles enough already?'[23] This encounter of the stiff Semira and the drooping Artaserse is faintly droll, and his aria must be called merely decorative; it makes much of a tiny ornamental figure from its second bar. But it has poise and charm and provides a relaxation, especially when compared to the previous aria.

A long scene for Semira and Megabise follows. It is virtually irrelevant except in that Semira learns of Serse's death, and the two characters are elaborated. Megabise displays outrageous sangfroid: 'Let the blood of the contending brothers be shed, let it inundate the throne, I am indifferent who wins', while Semira moralizes: 'In the disasters of a kingdom everyone has a part, and in a faithful subject indifference is culpable' (Ex. 13a). Her tone is not pathetic but very poised, the bass describing a calm cadential sequence, the key stable. Megabise later slights Semira's loyalty and seriousness—which seem in any case a bit heavy—by attributing them to her love for Artaserse. This is enhanced by his singing the jibe to the very music in which Semira had moralized (Ex. 13b). Her continuation was

Ex. 13

tame, in equal values, unaccented, falling to a docile close in C. Megabise already promises spicier things with his chromatic shift; in fact, he goes on to point out that Semira will lose Artaserse whether he defeats Dario or is killed by him. Their exchange of 'consigli' follows,[24] and Megabise sings his 'Sogna il guerrier le schiere', a bright piece with coloratura, the final affront to Semira and a truly comic touch, with a commonplace swaggering theme.

[23] 'Per pietà, bell'idol mio,/Non mi dir ch'io sono ingrato:/Infelice e sventurato/Abbastanza il Ciel mi fa.'

[24] See above, p. 255.

Semira's closing scene occupies the position which in later sections demands *stromentato*. Her noble resolve to renounce Artaserse so that he can ascend the throne is a sentiment not quite warm enough for this; nor should it be, coming in the midst of an act. The aria concluding the scene is neither an *aria di bravura* like that closing this act, nor an aria of high drama like that closing Act II. The entire scene is therefore in simple recitative (Ex. 14). Semira's

Ex. 14

You gods, protectors of Persia, preserve Artaserse for this empire. Ah! I lose him if he triumphs over Dario. As a subject he desired my hand, as a king he will disdain it. But what do I say? Is not so worthy a life worth more than my grief? May I lose my beloved, so that he may reign, and so that he may live. If I demanded that he die, so as not to be deprived of him, I should be wicked. No, I do not repent of my vow, O gods.

invocation to the gods of Persia, triadic and statuesque, is partially recapitulated at the end ('Per non esserne priva, / Se lo bramassi estinto'), and since the final cadence resembles the setting of 'conservate Artaserse' the whole final passage may be regarded as an extension of the opening, with the last key changed to match the succeeding aria. In between come two passages, each beginning with a figure like that on 'deità protettrici', that is, containing a falling fifth. Each refers to the loss of Artaserse, first in dread ('Ah! ch'io lo perdo, se trionfa di Dario') and afterwards with heroic resolve ('Si perda, / Purché regni il mio bene') the first leading to G minor, the second to G major, because of the contrast of sentiment. Between these are clearly related passages in D minor ('Bramò vassallo') and D major ('Forse non vale il mio dolor'), the change of mode again matching Semira's change of heart, which occurs at the precise moment of the mode change ('Ma che? Sì degna vita . . .'). The whole scene, apart from its tight structure, which may be represented as A B C (x) C B A, is admirably restrained and dignified, even expressive, especially at 'empia sarei', a figure which is external to the pattern. The two perverse cadences should be observed, too, since they mark psychological changes. The aria, 'Bramar di perdere', is a stately, melodious piece, what John Brown called an *aria di portamento*.[25] It halts the dramatic impetus and prepares the way for a new section.

Later Arbace's steadfastness causes the breakdown of his father's nerve, and he becomes a progressively more powerful character. In Act II scene 11, when Artabano, appointed judge of his son, begins to list the evidence against him, their developed relationship is typified (Ex. 15). Lists were often sung over a pedal, and here Artabano assumes a cool, dignified stance in D minor. But Arbace sweeps the argument out of his hands, continuing in a rush up the arpeggio and descending over an emotional and unexpected diminished seventh, ending with a pungent tritone in the cadence. Artabano can only go on tamely in E minor.

[25] Op. cit., pp. 57–67.

When the end of the act comes this development is underlined. Mandane has changed, too; from being a haughty lover she has tried to affect disdain, and failed. Now she turns on Artabano for condemning Arbace, though this was what she demanded. The last three arias of Act II consummate these character changes. The second section of the act proceeds entirely in simple recitative until the cluster of arias that ends it. Thus it matches the corresponding section of Act I. First Arbace masters his transport of feeling and with superb self-possession kneels to ask his father's forgiveness.

> Ah, genitor, perdona:
> Eccomi a' piedi tuoi; scusa i trasporti
> D'un insano dolor. Tutto il mio sangue
> Si versi pur, non me ne lagno; e, in vece
> Di chiamarla tiranna,
> Io bacio quella man che mi condanna.

> Ah, father, forgive me: see, I kneel to you; excuse the transports of my crazed grief. May all my blood be shed before I utter any complaint; and instead of calling it cruel I kiss the hand that condemns me.

Artabano is defeated. His facade of stern reproof cannot hold out against the true uprightness of his son. Beginning in E major he waves Arbace haughtily aside. But the harmony goes to pieces; in an access of tritones and false relations, he embraces his son (Ex. 16).

Ex. 16

> It is enough: arise: there is good reason for your grief. But take heed ... (Oh God!) let me embrace you, and you must go.

The way is clear for Arbace's lovely aria in E major, the key of sorrowful partings.[26]

[26] J. Mattheson, *Das neu-eröffnete Orchestre*, Hamburg, 1713, p. 250.

> Per quel paterno amplesso,
> Per questo estremo addio
> Conservami te stesso,
> Placami l'idol mio,
> Difendimi il mio re.
>
>> Swear by this fatherly embrace,
>> By this final farewell,
>> That you will preserve yourself, for my sake,
>> That you will console my beloved,
>> That you will defend my king.

Arbace is clearly the moral victor. Now Mandane comes forward to reinforce Artabano's regret and confusion. In the recitative her wrath mounts, the music pressing constantly upward, and her aria, textually conventional, is musically stupendous.

> Va tra le selve ircane
> Barbaro genitore,
> Fiera di te peggiore
> Mostro peggior non v'è.
>
>> There roams the Hyrcanian forests
>> No worse monsters,
>> No worse wild beasts
>> Than you, violent father.

A tremolando accompaniment begins; the first violins storm in, then the two horns; later come prickly coloratura, with concertante of horns and voice, and gruesome chromatic effects.

Metastasio had organised a small relaxation before Artabano's solo scene; in two short scenes Semira reproached Artaserse, and Artaserse sang a little sententiously of the comparative positions of Artabano and himself. Hasse's drama has gathered too much force for these slighter matters to tell, and he omits both arias, Semira's and Artaserse's. We are hustled into the masterly closing scene with its variant text, set almost wholly in *stromentato*. The final aria not only differs in spirit from Metastasio's original, but lacks the conventional pastoral reference which was often a chance for *gran' bravura*. The original text, set by Vinci and published in the editions of Metastasio, ran as follows.

> Così stupisce e cade,
> Pallido e smorto in viso,
> Al fulmine improvviso,
> L'attonito pastor.
>   Ma, quando poi s'avvede
> Del vano suo spavento,
> Sorge, respira e riede
> A numerar l'armento
> Disperso dal timor.

Thus the astonished shepherd, / When lightning flashes unforeseen, / Is stupefied and falls to the ground, / With pale and deathly visage. / But as soon as he sees / That his fear is groundless, / He arises, breathes again and returns / To count the flock / Dispersed by fear.

The adaptor, who may have been the poet himself, takes up the theme of the shepherd's pallor and produces a text of vibrant intensity.

> Pallido il sole, torbido il cielo,
> Pena minaccia, morte prepara,
> Tutto mi spira rimorso e orror.
> Timor mi cinge, di freddo gelo,
> Valor mi rende la vita amara;
> Io stesso fremo contro il mio cor.

> The sun is pale, the sky stormy,
> Trouble threatens, death awaits,
> Everything speaks to me of remorse and horror.
> Fear grips me, I freeze with cold,
> Honour makes my life seem bitter;
> I tremble with resentment against my own heart.

The gloomy susurration of muted strings, a chromatically descending bass, a mounting vocal part, all reveal the horror of the guilty father (Ex. 17). This is not a coloratura piece. In fact, it shows the composer at his most dramatic.

Ex. 17

In the final act the pattern is reversed. First comes a series of emotional scenes with arias; finally a long scene in simple recitative, in which the characters are brought on the stage one by one, the opera ending with a full stage for the brief *coro*.[27] To the modern listener Hasse's last act would be disappointing, for it reaches its climax early with an excellent *stromentato* in scene 2 and a stunning

---

[27] Sung by the assembled principals, not by a true chorus as some modern writers have said.

aria di bravura. The last number, a duet, is a cool piece, less memorable than Vinci's setting of the same words, and it is followed by the extensive closing scenes. These are mostly composed in historic recitative, and while this is full of individual traits it is clear that the emphasis has shifted to the text, for the plot must be untied; the poetry and its musical garment are of less importance. For example, when Arbace goes to drink of the sacred cup and Artabano blurts out that it is poisoned, the setting with its narrow intervals and simple harmonies is helter-skelter, only the question-formula causing a slight arrest.

Although the *stromentati* and many fine arias have not been discussed, this opera emerges as a delicately and minutely contrived pattern, in which dramatic tempo and contrast, characterization and the librettist's overall plan are all clarified and furthered by a continuous fabric of recitative and aria. This score and many others of the period show the *dramma per musica* to have been a coherent dramatic form of great power and refinement—so refined, indeed, that its subtleties have been overlooked by most modern commentators, who have assumed it was merely dull, especially the recitative. Worse still, they have resorted to typologies, as did the contemporary writers, in analyzing the *dramma*. Arias are classified according to the relation of poetic and musical metre or the melodic structure of the incipit.[28] Such typologies tell us no more about Neapolitan opera than do those of Goldoni and Brown.[29] They reflect a tendency to remove the arias from their contexts and study them as independent pieces. A recent German study has continued this approach.[30] Clearly arias must be examined alongside recitative after an initial study of the text in its dramatic and poetic aspects. This initial study may be based on the fine Italian essays on Metastasio, especially Binni on the poetic aspect and Varese on dramaturgy.

Naturally there can be no more than a sample of dramaturgical criticism of Neapolitan opera in this paper, concerned as it is chiefly with a single opera and especially with only one act thereof. The kind of rhythm described—peripeteia leading to sentimental reaction presented in an analytical *sfaccettamento*—is typical but not universal, and the reflection of the text in the recitative is particularly obvious in this opera. But there is much to be learnt from Hasse's *Artaserse*, and it would be odd if the other operas of the period were quite barren. Indeed, the works of these decades present an absorbingly varied panorama of experiments and successes in dramaturgy, recitative and aria.

[28] R. Gerber, *Der Operntypus J. A. Hasses und seine textlichen Grundlagen*, Leipzig, 1925; S. H. Hansell, *The Solo Cantatas, Motets, and Antiphons of Johann Adolf Hasse* (unpublished dissertation), University of Illinois, 1966.

[29] 'Mémoires', in *Tutte le opere di Carlo Goldoni*, ed. G. Ortolani, 5th edn., Milan, 1959, i. 129; John Brown, op. cit.

[30] R. Strohm, *Italienische Opernarien des frühen Settecento*, Cologne, 1976.

[3]

Opera Versus Drama: *Romeo and Juliet* in Eighteenth-Century Germany

THOMAS BAUMAN

SERIOUSNESS WAS A HIGHLY PRIZED QUALITY in eighteenth-century Germany, manifest in all corners of artistic and practical life. During the second half of the century, it united with the internationally pervasive taste for sentimentality to give German literature its distinctive character in the literary era now referred to as *Empfindsamkeit* [sensibility]. There were even attempts at infusing a seriousness of tone into the *Singspiel,* but these have remained obscured by easy generalizations which depict the genre as a trivial species for bad actors and worse singers, composed of simple-minded plots in which rubes invariably outwit courtiers and city folk, and featuring equally simple-minded ditties that properly belonged in the streets and taverns, and often wound up there.

No work suffers more from such misapprehensions than Jiří Benda's *Romeo und Julie,* a three-act music drama first performed at the Gotha court, where Benda was Kapellmeister, in 1776. At that time the designation *Singspiel* was not applied specifically to a spoken drama with interspersed arias, ensembles, and choruses, but was a generic term for any dramatic work employing music (Wieland referred to his opera seria *Alceste* as a *Singspiel*). What we use the word to betoken today was known then as a "komische Oper" —a term used by Hiller for almost all of his comic operas but never applied to *Romeo und Julie.* Benda's librettist, F. W. Gotter, called the work a "Schauspiel mit Gesang" in his printed libretto (Leipzig, 1779). The composer in his keyboard reduction (Leipzig, 1778, 2/1782) labeled it simply "eine Oper," and manuscript scores surviving at Berlin and Darmstadt use this as well as "eine ernsthafte Oper" and "ein ernsthaftes Singspiel."

In this context, "ernsthaft" carries a musical connotation—that of Italian opera seria. Although Benda's work utilizes spoken dialogue, even a cursory glance at the score's elaborate arias and affective obbligato recitatives will establish that *Romeo und Julie* has very little in common with the *Singspiel* popularized by Hiller. The musical precedents in Germany for Benda's work are obvious if one considers its basis in Italian opera style—Anton Schweitzer's setting of Wieland's *Alceste* (1773) and Benda's own melodramas *Medea* and *Ariadne auf Naxos* (1775). All these works are further related since they were written for the same theatrical company.

Yet Benda and Gotter did not seek simply to create another opera seria in German along the lines of *Alceste*. Already in his two melodramas, Benda had brought his musical talents to bear on texts conceived as spoken dramas, in effect huge monologues (or as one contemporary put it, the fifth act of a tragedy whose first four acts have been omitted). The literary traditions of Wieland's *Alceste* are those of Metastasio and Italian opera, but *Medea* and especially *Ariadne* derive from French classical tragedy transmuted by the new naturalism of Diderot and the *drame*. *Romeo und Julie* is also very much a product of the German spoken theater, but instead of confining music to instrumental accompaniment (as the melodrama does), it embraces the language and procedures of Italian opera. In choosing this subject, Gotter carried one step further not only the innovations in opera and melodrama just mentioned but also the progressive transformation of Shakespeare's tragedy at the hands of German translators and adapters.

The history of *Romeo and Juliet* in Germany during the second half of the eighteenth century begins in London and, perhaps fittingly, not with Shakespeare but with David Garrick. In 1750 *Romeo and Juliet* kindled a remarkable theatrical confrontation on the London stage. Beginning on 28 September Covent Garden and Drury Lane mounted their rival productions of the play in a series of performances unbroken by any other work until 12 October.[1]

Both Spranger Barry at Covent Garden and Garrick at Drury Lane used Theophilus Cibber's adaptation of 1744; Garrick made several alterations and additions of his own and published his version in 1751. His text influenced nearly all the German translations

---

[1] See George W. Stone, Jr., *The London Stage, 1860–1800*, 4 pts. (Carbondale, Ill., 1962), pt. 4, I, 208–11.

and adaptations of *Romeo and Juliet* published during the next quarter century. The first, issued at Basel in 1758, explicitly claims Garrick's version as its source on the title page. The anonymous translator, Simon Grynaeus (1725–99), may actually have seen Garrick as Romeo on a visit to England in 1749–50. Grynaeus' translation, literal and in blank verse, caused no great stir; the author never followed up on his intention, should *Romeo und Julie* be favorably received, to translate all of Shakespeare "and, as far as possible, word for word."[2]

A much more significant translation of the play appeared in the seventh volume of C. M. Wieland's *Shakespear Theatralische Werke* (Zurich, 1766).[3] Like the other twenty-one plays in this undertaking, *Romeo und Juliette* was not intended for performance. The adapter was more interested in the cultivated German reader in his armchair, anxious to acquaint himself with the bard. (Thus Wieland also included a life of Shakespeare in the last volume of the set.)

By and large Wieland follows Shakespeare's plot quite closely, but he does not hesitate to omit scenes and passages which he finds offensive or nonsensical. He cast his translation in prose, and indeed did not hold a very high opinion of Shakespeare's own poetry, which he found "mostly hard, forced, and dark; the rhyme forever forces him to say something other than what he intends—or else to express his ideas poorly." Shakespeare's couplet conjoining "maidenhead" and "wedding bed" (III.2, 136–37) particularly offended Wieland, who believed there was no nonsense or impropriety Shakespeare would stop at to find a quick rhyme.

Similarly, he objected to the surfeit of puns in Shakespeare—not only untranslatable but also tedious in his view. Hence, Mercutio ends up with very little to say (Wieland will not even grant him his dying pun on 'grave'), and Romeo's character suffers as well. The translator also condemned Lady Capulet's extended comparison of Paris to a book as the base broth of the most tasteless kind of wit

---

[2] Quoted by Hans Küry, *Simon Grynaeus von Basel, 1725–1799, der erste deutsche Uebersetzer von Shakespeares Romeo und Julia*, Basler Beiträge zur deutschen Literatur- und Geistesgeschichte, vol. II (Zurich and Leipzig, 1935), 64. The *Bibliothek der schönen Wissenschaften und der freyen Künste* complained of the translator's verses: "Sie sind bisweilen so holpricht, die Harmonie, und der Abschnitt so verabsäumt, kurz, so—schweizerisch, dass wir eine wohlklingende Prose, diesen Versen weit vorziehen würden" (6:1 [1760]: 61).

[3] Wieland used the Pope-Warburton and Theobald editions as the bases for his translations. He also translated and put at the head of his first volume of plays the preface written by Pope (1725) for the former edition.

and totally unworthy of the character of a mother. The crude interchange among Peter and the three musicians after Juliet's body is discovered (IV.5) is only summarized. Wieland conjectures that this "small *divertissement* of puns and pranks in the taste of the Viennese Harlequin" was included so that the preceding scene of lamentation would not touch the audience too deeply. In this Wieland reflected the taste of his age, for Garrick too had excised this comic incongruity in his adaptation of *Romeo and Juliet*.

Wieland obviously placed considerations of tone and propriety above those of characterization and dramatic construction. This is evident in his own plays and librettos as well. Herder saw the particular failing of *Romeo und Juliette* in the translator's lack of personal empathy with the star-crossed lovers. In the fall of 1770 Herder wrote to his wife:

Of all Shakespeare's plays, Wieland is never more unsuccessful than with *Romeo and Juliet*. The reason, perhaps, is that Wieland himself has never felt a Romeo's love, but has always inflated his head with Sympathies and Pantheons and Seraphim, without his heart ever feeling human warmth.[4]

There is an undeniable coldness in Wieland's translation. As a specimen one may offer his stiff reworking of the Prince's closing homily, which takes an entirely new direction at his hands, pounding with a pompous, sermonesque tone called "Kanzelberedsamkeit" [pulpit oratory] at the time:

Ihr aber, getreue Liebende, die ein allzustrenges Schicksal im Leben getrennt, und nun ein freywilliger Tod auf ewig vereiniget hat, lebet, Juliette und Romeo, lebet in unserm Andenken, und die späteste Nachwelt möge das Gedächtniss eurer unglücklichen Liebe mit mitleidigen Thränen ehren!

[A glooming peace this morning with it brings
The sun for sorrow will not show his head.
Go hence, to have more talk of these sad things.
Some shall be pardoned and some punished.
For never was there story of more woe
Than that of Juliet and her Romeo.]

By 1773 Wieland's set of translations had finally been sold out, and his publisher suggested a new edition to incorporate the many

---

[4] Quoted by August Koberstein, "Shakespeare's allmähliches Bekanntwerden in Deutschland und Urtheile über ihm bis zum Jahre 1773," in *Vermischte Aufsätze zur Litteraturgeschichte und Aesthetik* (Leipzig, 1858), p. 206, note 60.

errors critics had pointed out. Wieland refused, and J. J. Eschenburg, a distinguished scholar and Anglophile, undertook the task. Eschenburg not only restored all the passages suppressed or altered by his predecessor but also translated the plays omitted by Wieland —which included *Richard II, Coriolanus,* and *Cymbeline.* The new thirteen-volume edition, which appeared from 1775 to 1782, already belongs to a new chapter in German literary history. In his preface, Eschenburg could look back with scholarly perspective on the goals of Wieland's undertaking: "Its purpose was, insofar as it was possible, to cloak the English poet in German garb."[5] Yet, in spite of its flaws, Goethe preferred Wieland's translations even to Schlegel's and dated the widespread acquaintance of German readers with Shakespeare from its appearance.

Christian Felix Weisse, universally beloved in his own day for the *Singspiel* librettos he wrote or adapted for Hiller, earned the highest regard from his countrymen with his five-act version of Shakespeare's tragedy, a complete reworking which he claimed to be "ein ganz neues Stück." Weisse's *Romeo und Julie, ein bürgerliches Trauerspiel* (Leipzig, 1767) is as much a work for his own age as Shakespeare's was for his. Although Weisse was acquainted with the literary history of his subject, he draws on the story's various versions only to serve his own ideals (substantially those of Lessing, too), the spirit of bourgeois sentimentality framed by the constructive rules of French classical tragedy.

Weisse's indebtedness to Shakespeare and the Italian novellas of Bandello and Porto has been carefully studied by German scholars,[6] but the provenance of his alterations is less important than his artistic intentions in incorporating them. Unlike Wieland, Weisse was very much a man of the theatre and wrote his play to be performed as well as read. In his preface to the first edition, he relates how he had the play brought on stage (in the fall of 1767 at Leipzig) before offering the printed text to the public. As a result he cut the

---

[5] Quoted by Gisbert Freiherr von Vincke, "Zur Geschichte der deutschen Shakspere-Uebersetzung," in *Gesammelte Aufsätze zur Bühnengeschichte, Theatergeschichteliche Forschungen, vol.* VI (Hamburg and Leipzig, 1893), p. 68.

[6] Johanna Gruber, "Das Verhältnis von Weisses *Romeo und Julie* zu Shakespeare und den Novellen," *Studien zur vergleichenden Literaturgeschichte,* 5 (1905), 395–428; Walter Hüttemann, *Christian Felix Weisse und seine Zeit in ihrem Verhältniss zu Shakespeare,* Inaug.-Diss., Rheinische Friedrich-Wilhelms-Universität (Duisburg, 1912); and Artur Sauer, *Shakespeares* Romeo und Julia *in den Bearbeitungen und Uebersetzungen der deutschen Literatur,* Inaug.-Diss., Königliche Universität (Greifswald, 1915).

last two scenes, in which Montague and Capulet learn of the disaster and reconcile their families. He had realized that in performance they were expendible, since the spectator is overwhelmed with interest for the lovers. He retained the two scenes as an appendix in the printed text "for more tranquil readers."

In order to conform to the unities, Weisse begins his tragedy after Romeo and Juliet have met, fallen in love, and married, after Mercutio and Tybalt have been slain and a warrant has been issued for Romeo's arrest. Appropriately enough in terms of Weisse's concerns, his story opens with Juliet center-stage, alone and anxiously awaiting her Romeo. Much of the author's handling of her character is typical of the German sentimental drama. He seeks to imbue his heroine with the sweet and passive tenderness his age idealized in the female sex. Rather than respecting the growing sense of self-assurance and maturity which transforms Shakespeare's Juliet, Weisse draws a static, timorous soul. There are, however, a few exceptions. Juliet's soliloquy in which she summons up the horrors of the grave before taking the potion provided by Friar Laurence (the family doctor Benvoglio in Weisse) captures at least an echo of the fortitude of Shakespeare's heroine. The nurse (Laura in Weisse's version, as well as in Gotter's) and Lady Capulet, against whom Juliet's development was gauged by Shakespeare, also undergo alterations: both become sympathetic confidantes. Weisse also decided to blacken Capulet into a remorseless tyrant against whom the three ladies wage a common battle.

Romeo, stripped of the scenes with Tybalt and Mercutio in which he could display his manliness to advantage, matches Juliet's distaff languor with his own insipid whining. In his first appearance he seeks to justify his fleeing her and Verona. Where Shakespeare's hero had needed Juliet's urging to go, boldly asserting, "Let me be ta'en, let me be put to death!", Weisse's Romeo quails before the very thought: "As soon as morning breaks they will hear the rumor that I am still in Verona and come looking for me, and think what would happen if they found me! Think, Juliet!" She offers to flee with him, but he protests that then, if caught, he would be punished as her seducer as well. From this point, the middle of the first act, to the beginning of the last, Romeo disappears. When he returns he spins out a long monologue at Juliet's tomb which Weisse drastically shortened in later editions.

In these closing scenes the two do not die severally; rather Romeo lives on after taking poison to see Juliet awake, to curse his lack of trust in Providence, and to weep through a final dialogue. However much this alteration may have suited Weisse's goals, he cannot claim credit for the change. Again, Garrick had made exactly the same departure. Weisse's preface reveals that he knew of Garrick's revision,[7] although the farewell dialogue also occurs in another of his sources, Porto's novella. The differences between Garrick's scene and Weisse's reflect the German dramatist's preoccupation with his heroine. In Garrick's version Romeo takes the initiative. He suggests they flee "from this cave of death, this house of horror" —forgetting for a moment the fatal step he has already taken. Juliet wakes in confusion, not realizing at first where she is (as in Porto). Romeo tells her of the poison when he recollects his situation, and in the end he dies with an appeal to their parents on his lips. Weisse's Juliet, in contrast, comes immediately to her senses and takes charge, exhorting Romeo to flee with her. She stumbles upon the emptied vial—he has not been able to summon the fortitude to tell her himself that he is undone. Wrapped in morbid self-pity, Romeo can do nothing but expire in helpless anguish.

The suicide of Juliet after Romeo dies chilled Weisse's audiences. The poet Gleim wrote from Leipzig shortly after the première of the tragedy that "Juliet aroused not tears but shocks of horror."[8] This dark scene, rather than the lovers' reunion, was chosen for the play's frontispiece in the collected edition of Weisse's tragedies issued at Leipzig in 1776. By that date, the suicide scene was no doubt considered among the most "Shakespearean" in the tragedy. Yet it was not shudders of horror but rather sympathetic tears that expressed the approval Weisse sought for his drama, especially in adopting and expanding Garrick's final farewell for the lovers. Both men considered the absence of such a dialogue in Shakespeare an error in judgment. Weisse appeals to "the tears of the spectators, which have flown for Romeo and Juliet" as his vindication for departing so sharply from Shakespeare—and, indeed, his play went on to achieve a success never before equaled by a German tragedy.

While many of Europe's most beloved comedies and farces had

---

[7] Weisse refers in his preface to Garrick's criticism of Shakespeare's "jingle and quibble," a phrase used by the actor in the foreword to the printed edition of his adaptation.

[8] Carl Schüddekopf, ed., *Briefwechsel zwischen Gleim und Uz*, Bibliothek des litterarischen Vereins in Stuttgart, vol. 218 (Tübingen, 1899), p. 377.

been turned into musical works in the second half of the eighteenth century, librettists had completely avoided the domestic tragedy until Gotter decided to create a German opera out of the Romeo and Juliet story. Such a daring venture was only possible because he and Benda envisioned a new kind of music drama, one in which the emotionalism and seriousness of character essential to the domestic tragedy would be intensified by the most elevated musical language available, that of opera seria.

At the beginning of his preface to *Romeo und Julie,* dated October 1778, Gotter wrote, "Let Benda's music be the document in my defense against those who consider it a desecration to transplant a subject of the tragic muse to the opera stage." By then, Benda's music had already established the work's popularity throughout Germany. Yet voices had been raised against the libretto, and Gotter had been particularly stung by the criticism of Heinrich Leopold Wagner, who charged him with diluting Shakespeare to ninety-five percent water.[9] Against this the librettist made the inaccurate claim that he had indeed returned to Shakespeare in fashioning his text, which had nothing but title and plot in common with Weisse's tragedy.

It is true that many passages in Gotter's libretto stand closer to Shakespeare's language than to Weisse's. Compare, for example, the parting scene at Juliet's balcony in the three versions:

GOTTER:

Julie: Ach, ich habe eine Unglück weissagende Seele. — Sieh! wenn ich dich so betrachte, Romeo, glaub' ich einen Todten zu sehen, den sie in das Grab legen. — Sind meine Augen düster — oder bist du wirklich so bleich?
Romeo: Auch du kömmst mir bleich vor. Der Kummer trinkt das Blut in unsern Wangen auf.

WEISSE:

Julie: . . . Sieh mich immer noch recht an! — Du scheinst mir bleich wie das Grab! Scheine ich dir nicht auch so? O Romeo, lass mich meine Seele noch in die deinige atmen! (Sie fällt ihm um den Hals.) — und sterben —

SHAKESPEARE:

Juliet: Oh God! I have an ill-divining soul.
            Methinks I see thee, now thou art below,

[9] *Briefe, die Seylerische Theatergesellschaft und ihre Vorstellungen zu Frankfurt am Main betreffend* (Frankfurt, 1777).

> As one dead in the bottom of a tomb.
> Either my eyesight fails or thou look'st pale.
> *Romeo:* And trust me, love, in my eye so do you.
> Dry sorrow drinks our blood. Adieu, adieu!
> (III.v.54–59)

Constructively, however, Gotter follows Weisse in observing the unities and concentrating on the female characters. When his purposes deviate from Weisse's it is because of the medium in which he is working. For example, after the exchange just quoted, Shakespeare's Romeo leaves. Weisse, however, draws out the scene. He is forced to establish character here, having sacrificed Romeo's earlier appearances in order to compress everything into twenty-four hours. Gotter, of course, faced the same problem, but could call Benda to his aid.[10] In his libretto, a sort of operatic scena follows in which Romeo offers an aria of hope and love (its incipit suggested by a line from Weisse). Juliet counters that there is no hope, and only love remains. She suggests a double suicide and draws a knife. Romeo snatches it from her and they join Laura in a trio which closes the act. In such a situation Romeo makes a much stronger impression, and momentum builds toward the musical capstone of the act, the trio, rather than dissipating. Weisse, in contrast, has Romeo scurry off when Laura announces Lady Capulet.

Gotter's delineation of Juliet's character is instructive. She is still the unchallenged center of attention (one manuscript calls the opera *Julie und Romeo*) and also gains considerably in courage and resourcefulness over Weisse's heroine. To be sure, weakness is still valued highly, but especially where Gotter calls on Benda's obbligato skills Juliet gathers strength, as in her final monologue before taking Friar Laurence's potion. This musical complex culminates in an f-minor aria whose final line is drawn straight from Shakespeare: "Romeo, diess trink ich dir zu." Weisse avoids such an "operatic" flourish.

Capulet, one of Weisse's most unfortunate creations, is toned down considerably in the opera, perhaps partly for musical reasons.

---

[10] Because Romeo is forced to stay on in both versions, neither Weisse nor Gotter can take advantage of the splendid visual effect sought by Shakespeare—Juliet looking down to her Romeo at the foot of the rope ladder, standing "as one dead in the bottom of a tomb." It will be noticed that neither man translates Shakespeare's "now thou art below." Garrick, too, changes the line to "now thou art parting from me" (perhaps the ladder and balcony were not used in his production).

His big spoken monologue in Act II is not filled with the execrations and threats of Weisse's Capulet. At the close he cries, "I will use force if argument has no effect! I? Use force against the darling of my heart?" There follows an aria, "Schweres Amt," in which he reflects on the pangs of parenthood. In such instances Capulet's anger takes on an impulsive, more human character, and his grief in the last act is thus much more genuine. Had Gotter preserved Weisse's storming villain, a noisy bravura aria full of impassioned virtuosic passages would have come here by long-standing operatic custom. Yet the vocal demands on Capulet, here and throughout the opera, are not very great. In fact, the musical demands on the whole cast reflect conditions at Gotha, where first-rate female singers abounded, but good male singers were scarce (the best tenor and bass having both left in 1775). The most virtuosic role in *Romeo und Julie,* that of Juliet's confidante Laura, was written especially for Benda's own daughter. Capulet's solo numbers, on the other hand, approach the dimensions of the lied, as found in most *Singspiele* of the day.

Despite Gotter's more elliptic approach and shifts of emphasis in characterization in conflating Weisse's five acts to three, his departures in the first two of his three acts are not major ones. Benda's music, too, seldom shows much inspiration in these two acts—in Winton Dean's somewhat harsh judgment, it is "fluent and superficial, rich in period clichés and sparing of surprises."[11] Except for Juliet's recitative and aria at the close of Act II, most of the music is conventional and sentimental, although now and again Benda effects one of the astonishing harmonic sallies he used with such splendid results in his melodramas. More often than not, these moments come from the opera's three obbligato recitatives. For example, in the opening solo scene of Act 1, where as in Weisse Juliet anxiously awaits Romeo's arrival, jumping at every footfall, Benda portrays her unrest with a jarring shift from V of b minor to F major, a tritone away from the expected resolution (Musical Example 1).

Benda's arias are all well crafted and evoked from his contemporaries the age's highest praise for an artist—their tears. The most celebrated one in the opera was Juliet's "Ihn wieder zu seh'n," an aria with intermixed recitative elements which she sings in response

---

[11] "Shakespeare and Opera," in *Shakespeare in Music,* ed. Phyllis Hartnoll (London, 1964), p. 146.

MUSICAL EXAMPLE 1. Jiří Benda, Romeo und Julie, act 1, scene 1.

MUSICAL EXAMPLE 2. Jiří Benda, Romeo und Julie, act 2, scene 6

to Friar Laurence's suggestion that he may have a way to reunite the pair. J. F. Reichardt praised it as "the highest expression of rapture that art is capable of reaching,"[12] and Benda's necrologist transmitted the following anecdote concerning the aria:

> A librettist spoke at great length on the pains it cost him to make his verses musical. "That is no great favor to *me*," cried Benda, with whom the poet in general did not sit well; "for my best and most moving melodies I have unmusical verses to thank, which force me to bend my every effort in order to improve on the poet." In support he referred to his beautiful aria "Meinen Romeo zu sehn" and its verses:
>
> > Alle Gedanken verlieren sich
> > In dem Wonnegedanken:
> > Meinen Romeo zu sehn, etc.
>
> He sprang to the clavier and sang this splendid aria with such inner emotion that crystalline tears rolled down his cheeks and everyone present, in spite of his dreadful voice and his broad Bohemian accent and heavy gestures and facial expressions, was moved to tears.[13]

Benda may be allowed his pride in the declamatory merits of his setting (Musical Example 2, drawn from near the end of the aria's first part); but the passage has other, more significant virtues as well. The melisma on "seh'n" not only caps the long drive of the aria's first part to the dominant, A major, but also paints Juliet's joy at seeing her Romeo again, and the sudden shift back to D major at the brink of achieving the dominant offers a heart-wrenching musical jolt back to the reality of the lovers' present separation. The extent of the dominant preparation for A major and the long-awaited melodic climax on high a''' at the end of the melisma speak with a Mozartean breadth of conception.

Such moments arouse great expectations for the composer's acquittal of himself in the closing scene at the tomb. Yet here Gotter departs from the models before him and substitutes for the tragical close a happy ending (Juliet awakes before Romeo can poison himself)—an alteration that aroused much discussion at the time.

---

[12] *Allgemeine deutsche Bibliothek*, 40:1 (1780), 130. (A review of the printed keyboard reduction of 1778.)

[13] Friedrich von Schlichtegroll, *Musiker-Nekrologe,* ed. Richard Schaal (Kassel and Basel, n.d.), p. 29.

Reichardt cried out for the restoration of the ending as it stands in Shakespeare and Weisse (he also inveighed against the *lieto fine* in Wieland's *Alceste*). Eschenburg, on the other hand, found much to praise in Gotter's libretto. The plot develops quickly, he observes, adding: "How much more offensive, in contrast, are so many tedious scenes in our German tragedy of this name [Weisse's *Romeo und Julie* is meant]." He found nothing objectionable in the happy ending. "Presumably, the author was anxious to assemble all the characters at the close and to end the work with a chorus."[14]

A happy ending was standard in opera seria, but served in most of the genre's librettos as an excuse for the hero to display his magnanimity. The theme present here, reconciliation, was rather the property of the sentimental comedy and of comic opera. However, Gotter was not the first to transfer this theme to serious opera—or indeed to the Romeo and Juliet story. The Italian librettist Sanseverino wrote a *Romeo e Giulia* (unrelated to Weisse's tragedy) for the composer Schwanberg at the Brunswick court early in 1773 and added a happy ending. Gotter may possibly have known this work; a second edition of the libretto was published at Berlin in 1776.[15]

Gotter did not mention this direct precedent, however, when he set forth his reasons for altering the ending in the preface to his printed text. Two considerations, he claims, would not allow him to retain the "all-too-tragic catastrophe": musical economy and the abilities of the singers. A lexicon of the day notes that "Oekonomie" was used figuratively with reference to the disposition of ends and means within a work of art.[16] Gotter apparently held that the musical means of an opera were not appropriate to the tragic ending he found in Shakespeare and Weisse. He may also have felt that the singers were not equal to the dramatic demands of such a close.

It seems odd that Gotter would seek to put the blame on the composer and singers in circumstances where he had competent vocalists as well as the best dramatic composer in Protestant Germany. Only a year earlier, Gotter had provided Benda with a text of unquestionable tragic credentials—the melodrama *Medea*, in which

---

[14] *Allgemeine deutsche Bibliothek*, 39:1 (1780), 162–63.
[15] See O. G. T. Sonneck, *Catalogue of Opera Librettos Printed Before 1800*, 3 vols. (Washington, 1914), I, 949.
[16] [Johann Christoph Adelung], *Versuch eines vollständigen grammatisch-kritischen Wörterbuches der hochdeutschen Mundart*, 5 vols. (Leipzig, 1774–86), vol. III (1777), col. 911: ". . . so wird oft auch figürlich die ganze Einrichtung der Endzwecke und Mittel *die Oekonomie* genannt."

the jealous heroine slays her own children, then taunts her grief-stricken husband to suicide. The difference Gotter saw between *Medea* and *Romeo und Julie* reflects a mistrust, common in German literati of the period, of the abilities of the opera composer to discharge duties normally assigned to the tragedian. *Medea* had been written for an actress, not a singer; the text was spoken throughout, and music functioned as the drama's handmaiden. In *Romeo und Julie,* Gotter knew, the success or failure of the piece would depend principally on Benda's music, and thus the roles were reversed. It is bitterly ironic that later on Benda expressed in connection with this very opera his own artistic maxim: "Music itself suffers when one sacrifices everything for its sake."[17]

Dean ascribes the failure of Act III to its central episode, where the "deplorably false sentiment of Romeo's scene at the tomb" may well disgust the modern listener. Furthermore, the contrived and pallid closing scene of reunion and reconciliation belies the morbid forebodings of everything that precedes. Benda's music here is as workaday as the denouement is unmotivated. This dramatic disintegration is all the more offensive because the last act opens with unquestionably the finest, most impressive tableau in all of Benda's *Singspiele,* a funeral chorus at Juliet's grave. This chorus (more probably an ensemble of soloists, as the part writing will show) exists in two versions. Originally its dimensions were modest: a funeral procession led by Capulet enters the grove of cypresses and Babylonian willows where Juliet's casket lies; a quartet behind the scenes intones a dirge in c minor as Capulet and his followers pay their last respects to Juliet; he sings an expressive E-flat major duet with another mourner who seeks to comfort him; the last half of the quartet's dirge is repeated as the party withdraws.

When Gotter's friend Friedrich Ludwig Schröder mounted Benda's *Romeo und Julie* at Hamburg, he wrote to the librettist recommending to him some changes he had made in the last act, which included bringing the disembodied quartet on stage. Gotter incorporated these alterations in his printed text and also expanded the whole funeral scene, for which Benda provided additional music. In the new version the chorus bears Juliet's open casket to the crypt where it is placed next to Tybalt's. Capulet, after the c-minor

---

[17] The remark appears in an essay "On Simple Recitative" submitted by the composer to Carl Friedrich Cramer's *Magazin der Musik,* 1 (Hamburg, 1783), 751.

quartet, breaks free and kneels at her coffin. A few mourners follow him. After his E-flat duet with one of them he exits in despair. Laura, accompanied by maidens with burning candles, steps forward and sings a "Wechselgesang" (antiphonal duet) with one of these. She places a wreath on the coffin and leaves. During the repetition of the chorus the casket is closed, the crypt is darkened and shut, and the stage is emptied for the entrance of Romeo and his servant.

The scene gains much in the new version. The dignified and measured last exequies must have been of powerful theatrical effect when accompanied by Benda's quartet (Musical Example 3).[18] The combination of stark and unadorned harmonies (underscored dynamically) and a clear but distinctive progression announcing c minor establishes the scene's mood as the curtain rises. The quartet's pitiless unison descent of the tonic triad is truly Gluckian. But most astonishing of all is the unaccompanied, contrapuntal surge that follows. Whatever parallels one might be tempted to draw between Benda's funeral chorus and Schweitzer's choral tombeau in Act V of *Alceste* (also in c minor) quickly break down. Schweitzer writes mostly for the two soloists Admet and Parthenia; Benda's music recalls the North German motet, which after Bach turned to discreet polyphony and free combinations of voices within a homophonic context. While such an association must not be overlooked —a motet was a frequent adjunct to a funeral service—neither must the dramatic context in which Benda was working and its precedents in Italian opera. Several Metastasian librettos employ funeral choruses (for example, *Artaserse,* set as a quartet of soloists by Galuppi for Vienna in 1749); and, more important, Gluck's *Orfeo* opens with a strikingly similar scene—also in c minor.

Benda may have known Galuppi's *Artaserse*, and most certainly he knew Gluck's masterpiece. Yet, from the literary standpoint at least, it is the London stage of 1750 that once again offers a direct precedent for this German departure from Shakespeare. On the first evening of the *Romeo and Juliet* rivalry, Covent Garden added a funeral procession at the beginning of Act V which included a

---

[18] The high c''' in the first soprano part here, which makes the work highly unlikely for a chorus, is not found in all manuscripts. In these sources one also finds a rising chromatic line beginning on c'' an octave lower. Even in this form, the piece is so unusual for an opera chorus that there can be little doubt that it was intended for soloists. All the manuscripts refer to a "vierstimmiger Gesang" behind the scene, while the keyboard reduction calls specifically for "5 voci soli."

MUSICAL EXAMPLE 3. Jiří Benda, Romeo und Julie, act 3, scene 1

solemn dirge composed by Thomas Arne. Garrick quickly got Arne's competitor, William Boyce, to provide music for a funeral scene written by Garrick for his own production.[19] It is possible that Gotter's scene was inspired by one or the other of these funerary processions, although his text betrays no direct borrowings. But it is equally important to recognize an operatic model which lay much closer at hand—the choral lament which opens Act V of Wieland's *Alceste* (Weimar, 1773). The English funeral scenes themeselves no doubt took their lead from operatic traditions. Making a case for the precedents in either serious opera or the spoken theatre is less important, however, than recognizing this very ambiguity as a ratification of the dual heritage of Gotter's work. The choral scenes in all these works aspire to a common goal—a dignified moment of high seriousness investing the "death" of the heroine with the emotional reality the drama demands. Exactly the same may be said of the great opening chorus in Gluck's *Orfeo*. And there can be no ambiguity about the affinity of Benda's funeral tableau with this classic model.[20]

C. F. D. Schubart hailed Benda as an epoch-maker not just because of his melodramas but also because of his choruses in *Romeo und Julie*—and clearly he was thinking of this funeral tableau.[21] Reichardt, too, declared that with this chorus Benda had "harvested the highest praise: tears from an overflowing fullness of heart."[22]

---

[19] Arne's *Compleat Score of the Solemn Dirge in Romeo and Juliet* was published (London: Thorowgood, [1750?]), but Boyce's hasty effort (composed and prepared for performance in only two days) was apparently never printed and has not been traced. Charles Haywood, "William Boyce's 'Solemn Dirge' in Garrick's *Romeo and Juliet* Production of 1750," *Shakespeare Quarterly*, 11 (1960), 173-87, attributes to Boyce a setting of Garrick's text in a manuscript which belonged to the American statesman and composer Francis Hopkinson (1737-91). It is difficult to share Haywood's confidence, based solely on stylistic grounds, in this ascription. One readily grants him the music's simplicity; less readily, however, qualities of "subdued lyricism and unaffected poignancy"; and it is scarcely more than wishful thinking to lump Arne with purveyors of "exaggerated affections and ornamental artificialities."

[20] Serious opera as represented by Gluck and his reforms must not be construed as unrelated to the English stage. Burney remarks of Gluck, "He told me that he owed entirely to England the study of nature in his dramatic compositions." That the good doctor's statement bespeaks more than insular pride is made clear by Daniel Heartz, "From Garrick to Gluck: the Reform of Theater and Opera in the Mid-Eighteenth Century," *Proceedings of the Royal Musicological Association*, 94 (1967-68), 111-27.

[21] *Ideen zu einer Aesthetik der Tonkunst*, ed. Ludwig Schubart (Vienna, 1806), p. 112.

[22] *Allgemeine deutsche Bibliothek*, 40:1 (1780), 130.

Today one can still admire the quartet. Yet its intensification of dramatic demands which Gotter felt an opera libretto could not fulfill points up the fundamental problem in *Romeo und Julie*. Benda, both at Berlin and in Italy, had mastered the international language that was Italian opera and proved that it could still find fresh validity in the melodrama, in which operatic music and French classical tragedy created a new dramatic genre. Gotter failed to see the promise this held for their collaboration on *Romeo und Julie,* and retreated from the work's literary basis in the spoken theatre under cover of a false aesthetic which separated opera and drama. He failed to grasp that in this new context the literary traditions of serious opera were fundamentally inappropriate. This is perhaps what Reichardt had in mind when he complained, "If only the poet had not so irresponsibly cut up his material into well-mannered, everyday opera garb!"[23]

University of Pennsylvania

[23] Ibid.

[4]
Mozart's operas and the myth of musical unity

JAMES WEBSTER

Books discussed in this essay:

Wye Jamison Allanbrook. *Rhythmic Gesture in Mozart: 'Le nozze di Figaro' and 'Don Giovanni'*. University of Chicago Press, 1983. xii + 396 pp.

Thomas Bauman. *W. A. Mozart: 'Die Entführung aus dem Serail'*. Cambridge University Press, 1987. xiii+141 pp. (Cambridge Opera Handbooks).

Tim Carter. *W. A. Mozart: 'Le nozze di Figaro'*. Cambridge University Press, 1987. xii+180 pp. (Cambridge Opera Handbooks).

Daniel Heartz. *Mozart's Operas*. Edited with contributing essays by Thomas Bauman. University of California Press (forthcoming fall 1990).

Stefan Kunze. *Mozarts Opern*. Reclam, 1984. 687 pp.

Julian Rushton. *W. A. Mozart: 'Don Giovanni'*. Cambridge University Press, 1981. ix+165 pp. (Cambridge Opera Handbooks).

Andrew Steptoe. *The Mozart–Da Ponte Operas: The Cultural and Musical Background to 'Le nozze di Figaro', 'Don Giovanni', and 'Così fan tutte'*. The Clarendon Press (Oxford), 1988. [viii]+273 pp.

1

The privileged status of Mozart's operas is reflected not only in their prominence in the repertory and in the unceasing flood of publications devoted to them, but even more in their composer's iconic role as arguably our greatest culture-hero. Even if we disagree about their dramaturgy and ultimate meanings, or admit the occasional flaw, their talismanic role – their moving us not merely to delight and admiration but reverence and awe – seems unshakable.

And yet, they have received relatively little close or informed musical analysis. In view of the intense cultivation of theory since the Second World War, and the literally thousands of published analyses of Mozart's instrumental music, this neglect would be baffling indeed, if it did not reflect the traditional uncertainty about the status of opera as 'absolute music', and the lack of consensus about how to understand it in technical terms. In addition, recent operatic analysis has concerned itself more with the nineteenth-century giants Verdi and Wagner than with Mozart. This too can be explained: they composed little or no significant instrumental music; to study them is necessarily to study their operas. In addition (and this is only an apparent paradox), the dominance of analytical models based on the instrumental music of Mozart and Beethoven was a positive stimulus to Verdians and Wagnerites: although a battle had to be waged to overcome them, the cause was just and the enemy soon routed. Indeed, the critical thinking entailed by this effort led to the development of new and fruitful analytical paradigms, notably that of 'multivalence'. This holds that the various 'domains' of an opera (text, action, music, etc.; as well as, within the music, tonality, motives, instrumentation, etc.) are not necessarily congruent and may even be incompatible; and that the resulting complexity or lack of integration is often a primary source of their aesthetic effect. In Mozart studies, by contrast, the presence of his unsurpassable instrumental music has tended on the one hand to make close study of the operas seem unnecessary, while on the other hand those few who have attempted it have transferred 'instrumental' methods to the very different context of dramatic staged vocal music – uncritically, and without benefit of countervailing analytical traditions.

In 1987, I drew attention to these matters and called for concerted multivalent analysis of Mozart's operas: 'all we need to do is get on with it'.[1] This now strikes me as simplistic; my discussions were not always sufficiently attentive to the differences between opera and instrumental music. The enterprise will require a more nearly fundamental re-examination of paradigms and methods. As a first step, I review here a number of recent studies which include substantial analytical material.[2]

The volumes by Thomas Bauman on *Die Entführung aus dem Serail*, Tim Carter on *Le nozze di Figaro* and Julian Rushton on *Don Giovanni* appear in the useful Cambridge Opera Handbook series, which strikes a balance between 'Kenner' and 'Liebhaber' that Mozart himself would have admired. Each includes a detailed dramatic and musical synopsis which is everything other than a crutch for the uninitiated; in Rushton, it leads to fundamental new dramatic insights. A signal virtue of Carter's volume is the inclusion of a chapter on Italian prosody and its implications for Mozart's music, a vital aspect of any Italian opera which has been almost entirely ignored in the English-language Mozart literature.

The strength of Andrew Steptoe's *The Mozart–Da Ponte Operas* is his focus on the particular social-cultural milieu of each work. The Vienna of 1785–86,

[1] James Webster, 'To Understand Verdi and Wagner We Must Understand Mozart', *19th-Century Music*, 11 (1987–88), 175–93 (here, 179); the preceding paragraph summarises this item. On Verdi and Wagner analysis, see Carolyn Abbate and Roger Parker, 'Introduction: On Analyzing Opera', in Abbate and Parker, eds., *Analyzing Opera: Verdi and Wagner* (Berkeley, 1989), 1–24.
[2] In preparing this essay I have profited especially from discussions with Mary Hunter, Roger Parker and John Platoff. I also thank Thomas Bauman for making available the front matter to Daniel Heartz's volume.

he argues, was not the same as that of 1789–90, and Prague was another place altogether. The differences among the three works reflect Da Ponte's and Mozart's conscious attempts to please these various audiences:

Figaro was written for the sophisticated audience of a society in flux, one in which the conventions of the *ancien régime* coexisted with a new interest in egalitarianism. [...] A whiff of scandal was attached [...], and the audience expected to enjoy the *frisson* of contact with potentially inflammatory material. [...] Mozart wrote the work during a period of high optimism. [...]

The conditions surrounding *Don Giovanni* were quite different. [...] The project was hazardous because although the story was still guaranteed to win popular applause, more refined audiences were unlikely to be satisfied with the much-abused legend. However, Mozart and Da Ponte gauged that the piece would be suitable for the musically intelligent but provincial and somewhat unsophisticated tastes of Prague. [...]

When *Così fan tutte* reached the stage early in 1790, the situation had changed yet again. [...] Society in Vienna had retreated from its flirtation with egalitarianism, and fear of revolution had led to the ascendancy of conservative elements. [...] Mozart [...] responded by producing an opera specifically designed for his aristocratic audience [, who] would prefer an amusing exposition of more personal human foibles. (pp. 243–4)

If perhaps overly schematic, this orientation is a refreshing change from the usual art-for-art's sake approach to a genre which was explicitly rooted in social relations, and was covertly (if not indeed overtly) political.

The social element appears in a different light in Wye Jamison Allanbrook's *Rhythmic Gesture in Mozart*. Developing insights of Leonard Ratner,[3] she works out elaborate correlations between the so-called 'rhythmic topoi' (defined roughly by patterns of metre, tempo and musical phrasing) and 'the gestures of social dance' (see her introduction and Part I). She then employs this system as a framework for superb detailed analyses of *Figaro* and *Don Giovanni*, with particular attention to the literary and social aspects of the musical drama. Daniel Heartz's *Mozart's Operas* offers a welcome compilation of his many articles published over a period of more than twenty years, some of them in out-of-the-way places, together with four new essays, and two additional contributions by Bauman (who signs as editor) on the German operas *Die Entführung* and *Die Zauberflöte*. If the volume lacks a central thesis or consistent point of view, its variety, learning (not only about Mozart, but Italian opera in general) and sparkle will delight many readers. Stefan Kunze's *Mozarts Opern*, finally, is the first large-scale, comprehensive treatment of Mozart's operas since Hermann Abert and Edward J. Dent, nearly three generations ago. For that reason, and because it has so far excited little attention in the English-speaking world, I will devote considerable space to it in what follows.

2

All of these volumes depend on traditional paradigms drawn from the analysis of instrumental music. I will focus on the most problematical of these: the

---

[3] *Classic Music: Expression, Form, and Style* (New York, 1980).

search for 'unity'. The notion of artistic unity in the modern sense arose in the early nineteenth century as an aspect of Romantic aesthetics, based on organicism and evolutionism; it was thus linked with the rise of 'absolute' instrumental music.[4] Its analytical manifestations in theorists like Schenker, Schoenberg and Réti have been much discussed recently.[5] In operatic studies, this orientation flourished primarily in connection with Wagner, especially in the work of Alfred Lorenz. Although Lorenz's procrustean analyses are now widely ridiculed, his approach decisively influenced Mozart studies in at least four ways: by taking operatic music 'seriously' as a proper subject for analysis; through the belief in unity as the ultimate criterion of aesthetic value, and the concomitant tendency to hierarchical reductionism; by his assumption that, ideally, there exists a congruence or correspondence between music on the one hand, and text and stage action on the other; and by privileging Mozart's ensembles and finales (which is to say, his most nearly through-composed, his most nearly Wagnerian music) at the expense of arias, not to mention recitatives.[6]

Among postwar English-speaking critics, even the intelligent and undogmatic Joseph Kerman and Charles Rosen focused mainly on ensembles and finales, and explicitly invoked sonata form both as a primary constituent of Mozart's operas and as a criterion of value.[7] In his influential account in *Opera as Drama*, Kerman's paradigmatic example was Donna Elvira's trio 'Ah taci, ingiusto core' from Act II of *Don Giovanni* (no. 15), which he lovingly explicated in terms of sonata form's tonal and material rhythms: the exposition, contrasting themes, increasing tension and eventual resolution were seen to accommodate different personalities, to create a form analogous to the stage action, and most of all to reflect the characters' developing psychology. And yet, of the sixteen non-duet ensembles in the three Da Ponte operas,[8] 'Ah taci, ingiusto core'

---

[4] Bellamy Hosler, *Changing Aesthetic Views of Instrumental Music in 18th-Century Germany* (Ann Arbor, 1981); James Anderson Winn, *Unsuspected Eloquence* (New Haven, 1981), Ch. 5; Carl Dahlhaus, *Esthetics of Music*, trans. William W. Austin (Cambridge, 1982), Chs. 4–6; idem, *The Idea of Absolute Music*, trans. Roger Lustig (Chicago, 1989); John Neubauer, *The Emancipation of Music from Language: Departure from Mimesis in Eighteenth-Century Aesthetics* (New Haven, 1986).

[5] Vernon L. Kliewer, 'The Concept of Organic Unity in Music Criticism and Analysis', Ph.D. diss. (Indiana University, 1961); Dahlhaus, 'Schoenberg and Schenker', *Proceedings of the Royal Musical Association*, 100 (1973–74), 209–15; Ruth Solie, 'The Living Work: Organicism and Musical Analysis', *19th-Century Music*, 4 (1980), 147–56; Jamie Croy Kassler, 'Heinrich Schenker's Epistemology and Philosophy of Music: An Essay on the Relations between Evolutionary Theory and Music Theory', in David Oldroyd and Ian Langham, eds., *The Wider Domain of Evolutionary Thought* (Dordrecht and Boston, 1983), 221–60; William Pastille, '*Ursatz*: The Music Philosophy of Heinrich Schenker', Ph.D. diss. (Cornell University, 1985).

[6] A hint of this appears in Abbate and Parker (see n. 1), 4 n. 9, 13–16; it is developed in their essay 'Dismembering Mozart', published elsewhere in this issue.

[7] Kerman, *Opera as Drama* (1956; rev. edn. Berkeley and Los Angeles, 1988), Chs. 4–5; Rosen, *The Classical Style* (New York, 1971), 290–312. That the reissue of Kerman's New Critical work is essentially unaltered despite today's changed critical climate only emphasises its dated qualities.

[8] *Figaro*, nos. 7, 13, 18; *Don Giovanni*, nos. 1, 9, 15, 19; *Così*, nos. 1–3, 6, 9, 10, 13, 16, 22. I omit *Don Giovanni*, no. 3 (Elvira's 'Ah chi mi dice mai'), which is not a true trio, but an aria with occasional asides; in form it is a sonata without development.

is the only one which is unambiguously in sonata form! (Admittedly, a number of others are in sonata-without-development ['sonatina'] form, including Rosen's paradigmatic example, the sextet [no. 18] in Act III of *Figaro*.) The paradigm in question is located more in this critical tradition than in Mozart's musical drama.

It will be appropriate to begin with arias. Other things being equal, an aria entails fewer 'domains' than an ensemble or finale (which does not necessarily imply that it is 'simpler' or 'less dramatic'), and to this extent the task is easier. And a focus on arias will at least signal the need to redress the balance vis-à-vis the traditional privileging of Mozart's ensembles.

To a greater extent than his ensembles, Mozart's arias are indebted to the operatic traditions of his time. (Again, this must not be taken as implying a negative value-judgement.) Eighteenth-century opera was based on conventions of all sorts: plots, character-types, verse-patterns, key-associations, 'semantic' instrumental usages and so forth, onto which each city or company grafted its own local traditions. Even a Mozart could not escape them (nor is there evidence that he wanted to do so). In this respect Heartz's approach is exemplary; he vividly 'sets the stage' (see his Ch. 7) for the composition and production of a work, and his vast knowledge of eighteenth-century Italian opera repeatedly leads him to new insights. It would admittedly have been better to place less emphasis on one-to-one 'modelling', as for example Paisiello's *Il barbiere di Siviglia* with respect to *Figaro* (Ch. 8), and more on conventions as such, for example aria-types. From this point of view, Michael Robinson's chapter on opera buffa in Carter's *Figaro* handbook is preferable; Bauman, too, describes the much thinner *Singspiel* tradition within which Mozart composed *Die Entführung*. Rushton's handbook on *Don Giovanni* includes a superb analysis by Edward Forman of the various earlier Don Juan stories and Da Ponte's relation to them. Kunze also treats this subject illuminatingly (pp. 330–40; in 1972 he published a detailed monograph on *Don Giovanni vor Mozart*). Unfortunately, he adopts Abert's nationalistic stance that the 'Germanic' Mozart always transformed and transcended the Italianate *buffo* traditions. At times he goes even further: 'In *Figaro* Mozart was competing only against himself, not this or that model, nor any given tradition' (p. 297). As Heartz's discussion shows, this is absurd; it can be understood only in light of the Germanic ideology of 'Classical style'.[9] The most balanced approach so far to the topic of Mozart's arias in relation to their context has been adumbrated by John Platoff.[10]

Given the critical tradition, it is a signal virtue that Kunze devotes as much attention to the arias as to ensembles and finales, and that his treatment of them is equally sympathetic and rigorous. For example, in the chapter on *Figaro*,

---

[9] On this subject, see Webster, *Haydn's 'Farewell' Symphony and the Idea of Classical Style: Through-Composition and Cyclic Integration in his Instrumental Music* (Cambridge, forthcoming), conclusion.

[10] 'The buffa aria in Mozart's Vienna', elsewhere in this issue.

each group receives just under thirty pages of analytical treatment.[11] (Kunze does not mention or discuss the plausible hypothesis that eighteenth-century buffa duets resemble arias more closely than they do larger ensembles, as regards both internal construction and the fact of being based largely on 'types'.) Hence one is inclined to give him the benefit of the doubt, even though his selection of arias for analysis is biased towards those which accompany stage action (Susanna's 'Venite, inginocchiatevi', no. 12; pp. 288–94), represent actual music on stage (Cherubino's 'Voi che sapete', no. 11; pp. 295–7), or are overtly ironic (Susanna's 'Deh, vieni', no. 27; pp. 299–307), while others, equally important, are not discussed at all – the Count's 'Vedrò mentre io sospiro', no. 17; the Countess's 'Dove sono', no. 19; Figaro's 'Aprite un po' quegl'occhi', no. 26. This is the old privileging of 'dramatically flowing' or 'realistic' numbers over supposedly 'static' or 'conventional' ones. Allanbrook, by contrast, gives every aria its due, including those usually ignored, such as Marcellina's and Basilio's in Act IV (nos. 24–5).

Kunze's approach is multifarious, emphasising versification, tonality, phrase-structure, vocal-instrumental relations, relations to traditional aria-types and so on; although the choice of focus often seems arbitrary, the results are always worth study. The accuracy and pertinence of analytical detail, often related to broad historical and critical issues, and sustained across the entirety of Mozart's *oeuvre*, is genuinely imposing. Nothing like it has been seen since Abert; his only rival in this respect among our authors is Allanbrook, who had the luxury of limiting herself to only two operas. Especially for his chosen repertory of 'action' arias, in which the orchestra is largely independent of the vocal line, Kunze develops remarkably subtle and highly differentiated analyses.[12]

One must also admire the sheer weight of Kunze's analyses; indeed his programme is to 'understand the operas as theatre through music' (p. 5). As he puts it elsewhere, 'The character of the dramatic course as a whole is analogous to that principle which governs the music of each individual number' (p. 237);

---

[11] Ensembles and finales, 253–4, 258–71, 307–18; arias and duets, 279–307. Kunze's book is not easy to use. For 650 dense pages of text divided into very long paragraphs whose initial lines are not indented, the table of contents gives only the (eight) chapter titles (averaging eighty pages), and the text and running-heads offer only one level of subheadings (averaging perhaps twenty pages). Nor is there an index of works or of individual numbers (a necessity in a volume of this type, realised in every other book under review). The reader wishing to grasp the organisation, or merely to locate the discussion of a given number, must laboriously outline the entire volume.

[12] His methods are indebted to the late Thrasybulous Georgiades, whose provocative but eccentric system was founded on the belief that Classical-period music simultaneously projects two complementary rhythmic domains: a 'scaffolding' (*Gerüstbau*) based on the unchanging 'empty' measure; and the infinitely flexible tonal-metric shapes of motives and phrases, which 'fill' those measures with ever-varying content. This is not the same as our distinction between metre and rhythm, although there are points of contact. Its great advantage for opera is that it is inherently 'multivalent'. *Mutatis mutandis*, it also excels in disentangling the differentiated vocal parts of ensembles. Georgiades, 'Aus der Musiksprache des Mozart-Theaters', *Mozart-Jahrbuch*, 1950, 76–98; rpt. in Georgiades, *Kleine Schriften* (Tutzing, 1977), 9–32.

the principle in question is the dialectic between strict construction and dramatic freedom. To be sure, this is again the correspondence theory, and the 'dialectic' is often displaced to the level of philosophical abstraction. Thus Kunze expands the technical opposition between 'skeleton' and 'content' into an abstract one between 'necessity' and 'freedom': 'Already in structuring the libretto, Da Ponte allowed a polarity to become manifest which is equally a subject for resolution in Mozart's music: strict, complex construction vs. complete freedom of movement and action' (p. 236). Occasionally, this tendency leads to passages like the following, regarding the finale in Act II of *Figaro*:

> Two principles can be teased out, which have analogies in Mozart's compositional thought: the end- and goal-orientated, processive character of the musical construction; and equally the space-encompassing establishment of a temporal realm in comprehensible and, to this extent, motionless space-relations, the establishment precisely of the temporal and experiential space in which the work constitutes itself as permanent.[13]

When Gurnemanz explains these things to Parsifal just before the *Verwandlung* leading to the Grail scene at the end of Act I, he needs just six short words: 'Zum Raum wird hier die Zeit'.

Another of Kunze's leitmotifs is musical 'autonomy'. He asserts that Mozart was 'interested in operatic "reform" only to the extent that it did not endanger musical autonomy; that is, the possibility of allowing musical theatre to emerge from the technical construction' of the music (p. 192). This is not merely another example of critics projecting their concerns backwards onto artists, but leads to a denial of the dramatic function of Mozart's overtures (except in *Don Giovanni*): 'the overtures always remain independent, indeed autonomous instrumental compositions, even those which do not actually close; there is nothing whose intelligibility depends on a knowledge of the entire opera or the first scene.' This stance is rightly rejected by Heartz (Ch. 18) and Bauman (pp. 93–4).

More generally, Kunze's insistence on the 'autonomy' of musical detail often leads him to miss the forest for the trees. For example, his discussion of Figaro's 'Non più andrai' (no. 10; pp. 282–4) correctly emphasises its 'double' construction, as a rondo and as a process leading to the triumphant march at the end; but he says nothing about *why* this should be so, what it shows us about Cherubino's potential for love and Figaro's ability to turn sticky situations to his advantage.[14] Regarding Susanna's 'Deh, vieni', he goes so far as to claim that 'a precise description of the construction [in mm. 40–44] would lead to the same results even if the text were not taken into account' – with respect to her climactic envoi, no less, 'Ti vo' la fronte incoronar con rose'. In these

---

[13] 'daß [...] sich zwei Prinzipien herausschälen lassen, die ihre Analogie auch in Mozarts kompositorischem Denken finden, namentlich der finale, zielgerichtete und prozeßhafte Charakter des musikalischen Baus sowie gleichermaßen die raumumspannende Herstellung eines Zeitbezirks in überschaubaren und insofern stillgelegten Raumverhältnissen, die Herstellung eben des Zeit- und Ereignisraums, in dem sich das Werk als Bleibendes konstituiert' (311).

[14] See Allanbrook, 93–9, and Webster, 'To Understand ... Mozart' (n. 1), 181.

respects Allanbrook's analyses are a welcome corrective. Her insights into Mozart's characters and their social relations (which constitute the dramatic expression of the 'rhythmic topoi'), and her interpretations of *Figaro* as a sublime-comic version of pastoral, and of *Don Giovanni* as a society which 'No-Man' shocks into extremes of inauthentic passion, are the best we have.

But the ways Mozart's arias really function – the relations among text-form, 'type', instrumentation and key, formal design of the music, tessitura, voice vs. orchestra, characterisation, dramatic context and so on – remain mysterious. Even revisionists – I include myself in the indictment – have not fully overcome the methods and presuppositions derived from two hundred years of instrumental analysis. As Platoff argues, 'sonata form' itself is in many respects irrelevant: even if one modulates to and then prolongs the dominant, the concluding sections in the tonic often do not constitute a 'recapitulation', either motivically (the music may be varied beyond aural recognition, or totally new) or gesturally (the return to the tonic is often 'underarticulated' compared to what is always heard in instrumental movements). Hence, something like my concept 'free recapitulation' or Mary Hunter's more neutral 'tonal return section' is needed.[15] But even if one accepted the traditional categories, a catalogue of formal types in Mozart's Da Ponte operas would include precisely one aria in sonata form ('Venite, inginocchiatevi') – compare what was said above regarding ensembles. And even in this aria, the 'recapitulation' (mm. 82 ff.) has very little to do with the 'first group' (1–14); in dramatic terms it represents a new state (Susanna has finished dressing Cherubino, and she and the Countess marvel at the result), and this is heard in the music.

More fundamentally, to invoke instrumental formal types as the primary basis for understanding arias may be irrelevant, if not positively misleading. Even the hypothesis that most late-eighteenth-century operatic numbers begin with an 'exposition', defined neutrally as a paragraph in the tonic followed by one in the dominant – which all revisionists so far still accept – needs critical review. Does this tonic-dominant relation really function analogously to the structural, form-defining polarity of the first large section of a sonata or binary form? If this section leads, not to a 'development' and 'recapitulation' but to a return of 'A' in the tonic and then a faster concluding section, as in many rondòs (for example, 'Dove sono'), is it properly understood as 'expository'? The sectional division is often A | B | A or A | B | A || C, so that the putative exposition (A + B) does not even exist as a formal unit. Or it may be ambiguous, as in *Così*, no. 17, Ferrando's 'Un'aura amorosa'.[16] Perhaps 'the' form of many arias permanently oscillates among various potential groupings of its sections.

[15] Platoff, 'The buffa aria', §§2 and 4; Hunter, 'Haydn's Aria Forms: A Study of the Arias in the Italian Operas Written at Eszterháza, 1766–1783', Ph.D. diss. (Cornell University, 1982), Ch. 9.

[16] See the differing accounts of this aria in Sieghard Döhring, *Formgeschichte der Opernarien* (Marburg/Lahn, 1975), 97–8, and Hunter, 44–5.

3

We turn now to the 'unity' of larger spans. With its allies – 'tonal planning', the privileged position of ensembles and finales, and the dominance of instrumental formal models – its existence is assumed in all the volumes under review.

The paradigmatic example of a large, complex number interpreted as a 'unity' on the basis of instrumental formal models is of course the Act II finale in *Figaro*. Both the notion and the choice of example go back to Lorenz.[17] To this day it remains an obligatory ritual to praise it as Mozart's finest achievement. For Allanbrook it is

> perhaps Mozart's greatest single piece of dramatic composition. [...] In form the finale consists of eight smaller pieces laid out in a large key-area [sonata-form-like] plan.[18] [...] This key scheme shapes a closed form with its own harmonic drive and dynamic curve. (p. 119)

Kunze writes that

> the finale of Act II of *Figaro* [is] by far [*mit Abstand*] the longest of Mozart's great finale-compositions. [...] In the finale, the key-succession [of Act II] is united into a cycle. [...] Tonally, the finale itself is [...] constructed in virtual symmetry around C major in the middle, and gravitationally with respect to the tonal foundation E flat of the two pillar-sections, Allegro and Allegro assai. (pp. 307, 308, 310)

Kunze's account harbours a serious error. Several other Mozart finales are effectively as long as this one (which comprises 939 notated measures), including those in *Don Giovanni*/II (871) and *Die Zauberflöte*/II (920); if length in performance and dramatic complexity were taken into account, *Figaro*/IV, both finales of *Così* and *Don Giovanni*/I would count as well. Nor is Mozart's length unusual for Viennese operas of the 1780s; indeed, Paisiello's *Il re Teodoro in Venezia*/II and Dittersdorf's *Der Apotheker und der Doktor*/I, *Betrug durch Aberglauben*/II and *Die Liebe im Narrenhause*/I actually exceed it.[19] Kunze's failure to check this 'fact' indicates how deep-seated is the notion of *Figaro*/II's special character. His positing of a 'symmetrical' axis around the C-major section ('Conoscete, signor Figaro', when the Count interrogates Figaro about the letter of assignation, and he and the ladies ask permission for the wedding to proceed) is based both on the patterns of tempo changes and on supposed tonal relations

---

[17] 'Das Finale in Mozarts Meisteropern', *Die Musik*, 19 (1926–27), 621–32. His idea had been anticipated in Oskar Wappenschmidt, 'Die Tonart als Kunstmittel im ersten Finale von Mozarts "Die Hochzeit des Figaro"', *Die Musik*, 10 (1910–11), 2nd quarter, 272–84, 323–40, whose account however was purely descriptive, without invoking 'unity' or 'tonal forms'. In English, Rosen's assumption (301–5) of large sonata-form-like unities has been very influential.

[18] The term 'key-area plan' was coined by Ratner to denote the common ground of binary and sonata forms; see his *Classic Music* (n. 5), Ch. 13.

[19] Platoff, 'Music and Drama in the *Opera Buffa* Finale: Mozart and his Contemporaries in Vienna, 1781–1790', Ph.D. diss. (University of Pennsylvania, 1984), 21, 82–3; Paul Joseph Horsley, 'Dittersdorf and the Finale in Late-Eighteenth-Century German Comic Opera', Ph.D. diss. (Cornell University, 1986), 154–9.

to the remainder of Act II (see p. 212). But this is of little weight, compared to the lack of entries or exits within it, and its placement in the middle of other spans: the overall build-up towards the climax of complexity at the end; and the famous descending-fifth sequence of keys, which has begun in the preceding section in G. And despite his invocation of its 'axial' importance, Kunze oddly says almost nothing about this section. Only Allanbrook's interpretation of it as a pastoral hymn (pp. 127–31), a stage in the increasing intimacy between Susanna and the Countess – for her, one of the central aspects of the plot – begins to do it justice.

Steptoe explicitly invokes sonata form in describing both the finale as a whole, and the individual sections:

[In] the mighty Act II Finale [...] the sections all contribute to an organised key structure based on the tonic E^b major. [...] Figaro's entry in G] is in an axial position harmonically, since it is here that structural tension is greatest. [...] It is midway between the tonic (E^b) and the dominant of the whole Finale. The keys [to this point] pick out the E^b major tonic triad, reinforcing the home key while generating tension from it. [...]
The general organisation of the Finale into a harmonically balanced sequence is duplicated in the internal structure of sections. [...] The dramatic stimulus is presented in the exposition, worked through the central development, and resolved for [sic] the recapitulation. (pp. 175–6, 178–9)

Carter's comments are shorter but no less sweet:

The Act II finale (no. 15) is so constructed that the keys of its eight sections move through a clearly conceived arch. [...] The whole finale is a masterpiece of tonal planning that creates a firm structure through no less than 940 [recte 939] bars of music and despite all the twists and turns of the action. (pp. 118–19)

That the finale as a whole is orientated around E flat, nobody will dispute. But to assert that it is 'in' this key, as if it were no different from a symphony movement, is already premature. And to call it a sonata form is to take a single domain (tonal shape) as standing for the whole, ignoring every other aspect of both music and drama: its systematic increase in complexity, which points towards the end as a climax; its sheer sectionality, emphasised by the abrupt contrasts at the entry of each new character; the lack of cogent musical relationship between the putative 'exposition' (Sections 1–3) and the putative 'recapitulation' (Marcellina); and so forth. (No responsible analyst of instrumental music would dream of invoking 'sonata form' on the basis of tonal shape alone.) One might accept the notion as a kind of synechdoche – the tonal form standing for the musical-dramatic whole – if its votaries did not ignore its incompatibility with so many other aspects of the finale (and if the interpretation itself had not long since become reified). Again, a multivalent approach is essential. And one consequence of this approach is likely to be the realisation that, as we have already suggested for some arias, this finale does not exhibit any single 'form'. Allanbrook's original and detailed 'demystification' of what she calls the *ombra* music in the Act II finale of *Don Giovanni* is a step in the right direction; it describes both Mozart's invocations of ecclesiastical terror in the small and a 'key-area form' organising the whole.

Abbate and Parker ('Dismembering', p. 194) note one multivalent feature in the finale of Act II of *Figaro*. The very long concluding section in E flat, which as a whole provides tonal closure and whose two final subsections (Più allegro – Prestissimo) continually cadence, seems to stand in a non-congruent relation to the dramatic situation, which 'is wide open, at a moment of maximum instability'. They add that at the end of Act IV, when the action has reached a stable conclusion, the closing D major section is relatively brief, apparently creating the 'opposite' disjunction. But neither case is straightforward. Despite the repeated strong cadences, the end of Act II remains in important ways musically unstable: incessant contrasts in text, material, rhythm and dynamics between the four victorious characters *en bloc* and the three (internally differentiated) defeated ones;[20] Susanna's chromaticism, syncopations and unstable coloratura (mm. 825, 842, 880); harshly dissonant dominant sevenths over tonic pedals (892 ff.); and most of all, at 'Prestissimo', the losers' desperate new motive, sf–p–crescendo, entering on an unharmonised, syncopated G and rising chromatically a ninth to A^b.

What is more, in all these respects the final D major section of the Act IV finale is fundamentally different. Everyone sings the same text; there are no meaningful distinctions between groups of characters (they all generally sing in rhythmic unison). In the last sixty bars (from m. 460) there are no dissonances, save the cadential six-four in 495 and 505; no chromatic notes, save $G^\sharp$ in the lightning orchestral flashes in 465–7 and 508–10 (neither is in the slightest degree destabilising). To be sure, it is shorter than the Più allegro/Prestissimo sequence at the end of Act II, and has fewer V–I cadences. But this is appropriate: the drama is already resolved; we are in a state of harmony. Nor is this a question of dramatic closure allowing the music 'to be free' (Abbate and Parker, p. 195), as if Mozart's harping on E flat at the end of Act II somehow represented a state of comparative 'unfreedom'. Such a notion still perpetuates, by inversion, the old prejudice according to which sonata forms are 'tighter' than others. In fact, one might well feel that there are *too many* strong cadences at the end of Act II, too hectically cascading over each other, for effective closure; do not the victors 'protest too much'? No Mozart or Haydn instrumental movement would ever dream of such excess. Nor would the last section of any concluding finale; 'Corriam tutti' in Act IV of *Figaro* is by comparison a model of control. Thus tonality itself is multivalent at the end of Act II: the long 'grounding' of E flat functions differently from the dissonances, chromaticism, syncopations and rhythmic diversity. (For the possibility that E flat itself is dissonant with respect to the D of the overture and the end of the opera, and further discussion of the function of D at the end, see pp. 215–16.)

Don Giovanni and *Così* exhibit the same distinction as *Figaro*. Despite

---

[20] Hermann Abert, *W. A. Mozart*, 2 vols. (Leipzig, 1956), II, 277–8.

repeated tonal closure, their central finales end in a state of musical as well as dramatic confusion and dissonance, with opposed groups of characters, disjunct texts, rhythmic contrast, coloratura and/or patter for leading characters, dissonance and chromaticism; while their end-finales are harmonious on all levels, with at most an echo of past troubles overcome (most prominently in *Don Giovanni*). Even in the very different world of *Die Zauberflöte*, where Act I itself ends with a moralising hymn, the latter is lightly chromatic on the harmonic level and includes a striking tenfold augmented triad under $d^{\sharp'''}$ in the orchestral postlude; these have no counterpart in the final section of Act II. In fact, no other Mozart finale has a sonata-like tonal form like that in Act II of *Figaro*; it is no more typical of his finales in general than 'Ah taci, ingiusto core' of his ensembles, or 'Venite, inginocchiatevi' of his arias.

4

Even if one is unwilling to embrace the post-postmodernist image of 'dismemberment' as a way of understanding Mozart's operas, one dare not ignore their ineluctably multivalent character. This applies not merely to individual numbers, but to the relations among them as well. An aria or trio is a single unbroken span of music, with a clear beginning and end, sung by the same character(s), in a single key and with uniform instrumental forces; despite all difficulties, it may in principle be analysed as a coherent movement. Even a finale has a clearly defined beginning and end in the same key, and once under way proceeds without interruption. It too might in principle be analysed as a coherent musical-dramatic action – not as a 'sonata form', of course, but perhaps analogously to a through-composed symphony, or to non-operatic compound movements with voices like the finale of Beethoven's Ninth. (For the distinction between 'coherence' and 'unity' as analytical ideals, see §6.)

But what of discrete numbers? In an eighteenth-century opera, each number is not only independent, with its own character and form, but is separated from all the others: by recitative, action, entries and exits, dramatic reversals, changes of scene, even perhaps the fall and rise of the curtain. In the absence of strong 'corroborating' evidence (as Tovey would have insisted), the hypothesis that these independent pieces are related like the movements of a symphony, let alone that they articulate a 'progression' like the wholly interdependent sections of a single instrumental movement, is implausible, to say the least. And yet every one of these volumes takes it for granted.

Act I of *Figaro* ends with 'Non più andrai' in C (no. 9), following a chorus in G; Heartz (Chapter 8; quoted on p. 210), Carter (p. 119) and Kunze (p. 255) assume that this constitutes a 'progression' from a 'dominant' to a 'tonic'.[21] But these numbers are separated by a considerable recitative, which brings an

---

[21] In this, as in many other points to be taken up here regarding 'tonal planning' in *Figaro*, the authors under review explicitly or implicitly follow suggestions first made by Abert, in his introduction to the Eulenburg miniature-score edition (ed. Rudolf Gerber); and by Siegmund Levarie, in *Mozart's 'Le nozze di Figaro'* (Chicago, 1952).

important dramatic turn (the Count's pardon and banishment of Cherubino). Even to think of them as analogous to two successive movements of a symphony probably goes too far. Besides, in a classical-period symphony we do not think of the keys of the several movements as creating a *progression*; the 'Jupiter' is never described as a 'plagal' form, I–IV–I, nor the 'Eroica' as a 'weak' one, I–vi–I. (An exception occurs only if movements are run-on, as in Haydn's 'Farewell' and Beethoven's Fifth.) And how does one know that C rather than G is the 'tonic', unless on the assumption that the key in which an internal unit ends always exercises this function? This too is only a hypothesis, which (so far) is no more than an uncritical borrowing from instrumental analysis. Bauman, owing to the use of dialogue rather than recitative in *Die Entführung*, emphasises the discontinuity between musical numbers and non-music; see pp. 1, 26, 72–3, 93. But he does not explain why *Die Entführung* should be 'problematical' in this respect, while *Die Zauberflöte* remains beyond criticism. Nor do the discontinuities prevent him from asserting the presence of tonal unities spanning the entire opera.

To return to the opening of *Figaro*: the overture is in D, the first duettino between Figaro and Susanna in G. Not only the three authors just cited, but Allanbrook (p. 75) and Steptoe (p. 187) as well, interpret this as a move from 'tonic' to 'subdominant'. Allanbrook goes so far as to mistake this supposed tonal relation for a 'sign' of dramatic content: in the same sentence, she calls no. 1 a 'relaxed and leisurely scene', whereas it is nothing of the sort.[22] To be sure, nothing intervenes. But in important ways overture and duet are incommensurable: instrumental *versus* vocal music; curtain down (or empty stage) *versus* characters, costumes, scenery, action, dialogue, disagreement, drama; in the eighteenth century, audience entering or talking or woolgathering *versus* (perhaps) attending to what is happening; and so forth. What is the justification for calling this a 'progression'? And suppose we were to grant this point: how do we know that D is the 'tonic' and G the 'subdominant', rather than D the 'dominant' and G (the beginning of the action, after all) the 'tonic' – except by retrodicting from the end of the opera, three hours and four acts in the future, or by appealing to Mozart's general practice of ending an opera in the key of the overture? Nothing else in *Figaro* supports the hypothesis that D is 'the tonic'; it appears elsewhere only in Bartolo's and the Count's arias, nos. 4 and 17. (See §5 below.)

And if the overture and no. 1 do constitute a progression from I to IV, what then? How does B flat in no. 2 prolong or extend it? (One answer has been: 'further' into the 'subdominant realm', as Figaro's and Susanna's situation becomes increasingly difficult; this can only be called risible.) And where is the 'dominant'? Only in the duet no. 5 between Susanna and Marcellina,

---

[22] Levarie, 17–19; Frits Noske, *The Signifier and the Signified: Studies in the Operas of Mozart and Verdi* (The Hague, 1977), Ch. 2; idem, 'Verbal to Musical Drama: Adaptation or Creation?', in James Redmond, ed., *Drama, Dance and Music* (Cambridge, 1981), 143–52; Webster, 'To Understand ... Mozart' (see n. 1), 183–4.

arguably the least important number in the act (save possibly the chorus); what follows is not the tonic, but Cherubino's aria 'Non so più' in the (*a fortiori*) 'remote' key of E flat; indeed, neither D nor A is heard again until Act III. Admittedly (as Kunze, Carter and Heartz point out), the first two acts exhibit correlations between the use of closely related keys in contiguous numbers for a given group of characters, but remote relations between one group and the next: Bartolo and Marcellina (nos. 4 and 5) in D and A; Cherubino (nos. 6 and 7) in E flat and B flat; Figaro (nos. 8 and 9) in G and C; the Countess and Cherubino (nos. 10 and 11) in E flat and B flat; Susanna (and the others) in G and C (nos. 12–14). Even this scheme does not always apply: the opening scene for Figaro and Susanna begins in G, but continues in B flat and F; nobody enters or leaves between 'Voi che sapete' in B flat and 'Venite, inginocchiatevi' in G. Furthermore, these are primarily 'associative' uses of tonality: D for highborn sentiments (or parodies of same); the 'simple' keys C, F and G for 'buffa' numbers, E flat for deeply-felt utterances, A for love-duets (or parodies), and so forth. This does not add up to the presence of 'progressions'.

Still less can one defend the extension of such 'progressions' over larger spans such as an entire act, as do Heartz, Carter and Kunze regarding Act I of *Figaro*. I quote Heartz:

'Non più andrai' [in C] arrives with a sense of inevitability not only because Mozart planted its rhythm in the opening number, but more importantly because it has been set up as a tonal goal, both in short-range terms, being preceded by the twice-sung Peasants' Chorus in G (which serves as dominant preparation), and in long-range terms that reach back to the initial duettino in G.[23]

And Carter baldly states that 'the act elaborates a large-scale V–I progression'. But we are not told how G can be 'prolonged' through six intervening numbers in five different keys; only one of these (D) is closely related to it, and it appears only in no. 4, at a far temporal remove from both nos. 1 and 8. What is worse, their treatment of G harbours an unacknowledged inconsistency: how can the same key simultaneously be the 'subdominant' of D (following the overture), and the 'dominant' of C (at the end)? In the former case, the act ends in IV of IV (and no. 8 cannot be the 'dominant'); in the latter, it begins in V of V, which is not only senseless in its own right, but will not mesh with the ultimate goal of 'tonal planning', which is to establish D as the tonic of the entire opera. (This differs only in degree from the games analysts play with Wagner's *Ring*, in which the E flat at the beginning of *Das Rheingold* is said to function as V of V of the concluding D flat of Brünnhilde's immolation and the end of Valhalla; in a real-life production, the latter events are witnessed approximately one week later.) Hence if one takes G seriously in both its putative

---

[23] Heartz, Ch. 8; quoted from 'Constructing *Le nozze di Figaro*', *Journal of the Royal Musical Association*, 112 (1987), 90–1.

tonal functions, one must admit that the 'tonic' itself has changed during the course of the act, from D to C. But if this is so, the act cannot be 'in' any single key, and it would be a pretty puzzle to determine the *location* of this change.[24] It would seem that overall tonal progressions governing entire acts (as opposed to more or less consistent key-associations) do not exist in Mozart – not even in Act II of *Figaro* (see §5).

The tendency to posit links between separate, often distant numbers does not affect tonality alone. The hunter of motivic correspondences and derivations is a familiar figure on the analytical scene, who, after a period of ostracisation, is making something of a comeback. As regards Mozart, the most prominent exponent has been Noske, now seconded by Heartz and Carter.[25] Motivic development *within* a number is unquestionably one of Mozart's most important techniques for generating coherence, precisely in the supple, unremarkable ways that dramatic music requires (and in full compatibility with the lessened importance of tonal 'polarities' and 'resolutions' compared to instrumental music). Another potentially effective linking technique involves vocal tessitura, especially the consistent exploitation of prominent high pitches. Carter (110–13; following Levarie) links the Countess's two arias through their common feature of 'searching' for g''. He may however go too far in arguing that, owing to differences in the treatment of that g'', 'Porgi amor' 'closes on a question-mark that emphasises the uncertainty of the Countess's present position', whereas in 'Dove sono' her 'emotional maturity is established'.[26] He certainly does so in linking all this with the g'' following her forgiveness of the Count in the Act IV finale (mm. 436–7); among other things, in this scene she never sings g'' by herself, and its harmonisation gravitates towards the subdominant of m. 437. Still another vital linking technique is instrumentation. All this leads on the one hand to conventional 'types' of aria (etc.), and on the other to the idea of 'subplots' involving particular groups of characters or strands of the action. But in all these contexts, it remains essential to proceed multivalently, rather than to depend on tonality, or instrumentation, or motivic connections alone.[27]

---

[24] Admittedly, Edward T. Cone speculates about such matters in Verdi without assuming that they are nonsensical; see 'On the Road to *Otello*: Tonality and Structure in *Simon Boccanegra*', *Studi verdiani*, 1 (1982), 72–98.

[25] Noske, *Signifier* (see n. 22); Heartz, Ch. 14, 18; see also his 'Tonality and Motif in *Idomeneo*', *The Musical Times*, 115 (1974), 382–6; Carter, 115–18.

[26] My doubts depend on analytical considerations for which there is no space here; I discuss the topic in the context of a methodological study of the analysis of Mozart's arias, to appear in Cliff Eisen, ed., *Mozart Studies* (Oxford, forthcoming in 1991). For the 'high-note' organisation of Tamino's scene with the Priest in the Act I finale of *Die Zauberflöte*, see my 'To Understand... Mozart' (n. 1), 188–90.

[27] I have briefly sketched a subplot in *Die Zauberflöte*, involving Pamina, the Queen of the Night and the magic flute itself, in connection with Pamina's aria 'Ach, ich fühl's', in 'Cone's "Personae" and the Analysis of Opera', *College Music Symposium*, 29 (1989), 44–65. See also Allanbrook on Acts III–IV of *Figaro*, described later.

5

If it is dubious to interpret a finale as a single form based on tonality, it is downright dangerous to unite discrete numbers, separated not only by recitatives and action but often by intervening concerted numbers as well, in extreme cases even by the curtain and an interval, into large-scale 'forms'. Yet Allanbrook, Kunze, Carter and Steptoe all exhibit this tendency (which again derives from Lorenz *via* Rosen and others). For Carter, E flat in the Act II Finale of *Figaro* is 'the same as the key of the Countess's "Porgi amor qualche ristoro" (no. 10); thus the whole of Act II might be said to elaborate [this key]' (p. 119); and for Kunze,

the E flat finale (no. 15) is already prefigured in the E flat cavatina of the Countess; the tonal succession of the five numbers preceding the finale (E flat, B flat, G, C, G) is unified in the finale into a cycle. [...] The action which culminates in the finale begins with the trio no. 13 'Susanna or via sortite' in C, in the key of the Andante movement which forms the mid-point of the finale. (pp. 309–10)

Allanbrook goes even further, proposing for the end of *Figaro*

a separate and transcendent line of action, which begins to take shape in act III with the pastoral letter duet [no. 20], and which merits a climax [of its own]. The line to this climax plots out its own key-area plan in B-flat, arching from the B-flat letter duet through to the pastoral fourth act, where Barbarina's F-minor cavatina and Susanna's F-major aria 'Deh, vieni' stand both in key and in tone as a kind of dominant to the final B-flat resolution – the pastoral reconciliation of the happy couple. (pp. 173–4)

About the cogency of this 'line of action' (or subplot) there will be little dispute (save to puzzle over the omission of Figaro's 'Aprite un po' quegl'occhi', which involves one of the main characters of the subplot and is in E flat – the putative 'subdominant', immediately preceding the 'dominant' of 'Deh vieni'). But one cannot possibly sustain a 'key-area plan' – that is, a sonata-like form – across parts of two different acts, or imagine its dominant resolving to its tonic across the intervening 'public' music in D and G (the first two sections of the finale, with their excruciating confusion). For that matter, the reconciliation is immediately preceded by Figaro's Larghetto 'Vulcan' speech and the long, complex box-on-the-ear section, both in E flat; this is hardly compatible with a 'dominant' function of 'Deh, vieni' in relation to 'Pace, pace, mio dolce tesoro' in B flat. Kunze, as we have seen, says the same kind of thing about Act II; elsewhere (pp. 347–8), he argues that in Act I of *Don Giovanni*, the 'Champagne' aria in B flat and Zerlina's 'Batti, batti' in F (nos. 11–12) 'prepare' the C major of the finale, and hence already constitute part of it, because of the sequence of rising fifths. (He also mentions, with Allanbrook [220–3], a more cogent relation: in his aria, Don Giovanni invokes the musical-social breakdown which, in the finale, will be realised through the three simultaneous dances: 'Senza alcun ordine / La danza sia'.)

In *Don Giovanni*, Steptoe interprets the opening scene as a macro-sonata form: overture in D minor and major = exposition; *introduzione* in various keys = development; duet no. 2, 'Fuggi, crudele, fuggi' in D minor = recapitulation (pp. 186–7), his application of the sonata principle to successions of discrete numbers deriving from Rosen. Even granting everything possible – the single scene, the unbroken dramatic sweep, the beginning and ending in D minor, the close relation of the *introduzione* keys – this strains credulity to the breaking point. After all, we have to do with three separate and distinct movements, of which the second and third are separated by recitatives both *semplice* and *accompagnato*, by exits and entrances, and by a proper young lady's discovery of her father's bloody and still very warm corpse. The Molto allegro of the overture is not an 'exposition', but a complete sonata form in its own right; the *introduzione* does not at all resemble a development section in internal construction (it is sectional, Leporello's 'Notte e giorno' is if anything expository, and it breaks off following the Commendatore's death with no hint of preparing D or a 'return'), and bears no tangible relationship to the overture; Anna and Ottavio 'recapitulate' nothing, rather their oath of vengeance crystallises a new stage in the drama. The invocation of 'sonata form' is not merely superfluous; it betrays an unwillingness to attend to what is happening on stage and in the pit, masquerading under a veneer of analytical sophistication.

By contrast, Rushton's approach to large-scale organisation, while not comprehensive (an impossibility in the 'handbook' format), is the best of those here under review. He is the only writer on *Don Giovanni* who pays sufficiently close attention to the staging, particularly the alternation of half- and full-stage sets and the timing of scene-changes. For example, Allanbrook (pp. 245, 258), Steptoe (pp. 119, 193) and Kunze (p. 346) still perpetuate the notion that, following Leporello's 'Catalogue' aria (no. 4), the scene changes to a country locale for the peasant wedding-party with Zerlina and Masetto. But Rushton had already shown (as both libretto and autograph make clear) that a single (full-stage) set, showing both Elvira's lodgings and Don Giovanni's town house, is used without change from before Elvira's initial entry (no. 3) until after the Don's 'Champagne' aria (no. 11).[28] This is not pedantry; it leads to a convincing argument that the drama preserves 'temporal unity', in that the entire action takes place within roughly twenty-four hours – from Don Giovanni's attack on Anna near midnight one night, to his downfall shortly after midnight the next. This insight has wide-ranging dramaturgical implications.

Rushton's acuity and common sense are equally evident in his technical discussions. He does not shy away from proposing elaborate structural relations between the opening scene (agreeing with Steptoe that the overture must be included) and the catastrophe in the Act II finale (104–9, 111–21). But his methods are the opposite of reductive; he assumes no single principle, appeals to no formal types. Instead he points, according to the context, to dramatic parallels, tonal sequences, 'sensitive' sonorities and whatever else seems appropriate. His tracing of the effects of the destabilising pitch B (in the D-minor context),

[28] Ch. 2 and 49–53; Rushton implies (143 n.8) that the error originated in Otto Jahn's Mozart biography.

for example, is exemplary. Although *ad hoc* procedures applied to such unique music cannot be imitated, let alone suggest approaches to methodology or theory, Rushton's tact and insight should inspire emulation.

From Act II of *Figaro* being 'in' E flat and the overture and nos. 1–2 of *Don Giovanni* 'in' sonata form, it is but a step to the belief that an entire opera is in a key or exhibits a form. Bauman, many of whose musical discussions of *Die Entführung* are excellent, nevertheless titles his last section (pp. 89–98) 'Unity and Coherence', stating that the opera is a 'living organism' (89) and that it is 'in' C, prolonged throughout by 'tonal planning' (73–5). He even goes so far as to claim (p. 97) that the final Janissary chorus 'recalls and completes [...] falling fourths left unresolved by the opening phrases of the overture'! This would be difficult to credit even if the D in question, m. 13 of the overture, were not resolved in the immediate context, mm. 29 and 33.

Carter, who begins his discussion of unity in *Figaro* with some scepticism (pp. 115–6), becomes less and less sure of his stance as he adduces more and more links of various kinds, and eventually concludes that

the whole of Act II might be said to elaborate the Neapolitan (flat supertonic) area of the opera's main key, D major. [...] The opera [is] an extended i–bII(=IV)–V–I progression. [...] The 'folle journée' opens and closes in D and thus exists within a single tonal space.[29]

Steptoe goes so far as to locate, among the three Da Ponte operas, 'a progressive movement towards greater unity [...] reflected in the growing emphasis on tonal cohesion, linkage of disparate sections by thematic allusion, and the structural use of key'. Thus whereas *Figaro* exhibits merely 'a genial sequence of memorable but distinct musical experiences', *Don Giovanni*

is characterised by a powerful unity of purpose. [...] Several procedures [...] sustain the dramatic unity [...:] the elimination of musical numbers which impeded the flow [... and] the grouping of successive musical numbers into broader harmonic units. Numbers [...] are embedded within a larger arch. (pp. 185–6)

And in *Così*,

two unifying devices [...] – the linking of separate numbers by tonal progression and the technique of thematic reminiscence – were brought to a further level of refinement. [...]

The key structure penetrates beneath the text and surface plot to delineate the meaning behind actions, and the motivations of the protagonists. [...] The central key, and the axis around which the work revolves, is C major. [...] 'Flat' keys are used to depict false or shallow feelings, while authentic emotion is presented in dominant 'sharp' keys. Such a scheme is a logical extension of the application of classical sonata forms to the dramatic medium. (pp. 213, 232)

Quite apart from the fact that such a scheme, pretending to relate almost all the numbers in a very long opera, has nothing to do with sonata form (a principle of organisation governing single closed movements), the dichotomy of 'true'

---

[29] 119–20; the 'progression' in question was asserted by Levarie (see below).

and 'false' emotions will not hold up. For example, Fiordiligi's 'Come scoglio' (no. 14) in B flat is notoriously difficult to interpret (Steptoe himself elsewhere describes its ambiguity). Although the Guglielmo–Dorabella seduction duet (no. 23 in F) may be 'shallower' than 'Fra gli amplessi' (no. 29 in A) between Ferrando and Fiordiligi, it is hardly 'false' on that account. And no. 2 in E major is a problem; in Steptoe's scheme it would have to be notably 'sincere', whereas it is merely the middle member in the set of three short introductory trios, of which the other two are in the supposedly 'neutral' keys G and C.

Heartz treats the tonality of *Figaro* in equally schematic ways:

Choosing the key of the second finale meant choosing the keynote of the opera. [...] Every subsequent choice of key had to be calculated on [... its] relationship to the three act-ending keys.

The pairings [of B flat and G] occur in every act. [... They] occur after E-flat not only in [the finale to Act II] but also in the sequences of Nos. 6–8, Nos. 10–12, and one last time in the finale of Act 4, another indication of how schematic Mozart was in laying out the whole opera with regard to tonalities. [...] It probably pleased his sense of long-term symmetry that the 'folle journée' ended with the scampering motions of the overture ('Corriam tutti') and mirroring the relationship of the overture to Nos. 1 and 2.[30]

He means that the overture and nos. 1–2 proceed D–G–B flat, and the last three keys of the Act IV finale proceed B flat–G–D. But no evidence suggests that Mozart paid very much attention to such abstract 'long-term symmetries', least of all those separated by the three hours and four acts of a musical drama, intended for live performance before a primarily lay audience whom he wanted above all to delight and impress.

Besides, the apparently unanimous opinion that the end of Act IV moves 'from G to D' is erroneous. Following the Andante forgiveness music in G, the wonderful orchestral transition modulates to the *dominant* (the 'home' dominant, of course); and the Allegro assai not only begins on this sonority, but prolongs it at least through the end of the minor-mode shadow (m. 456), if not indeed all the way to the structural half-cadence in 471–5. The progression is thus not IV–I, but IV–V–I; and it is *through-composed*, bound together by the transition and the new beginning on V. This 'tight' construction gains additional significance by contrasting with this finale's tendency (from Section 3 in E flat onwards) to juxtapose keys and sections. (This tendency has often been noted, but most often in the context of its supposed inferiority to the Act II finale; here, the dominant does not appear as a key, and remotely related key complexes – D and G for the 'public' action at the beginning and end, *versus* E flat and B flat for Susanna's and Figaro's 'private' reconciliation in the middle – are juxtaposed, rather than merging into one another.[31]) The supposed parallelism between the overture and no. 1 and these two sections, dubious enough in

---

[30] Ch. 8; quoted from 'Constructing *Figaro*' (see n. 23), 83–4, 93–4. Compare his 'Tonality and Motif in *Idomeneo*' (see n. 25).

[31] Favourable interpretations of the Act IV finale can be found in Noske, *Signifier* (see n. 22), 16–7; Allanbrook, 173–94; and Platoff, 'Finale' (see n. 19), 418–22.

dramatic terms and in its dependence on 'symmetry' (which, with respect to tonal music, exists only in analytical diagrams), thus goes up in smoke. Indeed, this is yet another reason why the conclusion of *Figaro* is so satisfying, 'despite' the relative brevity of D major: we finally hear a key which is strongly prepared by its own dominant, and which not only articulates the requisite happy ending, but *resolves* the music of the final dramatic crux. (Of course, this resolution has nothing to do with sonata form.) This difference from the sectionality of the remainder of the finale (let alone of successions of independent numbers) creates a strong effect of culmination at the end of the opera. At the end of *Don Giovanni*, the keys of the last two stable sections are likewise G, for Anna's and Ottavio's dialogue and love-duet; and D, for the final pseudo-contrapuntal wind-up. And the dominant mediates between them here as well (mm. 744–55), although the passage is not as strongly through-composed as in *Figaro*.

All this is not to imply that associations of keys with particular characters, dramatic situations, instruments, textual features and so forth have no force, or that key-relations are irrelevant. It cannot be accidental that from *Idomeneo* on Mozart always ended his operas in the key of the overture, always articulated the central finale in a different key, and always ended a finale in the key in which it began (as did all Viennese composers in the 1780s). What must be avoided is the uncritical assumption that these features go together to make up a 'form', or that the opera is 'in' a key, as in Levarie's notorious interpretation (pp. 233–45) of the entirety of *Figaro* as a single, gigantic progression, I–bII–V–I. For example, it may be of little consequence that the key of the central finale is 'remote' from that of the overture and the ending. Mozart's primary reason for the choice was purely practical: he used trumpets and drums in only three keys – C, D and E flat.[32] Given that the central finale was to be in any key other than that of the beginning and ending, the relation was necessarily 'remote'. Thus, to cite the finale of Act II of *Figaro* for the last time, it is not clear whether the confusion and instability at the end have anything to do with the fact that, in the context of a single movement, the key of E flat could be heard as 'dissonant' with respect to the D major in which the opera begins and ends. In fact, the overall role of D in Figaro is far weaker than that of D in *Idomeneo*, C in *Die Entführung*, D minor/major in *Don Giovanni* or E flat in *Die Zauberflöte*. But even in these operas, the putative 'tonics' may represent little more than a network of associations, not so different in its way from what one finds in Verdi or Wagner. The real – that is, critically aware – discussion of whether, and if so how, a Mozart opera is 'in' a key has not yet begun.

6

The notion of 'unity' in Mozart's operas is doubly suspect: it originated in the historically-culturally delimited and un-Mozartean context of German

---

[32] Heartz, 'Constructing *Figaro*' (see n. 23), 83.

interwar Wagnerian aesthetics; and it leads to absurd results. We can but wish it well in retirement, where it may enjoy the more modest, but also more helpful, role of documenting a long and influential, but now passing, phase in the history of Mozart criticism.

Indeed, the search for 'unity', whose irrelevance to opera now seems obvious, is increasingly coming to seem unsatisfactory even in the realm of instrumental music – even that of the Classical period. The 'reductive' character of any unifying theory seems inadequate to the richness and complexity of all great musical artworks. The realisation that the paradigm of organicism (on which 'unity' depends) arose and flourished in the particular historical and cultural context of German Romanticism and its aftermath allows us to see that it is no more universal than the eighteenth-century doctrine of the affections or today's aesthetics of disjunction. And 'deconstruction' and other post-structuralist approaches reveal unacknowledged contradictions in the discourse of 'unifying' analyses (as well as an underlying dependence on the concept of unity even in most of those who attempt to escape it).[33] The fact that historical and analytical discourse about music can be deconstructed does not imply that music itself can be; a philosophy whose *raison d'être* is the use of language to probe the functioning of language is scarcely equipped to tell us very much about music. A strong irony, however, is that the best English-language analysts of Classical-period instrumental music, such as Tovey, Edward T. Cone, Leonard B. Meyer and Rosen (notwithstanding his sonata-principle orientation), have never set much store by 'unity'.

In all this, the distinction between 'unity' and 'coherence' (referred to at the beginning of §4) is crucial; in essence, it entails two fundamental differences of approach.[34] First, unifying analyses tend to be reductive: both in assuming that a single criterion or domain must be primary, and all others secondary; and that the aim is often literally to 'reduce' a work to some fundamental entity, such as a Schenkerian *Ursatz* or a Schoenbergian *Grundgestalt*. A belief in 'unity' also tends to entail the use of hierarchical methods, which reflect the organicist belief that a central or fundamental entity must be replicated in the detail of all subsequent levels. (The hierarchical paradigm is of all the aspects of organicist thinking one of the most misleading for musical analysis.) By contrast, a complex, non-reductive approach such as multivalence is in principle compatible with a differentiated analysis which comes closer to the complexity of great music. Secondly, a 'unifying' analysis usually underplays the experiential aspects of music (temporal succession, rhythm, timbre, musical processes, listeners' psychology, etc.), in favour of a more nearly abstract or 'ideal' mode of understanding. By contrast, a demonstration of coherence remains compatible with

---

[33] From this chorus I cite (more or less arbitrarily) Dahlhaus, 'Some Models of Unity in Musical Form', *Journal of Music Theory*, 19 (1975), 2–30; Arnold Whittall, 'The Theorist's Sense of History: Concepts of Contemporaneity in Composition and Analysis', *Journal of the Royal Musical Association*, 112 (1987), 1–20; and Alan Street, 'Superior Myths, Dogmatic Allegories: The Resistance to Musical Unity', *Music Analysis*, 8 (1989), 77–123.

[34] I broach this issue in a somewhat different manner in 'To understand ... Mozart' (see n. 1), 178–9, 191–2.

adequate attention to these matters. In principle, every analysis, of instrumental as well as vocal works, should account for them.[35]

But a programme of multivalent analysis will not be easy to realise. And in opera, even more than in other contexts, rigorous self-criticism remains essential, in proportion as the genre is more complex than any other, and viable paradigms and theoretical traditions have not yet emerged. A given number cannot be understood except in awareness of its dramatic and musical context, yet concepts for dealing appropriately with that context hardly exist. And in a genre so dependent on convention as eighteenth-century opera, not even *Figaro* can be discussed in a vacuum, without attention to the remainder of its composer's *oeuvre* and works by other composers. And so I can only conclude with an apparently simple question, to which however a satisfactory answer would speak volumes: how shall we understand a single Mozart number?

---

[35] I have attempted full-dress analyses along these lines in *Haydn's 'Farewell' Symphony* (see n. 9); and in 'Zur Form des Finales von Beethovens 9. Sinfonie', in the forthcoming report of a conference on the nineteenth-century symphony, held in Bonn, 1989, to be edited by Siegfried Kross.

Part II
Singers

[5]

RAAFF'S LAST ARIA: A MOZARTIAN IDYLL IN THE SPIRIT OF HASSE

By DANIEL HEARTZ

"Man muss aus der Noth eine tugend machen."

PRIOR to composing *Idomeneo* in 1780–81, Mozart had tailored his art to some of the greatest singers of the age, both in concert arias and in his several stage works. The castrato Giovanni Manzuoli comes to mind at once. For him Mozart wrote the title part of *Ascanio in Alba,* and he knew the voice well even earlier, from the singing lessons Manzuoli imparted when the Mozarts were in London in 1764–65. "Tailored" fits the case perfectly. It is the expression Mozart himself chose when expressing his function as composer. With regard to his *Mitridate,* written for Milan in 1770, he was reported by father Leopold as unwilling to compose much in the way of arias until he knew a voice firsthand, "so as to measure the garment exactly to the person."[1] Eight years later, when composing the

---

[1] "Um das Kleid recht an den Leib zu messen." Letter of November 24, 1770, No. 220, lines 6-7. Passages from Mozart's letters have been translated by the author from *Mozart Briefe und Aufzeichnungen. Gesamtausgabe,* ed. Wilhelm A. Bauer and Otto Erich Deutsch, 4 vols. (Kassel, 1962–63). Citations will be identified henceforth by date, number in this edition, and line, with the German text included where comparison with the original proves to be of particular interest.

aria "Se al labbro mio non credi" (K. 295) expressly to suit the voice and satisfy the taste of Anton Raaff (1714–1797), he used a similar formulation: "I like to measure an aria to a singer so accurately that it resembles a well-fitting garment."[2] Satisfying Raaff at this late stage of his long career proved no easy task. From his experience of Raaff in the theater at Mannheim, he knew exactly what he could and could not expect of the veteran tenor. He witnessed Raaff's performance in the title role of Holzbauer's *Günther von Schwarzburg* in November, 1777, and wrote to his father: "Whoever hears him begin an aria and fails to recall that this is Raaff, the old and once so famous tenor — he must certainly laugh wholeheartedly. For it is a fact, as I was thinking to myself, that if I didn't know it was Raaff singing, I'd double up with laughter; instead I take out my handkerchief and soil it. His life long, he was never anything of an actor, as people tell me even here, where they say he should be heard but not seen. He has no stage presence whatsoever. In the opera he has to die, and while doing so sing a /: long:/ slow aria; well, sir, he died with a grin on his face, and at the end of the aria his voice gave out so badly that one couldn't bear it any longer."[3] With this portrait in mind, it will be possible to appreciate all the more what a superb sartorial fitting Raaff both required and received in the role of Idomeneo.

Mozart left Salzburg for Munich in early November, 1780, in order to finish the composition of *Idomeneo* on the spot, in collaboration with the singers, players, dancers, and scenic artists. His first letter back to his father brings up the old problem anew: "Raaff is like a statue."[4] A week later it was a question of asking the librettist,

---

[2] Letter of February 28, 1778, No. 431, lines 26-27: "denn ich liebe dass die aria einem sänger so accurat angemessen sey, wie ein gutgemachts kleid." Compare also Mozart's words about "Non so, d'onde viene" (K. 294) written for Aloysia Weber, in a letter of December 3, 1778, No. 508, lines 44-45: "indemm sie ganz für sie geschrieben, und ihr so past, wie ein kleid auf den leib."

[3] Letter of November 14, 1777, No. 373, lines 61-68. I have preserved Mozart's use of repetition marks to emphasize a point. In the original he wrote in addition the word "ter" above "/: lang :/", i. e., "thrice-long."

[4] Letter of November 8, 1780, No. 535, line 46. In a subsequent letter (December 19, No. 565, line 53), Mozart referred to Raaff as a "schlechte acteur." There is no lack of corroborating evidence on Raaff's inadequacies as an actor. Metastasio referred to him as a "freddissimo rappresentante" as early as 1749; see Otto Michtner, *Das alte Burgtheater als Opernbühne von der Einführung des deutschen Singspiels (1778) bis zum Tod Kaiser Leopolds II. (1792)* (Vienna, 1970), p. 379, note 20. In the *Musikalisches Handbuch auf das Jahr 1782* ascribed to Carl Ludwig Junker there is another revealing picture of Raaff at the end of his career: "Nun hat er beynahe ausgedient

Abbé Varesco of Salzburg cathedral, to accommodate Raaff's request for a change at the end of the opera: "He is right moreover, and even were he not, some consideration should be shown his grey hairs. He was with me yesterday and I ran through his first aria, with which he was very content. Now the man is old and can no longer show himself to advantage in an aria such as he has in Act II, 'Fuor del mar, ho un mar in seno.' So, inasmuch as he has no aria in Act III, and his aria in Act I cannot be as cantabile as he'd like on account of the text, he wishes to have a pretty one to sing after his last speech, 'O Creta fortunata, O me felice,' instead of the quartet there. And thus another useless piece will be gotten rid of, and Act III will make a much better effect."[5] Only from these last remarks do we learn that the libretto originally included a second quartet, not to be confused, as is so often done, with the Great Quartet early in Act III, but a *licenza* of the perfunctory type that was so common, allowing the remaining principal singers to take their leave.[6] Raaff had a history of getting his way with composers and librettists when it came to final scenes. His death scene in *Günther* represented his fourth aria, as Mozart pointed out, noting the fact also that this gave him altogether some 450 bars of music to sing.[7] Earlier Raaff had the ending of one of Metastasio's most celebrated dramas altered so that he could sing an additional aria in place of the concluding *coro*. The case is instructive and warrants consideration here. In *Attilio Regolo*, which was Metastasio's own favorite among his dramas, the title hero is sent off the stage with a magnificent monologue, meant to be set as an obbligato recitative, without an aria.[8] This ending was so effective as composed by Jommelli for

---

und ist kalt. Ob er gleich mehr spricht als singt, oder obgleich sein Gesang meist singende Rede ist, so kann man doch aus den Ueberresten desselben und aus seiner meist guten Declamation schliessen, dass er ehmals gross müsse gewesen seyn. Von Action weiss er nichts." (This annual bears no place of publication and is not paginated; a copy exists in the Bavarian State Library, Munich, Mus. Th. 1654.)

[5] Letter of November 15, 1780, No. 538, lines 9-20. The first-act aria in question is "Vedrommi intorno l'ombra dolente" (No. 6).

[6] Confusion of the two quartet texts was made by Edward J. Dent, *Mozart's Operas: A Critical Study*, 2nd ed. (London, 1947), p. 37, and is encountered widely on Dent's authority.

[7] Letter of November 14, 1777, No. 373, lines 59-60.

[8] Metastasio expressed his preference to Casanova in a detailed and very informative interview accorded the latter in 1753, as related in Casanova's *Mémoires*, chap. 33 (Pléiade ed. [Paris, 1964], I, 713). Metastasio's instructions how to set *Regolo* were written to Hasse in a letter, which has been widely reprinted, dating from October 20, 1749.

Rome in 1753 that it was encored when sung at London the following year, according to Burney.[9] Perhaps Varesco had been emboldened to give Idomeneo a concluding monologue in recitative, without aria, on precisely this model. Raaff intervened similarly in both operas, at any rate. As given at Naples in 1761, Jommelli's *Regolo* was a pasticcio "accomodato dal Sig. Nicola Sala con arie di diversi," and the final aria for Raaff, composed by Domenico Alberti, was borrowed in text from Metastasio's *Temistocle*.[10] Raaff may well have suggested the text himself, as he was later to do with Mozart.

The new aria text requested of Varesco was quickly produced and sent off to Munich on November 25. Leopold was already skeptical as to its viability when he quoted the first two lines, which is the only reason they have survived:

> Il cor languiva ed era
> Gelida massa in petto
> . . .

He objected specifically to the "ed era" at the end of the first line. Infelicitous, to be sure, was a run-on line at this spot. In lyric arias the first line was usually set as a discrete statement, either a phrase or a half-phrase; it was also used at will in the subsequent course of the piece where needed to provide text for transitions and the like. Leopold sought to justify the verse with the rather lame remark: "admittedly the same thing does occur often in Metastasio, where it's up to the composer's skill; many dumb Italian composers would set the first line to one melody and then make a different and separate melody for the second."[11] Mozart replied to his father only four days later: "the aria for Raaff which was sent pleases neither him nor me at all. Concerning *ed era* I say nothing; for that is always an error in this kind of aria. Agreed, Metastasio also has it sometimes, but

---

[9] Charles Burney, *A General History of Music* (London, 1789), ed. Frank Mercer (1935), II, 852: "It seems, however, worth recording, that a scene of *recitative*, in the part of Serafini, was encored every night during the run of the opera, the only instance of the kind I can remember. . . . It was in the last scene of Jommelli's opera, which ends without an air, that Regulus, determined to return to Carthage, addresses the Roman people who endeavored to prevent his departure, in the recitative which had so uncommon an effect, beginning: 'Romani, addio, Siano i congedi estremi degni di noi' etc." The situation in Regolo's final monologue is not unlike that of Idomeneo, and Metastasio's famed nobility of language here may have been exemplary for Varesco.

[10] "Ah! frenate il pianto imbelle," Act II, scene 3, aria of Neocle. I am indebted to my student Marita McClymonds for this information and for a detailed comparison of the 1753 and 1761 versions of *Attilio Regolo*.

[11] Letter of November 25, 1780, No. 543, lines 13-18.

extremely seldom, and those are not his best arias. And what is the need for it? Besides this the aria is not at all what we wanted, namely, it should express peace and satisfaction, and this it does not do until the second part. Of the misfortunes he has had to bear throughout the entire opera we have seen, heard and felt enough; now is the time for him to talk of his present condition. We don't need a second stanza anyway. So much the better if there is none. In the opera *Achille in Sciro* by Metastasio there is an aria of this kind, and in the style that Raaff would have liked:

> Or che mio figlio sei,
> Sfido il destin nemico;
> Sento degli anni miei
> Il peso alleggerir."[12]

Mozart erred in believing this aria to be of one quatrain only. It has two, like the great majority of Metastasio's arias, the second providing a typical nature simile, in this case a lovely image of new shoots springing from old wood:

> Cosi chi a tronco antico
> Florido ramo innesta,
> Nella natia foresta
> Lo vede rifiorir.[13]

Again on December 1, Mozart restated his needs after saying how pleased Raaff was with his second-act aria. He quoted Raaff as telling him and others: "I was always in the habit of changing my roles, in arias as well as in recitatives, but here all remains as written because I find not a note that is unsuitable to me."[14] The truth of the matter was quite otherwise, as we shall see. Mozart continues: "Raaff wishes, as do I, to have the aria you sent altered a bit; he also takes exception to the 'era.' And then we want here a peaceful, contented aria. Even if it has but one part, so much the better. The second part must be taken in the middle anyway, and that often gets in my way. In *Achile in Sciro* there is such an aria of this kind. . . ."[15] What is probably meant here is this: Mozart does not want to be obliged to have a contrasting musical section in the middle, which is almost mandatory if the textual content of the second stanza is very substantial. There are examples of this ternary

---

[12] Letter of November 29, 1780, No. 545, lines 1-17.
[13] *Achille in Sciro*, Act III, scene 7, aria of Licomede.
[14] Letter of December 1, 1780, No. 549, lines 42-45.
[15] *Ibid.*, lines 45-50. Mozart then quotes Metastasio's first quatrain again.

aria structure in *Idomeneo*. "Fuor del mar" is one; of the four others, two were cut before the première by Mozart himself.[16] The predominating aria form in the opera is binary, wherein the second stanza is distributed over the second key area, followed by a restatement in the tonic, without intervening middle section, of both parts.

Leopold sent Varesco's second attempt at a final aria for Raaff on December 11; Andreas Schachtner's German translation of it followed later, at an unspecifiable date. Both were printed in Libretto I, an Italian-German text for the opera that represented its state in the first part of January, 1781, before Mozart started making extensive cuts and revisions.[17] The new text and its translation read as follows:

Sazio è il Destino al fine	Nur erst nach ausgeprüften Leiden
Mostrami lieto aspetto.	Ertheilt die Fügung reife Freuden
Spirto novello in petto	Der Geist und Muth, den ich verlor,
Vien mi a rinvigorir.	Steigt doppelt frisch in mir empor.
Tal Serpe in frà le spine	So lassen auch die weisen Schlangen
Lascia le antiche spoglie,	Die Haut gestreift an Dörnern hangen,
E vinte l'aspre doglie	Um sich nach solcher blut'gen Pein
Torna à ringiovenir.	Verjüngt in neue Tracht zu freun.

Contrary to Mozart's wishes, Varesco provided a comparison aria in two stanzas, indebted somewhat to the proffered Metastasian model, from which it copies the end rhymes "alleggerir" and "rifiorir," turning them into "rinvigorir" and "ringiovenir." But now the comparison is to a rejuvenated snake that has hung up its skin on a thornbush. Raaff had compared himself with a deal of natural phenomena during his forty years of singing simile arias in opera seria. It is to be doubted that he had ever been asked to compare himself with an old snake. Schachtner's translation carries this bizarre image to another degree of tastelessness by rendering "aspre doglie" ("bitter sufferings") as "blut'gen Pein" ("bloody Pain"). The words of the first stanza may speak of joy and fulfillment, but

---

[16] Arbace's "Se il tuo duol," No. 10a, and Idamante's "Non, la morte," No. 27a; the two ternary arias not cut were Ilia's "Zeffiretti lusinghieri," No. 19, and Arbace's "Se cola ne' fatti," No. 22. The numbers are those in my edition in the Neue Ausgabe sämtlicher Werke, of *Idomeneo*, 2 vols. (Kassel, 1972), referred to subsequently as the Neue Mozart Ausgabe.

[17] On the two librettos for *Idomeneo* see the Vorwort to the Neue Mozart Ausgabe, section d, "Letzte Münchener Revision," pp. xii-xvi.

the sounds are far from being lovely. Five elisions occur in the first line alone. "Sazio è il" is hard to sing because the difficult "z" consonant explodes into a string of four vowels that must be pronounced as a single syllable — otherwise the line would not scan properly and yield the requisite seven syllables to match the other lines. Varesco could not have been thinking of musical setting when he concocted this harsh opening. How mediocre a poet he was when working without Mozart's direct guidance is nowhere more evident.

The reaction in Munich to Varesco's second effort can well be imagined. Raaff became increasingly hostile. Mozart tried at first to defend Varesco, with the result that Raaff began questioning the professional competence of composer and poet alike. This is the moment when Raaff raised objections to his part in the Great Quartet because it was not cantabile enough. He also objected to the text-setting in "Fuor del Mar." I have suggested elsewhere that the real problem with "Fuor del Mar" was Raaff's inability to sing it, and that the shortened version without coloratura (No. 12b) was in fact made at Munich for him.[18] Mozart at first attempted to weather the new storm without making further demands on Varesco, who was already irate with both Mozarts. In his letter of December 27 he only mentions the problem, after describing his other difficulties with Raaff: "just now he was totally indignant about the words in his last aria — rinvigorir — and ringiovenir, especially 'vienmi a rinvigorir,' five 'eee' sounds! It is true that at the end of an aria this is very unpleasant."[19] How far Mozart got with the composition of this aria cannot be determined. He may have showed the text to Raaff even before playing for him what he had in mind as to the music. The failure of Varesco's first text perhaps suggested such prudence. In his next letter three days later Mozart spelled out the dilemma in more detail: "I am now in an embarrassing situation with regard to Raaff's last aria and you must help me out of it; 'rinvigorir' and 'ringiovenir' he cannot stomach and because of these two words he hates the whole aria. It is true that 'mostrami' and 'vienmi' are also not good, but the two last words are the worst of all. In order to avoid putting the final trill on the *i* in the first 'rinvigorir' I have to take it on the *o*." Rarely does any composer of the time get down to cases regarding such matters as does Mozart here. The "o" is a possible sound for the melismas and cadenza that figured

---
[18] *Ibid.*, p. xv.
[19] Letter 570, lines 60-63.

by tradition at the end of the first section; even preferable to it was the open "a." But melismatic extensions could not occur on the "ee" sound of *"i"* or upon any other closed vowel. The "o" was also unlikely in this case because it was an unaccented syllable. Mozart continued the same letter with a proposal that is not his own: "Now Raaff has discovered, I believe in [Metastasio's] *Natal di Giove,* which admittedly /: is very little known: / an aria that is suitable to the situation: I believe it is the *aria di licenza:*

Bell'alme al Ciel dilette,	Creta non oda intorno
Si, respirate ormai;	Non vegga in si bel giorno
Gia palpitaste assai:	Che accenti di contenti
E tempo di goder.	Che oggetti di piacer.

And this aria he wants me to compose for him. No one knows it, he says, and we won't tell. He is fully aware that it is hardly possible to ask the abbé to alter this aria again, and as it is, he will not sing it. I beg you for a quick answer. Wednesday I hope to have your reply, then I shall just have time enough to compose his aria."[20] Mozart sent this urgent request on Saturday the thirtieth of December, 1780. Act III had already been put into rehearsal a few days earlier. Leopold Mozart acted at once to wrest a new aria from Varesco. The result was in Mozart's hands by Wednesday, January 3, as he acknowledged in closing his letter the same day: "I am very happy to have received the aria for Raaff, for he was absolutely determined to have his own text substituted. I would have been forced /:NB with a man like Raaff:/to the solution of having Varesco's text printed and Raaff's sung."[21] It is ironic that Varesco's "Sazio è il destin" was in fact being printed at just this time, in Libretto I.

Raaff was a man who knew his Metastasio. Of course he had been singing the cantatas, operas, and oratorios of the Caesarean poet all his life, and when he finally died, he was reported as reading not only from the Bible but from his edition of Metastasio.[22] He possessed the sumptuous Paris edition that began to come out in 1780, as I was happy to ascertain from the list of subscribers at the end of Volume XII, where he is listed as "Signor Antonio Raaff di Manheim."[23] Perhaps he even had Volume I at the time of his

[20] Letter of December 30, 1780, No. 573, lines 28-49.
[21] Letter of January 3, 1781, No. 574, lines 52-55.
[22] Heinz Freiberger, *Anton Raaff (1714–1797): Sein Leben und Wirken als Beitrag zur Musikgeschichte des 18. Jahrhunderts* (Bonn, 1929), p. 61.
[23] *Opere del Signor Abate Pietro Metastasio* (Paris, 1780-82).

controversy with Mozart. It included *Il Natal di Giove,* from which Raaff extracted "Bell 'alme." Directly preceding this *aria di licenza* was a line of recitative that may have initially led Raaff to light upon the choice: "In di cosi felice e Creta, e il Mondo." Recall that Idomeneo's final words in recitative were: "O Creta fortunata o me felice." With this truly mellifluous aria text as a goad and a model, Varesco was able, probably with Leopold Mozart's prompting, to produce a truly viable piece of *poesia per musica*. It is short, consisting of only two tercets; each of the first three lines is a discrete thought; the imagery is beautiful and so is the language, which cannot be easily translated, except in a most literal fashion:

Torna la pace al core,	Peace returns to my heart,
Torna lo spento ardore	My exhausted ardor revives,
Fiorisce in me l'età.	Age is flowering within me.
Tal la stagion di Flora	Thus the season of Flora.
L'albero annoso infiora	Makes the ancient poplar bloom
Nuovo vigor gli dà.	And gives it new vigor.

For all its charm and grace the verse is but a composite of ideas and sounds from the previous ones, which agrees with Mozart's emphasis throughout the correspondence upon altering rather than inventing from nothing. Using "core" in the first line goes back to Varesco's earliest verse. The play on "Flora" and "fiora" occurs in the first Metastasian aria given him as a model, as does the simile of new shoots from old wood. Varesco salvaged "vigor" from the much maligned fourth line of his second text, and "torna" from its last line. And he finally learned from "Bell 'alme," it seems, the lesson that Metastasio had to teach all librettists: in a lyric aria the more open vowels and liquid consonants, the better.[24]

---

[24] Other possible textual models include Metastasio's early and very popular Canzonetta *La Primavera* (Rome, 1719), which begins as follows: "Già riede primavera / Col suo fiorito aspetto; / Già il grato zeffiretto / Scherza fra l'erbe, e i fior. // Tornan le frondi agli alberi / L'erbette al prato tornano / Sol non ritorna a me / La pace del mio cor."

"Torna la pace al alma" figures as the final piece in *Ippolito ed Aricia* (Parma, 1759), the first "reform" opera based on Rameau, with text by Frugoni and music by Traetta — see Daniel Heartz, "Operatic Reform at Parma: *Ippolito ed Aricia*," in *Atti del convegno sul settecento parmense nel 2° centenario della morte di C. I. Frugoni* (Parma, 1969), pp. 271-300. The opera was known to the circles that would eventually produce *Idomeneo;* Holzbauer set the same text, probably adapting some of Traetta's music (Mannheim, fall, 1759).

526

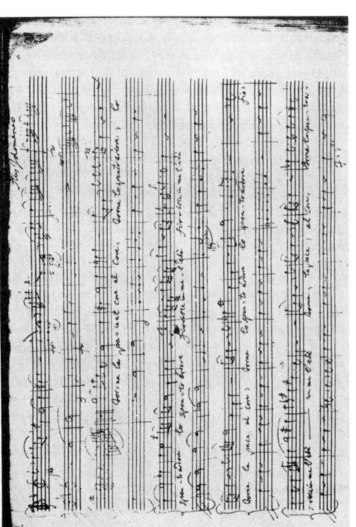

Plate I.

Draft-sketch for "Torna la pace" in Mozart's hand; the first page.

Raaff's Last Aria

Mozart set to work at once on the musical setting. He drafted a version in two voice-parts of the entire piece and it survives, by some miracle, along with the autograph of Act III at Berlin. It is reproduced here in facsimile for the first time. Plate I shows the first page, beginning with the nine-bar orchestral ritornello. On the top line Mozart writes in only what will become the first violin part, even though there are important motivic elements elsewhere, e. g., the introduction of the forte in measure 4 by a churning sixteenth-note figure in the second violins and violas, to which the first violins respond, and also in measure 6 the fluttering chromatic thirds of the clarinets and bassoons, against which the violins merely provide a pedal with their repeated F's. Omission of significant compositional detail like this suggests that Mozart is not sketching the piece for his own benefit, prior to scoring the orchestral version. This he does not need to do in any case: with him the whole piece is in his head, typically, as soon as the text is right. To what purpose, then, write out such a draft? Because Raaff needed something to study, and the time was short. Given the peculiar history of this case, it is also clear that Mozart was taking no chances on the possibility of another veto. From his earliest days he was loath to waste time or music paper until certain his efforts would meet requirements.

The fragile voice of Raaff required extraordinarily careful treatment. As the voice enters Mozart switched to the tenor clef, bringing him in on a sustained F, led up to by a little connecting passage in thirds by the clarinets and bassoons, which is in the vocal draft — Raaff needed to hear this. The F has no competition because all the strings, violins included, are scored under the voice. Later the violins climb up and help him by playing (no doubt very softly) in unison with the vocal line. His vocal part is confined to a very small range, from the fifth below middle C to the fifth above. What appears to be long and dull pedals in the bass line will be enlivened in the full orchestration by undulating thirds in the winds as already introduced in the ritornello — a lovely example of "Neapolitan zephyr music," and similar to what surfaces later in the terzettino "Soave sia il vento" of *Così fan tutte*.[25] But indeed Mozart had already used a similar texture and sonority for the middle section of Ido-

---

[25] For an example very similar to Mozart from a composer of the Neapolitan school, see Traetta's "Aure placide, che mormorate," illustrated in the article cited in the preceding note, p. 293.

96 Essays on Opera, 1750–1800

528

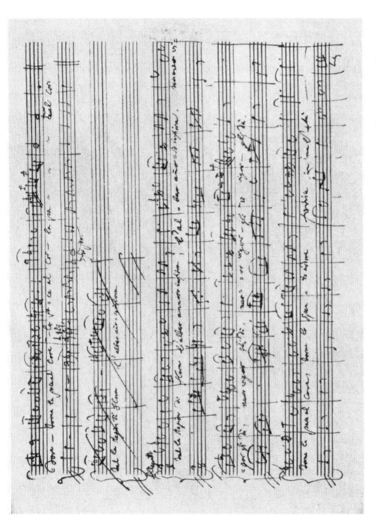

Plate II.

Draft-sketch for "Torna la pace"; the second page.

Courtesy of the State Library, Berlin.

meneo's Prayer, "Accogli o ré del mar," and not by chance does this section, to the text "Torni Zeffiro," share the same clarinet key of B-flat.

Plate II shows the draft approaching the end of the first part. From the spacing it is clear that Mozart tucked in an extra measure as an echo in the lower line after the third measure; it is an afterthought that will appear in the full score an octave higher, for the winds. He brings the initial line of the text back for the fourth time here. The reason must be because he wants to take the concluding melisma on the "ah" of "pace." He does not bother to notate the ensuing ritornello.

Mozart first began drafting the middle section with the melodic idea of the falling fourth, which had been prominent throughout the main section, but derives specifically from what may be called the second theme (the second measure in Plate II). He got no further than four measures, complete with text and the precise articulation of the melody. Even before writing in the accompanying bass another idea displaced the first. He crossed out the four measures and started over by transforming the melodic motive into an Allegretto in 3/8 time. The change in meter and tempo allows him to get away from the foursquare phraseology of his first attempt and to arrive at two three-measure phrases — a delightful example of how seven-syllable lines in Italian are apt to generate non-square phrases. Upon repeating the second line of the middle section he draws it out to four measures and a cadence on F. The process repeats itself for the last line, "Nuovo vigor gli da," set to the leap of a sixth, which certainly radiates vigor after all the conjunct motion preceding it. Raaff's high note of G is reached as the three-measure phrase is repeated in a rising sequence. This time the concluding phrase, with cadence on G minor, is stretched to six measures by means of an interrupted cadence with leap up to the high G. What happens next is contrary to all the "rules." Mozart, having repeated the last line of text four times, resorts to the first stanza, even though the middle section is not over. The textual anticipation of the reprise is very effective nevertheless, because the beginning of the tonal return to B-flat is already felt when the voice enunciates "Torna la pace." Mozart reinforces this rather subtle point by reintroducing the winds, heretofore excluded from the middle section, at precisely this juncture, prior to the first "Torna." Their presence confirms tonal indications that the reprise is near.

The change of compositional plan evident on this page makes it necessary to modify what was said above concerning draft versus sketch. This is surely a working version of the aria for Raaff's perusal. At the same time it is a working sketch, because Mozart was still making compositional decisions while jotting it down, important decisions at that, such as those involving the whole character of the middle section. Furthermore, the decision to change meter and tempo betrays Mozart's relentless effort to do everything in his power to please Raaff. Allegretto 3/8 middle sections in a common-time aria represent a fashion that was long out of date. They were, in fact, a trademark of the great J. A. Hasse, although not his exclusive property, it goes without saying. An example, one from an incredible number of Allegretto 3/8 middle sections that could be adduced, will show many features in common with Mozart. The aria is "Per pietà bell'idol mio," from Hasse's third setting of Metastasio's *Artaserse,* for Naples in 1760 (see Ex. 1). The melodic-harmonic sequences, the ambling gait of the bass line, and the canonic conduct between the voice and bass at "Sallo amor, lo sanno i Numi" are all typical. Coming back to the middle section of "Torna la pace" we find a similarly ambling bass line and, moreover, a similar canonic dialogue at "Nuovo vigor gli dà." Mozart changed this canonic passage in the full score, making it more euphonious and more chromatic, which had the effect of masking its old-fashioned prototype, at least slightly. He made another small change in the

Ex. 1

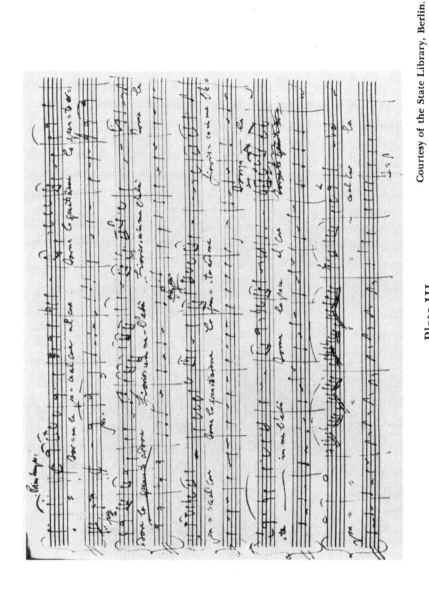

Plate III.
Draft-sketch for "Torna la pace"; the third page.

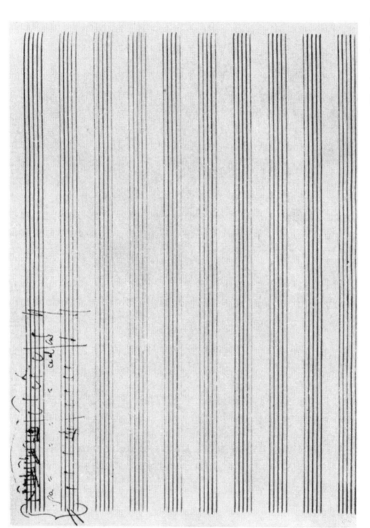

Plate IV.
Draft-sketch for "Torna la pace"; the fourth page.

bass line here which allowed him to avoid arriving at an open fifth between outer voices on the third "Nuovo vigor."[26] The case well illustrates how he continued to refine and polish his part-writing while orchestrating. It did not affect Raaff's part, and thus did not invalidate the purpose of the vocal draft.

The return of the Primo Tempo at the top of Plate III offers nothing remarkable until the transition section, when Mozart started recomposing. Keeping Raaff's voice within its narrow range did not allow the solutions of transposing up a fourth or down a fifth. Beginning with the "Torna" at the end of line 2, Mozart enriches the harmony with a wonderfully rich-sounding secondary dominant, to accompany the expressive leap of a seventh in the voice, then resolving in the next measure to a dominant ninth chord. These are new colorings and shadings. In the final version Mozart changed the leap from G up to G so that the voice struggles up the chord tones to the high G (measure 109). This change must have been imparted to Raaff at the last minute. The voice part is completely rewritten for the subsequent material, which must now appear in the tonic instead of the dominant. At the end of the second staff from the bottom on Plate III there is evidence of another change of tactic in the course of composition. Mozart first used the second line of text, "Torna lo spento ardore," but when he got to the long held F, with melisma ahead, he reverted to his first line, "Torna la pace." The reason can only be that he wanted to display Raaff's voice under the most favorable conditions of all, with the "ah" of "pace" rather than the "oh" of "ardore." There remained only the approach to the cadence, via a strong emphasis on the subdominant E-flat and a final melisma, again taken on "ah." Mozart must have felt that the cadence came too soon in his original version, especially after the busy and syncopated interlacings of the first measure on Plate IV. Comparison with the final version in full score shows that he extended the precadential tonic six-four to dominant from one measure to two, each harmony receiving an entire measure. Again Mozart did not bother to notate the orchestral ritornello. And there is no suggestion here as to the cadenza that Raaff was expected to improvise fol-

---

[26] Mm. 72-73 of the score. It is the same kind of change that Mozart often suggested to his English student Thomas Attwood. See *Thomas Attwoods Theorie- und Kompositionsstudien bei Mozart*, Neue Mozart Ausgabe, Series X/30, Vol. 1 (Kassel, 1964), especially the minuets that Attwood composed in late 1786, during the final months of his sojourn at Vienna.

lowing the orchestral pause on the tonic six-four chord towards the end of the final ritornello (measure 140). That was the singer's prerogative altogether.

Raaff was pleased with his last aria, as well he should have been. So were those who heard it in rehearsal, according to Mozart's last letter from Munich to Salzburg, with its stunning news that "Torna la pace" was to be cut. Without indignation or the slightest sign of self-pity, Mozart reported why all the troubles taken were to go for naught: "The rehearsal of the third act went excellently and people judged it far superior to the first two acts. But the text is far too long, and consequently the music /: which I have maintained from the beginning:/. Thus we are cutting Idamante's aria 'Nò, la morte io non pavento,' which is inept where it stands in any case, but over the loss of which those who have heard it in music lament, and also Raaff's last aria, over which they lament even more. Still, one must make a virtue out of necessity."[27] The aphorism applies as well to the whole composition of "Torna la pace." When Libretto II was printed shortly before the première of *Idomeneo* on January 29, 1781, it confirmed the cutting of both arias and also the elimination of Electra's third-act aria. Idomeneo's monologue ended with his last words of recitative "O Creta fortunata, o me felice," precisely as it had in the original version, some three months earlier.

The extraordinary lengths to which Mozart went to please his lead tenor actually began three years earlier at Mannheim, with the earlier aria written for Raaff, "Se al labbro mio," K. 295. Mozart explained in the greatest detail why he picked this text in a letter to his father: "Yesterday I was at Raaff's and brought him an aria that I composed for him recently. The words are 'Se al labro mio non credi, bella nemica mia etc.' I don't believe that the text is by Metastasio. The aria pleased him enormously. Such a man one must treat very gingerly. I sought out the text with care, knowing he already had an aria on the same, and would consequently sing mine with more ease and pleasure. I told him to tell me frankly if something doesn't suit him or please him and that I would alter it as he wishes, or even write another one. God forbid, he said, the aria must remain as it is, for it is very beautiful, only please shorten it a bit for me, for I can no longer sustain my notes. Very gladly, I answered, as short as you want. I made it a little long on purpose because it is always easy to cut, but not so easy to lengthen [note the possibility

[27] Letter of January 18, 1781, No. 580, lines 9-16.

that Mozart used a parallel strategy when composing, then cutting "Fuor del mar" in *Idomeneo*!]. After he had sung the second part he took off his glasses and looked at me with wide-open eyes and said, Beautiful! Beautiful!, that is a beautiful *seconda parte*, then he sang it three times. When I left, he thanked me most politely and I assured him that I would arrange the aria so that he would sing it very gladly, for I like to measure an aria to a singer so accurately that it is like a well-fitting garment."[28] Presumably Mozart prepared for Raaff a vocal score similar to that for "Torna la pace." It does not survive as such, but, then, such scores are among the greatest rarities today. The earlier aria shares with "Torna la pace" the key of B-flat and much more. It also has a main section marked Adagio, in common time, *alla breve*. The contrasting middle section, the *seconda parte* that so pleased Raaff, is an Allegretto in 3/8. Moreover, the main theme for the voice plays on the same range, even the same melodic turn.

Ex. 2

It could not have escaped Raaff that the cadential gesture of "Se al labbro" became the opening gesture of "Torna la pace" — an F prepared as a consonance, resolving as a suspension, by way of G, to E-flat. Even the spacing of the orchestral accompaniment is similar.

Mozart's inspiration for the beginning of "Se al labbro mio" raises an interesting question. The same text is set as an insert aria for Arbace in Hasse's 1760 setting of *Artaserse* for Naples.[29] Hasse

---

[28] Letter of February 28, 1778, No. 431, lines 9-27, cited briefly in note 2, above.

[29] Raaff sang at Naples in the 1760–61 season, as we saw above in connection with the mangled version of Jommelli's *Regolo*, but he did not sing in Hasse's *Artaserse*. The part of Arbace was written, moreover, for a soprano, Mozart's old friend Manzuoli. It was frequent practice at the time for soprano arias to be sung by tenors; see the Vorwort by Stefan Kunze to his edition of Mozart's concert arias, Neue Mozart Ausgabe, Series II/7, Vol. 2, pp. xx-xxi (Kassel, 1967). Kunze's edition of "Se al labbro

begins his melody by moving up the tonic triad to the fifth degree, then falling by stepwise motion (see Ex. 3). The correspondence with Mozart's opening (Ex. 2) may or may not be a coincidence, and the question is the more involved since we know Mozart was trying to capitalize on Raaff's affections for an older aria on the same text. For his middle section, that "seconda parte" by which Raaff evidently set such great store, Hasse reverted to his favorite 3/8 Allegretto style. He began in the parallel minor, no doubt prompted by a desire to express the words, "il cor dolente." After leaping via the triad to high A, the voice remains in a restricted ambitus and the leaping motion passes to the violins. Hasse's use of independent orchestral writing is remarkably fine throughout the Allegretto, which is quoted in its entirety (Ex. 4). By the time that the second line "ma d'ogni colpa privo" has begotten three phrases of three measures each, the long melodic extension on "innocente" comes as a surprise, a moment that is all the more intense for the long and partly chromatic rise in the voice, unaccompanied except by the violins in unison; the goal is the same high A of the initial measure. Canonic interaction between the voice and the bass begins at "ardor" but does not continue long; the descent of the bass line here seems to mirror the earlier ascent. After the cadence on F the voice intones the F major triad heard earlier in the first violins and the bass begins a chromatic rise that closes in on the pedal E of the voice and first violins. Or to put it another way, the E is reinterpreted several times, emotional intensity rising to a height with the diminished chord of the penultimate measure, before the release that comes with the cadential six-four chord and its resolution, with the fall of the voice through an octave to the lower E. It is not difficult to imagine that Raaff might have fallen in love with such a piece.

Mozart, not surprisingly, turned to an Allegretto in 3/8 for the middle section of his "Se al labbro." He chose G minor, the relative minor in this case, and began by outlining it triadically, while the bass jogs along in the old-fashioned style noted above in connection with "Torna la pace." A comparison with Hasse's middle section

---

mio non credi" is found in the same volume, No. 20, and his speculations as to the possible author of the text on pp. xiv-xv. Raaff sang Hasse to good effect on an occasion related in *Anecdotes du xviiie siècle* (London, 1787) according to the article "Raaff" in *Enciclopedia dello Spettacolo*: the Principessa di Belmonte, inconsolable at the loss of her husband, was brought out of her torpor by Raaff's admirable execution of an aria by Hasse.

gives the impression that Mozart is trying to be different, but not too different, that is, not too unlike what Raaff was used to singing. When towards the middle of his Allegretto Mozart closes in on a cadence by a chromatically rising bass line, the suspicion arises again that he was paying the older composer the sincerest kind of flattery.

Ex. 5

A colored drawing of Raaff in stage costume has been preserved, along with some other mementos of the Mannheimer Kappelle, in the Theater Museum at Munich (Plate V).[30] His sartorial finery is bright red in the original, while his armor is colored silver. The drawing is sometimes referred to as Raaff playing the role of Idomeneo, but there is no basis for such an ascription. In fact, the drawing could represent Raaff in any of his numerous heroic roles,

---

[30] For details on this drawing, see Daniel Heartz, "Idomeneus Rex," *Mozart-Jahrbuch*, 1973, p. 9, note 6.

540

Courtesy of the Theater Museum, Munich.

Plate V.

Raaff in heroic costume.

after his return to Germany and engagement at Mannheim in 1770. It could even represent his costume as Günther in Holzbauer's masterpiece — we do not know that the German subject of the opera entailed a corresponding departure from the conventional operatic costume, which was modeled, however loosely, on Roman antiquity. More likely, the costume is earlier still. Bustle, cloak, and feathers were already going out of style on advanced operatic stages by the 1760s. On the other hand, it is just possible that Raaff, as an honored relic from the fabled generation of mid-century singing "stars," obtained his way with costumers quite as much as he did with librettists and composers. He may have insisted upon wearing similar frippery at the first production of *Idomeneo*. If so, his appearance can hardly have matched the sets designed by Lorenzo Quaglio, an artist noted for his neoclassic sobriety and Piranesi-like somberness.[31]

A more impressive portrait of the old singer now graces the Beethoven House in Bonn, near which town Raaff was born (Plate VI). The painter, C.-A.-J. Philipart, rendered his likeness in oil at some time after 1777, date of *Günther*, a score of which Raaff holds in his hands. It is not a full score, to be sure, but only the "Tenor Arien," which were probably written in a two-part working version prepared for his benefit, such as Mozart made for "Torna la pace." Raaff looks out at us with the proud mien and noble stance of a Primo Tenore, his grey hairs dressed to a fault, his eyes unbedimmed by the years and unencumbered, moreover, by his eyeglasses, although we know these were necessary when he read music. Holzbauer's *Günther* preceded Mozart's *Idomeneo* by a scant few years, albeit the composers were separated by two generations in age. If Philipart's portrait was done later than 1780, a possibility that cannot be dismissed, Raaff's choice of music reveals in telling fashion where his sympathies lay: with the generation of Holzbauer and Hasse.

Mozart, too, venerated both older masters. In this respect he was quite unlike Leopold, who lost few opportunities to disparage music other than his son's. Witness his remark that *Ascanio in Alba* had

---

[31] The gloom of Piranesi's "Carceri" weighs upon the massively framed harbor with ships designed by Quaglio, possibly for *Idomeneo,* Act II; see Daniel Heartz, "The Genesis of Mozart's *Idomeneo,*" *The Musical Quarterly,* LV (1969), 1-19, Plate III. The well-known design by Quaglio representing Neptune's temple shows his more neoclassic side; although often ascribed to *Idomeneo,* it does not match what the libretto calls for at all, and must have been done for some other opera.

542

Courtesy of the Beethoven House, Bonn.

Plate VI.

Philipart's portrait of Raaff.

Raaff's Last Aria

"quite beaten" Hasse's *Ruggiero* at Milan in 1771.[32] What a different attitude emerges from the words written by the young genius of the operatic stage! Unable to attend all the performances, as he would have liked, he was nevertheless present in spirit: "Today is Hasse's opera, but since Papa is not going out, I can't go; luckily I know all the arias by heart, and thus I can, even at home, hear them and see them in my mind."[33] Twenty years later, in November, 1791, Mozart would follow the performances of *Die Zauberflöte* from his deathbed with watch in hand. His heart was in the theater then as always. Cutting Raaff's last aria, in spite of its undeniable beauties, was wise in terms of theater, and Dent draws a proper comparison with Beethoven's unyielding stubbornness in such matters, writing of Mozart: "he thinks only of the stage and the general dramatic effect . . " and "is his own physician and surgeon."[34] For all that the two "Viennese" masters had in common, Mozart was in some ways more attuned in temperament to a grand old figure like Hasse, although separated from him in age by more than half a century. Like "il caro Sassone," he never questioned the fundamental Italian premise that an opera composer's first duty was to enhance the human voice, and treat it individually. In this respect Mozart was at one, in the deepest sense, with the spirit of Hasse.[35]

---

[32] Letter of October 19, 1771, No. 250, lines 7-9: "mir ist Leid, die Serenata des Wolfg: hat die oper von Hasse so niedergeschlagen, dass ich es nicht beschreiben kann." Leopold's unabashed glee is all the more inexcusable because the commission for Mozart's Milanese operas was passed by way of Hasse.

[33] Letter of November 2, 1771, No. 254, lines 23-26.

[34] *Mozart's Operas*, 2nd ed., p. 63.

[35] This paper was read at the Annual Meeting of the American Musicological Society, Dallas, Texas, 1972.

[6]

GALUPPI, TENDUCCI, AND *MOTEZUMA*: A COMMENTARY ON THE HISTORY AND MUSICAL STYLE OF OPERA SERIA AFTER 1750

DALE E. MONSON

Baldassare Galuppi's serious operas, like Haydn's symphonies, spanned a vast period of changing musical styles and aesthetics. Galuppi's first tentative efforts were mostly substitute arias and collaborations in pasticci for Venetian productions of the 1720s and 1730s,[1] dating from the time Pergolesi (whose *L'Olimpiade* was first staged in Rome in 1735), while Galuppi's last works are contemporary with Mozart's travels and opera productions for Milan. Over the approximately 50 years covered by Galuppi's serious operas, much, of course, changed.

Many important questions about the changes and influences of Galuppi's lengthy and prolific career in serious opera, as well as about 18th-century Italian opera in general, have not yet been seriously considered, because, until recent breakthroughs in the sophistication and availability of new technology, the sheer quantity of information that had to be located, sorted, indexed, and evaluated, just to establish the initial criteria for judgment, dissuaded all but the most dedicated.[2] One of these problematic, yet crucial issues, concerns the symbiotic relationship of composers and singers in the composition of opera seria.[3] As an illustration of this issue, and the way in which this relationship flourished, this paper will explore the career and

---

[1] Cf. R. WIESEND, *Il giovane Galuppi e l'opera - materiali per gli anni 1722-1741*, «Nuova Rivista Musicale Italiana», XVII, 1983, pp. 383-397.

[2] Issues such as the establishment of a singer's career have been, until now, particularly difficult to determine. Much of the methodology for sorting data for this current paper comes from the ECOD (Eighteenth-Century Opera Database) project of the University of Michigan, supported by the University's Amdahl computer. For futher information on this project, contact the author at the School of Music, U of M, Ann Arbor, Michigan 48109.

[3] My thanks are extended to Dr. Dennis Libby, whose research and advice concerning the importance and careers of eighteenth-century singers inspired this paper.

singing technique of the well-known castrato singer, Giusto Ferdinando Tenducci, and will discuss the music composed for him by Galuppi against the background of other contemporary composers. By commenting on the nature of the Tenducci/Galuppi music, much can be said about how their collaboration played an important role in the creation of the music.

Giusto Ferdinando Tenducci was probably born in Siena, around 1735, since throughout his career he carried the pseudonym « Il Senesino ».[4] Nothing about his early life and education is known. Details about his singing career are given in the Table.

Date		City	Title	Composer	Role
17 Nov	1750	Cagliari	*Giunone placata*	Bollano	[?]
	1750	Cagliari	*Artaserse*	[?]	Artaserse
Aut	1752	Palermo	*La serva bacchettona*	(*Pasticcio*)	Don Sancio
Car	1753	Palermo	*La finta sposa*	Fischietti	Camillo
29 Aug	1753	Lucca	*La clemenza di Tito*	[?]	Annio
Aut	1753	Venezia	*Ginevra*	Bertoni	Ariodante
Car	1754	Venezia	*Adriano in Siria*	Scolari	Farnaspe
Car	1754	Venezia	*La clemenza di Tito*	(*Pasticcio*)	Annio
Car	1754	Venezia	*Tamerlano*	Cocchi/Pescetti	Andronico
12 Mar	1755	Wien	*Gioas re di Giuda*	Wagenseil	Gioas
	1755	Dresden	*Il conte caramella*	Galuppi	Ripoli
	1755	Dresden	*Il filosofo di campagna*	Galuppi	Rinaldo
26 Dec	1756	Milano	*Artaserse*	Q. Gasparini	Artaserse
Car	1757	Milano	*Ezio*	Galuppi	Valentiniano
8 May	1757	Napoli	*Farnace*	Perez/Piccinni	Pompeo
4 Nov	1757	Napoli	*Nitteti*	Piccinni	Amenofi
18 Dec	1757	Napoli	*Temistocle*	Jommelli	Lisimaco
20 Jan	1758	Napoli	*Arianna e Teseo*	Mazzoni	Alceste
Jun	1758	Padova	*Demofoonte*	Galuppi	Cherinto
11 Nov	1758	London	*Attalo*	(*Pasticcio*)	Idaspe
16 Dec	1758	London	*Demetrio*	(*Pasticcio*)	[?]
16 Jan	1759	London	*Il Ciro riconosciuto*	Cocchi	Cambises

---

[4] Information on Tenducci's career and biography is scattered through a wide variety of secondary sources. The most important of these include: T. J. WALSH, *Opera in Dublin 1705-1797: The Social Scene*, Dublin 1973; C. TERRY, *Johann Christian Bach*, London, Oxford University Press 1929; 1967[2]; and C. B. OLDMAN, *Mozart's Scena for Tenducci*, « Music and Letters », XLII, 1961, pp. 44-52. Many details concerning Tenducci's performance career have been gathered (with assistance from Dr. Libby) from Claudio Sartori's catalogue of libretti, as well as references found in *The London Stage*, and D. J. REID's, *Some Festival Programmes of the Eighteenth and Nineteenth Centuries*, « RMA Research Chronicle », V, 1965, pp. 51-79. Tenducci should of course not be confused with the other « Senesino », Francesco Bernardi, who sang for Handel in the King's Theatre of London, in the 1720s.

GALUPPI, TENDUCCI, AND « MOTEZUMA »

Date			City	Title	Composer	Role
21 Apr	1759	London	*Farnace*	(*Pasticcio*)	[?]
13 Nov	1759	London	*Vologeso*	(*Pasticcio*)	Aniceto
15 Jan	1760	London	*La clemenza di Tito*	Cocchi	Annio
1 Mar	1760	London	*Arminio*	(*Pasticcio*)	Sigismondo
13 Mar	1760	London	*L'isola disabitata*	Jommelli	[?]
17 Apr	1760	London	*Antigona*	Cocchi	Learco
5 Jun	1760	London	(a concert of arias)		
28 Jan	1761	London	(a concert of arias)		
27 Feb	1761	London	*Judith*	Arne	[?]
12 Jun	1761	London	*The Judgment of Paris*	Arne	[?]
2 Feb	1762	London	*Artaxerxes*	Arne	Arbaces
26 Feb	1762	London	*Alexander's Feast*	Handel	[?]
			Beauty and Virtue	Arne	Wisdom
5 Mar	1762	London	*The Sacrifice*	Arne	[?]
16 Mar	1762	London	(a concert of arias)		
3 Apr	1762	London	(a concert of arias)		
22 Apr	1762	London	(a concert of arias)		
18 May	1762	London	(a concert of arias)		
20 May	1762	London	(a concert of arias)		
11 Jun	1762	London	(a concert of arias)		
30 Sep	1762	Salisbury	(sacred concert)		
1 Nov	1762	London	*The Harlequin Sorcerer*	[?]	Shepherd
15 Nov	1762	London	*The Royal Convert*	[?]	(chorus)
24 Jan	1763	London	*Romeo and Juliet*	[?]	(chorus)
24 Feb	1763	London	*Artaxerxes*	[Arne]	[Arbaces]
27 Apr	1763	London	*The Cure of Saul*	(*Pasticcio*)	[?]
3 May	1763	London	*Artaxerxes*	[Arne]	[Arbaces]
9 Jun	1763	London	(a concert of arias)		
3 Oct	1763	London	*The Royal Convert*	[?]	(chorus)
21 Sep	1763	Salisbury	(sacred concert)		
12 Dec	1763	London	*Artaxerxes*	[Arne]	[Arbaces]
29 Dec	1763	London	*Romeo and Juliet*	[?]	(chorus)
29 Feb	1764	London	*Judith*	Arne	[?]
5 Apr	1764	London	*Pellegrini*	(*Pasticcio*)	[?]
2 May	1764	London	*Artaxerxes*	[Arne]	[Arbaces]
22 Aug	1764	Salisbury	(sacred concert)		
23 Nov	1764	London	*Artaxerxes*	[Arne]	[Arbaces]
24 Nov	1764	London	*Ezio*	(*Pasticcio*)	Valentiniano
1 Jan	1765	London	*Berenice*	(*Pasticcio*)	[?]
26 Jan	1765	London	*Adriano in Siria*	Bach	Adriano
15 Feb	1765	London	*Judith*	Arne	[?]
2 Mar	1765	London	*Demofoonte*	Vento	[?]

281

DALE E. MONSON

Date			City	Title	Composer	Role
7 Mar	1765		London	*Il re pastore*	Giardini	Agenore
28 Mar	1765		London	*Antigonus*	Pasticcio	Alexander
27 Apr	1765		London	*L'Olimpiade*	Arne	Licida
1 May	1765		London	*Artaxerxes*	[Arne]	[Arbaces]
14 May	1765		London	*Il Solimano*	(Pasticcio)	[?]
18 July	1765		Dublin	*The Royal Shepherd*	(Pasticcio)	Amyntas
30 July	1765		Dublin	*Artaxerxes*	Arne	Arbaces
	1765		Dublin	*Farnace*	(Pasticcio)	[?]
3 Dec	1765		London	*La clemenza di Tito*	(Pasticcio)	Annio
31 Jan	1766		Dublin	*Comus*	(Pasticcio)	Ariel Spirit
3 Mar	1766		Dublin	*Love in a Village*	Arne	Young Meadows
24 Apr	1766		Dublin	*Love in Disguise*	Giordani	[?]
7 May	1766		Dublin	*L'eroe cinese*	Giordani	Siveno
Jun	1766		Dublin	*Pharnaces*	[?]	[?]
Jun	1766		Dublin	*The Royal Shepherd*	[?]	[?]
15 Dec	1769		London	*Amintas*	(Pasticcio)	Amintas
2 Feb	1770		London	(a concert of arias)		
9 Mar	1770		London	*The Resurrection*	Arne	[?]
12 Mar	1770		London	(a concert of arias)		
29 Mar	1770		London	*Gioas re di Giuda*	Bach	Gioas
7 Apr	1770		London	*Artaxerxes*	[Arne]	Arbaces
3 May	1770		London	*Amintas*	(Pasticcio)	Amintas
4 May	1770		London	*Artaxerxes*	[Arne]	Arbaces
5 Sep	1770		Winchester	(sacred concert)		
3 Oct	1770		Salisbury	(sacred concert)		
24 Nov	1770		London	*Cosroe*	[?]	[?]
13 Dec	1770		London	*Astarto*	[?]	[?]
	1770		London	*Orfeo ed Euridice*	Gluck/Bach	Orfeo
10 Jan	1771		London	*Gioas re di Giuda*	Bach	[Gioas]
8 Feb	1771		London	(a concert of arias)		
9 Feb	1771		London	*Semiramide riconosciuto*	Cocchi	Scitalce
28 Feb	1771		London	*La passione*	Jommelli	[?]
13 Sep	1771		Firenze	*Orfeo ed Euridice*	Gluck/et al.	Orfeo
Car	1772		Roma	*Farnace*	De Franchi	Farnace
Car	1772		Roma	*Motezuma*	Paisiello	Motezuma
14 Mar	1772		Roma	(academy)		
27 May	1772		Venezia	*Motezuma*	Galuppi	Motezuma
18 Sep	1772		Firenze	*Armida*	Sacchini	Rinaldo
Aut	1772		Firenze	*Enea in Cartagine*	[?]	Enea
9 Jan	1773		Roma	*Armida*	Gazzaniga	Rinaldo
6 Feb	1773		Roma	*Demofoonte*	Anfossi	Timante
Apr	1773		Genova	*Antigono*	Alessandri	Demetrio

282

GALUPPI, TENDUCCI, AND « MOTEZUMA »

Date	City	Title	Composer	Role
May 1773	Genova	Armida	[?]	[?]
9 July 1773	Pisa	(cantata)		
Aut 1773	Firenze	Demofoonte	Anfossi	Timante
Aut 1773	Firenze	Telemaco nell'isola di Calipso	Meucci	Telemaco
26 Dec 1773	Milano	Tolomeo	Colla	Tolomeo
Car 1774	Milano	Andromeda	Paisiello	Perseo
30 May 1774	Napoli	L'Olimpiade	Piccinni	Megacle
13 Aug 1774	Napoli	Artaserse	Myslivecek	Arbace
4 Nov 1774	Napoli	Orfeo ed Euridice	Gluck/Bach	Orfeo
1774	Napoli	Araspe	Monza	[?]
20 Jan 1775	Napoli	Demofoonte	Myslivecek	Timante
Aut 1775	Venezia	Rinaldo	Tozzi	Rinaldo
17 Oct 1775	Alessandria	Antigona	Bertoni	Euristeo
Car 1776	Modena	Armida	Mortellari	Rinaldo
27 Jan 1776	Modena	Creonte	Bertoni	Euristeo
1776	Modena	La contesa	Anfossi	Apollo
1776	Reggio	Motezuma	Anfossi	Motezuma
10 Feb 1777	London	The Maid of Oakes	[?]	(songs)
14 Feb 1777	London	Judas Maccabaeus	[Handel]	[?]
19 Mar 1777	London	Acis and Galatea	[?]	[?]
Sum 1777	Paris	(concert of arias)	Piccinni	
15 Dec 1777	London	Comus	(Pasticcio)	2nd spirit
5 Sep 1781	Winchester	(sacred concert)		
19 Sep 1781	Salisbury	(sacred concert)		
18 Sep 1782	Salisbury	(sacred concert)		
25 Sep 1782	Winchester	(sacred concert)		
25 Feb 1783	Dublin	Artaxerxes	[Arne]	Arbaces
29 Mar 1783	Dublin	Amintas	(Pasticcio)	[Amintas]
8 May 1783	Dublin	Pharnaces	[?]	Pharnaces
15 Nov 1783	Dublin	Artaxerxes	[Arne]	[Arbaces]
19 Nov 1783	Dublin	Il castello d'Andalusia	(Pasticcio)	Alphonso
29 Nov 1783	Dublin	Amintas	[?]	[Amintas]
5 Jan 1784	Dublin	Orfeo ed Euridice	Gluck/Bach	Orfeo
1784	Dublin	The Campaign	(Pasticcio)	[?]
22 Sep 1784	Salisbury	(sacred concert)		
May 1785	London	Esther	Handel	[?]
12 May 1785	London	Orfeo	(Pasticcio)	Orfeo

DALE E. MONSON

Tenducci's public singing career apparently began in Cagliari in 1750, in festivities celebrating the royal wedding of Vittorio Amedeo, Duke of Savoy, and the Infante Maria Antonia of Spain. Like that of many of his contemporaries, Tenducci's early singing career was unstable, both in his ability to command *primo uomo* roles in serious opera, and in his willingness to sing comic opera. His next known performances, in fact, occurred in Palermo, in two comic operas, which included the premier of Fischietti's *La finta sposa*. He subsequently appeared in Lucca as *primo uomo*, and then travelled to the San Samuele in Venice for the 1754 carnival season. Tenducci turns up in the Vienna court pay records from 1752-54, although his only confirmed appearance there occurred in Wagenseil's *Gioas, re di Giuda*, in March 1755. From 1755 until later 1756 his travels are uncertain. Giazotto suggested that he was in Genoa, although no extant libretto supports this.[5] He apparently travelled in Germanic countries, as he appeared in productions of two Galuppi/Goldoni comic operas in Dresden in 1755, and upon his return to Italy he carried the title of « Virtuoso di camera dell'elettore di Baviera », Maximillian III.

Tenducci's Italian singing career held little promise in the late 1750s. He appeared only as *secondo uomo* for the next two years, first in the Milan carnival season of 1757 (which included Galuppi's *Ezio*), and then in Naples, where he sang with Manzuoli, with whom he was frequently to share the stage later in England. Tenducci left Italy for London late in 1758, after a farewell appearance in the June festival of Padua, when he appeared in one of Galuppi's *Demofoonte* settings. He sang in London, and later Dublin, for the next 13 years.

Tenducci reappeared in Italy in the early 1770s in the title role of a Florentine revival of Gluck's *Orfeo* (now a *pasticcio*), which had brought him so much acclaim in London. It seems this role was also instrumental in launching his revived and now successful Italian career. Thereafter he was engaged as *primo uomo* for the carnival season of the Teatro delle Dame in Rome, 1772, where he appeared in two productions and carried the title of « Virt. di camera dell'Arciduca d'Austria, granduca di Toscana ». Following his appearance in Galuppi's *Motezuma* for Venice, he was *primo uomo* for the Ascension opera of the San Benedetto in Venice.

For the next four and a half years, Tenducci was seen, primarily as *primo uomo*, in many of the most prestigious theaters in Italy, including

---

[5] Cf. R. GIAZOTTO, *La musica a Genova: nella vita pubblica e privata dal XIII al XVIII secolo*, Genoa, Comune di Genova 1851. Giazotto lists Tenducci among the casts performing in the Falcone for three works: *Erasistea* (spring of 1755) of unknown composer, *Antigona* (carnival 1756) by Galuppi, and *L'isola disabitata* (spring 1756) with music by Bonno.

GALUPPI, TENDUCCI, AND « MOTEZUMA »

regular seasons with the Teatro di Via del Cocomero in Florence, the Teatro Argentina in Rome, as well as in Genoa and the Falcone. He sang in the theaters of Pisa, Milan, Naples (where he appeared for an entire year in the San Carlo), Venice, and was honored to be first man for the opening of the new opera house in Alessandria, 1775.[6] His last carnival season in Italy was passed in Modena, 1776, and his final public appearances in Italy were in Anfossi's *Motezuma*, staged in Reggio sometime later that year.

It is unclear why Tenducci left Italy at that time. Perhaps the most likely motivation may have been the final anullment of his 1766 marriage to the daughter of a Dublin lawyer. Understandably a scandal of large proportion, this elopement had been widely discussed and attacked from the beginning.[7]

Although Tenducci appears to have gone directly back to England from Italy, Johann Christian Bach was apparently reunited with his close friend, Tenducci, in Paris in 1778. Mozart, who was also in Paris, on the fateful visit during which his mother died, had known Tenducci in England years before, while Mozart was yet a small boy. He now commented on the friendship these two men shared, and wrote: « Tentuci ist auch hier – der ist der Herzensfreund von Bach – der hat die grösste freude gehabt mich wieder zu sehen ».[8]

Tenducci continued to sing in London until his announced retirement to Dublin in March of 1784 to teach singing. This apparently didn't work out, and he returned to London in December, where he was Director of the Handel Festivals in Westminster Abbey. Nothing about his date and place of death is known.

Tenducci's voice was described by several of his contemporaries. Frequently quoted is the reference found in Tobias Smollett's novel, *The Expedition of Humphrey Clinker* (Dublin, 1771):

At Ranelagh I heard the famous Tenducci, a thing from Italy; it looks for all the world like a man, though they say it is not. The voice to be sure is neither man's nor woman's, but it is more melodious than either, and it warbled so divinely, that the while I listened, I really thought myself in Paradise.[9]

In was this « melodious » character of Tenducci's voice that was apparently its greatest virtue. Tenducci's arias consistently reflect this ideal, and focus

---

[6] See the discussion in OLDMAN, *op. cit.*
[7] Mrs. Tenducci published her own version of this story in 1768: « A True and Genuine Narrative of Mr. and Mrs. Tenducci ».
[8] W. A. MOZART, *Briefe*.
[9] Quoted in WALSH, *op. cit.*, p. 140.

on the cantabile singing style attributed to him in the *ABCDario*, published in London in 1780. Here we find that Tenducci was:

deservedly of the greatest reputation for cantabile singing of any castrato that has appeared in this country. His style is formed on that of Caffarelli, by whom he was instructed. Tho' his notes are few, he has not been exceeded by Egiziello nor any other of his contemporaries.[10]

It is indeed possible that Tenducci studied with Caffarelli in Naples during his early career there, although no other evidence of this relationship exists, and the comparison of singing styles is rather suspect. The analogy drawn for Tenducci with Gizziello, on the other hand, is particularly flattering, since Gizziello was so universally regarded as a master of the cantabile, lyric singing style in 18th-century Europe.

With this lyrical, expressive style of singing as Tenducci's strong suit, it is easy to see why he was able to capitalize so convincingly on Gluck's attempt to strip ostentacious display from arias, and to concentrate rather on simple melody – at least in the so-called « reform » operas. This style of singing was reportedly what Tenducci did best. It is little surprise that his greatest success for the London public, as well as his triumphal reentry into Italy, was intimately intertwined with his rendition of the famous aria *Che farò senza Euridice*.

One of the most significant of sources for information on Tenducci's vocal technique comes from Tenducci's own pen. Upon retiring to England he published a work in 1782 entitled, *Instruction of Mr. Tenducci to His Scholars*. In the first place, Tenducci, like Tosi before him, felt that the heart and expression were of the greatest necessity in music.

It is my intention at some future time farther to illustrate the rules here laid down, and to explain at greater length the requisites necessary for making the song accord with ye sense, and the variations of the voice with the fluctuation of passion, without which music is but harmonious trifling and unmeaning noise.[11]

This work, which is actually a collection of vocal exercises, includes an appendage of 21 preliminary « rules » of vocal music. The vocal exercises, although informative, do not themselves seem to give much insight into the character of Tenducci's own voice.

---

[10] *ABCDario*, Bach, the authors 1780, p. 45.
[11] From the dedication (p. 1), « to the professors of music in London ».

GALUPPI, TENDUCCI, AND « MOTEZUMA »

Necessary rules for students and dilettanti of vocal music

I. The first and most necessary rule in singing, is to keep the voice steady.

II. To form the voice in as pleasing a tone, as is in the power of the scholar.

III. To be exactly in tune; as without a perfect intonation, it is needless to attempt singing.

IV. To vocalise correctly; that is, to give as open and clear a sound to the vowels, as the nature of the language in which the student sings, will admit.

V. To articulate perfectly each syllable.

VI. To sing the scale, or gamut, frequently; allowing to each sound one breve, or two semibreves, which must be sung in the same breath; and this must be done, in both, a *messa di voce*: that is, by swelling the voice, beginning *pianissimo*, and encreasing gradually to the end of each note, which will be expressed in this way,

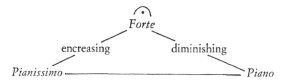

VII. To exercise the voice in *solfegio* every day, with the monosyllables Do, Re, Mi, &c.

VIII. To copy a little music every day, in order to accustom the eye to divide the time into all its proportions.

IX. Never to force the voice, in order to extend its compass in the *voce di petto* upwards; but rather to cultivate the *voce di testa* in what is called *falsetto*, in order to join it well and imperceptibly, to the *voce di petto* for fear of incurring the disagreeable habit of singing in the throat, or through the nose: unpardonable faults in a singer.

X. In the exercise of singing, never to discover any pain or difficulty, by distortion of the mouth, or grimace of any kind; which will be best avoided by examining the countenance in a looking glass, during the most difficult passages.

XI. It is recommended to sing a little at a time, and often; and, if standing, so much the better for the chest.

XII. That scholars should appear at the harpsichord and to their friends with a calm and cheerful countenance.

XIII. To rest or take breath between the passages, and in proper time; that is to say, to take it only when the periods, or members of the melody, are ended; which periods, or portions of the air, generally terminate on the accented parts of a bar. And this rule is the more necessary, as by dwelling too long upon the last note of a musical period, the singer loses the oppertunity it affords of taking breath, without breaking the passages, or even being perceived by the audience.

XIV. That without the most urgent necessity, of either a long passage, or of an affecting expression, words must never be broken, or divided.

XV. That a good *messa di voce*, or swell of the voice, must always precede the *ad libitum* pause and cadenza.

XVI. That in pronouncing the words, care must be taken to accord with the sentiment that was intended by the poet.

XVII. That the acute and super acute sounds must never be so forced as to render them similar to shrieks.

XVIII. That in singing, the tones of the voice must be united, except in the case of staccato notes.

XIX. That in pronouncing the words double consonants in the Italian language, must be particularly enforced, and care taken not to make those that are single seem double.

XX. To practice the shake with the greatest care and attention, which must generally commence with the highest of the two notes, and finish with the lowest.

XXI. That the ornaments and embellishments of songs should be derived from the character of the air, and passion of the words.

Of the many opera productions documented for Tenducci's singing career, a significant number still exist in score, and give a good portrait of Tenducci's singing style. For this study, 19 Italian arias by 7 different composers (10 of these 19 works from Galuppi's serious operas), and a collection of Tenducci's favorite English songs, collected and apparently edited by Tenducci, were examined. A few examples taken from Tenducci's early career will first be taken, beginning with his last work from this period, Galuppi's *Demofoonte*.

There are seven known productions of a Galuppi/Metastasio *Demofoonte*, scattered over a 20 year span. These seem to represent at least two rather distinct settings, with some evidence for portions of a third. The first time Galuppi set the libretto was for Madrid in December of 1749, followed by revivals of this production, first in the same theater in 1755, and then in Bologna in 1756. Galuppi then made a mostly new setting of this Metastasio libretto for Padua in 1758. A libretto substantiates another production in Venice in 1759. A revival in Palermo in 1768 includes elements of both earlier productions, and another libretto, printed for Prague, carries no date.

These productions were, in general, supported with good casts, including repeat performances in leading roles by such as Manzuoli in 1750/

GALUPPI, TENDUCCI, AND « MOTEZUMA »

1755, Catarina Gabrielli 1758/1768, Carlo Carlani 1750/1756, and single appearances by such as Anton Raff and Tedeschi (also known as Amadori). It was in the 1758 production, at the end of his first Italian career, that Tenducci sang the role of Cherinto, second man, his final role before departing for England.

There are five known full scores of a Galuppi *Demofoonte*, and scattered single arias. Three of these manuscripts represent the same production, with occasional minor differences, and correspond, in the main, to the Padua 1758 production. Tenducci only had two arias in this production. The aria provided by Metastasio for Cherinto in the first act was cut, which left only the second and third act arias. That for the second act has this text:

> No, non chiedo, amate stelle,
> se nemiche ancor mi siete,
> non è poco, o luci belle,
> ch'io ne possa dubitar.
>
> Chi non ebbe ora mai lieta,
> chi agl'affanni ha l'alma avezza,
> crede acquisto una dubiezza
> ch'è principio allo sperar.

The vocal range of this aria (lying between c♯', and a"), and particularly the *tessitura* (approximately a' to e"), is rather narrow and low, more the range of a mezzosoprano than a true soprano. The top a" is sung only once, at the climax of the principal coloratura section. The melodic lines are, in the main, conjunct, and almost always uniformly fashioned in a smooth arch: from low in the tessitura (around a'), rising in mid phrase, and then falling towards the end. The opening phrase of *No, non chiedo amate stelle* bears this out (see the following example). The cantabile character of Tenducci's voice has been carefully observed by Galuppi. The aria begins with the main motive, in a fiery violin ritornello marked « Allegro assai », yet when the voice enters, the melody becomes lyrical and conjunct, with the fire all confined to brief counterpoint in the strings.

---

[12] The 1758 scores are *B-Bc* (MsM 2091), *D-Dlb* (Mus. 2973/F8), and *P-La* (44-II-12 to 14).

Galuppi, *Demofoonte: No, non chiedo amate stelle*, mm. 1-47.

GALUPPI, TENDUCCI, AND « MOTEZUMA »

To say that the coloratura is reserved is conservative. The most florid vocal treatment, as expected, comes at the end of the second solo of the first part:

Galuppi, *Demofoonte: No, non chiedo amate stelle*, mm. 78-85.

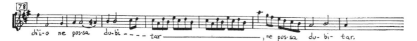

This is nothing more than eighth note thirds, up and down within the range of a fifth, and a descending scale, from a" to a', and all this doubled by the violins.

T'intendo ingrata, the second aria, follows this pattern. The emotional text is set here as a 3/8 « Andantino »; the coloratura is mostly short, conjunct in character, with a reserved *tessitura*. Like the former aria, the lyric quality of the vocal part seems the most important element.

Previous to Tenducci's appearance in Padua for Galuppi's *Demofoonte*, he sang during the carnival season in the San Carlo Theater in Naples, which included Jommelli's *Temistocle*. He again sang two arias, now in the role of Lisimaco to Manzuoli's Serse. Since the work is contemporary with Galuppi's *Demofoonte*, and exists in numerous manuscript copies, a few comments in comparing the aria styles seems in order.

The basic design of Jommelli's arias for Tenducci is identical to that of Galuppi's outline.[13] The vocal range is the same: both Jommelli arias extend from e' to a", with a *tessitura* lying in the upper half of the treble clef, as did Galuppi's. The first aria (I.8) is a 3/4 « Andante » in A major, with very conjunct, simple, lyric lines, short phrases and limited coloratura. The second aria, *Vicino al tuo sembiante*, is more vigorous, in duple meter with a B section in contrasting meter. In the second solo part of the A section we find a four measure held c", probably performed *messa di voce*, a feature of cantabile singing, and a vital element of the singer's art, as Tenducci stresses himself in his « Rules » (nos. 6 and 15) for singing mentioned above.

The similarity of style between the Jommelli and the Galuppi examples is striking. In both operas, the arias for Tenducci are constructed of short, arched, conjunct, diatonic phrases, supported lightly with either string configuration or unisono string passages, reinforcing the character of Tenducci's lyric, cantabile voice.

---

[13] The copy examined here is the *US-Wc* 1910 copy of the manuscript in *GB-Lbl*.

Before proceeding to the later career of Tenducci and Galuppi, a few comments on one additional early collaboration must be made. Unlike *Demofoonte*, which Galuppi set at least twice and which was repeatedly staged, his setting of *Ezio*,[14] for the Milan carnival season in 1757, was apparently never revised or reset, with the exception of a London pasticcio that included a single aria by Galuppi.[15] This was the first time that Galuppi was asked to write for Tenducci.

In *Ezio*, Tenducci, singing second man, again had two arias. The Naples Conservatory manuscript of this production, however, reveals that, at this point in the singer's career, Galuppi felt Tenducci capable of rather more technique, range, and general ability than he would afford him a year and a half later, with *Demofoonte*, which rather serves to illustrate Tenducci's fading Italian career.

The first aria, *Se tu la reggi al volo*, is a brilliant, C major « Allegro », with strings, oboes and horns. Although the principal motives of the ritornello and first solo section are conjunct and fluid, as before, the overall character of the aria is rather more virtuosic than the later arias already discussed. The range, while similar on the bottom (e'), extends a minor third higher, up to c''', which is reached several times in the coloratura of both the first and second solo sections. Still, when compared with Manzuoli's coloratura in Jommelli's *Temistocle*, or Catarina Gabrielli's display in Galuppi's *Demofoonte*, these sections are rather more subdued. As with the Jommelli, Galuppi supplied Tenducci with a sustained, *messa di voce* passage in the second solo of the first part, as, for example, in the second solo of this first aria:

Galuppi, *Ezio: Se tu la reggi al volo*, mm. 68-104.

[14] The copy examined is *I-Nc*, Rari 6.5.21.
[15] London, King's Theatre, 1764. Other composers for this production included Pescetti, J. C. Bach, De Majo, and Vento. Copies of the libretto for this production are found in *US-Wc*, *GB-Lbl*, and *F-Pc*.

GALUPPI, TENDUCCI, AND « MOTEZUMA »

The second aria, *Che mi giova Impero e Soglio*, is likewise scored for strings, oboes, and horns. Like the later *Demofoonte* aria, *No, non chiedo amate stelle*, this aria is full of brilliant bravura writing in the instrumental parts, while the vocal line is more subdued, narrow, and full of moderate scalar passages and mild coloratura, although the range is still larger than it will become. The most substantial solo sections of this aria include primarily two elements: sustained tones (as before), and descending octave scales – both of which seem to be very popular configurations for Tenducci's voice.

These arias are different than those of *Demofoonte* and Jommelli's *Temistocle* for Tenducci in regards both to range and overall difficulty. It seems likely, then, that Tenducci's voice was changing over this period of a year and a half, and that Galuppi took notice of this later on, when he wrote for him again. His voice became less agile, more lyric, and a couple of the top notes were lost.

Tenducci's London career will be passed over with only a brief comment, since Galuppi was involved here only peripherally, and very few scores are extant for Tenducci over these years. In brief, Tenducci seems not to have changed his preference much for cantabile writing. Typical of his predilection for simple melodies is his publication for the « Haberdashers Hall » ca. 1770, just before he left London for Italy, a collection of popular English airs, scored for strings and winds. These tunes feature simple, diatonic, conjunct phrases, often accompanying rather mediocre poetry about love, rejection, and ill-deserved death of a broken heart.[16]

As previously mentioned, Tenducci's reentry into the Italian performance circuit in September of 1771 was in the title role of Gluck's *Orfeo ed Euridice*, the role that had brought him such enormous success in London from his first performance of the role there, in 1770. His lyric rendition of *Che farò senza Euridice* was long remembered by the London audience,[17] and its impact on the Italian public seems to have been the key to his new success as *primo uomo* over the next 5 years in Italy.

It must be stressed that this was not the first or only time that Tenducci favored some libretto or musical setting and then succeeded in having the work produced elsewhere, with him in the cast. In 1757, for example, he had appeared in a Piccinni adaptation of David Perez's *Farnace* in Naples. Shortly thereafter, in London, the same work was produced

---

[16] *A Collection of Favorite Airs in Score Sung at Haberdashers Hall*, London, Welcker [ca. 1770].

[17] Attested by repeat performances of the work in both Dublin and London after Tenducci's reappearance on stage there in the 1780s.

with Tenducci for the King's Theatre. Likewise, he later appeared as first man in Anfossi's *Demofoonte* in Rome in February of 1773. Later that year the same work was given in Florence, a production with an all new cast, except, of course, for Tenducci.

One of the most interesting of these operas that Tenducci seems to have promoted actually concerns a libretto. Following *Orfeo*, two of the next productions that Tenducci joined (as *primo uomo*), as well as his last production before departing for England in 1776, had a libretto based on the story of Cortez and his conquest of Mexico and its emperor, Motezuma.

General interest in the tale of the conquest of Mexico had run high in Europe for many years by the mid 18th century. The principal reason for this fascination, and many of the prefaces included in the libretti for these productions acknowledge this debt, was the *Historia de la conquista de Mexico*, written by Antonio de Solis y Rivadeneyra, and published in Madrid in 1684, a book of remarkable historiographical significance. Solis sorted through the many confused reports, histories, diaries, and other accounts concerning Cortez, and wrote what he felt to be a truly objective history – although his own peculiar bias of pro-European/Catholic interests is only too clear. The book was enormously successful, with over 31 new Spanish editions before the end of the 18th century. It was repeatedly translated into other languages as well, with 18 French editions in the 1700s, and numerous others in English, German, Italian, etc.[18]

In opera composition, fascination with the exotic setting of the new world extended far beyond Motezuma, of course. The number of libretti on this and similar topics is large. For example, after interest in the Motezuma story seems to have run its course, operas and ballets on the theme of Pizzaro began to appear – there were at least seven in the 1780s.

There were as many as 12 different productions of an opera with the title of *Motezuma* in the 18th century, and essentially three different libretti. The most popular of these was by Vittorio Amedeo Cigna-Santi,[19] first set by De Majo for Turin in 1765. It was adapted (sometimes drastically) and reset by Mislivecek, Paisiello, Galuppi, Sacchini, Anfossi, Insanguine,

---

[18] ANTONIO DE SOLIS Y RIVADENEYRA, *Historia de la conquista de Mexico, poblacion, y progressos de la America Septentrional, conocia por el nombre de nueva Espana*, Madrid, B. de Villa-Diego 1684. A continuation of this work, entitled *Historia de la conquista de Mexico [...] segunda parte*, was written by I. de Salazar y Olarte, and was published in Cordoba in 1743.

[19] Cigna-Santi, 20 years younger than Galuppi, had been writing and publishing poetry from the middle of the century. From 1754-55 he was the principal librettist of the Regio Teatro of Turin. Of his numerous libretti, the most successful was *Motezuma*. Cf. *Dizionario biografico degli Italiani*, XXV, Rome 1981, pp. 500-501.

GALUPPI, TENDUCCI, AND « MOTEZUMA »

and Zingarelli, over the next 16 years. The libretto proved enormously popular (the Zingarelli version, for example, was revised and restaged at Esterhaza by Haydn in 1785). Of the three Italian productions of 1772-76, Tenducci appeared in them all. These were by Paisiello, Galuppi, and then Anfossi.

The political context of a libretto on the story of Cortez is itself of interest. As Solis himself made clear, a noble Catholic representative of the Spanish throne undermines, frequently by deception, the empire of Motezuma. Where is the noble display of virtue so much desired in Arcadian aesthetics? Frederik the Great, after having written his own libretto on Motezuma for Graun somewhat earlier, did not hesitate to point this issue out to the well known Italian reformer, Algarotti, in 1753:

> Si vos opéras sont mauvais, vous en trouverez ici un nouveau qui peut-être ne les surpassera pas. C'est Montézuma. J'ai choisi ce sujet, et je l'accomode à présent. Vous sentez bien, que j'intéresserai pour Montézuma, que Cortès sera le tyran, et que par conséquent on pourra lâcher, en musique même, quelque lardon contre la barbarie de la R. Cr. (rélLigion chrétienne). Mai j'oublie que vous êtes dans un pays d'inquisition; je vous en fais mes excuses, et j'espere de vous revoir bientôt dans un pays hérétique où l'opéra même peut servir à réformer les moeurs et à détruire des superstitions.[20]

Cigna-Santi's libretto includes three main characters: Motezuma (the role of the first man, sung by Tenducci in this instance), emperor of Mexico; his betrothed, Guacozinga (or, as renamed in Galuppi's version, Erismena), and the conquering Spaniard, Ferdinando Cortez. The other three characters are all servants, two of whom are engaged to be married.

The entire first act merely sets the stage for the confrontation of Cortez and Motezuma. Motezuma, in his temple, laments that the Gods have forsaken him, and that evil omens have appeared, despite heavy human sacrifice of innocent victims. Cortez approaches the palace, although servants of Motezuma try to dissuade him with gifts from advancing further. Motezuma will not fight Cortez, for fear of the omens.

In act two, Motezuma and Erismena greet Cortez within the palace, and Cortez delivers his ultimatum: Motezuma must pay homage to Spain, and he must renounce his false Gods. This last demand Motezuma vows angrily never to do. Suspicious of Motezuma's actions, Cortez confronts Motezuma in his Temple and puts him in chains.

---

[20] As quoted in H. J. MOSER's *Vorwort*, to his edition of Graun's *Montezuma*, « Denkmäler der deutschen Tonkunst », 1st series, vol. 15, Wiesbaden, Breitkopf und Härtel [1904], p. IX.

DALE E. MONSON

In the last act, Erismena attempts to free Motezuma, while a general uproar of mob violence reigns within the city. Cortez summons the emperor and, now fearing for his own safety, entreats him to show himself to the people to calm them. Since Cortez holds Erismena hostage, and Motezuma values his love for Erismena more dear than any duty to his country, he obeys. The opera ends as Cortez restores Erismena to Motezuma, who is surprised, having suspected only treachery, and Motezuma is gratified to see this display of honor and virtue.[21]

From what we have seen of the music written for Tenducci in his early career, what do we expect to find now? This question is particularly pertinent since, of a single libretto, we have two settings, one by Paisiello, the other by Galuppi, just months apart in 1772. The first major aria for Motezuma (Tenducci) in the libretto (although a short Cavatina preceeds it) is sung to reassure Erismena of his constancy. The text reads:

> Cara fiamma del mio seno,
> sempre, o dio, del t'amai,
> e costante mi vedrai
> per te sempre sospirar.
>
> Pria ch'io lascio o mio tesoro
> d'avvampare quei bei lumi
> torneranno indietro i fiumi
> resterà senza aqua il mar.

The character of the vocal line in Paisiello's *Cara fiamma del mio seno* reveals that the range of Tenducci's voice continued to fall over his career.[22] From the time of Galuppi's *Ezio*, when Tenducci several times reached c''', to that of his *Demofoonte*, where his range fell to a'', we now find that his range in this aria only once goes above an f#'', to a g''. The bottom of his range also dropped from the e' and occasional d' of his early years, to a c#' in this aria. The tessitura of his aria has changed as well, now sinking to the middle-to-lower half of the treble clef.

The first vocal entrance, however, reinforces yet again our estimation of Tenducci's cantabile voice. Paisiello elects to drop the orchestra out all together, while Tenducci sustains two pitches, dominant and tonic. It is

---

[21] The most divergent rendition of this libretto is that set by Sacchini in London in 1775, to this same Cigna-Santi libretto, as adapted by Bottarelli. Here Motezuma likewise shows himself to the crowd at the end of act III, but is filled full of arrows. His death drives his bride insane.

[22] This aria is found in *Six Favorite Italian Songs*, London [1778].

the simple, clear beauty of the voice that is on display here, not bravura technique.[23] As the first statement of the text then unwinds, we see the short, conjunct lines we found typical of his singing earlier.

Jommelli, *Motezuma: Cara fiamma del mio seno*, mm. 21-37.

The embellishment of the second solo in the first part is only slightly more adventuresome than Tenducci's *Demofoonte* style. Long sixteenth note runs are present, although generally only scales or melodic sequences of conjunct motives. These are, as we expect, coupled with another *messa di voce*. This seems to be one of Tenducci's important trademarks of style.

Jommelli, *Motezuma: Cara fiamma del mio seno*, mm. 109-125.

---

[23] See Tenducci's Rule no. 3.

GALUPPI, TENDUCCI, AND « MOTEZUMA »

Galuppi's aria for Tenducci with the same text is remarkably similar to Paisiello's, in several ways.[24] As expected, the opening phrase is lyric and simple in outline, broken into short phrases, with largely conjunct motion. The range is also like that found in Paisiello's aria, from a low of b, to a brief high of g♯″. We similarly find more generous coloratura in Galuppi's writing for Tenducci here than we did earlier in *Demofoonte*, although, again, it is relatively reserved in character, with descending or ascending scale runs and repeated conjunct motivic sequences. We do see a few leaps of an octave, although no rapid leaps are required. Although no lengthy, sustained tones are found, some portions, such as the closing of the first solo, mimic this style, by repeating a single note over the recited text. Here, in the last example, is the first solo (the modulation from tonic to dominant) of Galuppi's aria *Cara fiamma del mio seno*.

Galuppi's aria for Tenducci obviously has more than just stylistic similarities to Paisiello. It is practically the same tune. The most likely reason for this was inferred earlier: Tenducci's portrayal of Motezuma for Paisiello in Rome was during carnival of 1772, and his portrayal of the same character for Galuppi in Venice was in May. We already know Tenducci carried scores and arias with him to produce the music elsewhere, perhaps in copies made in his own hand.[25] It is quite likely that he showed the Paisiello aria to Galuppi – and the rest is history.

So what does all this tell us about 18th-century aria composition? Most importantly, it focuses our attention on an issue we are already aware of, but have been, as yet, reluctant or unable to integrate properly into our evaluation of opera seria. Traditional western scholarship still finds it difficult to release its tenacious grasp on the concept of a singular « authorship », particularly as this relates to musical composition. It is true, that one man, generally, wrote the notes on the paper, but the issue is often more complex. We have long acknowledged that composers had to know their singers before writing the arias of an opera in the 18th century. This is cited in every secondary text, but why was it so necessary? Indeed, the metaphor of the 18th century that an aria had to be tailored for the singer, to fit him like a suit of clothes, was almost a cliché. What this meant was this: much of the nature of the composition was determined by the singer. From simple things, like range and tessitura, to more complex aspects, like preferred kinds of ornaments, and the shape, expression, and contour of

---

[24] The copy examined is the *Us-Wc* 1912 copy (M1500.G2M) of the now lost manuscript of *D-Dlb*.

[25] See Tenducci's Rule no. 6.

DALE E. MONSON

Galuppi, *Motezuma: Cara fiamma del mio seno*, mm. 15-56.

the vocal line, all this could be influenced or determined by the singer's desires. It was only a natural result that the pasticcio, a work with often irreconcilable authorship problems, and today often viewed as the poor sister of better, single composer operas, was, in reality, the archetypical example of the sociological state of opera in the 18th century.

To say that arias for Tenducci composed by Galuppi, Paisiello, and Jommelli share many style traits does not negate the importance of composer innovation and creativity, but allows, rather, a more complete perspective for our evaluation of a composer's works. Galuppi's characterization for the role of Motezuma, for example, cannot be properly understood without understanding the musical style of the singer, in this case, Tenducci. This is true for all important singers and composers. The study of the repertoire and singing style of influential singers of the 18th century is as important, at least for opera seria, as is the study of the careers and music written by single composers.

[7]

'Ich bin die erste Sängerin'
Vocal profiles of two Mozart sopranos

Patricia Lewy Gidwitz

1   Johann Hieronymus Löschenkohl, Silhouette of Caterina Cavalieri (1785)

Every opera composer and poet during the late 18th century was a pragmatist—continually reworking his conceptions to fit constantly fluctuating conditions. Solo numbers were regularly adapted to suit the particular singer participating in local premières and revivals. The number of emendations to the manuscripts of operas makes clear just how often such changes occurred. Markings for transpositions, for interpolations within a piece, for the reordering and cutting of numbers, and for the additions or substitutions of complete compositions as well as shorter passages of music attest not only to the adaptability of the medium but also to the expectation on the part of composers and poets that these works would not be performed the same way throughout a single run, much less from year to year.[1]

The professional singer was specific and forthright in his or her demands. To venture onto the stage unarmed with a piece expressly written for oneself to sing was a risk. When a singer fell into the hands of an unskilled composer, or was miscast, the results could be disastrous.[2] For this reason, if a singer was incapable of singing the piece, or uncomfortable with it in any way, most late 18th-century composers willingly changed it. In an oft-quoted passage concerning an aria composed for the tenor Anton Raaff, Mozart expresses unmistakable professional pride in his musical tailoring.

2   Anon., Portrait of Aloysia Lange (private collection)

I told him that he should tell me honestly if [the aria] didn't suit him, or if he didn't like it. I'll alter it for him however he wants, or even write another . . . I'll arrange the aria for him so that he will be sure to enjoy singing it, for I like an aria to fit the singer like a well-made garment.[3]

If the testimony of letters and other written documents points so explicitly to the great influence wielded by singers, it should be possible to discover direct evidence of such influence in the music itself. And, indeed, by examining a sufficient quantity of music known to have been written or adapted for a particular identifiable singer, clear evidence of this kind can be found. Within the confines of the present brief study, I shall look for signs of the musical influence exerted by two leading sopranos of Vienna in the 1780s, Caterina Cavalieri and Aloysia Weber Lange.[4] Their vocal styles are richly documented in composers' autographs, the fair copies and especially the working manuscripts for operatic productions of the day.[5]

With singers such as Cavalieri and Lange, identifiable vocal personalities emerge that may then be seen to act in various ways on the making and shaping of their music. Identifying their distinctive vocal styles may go far to explain aspects of operatic composition that are usually overlooked or inadequately accounted for. For example, the singer's perspective is often quite sufficient to explain why an aria written for another, even an uncommonly fine one, is rejected or undergoes thorough rewriting. In the case of arias for which we do not know the intended singer, it is reasonable to consider whether they would, or even could, have been performed by a particular singer whose voice we have come to know through evidence of his or her music. And then there is the reverse situation in which an attributed aria is so at odds with a singer's 'vocal profile' that one is tempted to disbelieve the extramusical evidence that links a particular singer with a role and perhaps look for another, more likely, candidate. Finally, a singer's vocal style can determine the character of a specific role and on occasion, as we shall see, a composer might turn the spirit of the drama on the vocal style of the singer.

The physical characteristics of the vocal instrument—its range, tessitura and weight—make up one dimension of a singer's profile. If there is sufficient attributed music available, these characteristics may be determined with some confidence. Lange's known arias, for example, reveal an upper range extending regularly to the third octave (on occasion to g''' or a''').[6] Cavalieri, though she was endowed with an admirable top voice, could not match Lange here; in her prime her range may have extended to e''' though earlier her limit was d'''.[7] The tessitura of their music was different: Lange's most characteristic range was between b' and $f''\sharp$ while Cavalieri's was somewhat lower, between g' and d''. The care that Mozart always took to provide Lange with transparent accompaniment suggests that hers was a light voice, whereas in the arias for Cavalieri there is much instrumental doubling of her line, and vigorous concertante treatment of strings and/or winds—all indications of her vocal power, and perhaps a sign of insecure intonation as well. Lange was rarely required to remain in her chest voice, whereas Cavalieri usually sang throughout her range with apparent ease.

A second dimension of vocal style involves characteristic vocal gestures. A composer was expected to write these into the music, particularly at certain signal points for bravura display within the composition, notably the approaches to sectional cadences (half-closes) and especially in the climactic passages of tonic confirmation and elaboration. Not merely by means of actual improvisation was this accomplished. The fully written-out music in these parts of an aria were also designed to allow a singer opportunities for display; that is, the composer wrote them with the singer's particular proclivities in mind. This attitude on the part of the composer becomes clear from the fact that, generally speaking, music written for a particular performer exploits a limited number of vocal devices available while avoiding others. One might well imagine the composer responding to a vocal style perceived in terms of a limited repertory of vocal gestures that a particular singer was known to prefer. The aria was then composed using these gestures, assembled in the composer's personal manner.

The following series of examples from music written for Lange and Cavalieri is intended to suggest their rather dissimilar vocal styles.[8] Those for Lange (exx.1–3) hint at a voice of great flexibility, with a predilection toward portamento singing. As Mozart appreciated from the very first, she seems to have been particularly at ease in the upper reaches of her range over light scoring, while the chest voice is generally avoided. Especially characteristic are scales rising effortlessly into the third octave. *Salti* often introduced by *gruppetti* are carried out within a sustained line. Her style embodies what we think of as Mozartean cantabile.[9] But if this approach to singing is so perfectly memorialized in the arias that Mozart wrote for her, it is also present, less memorably, in music others provided for Lange.

Cavalieri presents a contrasting vocal portrait (exx.4–6). Her singing is essentially athletic, her color-

Ex.1 Mozart, 'Alcandro lo confesso . . . Non so d'onde viene', K294, bars 146–66

Ex.2 Mozart, 'Popoli di Tessaglia . . . Io non chiedo, eterni Dei', K316/300b, bars 67–86

Ex.3 Umlauf, *Das Irrlicht*, Act 1, scene i, no.2. Blanka: 'Senkt, kühle Schatten!', bars 10–26

atura tending to elaborate more or less routine scales or triplet figures in extended sequences. Whereas Lange can reach almost casually into the third octave and remain aloft, Cavalieri has an earnestness about her upper range, which she attains with scales that push upward powerfully and terminate with a final quick high note. Her approach is proclamatory; her texts are often syllabically declaimed in minims which then yield to pairs of quavers. Cavalieri is comfortable using the chest voice and resorts to a device referred to by contemporary theorists as *cantar di sbalzo*, that is, a series of large leaps (*salti*) intended to contrast dramatically a singer's regis-

ters.[10] More generally, Cavalieri did not have Lange's ability to spin out a long line, integrating a variety of *abbellimenti*; rather, she impressed by strenuous displays of a few vocal patterns, often in the style of a vocal exercise. The fact that her line is often doubled or heavily scored suggests not only that her voice was powerful but also that she may have been disinclined to introduce genuinely extempore elements.

Contemporary sources, too, are suggestive as regards these sopranos' voices. A report in the *Deutsches Museum* from 1781 states that '[Lange] has a very pleasing voice, though it is too weak for the theatre.' Not less

Ex.4 Umlauf, *Die Bergknappen*. Sophie: 'Himmel, hör isst meine Bitte', bars 24–31

Ex.5 Aspelmayr, *Die Kinder der Natur*, Act 2, no.22. Therese: 'So gut wie er mir schiene': (a) bars 44–9; (b) bars 55–67
(a)

(b)

Ex.6 Cimarosa, *Il falegname*, Act 2, no.4. Lindane: 'Voi notturne aure serene . . . Mà ritorna nel mio petto', bars 138–53

emphatic is Gerber's pronouncement that her voice was 'more suited for an ordinary room [Kammer] than for the theatre'. And Count Zinzendorf complains of a fading of her voice in a performance of *I viaggiatori felice* on 14 July 1784.[11] This seeming liability is addressed by Leopold Mozart in a letter to his daughter of 25 March 1785:

It can scarcely be denied that she sings with the greatest expression: only now I understand why some persons I frequently asked would say that she has a very weak voice, while others said she has a very loud voice. Both are true. The held notes and all expressive notes are astonishingly loud; the tender moments, the passage work and embellishments, and high notes are very delicate, so that for my taste the one contrasts too strongly with the other. In an ordinary room the loud notes assault the ear, while in the theatre the delicate passages demand a great attentiveness and stillness on the part of the audience.[12]

Cavalieri, on the other hand, might on occasion drown out other singers, as allegedly happened in a performance of Sarti's *Giulio Sabino*. In a diary entry of 29 July 1785 Zinzendorf reported that 'dans le duo la Cavalieri étouffa la voix de Marchesini par ses cris'. And she was compared specifically with Lange in an article in the *Deutsches Museum* (Leipzig, 1781), in which her voice is described as 'incomparably more powerful but of a very unusual character'.[13] Of course, the exact nature of this individual quality we can never know, but the writer was obviously alluding to a singer who had no need to fear contemporary orchestral resources.[14]

If the foregoing examples are sufficient to suggest distinctive vocal styles for Cavalieri and Lange, they may also serve as a frame of reference for an examination of several recurring problems in the study of 18th-century opera. In the first place, purely vocal factors must be given pride of place in the consideration of insertion arias. Let us begin with the case in which both old and new arias for a particular scene exist and may be clearly identified with a role. Usually it is easy to see that new music conforms to a singer's requirements more fully than does the music it is replacing. Generally, letting the vocal personality enjoy optimum display would have been grounds enough for introducing new music of very different character, for vocal display was an aspect of the theatrical experience appreciated as much or more than any dramatic 'integrity' of the opera *per se*, and was regularly satisfied at the expense of the latter. Two examples, one each for Cavalieri and Lange, illustrate a normative practice.

Cavalieri appeared regularly with the new Italian company when, after the popular failure of the German National Opera, Joseph II inaugurated *opera buffa* at the Burgtheater in 1783. In the inaugural production, Salieri's *La scuola dei gelosi* (22 April 1783), she took the *buffa* role of Ernestina.[15] For her Act 2 solo, Salieri composed a new *aria di bravura*, 'Staremo in pace', replacing Ernestina's original modest single-tempo aria, 'Queste donne sussiegate'. Perhaps Cavalieri was especially anxious to outshine Nancy Storace, a rival prima donna newly arrived from Italy who was appearing with her.[16] Whereas 'Queste donne sussiegate' is in a single tempo, carried out in *nota e parola* style,[17] and does not exceed *a''* in range—a vocal style that, on the face of it, would seem better suited to a seconda donna—the new aria is on a grand scale, and fully realized Cavalieri's particular talent for straightforward, athletic vocal display. The hard-hitting proclamatory opening, extensive use of triplet quavers, *salti* of more than two octaves—all are reminiscent of previously cited examples of her vocal style (ex.7).

Yet the style of 'Staremo in pace' does not seem appropriate for its dramatic context. Its dimensions threaten to spring the dramatic framework altogether by inter-

Ex.7 Salieri, *La scuola dei gelosi*, Act 2, no.5. Ernestina: 'Staremo in pace': (a) bars 7-15; (b) bars 42-54

rupting the action. There is no motivation here for a climatic expression such as this defiant, almost manic pronouncement of retaliation.[18] The only reason, then, for its presence in the opera would have been to display Cavalieri's prowess in bravura.[19]

In his letter of 2 July 1783 Mozart reports to his father that: 'Lange was here at our house to try the 2 arias, and she and I discussed how to outwit our enemies—because I have enough of them, and now Lange does, too, on account of Storaci, the "new singer".'[20] One of the new pieces, 'Vorrei spiegarvi, oh Dio!' (K418), Mozart completed for Lange on 20 June.[21] The opera was a revival of Anfossi's comic opera *Il curioso indiscreto*, and Lange was making her debut with the new Italian company at the Burgtheater, in the role of Clorinda.[22] From what we already know of Lange's voice, it is easy enough to explain why Anfossi's original rondò, 'Ah, spiegarti, oh Dio', would not have pleased her.[23] In it, Lange's effortless high notes, the most singular feature of her vocal style, would have found no employment whatsoever; the music remains nearly the whole time between a' and f'', with only a few extensions to a'' and a single b'', the latter in the only flourish in the aria.[24] What is more, these high notes are never sustained, and one senses that they indicate a ceiling for the original singer. Even more telling of the very limited nature of Anfossi's setting is the choice of e'' for the single long-held note. As a whole the aria lacks a distinctive characterization, its indifferent moods devoid of the nuance in Mozart's work. Finally, the heavy accompaniment of the Allegro section provided by the strings and frequently the full ensemble (with much doubling of the voice) would certainly have taxed Lange, so that we may say that Anfossi's setting not only offered little scope for her virtues but would have exposed her principal deficiency.

Mozart's setting is introspective, quiet and poignant. As Clorinda guardedly reveals her love to Count Ripaverde, the delicate, almost tentative quality of the string figures, the pressing, rather urgent solo oboe vividly conjure Clorinda's disturbance over her growing love for a man pledged to another woman. Mozart provides Lange with a singularly soaring melodic line. Here is portamento singing—connected, shaped, carried on the breath—that must have been both inspired by Lange's abilities and realized to Mozart's satisfaction (ex.8a). For the return of the opening melody before the second section, Mozart takes the voice to e'' a secure and much prized note in Lange's voice (ex.8b). Within the Allegro there occurs a leap of extraordinary proportions from b to d''' (ex.8c). Each pitch is left almost unaccompanied

Ex.8 Mozart, 'Vorrei spiegarvi, oh Dio!', K418: (a) bars 12–20; (b) bar 67–73; (c) bars 131–41

Ex.9 Gazzaniga, *Le Vendemmie, ossia La dama incognita*, Act 2, scene ix. Agatina: 'Alma grande altiera ardita': (a) bars 19–27; (b) bars 65–73

to guarantee that Lange's slight instrument will be easily heard. In a characteristically self-serving comment, Mozart pronounced the opera a failure but for the music he wrote for Lange.[35]

Attention to specific vocal style can sometimes call into question a specific role attribution. We know that for the Burgtheater production of Gazzaniga's *La dama incognita, ossia La vendemmia*, which opened 11 February 1784,[26] the *prima seria* role, Donna Artemesia, was taken by Aloysia Lange.[27] It is uncertain who sang Agatina, the *prima buffa* role, although both musical evidence and other circumstances point to Nancy Storace.[28] In KT459, the main working manuscript for this production, one finds an insertion aria for Act 2, scene ix, assigned in the preceding recitative to 'Agatina'. However, the *prima buffa* has another large aria in this version of the act, and two such pieces so close together would be puzzling.[29] But 'Alma grande', the insertion aria, is unlike the other music for Agatina, which requires a soprano of only modest capacity, that is, a rather light instrument of limited range and flexibility. 'Alma grande' is extraordinarily demanding, and calls for an exceptional voice.

Its opening vocal motto signals a distinctive vocal instrument, since this entrance takes place on an exposed g'' which must carry the sustained swelling and receding of a *messa di voce*[30] (ex.9a). Every sort of semiquaver configuration is pressed into the service of vocal pyrotechnics as the piece moves toward the dominant close of the exposition. Just before the transition to the tonic return there is an impressive *volatina* up to a sustained d''', then an e''' followed by a two-octave plunge to e', accompanied only by strings (ex.9b). The orchestration remains transparent during every such passage. Another such startling leap occurs in the closing vocal cadence: a descent through a dominant-chord arpeggio into the chest voice suddenly springs up two octaves from b' to b''. This extreme use of the technique of *cantar di sbalzo*—like almost every other feature of 'Alma grande'—corresponds to what we have seen in Mozart's writing for Lange.[31]

One must not discount the possibility that 'Alma grande' was entered into the working manuscript some time after the 1784 production. During the years when KT459 was presumably in use (that is, the middle and latter 1780s), no one on the roster of the Italian company would have attempted such a piece.[32] Therefore, on the basis of the vocal writing of this piece and its similarity to her style, it seems reasonable to reassign 'Alma grande' to Lange, who is known to have been involved in the production.

If the physical evidence of the manuscript is used to connect a working copy of an opera score with a particular production, and something is known about the cast for that production, examination of vocal style can offer significant corroboration. There is a working copy of *Le nozze di Figaro*, now in Florence, that Alan Tyson has tentatively associated with the 1789 revival in Vienna, and therefore with Mozart himself.[33] This source is one of many manuscripts of Viennese origin from the period that contains a revised version of 'Dove sono', the Countess's Act 3 aria (this version is not transmitted in sources that can be dated to 1786 or 1787).[34] Since it is known that Cavalieri took the role of the Countess in the 1789 Vienna production, an examination of the revisions to the music may indicate whether they are prompted by Cavalieri's vocal style.

Two sections of this rondò have been rewritten. First, the return of at least part of the opening material that one expects at the close of the slow section has been

Ex.10 Mozart, *Le nozze di Figaro*, k492, Act 3, no.21 (variant). Countess: 'Dove sono': (a) bars 28–43; (b) 68–84

eliminated entirely, and the beginning of the ensuing Allegro section has been recomposed in the wake of this adjustment (ex.10a).[35] By dispensing with a return to the opening tune as well as the full stop of an interpolated vocal cadenza (the vocal *Eingang*), the composition is compressed, as it were, and moves more swiftly through a dramatic and musical crescendo into the inevitable fast second half. This change alone alters the whole character of the piece. Now there is continuous progression and development of material from the beginning to the end, with no real break; the poignant hesitations and questionings of the 1786 version have been swept away, and any suggestion that the Countess is contemplating her bleak predicament is lost.[36] The second difference in this version of 'Dove sono' does not affect the formal design, but, as we shall see, is in keeping with the first: bars 84–98 of the original—that is, the passage in which the tonic is confirmed, towards the climax of the Allegro section— are here replaced by 13 bars of new music (ex.10b).

If the two passages at this place are compared, it is apparent that a bravura element lacking in the 1786 version has been introduced. Mozart originally shaped the passage around two protracted occurrences of a'', and connected them with uncomplicated material; the later version substitutes a broader gesture in which three and a half bars of paired quavers lead to a second-octave g that is held for two and a half bars, after which there is a semiquaver scalar ascent to a'' (not held).

When this music is compared with earlier music by Mozart for Cavalieri its essential kinship cannot be doubted. For example, in 'Tra l'oscure ombre funeste', from the cantata *Davide penitente*, k469, composed for Cavalieri in 1785, there are passages strikingly similar to the new material in 'Dove sono'—the emphasis on paired quavers, vigorously executed in the middle range—are almost Cavalieri's vocal signature. Temperamentally, the new passage fits with the compression and elision of the revised sectional design, making for a more headlong rush of simplified feeling that dispenses with the nuances of the original. It may be pointed out that there is a certain consistency in the revising process—a singleness of purpose—that points to Mozart himself. But one might go further. The new character of 'Dove sono' as found in the Florence manuscript, and with it the new side that is revealed of the Countess's character, is in keeping with the vocal personality that Cavalieri revealed on other occasions. We sense a heightened Mozartean responsiveness to the possibilities of writing the inherent vocal style of a singer into the drama. The clearest example of this musical and dramatic synergy between Mozart and singers can be seen in *Der Schauspieldirektor*.

Within the modest frame of Mozart's one-act entertainment of 1786 the contrasting vocal personalities of Cavalieri and Lange, as Mademoiselle Silberklang and Madame Herz respectively, are displayed as rival prima donnas contending for vocal supremacy. Their very names must be intended to reveal something of the differing nature of their vocal styles; Cavalieri's voice must have been comparatively bright and incisive, while Lange's would have more readily conveyed warmth and sentiment. During the action, each executes a display piece in which her voice is shown to advantage—but the contrast between them is also a source of much amusement.

Lange's two-tempo arietta ('Da schlägt die Abschiedsstunde . . . Ein Herz, das so der Abschied kranket') immediately reveals Mozart's wish to highlight the soprano's cantabile. This diminutive G minor Larghetto is set, for the most part, above $b'b$, and rides along on undulating semiquavers in triple time. Ample opportunity is given the singer to draw out and shape the line with portamento. The *passaggi* of the G major fast section cascade over a transparent orchestration of sustaining wind instruments and strings marking in quavers (ex.11). Cavalieri counters with a high-spirited, robust, two-tempo rondò in E♭ major ('Bester Jüngling') that features mostly syllabic writing; the tune is asserted in forceful gestures and pitches above the staff are saved for climactic moments. In the Allegretto second section, after several bars of paired quavers, we arrive at an open syllable on 'Pfand' (ex.12), which features distinctive two-note divisions and repeated pitches called *martellato* by 18th-century theorists.[37] The contrast between the two sopranos finds even more trenchant expression in the trio 'Ich bin die erste Sängerin'. Mozart first gives to Madame Herz a ravishing moment of portamento, when, after Herr Vogelsang exclaims, 'Ei, ei, ein jedes hat besondern Wert', she soars above a transparent orchestral texture (repeated crotchets in the strings and quiet semibreves in the winds), uttering 'Adagio, adagio' (ex.13a). The range extends to $e'''b$, from which high note a graceful arpeggio descends and is then completed by a delicate leap. Interrupting, Mademoiselle Silberklang countercharges with 'Allegro, allegrissimo' in Cavalieri's familiar style. Her outburst ends with forceful exercise-like triplet divisions (ex.13b). Tempers are soon checked by Vogelsang, who asserts that no artist may censure another. Ostensibly placated (they sing in 3rds at this point), they are in fact still seething. Lange begins to pull away from Cavalieri, to outdo her in

Ex.11 Mozart, *Der Schauspieldirektor*, K486, no.1. Madame Herz, arietta: 'Da schlägt die Abschiedsstunde', bars 60–67

Ex.12 Mozart, *Der Schauspieldirektor*, no.2. Madame Silberklang, rondò, 'Bester Jüngling!', bars 59–73

Ex.13 Mozart, *Der Schauspieldirektor*, no.3. Terzett, 'Ich bin die erste Sängerin': (a) bars 90–97; (b) bars 98–109; (c) bars 129–35

tirata gestures extending first to d''' and then $e'''b$ (ex.13c). Cavalieri joins in as Lange heads for f'''; settling, however, a 3rd lower, on d'''. The rival singers fall back in 3rds, but the tensions of the opening section return, only half-suppressed, at the end.

Here at the crux of Mozart's slight comedy one must sense that much of the humour turns on the fact that the two singers are playing themselves. *Der Schauspieldirektor* is best approached in light of the 18th-century vocal style. This style would have expressed itself by means of a repertory of distinctive vocal gestures respected by the composer and immediately recognizable as such by an audience.[38]

So, while we can never recapture the actual sound of the voices for which Mozart composed his operas, a study of musical and extra-musical sources can provide us with considerable insight into his singers. Mozart composed his music specifically for the singers: at the least, the vocal line was crafted to their needs; at the most, the singer could provide the inspiration that determined the character of the music. As much as the libretto, the singers were the material out of which the operas were composed. Mozart was not unique in this manner of creating an opera, yet in his hands such compositional practice was perhaps given its greatest scope and acquired a lasting significance.

Patricia Lewy Gidwitz recently completed her doctoral dissertation Vocal Profiles of Four Mozart Sopranos *at the University of California, Berkeley.*

[1]The responsibilities undertaken by the poet and composer in charge of producing an opera in Vienna are codified in a short document addressed to the Imperial Direction of the Burgtheater by Lorenzo Da Ponte. The poet must 'change the arias which, in the musical director's opinion do not compliment the singer's voice'. And the composer is 'to set all the recitatives that have been changed or lengthened by the poet and to assist with the insertion of those pieces that, in agreement with the poet, might be judged useful to the opera'. Da Ponte insists that a singer must sing the role assigned, that he or she may not arbitrarily order the poet to rewrite an aria or to introduce an alternative piece, and finally, that he or she 'shall be obliged to perform the music as ordered by the maestro.' Document in the Österreichisches Haus- und Staatsarchiv entitled 'Ordine necessarissimo in una Direzione teatrale. Scelta ed approvata un' opera dalla Direzione Imperiale.' In O. Michtner, *Das alte Burgtheater als Opernbühne* (Vienna, 1970), p.439. Also see D. Heartz, *Mozart's Operas,* ed. T. Bauman (Berkeley, 1990), pp.104-5.

[2]We have Mozart's comments as evidence. See, for example, his letter to Leopold Mozart of 11 September 1778, no.487, lines 179-88. As Daniel Heartz has pointed out, Mozart is surely pleading Weber's case for his own purposes.

[3]All translations of German text by Carl Skoggard. 'Ich habe ihm gesagt, er soll mir aufrichtig sagen, wenn sie ihm nicht taugt, oder nicht gefällt; ich will ihm die arie ändern wie er will, oder auch eine andere machen ... ich ihm die aria so arangieren werde, dass er sie gewis gerne singen wird; denn ich liebe dass die aria einem sänger so accurat angemessen sey, wie ein gutgemachtes kleid.' Letter of 28 February 1778, no.431, lines 14-16, 25-7.

[4]Caterina Cavalieri [Franziska Helena Appolonia Kavalier] (1760-1801) sang almost exclusively in Vienna both as a serious and comic lead in German and Italian opera during the 1780s. Not only Mozart (Konstanze in *Die Entführung* and Mlle Silberklang in *Der Schauspieldirektor*), but many composers of the day, most notably Salieri, Umlauf and Cimarosa composed specifically for her. Aloysia Weber Lange (*b* between 1759 and 1761, *d* 1839) was Mozart's sister-in-law. Active primarily at the Burgtheater in Vienna during the 1780s in both German and Italian comic opera, she married the court actor and painter Joseph Lange on 31 October 1780. Her long association with Mozart produced seven concert arias and a role in *Der Schauspieldirektor.* Her career in Vienna was primarily as a leading singer in revivals of Italian operas. After 1785, she was removed with other German singers to the neighbouring Kärntnertortheater, where she appeared in German translations of Italian opera currently in the repertory of the Italian company at the Burgtheater and translations of *opéra comique* from the earlier repertory of the defunct German National Opera.

[5]Opera manuscripts are records, generally, of three types of activity related to mounting a production. They are either fair copies made at the request of the management by a copy firm for purposes of future productions or they may be conflations of the fair copy and the changes made both in anticipation of a production and during rehearsals. They may contain changes made during a run of performances and in some cases a single manuscript copy may reflect changes associated with more than one production of the opera. For a larger study of Viennese operatic productions see P. L. Gidwitz, *Vocal Profiles of Four Mozart Sopranos* (Ph.D. diss., U. of California, Berkeley, 1991), in which vocal evidence for four singers, Aloysia Weber Lange, Caterina Cavalieri, Anna Selina Storace and Adriana Ferrarese del Bene, is examined in sources related to the repertory of German and Italian opera at the Burgtheater during the 1780s. These singers were part of an operatic troupe whose constituency of German and Italian singers remained fairly stable for the period under discussion. For them Mozart composed *Die Entführung aus dem Serail* (1782), *Le nozze di Figaro* (1786), *Der Schauspieldirektor* (1786) and *Così fan tutte* (1790). *Don Giovanni* (1787), originally written for the Bondini troupe in Prague, was altered in 1788 to accommodate the new singers in the Viennese production. *Le nozze di Figaro* was changed for a Viennese revival three years after its première.

[6]The note g''' occurs in 'Popoli di Tessaglia ... Io non chiedo', K316 (300b) (the compositional date is recorded on the manuscript as 8 January 1779), see NMA II/7/2, p.85. An a''' is found in Umlauf's aria conceived for her, 'Senkt, kühle Schatten', Act 1, scene 1, no.2 of *Das Irrlicht* (January 1782); the source cited is from a fair copy, A-Wn: Cod.16.521.

[7]Salieri wrote an e''' for Cavalieri in his single German opera for Vienna, *Der Rauchfangkehrer* (A-Wn: Mus. Hs. 16.611). The aria 'Basta vincesti ... Ah non lasciarmi', is a small-scale piece sung as an Italian song within the Singspiel. The autograph, however, transmits a version of the aria with a marking to transpose the piece downward a major 2nd, an indication that she was losing her top notes or that Salieri had initially miscalculated her capacities. A well known example of such downward transposition later in her career is 'Mi tradì', which Mozart wrote for her to sing in E♭ in the Viennese production (1788) of *Don Giovanni* but transposed to D.

[8]Lange's long association with the role of Konstanze, undertaken when she became a leading singer with the German troupe in residence at the Kärntnertortheater from 1785 to 1788, has caused recent scholars to suggest the possibility that the role was originally conceived for Lange rather than Cavalieri. Even Michael Kelly, singer, composer, publisher and friend of Mozart, comments that 'the songs which Mozart composed for her in "L'Enlèvement du Sérail," shew what a compass of voice she had.' See Michael Kelly, *Reminiscences,* p.250. Compass was, as we point out, only one aspect of a vocal portrait.

[9]Mozart's letter to his father of 19 February 1778 (lines 51-65) offers a defence of Aloysia Weber by stating what sort of singer she was not. The passage expressly identifies her with cantabile and cantabile with the art of singing. Also in Gidwitz, *Vocal Profiles,* chap.2, n.4, p.43.

[10]Giovanni Battista Mancini defines the technique of *cantar di sbalzo* in *Pensieri, e riflessioni pratiche sopra il canto figurato* (Vienna, 1774), pp.140-41:

' ... cantar di sbalzo, sia questo formato con note di volare, oppur di minor volare, è sempre un cantar d'agilità nel genere il più difficile, e penoso per ben impossessarsene ... Nel già proposto genere di cantare, per esser bene appropriato, si ricerca una voce robusta, sonora, agile, e ricca di profondi gravi, ed acuti, quantunque sia voce si soprano; non ritrovandosi unite tutte queste prerogative non si deve assolutamente neppur tentare di apprenderlo.

Il cantar di sbalzo richiede uno studio particolare, e totalmente separato da tutti gl'altri. L'intonazione, per esempio, quantunque ridotta perfetta in ogni altro metodo, in questo deve essere studiata di nuovo per accostumar la voce a sbalzare da quel grave a quell' acuto, intonandolo a perfezzione.

Si crederà da taluni esser ciò facile, ma in realtà non è, perchè oltre lo sbalzare con perfetta intonazione è necessario di dare una bilanciata misura alla voce sì nel sbalzare salendo, come discendendo; è naturale, che in se stessa la corda grave deve esser vibrata, oppur sostenuta con forza secondo il bisogno, eppure anche l'acuto, comunque si adopera, convien sempre trattarlo con dolcezza, purchè fra l'uno, e l'altro resti sempre conservata una proporzionata corrispondenza. Necessario anch' è, che l' esecuzione perfetta vada unita col portamento di voce . . .'

[11][Lange] hat eine sehr angenehme Stimme, die aber fürs Theater zu schwach ist.' *Deutches Museum* (Leipzig, 1781). In Deutsch, *Dokumente*, p.172. '[Lange's] Stimme gehört mehr für die Kammer als für das Theater'. For Gerber see his *Musiklexicon*, i, column 785, quoted in Michtner, *Das alte Burgtheater*, p.368; for Zinzendorf Michtner, p.390, n.57: 'I viaggiatori felice . . . Marchesi plut, la Weber fane sa voix.'

[12]'Es ist gar nicht zu widersprechen, dass sie mit der grössten expression singt: allein itzt erkäre ich mir, warum mir einige, die ich öfters fragte, sagten, sie habe eine sehr schwache Stimme—und andere sagten mir, sie habe eine sehr laute Stimme. beydes ist wahr: die Haltung, und alle Noten des Ausdrucks sind erstaunlich stark; die zährtlichen Sachen, die Passagen und auszierungen und die hohen Töne sehr fein, so dass, nach meiner Empfindung eins gegen den anderen zu sehr absticht, und im Zimmer die starken Töne die Ohren beleidigen, im Theater aber die feinen Passagen eine grosse Stille und aufmerksamkeit der Zuhörer vorrausstezen.' Letter of Leopold Mozart, 25 March 1784, no.854, lines 42–51.

[13]' . . . unvergleich stärker, aber ganz besonderer Art . . . ' In *Deutsches Museum* (Leipzig, 1781). In Deutsch, *Dokumente*, p.172. For Zinzendorf quoted directly above see Michtner, p.397, n.30.

[14]Even so, there is some contemporary testimony to the contrary. On 1 April 1783 the composer Joseph Martin Kraus travelled to Vienna and that same evening heard Cavalieri at the Burgtheater. Kraus had this report: 'Signorina Cavalieri has adequate skill and a small, yet well-sounding voice. The first aria in A major was by Salieri. The bravura was well-composed and well-sung. The place did not strike me as well endowed for the music.' Bertil Van Boer, 'The Travel Diary of Joseph Martin Kraus: Translation and Commentary', *Journal of Musicology*, viii (1990); p.283. The Burgtheater began its life as a tennis court.

[15]Salieri's and Casti's *La scuola dei gelosi* was first produced in Venice at the San Moisè on 27 December 1778. The autograph, which was also used as a working score for the 1783 Viennese production, is housed in the Musiksammlung der Österreichisches Nationalbibliotek, A-Wn: 16.615. Also in this collection is another working manuscript, KT410, the second folio of which contains the characters and names of the 1783 cast. An additional trio and new solo arias for Michael Kelly, Cavalieri, Francesco Bussani, Pugnetti and Therese Theyber are contained in this manuscript. No new pieces were written for Francesco Benucci.

[16]Anna Selina Storace (1765–1817) arrived in Vienna after great successes on the Italian stage primarily as a *buffa* singer. Trained in London in the Italian singing style, she first attempted to put her abilities to use in Vienna in serious singing. The vehicle was the role of the Countess, the *prima seria*, in Salieri's *La scuola dei gelosi* (22 April 1783). Competition in this style from the local native pool—with Lange and Cavalieri chief among her rivals—forced Storace to reclaim her successes as a *prima buffa*. This she did splendidly and was celebrated as among the greatest comic actresses of her age, inspiring the creation of roles such as Susanna in Mozart's *Le nozze di Figaro* (1786) and Lilla in Martin y Soler's *Una cosa rara* (1786).

[17]*Nota e parola* style is characterized by its declaimed quality in which, literally, one syllable is assigned to one note. See John Brown, *Letters on the Italian opera: addressed to a friend. By the late Mr John Brown, painter* (Edinburgh, Bell and Bradfute; [etc., etc.] 1789), p.39. 'Aria parlante—speaking Air, is that which, from the nature of its subject admits neither of long notes in the composition, nor of many ornaments in the execution. The rapidity of the motion of this Air is proportioned to the violence of the passion which is expressed by it. This species of Air goes sometimes by the name of aria di nota e parola, and likewise of aria agitata; but these are rather sub-divisions of the species, and relate to the different degrees of violence of the passion expressed'.

[18]Throughout the opera Ernestina has been angry with her husband for his overbearing jealousy. Just before this moment (Act 2, scene v) he has attempted to redress the situation, by making her jealous in return.

[19]Salieri seems to have overshot the mark here; the aria as it was first written and copied into KT410 is in E major, but has been transposed down to D major. We may suppose that Cavalieri importuned composers for the most impressive opportunities, but then was not always able to deliver on what she was given.

[20]'es war die Langin bey uns um die 2 arien zu Probieren, und wir hielten Rath um feiner zu seyn als unsere feinde—denn Ich habe ihrer genug, und die Langin hat wegen der storaci der *Neuen Sängerin* auch nun genug.' Letter of 2 July 1783, no.754, lines 4–6. Daniel Heartz, cautions that Mozart's words must not be taken at face value. A certain paranoia invades Mozart's reactions to the circumstances surrounding the composition of the two insertion arias K418 and K419: he was at this time still an outsider in Vienna, with no position and no access, and was attempting, probably in part by the composition of these insertion arias, to make a name for himself in opera. Heartz casts doubt on whether Storace was perceived as either antagonistic or threatening to the success of Lange or Mozart, although Mozart's mention of Storace bears consideration. Mozart would not have included Storace's name gratuitously. She must have figured in some way, either real or imagined, in the conception of K418.

[21]The manuscript of 'Vorrei spiegarti, oh Dio', transmits 20 June 1783, indicating that it was probably completed ten days before the production of Anfossi's *Il curioso indiscreto* on the stage of the Burgtheater. See NMA II/7/3, p.25.

[22]Anfossi's *Il curioso indiscreto* received its première at the Teatro delle Dame in Rome during carnival of 1777.

[23]Mozart's efforts with regard to this aria survive in two versions, the first an attempt to reset the existing text, 'Ah, spiegarti, oh Dio! Vorrei quel desio'. Transmitted in keyboard reduction (see NMA II/7/iii, p.210), the aria seems to show Mozart tinkering, in effect, with Anfossi's original version. Mozart ultimately reworked both text and music in the final version of the aria, 'Vorrei spiegarvi, oh Dio', with optimum results.

[24]Even if Lange extemporized additional high notes in the original aria (certainly standard practice of the day) the full effect of her abilities might have gone imperfectly realized.

[25]The success of Mozart's arias is corroborated by Count Zinzendorf, who recorded that 'La Lang chanta des airs de bravoure et joua avec Adamberger d'une fraischeur admirable'. Michtner, p.388, n.26. The career of Count Johann Karl Zinzendorf (1739–1813), the tireless chronicler of Viennese theatrical life, is detailed in Michtner, p.357, n.21.

[26]The work was first given on 12 May 1778 at the Teatro di Via della Pergola, Florence.

[27]The source for the cast list is Michtner, p.168. The following manuscript scores were consulted: *Fair copies:* (1) D-Dlb: Mus. 3491-F-502, Bd. 1, 2. La Vendemia/Musica/del/Sigl Giuseppe Gazaniga; (2) US-Wc: M1500 G 29 v, case; before 1780 (see Barthà/Somfei, *Haydn als Opernkapellmeister* (Budapest, 1966), p.219, for a complete description of this source). *Working copies:* (1) A-Wn: anonymous score, S.M.30.108 2 Bks. 381.117; identified by the author as such, May 1989; (2) A-Wn: KT459: *Le Vendemie ossia La dama incognita/Drama giocoso per Musica/in due Atti/Del Sigl.: Giuseppe Gazaniga;* although there is no date on the manuscript, it was probably copied in 1784. *Libretti:* (1) A-Wst: W 200.412. LA VENDEMMIA/DRAMMA GIOCOSO/PER MUSICA/DA RAPPRESENATARSI/Nel Teatro nuovamente erretto in parte/piccola della Regia Città di Praga, nella/Casa del Conte Thun . . . 1782; (2) US-Wc: Schatz no. 3675, Dresden, 1783; (3) G-Lbm: 907.K.2. Tract six. LA VENDEMMIA./ A/NEW COMIC OPERA,/IN TWO ACTS./As performed at the KING'S THEATRE, in the /HAY MARKET./THE MUSIC ENTIRELY NEW/By SIGNOR GAZZANIGHA/. . . LONDON: . . . 1789.

[28]See Gidwitz, *Vocal Profiles*, chap.2, pp.77–8.

[29]In the preface to his collected libretto edition of 1792, Stephanie argues on behalf of an even distribution for solo numbers. Stephanie

der Jüngerere, *Sämmtliche Singspiele* (Liegnitz, 1792), pp.iii–xx. 'Man macht oft eine blosse Komödie, setzt nach Laune da oder dorthin eine Arie; sieht nicht drauf, ob eine und die nämliche Person zwey oder mehrere Arien nach einander zu singen habe; . . . Mehr als zwey Arien müssen selten auf einander folgen, und diese nicht von einer Person gesungen werden; ein Duett, Terzet oder Quartet, muss dann gleichsam einen Abschnitt machen.' Printed in R. Schusky, *Das deutsche Singspiel im 18. Jahrhundert, Quellen und Zeugnisse zu Ästhetik und Rezeption* (Bonn, 1980), pp.93-4.

[30]The Italian vocal method was based on the cultivation of a pure, clear, even tone. This quality was expected in every note of a singer's voice, in every dynamic and in every style. To this end, a vocal exercise was introduced and adapted that would ensure evenness, control and consistency of tone quality throughout the range. The exercise was based on the 16th-century ornament the *messa di voce* and involved the protraction of a single note during which the tone begins softly, gains volume, and finally returns to the original quiet tone. To accomplish this smoothly throughout the range represented the ultimate test of tone production. Caccini describes the *messa di voce* in *Le nuove musiche* (Florence, 1601-2, repr. 1930, 1934 and 1973; Eng. trans., ed. H. Wiley Hitchcock, *Recent Researches in the Music of the Baroque* (Madison, 1970), p.55-6.

[31]Close parallels are 'Vorrei spiegarvi, oh Dio!', K418, bars 133ff. and 'Ah se in ciel, benigne stelle', K538, bars 96ff. NMA II/7/3.

[32]Indeed, none of the other candidates—one thinks immediately of Rosa Manservisi, the Sandrina in Mozart's *La finta giardiniera* and Theresa Teyber, the first Blöndchen in *Die Entführung*—are known to have undertaken an aria in this particular style. No contemporary journalistic evidence speaks to this question: the only extant criticism of Lange in *La vendemmia* is from Zinzendorf's diary (13 April 1785), a year after the première: 'La dama incognita ou la Lang chevrota.' Quoted in Michtner, p.391. Lange became ill shortly after; there is a report in the *Wiener Zeitung* of 3 December 1785 that she reappeared for the first time in *Die Entführung aus dem Serail*, at the Kärntnertor, on 25 November 1785, ' . . . nach ihrer grossen Krankheit . . . ', Deutsch, *Dokumente*, p.225. 'Chevroter' means to sing in a tremulous voice. Zinzendorf is noting, no doubt, the effects of illness on her vocal production.

[33]See A. Tyson, 'Problems in the text of *Le nozze di Figaro*', *Mozart: Studies of the Autograph Scores* (Cambridge, Mass., 1987), p.317. The manuscript is Conservatorio di Musica Luigi Cherubini, Florence F.P.T. 262.

[34]Tyson, p.321. This revision of 'Dove sono' is reproduced in Mozart, *Le nozze di Figaro: Eight Variant Versions*, ed. A. Tyson (Oxford, 1989), pp.31-8.

[35]Traditionally, the anticipation of the reprise was seen as an important display moment for the singer. It was the occasion for the vocal *Eingang*, or lead-in, to the return of the initial material; it occurs as a cadenza on the dominant before the tonic return. In his revisions of this piece Mozart eliminated the vocal *Eingang*, replacing it with abbreviated material that leads directly into the Allegro. Such a procedure, the substitution of an orchestral *Eingang* for a vocal one, can be seen as a dramatic stroke, one that impels the aria forward, heightening the pace toward the emotional release brought on by the Allegro. There are precedents in Mozart for the more radical abridgment of the rondò form that is found here, for example 'Mentre ti lascio, o figlia', K513.

[36]From an objective standpoint—that of the integrity of the opera as drama—it cannot be claimed that the revised version maintains the level of the original.

[37]See, for example, Mancini, *Pensieri, e reflessioni*, pp.138-40. *Martellato* 'consiste nel battere alcune note simili. Deve dunque la voce ripercuotere le medesime note più vole, e delle quattro la prima dev' essere più acuta delle altre tre scritte nella medesima linea.

Questo genere di agilità è dificilissimo ad eseguirsi a perfezzione, poichè per ben riuscirvi fa' d' uopo avere una voce agilissima, un genio perticolare per applicarvisi, ed uno studio indefesso. Sopra ogni cosa . . . bisogna possedere una purgatissima intonazione, acciò ogni nota martellata sia distintamente intonata.'

[38]A well known example is Salieri's and Nancy Storace's send-up of the celebrated soprano castrato Luigi Marchesi in the role of the dramatische Sängerin, Eleonora, for *Prima la musica poi la parola* (1786). In all contemporary accounts of her singing in *Prima la musica*, Storace was praised for her imitation of Marchesi's style. The *Realzeitung* of Vienna, for example, announced that 'Madame Storace excited universal enthusiasm; she imitated the famous Sr. Luigi Marchesi in singing arias from *Giulio Sabino* so well that one imagined one was hearing Marchesi himself, and she even mimicked his acting with real skill.' Quoted in Michtner, pp.200-201 and p.400, n.55. The cast list cited in Michtner (p.200) erroneously reverses the roles taken by Storace (Eleonora) and Celeste Coltellini (Tonina).

[8]

Mozarts's Ilia and Elettra: New Perspectives on *Idomeneo*

Paul Corneilson

In discussing Mozart's vocal music, Franz Niemetschek was among the first to suggest that *"Darum müßte man immer die Sänger kennen, für die er schrieb, wenn man ein richtiges Urtheil über seine [i.e., Mozart's] dramatischen Werken fällen wollte"*.[1] A good case in point are the sisters-in-law Dorothea Wendling and Elisabeth Wendling, who shared the stage as the leading sopranos for almost twenty years, from 1762 to 1781, first at Mannheim and later at Munich. Mozart met the Wendlings while visiting Mannheim in the winter of 1777–78 and later composed for them the roles of Ilia and Elettra. While their respective roles in *Idomeneo* are undoubtedly their most famous, these two sopranos made tangible contributions to the operas they performed at Mannheim in the 1760s and 1770s. The arias written specifically for Dorothea and Elisabeth not only reveal much about their vocal abilities and tastes, but also much about the way composers, including Mozart, adapted roles for individual singers.

In the eighteenth century composers depended on singers to win them success, just as singers depended on composers to write stylish and effective arias for them to display their talents. The modern notion of a composer writing music and then finding a singer who could sing it was a foreign concept to Mozart and his contemporaries. In most cases singers were selected before the composer began to write an opera. An opera's success depended on matching a singer's acting and musical talents to a particular role, and opera subjects and texts were chosen with the strengths of particular singers in mind. It is no accident, for instance, that Anton Raaff, who was sixty-six at the time of the premiere of *Idomeneo*, had portrayed elder statesmen in other seria roles, including Catone, Temistocle, Lucio Silla, and Günther von Schwarzburg.[2] Of course Homer himself makes a passing reference to Idomeneus' old age in book 13 of the *Iliad*.[3]

Music written for a particular voice, when written by a sensitive composer, illuminates the basic abilities of the singer; contemporary descriptions of a voice also help us imagine the singer's strengths and weaknesses. Mozart and other composers prided themselves on their ability to tailor their music to a particular voice. Although it can be difficult to document a singer's entire career, it is possible to sketch the "vocal profile" of singers based on the types of arias they performed, their range and tessitura, their characteristic *fioritura*, and certain recurring vocal gestures, such as *cantar di sbalzo* and *portamento*, that inhabit the arias.[4]

---

[1] Franz Niemetschek, *Lebenbeschreibung des k. k. Kapellmeisters Wolfgang Amadeus Mozart*, 2d ed., Prague 1808, p. 76n. As an example in the first edition, Niemetschek mentions the two arias of the Queen of the Night, which were written specially for Mozart's sister-in-law Josepha Hofer, but this reference was cut in the second edition, presumably because ten years later, in 1808, few of his readers would have heard Hofer sing this role.

[2] See Daniel Heartz, "Raaff's Last Aria: A Mozartian Idyll in the Spirit of Hasse", in: *Musical Quarterly* 60 (1974), pp. 517–43.

[3] *"And there, grizzled gray as he was, he spurred his men,/Idomeneus ramping amidst the Trojans, striking panic"*; Iliad 13 420 (translated by Robert Fagles). Considering the destruction that Idomeneus caused that day, it is no wonder that Poseidon struck back at his ships when he returned to Crete (cf. *Odyssey*).

[4] Pat Lewy Gidwitz has developed a method for describing eighteenth-century singers in *Vocal Profiles of Four Mozart Sopranos*, Ph.D. diss., University of California, Berkeley 1991.

Fortunately, in looking at the sopranos Dorothea and Elisabeth Wendling, we have two singers whose careers are relatively well documented. Born at Stuttgart in 1736 – twenty years before Mozart – to a family of musicians named Spurni, Dorothea married the flautist Johann Baptist Wendling on 9 January 1752. Later that year she was appointed a singer at the Mannheim court.[5] At the age of sixteen she made her debut as Ermione in Galuppi's *Antigona* (1753). She appeared as prima donna for the first time in 1758 in Ignaz Holzbauer's *Nitteti*. (A list of her roles is given in table 1). For the next twenty years Dorothea was one of the most celebrated sopranos in Germany, gaining wide recognition for her performances in the title roles in Tommaso Traetta's *Sofonisba* (1762) and Gian Francesco de Majo's *Ifigenia in Tauride* (1764). The novelist Wilhelm Heinse, who has many perceptive comments about eighteenth-century opera, including a few of the Mannheim-operas in *Hildegard von Hohenthal* (1795–96), called her the "Deutsche Melpomene der goldnen Zeit zu Mannheim".[6] She was well paid for her efforts: the surviving *"Besoldungs Status"* of 1776 shows that she earned 1500 fl., 500 fl. more than her husband and only 400 fl. less than Ignaz Holzbauer, the Hofkapellmeister.[7]

According to a local commentator, Dorothea Wendling *"brought together a very attractive appearance, the most beautiful voice, the art of singing to perfection in all genres, and the most accomplished acting on stage"*.[8] She was an effective actress, and she excelled at cantabile singing. She had an effective range from e-flat^1 to b-flat^2 and only rarely sang c^3 and never above it. Over the course of her career, composers exploited the strength of her tessitura (b-flat^1–f^2), and, as we shall see, a striking number of arias written specifically for her are in flat keys (especially B-flat, E-flat, and G-minor). When necessary she could sing *passagi*, although the brilliant style of *fioriture* embellishment was not one of her strengths. Her specialty was the pathetic style and its attendant rhetorical gestures: "sighing" melodic figures, sudden chromatic shifts to minor harmonies or tonalities, and a vocabulary rich in pathetic discourse.[9]

Christian Friedrich Daniel Schubart heard Dorothea sing probably near the end of her career, since he mentions a technical flaw.

"[Dorothea] hat sich als eine unsrer besten Theatersängerinnen ausgezeichnet. Sie figurirte im französischen, welschen und deutschen Spiele; doch im komischen Fache weit mehr als im tragischen. Sie fing zu früh an zu schettern – was im ernsthaften Vortrag die widrigste Wirkung macht".[10]

---

[5] Electoral decree, dated 19 February 1753, in Karlsruhe, Badisches Generallandesarchiv, 77/1665. The brief entry on Dorothea Wendling in Felix Joseph Lipowsky's *Baierisches Musik-Lexikon*, Munich 1811, pp. 386–87, although somewhat inaccurate in details, provides a fairly complete list of operas performed at the Mannheim court between 1742 and 1777.

[6] Wilhelm Heinse, *Sämmtliche Werke*, Bd. 5, *Hildegard von Hohenthal*, ed. Carl Schüddekopf, Leipzig 1903, p. 171. Heinse clearly admired Dorothea's interpretations and singled out arias written especially for her. The novel's protagonist, Herr Lockmann, says her aria ("Tutti gl'affetti miei") in act 2 of *Cajo Fabrizio "gehört unter die schönsten weiblichen Sachen von Jomelli"* (p. 225); her aria ("Sventurata in van mi lagno") in act 3 of Traetta's *Sofonisba* is *"vortrefliche leidenschaftliche Melodie, und eine der schönsten Bravourarien"* (p. 173); and the aria ("Ombra cara, che intorno t'aggiri") in act 2 of *Ifigenia in Tauride* "hat Majo's Iphigenia den wahren Ausdruck einer bis zur Schwärmerey tief gerührten und ergriffnen Seele; die Töne der Melodie sind eigentlicher Accent Griechischer Grazie" (p. 293).

[7] Munich, Bayerisches Hauptstaatsarchiv, HRI Fasc. 457/13; reproduced in: *Die Mannheimer Hofkapelle im Zeitalter Carl Theodors*, ed. Ludwig Finscher, Mannheim 1992, pp. 40–43.

[8] "[Dorothea] joignoit a une figure trés interessante, la plus belle voix, l'art de chanter, dans tout les genres, en perfection, et l'action au theatre la plus complette". In the Traitteur Nachlass in Munich, Geheimes Hausarchiv, Korr. Akt. 882/V b.

[9] I use the word "pathetic" in the sense of Rousseau's definition in his *Dictionnaire de musique*, Paris 1768, p. 367: "*PATHETIQUE. Genre de musique dramatique & théâtral, qui tend à peindre & à émouvoir les grandes passions, & plus particulièrement la douleur & la tristesse. ... Le vrai pathétique est dans l'Accent passionné, qui me se détermine point par les règles; mais que le génie trouve & que le cœur sent, sans que l'Art puisse, en auceune manière en donner la loi*".

[10] Schubart, *Ideen zu einer Aesthetik der Tonkunst*, Vienna 1806, p. 144. The verb "schettern" is defined by Jacob and Wilhelm Grimm, *Deutsches Wörterbuch*, rev. Moriz Heyne, Leipzig 1893, as "klingen, klirren, tonmalend". It

Did Schubart hear her on a bad night, or were other commentators able to overlook her "warbly tone" in the same way modern critics forgave Maria Callas's expressive but sometimes raw singing? Schubart is correct in pointing out that Dorothea performed in a variety of different roles at the Mannheim theater, and in the period 1769–77, she actually did sing more comic roles than seria roles. But since most of the comic operas were imported from Vienna or Italy, it is possible that Schubart heard her sing arias less well suited to her voice.

In the 1770s she sang a series of roles in which she was cast as the unfortunate daughter or unhappy lover: as Marzia, daughter of Catone (who is defeated and commits suicide); as Aspasia, daughter of Temistocle (who is banished from Greece and condemned to die); and as Giunia, daughter of Gaius Marius (enemy of Lucio Silla, who now wants to marry her). Her last major role, Ilia, is in the same vein. Following her retirement from the stage she continued to sing in "Concerts de M^{rs} les Amateurs" in Munich, occasionally appearing with her daughter Elisabeth Augusta. For instance, on 20 January 1786, she sang a "Quatuor de Mr. Mozart," with her daughter, Franz or Anton Ludwig Danzi, and the tenor Friedrich Epp (see plate 1).[11] In 1798 she applied for a pension, and in her later years gained renown as a singing teacher.[12]

Elisabeth Wendling was ten years younger than Dorothea. Her parents, Pietro and Carolina Sarselli, were singers at Mannheim. She traveled to Italy in 1760 and after her return to Mannheim the following year was appointed a court musician. Like Dorothea, Elisabeth was sixteen at the time of her stage debut, singing Cirene in *Sofonisba* (1762). (See table 2 for a list of her roles.) On 21 November 1764, she married Franz Anton Wendling, a violinist in the orchestra and a brother of Johann Baptist. Throughout most of her career she took supporting roles behind her sister-in-law, and this was reflected in her annual stipend. In 1776 she received 1000 fl., that is, 500 fl. less than Dorothea. Elisabeth also gained distinction in a variety of comic and serious roles at Mannheim, although there are fewer descriptions of her voice.[13] Mozart heard Elisabeth sing the role of Anna in the revival of Holzbauer's *Günther von Schwarzburg*. In a letter of 14 November 1777, Mozart writes, *"die Prima donna war die Mad: Elisabeth Wendling, nicht die flutraversisten frau, sondern des geigers. sie ist immer kränklich, und zu demm war auch die opera nicht für sie, sondern für eine gewisse [Franziska] Danzi geschrieben, die jezt in England ist; folglich nicht für ihre stimme, sondern zu hoch"*.[14] In 1778 she accompanied Carl Theodor to Munich, where she appeared in *Telemaco* (1780) and *Idomeneo*

---

is also related to "schättern", meaning "tonmalend, meist von hellen, kurzen, klappernden, knarrenden klängen". The word is also used in a derogatory way, as in "krachend, dumpfklingend töne, wie z. B. zerbrochenes töpfergeschirr, auch laut lachen". Perhaps Schubart means that her voice broke or cracked on certain notes, or perhaps that she used excessive vibrato.

[11] Munich, Geheimes Hausarchiv, Korr. Akt. 882/V b. I am very grateful to the Director, Herr Dr. Immler, for allowing me to examine these programs and to reproduce one of them here. Cliff Eisen cites this programme in *New Mozart Documents: A Supplement to O. E. Deutsch's Documentary Biography*, Stanford 1991, p. 102, but he incorrectly gives the place as Mannheim and suggests one of the six 'Haydn' quartets as the piece performed. However, this almost certainly must refer to the quartet from *Idomeneo*, with Danzi presumably singing the part of Idamante down an octave. It is possible that Mozart himself sent a copy of his revision for tenor, which was performed only two months later in Vienna.

[12] Munich, Bayerisches Hauptstaatsarchiv, HRI Fasc. 473/922. According to Lipowsky, *Baierisches Musik-Lexikon*, p. 386, *"Jedes Individuum, das aus der Wendling Schule kam, zeichnet sich durch eine gute Methode aus, und beweiset deutlich bei einer der esten Sängerinnen Unterricht erhalten zu haben"*.

[13] Traitteur mentions her briefly: *"Entre les voix il y avait aussi Tonarelli, et Roncaglio, qui ont fait les pres Roles, avec succès, a la cour, comme allieurs. La fille de Sarselli, epouse de Francois Wendling, s'est également distinguer"*. Traitteur Nachlass in Munich, Geheimes Hausarchiv, Korr. Akt. 882/V b.

[14] *Mozart: Briefe und Aufzeichnungen*, ed. Otto Erich Deutsch and W. A. Bauer, Kassel 1962–1975, vol. 2, p. 125.

(1781); in 1782 Elisabeth created the title role in Antonio Salieri's *Semiramide*. Her last role would have been Zelmira in Alessio Prati's *Armida abbandonata* (1785), and she died the following year.[15]

Elisabeth Wendling must have been a good actress, capable of fiery declamation, although not all her roles displayed her abilities to the extent of the jealous fury of Elettra's "Tutte nel cor vi sento". She had a somewhat wider range than Dorothea (d^1 to d^3 and a higher tessitura. In general, Elisabeth's aria have more coloratura and *passagi*, but she was not in the same league as Franziska Danzi-Lebrun or perhaps not even Aloysia Weber-Lange in her prime. Nevertheless, Elisabeth Wendling did appear as prima donna in a few operas, and she occasionally has a concertante aria or a solo scena, as in act 2 of *Temistocle* ("Or a' danni d'un ingrato"). But as a rule Elisabeth's arias tend to be shorter and less substantial than Dorothea's.

Elisabeth often played rivals to her sister-in-law's roles. As Cirene, she thwarts Sofonisba's plans to marry Massinissa, thus causing her to commit suicide. Elisabeth is similarly pitted against Dorothea in *Catone*, *Temistocle*, *Lucio Silla*, and most strikingly in *Idomeneo*. Although Elisabeth played the antagonist in some operas, in *Ifigenia* she portrayed Tomiri, princess of Taurus, who for complicated and inexplicable reasons is in love with the despot Thoas. In other works, like *Alessandro* and *Adriano*, the women had approximately equal parts, although in each of these works Dorothea sang one aria more than Elisabeth.[16]

Many late eighteenth-century theorists and composers discussed the contrasting qualities of sharp and flat ("hard" and "soft") keys.[17] Pathetic arias tend to be written in flat keys, while more brilliant arias are usually in sharp keys. For instance, Schubart believed that *"Jeder Ton ist entweder gefärbt, oder nicht gefärbt...Unschuld und Einfalt drückt man mit ungefärbten Tönen aus. Sanfte, melancholische Gefühle, mit B Tönen; wilde und starke Leidenschaften mit Kreuztönen"*.[18] Georg Joseph Vogler, an influential teacher and composer at Mannheim, was among those who held a similar view: *"Die Karakteristik der Töne besteht in der Sonderung der schärfern und weichern Dur-Tonarten. Wenn A-Harmonie klingen sollte, wie Es-Harmonie; H-Harmonie wie As; E wie B: so wär es um unsere Mannichfaltigkeit gethan."*[19]

Composers chose particular keys not only for their affect but also to suit the voice of an individual singer. The two sopranos, Dorothea and Elisabeth, were often distinguished by key (see tables 3 and 4). Since the characters they portrayed often sang arias in successive

---

[15] She is sometimes confused with her niece Elisabeth Augusta Wendling, daughter of Dorothea and Johann Baptist. Although the role of Zelmira was intended for Elisabeth, she was not able to sing it. Gerber, *Neues historisch-biographisches Lexikon der Tonkünstler*, 4, pp. 543–44, remarks *"so weit lassen sich die in diesen Artikeln vorkommenden Nachrichten gar wohl vereinigen, bis auf das daß Dorothea eine Schülerin von Madame [i.e., Dorothea], also von sich selbst, gewesen sey. Aber kein Wunder, wenn das [alte Lexikon] von dergleichen Verirrungen wimmelte; da ich aus so manchen Druckschriften die verwirrtesten, ja widersprechendsten Notizen und Angaben von einer und der nämlichsten Person eben so oft in einem einzigen Artikel zu vereinigen, als auf zwey verschiedene Personen anzuwenden mich genöthigt war"*.

[16] Metastasio himself admits that it is difficult to say who the leading character is in Adriano: *"It seems a matter of choice whether Adriano and Sabina [sung by Dorothea] or Farnace and Emirena [Elisabeth], are regarded as the principal parts... But in fact, Adriano is the title of the opera, and between him and Sabina the principal business is transacted"*; translated by Charles Burney, *Memoirs of the Life and Writings of the Abate Metastasio*, 3 vols., London 1796, 2, pp. 75–76.

[17] For late eighteenth-century theorists who codified the characteristics of keys, E-flat was a key of "devotion and love", "gentle majesty", or "religious solemnity". While this might seem subjective or naive today, these theories were evidently taken for granted by many musicians. Among theorists, there was more agreement about a key's particular character than one might expect. See Rita Steblin, *A History of Key Characteristics in the Eighteenth and Early Nineteenth Centuries*, Ann Arbor 1983.

[18] Schubart, *Ideen*, p. 377.

[19] Abt Vogler, *Choral-System*, 2 vols., Offenbach 1800, 1, p. 17.

scenes, the contrast in tonality would have been noticable. To summarize, of the 39 arias written for her in Italian *opere serie* between 1760 and 1781, Dorothea has 20 arias in flat major keys (F, B-flat, and E-flat) and 9 arias in minor keys (g, c, and f minor); that is, 29 of 39 arias are in flat keys. In contrast, Elisabeth sang six arias in flat major keys and only four in minor keys (two of these occur in *Idomeneo*), in other words, 10 of the 31 arias written for her are in flat keys. Dorothea has significantly fewer arias (9) in sharp major keys (G, D, A, and E major) and only one aria in C major; but Elisabeth has 16 arias in sharp keys and five in C major.

These tables do not include the duets, trios, and quartets in which these sopranos appeared, because in ensembles the composer had to have his way.[20] My point is not to suggest that Dorothea sang exclusively in flat keys and Elisabeth in sharp keys, but it is no doubt significant that Dorothea sang an aria in E-flat major in each of her seria roles between 1760 and 1781, as well as Mozart's concert aria for her, *Ah non lasciarmi no*, K.295 a.[21] Dorothea also sang an extraordinarily high proportion of minor-key arias, especially G minor, which is characteristic of the types of roles she created (see examples 1–4 below).[22] The difficult question here is did the qualities of Dorothea Wendling's voice influence the various composers' choice of key, or did she simply happen to play characters who were required to express such qualities in their arias?[23] The high proportion of arias written for her in flat keys, both in major and minor mode, is surely no coincidence.

For some time Mozart scholars have speculated about who chose the subject for *Idomeneo*. While the subject matter must have been attractive to Mozart, it is unlikely that the organist from Salzburg would have been given a choice. Surely, it is no coincidence that three of the first four carnival operas commissioned by Carl Theodor in Munich were based on French tragédies: Fénelon's *Les aventures de Télémaque* (1699), and Danchet's *Idomenée* (1712) and *Tancrède* (1702), in adaptations set by Paul Grua (1780), Mozart (1781), and Holzbauer (1783), respectively.[24] In any event, the opera seria at Munich were all given "per comando" of Carl Theodor, and although Mozart's Mannheim friends, including Cannabich, Raaff, and the Wendlings, probably lobbied for him, the contracts issued by the Intendant specified the libretto or at least the subject to be set.[25]

---

[20] Mozart makes this clear in his letter of 27 December 1780, regarding the Quartet in act 3 of *Idomeneo*: *"aber was terzetten und Quartetten anbelangt muß man dem Compositeur seinen freyen Willen lassen – darauf gab er sich zufrieden"*; see Mozart, *Briefe*, 3, p. 73. Although Mozart is not explicit here, duets must represent the middle ground, where the composer had to accommodate the two singers more so than the larger ensembles but to a lesser extent than solo arias.

[21] See Paul Corneilson, "An Intimate Vocal Portrait of Dorothea Wendling", in: *Mozart-Jahrbuch 2000*, forthcoming.

[22] Schubart, *Ideen*, p. 377, defined the key of G minor as follows: *"Missvergnügen, Unbehaglichkeit, Zerren an einem verunglückten Plane; missmuthiges Nagen am Gebiss; mit einem Worte, Groll und Unlust"*. See also Gretchen A. Wheelock, "*Schwarze Gredel* and the Engendered Minor Mode in Mozart's Operas", in: *Musicology and Difference: Gender and Sexuality in Music Scholarship*, ed. Ruth A. Solie, Berkeley and Los Angeles 1993, pp. 201–21.

[23] For a summary of the some of the recent secondary literature, see John Platoff, "Myths and Realities about Tonal Planning in Mozart's Operas", in: *Cambridge Opera Journal* 8 (1996), pp. 3–15.

[24] For further information on the sources of Grua's *Telemaco*, see Karl Böhmer, *W. A. Mozarts "Idomeneo" und die Tradition der Karnevalsopern in München*, Tutzing 1999, pp. 176–81. On the sources of *Idomeneo*, see Kurt Kramer, "Das Libretto zu Mozarts «Idomeneo»: Quellen und Umgestaltung der Fabel", in: *Wolfgang Amadeus Mozart: Idomeneo 1781–1981. Ausstellungskatalog der Bayerischen Staatsbibliothek*, Red. Robert Münster and R. Angermüller, Munich 1981, pp. 7–43.

[25] See Daniel Heartz, "The Genesis of *Idomeneo*", in: *Musical Quarterly* 55 (1969), pp. 1–19; repr. in *Mozart's Operas*, ed. Thomas Bauman, Berkeley and Los Angeles 1990, pp. 15–35; Ders., "Hat Mozart das Libretto zu 'Idomeneo' ausgewählt?", in: *Wolfgang Amadeus Mozart: Idomeneo 1781–1981*, pp. 62–70.

There is a missing link that has gone virtually unnoticed until now. In August 1780, about the time Mozart would have received his *scrittura*,[26] an azione teatrale titled *Laodamia* was performed at the Electress's summer residence in Oggersheim. The text was by Mattia Verazi, the Mannheim court poet, was set to music by his son, Giovanni Battista Verazi.[27] A copy of the libretto survives in the Reiss-Museum der Stadt Mannheim, but the music is lost. (See plate 2. The page before the title page bears a handwritten place and date, "Oggersheim/den 3 August 1780".) There are two different women named Laodamia referred to in *The Iliad*. The first Laodamia was a daughter of Bellerophon, and mother of Sarpedon by Zeus, who was killed by Artemis (goddess of hunt). The second Laodamia (not mentioned by name in Homer) was the wife of Protesilaus, who was the first of the Greeks to disembark and to be killed at Troy, and "his wife was left tearing her cheeks and his house half-built". This Laodamia, according to commentators (Ovid, *Heroides Epistola* XIII), was so grieved by her husband's death that the gods allowed her to see him for three hours, after which she killed herself. (For her irrational loyalty, she made Chaucer's list of "good women").

Verazi's libretto has nothing to do with either of these characters, although the "faithful" Laodamia probably served as a model. Rather, his Laodamia is the Queen of Crete, consort of Idomeneo, and mother of Idamante! The "argomento" (see the appendix) gives a summary of the plot. The work tells the post-Trojan-war episode from the mother's perspective, and the action takes place after Idomeneus has left the island of Crete. Idamante is betrothed to Asteria, rather than the Trojan princess Ilia, and there is a High Priest of Neptune called Corebo as well as a "Coro di sagri ministri". Neither Elettra nor Arbace appear in Verazi's libretto. The title role was sung by Dorothea Wendling, with the tenor Franz Hartig as Idamante, Maria Josepha Schäfer as Asteria, and Giovanni Battista Zonca as Corebo – all were former Mannheim court singers except Schäfer, who was one of Dorothea Wendling's pupils.

A summary of the scenes and aria incipits are given in the appendix, mainly in the hope that someone will be able to identify one or more of the arias by Verazi's son. One of the arias sung by Idamante in scene vii of *Laodamia* is virtually identical to the aria text for Asterio in act 2, scene vi of Verazi's *Europa riconosciuta*, set by Antonio Salieri.[28] Verazi had been invited to write four "drammi in azione" for the opening of the Teatro alla Scala in Milan, during the 1778–79 season, and had lately returned to the electoral court. Therefore, it is only natural that he borrowed this melancholy text for a similar situation in *Laodamia*. In *Europa*, the character Asterio (King of Crete!) addresses his spouse Europa (Princess of Tyre), and in *Laodamia*, Idamante addresses his betrothed Asteria. Verazi only needed to make two minor changes to fit the slightly different context: "figlio infelice" in line 5 of the original was altered to "sposa infelice", and "Sposa, addio" in the penultimate line became "Madre, addio". (The complete text of the aria in *Laodamia* is given below.) Although the two dramas are otherwise unrelated, it is worth noting that both involve sovereigns of Crete.

---

[26] According to an entry in Nannerl Mozart's "Tagebuch", Abt Varesco came to visit the Mozarts on 22 August 1780, probably to work on the scenario for *Idomeneo;* see Mozart. *Briefe,* no. 533, line 54.

[27] According to the libretto in the Reiss-Museum der Stadt Mannheim, Mh 1788, "La musica è nuova composizione del VERAZI FIGLIO". RISM B/1 lists two sets of "Trois sonates pour le clavecin ou pianoforte" with violin or flute accompaniment by Giovanni Battista Verazi; see V1213 and V1214. Vogler, who published a Lied by Verazi in *Betrachtungen der Mannheimer Tonschule,* 4 vols., Mannheim, 1778–81, 4, pp. 345–48, was probably his teacher.

[28] I am grateful to John A. Rice for bringing this to my attention. He discusses Salieri's setting of this aria in his recent monograph, *Antonio Salieri and Viennese Opera,* Chicago 1998, pp. 261–63.

Scena vii (Aria for Idamante)

> Del morir l'angoscie adesso,
>   Tutte io provo a voi dappresso.
>   Sventurato! ah quest'amplesso
>   Sarà l'ultimo per me.
>
> Lascia oh Dio! – sposa infelice,
>   Lascia ch'io – ti stringa al seno.
>   La dolente Genitrice
>   Mi ritrovi almeno – in te.
>
> Ah dov'è quel cuor di sasso,
>   Che non pianga al pianto mio?
>   Madre, addio . . . Più amaro passo,
>   Duol più barbaro non v'è.

The extensive scena for Laodamia in scene ix is exactly the type of dramatic situation in which Dorothea Wendling excelled. This text calls for an alternation of obbligato recitative and contrasting numbers, both cavatina and multi-movement aria; perhaps concluding with a rondò. Mozart's concert aria K.272, the scena of Andromeda, would have been a good model for Verazi.

Scena ix (Laodamia *sola*)

> Deh t'arresta: sospendi . . . Ah più non sente!
> Raggiungerla degg'io . . . Ma il piè s'arresta!
>   Qual'orrore in me si desta!
>   Chi ritiene I passi miei?
>   Figlio, oh Dei! – chi a me t'asconde? . . .
>   Mi confonde – il mio martir.
>
> Numi! Tutti già parmi
> I suoi gemiti udir, le sue querele.
> Già un acciaro crudele . . . Ah no: fermate,
> Barbari. Se bramate
> Il sangue, eccovi il mio . . .
> Misera, oh Dio! Che parlo? A chi ragiono?
> Forse in questo momento,
> Ch'io bagno invan d'inutil pianto il ciglio,
> Non son più madre, oh Dei! non ho più figlio.
>   Del figlio, che muore
>   Gli estremi son questi
>   Funesti – lamenti.
>   Quei flebili accenti,
>   Che barbara sorte!
>   Che strano martir!
>   L'affanno – di morte
>   Mi fanno – soffrir.
> Figlio, aspetta. Di Lete ombra dolente
> Varcar teco vogl'io le torbid' onde . . .
>   Ma di Lete dalle sponde

> Volgi a me turbato il ciglio!
> Figlio, – almen. Più non risponde . . .
> Mi confonde – il mio martir.
> Ah sì: mi risponde
> Co' flebili accenti
> Il figlio, che muore.
> Quei mesti lamenti,
> Che fato severo!
> Che fiero – martir!
> Di morte l'affanno
> Mi fanno – soffrir.

Laodamia ends with an honorific text, which functions at various levels: first, Idamante sings the praise of his mother, the "Augusta Donna", echoed by the others, and finally Laodamia acknowledges the "Genitor" (a reference to their patron, the Electress). Thus, the work celebrates "good women", and indirectly the prima donna, Dorothea Wendling, and the Electress Elisabeth Auguste.

> Scena xii (Final Ensemble)
>
> Idamante: Al Genitore accantò
>   Ah se felici siamo;
>   Dovuto è un sì bel vanto,
>   AUGUSTA Donna, a te.
> *Tutti, alla riserva di Laodamia.*
>   Dovuto è un sì bel vanto,
>   AUGUSTA Donna, a te.
> Laodamia: Dovuto un sì bel vanto,
>   Al Genitor sol'è.

For the carnival opera in Munich, Dorothea Wendling was given the "daughter" role, rather than the "mother" role, since Raaff as Idomeneo was old enough to be her "father". Elettra of course is pure poetic invention: she had to land on Crete so that Elisabeth Wendling would have an interesting role to sing. Varesco and Mozart could have introduced a local Cretan girl to be the rival of the foreign princess; but troubled Elettra, daughter of Agememnon and brother of Orestes (and sister of Iphigenia), gave the composer an opportunity to exploit the melodramatic qualities of the character. The passionate energy of Elettra makes for a striking contrast with the self-sacrificing nature of Ilia.

Idomeneo was one of the happiest collaborations of Mozart's career, and it must have been one of the best experiences for his prima and seconda donna. From Munich, Mozart wrote to his father: *"Nun aber etwas gutes. Madme Wendling ist mit ihrer Scene Arcicontentissima. Sie hat sie 3 mal nach einander hören wollen"*.[29] A week later, on 15 November, he mentions: *"ich habe es von einer dritten hand, dass die 2 Wendlinge [Dorothea and Elisabeth] ihre Arien sehr gelobt haben"*.[30] Niemetschek's brief summary of Mozart's *Idomeneo* is *a propos*:

> *"Idomeneo ist eines seiner größten, und gedankenreichesten Werke; der Stil ist durchgehends pathetisch und athmet heroische Erhabenheit. Da er diese Opera für große Sänger und für eines der besten Orchester von Europa schrieb, so fühlte sein Geist keinen Zwang, und entfaltete sich darinn am üppigsten. Aber Idomeneo muß besser aufgeführt werden, als es zu Prag vor eini-*

---

[29] *Mozart, Briefe*, 3, p. 14.
[30] *Mozart, Briefe*, 3, p. 20.

gen Jahren in Sommer geschah, wo ihn der Opern-Unternehmer im eigentlichen Verstande prostituirte. Es war ein drolligrer Gedanke eine der größten Opera ohne Sängerinnen und Orchester aufzuführen. Denn beydes fehlte, und ward durch Substituten ersetzt".[31]

Apparently, Prague did not possess a pair of sopranos as gifted as Dorothea and Elisabeth Wendling.

As an epilogue to my paper, I want to make one other point. Mozart's bravura concert aria, *Sperai vicino il lido* K.368, possibly written at Munich in 1780–81, was certainly not intended for Elisabeth Wendling, as Alfred Einstein suggested years ago and which is now often passed on as "fact". The range (up to high f^3) and difficulty of the coloratura were beyond her scope. The bravura arias in her other roles, including Elettra, make less stringent demands on the singer's range and agility. The aria was more likely written for Josephine Dussek, who had requested an aria from Mozart. Leopold mentioned this in his letter of 15 December 1780, to which Mozart responded on 19 December 1780: Madame Duschek will have to wait until *Idomeneo* is finished.[32] Later in a postscript to his letter of 5 September 1781, Mozart asked his father, *"bitte mit gelegenheit mir die aria die ich für die baumgarten gemacht, – das Rondeau für die Duscheck – und dem Ceccarelli seines zu schicken".*[33] That is, K.369, possibly K.368 (certainly not K.272, which is a large-scale scena not a rondeau), and K.374 (which actually is a rondeaux for the castrato Ceccarelli). Although Mozart did not label K.368 "Rondeau", it does have some of the characteristics of the Italian, two-tempo rondò (Andantino–Allegro).[34]

The only problem with this theory, however, is that Josepha Duschek would probably not have been able to sing *Sperai vicino il lido* either. Although the other two concert arias Mozart wrote for her, K.272 and K.538, are ambitious and challenging pieces, neither has as high a range and tessitura as K.368. Of course, it is possible that Mozart sent K.368 to Duschek, knowing full well that it would be too high for her. A more likely possibility is that he wrote the aria for Aloysia Weber during the summer or autumn of 1778 on his way back home from Paris.[35] There are limits to such analysis, but it can provide clues and insight into some of our unsolved mysteries surrounding Mozart.

---

[31] Niemetschek, *Lebenbeschreibung*, p. 110.

[32] Leopold wrote: *"aber ich hatte wohl unter dieser Zeit ein schreiben von M.me Dussek mit einem Text zu einer Aria bekommen, hab ihr auch schon geantwortet, dass vor dem neuen Jahre nichts möglich sey. Sie schrieb, dass sie noch ein Schuldnerin wegen der vorigen Aria wäre, und da sie es zimmlich pressant machte, so musste ich ihr mit aller Höflichkeit die dermalige unmöglichkeit alsogleich umständlich schreiben".* Mozart responded: *"wegen Mad:me Duschek ist es freylich dermalen ohnmöglich – aber nach geendigter opera mit vergnügen – unterdessen bitte sie ihr mein Compliment zu schreiben"*, Mozart, *Briefe*, 3, pp. 57 and 65.

[33] Mozart, *Briefe*, 3, p. 156.

[34] See Don Neville, "The Rondò in Mozart's Late Operas", in: *Mozart Jahrbuch* 1994, pp. 141–55.

[35] This latter scenario would fit better with the paper and handwriting studies of Alan Tyson and Wolfgang Plath, who have assigned the aria to the summer of 1780.

Appendix

Argomento to Verazi's *Laodamia*

Ritornava dalla guerra di Troja vincitore al suo regno Idomeneo, re di Creta, quando assalito da una fiera tempesta, si vide in periglio di restar miseramente sommerso. Per sottrarsi al rischio dell'imminente naufragio, sè però voto di sagrificare a Nettuno il primo vivente, che a lui si presenterebbe nell'approdar salvo alle sponde. Ma riconosciuto nella promessa vittima il suo figlio Idamante, piutosto che spargere ad onta della paterna tenerezza l'innocente suo sangue, solo in mare nuovamenta si espose a'minacciati risentimenti dell'irritata Divinità. Ridusse la sua nuova partenza nell'ultima desolazione gli abbandonati suoi sudditi. Ma confortati dalla virtuosa Laodamia, sua consorte, ch'era in Creta con essi rimasa, vider sua mercé in breve cangiato il funesto aspetto dell'avversa loro fortuna. Pago a render Nettuno bastò l'intrepida costanza dell' Augusta Donna, che a costo de'suoi giorni medesimi si propose di conservar quelli dell'amato figlio, presentandosi vittima volontaria per essere in sua vece immolata. Commosso il Nume dall'eroico sforzo di sì gloriosa risoluzione, si dichiarò per mezzo del gran sacerdote Corebo intieramente sodisfatto, e placato. Reso quindi alla Creta il sospirato Regnante, mise il colmo alla felicità de' suoi popoli coll'avventuroso compimento della desiderata unione d'Idamante, e d'Asteria, principessa del regio sangue Cretense, che per invariabil disposizion de' fati avea già ne' suoi decreti il cielo a lui destinata.

Il fondamento di quest'azione drammatica si troverà in Omero, ed in Servio.

La scena si finge nell'isola di Creta, e rappresenta un verde recinto vicino alla spiaggia, con antro da un lato, ed ara nel mezzo consagrata a Nettuno.

Outline of *Laodamia* with Aria Incipits (Character)

Scena i. Laodamia, Idamante, ed Asteria
  „Rasserena il mesto ciglio" (Laodamia)
Scena ii. Idamante ed Asteria
Scena iii. Corebo, *e detti*
  „In grembo alla calma" (Corebo)
Scena iv. Idamante ed Asteria
  „D'un Padre, e d'un Regnante" (Idamante)
Scena v. Asteria *sola*
  „Fedel mi adora" (Asteria) [rondò?]
Scena vi. Corebo, Laodamia, ed Idamante
  „Come ritorna in vita" (Corebo)
Scena vii. Asteria, *e detti*
  „Del morir le angoscie adesso" (Idamante)
Scena viii. Asteria e Laodamia
  „D'un debole affetto" (Asteria)
Scena ix. Laodamia *sola*
  „Deh t'arresta: sospendi" – „Qual'orrore in me si desta!"
Scena x. Idamante e Corebo, *con seguito di sagri ministri, che al suono lugubre di flebili istrumenti accompagnan lentamente verso l'ara la vittima.*
  „La sagra vittima" (Corebo, Idamante, and Coro)

Scena xi. Asteria, *che accore ansante, e detti*
   „Fermate: sospendete" (Asteria)
Scena xii. Laodamia, *che viene affannosa, e detti*
   „Crudeli, oh Dio! Che fate?" (Laodamia, Idamante, Asteria, Corebo)

Ex. 1: Aria (Sofonisba) from Traetta's *Sofonisba* (1762)

Ex. 2: Aria (Marzia) from Piccinnis's *Catone in Utica* (1770)

Ex. 3: Aria (Aspasia) from J. C. Bach's *Temistocle* (1772)

Ex. 4: Aria (Illia) from Mozart's *Idomeneo* (1781)

Table 1
Dorothea Wendling's Opera Career*

Date	Role	Opera	Composer
1753	Ermione	Antigona	Galuppi
	Barsene	Demetrio	Jommelli
1754	**Silvia**	L'isola disabitata (azione comica per musica)	Holzbauer
1755	**Dorotea**	Don Chisciotte (opera serio-ridicola)	Holzbauer
1756	**Lisinga**	I cinesi (componimento drammatico)	Holzbauer
	Fedra	Le nozze d'Arianna (festa teatrale)	Holzbauer
	[Aristea]	L'Olimpiade	Galuppi
1757	[Servilia]	La clemenza di Tito	Holzbauer
1758	**Beroe**	Nitteti	Holzbauer
1759	**Aricia**	Ippolito ed Aricia	Holzbauer
1760	**Giunia**	Cajo Fabrizio	Jommelli
1762	**Sofonisba**	Sofonisba	Traetta
1764	**Ifigenia**	Ifigenia in Tauride	Majo
1766	**Cleofide**	Alessandro	Majo
1768	**Emirena**	Adriano in Siria	Holzbauer
1769	Lucinda	La buona figliuola zitella (dramma giocoso)	Piccinni
1770	Clarice	L'amante di tutte (dramma giocoso)	Galuppi
	Marzia	Catone in Utica	Piccinni
1771	Eugenia	Il filosofo di campagna (dramma giocoso)	Galuppi
	Elmira	Il figlio della selve (favola pastorale)	Holzbauer
	Arminda	Gli stravaganti (azione comica)	Piccinni
1772	Mme Costanza	L'amore artigiano (dramma giocoso)	F. L. Gassmann
	Isabella	Le finte gemelle (operetta giocosa)	Piccinni
	Belinda	L'isola d'Amore (azione comica)	Sacchini
	[Diana]	Endimione (azione drammatica teatrale)	J. C. Bach
	Aspasia	Temistocle	J. C. Bach
1774	[Renoppia]	La secchia rapita (dramma eroicomico)	Salieri
	[Dalisa]	Amore vincitore (azione teatrale)	J. C. Bach
1775	**Giunia**	Lucio Silla	J. C. Bach
1778	**Rosamund**	Rosamund	A. Schweitzer
	Didone	„Ah non lasciarmi, no" K.295a	Mozart
1779	**Didone**	La morte di Didone	Holzbauer
1780	**Laodamia**	Laodamia (azione teatrale)	G. J. Verazi
	Calipso	Telemaco	P. Grua
1781	**Ilia**	Idomeneo	Mozart

* Dates given are generally those of the first performance at the Hoftheater, Mannheim (through 1777) and the Residenztheater, Munich (1780–81). Roles in bold type were written specifically for her; roles in brackets are conjectural. All are "dramma per musica" unless otherwise stated.

For further information on the dates of performance and sources of these operas, see the following works: Paul Corneilson, *Opera at Mannheim, 1770–1778*, Ph. D. diss., University of North Carolina Chapel Hill, 1992; Paul Corneilson, "The Case of J. C. Bach's Lucio Silla", in: *Journal of Musicology* 12 (1994): pp. 206–18; Paul Corneilson and Eugene K. Wolf. "Newly Identified Manuscripts of Operas and Related Works from Mannheim", in: *Journal of the American Musicological Society* 47 (1994), pp. 244–73; Bärbel Pelker, "Theateraufführungen und musicalische Akademien am Hof Carl Theodors", in: *Die Mannheimer Hofkapelle im Zeitalter Carl Theodors*, ed. Ludwig Finscher, Mannheim 1992, pp. 219–59; Claudio Sartori, *I libretti italiani a stampa dalle origini al 1800*, 7 vols., Cuneo 1990–94.

Table 2
Elisabeth Wendling's Opera Career*

Date	Role	Opera	Composer
1762	**Cirene**	Sofonisba	Traetta
1764	**Tomiri**	Ifigenia in Tauride	Majo
1766	**Erismena**	Alessandro	Majo
1768	**Sabina**	Adriano in Siria	Holzbauer
1769	Sandrina Contadina	La buona figliuola zitella (dramma giocoso)	Piccinni
1770	Lucinda	L'amante di tutte (dramma giocoso)	Galuppi
	Emilia	Catone in Utica	Piccinni
1771	Lesbina	Il filosofo di campagna (dramma giocoso)	Galuppi
	Arsinda	Il figlio della selve (favola pastorale)	Holzbauer
1772	Falsirena	La fiera di Venezia (dramma giocoso)	Salieri
	Marina	L'isola d'Amore (azione comica)	Sacchini
	Rossane	Temistocle	J. C. Bach
1774	[Gheranda]	La secchia rapita (dramma giocoso)	Salieri
1775	**Celia**	Lucio Silla	J. C. Bach
1777	Anna	Günther von Schwarzburg	Holzbauer
1780	**Eucari**	Telemaco	P. Grua
1781	**Elettra**	Idomeneo	Mozart
1782	**Semiramide**	Semiramide	Salieri

* Dates given are generally those of the first performance at the Mannheim Hoftheater (through 1777) and the Munich Residenztheater (1780–85). Roles in bold type were written specifically for her; roles in brackets are conjectural. All are "dramma per musica" unless otherwise stated.

For further information on the dates of performance and sources of these operas, see the works cited in Table 1 above.

Table 3:
Arias Written for Dorothea Wendling, 1760–1781
(Arranged by Key)

A-flat/f	E-flat/c	B-flat/g	F	C	G	D	A	E
„Frà i pensier più funesti di morte" *Lucio Silla*	„Parto: ma attendimi" *Cajo Fabrizio*	„Tutti gl'affetti miei" *Cajo Fabrizio*	„Il padre crudele" *Cajo Fabrizio*	„Dalla sponda tenebrosa" *Lucio Silla*	„Se mai turbo il tuo riposo" *Alessandro*	„Per te d'eterni allori" *Adriano*	„Digli ch'io son fedele" *Alessandro*	„Zeffiretti lusinghieri" *Idomeneo*
	„Sventurata invan mi lagno" *Sofonisba*	„Intesi: ti basti" *Sofonisba*	„Se il labbro si lagna" *Ifigenia*		„Che fa il mio bene?" *Adriano*		„Tu fedel sarai" *Telemaco*	
	„Darti, o figlio" *Sofonisba*	„Crudeli, aimè! Che fate?" *Sofonisba*	„Se troppo crede al ciglio" *Alessandro*		„Non ti minaccio sdegno" *Catone*			
	„Ombra cara, che intorno t'aggiri" *Ifigenia*	„De' tuoi mali esultarei" *Ifigenia*			„Ah si resti... Onor mi sgrida" *Temistocle*			

Table 3 continued

A-flat/f	E-flat/c	B-flat/g	F	C	G	D	A	E
	„Se il Ciel mi divide" *Alessandro*	„E follia, se nascondete" *Catone*			„Va crescendo il mio tormento" *Didone*			
	„Prigioniera, abbandonata" *Adriano*	„In che ti offende" *Catone*						
	„Quell'amplesso, e quel perdono" *Adriano*	„Chi mai d'iniqua stella" *Temistocle*						
	„Oh, Dio! Mancar mi sento" *Adriano*	„Va lusingando amore" *Didone*						
	„Confusa, smarrita" *Catone*	„Padre, germani, addio!" *Idomeneo*						
	„E specie di tormento" *Temistocle*							
	„Dalla sponda tenebrosa" *Lucio Silla*							
	„Ah non lasciarmi, no" (K.295a)							
	„Vado, ma dove, o Dio" *Didone*							
	„Tradita... sprezzata" *Telemaco*							
	„Ah s'accenda in quest'istante" *Telemaco*							
	„Se il padre perdei" *Idomeneo*							

Table 4
Arias Written for Elisabeth Wendling, 1762–1785
Arranged by Key

A-flat/f	E-flat/c	B-flat/g	F/d	C	G	D	A	E
„Assai m'ingannasti" *Adriano*	„Nacqui agli affanni in seno" *Catone*	„L'istesso tormento" *Sofonisba*	„Per te spero e per te solo" *Catone*	„Chi d'insano amor delira" *Sofonisba*	„Son confusa pastorella" *Alessandro*	„Ah lo sdegno degli amanti" *Ifigenia*	„Senti: aspetta" *Sofonisba*	
	„Scherzi l'aura" *Telemaco*	„Torni al labbro" *Telemaco*	„Tutte nel cor vi sento" *Idomeneo*	„Chi vive amante, sai che delira" *Alessandro*	„Numi, se giusti siete" *Adriano*	„Di rendermi la calma" *Alessandro*	„E specie di follia" *Ifigenia*	
	„D'Oreste, d'Ajace" *Idomeneo*	„Non so, se più t'accendi" *Semiramide*		„Volga il Ciel, felici amanti" *Adriano*	„Strider sento la procella" *Lucio Silla*	„Se lusinghiera speme" *Lucio Silla*	„Digli ch'è un'infedele" *Adriano*	
		„Sente l'amica speme" *Semiramide*		„O nel sen di qualche stella" *Catone*	„Del mio ben nelle pupille" *Telemaco*		„Un certo no so che" *Catone*	
				„Or a' danni d'un ingrato" *Temistocle*	„Idol mio" *Idomeneo*		„Basta dir ch'io sono amante" *Temistocle*	
					„Ah non è vano il pianto" *Semiramide*		„Il labbro timido" *Lucio Silla*	
							„Fuggi dagli occhi miei" *Semiramide*	

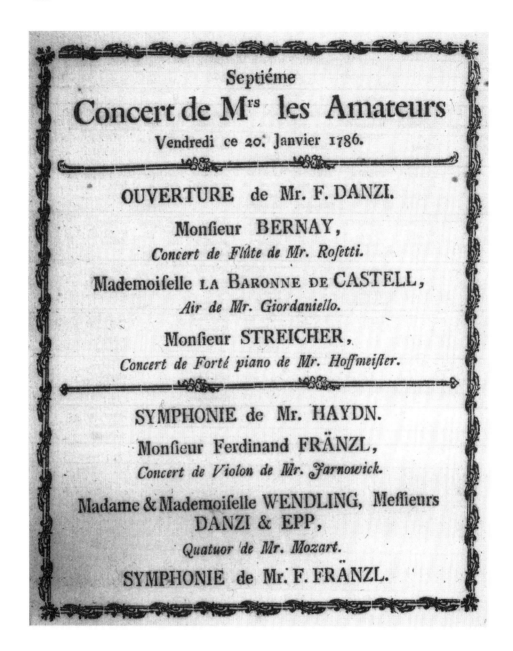

Plate 1: Concert Program (Courtesy of The Geheimes Hausarchiv, Munich)

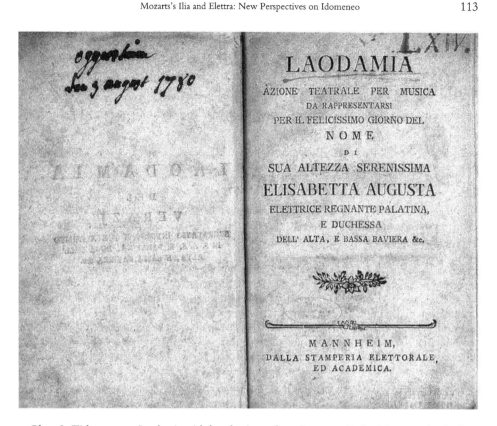

Plate 2: Title page to *Laodamia* with handwritten date. (courtesy Reiss-Museum der Stadt Mannheim)

Part III
Sensibility, Sentiment and the Pastoral

[9]
"Pamela": The Offspring of Richardson's Heroine in Eighteenth-Century Opera

MARY HUNTER

While *Pamela*'s career in the literary world has been examined in some detail, the novel's effect on works in other artistic domains is less well-known. In the present essay I propose to explore the influence of Richardson's novel on Italian comic opera from 1760 to 1793, starting with Goldoni's famous adaptation of the work as *La buona figliuola*. Set by Niccolo Piccinni in 1760, this opera rivalled the success of the original novel, playing regularly throughout Italy in the 1760s and '70s, and across Europe, in Italian and in translation, until the late 1780s. The latest recorded production until its revival in the twentieth century was in London in 1810.[1] Goldoni and Piccinni collaborated on a sequel, *La buona figliuola maritata* (Bologna, 1761); and for several decades after, *opere buffe* on similar themes and with similar devices of characterization appeared both in Italy (principally north of Naples) and in other European operatic centers.

Although Alan D. McKillop argues that "in Goldoni's own reworkings of the [*Pamela*] theme to the ends of comic opera...Richardson's influence is attenuated to the vanishing point,"[2] closer examination of both Goldoni's and succeeding operas based on the *Pamela* theme suggests that many of the significant features of these musical works do in fact relate directly to elements of Richardson's novel. More particularly, what we find in examining the "canon" of *Pamela*-like operas is that the features of Richardson's novel which Goldoni and Piccinni either retained or recalled in *La buona figliuola* are those which become standardized in the succeeding works.

62   Mary Hunter

The first, and perhaps most obvious, point in comparing *Pamela* and *La buona figliuola*[3] is that Goldoni's adaptation of the story as a libretto puts it squarely within the contemporary conventions of *opera buffa*, both in its practical aspects and as regards its esthetic and moral status. Goldoni's cast for his libretto differs considerably from Richardson's novel, and, for that matter, from that of his own earlier stage play on the same theme, *Pamela nubile* (1750). His changes for the libretto version made the work easily performable by a troupe accustomed to other *opere buffe*. Not only is the number of characters commensurate with other works in the genre, but the characters themselves are almost all recognizable "types." Sandrina and Paoluccia, the spiteful and jealous serving girls, for example, represent a well-established comic type, deriving quite directly from the *commedia dell'arte*. Mengotto, the ingenuous country lad, has many cousins in libretti by Goldoni and others; and Tagliaferro, the pugnacious, fleshly, ill-spoken German soldier is another character who turns up in many contemporary *opere buffe*, saying "*Trinche vain, paesan*," and "*Ja main Herr*," wherever he goes. The use of a pair of noble lovers (here, the Marchesa Lucinda and the Cavalier Armidoro) is also a *commedia* convention.[4] Never for a moment forgetful of their upper-class origins, conversing in rarefied, often metaphorical, language, and singing in idioms derived from contemporary *opera seria*, these lovers present a striking contrast to the *buffa* figures, and perfectly embody the conservative impulses of Richardson's upper-class figures.

A second point of interest to emerge from a comparison of the novel and the opera is that Goldoni's use of well-established operatic stock types to represent the various attitudes and positions taken by groups of people in *Pamela* focuses the inherently operatic themes of the story in telling and economical ways. Cecchina herself derives from the type of the female *ingénue*, though she is in fact further removed from her *commedia* origins than most of the other members of the cast. Her apparently purposeless transformation from chambermaid (her position in both the novel and the play) to gardener is particularly interesting in the context of operatic character types. It immediately dissociates her from the figure of the worldly-wise, ambitious serving maid, of which Serpetta in Federico's and Pergolesi's *La serva padrona* (Naples, 1733) is only the most famous example, and of which Sandrina and Paoluccia are direct descendants. The transformation also symbolically, and by association with the idea of the flower garden, suggests the fresh and natural, but by no means uncultivated sweetness, which characterizes both Pamela and Cecchina. While Richardson could convey Pamela's blend of earthiness and airy sweetness over the course of hundreds of pages, however, the limited scope of a libretto may have forced Goldoni to find a more immediately suggestive image for his heroine. Another example of this concentration in the libretto is the figure of Mengotto, whose persistent and hopeless love for Cecchina directly and simply suggests her general appeal — an appeal which both *Pamela* and *Pamela nubile* can convey by more complex or diffuse means. Sandrina and Paoluccia, being of similar age and station to

Cecchina, vividly represent what she might have been, in addition to providing the invective which fuels the plot.

The concentration of means in Goldoni's libretto also extends to his choice of events and moments to include. One of the richest and most crucial moments in the novel is, of course, the scene where Pamela escapes out of her closet in Lincolnshire to the pond, where she contemplates suicide. Cecchina thinks of nothing so violent as killing herself, and is not prey to the ultimate temptation of despair, but she does flee from her persecutors to an orchard behind the Marchese's house, where she picturesquely falls asleep. The device of flight to natural surroundings (which, significantly, does not appear in the play) provides Goldoni with a perfect opportunity for a soliloquy by Cecchina in surroundings which underscore her natural beauty and emphasize her isolation from the divided society she has left behind.

The third major point in this comparison of *Pamela* and *La buona figliuola* is that isolation, both physical and structural, is a crucial feature in the characterization of both heroines. Most sympathetic critics of the novel have noted the advantages of its epistolary form for our knowledge and understanding of Pamela. As Mark Kinkead-Weekes remarks, this form allows us to "live in a mind and [to come] to know it intimately in its day to day fluctuations."[5] At the same time, the fact that the form has a "single focus" (even though more than one point of view is actually available through the single focus of Pamela's letters) means that Pamela is isolated in relation to the other characters, and in particular in relation to the other major figures in the work. Only she presents us with the complexities and subtleties of emotion and motivation which make a character come alive, with the result that Mr. B is a shadowy figure. Interestingly, both the immediacy of Pamela herself and the relative neutrality of Mr. B are reflected in *La buona figliuola*. Like Pamela, Cecchina is central, not only because the story is about her, but also because she projects so much more strongly than the other characters who then exist solely in her orbit. Also like Pamela, Cecchina is isolated both by the mechanisms of the plot and by the very vividness which makes her central.

Indeed, the affective immediacy of the heroine and the use of distinctions in social class for emotive purposes are the main points of agreement between the novel and the opera, so that what has been said of Richardson's work applies equally well to Goldoni's: "With Richardson, we slip, invisible, into the domestic privacy of his characters, and hear and see everything that is said and done among them, whether it be interesting or otherwise, and whether it gratify our curiosity or disappoint it."[6] Of course opera does not permit the accumulation of vast numbers of apparently irrelevant details for the purposes of characterization; nor did eighteenth-century operatic conventions allow for singing "to the moment" in pseudo-epistolary style. Nevertheless, it is precisely the illusion of having made no "visit by appointment," of "slipping, invisible," into the privacy of Cecchina's thoughts, which most vividly attends her first aria, "*Che piacer, che bel diletto:*"

64 Mary Hunter

(Source: *I classici musicali italiani*, vol. 7, ed. G. Benvenuti)

Although this aria is not in itself particularly exciting in language or content, Goldoni deployed it with genius. Cecchina is alone in her garden as she sings this, the first sung number of the opera. It comes immediately after the overture, unannounced by recitative or by a chorus. This placement purifies and magnifies its emotional effect, since our reaction to it is uncomplicated by residual interest in other characters, in recent developments in the plot, or in Cecchina's previous speeches or actions. The clarity of the image presented in this aria informs our perception of Cecchina throughout the rest of the opera.

"Pamela" and Opera 65

The use of a low-born or *buffa* character to open an opera with an aria was not new *per se*. Among Goldoni's earlier libretti, for example, *Lo Speziale* (1752) opens with Mengone, the pharmacist's assistant, singing a funny number about the reasons for, and effects of, the various remedies he spends his days grinding. And, as Piero Weiss has recently shown, many early Neapolitan *opere buffe* opened with one member of the pair of young lovers singing a pre-existent popular song.[7] These examples, however, differ from the opening of *La buona figliuola* in the concrete specificity of their textual or contextual references, and in the ways they establish their singers as familiar middle- or lower-class types. Cecchina's aria is much more like a *seria* character's utterance in its relatively generalized and pretty content and in its inwardness; and it is precisely the combination of *seria*-like content and *buffa*-like placing which is so striking. This combination suggests simultaneously that Cecchina is a familiar and approachable sort of figure and that she is to be taken seriously. Also, in its projection of both seriousness and familiarity, *"Che piacer"* allows the audience the illusion of "privileged access" to Cecchina's thoughts which is in some way analogous to the sense of participation engendered in the readers of Richardson's novel.

Piccinni's music for *"Che piacer"* crystallizes and intensifies the emotional tone of Cecchina's first appearance in ways which reinforce both her affective immediacy and her ambiguous social position. The natural-sounding symmetry of her opening phrases, with their arch-shaped melodic line and their "sighing" suspensions (evident in the previous example), all vividly suggest Cecchina's affecting sweetness. It is, in short, an unusually beautiful and touching number, of a similar type to Orfeo's much celebrated lament in Act II of Gluck's *Orfeo* (1762), *"Che farò senza Euridice."* Perhaps more striking than the absolute quality of Piccinni's music here, however, is the fact that it is sung without parodistic intent by a character who seems otherwise to be a classic *buffa* type. The only other character in *La buona figliuola* who sings in anything like this style is the Cavalier Armidoro, the middle of whose first *da capo* aria and whose last number have the same graceful *Affettuoso* character:

[Andante]

Che più di me- con-ten- to vi-der le stel- le a- mi- che

It is generally true in the *opere buffe* of this period that this apparently very simple but affecting melodic style is reserved for *seria* characters in their tender moments. Cecchina's appearance in garden clothes, then, singing this sort of text to this sort of melody, calls both her character type and the conventional associations of this melodic style into question. Indeed, throughout the opera, Cecchina's arias are poised subtly between *buffa* and *seria* idioms, just as she herself is suspended between the upper and lower classes. While *"Che piacer"* puts certain linguistic and musical idioms from *opera seria* into new contexts, Cecchina's next aria, "*Una povera ragazza*," uses the short phrases and fragmented melodies characteristic of *buffa* style, but lends these an uncharacteristic pathos and seriousness.

Perhaps the chief factor in the heightened seriousness of this aria is the accompaniment, which continues in the above vein for the duration of the aria. This accompaniment, unlike most accompaniments to *opera buffa* arias, is both prominent and functionally distinct from the vocal line. It adds to Cecchina's self-pitying description of her condition a gestural suggestion of her halting speech and faltering demeanor, and, as with all such prominent and functionally distinct accompaniments, it provides a continuous emotional context for her speech. Two of Cecchina's four full-scale arias are enriched by such an accompaniment; of the other characters' arias, only Mengotto's "suicide" aria, "*Ah Cecchina*," (II, vi) exhibits this texture, and even this is perhaps best heard as parodistic.

Thus, while Pamela's centrality is assured by her constant presence in the novel, Cecchina's is created by the striking placement of her opening number and the extraordinary sweetness and immediacy of all the music she sings. Her isolation, like Pamela's, is emphasized by the persecution she endures from the other characters, and by her flight to natural surroundings. And whereas Pamela's isolation is created in part by the single focus of Richardson's epistolary form, Cecchina's is suggested by the uniquely complex interlocking of *buffa* and *seria* idioms and devices in her dramatic presence, her language and her music.

Yet finally, it is in its moral content, and in the relation between its vivid characterization of the heroine and the moral message it conveys, that *La buona figliuola* differs most profoundly from *Pamela*. Whereas the vitality and verisimilitude of Pamela's characterization is the essential and effective means toward Richardson's moral ends in the novel, Cecchina's immediacy is more or less an end in itself. Cecchina is, to adapt Robert D. Hume's useful distinctions, a sentimental character without being exemplary.[8] Not only does Cecchina not endure Pamela's moral persecution and crisis of faith but she does not even, properly speaking, enjoy virtue's reward of social advancement, since she turns out to be the long-lost daughter of a German Baron, equivalent in rank to her love, the Marchese. We need the immediacy and effect of her characterization to make plausible the Marchese's love for her in her lowly state, but those qualities in her which we find most touching are dramatic rather than moral necessities.

Goldoni has changed the denouement in his play as well, though in a slightly more plausible fashion—making Pamela's father a nobleman in hiding from the supposedly hostile king. In his preface to the play he took pains to assert the moral value of his change: "The reward of virtue is the aim of the English author; such a purpose would please me greatly, but I would not want the propriety of the family to be sacrificed to the merit of virtue."[9] And in fact much of the play is taken up with discussions of the pros and cons of socially mixed marriages. There is no such overt assertion of moral or didactic purpose either in or around *La buona figliuola*. Indeed, the endings to the two works very clearly indicate the differences in moral intent between the play and the opera. At the end of the play, Pamela says, "Let the world learn that virtue is not dead, that it struggles and suffers, but finally overcomes, conquers, and gloriously triumphs" (III, xvii). At the end of the opera the chorus sings "And the lovely delight of a true affection shall never end" (III, xiii).

Insofar as *La buona figliuola* makes a moral point (and it is certainly neither an immoral, nor even an amoral work), that point is that constancy in love brings its rewards, as long as those rewards are socially appropriate. But in part because this is a rather ordinary and totally unexceptionable message, and partly because open didacticism was not the rule in *opera buffa* in the 1760s and '70s, the moral "lesson" of *La buona figliuola* is subordinated to its entertainment purposes.

The virtue of constancy and its eventual reward form the moral meat of all the operas in this subgenre. They all also feature a heroine who either is or seems to be from the lower orders of society, and who sings in the "sentimental" style just described for Cecchina. For example, there is the following sleep scene in *La buona figliuola*:

68   Mary Hunter

Obviously deriving from the above, and indicative of the continuity of the "sentimental" style in this subgenre, is the beginning of Giannette's *"Vieni, o sonno,"* from Anfossi's setting of *L'incognita perseguitata:*

(Source: Us: Wc bound ms., 1765 [*sic*])

Before moving on to *Nina* and *Griselda*, the twin "apotheoses" of this subtype of comic opera, I would like briefly to comment on Antonio Sacchini's setting of *La contadina in corte*, which is a particularly interesting treatment of the *Pamela* theme, in that it shows how older operatic material was adapted for new enthusiasms. The story derives from Goldoni's adaptations of certain *commedia dell'arte* routines in *Berto, Bertoldino e Cacasenno*, which deals with the adventures of Bertoldino at court as he tries to rescue his wife from the amorous clutches of the king. Ridicule of lower-class pretensions to nobility forms the main substance of the plot, and everything ends happily when the status quo is restored, and Bertoldino gets to keep his wife. In the libretto set by Sacchini, however, Berto's (=Bertoldino's) *innamorata* Sandrina does in the end marry the nobelman Ruggiero (or, in some versions, Rinaldo). Sandrina is as attracted to the ease and comfort of noble life as to Ruggiero himself, however, and her one truly touching moment, which strongly resembles the sentimental utterances of our previous heroines, is her farewell to Berto (see below). In Sacchini's Sandrina we may very clearly see the link between the well-established figure of the ambitious and worldly servant girl, and the newer type of the young woman of sensibility whose merits enable her to marry above her station.

70 *Mary Hunter*

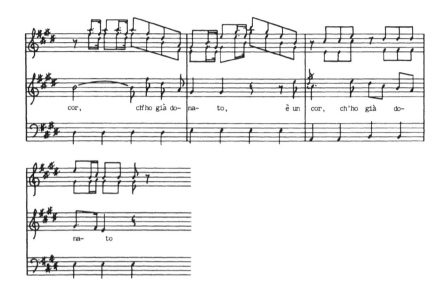

(Source: Us: Wc bound ms., 1765 [*sic*])

Paisiello's *Nina, o sia La pazza per amore* (*Nina, or the Girl Stricken Mad by Love*) and Piccinni's *Griselda* are interesting both individually and in conjunction in the ways they demonstrate different but related developments of this subgenre of *opera buffa*. *Nina* is based on a French *opéra comique* libretto by Joseph Marsollier, which was set to music originally by Nicolas Dalayrac. The libretto which Paisiello set was a fairly literal translation of the French work, made by Giuseppe Carpani, with arias added and adapted by Giambattista Lorenzi. *Nina* derives from the *comédie larmoyante* tradition rather than from farce or from comedies of manners, and concentrates on the fragile emotional condition of the heroine almost to the exclusion of everything else. The plot is devoid of intrigue, and the events which cause Nina's madness occur before the opera begins, being simply narrated by her maid Susanna at the beginning of the work. The librettists focused the story on the heroine partly by having her sing more than the other characters, but also partly by having them—and particularly the servants—sing primarily about her, and thus define themselves only in relation to her. Nina's major aria, indeed the central musical number of the work, is her opening number, "*Il mio ben, quando verrà*":

(Source: piano-vocal score, Paris: Pacini, 1830)

In this aria Nina obsessively anticipates the return of her lover Lindoro, who was left for dead after a duel with a rival for Nina's hand, a man of standing preferred by her father. This aria unites and intensifies all the sentimental characteristics noted above. It is a reflective soliloquy; and Nina has fled both physically, to natural surroundings, and emotionally, to a "state of nature" in which the only people she will respond to are the local peasants. The aria uses the simple lyrical style mentioned above, though here it is even more "pared down" than in earlier examples, and the melodic line is accompanied by prominent, continuous and functionally distinct triplet figuration. The other characters in the work are attractive but lightly-drawn *buffa* and *seria* stereotypes. The superficiality of characterization in the lesser roles has a positive dramatic function, however, in that it serves by contrast to bring Nina forward in the listener's consciousness and to intensify the impression she makes.

Nina was a phenomenal success; indeed, it was the first comic opera since *La buona figliuola* to enjoy truly comparable enthusiasm and dissemination. However, in one respect at least, the reception of *Nina* was closer to that of *Pamela* than to that of *La buona figliuola*. The audience responded not only to the extraordinary "presence" of the heroine, as they did with *La buona figliuola*, but, in large part because of that presence, also to the moral message of the whole. Two incidents cited by Andrea della Corte in his biography of Paisiello illustrate these responses. The first was reported by Francesco Florimo, who noted that during the opera's first run in Naples in 1790, the men in the audience leapt off their seats during "*Il mio ben*," shouting to the singer, "Don't worry, you will see your lover!" The second is that in 1794 a group of Turinese citizens sent a letter to Paisiello, saying that since the production of the opera, parents were promising never to oppose the virtuous desires of their children, lovers were becoming dearer to one another, and everyone was more desirous of the simple pleasures of innocent nature. They also noted that if all operas were like *Nina*, composers should be generally honored as extirpators of vice, producers of virtue, and correctors of customs.[10]

Nina, then, uses and magnifies what we might call the identifying characteristics of the sentimental, or Pamela-like, heroine in the context of a story that does not, on the face of it, resemble *Pamela* in any significant respects. However, *Pamela*, or, more exactly, the "Pamela" archetype, is recalled in *Nina* in three primary ways. First, the situation which gives rise to Nina's madness is her father's discomfort with the uncertainty of Lindoro's origins, so that even though we do not see the class conflicts played out in front of us, they nevertheless underpin the work as a whole. Second, it is precisely the social difficulty which gives Nina the opportunity to manifest her sensibility. And third, the moral of the libretto explicitly notes that the happy resolution of the story depends on Nina's demonstration of her merit. The five main characters join together at the end to sing, "And every lover should learn how Love, in the space of a few moments, is in the habit of rewarding the long complaints of a dear [or costly] fidelity" (II, vii, Finale). In other words, once fidelity has been proven by a certain length and depth of despair, love rushes in to repair the wounds. Constancy is, of course, rewarded by love in all the operas in this sub-tradition, but not until *Nina* is that constancy presented in a specifically and overtly moral light.

Pamela's constancy of purpose and Nina's fidelity to a lover are united in the story of Griselda. She remains faithful to her nobly-born husband who puts her through endless public humiliation in order to prove her worth to his arrogant sister. The story played out in this opera is closer in many ways to *Pamela* than is the story of *Nina*. Class conflict is the meat of the tale, and the heroine proves herself in response to overt persecution by both rich and poor. However, it is apparent from the librettist's preface to the first publication of the work that it was in part the success of *Nina* which prompted him to revive the *Griselda* story once more as an opera: "[I am] well persuaded that this wise and respectable [Venetian] public which has approved of the productions of *Nina*, of *Eugenia*, and of other dramas which the French call sentimental, could be similarly moved by the misfortunes of my Griselda."

Although Griselda's situation resembles those of Cecchina and Giannetta in terms of social and physical isolation, and as regards the persecution she suffers from all sides, I think it is more illuminating to describe *Griselda*, like *Nina*, as a "drama of sentiment" rather than as a comic opera with one or two sentimental characters. *Nina* qualifies as a drama of sentiment despite the presence of some genuinely comic elements, because of the extraordinary intensity of Nina herself, and also because of the exclusive focus of the work on the heroine's emotional condition. *Griselda* (interestingly designated *dramma eroicomico* on the title page) shares with *Nina* the heroine's intensity of characterization and the prolonged treatment of moments of strong emotion.[11] In addition, both works treat the rural poor (Nina's villagers, Griselda's father and brother) in distinctly pastoral and sentimental ways, rather than as the boorish bumpkins of earlier "sentimental comedies in music."

Whereas the focus of Nina's characterization is her opening soliloquy, Griselda's most important moment is the scene where she first sees Doristella, her long-lost daughter, who is introduced as her husband's future bride (I, vii). She immediately recognizes the now-adolescent girl, and faints. A chorus of chambermaids comments on Griselda's condition:

(Source: I: Fc FPT 388)

When Griselda regains consciousness, she uses the same melody, now in the major mode, to comment on Doristella's beauty:

74 *Mary Hunter*

Eventually, however, she decides that her daughter's return after so long an absence (she believed her dead) must be an illusion, and she utters a long lament, back in the minor mode, which exhibits the now familiar "sentimental" texture of a simple, long-breathed melody over an active and functionally distinct accompaniment:

At the end of this she faints again, and the chorus of chambermaids resumes. In Griselda's interaction and musical identification with the chorus, in the extended use of the minor mode, and in the dramatic intensity of the music here, this scene strongly resembles Nina's second appearance in Paisiello's opera (I, viii), singing "*Lontano da te.*"

It is important to note here that Griselda and Nina, like Pamela, but unlike Cecchina and her most immediate successors, are what they seem to be; and this absence of disguise allows their affective immediacy to communicate meanings with social and moral, as well as dramatic, weight. The "moral" of *Nina* has already been noted. Griselda ends with an injunction to all wives to behave with Griselda's patience, obedience and fortitude, and in both works the effective communication and apprehension of the moral or didactic element of the opera is entirely dependent on the psychological and emotional plausibility of the heroine.

Such heroines are not the only sentimental protagonists in late eighteenth-century *opera buffa*, just as this subgenre of *opera buffa* is not the only locus of sentimental comedy in music. Yet, what was new about *La buona figliuola* in 1760, and what distinguishes this group of operas (including *Nina* and *Griselda*) from others on similar plots or with similarly affecting characters, is the way distinctions in social class (which, after all, form the basic material for all sorts of comedies, both with and without music) provide the occasion for the development of, and concentration on, an unusually sympathetic, plausible and sentimental character-type. And it is the structural relation between class-distinctions and the manifestation of sensibility that Goldoni's libretto borrows from Richardson's novel, and which is transmitted through three decades to *Nina* and *Griselda*. Interestingly, it is in the ways that the latter differ most from *La buona figliuola* that they most resemble *Pamela*: in the intensity (rather than simple sweetness) of their heroines, in their serious and explicit moral and didactic tones, and in the introduction of other sentimental characters. One might suggest, then, that although *La buona figliuola* was historically and culturally the most direct adaptation of Richardson's novel, and although it resembles that work more than most critics have been willing to admit, it nevertheless took another three decades before Richardson's combination of "low" subject matter, psychological verisimilitude and didacticism could be absorbed into a genre with such different origins and constraints.*

NOTES

1/ Alfred Loewenberg, *The Annals of Opera* (1955), 3rd ed., rev. by Herbert Weinstock (Totowa, N.J., 1978).

2/ Alan D. McKillop, *Samuel Richardson: Printer and Novelist* (Chapel Hill, 1936), p. 106.

3/ The two works have been contrasted with regard to plot and action by Andrea della Corte, *L'opera comica italiana nel 1700* (Bari, 1923), pp. 175-79, and William C. Holmes, "Pamela Transformed," *The Musical Quarterly*, 38 (1952), 581-94.

4/ Patrick J. Smith, *The Tenth Muse: A Historical Study of the Opera Libretto* (New York, 1975), p. 108.

5/ Mark Kinkead-Weekes, *Samuel Richardson: Dramatic Novelist* (Ithaca, N.Y., 1973), p. 95.

6/ Francis Jeffrey, in *The Edinburgh Review* (1804), quoted in Ian Watt, *The Rise of the Novel* (Berkeley, 1957), p. 25.

7/ Piero Weiss, "The Role of Dialect in Early Opera Buffa," paper read at the 50th Annual Meeting of the American Musicological Society, Philadelphia, October 1984.

8 Robert D. Hume, "Goldsmith and Sheridan and the supposed revolution of 'laughing' against 'sentimental' comedy," Chapter 20 of *The Rakish Stage* (Carbondale, 1983), esp. p. 320.

9/ Preface to *Pamela nubile*, in *Carlo Goldoni: Tutte le opera*, ed. G. Ortolani (Milan 1964), III, 331. Citations from *La buona figliuola* are also from this edition. All translations are mine.

10/ Della Corte, *Paisiello (Settecento Italiano)* (Bari, 1922), pp. 175-77.

11/ Arthur Sherbo, *English Sentimental Drama* (East Lansing, 1957), notes that prolongation of strongly affecting moments or events is a characteristic of sentimental dramas in the eighteenth century.

*An earlier version of this essay was read at the 50th annual meeting of the American Musicological Society, Philadelphia, Oct. 1984. I acknowledge with gratitude a grant from the National Endowment for the Humanities, which allowed me to spend the academic year 1983-84 doing some of the research toward this essay.

[10]

Human Nature in the Unnatural Garden: *Figaro* as Pastoral[†]

By Wye J. Allanbrook

The genre named pastoral had a long and rich history before the eighteenth century: it was invented by the Sicilian poet Theocritus for the sophisticated court of Alexandria, inherited and transformed by Virgil in his Eclogues, and finally reshaped by Renaissance poets into a fictive world of extraordinary evocative power—Andrew Marvell's "green thought in a green shade." By the eighteenth century, however, it had clearly fallen into disrepute, witness this satirical "Recipe for a Pastoral Elegy," that appeared anonymously in the *London Magazine* in 1738:

> Take *Damon* and *Thyrsis*, both which Virgil will lend you with all his Heart, put them in a Cave together; be sure it be garnish'd well with Cypress, and don't forget a murmuring Stream, which may help you to a Rhyme or Simile upon Occasion. Let them lament *Daphnis* or *Pastorella;* or take any other Name, which you think will run off smoothly in your Verse. . . . Blast an old Oak or two, wither your Flowers *secundum Artem*, season it with Prodigies *quantum sufficit*, and 'twill make an excellent *Elegy*.[1]

Critics of the pastoral complained of the inherent artificiality of the genre and its tendency to false idealization: country life is not simple, nor are shepherds natural philosophers. In the pastoral at its most trivial, ennui led the sophisticate to dabble in these arrant falsifications, one notorious example being, in Mozart's own lifetime, the mock dairy farm of Marie Antoinette, *le Petit Trianon*, where aristocrats dressed as milkmaids indulged themselves in sentimental fantasies of rusticity. The French nobles even exalted the humble instruments of rustic music, decking the simple bagpipe or musette out in velvets and silks, and taking private lessons on it in order to excel in court pastoral entertainments.

Thus it is not immediately obvious what connection the pastoral could have with *Le mariage de Figaro*, Beaumarchais's witty Parisian's challenge to the *ancien régime;* that work seems to be one with the very eighteenth-century temper that rejected the pastoral as a hollow masquerade. In fact, if there is a desire for escape in the play, it would seem to be back to the city, away from the tyranny of the rural. When we view city life through

Figaro's eyes in his celebrated Act-V monologue about social injustice, the city seems the expansive arena of possibility—the seedbed of the cleverness and resource that will finally put things right in the country. Why, then, a pastoral?

It may help to remember that da Ponte and Mozart cut Figaro's biting monologue entirely from their libretto. Works often suffer a sea change in the transformation from stage play to opera, and this one is no exception. The monologue is occasioned by a plot turn that leaves Figaro with the false conviction that his beloved Susanna is about to betray him with the Count, making him a cuckold on the very day of his marriage. In the original, Figaro's doubts about Susanna merely served as a springboard for a lengthy tirade about his scrambles to survive in a social system that prizes rank above wits. The deletion of the monologue leaves him to focus instead on unrequited love, an appropriately pastoral subject. He gives vent to an angry diatribe against women, delivered at the very moment when the three women in Figaro's life—his newly disclosed mother Marcellina, his bride Susanna, and the Countess her mistress—have banded together to perform the task that Figaro himself had after great fanfare failed to accomplish: to discomfit the Count in his efforts to bed Susanna. The women have shown themselves united, capable, and determined; Figaro's anger is misdirected and futile. In the course of the transformation from play to libretto the emphasis has shifted from Figaro to the women and to their union of mutual affection and respect. Here in the last act of the opera Figaro has momentarily fallen from grace, and it will be up to Susanna to show him the way back.

This shift of subject matter—from the public to the private, from a preoccupation with issues of social injustice to one with issues of the human heart—makes the pastoral sound more plausible as a ruling metaphor for the opera. Furthermore, Beaumarchais's play already contained a significant suggestion of the pastoral on which to build: in its last act the Aguas Frescas garden with its spreading chestnuts (turned into pines in da Ponte's libretto) figures importantly; it provides a quasi-magic retreat like Shakespeare's Forest of Arden in *As You Like It*, where couples are shuffled and reshuffled until they find their proper order and relation. This green and twilight shelter offers a toehold for the notion of the pastoral; da Ponte and Mozart acted on the suggestion to create a psychological garden, a fictive enclosure that is contained by, yet transcends, the workaday world of the opera. Literary critics have written persuasively of Renaissance poets' use of the pastoral as a "second world," a "green world," where they constructed a counterfactual, alternative cosmos, a model for the world as it should or could be.[2] Although the green world is only a feigned world, and return from it to the enclosing world is always inevitable, things can happen in this unnatural world that could never take place in the so-called natural one. Although Shakespeare was aware of the limitations of his artificial Eden—not all of his shepherds are courtly innocents—it was there that he resolved enmities and fashioned appropriate marriages. The very "unnaturalness" of the pastoral world—in it one makes no distinction between the lowly and the exalted, the noble and the shepherd—allows human relations to flourish in a manner that is "natural" in another sense, natural if one believes that there ever existed a State of Nature in which human beings could form their most important bonds innocent of the "unnatural" distinctions of rank and class. In Mozart's opera the "green world" offers a withdrawing place to Susanna and the Countess where their friendship may flourish despite their social inequality; this friendship in turn offers to other characters in the opera a paradigm of natural human affection that transforms their behavior, at least for a moment, at the end of the long Mad Day.

This is the way I see the transformation that da Ponte and Mozart worked on Beaumarchais's *The Marriage of Figaro* to turn it into their own version, a version we could call, to solemnize the change, *The Marrying of Figaro*. Poet and composer each had at hand a thesaurus of conventional references with which to implement the change: da Ponte the whole panoply of the Italian poetic tradition and Mozart a set of characteristic musical styles that could be called "country music." These two modes of discourse penetrate the opera gradually, appearing at first to be a chance precipitate from the workaday world; their frequency and conjunction intensify, however, as the opera moves toward the twilight zone of the fourth act and the mysteries of the garden.

Lorenzo da Ponte was a well educated man; in the process of revising the play he introduced into it copious references to the myths of Roman antiquity, to the tropes of Italian pastoral poets like Tasso and Ariosto, and to the language of Dante. For example, da Ponte has Figaro call the page Cherubino a "little Narcissus, little Adonis of love"; later, in his anger at Susanna, Figaro pictures himself as one of the most famous cuckolds in literature, Vulcan surprising his wife Venus in the toils of love with Mars. In the fourth act Marcellina, newly reconciled to Susanna as the fiancée of the son she herself almost married, sings to the jealous Figaro of the amity in which the beasts of the field live with their significant others—if the lion will not lie down with the lamb, as in the Biblical pastoral, at least he keeps peace with the lioness; Marcellina's words, it has been pointed out, are a near-quotation from Ariosto.[3] Instead of the ballad Beaumarchais provided Cherubino, da Ponte has the boy sing a text reminiscent of a sonnet by Dante about the special intelligence of love possessed by women:

> Voi che sapete
> Che cosa è amor,
> Donne, vedete
> Si l'ho nel cor.[4]

I think in fact that da Ponte turns this anomalous, androgynous, ubiquitous adolescent into a figure for Eros, the presiding deity of the green world, and through him points up the centrality of the women in the opera and their gift of grace—but this is a theme for another occasion.[5]

As for Mozart's "country music," he inherited the court's own notion of the country, which included conventional musical "tag-lines" whose sounds transported one directly into a rural setting. I have already mentioned the bagpipe or musette, with its drone bass, and skirling solo in the treble; it represented the ultimate, unmediated country sound. A musical meter that often accompanied the musette was 6/8, a lilting rhythm consisting of groups of three beats bound into pairs; the feet move quickly to the triple pulse, the upper body more slowly to the duple. Eighteenth-century musicians believed that these 6/8 patterns reflected the actual dances of shepherds, and recognized a faster and slower version, the *pastorale* and the *siciliano*, wistfully considered true artifacts of the Arcadian *temps perdu*.[6] These gentle bucolic rhythms, which saturate the music of the last acts of *Le nozze di Figaro*, appear together with the drone in the peasant choruses of Acts I and III of *Figaro* in order to set the scene; here, for example, is the orchestral introduction to the second chorus (example 1).

In the third and fourth acts, as the twilight deepens and the aura of the "green world" increasingly dominates the opera, the rhythms of the 6/8 *pastorale* emerge as thematic, and a private drama is acted out in the interstices of the public world. The main action of the last two acts is to humble the Count, and it is played out in the full glare of publicity, ending with his apology to the Countess in front of the assembled *dramatis personae*. This action is set in martial duple rhythms, rather than the lilting Arcadian triple. But the private drama ends in a reconciliation also, one that to my mind is more genuine, namely, the reconciliation between Susanna and Figaro. To chart its course across the grain of the original play, da Ponte made the cuts and interpolations I have mentioned, and Mozart set five pieces in the gentle rhythms of the *pastorale*—the greatest concentration of a given characteristic musical style I know of in the operas. These pieces are the duet between Susanna and the Countess in Act III, when they compose a note to the Count about a rendezvous in the garden, the peasant chorus cited above, Barbarina's mock-tragic aria that opens Act IV and fortuitously triggers Figaro's jealousy, Susanna's "Deh, vieni," and the actual moment of reconcilation between Susanna and Figaro near the end of the fourth-act finale.[7]

Example 1. "Ricevete, oh padrone" (Wind doublings omitted).

* * *

Three of the pastorale numbers are particularly significant; they trace out the beginning, middle, and end of this private drama: the so-called letter duet, "Deh, vieni," and the moment in that finale when Susanna and Figaro, quickly reconciled, tease the Count with the image of their concord. I will close by taking a closer look at these three pieces.

The letter duet, "Che soave zefiretto," marks the moment when the two women finally resolve to take matters into their own hands. The Countess dictates to Susanna a letter for the Count that suggests a rendezvous, ostensibly with Susanna, that evening in the garden. The Countess intends to go instead, disguised as Susanna. She deliberately chooses a bucolic text for her note, a scrap of a song lyric: "What a gentle little zephyr will sigh this evening beneath the pines of the grove." This is the text in its entirety:

CONTESSA: Canzonetta sull'aria:

"Che soave zeffiretto
Questa sera spirerà
Sotto i pini del boschetto."

Ei già il resto capirà.

SUSANNA: Certo, certo il capirà.[8]

The duet is the image of an act of concentration: the two women completely unself-conscious in their attention to their task. The orchestra organizes the beginning, the Countess taking her cue from the melody first offered by the winds (example 2).

Example 2. "Che soave zeffiretto."

Susanna repeats each fragment of the text reflectively, to assure them both it is penned correctly, once even asking for a confirming repetition. When the note is completed, the Countess says, "Now he'll understand the rest," and Susanna answers, "Certainly." Singing together for the first time, in parallel thirds, they bring the section to a close (example 3).

Example 3.

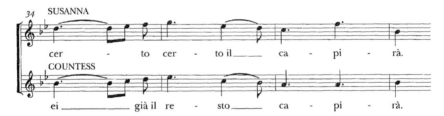

Now the Countess leans over Susanna's shoulder (note the disregard of the appropriate postures for mistress and maidservant; their exchange of costumes in the fourth-act finale has the same equalizing effect). They reread the text together, each taking a phrase, orchestra and voices overlapping. The original music is also repeated, but cunningly truncated so that the rereading of the note takes about one third the time of its dictation. The remaining time is given to extended cadences on that suggestive phrase "He'll understand the rest" (il capirà), Susanna first imitating the

Countess at a measure's distance. When they ornament the phrase with a measured trill on quicker note values, the effect of the echo is breathtaking (example 4).

Example 4.

All in all, at the close *il capirà* is heard twelve times. It is worth noting, by the way, how well *dramatic* and what one might call purely *musical* values work together here: the somewhat diffuse beginning—the hesitant composing of the note—leads to a strong structural downbeat on the first set of cadences; on repetition the contraction of the beginning material—the reviewing of the note—makes way for the much expanded cadential section, on that meaningful phrase, "He'll understand."

The duet is the eye of the opera's storm, showing the two women calm and secure in their friendship, meeting in the classless, timeless meadow figured by the pastoral. Their mutual trust and affection are all the more remarkable because the moment is objectively a humiliating one for the Countess: she is reduced to plotting with her servant to win back her husband. Their gentle but emphatic assertion of the phrase "He'll understand" is emblematic of their unity, and its repetition forces the casual phrase to significance. They rightly understand, and in this duet tacitly acknowledge to one another, that the understanding the Count will come to—both the trivial one about the rendezvous, and the deeper one, about the power of human affection—has been brought about by their own deep mutual understanding. That understanding is inviolable, and this duet with its interwoven garlands of female voices offers us an enduring image of it.

The second *pastorale*, Susanna's famous "Deh, vieni," is a serenade ostensibly intended for the Count, in truth directed to Figaro, and ultimately—if this is not too fanciful—dedicated to all lovers who are willing to receive the grace of the green world; it is finally a celebration of the pastoral mode. The aria is on the surface rendered by Susanna in retaliation for Figaro's mistrust of her. She pretends to sing with tremulous expectation of her tryst with the Count, knowing full well the effect her words will have on Figaro. The text of the introductory *recitativo accompagnato* is a sensuous invitation, firmly committed to the pathetic fallacy of the pastoral: "Oh, how it seems that this pleasant place, the earth and sky, responds to the fires of love! how the night supports my secrets!" ("Oh come par che all'amoroso foco / L'amenità del loco / La terra e il ciel risponda! / Come la notte i furti miei seconda!") Later the breeze "teases," the flowers "laugh"—the lover's version of the "tongues in trees, books in the running brooks" that the good Duke finds in Shakespeare's Forest of Arden. But the pathetic fallacy also works in reverse: just as natural elements in the magic garden take on human habits, humans merge naturally with the landscape. Susanna seems to be a nymph or dryad, a local deity murmuring incantatory promises. She lures her lover into the garden by offering to crown his forehead with roses—to make him one with the pastoral landscape as well.

The rhythms of the piece are the gentle legato 6/8 of the *pastorale*, with the occasional dotted figure. Its languorous eleven-syllable lines are strummed out on pizzicato strings as if on a guitar; the piece is, after all, as much a performance as Cherubino's "Voi che sapete," which also has a guitar-like accompaniment. The front-stressed dactyllic feet, organized into three-measure phrases, are hypnotic and enervating (example 5).

Example 5. "Deh vieni non tardar."

The regular cadences of the poetry predominate over harmonic events to the extent that they seem more like idle inflections than an intentional trajectory: the tonic is slipped back into place almost offhandedly at the end of a phrase. It takes the giant iamb of Susanna's "cadenza" ("Ti vo la fronte incoronar di rose") to prevail against these swooning rhythms and bring the aria to a cadence (example 6).

Example 6.

The sensual invitation of "Deh, vieni" is direct and immediate, but the dramatic situation allows Susanna to cloak her passion in sport, avoiding dull sentiment. Her punishment for Figaro is also a loving gesture to him, if he should be clever enough to recognize it—an invitation to shake off his heavy anger and join her in the twilit and uncorrupted garden. To his credit, he will understand this invitation in retrospect, when all disguises are removed; the *pastorale* is the couple's true nuptial song, and he will finally need no prompting to join Susanna in it. Now, however, he is left in a trancelike state between trust and suspicion, intensely moved by her beauty and grace, but stung to the quick by what he supposes to be her intentions.

The last *pastorale*, in which Susanna and Figaro are reconciled, is embedded in the fourth-act finale as part of the on-going action; it is perhaps the shortest reconciliation scene in opera, the theme of reconciliation being a natural invitation for an opera composer to indulge himself in extended harmonies. The movement is over in just under two minutes, and the couple is actually *alone* for less than half that time. For the Count stumbles in on them in their brief moment of private harmony, and they repeat it again for his benefit, this time with Susanna pretending to be the Countess responding to Figaro's amorous overtures. The imbroglio is here at its most taut, involving multiple cases of mistaken identity due to the characters' disguises and the cover of the pastoral twilight. Figaro recognizes Susanna dressed as the Countess when just for a moment she forgets to speak in her disguised voice; overjoyed, he cannot resist teasing his beloved by pretending to make love to her in her guise as the Countess. He accepts Susanna's angry slaps with dizzy rapture, and then in 6/8 *pastorale* rhythms confesses that he knew who she was all along: "I recognized the voice that I adore," he says, "and that I carry always engraved on my heart." ("Io conobbi la voce che adoro / E che impressa ognor serbo nel cor.") Moved by the figure of his beloved, he is immediately drawn back into the pastoral orbit. Susanna needs no time to contemplate the new development; she joins him in the close harmonies of true love, and they sing an eight-measure phrase to the text:

> Pace, pace, mio dolce tesoro,
> Pace, pace, mio tenero amor.[9]

That constitutes their time alone.

The Count enters, and they decide to continue the masquerade for him, confirming their decision with the harmonious eight-measure phrase that just constituted their brief reconciliation. Watching Figaro make love to the woman he supposes is the Countess provokes the Count to an angry outburst. Delighted with their mischief, the couple departs arm in arm, singing that same blissful strain for a third time. Their parting words are both a further irritant for the enraged Count and the proper sentiment to put the period to their reconciliation: "Corriamo, corriamo, mio bene . . ." "Let us hurry off, my love, and let pleasure make up for our pains" (example 7).

Example 7. Act-IV finale.

This pastoral duet is in one sense the end of the opera. Of course the opera cannot in fact end with Figaro making love to Susanna disguised as the Countess in order to humiliate the Count—that would strain the sense of fitness in the most modern among us. And there *is* one more reconciliation to come, that of the Countess with the Count, which occurs in the last moments of the opera and occasions its jubilant close. The hushed and hymn-like music of the second reconciliation is justly celebrated, but its public solemnity has always caused me to question whether on the

Count's part we are witnessing behavior straight from the heart. In contrast we have this extraordinarily modest private moment, embedded in the midst of imbroglio, when two human beings who know each other through and through are reconciled just as they courted one another, with passion, but under the guise of play; they have no need of public ceremonies and protestations of fidelity. Only two *enduring* relationships are portrayed in *Le nozze di Figaro:* that between Susanna and the Countess, and that between Susanna and Figaro. The imaginary garden of the pastoral exists to protect the first one, and to help bring the second to fullness. The very unreality of this green world is a guarantee of its possibility: it is merely a state of mind, called into being by a tacit understanding and defined by a nostalgic and otherworldly musical gesture. Its shelter is substantial precisely because it can coexist with the harsher realities of the daylight world. I like to think that Mozart took the same delight as Shakespeare in the sometimes dizzying paradoxes intendant on the words "nature" and "natural." In the conventional garden, where the poets' delight is to have rendered nature unnatural, human nature can discover— or is it rediscover?—the dim traces of its most natural bonds.

NOTES

* The following three articles are adapted from papers first delivered at a session of a symposium entitled "Mozart's Nature, Mozart's World," held at the Museum of Fine Arts, Boston, 28 February–3 March 1991. The authors wish to acknowledge the Westfield Center for Early Keyboard Studies and the Museum of Fine Arts, Boston, for their generous sponsorship of this conference.

† Some of the matters discussed here are taken up at greater length in my book *Rhythmic Gesture in Mozart: "Le nozze di Figaro" and "Don Giovanni"* (Chicago: University of Chicago Press, 1983), *passim.*

[1] Quoted in *The Pastoral Mode: A Casebook,* ed. Bryan Loughrey (London: Macmillan, 1984), 66.

[2] See especially Harry Berger Jr., "The Renaissance Imagination: Second World and Green World," *Second World and Green World: Studies in Renaissance Fiction-Making* (Berkeley: University of California Press, 1988), 3–40.

[3] See Edward J. Dent, *Mozart's Operas: A Critical Study,* 2nd ed. (London: Oxford University Press, 1947), p. 110, n. 1.

[4] "Ladies, you who know what love is, see if I have it in my heart."

[5] See *Rhythmic Gesture in Mozart,* 96–99, 109–12.

[6] It is not clear that the *pastorale* was ever strictly a dance, but rather a musical style, one documented from the early seventeenth century (see "Pastorale," *The New Grove Dictionary of Music and Musicians,* ed. Stanley Sadie [London: Macmillan, 1980], 14:290–96). Some later eighteenth-century writers, however, liked to think of it as the music to which shepherds once had danced; see, for example, Johann George Sulzer, *Allgemeine Theorie der schönen Künste,* 2nd ed. (Leipzig, 1786-87), 3:60, and Daniel Gottlob Türk, *Klavierschule,* trans. Raymond H. Haggh (Lincoln: University of Nebraska Press, 1982), 395. Koch does not accept that notion, defining the pastorale simply as "a piece . . . that expresses the song of the idealized world of shepherds" ("ein Tonstück, . . . wodurch der Gesang der idealischen Hirtenwelt ausgedrückt werden soll"). Heinrich Christoph Koch, "Pastorale," *Musikalisches Lexikon* (Frank-

furt am Main, 1802; reprint, New York: Georg Olms, 1985), col. 1142. For a further discussion of the *pastorale,* and the other dance types in compound duple meter, see Allanbrook, *Rhythmic Gesture in Mozart,* 40–45.

[7] There are, by the way, other collaterally pastoral pieces in Act IV—Marcellina's Ariostan aria, and Basilio's anti-pastoral that follows, wherein the basest character in the opera counterstates Marcellina's peaceable animals with a cartoon of the Forest of Arden scourged by a ravening lion. Figaro stages another anti-pastoral in the finale to the fourth act, when with grim sarcasm he styles himself as Vulcan the hunter; hunters disturb the ecology of the pastoral, and are not traditionally welcome there, as Figaro must learn. Briefly da Ponte has Figaro ally himself with those who mock the pastoral world, in order to underline his momentary alienation from the women, its natural residents.

[8] COUNTESS: A little song on this tune:
"What a gentle little zephyr / Will sigh this evening / Beneath the pines of the grove."
The rest he'll understand.
SUSANNA: Of course he'll understand.

[9] "Peace, peace, my sweet treasure, / Peace, peace, my gentle love."

[11]

From *Nina* to *Nina*:
Psychodrama, absorption and sentiment in the 1780s

STEFANO CASTELVECCHI

Paisiello's *Nina* 'is sentimental comedy at its worst.... Its sentimentality is to modern ears perfectly unbearable, and we cannot understand how the whole of Europe was reduced to tears by these infantile melodies.'[1] Edward Dent's opinion might well be shared, though perhaps less frankly expressed, by more than one musicologist of following generations. Yet the fact remains that eighteenth-century Europe was indeed reduced to tears by operas on the story of Nina: an attempt to 'thicken' our understanding of that cultural phenomenon is the aim of the present essay. In its first part – focusing on Marsollier's and Dalayrac's *Nina*, the source for Paisiello's opera – I try to reconstruct a web of relationships between the practices of psychiatry emerging in the late eighteenth century and the theatrical and aesthetic cultures of the time. In the second part, aspects of Paisiello's setting are read as a composer's effort to create an operatic language responsive to the culture of 'sensibility' shared by eighteenth-century humanists and physicians.

Nina, ou la Folle par amour (*Nina, or The Love-Distressed Maid*), a one-act *opéra comique* by Benoît-Joseph Marsollier and Nicolas Dalayrac, received its Parisian première at the Comédie Italienne on 15 May 1786. The work was extremely successful in Paris (where it was staged until the mid-nineteenth century), and started a trend with broad consequences for the European stage. *Nina* crossed the Alps as early as Autumn 1788, when an Italian translation by Giuseppe Carpani was staged in Monza. The most successful Italian version of *Nina*, however, was that set to music by Giovanni Paisiello and first performed on 25 June 1789 near Caserta (seat of a royal palace of the Neapolitan Bourbons). On this occasion, Paisiello set Carpani's translation of Marsollier's text, with a few changes and additions by Giambattista Lorenzi.[2]

---

[1] Edward J. Dent, *The Rise of Romantic Opera*, ed. Winton Dean (Cambridge, 1976), 111.
Earlier versions of this article were presented in Autumn 1995 in two workshops at the University of Chicago: at the Fishbein Center for the History of Science and Medicine, and in the Eighteenth-Century Workshop of the Division of Humanities. I wish to thank the participants in both workshops for their stimulating comments.

[2] *Nina o sia La pazza per amore. Commedia di un atto in prosa, ed in verso per musica* [...] (Naples: Flauto, 1789). Paisiello's *Nina* preserves one important feature of its sources: it employs spoken dialogue instead of recitative. For an early revival in Naples (Teatro dei Fiorentini, 1790), Lorenzi and Paisiello added a few new pieces in order to make two acts from the original one (this two-act version still employs spoken dialogue). The two versions are collated in Giovanni Paisiello, *Nina o sia La pazza per amore*, ed. Fausto Broussard (Milan, 1981).

One of the greatest operatic hits of the century,[3] Paisiello's *Nina* was to become a paradigm of sentimental opera – the musical version of that new, bourgeois drama that bestowed tragic dignity on events and characters from contemporary life.[4] Works in this genre owed much of their impact to the way they responded to a deep social need: the desire of eighteenth-century audiences to be projected on stage in serious, even tragic ways, something that would be impossible within the comic modes, or with the remote heroes and distant settings of tragedy. Indeed, in reviewing the Parisian première of Marsollier's and Dalayrac's *Nina*, the *Correspondance littéraire* attributed much of its success to the subject, which was found new for the stage and extremely touching.[5] Here, in brief, is the story in question:

Nina and Germeuil love each other, and are betrothed with the consent of Nina's father, the Count. Yet, when Nina's hand is requested by a wealthier suitor, the Count favours the latter, thus breaking the pact with Germeuil. A duel between the two suitors ensues; when Nina sees her beloved lying in his own blood, and her father asks her to accept as her spouse Germeuil's slayer, she loses her reason. The Count cannot bear the sight of his daughter's sorry state: he leaves Nina in his country estate, entrusting her to the benevolent care of the governess Elise.

Nina – having lost all memory of the recent, tragic events – spends her days thinking of Germeuil and waiting for his return, surrounded by the affection and compassion of servants and peasants. (On one occasion she falls into a delirium, and believes she sees Germeuil.) Some time later the Count comes back, stricken with sorrow and remorse; but his daughter does not recognise him. When Germeuil, whom everyone thought dead, returns, the Count welcomes him with open arms, and calls him son. At first, Nina does not recognise Germeuil. Father and lover 'cure' Nina by showing her that Germeuil is back and still loves her, and that she can marry her beloved with her father's consent.

Marsollier's and Dalayrac's *Nina*, however, stages only the events in the second paragraph of this summary, those in the first being simply recalled in a passage of dialogue. It is, then, a drama with very little staged plot: as the curtain rises Nina is already deranged, and she regains her reason only in the very last scene of the opera. There are no subplots, and the words and deeds of each character focus exclusively on the protagonist and her changing mental states.

The absence of narrative complexity – and the concomitant emphasis on emotions – is one of many key features that *Nina* shares with much sentimental literature and theatre of the eighteenth century. Indeed, the text of *Nina* – with its insistence on sentiment as a guiding force over reason – is in many ways an explicit advocate for a sentimental ideology. In particular, it is obvious that even Nina's

---

[3] By the 1790s Paisiello's *Nina* had reached many Italian and European centres. It was produced in Barcelona (1789), Vienna (1790, with a text revised by Lorenzo Da Ponte), Paris (1791, with musical additions by Cherubini) and London (1797). The opera also received many translations.

[4] In the 1770s and 1780s Neapolitan audiences had welcomed with growing enthusiasm spoken dramas of the bourgeois and sentimental genre, mostly of French origin. See Benedetto Croce, *I teatri di Napoli dal Rinascimento alla fine del secolo decimottavo*, ed. Giuseppe Galasso (Milan, 1992), 258–61.

[5] *Correspondance littéraire, philosophique et critique par* [Friedrich Melchior] *Grimm, Diderot* [. . .], ed. Maurice Tourneux, XIV (Paris, 1880), 401–3.

illness is merely the result of what is by itself a positive trait in a human being – *sensibilité*:

LE COMTE: Par-tout, le bruit de ta mort s'est répandu, & Nina ...
GERMEUIL (*avec joie*): Y a été sensible? Quel bonheur!
LE COMTE: Qu'oses-tu dire? frappée d'un coup si inattendu, sa raison ...[6]

[THE COUNT: The rumour of your death was spread everywhere, and Nina ...
GERMEUIL (*with joy*): She was responsive to it ... oh happiness! THE COUNT: What dare you say? Struck by such a sudden blow, her reason ...]

This is hardly surprising: the opera has its literary source in the work of a best-selling author of sentimental fiction. The review in the *Correspondance littéraire* mentioned this source, and – in line with its ideology – confirmed the supposed historical truth of the episode it recounts:

Le fonds de ce nouveau drame est un anecdote dont nous pouvons garantir l'authenticité, que nos papiers publics ont rapportée il y a quelques années, et que M. d'Arnaud a déjà employée dans ses *Nouvelles*, ou *Délassements de l'homme sensible*, sous le nom de *la Nouvelle Clémentine*.[7]

[The substance of this new *drame* is an anecdote whose authenticity we can guarantee, an anecdote reported by our newspapers a few years ago, and already employed by M. d'Arnaud in his *Délassements de l'homme sensible*, under the title *La Nouvelle Clémentine*.]

Generations of opera historians have referred to this literary filiation, but apparently never looked at Baculard d'Arnaud's short story (Edward Dent even believed it a novel).[8] The most remarkable trait of this brief 'anecdote' is that its protagonist (allegedly a living person) never recovers, and in old age goes every day to a place where she waits in vain for her dead lover's return.[9]

Thus, aside from other discrepancies, Marsollier introduced major narrative changes when he transformed Baculard d'Arnaud's tale into an *opéra comique* in which the lover does come back, and the sanity of Nina is restored. Such changes probably have to do with a problem of genre – the need for a happy ending more appropriate to an *opéra comique*. Yet something more could be said about the details of Marsollier's story: the text of *Nina* resonates in many ways with contemporary theories of the mind and practices of the 'moral cure'; more remarkably, the finale of the opera can be read as a staging of a specific therapeutic technique apparently emerging in medical practice of the very same years.

---

[6] *Nina, ou La folle par amour; Comédie en un acte, en prose, mêlée d'ariettes. Par M[onsieur] M[arsollier] d[es] V[ivetières] Musique de M[onsieur] Dal[ayrac]* [...] (Paris: Brunet, 1786), scene 12. All translations are mine, unless otherwise specified.

[7] *Correspondance littéraire*, 401.

[8] Dent, 110.

[9] F. T. M. Baculard d'Arnaud, *Délassements de l'homme sensible, ou Anecdotes diverses*, 6 vols. (Paris: chez l'Auteur et la Veuve Ballard, 1783–5). Arnaud published a second set of anecdotes in 1786–7; the two collections add up to over five thousand printed pages. 'La Nouvelle Clémentine' is found in vol. I (1783) of the first set, pp. 50–8: its title and text make explicit reference to the character of Clementina in Richardson's *The History of Sir Charles Grandison* (1753–4).

Psychodrama and absorption

The idea that insanity could often have a 'moral' (that is, mental) aetiology – as opposed to anatomic, organic causes – and that the insane could therefore be given a 'moral' treatment (through intellect or emotion, not through physical means such as purges, bleedings, showers and drugs) gained ground in the eighteenth century, and was accorded scientific status through the work of the French physician Philippe Pinel.[10] Many details in the text of *Nina* show Marsollier's quite remarkable awareness of contemporary views of the mind and mental therapy:

(1) Nina's illness has obvious 'moral' (psychogenic) origins in a set of traumatic events: her malady is her way out of a frightful inner conflict she cannot withstand.[11]

(2) Nina passes from fits and faints to memory loss and hallucinations (all symptoms of 'vapours' listed, for instance, by the British physician George Cheyne).[12]

(3) She recalls Pinel's portrayal of those melancholics who show a deep, concentrated sadness, are dominated by an exclusive idea, and tend to lead a monotonous life with their phantoms.[13]

(4) She is kept in an enclosed, quiet, extra-urban retreat (with a walled garden) – the rich people's madhouse of the time. Opera scholars may have overlooked the fact that Nina does not simply live in this estate, but is actually enclosed in it: an eighteenth-century engraving (see Fig. 1) shows Nina against the garden wall and gate (the image portrays Irene Tomeoni, who sang the title role in a Viennese revival of Paisiello's *Nina* in 1794).

(5) Nina is kept under constant surveillance, even when she believes herself to be alone.

(6) She is always treated with gentleness.

(7) She is given canonical distractions and diversions such as walks in the open and music.[14]

(8) Trained servants and confidants take part in the healing process, communicating information about the patient to family members.

(9) Even the relationship between sanity and insanity is portrayed in ways that seem consonant with eighteenth-century views of the mind.

---

[10] In Roy Porter's words, 'the moral therapy ... was in practically all respects a commonplace of certain strands of eighteenth-century psychiatric thought'. Roy Porter, 'Was There a Moral Therapy in Eighteenth-Century Psychiatry?' *Lychnos: Annual of the Swedish History of Science Society* (1981–82), 12–26, here 20. On Pinel see Jan Goldstein, *Console and Classify: The French Psychiatric Profession in the Nineteenth Century* (Cambridge, 1987), in particular 'Scientizing "the treatment"', 89–105. Philippe Pinel's fundamental work is the *Traité médico-philosophique sur l'aliénation mentale, ou la manie* (Paris: Caille et Ravier, An VIII [1799–1800]). This first edition is mentioned in Dora B. Weiner, *The Citizen-Patient in Revolutionary and Imperial Paris* (Baltimore and London, 1993). I read the book in an early reprint (Paris: Richard, Caille et Ravier, An IX [1800–1801]), to which all following quotations refer.

[11] '[N]e peut résister au combat affreux qu'elle éprouve': Marsollier, *Nina*, scene 1.

[12] George Cheyne, *The English Malady* (London, 1733), 199–200.

[13] Pinel, *Traité*, 143–5.

[14] '[L]e Berger ... n'attend qu'un signal pour jouer des airs, qui tirent toujours Nina de sa sombre tristesse': Marsollier, *Nina*, scene 9.

Fig. 1 The singer Irene Tomeoni portrayed as Nina

This last point needs some elaboration. The eighteenth-century person of 'sensibility' is one gifted with a particularly receptive sensory apparatus that renders her or him especially susceptible to refined emotions and human compassion. Such apparatus is almost infallibly revealed by a family of signs, most often bodily ones, that might be called a symptomatology of sensitivity: the sensitive person will be prone to tears, blushes, tremblings, palpitations and swoons. Even more important is the insistence on non-verbal expression: silence and interrupted speech are often the appropriate responses of a sensitive person overwhelmed by emotion. In Marsollier's and Dalayrac's *opéra comique* – and even more in Paisiello's opera – the emotional states of sensitive characters are revealed by these 'symptoms' of verbal and musical disruption, markers of a sentimental style. In her mental derangement, Nina reaches the extremes of such disruption: her 'symptoms' are the hypertrophical version of those found in other characters, just as her illness is the result of an excess of *sensibilité*. In fact, these operas seem to show that between sensitivity and folly, as well as between their respective manifestations, the difference is only one of degree. In a similar way, Pinel's *aliéné* is quite other from the 'Other' so easily invoked in recent literature: indeed, it is the very continuity between the sane and the insane that allows for some communication between the two and, eventually, for a recovery.[15]

Yet the most striking resonance between the text of Marsollier's *Nina* and early psychiatric practices is found in the finale of the work. The very process through which Nina regains her sanity corresponds to one of Pinel's therapeutic solutions: shocking the patient's imagination through what amounts to the staging of a theatrical scene. An example is given by Pinel: during the Revolution, a man obsessed with the idea of having been sentenced to the guillotine for lack of patriotism was (temporarily) cured through a staged trial in which three physicians dressed as magistrates interrogated and eventually acquitted him.[16] Mind-curers had long been making use of generically 'theatrical' expedients and skills, but the practice Pinel describes here is more specific, resembling a therapeutic technique that, in our times, would be defined as a 'psychodrama' – a scene that dramatises the problematic or traumatic contents of the patient's mind. The finale of *Nina* works in a very similar way. Germeuil and the other characters re-enact Nina's past and give a positive turn to its traumatic contents: Nina finds herself between Germeuil, who is alive, and her father, who approves of their wedding. Only now does Nina feel well, and recognise father and lover. The process, as in Pinel's 'trial', involves a degree of staging: in *Nina*'s final 'psychodrama' the characters act as though the traumatic events – the father's refusal, Germeuil's supposed death – never took place.

Pinel published his treatise on 'mental alienation' only in 1799–1800, but his interest in mental illness dates back to the 1780s. He started thinking about these issues in 1783, shocked by the suicide of a depressed young friend;[17] his first experiments with the moral cure, in Paris, have been dated to 1786 (the very year of the Parisian première of *Nina*).[18]

In a general sense, Pinel's web of relationships between mental illness and theatre is 'thick' from the outset. In Pinel's account, his unfortunate friend had the last relapse into depression (leading to suicide) after attending a performance of *Le Philosophe sans le savoir*, Sedaine's masterpiece of bourgeois drama; and it is in theatrical terms that Pinel described his own pain during the friend's illness ('I was reduced to the role of spectator').[19] In 1784 Pinel recommended a comedy as an

---

[15] 'The lunatic is not consigned to total "otherness" but is located on a continuum with the sane person': Goldstein, *Console*, 109. 'Pinel breaks through the clear division between pathology and normality. The insane are seen as driven by motives that linger in everyone's heart. The difference is only one of degree': Patrick Vandermeersch, ' "*Les mythes d'origine*" in the History of Psychiatry', in *Discovering the History of Psychiatry*, ed. Mark S. Micale and Roy Porter (New York and Oxford, 1994), 219–31, here 223.
[16] Pinel, *Traité*, 233–7.
[17] *Ibid.*, 54–7.
[18] Jacques Postel, *Genèse de la psychiatrie: Les premiers écrits psychiatriques de Philippe Pinel* (Paris, 1981), 161.
[19] See Goldstein, *Console*, 68.

effective remedy against melancholy (the comedy was, by the way, *Les Docteurs modernes*, a parody of Mesmerism: apparently, the interest of curers in the theatre was reciprocated).[20] Finally, in a seminal public speech of 1794, Pinel would describe – with a term central to contemporary theories of theatre – the emotion aroused by the sight of the insane as a tender *intérêt*.[21]

In a more specific sense, historians of psychiatry have underlined the theatrical component in Pinel's therapeutic techniques, a component particularly apparent in the case of the staged trial.[22] Yet, in calling these techniques 'theatrical', we use the term with its modern meaning, quite opposite to that found in several writers of Pinel's time. According to Michael Fried's famous thesis, in the 1750s French art and aesthetics start moving away from 'theatricality' – a dimension in which the figures acknowledge the presence of, and clearly act for, the beholder.[23] (It is in this sense that Diderot frequently makes a deprecatory use of such terms as *théâtre*, *théâtral* – meaning 'mannered', 'false' – in relationship to this consciousness of being beheld.) Again, according to Fried, the new, 'de-theatricalised' dimension involves one of two techniques:

(a) denying the presence of the beholder, establishing the fiction of his/her nonexistence (the figures of the painting are so fully absorbed in their activity that it is impossible to 'distract' them);

(b) establishing the fiction of the beholder's physical presence in the painting (by drawing her or him inside the work).

The aim is, in both cases, that of *eliminating* the beholder from in front of the work, often with the side-effect of creating a higher degree of illusion and a stronger emotional impact. And indeed, Diderot's contemporaries were literally moved to tears by works such as those by the celebrated painter Jean-Baptiste Greuze; both Diderot and Mathon de la Cour described their desire to console the figure portrayed in Greuze's *Jeune Fille qui pleure son oiseau mort* (*Girl Mourning Her Dead Bird*, 1765), a desire made all the more painful by the weeping girl's refusal to acknowledge their presence.[24]

In the 1750s, Diderot explicitly articulated a similar theory for the theatrical stage: playwrights and actors should ignore the audience; they should write and act as

---

[20] Indeed, Sébastien Mercier – an influential playwright and theoretician of the new bourgeois drama – had planned as early as 1773 to bring Bicêtre (the Parisian hospital for 'incurable' madmen) on stage. Louis-Sébastien Mercier, *Du Théâtre, ou Nouvel Essai sur l'art dramatique* (Amsterdam: Harrevelt, 1773), 136. On Marsollier's early interest in psychiatry, see below.

[21] Philippe Pinel, 'Observations sur la manie pour servir l'Histoire naturelle de l'Homme' (1794), in Postel, *Genèse*, 233–48, here 234. Engl. transl. in Dora B. Weiner, 'Philippe Pinel's "Memoir on Madness" of 11 December 1794: A Fundamental Text of Modern Psychiatry', *The American Journal of Psychiatry*, 149/6 (June 1992), 725–32. Here, as in many eighteenth-century texts, 'interest' is to be understood in a broad sense, including an element of emotional involvement and empathy: an investment beyond the simply intellectual.

[22] Goldstein, *Console*, 84–5.

[23] Michael Fried, *Absorption and Theatricality: Painting and Beholder in the Age of Diderot* (Berkeley, 1980; rpt. Chicago, 1988, to which my page numbers refer).

[24] Fried, *Absorption*, 57–9.

though spectators did not exist.[25] More generally, the separation between stage and audience – the importance of absorption in the actor, of involvement and illusion in the spectator – is central to theatrical changes in the second half of the eighteenth century (as it is to subsequent theatrical developments).[26] Marmontel and Grétry would later contrive a most impressive operatic representation of such ideas. In their *comédie-ballet*, *Zémire et Azor* (1771), Azor (the Beast) shows Zémire (Beauty) a 'magic picture' that allows her to see her father and sisters at home, in despair over her disappearance – the 'canvas' was a gauze curtain, beyond which one could see the three actors singing on a stage within the stage (see Fig. 2):

AZOR: [. . .] si vous approchez, tout va s'évanouir.
ZEMIRE: [. . .] Si du moins il pouvoit m'entendre!
AZOR: Cela n'est pas possible.
[. . .]
ZEMIRE (*se précipitant vers le Tableau*): Ah, mon père! (*Tout disparoit*).
ZEMIRE (*à Azor*): Ah, cruel!
AZOR: Je vous l'avois prédit;
   Vous même avez détruit le charme.[27]

[AZOR: If you get close, everything will vanish. ZEMIRE: If [my father] could at least hear me! AZOR: That is not possible. ZEMIRE (*rushing towards the picture*): Ah, father! (*Everything disappears.*) ZEMIRE (*to Azor*): Ah, cruel one! AZOR: I had forewarned you; you destroyed the enchantment yourself.]

The scene displays the link between spectatorial exclusion and emotional involvement: the magic picture (a 'television' in the root sense) has such a painful effect on Zémire because she cannot reach the figures, be perceived by them, console them. While embodying a conception of the visual arts, the scene works as a pedagogy of the theatre: the ideal stage–spectator relationship is encapsulated within the play (a device not unusual at the time) by the relationship between the magic picture and Zémire.

Pinel's sense of spectatorial impotence in front of his insane friend's tragedy ('I was reduced to the role of spectator') resonates with the same, 'anti-theatrical' conception of theatre, and recalls Fried's first technique (cutting off the spectator). Pinel's 'psychodrama' (the staged trial), on the other hand, is somewhat analogous to Fried's second procedure: the spectator (the patient) is drawn inside the representation (the 'trial'), unaware of its fictive nature.

As for Nina, her state of absorption is evident from her first appearance on stage; indeed, it is underlined right before her entrance, when Elise informs the Count:

---

[25] 'Soit donc que vous composiez, soit que vous jouiez, ne pensez non plus au spectateur que s'il n'existait pas.' Denis Diderot, 'De la Poésie dramatique' (1758), in *Diderot: Le drame bourgeois: Fiction II*, J. Chouillet, A.-M. Chouillet, eds., vol. X of Diderot, *Œuvres complètes* (Paris, 1980), 373.

[26] See Daniel Heartz, 'From Garrick to Gluck: The Reform of Theatre and Opera in the Mid-Eighteenth Century', *Proceedings of the Royal Musical Association*, 94 (1967–68), 111–27; and James H. Johnson, *Listening in Paris: A Cultural History* (Berkeley, 1995).

[27] Jean-François Marmontel, *Zémire et Azor*, Act III scenes 5–7. See *Collection complète des œuvres de Grétry. Publiée par le Gouvernement belge*, XIII (Leipzig: Breitkopf & Härtel, n. d.), xx–xxi.

Fig. 2 The 'magic picture' in Marmontel's and Grétry's *Zémire et Azor*, engraving by Pierre-Charles Ingouf

Elle vient, la tête penchée, l'œil fixe, son bouquet à la main; elle cherche à être seule [. . .] *NINA, entre; ses cheveux sont sans poudre, bouclés au hasard; elle est vêtue d'une robe blanche; elle tient un bouquet à la main; sa marche est inégale; elle s'arrête, elle soupire, & va s'asseoir, en silence, sur le banc, le visage tourné vers la grille.*[28]

[She is coming here, with her head falling on her chest, her eyes enraptured, her bunch of flowers in hand; she is seeking solitude [. . .] *NINA enters; her hair is unpowdered, curled in a*

[28] Marsollier, *Nina*, scenes 5–6.

casual manner; she wears a white dress, and keeps a bunch of flowers in her hand. Her step is uneven; she stops, sighs, and goes to sit, silently, on the bench, staring out of the gate.]

Nina's disordered state is a clear sign of her forgetfulness of the surroundings (there are at this point spectators both among the play's characters and, obviously, in the audience). In their theories of drama, both Diderot and Mercier had claimed, against the rules of *décence*, that the attire of a desperate woman on stage should be consistent with her inner discomposure;[29] and Mathon de la Cour's comment on Greuze's weeping girl may also apply to Nina: 'The appearance of her dress no longer concerns her; she is preoccupied only by her sorrow'.[30] The greatest English actor of the time, David Garrick, must have been a master of such effects: a German traveller's report on Garrick's *Hamlet* reveals the clear correspondence between the involvement of the spectators, 'quiet' and 'motionless' in a darkened theatre, and the actor's signs of self-absorption and exclusion of the audience (Garrick 'turns his back on the audience', 'his hat falls to the ground', his eyes are 'fixed on the ghost', his 'hair disordered').[31]

The shock experienced by a spectator of the Parisian première of *Nina* has to do, again, with aspects of absorption and illusion (the spectator in question is the playwright Carlo Goldoni):

Madame *du Gazon* ... rendit avec tant d'art, et avec tant de vérité le rôle extraordinaire de *Nina*, qu'on a cru voir une nouvelle Actrice, ou, pour mieux dire, on a cru voir la malheureuse créature dont elle représentoit le personnage et imitoit les délires.[32]

[Madam de Gazon ... displayed such skill and truth in the extraordinary part of Nina, that we imagined we beheld a new actress, or rather the unfortunate wretch whose character and ravings she imitated.]

Goldoni's impression is remarkably similar to Baculard d'Arnaud's comment on Richardson's novels ('c'est l'original même qui est sous nos yeux, dans ses immortels écrits, & non la représentation' [his immortal writings put the original itself under our very eyes, and not its representation]),[33] or to the feeling described by Diderot in the 'Entretiens sur *Le Fils naturel*':

La représentation en avait été si vraie, qu'oubliant en plusieurs endroits que j'étais spectateur, et spectateur ignoré, j'avais été sur le point de sortir de ma place, et d'ajouter un personnage réel à la scène.[34]

[The performance had been so true, that forgetting at several points that I was a spectator, and an ignored one, I had been on the point of leaving my place and adding a real character to the scene.]

---

[29] Denis Diderot, 'Entretiens sur *Le Fils naturel*' (1757), in *Diderot: Le drame bourgeois*, 83–162, here 93. Mercier, *Du Théâtre*, 371.
[30] Fried, *Absorption*, 57.
[31] See the passage by G. C. Lichtenberg, quoted in E. J. Clery, *The Rise of Supernatural Fiction, 1762–1800* (Cambridge, 1995), 38–9.
[32] Carlo Goldoni, *Mémoirs* (Paris, 1787), Troisième Partie, chapter 39. The English translation is by John Black in *Memoirs of Goldoni* (London: Colburn, 1814), II, 333–4.
[33] Arnaud, 'La Nouvelle Clémentine', 50n.
[34] Diderot, 'Entretiens', 83–4.

Even more surprising to modern ears are reports about Paisiello's *Nina*. In a Neapolitan production of the opera, spectators screamed at the protagonist on stage in the vain attempt to console her, actions that call to mind the drive to console experienced by critics of Greuze's paintings.[35] In the finale of the opera, Nina's absorptive state is instrumental to the 'psychodramatic' situation: she is drawn inside the scene staged for her by the other characters, to the point of believing it true and regaining thereby her sanity. (Indeed, Nina lives happily thereafter within the delusion that her traumatic past never existed.)

If the libretto of *Nina* suggests Marsollier's awareness of contemporary psychiatric ideas and practices, an earlier text of his confirms such a link. As early as 1782, Marsollier had written for the Comédie Italienne *Le Vaporeux*, a play entirely devoted to staging the mental illness and recovery of its protagonist.[36] Aside from its largely comic tone, *Le Vaporeux* shows Marsollier's interest in early psychiatry, and rehearses some of the themes later found in *Nina*: most notably, the drama displays a 'moral' therapy effected through a *theatrically set* shock of the imagination, and contains explicit theoretical statements about it. M. de St Phar, the protagonist, is afflicted with 'vapours' (a rather general term, akin to *hypochondria*, or twentieth-century *depression*); he withdraws to his *château* in the countryside, where he seems to plan suicide. As in *Nina*, there is no physician on stage, only a character who fulfils a therapeutic function. Here, it is the vapourish man's close friend Blainville who seems best informed: he introduces the technical term *vapeurs*, explaining how they can have 'moral' causes, and how they are afflicting half of Europe;[37] he gets information about the conditions and habits of St Phar from a servant (the gardener); he devises the 'psychodrama' that will eventually rescue his friend. Since St Phar's imagination is still lively and responsive, there is hope for his recovery. Blainville asks St Phar's wife to 'play the part' ('jouer le rôle') of a deranged woman: she must pretend that she has gone insane from despair of ever regaining her husband, and that she wants to take her life. When Madame de St Phar 'enters the stage' for her husband, she shows an apt mixture of self-absorption and discomposure (with an 'absent and preoccupied look' and 'somewhat disordered hair').[38] In the ensuing dialogue between the two, St Phar tries to restore his wife's interest in life: he may believe he is 'treating' her with a moral cure; in fact she is

---

[35] Francesco Florimo, *La scuola musicale di Napoli*, II (Naples, 1882), 268. Florimo mentions the singer Celeste Coltellini and the Teatro di San Carlo. The report in question most probably refers to the 1790 revival at another Neapolitan theatre, the Teatro dei Fiorentini (where Coltellini sang); *Nina* was not produced at the San Carlo until 1820. See *Il Teatro di San Carlo. La Cronologia 1737–1987*, ed. Carlo Marinelli Roscioni (Naples, 1987). Coltellini was praised for her gifts, more exceptional in acting than in singing: 'nella *Nina*, poi, mi fu detto ch'era sublime, che faceva piangere e che toglieva quasi il respiro a chi l'ascoltava e la vedeva': G. G. Ferrari, quoted in 'Coltellini, Celeste', *Enciclopedia dello spettacolo*, III (Rome, 1956). On such 'literal' interpretations of the stage, see also Clery, *The Rise of Supernatural Fiction*, 40–1.

[36] *Le Vaporeux, comédie en deux actes et en prose, par M. M[arsollier] D[es Vivetières], Représentée pour la première fois par les Comédiens Italiens ordinaires du Roi, le 3 Mai 1782* (Toulouse: Broulhiet, 1784).

[37] Marsollier, *Le Vaporeux*, Act I scene 2.

[38] Ibid., Act II scene 6.

treating him with a 'psychodramatic' technique not dissimilar to that later described by Pinel. Predictably, there is little doubt as to the faculty that made St Phar's healing possible: 'un instant de sensibilité a plus fait que tous les arguments de la raison' (a moment of sensitivity did more than all of reason's arguments).[39]

In a general sense, Pinel seems to have learned many of his rhetorical devices, lexicon and ideology from extra-medical sources. More than the systematic exposition of a theory, his *Traité* is a chain of anecdotes, of allegedly real stories meant to function as *exempla* (and the reason for this procedure is expressed, again, in terms of a sentimental ideology: general propositions may be true and fruitful, but 'in order to *feel* them vividly, one needs examples').[40] Pinel's *Histoires* show a literary nature and a degree of human sympathy apparently unique in contemporary medicine.[41] With its insistence on extremes of sensitivity, with its touching scenes of domestic and familial misfortunes peopled by tender fathers and unfortunate lovers, by youngsters who die in war or commit suicide, Pinel's treatise bears more than a passing resemblance to much literature of his age, and may constitute as good a survey of eighteenth-century sentimental themes as Baculard d'Arnaud's *Délassements de l'homme sensible*.

In particular, it is tempting to suggest that Pinel may have derived his idea of 'psychodrama' from the stage – and most notably from *Nina*, an opera that was triumphing in the same city and year in which he started experimenting with the moral therapy. It may instead seem more likely that playwrights such as Marsollier took over the idea from contemporary medical experiments; and, of course, a strict question of paternity does not make much sense here: the idea and the practice were generally emerging in those years, and the story I am trying to tell allows us to catch a glimpse of the interaction between theatrical and medical practices in such a formation. But it is possible to suggest that the 'psychodramatic' therapy of mind curers would not have been quite thinkable without the conditions created by a new, 'anti-theatrical' culture of representation; and that the emergence, effectiveness and credibility of the therapy may well have been reinforced by the presence of such a powerful and lasting cultural icon as that provided by the story of Nina.[42]

To listen for the sentiment

The experience of *sensibilité* seems to have a fragmentary and incomplete quality, reflected in the tendency to fragmentation and incompleteness within sentimental texts. The person overwhelmed with emotion is often incapable of continuous

---

[39] *Ibid.*, Act II scene 9.
[40] Pinel, *Traité*, 100 (italics mine).
[41] 'No physician had yet written case histories as sympathetic and eloquent', Weiner, 'Philippe Pinel's "Memoir"', 727.
[42] It is perhaps not without meaning that such an archetype exerted some influence for almost a century. The acknowledged master of nineteenth-century sentimental literature in Italian, Edmondo De Amicis (1846–1908), wrote a short story about a woman who goes insane when her beloved marries someone else – and is cured through a final 'psychodrama' in which her traumatic past is re-enacted with a positive turn; see Edmondo De Amicis, 'Carmela', in *La vita militare* (1868).

discourse; the amount of the unspoken (interrupted speech, silence, bodily signs) unveils the communicative limits of verbal and rational language. Aside from the direct verbal description of tears, blushes and swoons, sentimental literature exploits a whole set of devices in order to stress the emotional inadequacy of words: interrupted phrases, broken syntax, repetition, typographical exuberance (ellipses, dashes, exclamation points, italics). This is a way to address *within* the only means available to literature – written language – the limits of language itself, while at the same time alluding to physical gestures (the silences built within the text may well be filled by gasps, sighs, etc.).

Theatre is, of course, an ideal venue for the expansion of such techniques: here, the tension between organised prose and physical gesture can be rendered much more explicit by the bodily presence of the actor (a presence that could, as we saw, inflame the audience).[43] The theatrical text will open extra-verbal dimensions not only through the literary devices described above, but also through stage directions (and, in the case of opera, through music). In this regard, the translator's foreword in the libretto for the first Italian *Nina* (Monza, 1788) deserves to be quoted at some length:

Qui tutto è natura, semplicità, e sentimento. Una bennata, ed ingenua Fanciulla, cui rapito venendo d'improvviso il legittimo amante perde l'uso della ragione, e lo riacquista riacquistando l'amante, forma tutto il soggetto della presente Commedia di nodo, se pur ve n'ha uno, semplicissimo, ma di una finezza poi senza pari; tutto è interessante nella Nina, un volger d'occhio, un gesto, una parola tronca può importar molto; perciò è brevissima, non si potendo per lungo tempo sperare nelle numerose adunanze quella attenzione scrupolosa, che è tanto necessaria a simil sorta di rappresentazioni.

[Here all is nature, simplicity and sentiment. A well-born and ingenuous maiden who – being suddenly bereft of her legitimate lover – loses her reason, then to regain it when she regains the lover, constitutes the whole subject of the present comedy; a comedy with a plot, if any, most simple – yet of a refinement without equal. Everything is significant in *Nina*: a glance, a gesture, a truncated word can be of the utmost importance; and the work is so brief because one cannot hope to obtain from large audiences that scrupulous attention so needed with this kind of play.]

The passage shows, again, the relationship between the simplicity of the plot and the richness of emotional detail: noteworthy are the emphasis on minimal gestures and truncated words, and the need for attentive behaviour in the audience. Predictably, the text of *Nina* is filled with physical symptoms of sensitivity (tears, sighs, etc., are mentioned and discussed in the lines for the characters, or prescribed in the stage directions) and with stylistic markers of the sentimental mode (fragmented discourse, typographical exuberance). In addition, Paisiello's music contributes in several ways to second and enhance those aspects of the text.

---

[43] On the 'ungrammatical' breaches in David Garrick's delivery, and their relationship to gestural expressiveness, see Laurence Sterne, *The Life and Opinions of Tristram Shandy, Gentleman*, vol. III, chapter 12, and its discussion in John Mullan, *Sentiment and Sociability: The Language of Feeling in the Eighteenth Century* (Oxford, 1988), 174–5.

The first quatrain for the entrance aria of the Count, for instance, contains none of the typographical excesses often found in conjunction with outbursts of sentiment; yet it invites them by virtue of its content:

> È sì fiero il mio tormento,
> È sì grave il mal ch'io provo,
> Che m'aggiro incerto, e movo,
> Né so dove, né perché.

[My torments are so fierce, my sorrows so grave, that I wander uncertain, and move knowing neither where, nor why.]

The opening of Paisiello's setting (see Ex. 1) conveys, with its short-breathed phrases, and the nervous line in the violins, the agitation of the text; more impressively, well-placed rests open gaps even *inside* the words ('fie-ro', 'gra-ve') from the very first two lines. Thus, the phrase the audience hears could be written as:

> È sì fie ... ro il mio tormento,
> È sì gra ... ve il mal ch'io provo,
> Che ... m'aggiro ... incerto, e movo,
> Né ... so dove, né ... perché.

Similar markers of a sentimental mode can be found at various levels of verbal and musical organisation in Paisiello's *Nina*. An example is 'Lontana da te' (for Nina and chorus), No. 7 of the opera. The day before, Nina taught the women of the village a song of her own invention, which she had wanted them to sing for Lindoro (Germeuil) on his return. But she has since forgotten the song entirely. In No. 7, the women teach the song back to Nina; she, in turn, shows them how to sing it, thus starting to remould the piece. While doing so, '*Nina, riscaldandosele la mente, segue da se sola, dando in un delirio*' (Nina, as her mind gets heated, goes on by herself, falling into a delirium):[44] the maid believes she sees Lindoro and talks to him; when the apparition vanishes, Nina desperately invokes Heaven (in Marsollier's libretto this entire section was set apart by the title 'Délire').

One could then say that Paisiello's No. 7 contains, one inside the other, the song 'per se' (what Nina taught the women the day before, or what they remember of it) and its 'performance'. The latter, No. 7 proper, includes two operations on the song: Nina's improvised singing lesson, and her equally unforeseen delirious interruption. Both operations are revealing in terms of the kind of musical language Nina introduces.

In the 'lesson', the women sing the first strophe (see Ex. 2). Nina asks them to sing with 'più d'espressione' ('*plus tendrement*' in Marsollier's stage direction), which she then proceeds to demonstrate (see Ex. 3). In a similar way, the second strophe is sung by the women first, and then by Nina. The peasants finally sing both strophes in the version they have just learned from Nina. What the women on stage, and presumably

---

[44] Scene 8.

Ex. 1 Aria 'È sì fiero il mio tormento' (Conte)

the people in the audience, have learned here may well be called a lesson in the style of *sensibilité*. Nina has added to the song some expressive touches (the tritone-appoggiatura at bar 20, the flattened second scale degree at bar 23) and, most tellingly, several of the interruptions that signal a broken discourse: the deep sigh (a fermata on a rest in all parts) before the pathetic Neapolitan inflection of bar 23, the gasps starting within the very first word (added rests at bar 17). Thus, with a technique similar to what we noted in the Count's aria, the 'Lontana da te' (sung legato by the women in their first statement) results in Nina's version as 'Lonta . . . na . . . da te'.

Following the turns of the text, the setting of the delirium gradually enters a series of disjointed passages alternating very different textures, and also including material from the initial song. At the peak of her distraction, Nina forsakes even higher levels of musical syntax: in the conclusion of the piece, the music of what began as a simple song dissolves into recitative (see Ex. 4), and then into spoken dialogue. In fact, the 'lesson' and the delirium of No. 7 show the continuity between the manifestations of sensitivity and those of folly.

The agitation excited in eighteenth-century audiences by scene 6 – which includes No. 5, Nina's famous entrance aria 'Il mio ben quando verrà' – is hardly understandable in our time (this is the scene, mentioned above, that drove Neapolitan spectators to scream at the protagonist). Nina does not appear on stage until this scene; and yet, given the opera's exclusive focus on the title role, her entrance is prepared by the emotional crescendo of all the preceding scenes, in which the sorry state of the maid is variously described and lamented. Nina's

Ex. 2 'Lontana da te' (Nina, Chorus). Translation: Away from you, her beloved Lindoro, Nina pined with love.

opening monologue introduces her through a textbook example of the extreme sentimental style; if the literary devices (dots, exclamation points, repetitions) usually allude to gestures, in a text for the theatre they must have worked as stage directions for the actress:

NINA: È questa l'ora in cui deve arrivare ... sì ... verrà ... oggi ... stasera ... certo. Me l'ha promesso. E dove potrebbe star meglio di qui? Vicino a lei che ama, e da cui è sì teneramente riamato? ... Questi fiori ... per lui ... Questo cuore ... per lui ... (*Vede passare per la strada un pastore, e credendo che sia il suo Lindoro, corre al cancello.*) E non viene! Che giornate lunghe! ... Oggi la natura è più trista dell'usato ... Io non esisto più ... No. Allora solo riviverò, che gli sarò vicina. (*Come sopra.*) E ancor non viene! ... Glielo impedissero mai? ... Chi? ... Essi! i scellerati ... Ah! come mi sento male! ... Qui ... da per tutto ... Ma se Lindoro, se Lindoro giungesse, come tutto anderebbe felicemente.

[NINA: This is the time he should arrive ... yes ... he will come ... today ... this evening ... certainly. He promised. After all, where could he feel better than here, close to the one

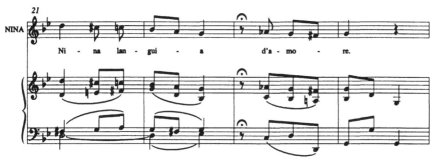

Ex. 3 'Lontana da te'

he loves, and who loves him so tenderly? ... These flowers ... for him ... This heart ... for him ... (*She sees a shepherd passing on the road, and, believing him to be her Lindoro, runs to the gate.*) And he does not come! What long days! ... Today nature is sadder than usual ... I do not exist any longer ... No. Only then will I live again, when I am close to him. (*Again as above.*) And still he does not come! ... Are they perhaps keeping him? ... Who? ... They! The scoundrels ... Ah! how ill I feel! ... Here ... everywhere ... Yet if Lindoro, if Lindoro were to come, how happily would everything go.]

The emotional impact of the subsequent aria is due, no less than to this preparation, to the inner functioning of the piece. The aria opens as a strophic song with a regular phrase structure, which undergoes a striking process of verbal and musical dissolution. As with No. 7, we may again detect in No. 5 two levels: the three-stanza strophic song with its hopeful text and its 'performance', interrupted by Nina's vain attempts to see and hear her beloved and eventually drowning in disillusion. The text for the aria already hints at such distinction (I have isolated the 'interruptions' from what I see as the three strophes of the song 'proper' by indentation – and italics in the translation):

> Il mio ben quando verrà,
> A veder la mesta amica,
> Di bei fior s'ammanterà
> La spiaggia aprica.

Ex. 4 'Lontana da te', concluding section. Translation: If only I could see him once more ... for one day ... one hour ... and tell him: 'I love you ... Lindoro ever reigned here, triumphing over everything ...' Then let my destiny be fulfilled, let Nina die. (*She collapses into the arms of the peasant women.*)

> Ma nol vedo . . .
> Ma sospiro . . .
> E il mio ben,
> Ahimè, non vien!
> Mentre all'aure spiegherà
> La sua fiamma, i suoi lamenti,
> Mille, o augei, v'insegnerà
> Più dolci accenti.
> Ma non l'odo!
> E chi l'udì?
> Ah! il mio bene
> Ammutolì.
> Tu, cui stanca omai già fè
> Il mio pianto, Eco pietosa,
> Ei ritorna, e dolce a te
> Chiede la sposa!
> Pian . . . mi chiama . . .
> Piano . . . ohimè!
> Non mi chiama:
> Oh Dio! non c'è.

[When my beloved comes to see his disconsolate friend, the sunny land will be clothed with lovely flowers. *Yet I do not see him . . . And I sigh . . . And my beloved, alas, does not come!* As he unfurls to the breezes his ardour and his woe, he will teach you birds a thousand sweeter sounds. *Yet I do not hear him! And who did hear him? Ah! My beloved fell silent.* You, merciful Echo, wearied by my plaint, he will come back and sweetly ask you to be his bride! *Softly . . . he calls me . . . softly . . . alas! No . . . he does not call: oh God! he is not there.*]

In the final interruption, the future of Nina's wishes is overwhelmed by the hopeless present of her reality. Paisiello set it into a concluding passage of over fifty bars (97–150) through the obsessive repetition of its words and of fragments from the earlier interruptions:

Pian . . . mi chiama . . . piano . . ahimè! piano . . . ahimè! No . . . non mi chiama: oh Dio! oh Dio! non c'è. Pian . . . mi chiama . . . piano . . ahimè! piano . . ahimè! No . . . non mi chiama: oh Dio! oh Dio! non c'è. Ma nol vedo . . . ma sospiro . . . ahimè, non vien! no . . . ahimè, ahimè, non vien! Ah! ammutolì . . . Ah! . . . Ah! . . . ammutolì! . . . Oh Dio! Non c'è . . . No . . . oh Dio! oh Dio! . . . non c'è.

The text repetition in the passage is not as unusual in degree (much text repetition is found, for instance, in opera seria arias) as it is in kind: the practice is not explicable here in terms of conventional musical needs such as virtuosic vocal display or phraseological-formal construction.

Nina's vocal manner here is equally fragmented, and she eventually manages to interrupt any melodic flow in the orchestra as well: the impressive ending of the piece (bars 128–45) is an exhausting passage in which voice and instruments proceed by quasi-pointillistic gestures (see Ex. 5). The situation, though unusual, is not as unstructured as it might seem: this last page is made up of three statements of the same material (bars 129–34, 135–40, 141–6) that echo the main melody of

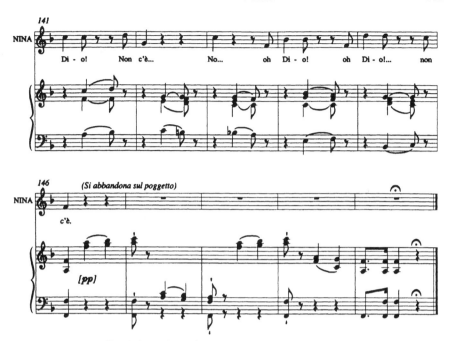

Ex. 5 Aria 'Il mio ben', concluding section (Nina)

Nina's song. In her distraction, Nina is using and reiterating in a free manner materials, musical and poetic, from earlier in the piece.

It is important to stress that we have, once again, gone far beyond simple matters of declamation or text delivery: if the song 'Lontana de te' dissolved into recitative and spoken dialogue, in the final page of 'Il mio ben' the strophic aria is shattered. Such unusual procedures seem to question the formal status of these pieces as closed numbers: spectators accustomed to the conventions of Italian opera could not miss this 'inappropriate' behaviour of Nina on stage as a sign of the character's distraction and obliviousness to the surroundings – the correlate at the level of musical form of such signs of absorption as her dishevelled and unpowdered hair.

The disturbing conclusion of 'Il mio ben' is hardly comprehensible in 'purely' musical terms, just as it is inexplicable in terms of eighteenth-century operatic conventions (not by chance has the page been excised in so many performances of the aria).[45] Yet we can begin to understand the rapture of eighteenth-century audiences by placing this piece in the textual and performative context of *Nina*, and

---

[45] Bars 120–45 are absent in the first volume of Alessandro Parisotti's *Arie antiche* (Milan, 1885 and ever after), where the aria is refashioned as a conservatory or salon piece. This may be the main reason the passage has been so often expunged in recent performances (and in all four recordings I know), even when the aria is sung as part of the entire opera. Similar cuts can be documented in earlier editions of the piece, starting in the late eighteenth century.

by setting the opera against the broader background of European sentimental culture. Analogously, the pathetic elements and theatrical gestures contained (or alluded to) in *Nina*'s text may help explain the success of a prima–donna opera with no grand vocal display: in this context – as the 1788 preface suggests – a performer's greatness could be manifest in realms other than that of vocal virtuosity (in 1811 Paisiello would congratulate the celebrated singer Isabella Colbran for her unadorned performance of this part).[46]

The question, then, is of the extent to which we can understand the success of eighteenth-century sentimental operas without some degree of empathy, or at least without trying to develop a critical ear for them – an ear sensitive to the realm of meanings, practices and stylemes of a sentimental mode. Samuel Johnson had warned that Richardson should not be read 'for the story', but 'for the sentiment';[47] in a similar way, to listen 'for the melody' in *Nina* is a way to forget that this work presupposes cultural references and invites spectatorial attitudes that may be lost for us.

---

[46] See Broussard, 'Prefazione', in Paisiello, *Nina*, v–vi.

[47] 'Why, Sir, if you were to read Richardson for the story, your impatience would be so much fretted that you would hang yourself. But you must read him for the sentiment, and consider the story as only giving occasion to the sentiment.' James Boswell, *Life of Johnson*, ed. G. B. Hill, rev. L. F. Powell (Oxford, 1934–64), II, 175.

[12]

L'arbore di Diana: a model for *Così fan tutte*

DOROTHEA LINK

REPEATED attempts at finding a literary model for *Così fan tutte* have so far produced not a single source but several plausible ones, each of which lends a component to Da Ponte's libretto. The wager theme, the Ovidian tale of Cephalus and Procris and the quartet of mismatched lovers have been traced to a number of other works.[1] I should like to add yet another source to this list by pointing out the kinship of *Così fan tutte* with an earlier Da Ponte libretto, *L'arbore di Diana* ('The Tree of Diana'),[2] and further to demonstrate that both librettos follow the conventions of the pastoral drama.[3] The pastoral element in *Così* has been noted before,[4] but, to my knowledge, no-one has explored the idea in any depth, or considered it in the context of Da Ponte's oeuvre.

When he began his career as librettist in Vienna in 1783, Lorenzo da Ponte relied for models on existing librettos and plays. The play from which in 1786 he fashioned his sixth libretto, *Una cosa rara*, for Vicente Martín y Soler, contains a large pastoral scene.[5] Da Ponte recognized in the pastoral mode the perfect vehicle for Martín's lyrical style and

---

[1] A. Steptoe, 'The Sources of "Così fan tutte": a Reappraisal', *Music & Letters*, lxii (1981), 281–94; J. Stone, 'The Background to the Libretto', *Così fan tutte*, ed. N. John (London, 1983), 33–45; D. Heartz, *Mozart's Operas*, ed., with contributing essays, by T. Bauman (Berkeley and Los Angeles, 1990).

[2] Steptoe briefly compares the librettos of *L'arbore di Diana* and *Così* in *The Mozart–Da Ponte Operas* (Oxford, 1988), 123.

[3] The pastoral, not well known as a genre, dropped out of fashion at the beginning of the 19th century and has only recently been rediscovered by modern scholarship: 'The revival of scholarly interest in the pastoral really began in the late 1950s', according to R. Poggioli, *The Oaten Flute: Essays on Pastoral Poetry and the Pastoral Ideal* (Cambridge, MA, 1975), 315. The most significant scholarly work on the pastoral in music is E. Harris, *Handel and the Pastoral Tradition* (London, 1980).

[4] P. Smith, *The Tenth Muse* (New York, 1970), 175, calls the opera 'a light divertissement with strong pastoral overtones'. T. Carter, 'Da Ponte, Lorenzo', *The New Grove Dictionary of Opera*, ed. S. Sadie (London, 1992), observes 'Da Ponte clearly places the drama in the time-honoured tradition of the pastoral' (i, 1075), while G. Chew, 'Pastoral', ibid., considers *Così* a parody of the pastoral: 'Of later 18th-century parodies, this time of the traditional Italian Platonic love pastoral, Lorenzo da Ponte's libretto for Mozart's opera *Così fan tutte* (1790) particularly deserves mention' (iii, 912).

[5] *La luna della Sierra*, by L. Vélez de Guevara, from after 1614; the author juxtaposes several dramatic modes, including the historical, the farcical and the pastoral. Da Ponte attenuates the first two and makes the pastoral predominant in his libretto.

accordingly cast the entire libretto in a pastoral hue. The opera was an immense success. The following year, confident of repeating that success, he provided Martín with a thoroughly typical pastoral libretto, *L'arbore di Diana*.[6] Nothing illustrates his confidence better than the fact that this was his first original libretto. He was proud of it, referring to it in his memoirs as 'the best of all the operas I ever composed'.[7] Adaptations of two further pastoral librettos followed: *Il pastor fido* for Salieri in February 1789 and *La cifra*, also for Salieri, in December that year. Hard on the heels of *La cifra* came *Così fan tutte*, to all appearances Da Ponte's second original libretto.

In *L'arbore di Diana*, Diana, the goddess of chastity, lives with her three nymphs on a beautiful island. She regularly tests their chastity by having them pass beneath a magic apple tree which either emits exquisite sound, for the virtuous, or drops black apples, on the guilty. Amore (or Cupid), incensed by this invention, undertakes to make Diana fall in love. He enters her garden in the form of a shepherdess, engages three youths to seduce the nymphs, gives Endimione one of his magic arrows with which to wound Diana, and frustrates Diana's rule at every turn. The raging Diana repeatedly tries to drive out the intruders but eventually yields to Endimione, whereupon Amore dissolves her realm and establishes a garden of love.

The parallels with *Così* are not hard to find. Both stories deal with the seduction of women, willing in the case of the nymphs and Dorabella and unwilling in the case of Diana and Fiordiligi. Both use the same dramatic structure. The respective first acts open with the formulation of the plan (in *L'arbore di Diana* it occurs offstage in the libretto's prologue, in *Così* it takes place in the initial scene) and end with its first significant advance (Endimione nicks Diana with the arrow, Ferrando and Guglielmo elicit sympathy from Fiordiligi and Dorabella). The climax in each drama occurs in Act 2 where Diana and Fiordiligi capitulate to their lovers. The dénouement in each involves the resolution of the impasse by the instigator of the trouble, Amore in the first case, Alfonso in the second. Finally, the central pair of lovers in both librettos (Diana and Endimione, Fiordiligi and Ferrando) are identical dramatic-vocal types. Diana is bound by her vow of chastity, Fiordiligi by her vow of fidelity. Both assert their steadfastness in a virtuoso aria in Act 1, express remorse or renunciation in a two-part rondò in Act 2[8] and give in to their lovers in duets close by the rondòs. Both Endimione and Ferrando are ardent, pleading lovers. (That the lovers in both operas had the same personae would have been obvious to the Viennese, for Adriana Ferrarese and Vincenzo Calvesi played Diana and Endimione respectively before being cast as Fiordiligi and Ferrando.)[9]

---

[6] First given on 1 Oct 1787, this was the most frequently performed Italian opera of the 75 produced in the court opera house from 1783 to 1792. Its success repeated that of *Una cosa rara* in 1786 (which Mozart acknowledged with a quotation from that opera in *Don Giovanni*). See D. Link, *The Da Ponte Operas of Vicente Martín y Soler* (diss., U. of Toronto, 1991).

[7] *Memoirs of Lorenzo da Ponte*, ed. A. Livingston, trans. E. Abbott (Philadelphia, 1929), 177–8.

[8] The two-part rondò in Act 2, however, is common to many operas of the period. See J. A. Rice, *Emperor and Impresario: Leopold II and the Transformation of Viennese Musical Theater, 1790–1792* (diss., U. of California, Berkeley, 1987), 92ff.

[9] *L'arbore di Diana* was still playing at the time of the première of *Così* on 26 Jan 1790. The season's

The similarities between the plots are reinforced by the pastoral features that they have in common. The pastoral tradition to which Da Ponte belongs originated in late sixteenth-century Italy and continued in waves of popularity to the end of the eighteenth century. It started with the literary play, the most distinguished examples of which are Tasso's *Aminta* (1573) and Guarini's *Il pastor fido* (1590). The pastoral was soon taken up by the new *dramma per musica* to which it was especially well suited because of its lyrical nature.[10] At about the same time, the pastoral found its way into the repertory of improvised plays cultivated by the *commedia dell'arte*.[11] In all three art forms – literature, opera, improvised theatre – the pastoral took root and flourished. It is this composite tradition that Da Ponte inherited.

Although *Aminta* and *Il pastor fido* came to represent the literary pastoral, neither is typical of the genre as found in the plays contemporary with them. These, for the most part forgotten, exhibit a mixture of disparate, often contrasting elements; they contain 'magic, gods, and combinations of high style with low, clowning with idealized love'.[12] Under the influence of the Tasso and Guarini masterpieces, the motley composition of the early literary pastoral eventually disappeared from the plays but continued in opera and the *commedia dell'arte*. In the scenarios of the latter it was soon reduced to a formula, which has been described as follows: 'The three sources of dramatic interest in the pastorals of the commedia dell'arte are the love affairs of the natives of Arcadia, the power of the Magician, and the horseplay of the ship-wrecked buffoons'.[13] We may follow these three topics in *L'arbore di Diana* and *Così fan tutte*.

The first, 'the love affairs of the natives of Arcadia', contains two components, Arcadia and romantic love. The historical Arcadia was in central Greece. Its inhabitants 'were renowned for their rustic virtue, their hospitality, and primordial simplicity, as well as for their complete ignorance of what was happening in the outer world'.[14] In the literary imagination of the Ancients, Arcadia became the locus of 'unbroken sweetness and innocent freedom'.[15] Eventually, it came to stand for any rural idyll distant in time or place from

performances preceding the opening of *Così* were relatively frequent: 27 and 29 June 1789; 1, 5, 11, 21 and 31 July; 6, 12, 19, 23 and 27 Aug; 9 and 29 Sept; 30 Oct; 19 Nov; and 10 Jan 1790. Calvesi was the original Endimione; Ferrarese, not the original Diana, took over the part in Oct 1788. Another casting parallel between the two operas left a permanent trace on *Così*. Louise Villeneuve, who created Dorabella, sang Amore in *L'arbore di Diana* the same season. Dorabella's aria 'È Amore un ladroncello' is a play on Villeneuve's role of Amore. See D. Link, '*Così fan tutte*: Dorabella and Amore', *MJb 1991*, 888–94.

[10] 'The Arcadians were renowned for... their musical accomplishments; for theirs was the only land where "music was considered an indispensable thing instead of a merely desirable one", to speak in the words of the historian Polybius, Arcadia's most famous son' (E. Ponofsky, '*Et in Arcadia Ego*: on the Conception of Transience in Poussin and Watteau', *Philosophy and History: Essays Presented to Ernst Cassirer*, ed. R. Klibansky and H. J. Paton, Oxford, 1936, p. 225). 'Arcadians are the only ones who know how to sing' (Poggioli, 23).

[11] While comedies make up the bulk of scenarios, pastorals form a small but distinct category within the *commedia dell'arte* repertory. For a specimen of a pastoral scenario, see 'The Enchanted Arcadia' in G. Oreglia, *The Commedia dell'Arte*, trans. L. Edwards (London, 1968), 36. For a composite scenario assembled from several scenarios, see K. Lea, *Italian Popular Comedy* (Oxford, 1934), 201.

[12] L. G. Clubb, 'The Making of the Pastoral Play: some Italian Experiments between 1573 and 1590', *Petrarch to Pirandello*, ed. J. Molinaro (Toronto, 1973), 70.

[13] Lea, 201.   [14] Ponofsky, 225.   [15] Ibid., 231.

reality in the normal sense of the word. Its sense of unreality was heightened even further in the Renaissance courtly pastoral, in which the nobility amused itself by playing shepherd and shepherdess while retaining the comportment of its own class.[16] The courtly pastoral also brought with it mythological pageantry.[17] Hence shepherds, both the simple and the refined kinds, are equally at home in Arcadia as princes and gods.

L'arbore di Diana readily fits the convention of the pastoral both as to locale and to characters. The drama takes place in the mythological garden of Diana, located on an island, a favourite setting for Arcadia. It is inhabited by nymphs, shepherds and gods.[18] *Così fan tutte* may not appear initially to fit the prescription. The setting is urban, specifically Naples, and the characters wear contemporary dress. However, the sisters' residence exhibits Arcadia's most essential feature: it is cut off from the real world. The sisters' independence, social and financial, is a fantasy. In eighteenth-century society, as in most of history, a woman, especially of marriageable age, lived a guarded life under the strict eyes of a father, guardian, brother or aunt. Fiordiligi and Dorabella have no dealings with the mundane world but can give themselves wholly to their amatory concerns, just like Diana's lovelorn nymphs. The men's exotic attire as Albanians, which they don only in the sisters' residence, adds to the picture of unreality. The pastoral nature of the setting is made explicit when the scene shifts to the garden (the serenade, no. 21, 'Secondate aurette', the glowing lyrical centrepiece of the opera). Amid the lawns and shrubs and ornamental cupids, the men disembark from a boat and woo with song their ladies, who timidly receive them as lovers.

Next, the love affairs of the Arcadians: and indeed the Arcadians of Italian invention are preoccupied with love.[19] The courtly pastoral, for example, made the inquiry into the nature of love its favourite pastime. '[The shepherds and nymphs] held forth in various meters, singly, in duets, trios and a final octet, on love, nature, illusion, love of nature, the nature of love, the illusion of love, the nature of illusion, and so forth'.[20] This description of a play from 1581 conveys exquisitely the spirit of elegant game-playing in which the inquiry was conducted. That strain of inquiry may be recognized in *Così*; running through the opera is the unarticulated question, 'What is love?', posed in myriad ways. What is the nature of the love between the betrothed couples at the beginning of opera, and at the end? how does Fiordiligi love Guglielmo, and how does she love Ferrando? how does Dorabella's love compare with Fiordiligi's? The inquiry has been updated with an eighteenth-century

---

[16] 'The courtly pastoral is but a costumed garden party, where even the great personages of the world play for a while, if only in emblematic fashion, the conventional role of shepherd and shepherdess' (Poggioli, 23).

[17] Clubb, 67.

[18] Amore and Diana, both equipped with bow and arrow, are two common pastoral deities. E.g., Diana figures in such *commedia dell'arte* scenarios as *Diana vinta* and *L'arcadia travagliata per l'ira di Diana contro Enea*, mentioned by Lea, 205 and 209. W. Greg, *Pastoral Poetry and Pastoral Drama* (London, 1906), 185, in a discussion of the recurring figure of Amore, cites an example entitled *Amore fuggitivo*, 'in which Venus comes to seek her runaway among the ladies and gallants of the court'.

[19] 'The central vision of the Italian Renaissance idyll [is one in which] any pastoral retreat is a retreat into love, or at least into love's dream' (Poggioli, 169).

[20] Clubb, 46, of Luigi Pasqualigo's play *Gl'Intricati: pastorale* (Venice, 1581); see also p. 53.

pedagogic gloss and made into a 'School for Lovers': the schoolmaster is Alfonso, the lesson that it is dangerous to test fidelity.[21] The lesson is learnt at great price, for the restoration of the *status quo* at the end barely masks the fact that a tragedy has occurred, that of broken trust all round.[22]

By having the lovers put on a brave face and pass over the disturbing incident, Da Ponte achieves the *lieto fine*, albeit a little forced. This has a precedent in Tasso's *Aminta*, which is essentially a tragedy with a happy ending tacked on.[23] The shepherd Aminta loves Silvia, who however does not reciprocate his love. Driven to the point of suicide by his despair, he hears a false report of her death and leaps from a cliff. Silvia, on receiving this news, is overcome with grief. There the stage action ends, and the story is continued as a narrative. It is related how Aminta turned out to be miraculously unhurt, how Silvia's love awoke, and how all ended happily.[24] Similarly, if less extreme, *Così* lacks a transition from tragic to happy ending. The audience, having witnessed the gradual awakening of love in Fiordiligi, is suddenly confronted with having to accept the rightness of her returning to Guglielmo.

The Italian pastoral vision of love focusses almost exclusively on wooing or courtship.[25] Interest ends with the consummation of love and almost never extends to children or conjugal love.[26] In *Handel and the Pastoral Tradition*, Ellen Harris illustrates this with examples from the operatic repertory:

The lack of marital subjects and the concept of duty in pastoral plots may explain why the apparently similar stories of Orpheus and Euridice and Admetus and Alcestis have traditionally been treated so differently; Orpheus has become in some ways the patron saint of the pastoral whereas Admetus and Alcestis remain outside the genre. Aside from the fact that Orpheus is a shepherd and Admetus a king (in the Golden Age shepherds were kings), the story of Orpheus is about a couple in love, a sudden loss, a bereavement, and a decision to regain the initial idyllic state against all odds. It is a selfish decision. The story of Alcestis is about a married couple, illness, the needs of society, and a sacrifice.[27]

Renato Poggioli, in *The Oaten Flute*, makes the interesting observation that the Italian pastoral is a male fantasy.[28] This fantasy of irresponsible love is laced with eroticism; one has

---

[21] S. Sadie, notes to the L'Oiseau-Lyre recording of *Così fan tutte*, conducted by Arnold Östman, Drottningholm Court Theatre, 1985 (p. 16).

[22] K. Küster, *Mozart: eine musikalische Biographie* (Stuttgart, 1990), 370.

[23] 'Insofar as it may be described as a dramatic genre, *Aminta* is a tragedy. More precisely, it is a series of eclogues grouped around a single situation, leading to a simple tragic denouement, on which a happy ending is superimposed' (Clubb, 48).

[24] 'The shortness, as well as the dramatic weakness of the fifth act is conspicuous' (Greg, 183).

[25] Harris, 2.

[26] 'Strangely enough, the eclogue looks with sympathy at conjugal love only when the marriage, as well as the pair, is an old one. From this standpoint, the fable of Philemon and Baucis is so exemplary as to become an archetype. According to such an archetype, the pair must be not only old, but also childless' (Poggioli, 253).

[27] Harris, 6.

[28] 'The pastoral remains a masculine dream world even when it abandons the realm of sex' (Poggioli, 22).

only to read *Aminta* and *Il pastor fido*, and perhaps also Ariosto's *Orlando furioso*, to find the most influential examples.[29]

L'arbore di Diana displays a degree of eroticism apparent even to a twentieth-century reader, although it hardly merits the resounding condemnation it received from an anonymous Viennese gentleman: 'The play from beginning to end is nothing but an abominable patchwork of equivocations, of obscenities and of horrors ... The poet and the composer must have conceived their ideas in a brothel since the piece talks of nothing but f . . . .'.[30] While the outrage seems not to have been shared by others,[31] it may have been provoked by passages such as the following. When Diana's nymphs encounter Amore's youths, they see boys for the first time in their lives, and this conversation ensues:

BRITOMARTE   Good gracious! What snouts!
                  Pardon, chaste Diana, such beautiful animals are found in neither fields nor woods.
                  Pretty youths, come a little closer.

...

SILVIO   What do you want?
BRITOMARTE   We don't want to spend time talking. Are you fond of women?
DORISTO   Very fond.
BRITOMARTE   Then come with us. You are three, we also are three. It could not be better. Let us
                  go. While the goddess bathes, let us make love.[32]

While Britomarte could hardly have been more direct, there is a certain innocence in her manner. A child of nature, she views the strange creatures with delight and enchantment and then follows her instincts shamelessly and unselfconsciously.

Another passage occurs in the conversation between Amore, in the guise of shepherdess, and the amorous Doristo:

AMORE   Roguish eye. What did you mean to tell me as you kissed my hand?
DORISTO   If you are quick-witted, you will understand.
AMORE   Yes, yes, I understand.
DORISTO   Well then, what did I say?
AMORE   That I adore you.
DORISTO   And then ...
AMORE   That you would like ...

---

[29] 'One of the tasks of European 17th-century literature was to ... liberate the pastoral from that excessive or exclusive concern with passion and sex which had shaped the bucolic vision of the Italians' (ibid., 167). Subsequent non-Italian pastorals discussed by Poggioli on pp. 58ff and 166ff include the pastoral of innocence and the pastoral of the self.

[30] 'Lettre d'un habitant de Vienne à son ami à Prague, qui lui avait demandé ses reflexions sur l'opéra intitulé L'Arbore di Diana', printed in the original French in O. Michtner, *Das alte Burgtheater als Opernbühne* (Vienna, 1970), 435ff.

[31] Count Karl von Zinzendorf considered the opera an inappropriate choice for a state wedding, as he did *Le nozze di Figaro* in Prague for the same occasion, but he did not find anything offensive in the opera itself. His diary entry of 19 Oct 1787 reads: 'Le soir a l'opera *L'arbore di Diana* ... Il etoit peu decent pour feter une jeune epouse—a Prague on lui a donné le *nozze di Figaro* aussi peu decent'.

[32] Act I scene v, recitative.

| DORISTO | Go on … |
| AMORE | That you wanted … Ah silence my dear, enough …[33] |

The effect was created by what was left unsaid. Could that have been offensive? Da Ponte maintained that in *L'arbore di Diana* he had stayed within the boundaries of good taste: 'It is voluptuous without overstepping into the lascivious'.[34]

The eroticism is much less overt in *Così*, although it is implied by the very situation of unchaperoned wooing. A change of text was made shortly before the première to tone down the erotic.[35] In the autograph score the conversation between Alfonso and Despina runs as follows:

ALFONSO	My dear Despina	Despina mia
	I need you.	Di te bisogno avrei.
DESPINA	And I don't need you.	Ed io niente di lei.
ALFONSO	I can do you a bit of good:	Ti vo fare del ben:
DESPINA	An old man like you cannot do very much for a young woman.	A una fanciulla un vecchio come lei non può far nulla.

In the subsequently published libretto, Despina's reply is less explicit.

| DESPINA | I don't need anything | Non n'ho bisogno |
| | A man like you cannot do very much. | Un huomo come lei non può far nulla. |

For whatever reason the change was made, the issue was clearly the degree of eroticism.

Da Ponte passed up an opportunity for eroticism provided by a pastoral device contrived for just that purpose, the ruse of the kiss. This occurs in the mock-suicide scene in the first finale, set, significantly, in the garden. The rejected Albanians swallow false poison, are revived through magnet therapy, and then, supposedly under the influence of the poison, ask for kisses. In the prototypical scene in *Aminta*,[36] 'the lovelorn protagonist pretends to be stung by a bee. Silvia, out of pity and naively unaware of her power over him, heals his swollen lip by applying repeated kisses'.[37] Da Ponte makes a comic travesty of this scene. The Albanians' plea for kisses is far from erotic and moreover far from successful; on the contrary, it undoes the progress made with the previous love-death, another pastoral device which Da Ponte combines with the ruse of the kiss. The love-death is a dramatic ploy in which an attempted suicide provides the shock that rouses feelings of love in the previously unresponsive lover.[38] In *Aminta*, as we have seen, the love-death formed the climactic turning-point in the story. Da Ponte's playing with the device in *Così* reveals the men's

---

[33] Act I scene x, duet 'Occhietto furbetto'.

[34] *Memoirs of Lorenzo da Ponte*, 178.

[35] A. Tyson, 'Notes on the Composition of Mozart's *Così fan tutte*', *JAMS*, xxxvii (1984), 379; repr. in *Mozart: Studies of the Autograph Scores* (Cambridge, MA, 1987), 198.

[36] This erotic scene inspired many imitations, but it in turn was borrowed from Achilles Tatius; see Greg, 184. Guarini produces a version of the ruse of the kiss in *Il pastor fido*. The protagonist disguises himself as a girl in order to gain admission to the girls' kissing-game where he is then able to kiss his beloved.

[37] Poggioli, 53.

[38] Clubb, 61.

lighthearted attitude to what is ultimately serious business. Later in the opera, in the love duet no. 29, the love-death is called up again by Ferrando in a threat, this time apparently heartfelt, and this time it elicits the classic response from Fiordiligi. However, even parodied as in the mock-suicide scene, the device of the love-death retains its power, for the sisters are moved to cradle the Albanians' heads. More importantly, their resistance has been broken down, as we see in the very next scene.

Da Ponte again downplays the potentially erotic in favour of the comic in the serenade scene. The serenade itself initiates a classic seduction scene; but then the tomfoolery begins. Alfonso and Despina speak for the dumbstruck lovers and, mimicking courtly shepherds, exchange fine poetic speeches.[39] Comical in itself, this action contrasts with the lovers' own awkward attempts at conversation that follow. Having successfully broken the pastoral spell, Da Ponte turns around and revives it. For the first time in the opera, the lovers pair into couples. Like Diana's errant nymphs, Dorabella playfully succumbs to Guglielmo. Like Diana and Endimione, Fiordiligi and Ferrando are intensely serious. Fiordiligi resists strongly and the seduction breaks off; it resumes after an interval, and she falls utterly and completely. The seductive power of the pastoral scene manifests itself in the end, despite the interposing of the comic and the sidestepping of the erotic.

The second topic, 'the horseplay of the ship-wrecked buffoons', addresses the comic element.[40] Comedy was an integral ingredient in the Italian literary pastoral, although its treatment varied widely.[41] At one end of the spectrum was the play that cultivated the juxtaposition of extreme contrasts. In this type of pastoral, found mainly in the early phase of the genre, there obtained an 'extraordinary encounter of literary shepherds with local rustics and witches and gods, and perhaps burghers and princesses as well'.[42] Great comic effect was drawn from the contrast between the Arcadians and the comic visitors, whose 'language, manners and grasp of life crazily reflect and comment on the shepherds'.[43] This contrast springs from the fact that the 'rustic pastoral types did not derive from the pastoral tradition at all, but from the rustic stereotypes found in the commedia dell'arte'.[44] At the other end of the spectrum was the play that followed the example of *Il pastor fido* and smoothed out the contrasts. Its author claimed to have closed the gap between comedy and tragedy by diluting 'the extremes of [the] two strains to produce a middle third'.[45] In such a work, the comic element is neither farcical nor confined to the clowning class but generally distributed.

The use of comedy in *L'arbore di Diana* and *Così* places these librettos in the latter group. This is evident, for example, in Da Ponte's treatment of such a stock comic figure as the

---

[39] Alfonso, apologizing on behalf of the tongue-tied Albanians for their improper behaviour in asking for kisses, says, 'Non può quel che vuole, vorrà quel che può' ('He cannot have what he wants, he'll want what he can have'). This is a play on a controversy between Tasso and Guarini revolving around the question of immorality. In *Aminta* Tasso writes, 'S'ei piace, ei lice' ('What delights, is lawful'). Disagreeing with Tasso, Guarini writes in *Il pastor fido*, 'Piaccia s'ei lice' ('May it please if it is lawful'). See Poggioli, 224.

[40] The phrase itself refers specifically to the comic routines practised by the masks in the *commedia dell'arte*.
[41] 'Italian pastoral drama in the mass ... is essentially a comic genre' (Clubb, 48).
[42] Ibid., 56. [43] Ibid., 54. [44] Harris, 10. [45] Clubb, 48.

servant. His servants are neither boorish nor vulgar. Like his predecessors, Doristo, guardian of the magic apple tree, keeps up a jocular commentary throughout *L'arbore di Diana*. Sometimes he contrasts jarringly with the pastoral characters, for example when he presumes to court the goddess Diana. He also avails himself of the well-worn jest of offering to become a common husband to all three nymphs, and in another familiar trick he receives a slap from Amore in place of the expected kiss from Britomarte. Despite the clowning, however, Doristo is sufficiently genteel to participate in the general love-making. Similarly, Despina remains respectable while exemplifying the conventional comic servant. She first appears sampling the hot chocolate intended for her mistresses, an allusion to the ever-hungry servant.[46] She acts as a foil to the sisters when she gives her opinions on love. She also assumes a disguise, another of the stock-in-trade of the *commedia dell'arte*, not once but twice.

If comedy lent character types to the pastoral, it also lent what Clubb calls 'intrigue structure'.[47] This term refers to a plot in which several strands are interwoven to produce an integrated complexity. In pastorals, intrigue structure is commonly applied to the progress of the love affairs.[48] A favourite constellation of intertwined love affairs is the quartet of mismatched lovers in which 'Silvio loves Chloris who loves Fileno who loves Phyllis who loves Silvio'.[49] The reversed pairing of the lovers in *Così fan tutte* is a variant of the classic merry-go-round pattern. *L'arbore di Diana*, by comparison, has an untidy arrangement of lovers. Endimione loves Diana, but so does Silvio. Britomarte flirts with both Silvio and Doristo, and Doristo woos all the women, including Amore disguised as the shepherdess. None of the love actions leads anywhere, except for that between Diana and Endimione, the sole serious couple.

The third topic, 'the power of the Magician', points to the use of magic as an element of plot. Indeed, in *L'arbore di Diana* magic constitutes a normal part of reality. There is the magic apple tree, as well as the ring that Amore gives Doristo to protect him from the tree's power. There is Amore's arrow with which Endimione pricks Diana, but which can also break down walls of caves, open doors at a touch and change inscriptions. Amore uses his power to freeze the three youths to the spot in Act 1; Diana freezes them in Act 2. In addition to these feats of magic, there occur what Clubb calls Ovidian metamorphoses.[50] Diana turns Doristo into a tree; Amore returns him to his human shape. Amore turns Doristo and the nymphs into stones and shrubs and Silvio into Diana's high priest. These are not disguises but transformations. Disguise is the property of comedy and, by extension, of comic pastorals, but transformations are found only in true pastorals.[51] Thus Despina is

---

[46] The hungry servant is Harlequin; Leporello is one of his manifestations. See Oreglia, 56ff.

[47] 'Dynamic use of intrigue structure was a comic ideal and is characteristic of many of these pastorals . . . including . . . Guarini's' (Clubb, 58).

[48] 'Instead of the single case of love proceeding along an episodic line to its end, as in *Aminta*, . . . [all the other surveyed] plays contain multiple love affairs' (ibid.).

[49] Oreglia, 38; for another example, see Lea, 203.   [50] Clubb, 67.

[51] 'Although mere disguise became common to pastoral drama under the influence of comic practice, genuine transformation was never permitted in regular comedy' (Clubb, 68).

disguised as a doctor, but Doristo is transformed into a tree; Cherubino is at one point disguised as a girl, but Amore actually changes shape and sex to become a shepherdess.

Under the influence of the urban *commedia erudita* of the late sixteenth century, some pastorals, including *Aminta* and *Il pastor fido*, aimed for verisimilitude and hence rationalized magic, or eschewed it altogether.[52] *Così* fits into this mould, for there is no trace of the grab-bag of magic tricks found in *L'arbore di Diana*. On the contrary, *Così* debunks magic[53] when it presents Dr Mesmer's magnetic cure in the same equation as the pretended arsenic, in other words, as a fake remedy for a fake malady. However, as in *L'arbore di Diana*, where the seduction of Diana depends on the magic of Amore's arrow, the men's seduction cannot work without the agent of transformation. The objection has often been raised that it is difficult to accept that Fiordiligi and Dorabella, as well as Despina who after all is party to some of the plot, do not recognize their lovers. However, the objection disappears when the men's disguise is understood in terms of a genuine transformation. In the second finale Da Ponte shifts back to the rationalists' camp and tries to explain away the transformation by pulling out in full view the moustaches and other props of disguise, but that occurs after the seduction has taken place and the pastoral equipment to bring it about is no longer needed.

Daniel Heartz puts his finger on an important characteristic of *Così* when he comments that ' "*Mutability* of character" could, in fact, be the title of the opera'.[54] The capacity for character development resides in the genre. Unlike tragedy and comedy, which were bound by rules governing unity of time and the decorum regulating fixed character types, the pastoral play was able to represent development in character through the symbolic use of magic and metamorphosis to represent psychological change.[55] Hence in *Così* one relic of magic, the transformation, persists. The lovers are initially shown to have an immature understanding of love. The men insist with one voice that their sweethearts are as faithful as they are beautiful because of the promises they have made and because they are well brought up. The women declare with one voice that they are happily in love because of their lovers' noble faces, beautiful mouths and fiery eyes. With the plan to test the women's

---

[52] 'Some pastoralists tend to draw nearer the plausibility expected of urban *commedia erudita* by banishing magic' (ibid., 54).

[53] The practice of magic, along with the judiciary arts, were under Inquisitional ban during the Counter-Reformation. When confronted with magic and other unexplainable phenomena, writers in this sphere of influence provide rationalizations that ultimately lead to God as the final explanation. See Clubb, 69, and also R. Cody, *The Landscape of the Mind: Pastoralism and Platonic Theory in Tasso's 'Aminta' and Shakespeare's Early Comedies* (Oxford, 1969).

[54] Heartz, 236.

[55] 'The pastoral device best suited to dramatic demonstration of the nature of love was one utterly forbidden even to the most romantic *commedia grave* . . . Real magic and Ovidian metamorphosis were stock elements of the genre' (Clubb, 67). Also (70), 'Development in character was uncommon in other regular genres of Italian drama, owing to the demands of unity of time and of the decorum regulating fixed types . . . The countless shifts and conversions of pastoral lovers, however, with or without magic and metamorphosis, opened new possibilities of characterization. And when magic and metamorphosis are subsumed into this more verisimilar psychological alteration, the impression of something like growth or at least mutability in character is heightened'.

fidelity, the men are challenging, unintentionally perhaps, their assumptions; here begins the road to self-discovery for all four lovers. This change is signalled by the men's transformation.

The magic in the pastorals is commonly wielded by the Magician who, although resident in Arcadia, exists apart from its other inhabitants. He often takes an active role in their love affairs, sometimes to amuse himself, occasionally to thwart them.[56] He may employ an assistant. Eventually, he untangles the lovers' imbroglio[57] in a large ceremonial scene built around gods or impersonated gods,[58] rituals in temples or on altars and disclosures that change the lives of the principal characters.

In *L'arbore di Diana* Amore fills the role of Magician. He initiates and directs the plan to make Diana fall in love, occasionally apprising the audience of its progress. He resolves the ensuing crisis in a large ceremonial scene to which the Olympian gods have been summoned as witnesses and in which Diana is judged by her own high priest, in reality the transformed Silvio acting as Amore's assistant. The judgment is rendered to the accompaniment of thunder and lightning, after which Amore appears in his true form and imposes a new order.[59]

The Magician in *Così*, of course, is Alfonso.[60] He sets up the wager, coaches the men, makes suggestions to the women, either directly or through Despina, who acts as his assistant, and then resolves the lovers' impasse by recommending marriage between the original couples. In the final ceremonial scene the wedding rites are under way—a toast is drunk, the contract is being signed—when the ceremony is interrupted by a revelation that changes the women's fate and restores the original order.

The implicit magical elements in *Così* were made explicit in an 1814 German production of the opera in the Theater an der Wien. Georg Friedrich Treitschke, a librettist of *Fidelio*, had translated *Così* into German in 1804 but for the production ten years later made a new translation that included a number of small changes to the plot.[61] Alfonso is portrayed as a real magician, with gown and magic rod. His accomplice is a jinni who appears alternately

---

[56] Lea, 199.

[57] 'The Magician marries Silvio to Chloris, Fileno to Phyllis and Silvano to Dameta. Upon which the comedy ends' (Oreglia, 42).

[58] Oreglia, 41. 'The Enchanted Arcadia' ends with a scene in which the comic characters appears disguised as Jove, Venus, Cupid and a priest.

[59] Like many pastorals, *L'arbore di Diana* has an allegorical dimension to its plot. Emperor Joseph II had recently taken the highly controversial step of liquidating the contemplative monasteries and directing the funds into social welfare programmes. In all, he closed over 700 monasteries and convents. In Da Ponte's allegory, Diana represents the contemplative monasteries that exist to promote the spiritual development of its members. Insofar as personal development can be seen as a selfish pursuit to the exclusion of fellow human beings, it is analogous to chastity. Amore, on the other hand, maintains that true happiness can be attained only through loving one's fellow human beings, which in social terms translates into helping them. Hence, from the perspective of a ruler concerned with the welfare of his subjects, love is the higher good.

[60] E. J. Dent, *Mozart's Operas: a Critical Study* (London, 2/1947), 192, perceptively portrays the lovers as marionettes manipulated by Alfonso, but without apparently recognizing the pastoral ancestry of this relationship.

[61] R. Angermüller, *Mozart: die Opern von der Uraufführung bis heute* (Fribourg, 1988); trans. as *Mozart's Operas* (New York, 1988), 204.

as himself and as Despina. Ferrando and Guglielmo's transformation into Albanians is achieved through the power of magic rings. The visibility of so much magic reduces the culpability of the women in the eyes of an audience that apparently no longer recognized the opera's pastoral conventions. Even more telling of this change in reception is Treitschke's handling of the only unambiguous pastoral scene in the opera, the serenade. He transferred it from the garden to the magician's conjured-up palace. For this audience, it seems, an outdoor love-nest was no longer the supreme erotic setting. Instead, magic was again called upon to help explain what transpired. Treitschke's alterations to the libretto may indicate the demise of the pastoral, or changes in audience attitudes, or both.[62]

Also of interest is a travesty of *L'arbore di Diana* put on by Joachim Perinet for the Theater in der Leopoldstadt in 1813.[63] Typically for the genre, humour is obtained from stepping outside the conventions of the targeted work. At one stroke Perinet wipes out the remoteness of setting and character essential to the pastoral by transposing the story from Diana's nameless island to Dornbacher Park zu Neuwaldegg on the outskirts of Vienna. Amore and Diana are no longer deities but become the girl-next-door; when Perinet's Diana expresses her anguish at realizing she is in love, she also casually remarks that her cloak needs mending. The awe before godly inscrutability and life's mysteries is similarly jettisoned in Perinet's handling of the magic, which is reduced to comic nonsense and feats of stagecraft.[64] While on the one hand the parodying of the pastoral conventions in *L'arbore di Diana* reinforces those conventions, on the other it may also signal a lack of comprehension or appreciation of them. Perinet's travesty, coming near the end of the opera's popularity, happens to sound its death knell.[65] However else the 1813 and 1814 productions of *L'arbore di Diana* and *Così fan tutte* may be understood, it is clear that both librettos were interpreted in ways that made sense to their audiences and that involved the explanation of the pastoral elements.

---

[62] The influence of the Viennese local tradition of magic opera should not be overlooked, although the exact nature of this influence awaits further study of that repertory.

[63] The title-page of the libretto (a copy is in the Theatersammlung of the Österreichische Nationalbibliothek) reads as follows: 'Der/ Baum der Diana/Eine/travestirte Oper in drey Aufzügen/für das/k.k. privil. Theater in der Leopoldstadt/in Knittelreimen/verfasst/von/ Joachim Perinet/Die Musik ist ein Quodlibet, zusammengesetzt von Hrn./Ignaz Schuster usw./Die Dekorationen von Hrn. Neefe./Die Maschinen von der Erfindung des Hrn. Roller,/Maschinisten dieser Schaubühne./Wien, 1813/Bey Joseph Tendler, k.k. privil. Buchhändler.' The opera was given on 19, 20, 21, 26 and 29 Dec 1812 and 15 Jan 1813.

[64] Again, this may reflect the influence of Viennese magic opera.

[65] *L'arbore di Diana* played in the Burgtheater in Italian from 1 Oct 1787 to 3 March 1791 and was revived in German in the same theatre on 29 Aug 1802, playing until 20 July 1804. Within months of the première in the Burgtheater, *L'arbore di Diana* was produced in German in the Theater in der Leopoldstadt (17 July 1788). This production played until 1796, and again in 1809 and 1810, with its final performance on 28 July 1810. Productions elsewhere in Europe became fewer about 1800. By 1811, in a revival in Moscow, a reviewer found the libretto incomprehensible: 'This once popular opera was now revived for the pleasure of many musical amateurs ... As is well known, the subject of this opera is drawn from that storehouse of absurdities from which almost all the European authors drew their material for the theatre' (*Le messager de l'Europe*, 1811, trans. from the French in R.-A. Mooser, *Annales de la musique et des musiciens en Russie au XVIIIe siècle*, ii, Geneva, 1949, p. 544).

[13]

The sentimental muse of opera buffa
Edmund J. Goehring

Comedy was created to correct vice and ridicule bad habits, and when the comedies of the ancients were written in this manner, the entire populace opted for them because, seeing the copy of a character on stage, each found the original either in himself or in someone else. But when comedies became merely ridiculous, no one paid attention any more, because with the pretense of making people laugh, they admitted the highest, loudest blunders. Now that we have returned to fish for comedies in nature's *Mare magnum*, however, men feel their hearts touched again (II. I).[1]

These words, delivered by a character in Carlo Goldoni's *Il teatro comico* (1750), may be taken to speak for the author himself, and they signal a manifesto for one of the most important developments on the eighteenth-century stage: the reform of comedy. There is little doubt about the popularity and influence of Goldoni's reformed works; their success in reconciling aims with achievement is less clear, as is their effect on the world of comic opera. The difficulty in assessing Goldoni's reform is in part a function of his eclecticism as a playwright. Not all of his comedies obediently line up under one definition of comedy, nor is there an ineluctable chronological movement toward reform. Even a work like *Il servitore di due padroni* (1745), sometimes heralded as the "crowning glory" of the very commedia dell'arte that Goldoni later repudiated, has an ethos arguably more characteristic of the later reform comedies than of the commedia dell'arte.[2] At the same time, works written during and after the reform do not always

---

1 Goldoni, vol. 2, pp. 1066–67.
2 For *Il servitore di due padroni* as the "crowning glory" of the commedia dell'arte, see Heinz Riedt, *Carlo Goldoni*, trans. Ursule Molinaro (New York: Ungar, 1974), p. 19. Elizabeth Blood, however, argues convincingly that the influence of the *Théâtre italien* significantly altered the character of *Il servitore*. See "From *canevas* to *commedia*: Innovation in Goldoni's *Il servitore di due padroni*," *Annali d'italianistica* 11 (1993), 111–19.

embrace the aims Goldoni articulated so forcefully in *Il teatro comico*.³

Reception and differences in regional taste further complicate the picture. The following account from a German periodical of 1768 shows a public caring little for poetics, far more for amusement:

> This part of the public – by far the largest, and that which values Goldoni not for his service in reforming the stage but rather for the comic elements of his works – brought in the most money, a fact no director of a German theatre overlooks. Indeed, *Un curioso accidente*, his most rulebound [*regelmäßigste*] comedy, had the poorest attendance; *Il servitore di due padroni* pleased more than *L'adulatore*.⁴

An essential aspect of Goldoni's reform was his intention to create a more natural representation, once again "fishing for comedy in Nature's great sea." "Natural" means many things in the eighteenth century; in this context, it indicates a rejection of Aristotelian poetics, which holds that comedy depicts men as worse than they are in real life, in favor of something truer to life. For Goldoni, the abandonment of the ridiculous in comic representation was the precondition of a theatre that not only permitted but positively encouraged the audience's emulation of the behavior on stage. The idea of comedy as a moral agent was an old (if not always convincing) way of defending the genre from its detractors. What was new with Goldoni was the desire to instruct by positive example.

This aspiration enjoyed support from many quarters. Here, for example, is an excerpt from the entry on comedy in Sulzer's *Allgemeine Theorie der schönen Künste*:

---

3 Ted Emery, in particular, identifies categories, like "arcadian" or "satire-fantasy," that either modify or stray significantly from the aims of the reform. *Goldoni as Librettist: Theatrical Reform and the "Drammi giocosi per musica"* (New York: Lang, 1991). He also addresses (as do others) the question of genre and its relation to the reform, pointing out that opera and its librettos have different aims and audiences than spoken plays.

4 *Deutsche Bibliothek der schönen Wissenschaften Halle* 2 (1768), 449. Cited in Arnold E. Maurer, *Carlo Goldoni: seine Komödien und ihre Verbreitung im deutschen Sprachraum des 18. Jahrhunderts* (Bonn: Herbert Grundmann, 1982), p. 165.

It can be exceedingly useful to show us the absurdities of men in their true light. Should it, however, be less useful to touch us through examples of sensible [*vernünftigem*] conduct, of noble disposition, of honesty, of every necessary virtue in daily life in such a way that we receive lasting impressions from them? . . . One therefore acknowledges the value of mocking and laughing comedy, yet also keeps the stage open for that which entertains without laughter, through noble portraits – for all that shows us human nature in its beautiful and charming sides.[5]

This theory differs from Goldoni's only in its tolerance of Aristotelian poetics. In most other respects, it coincides nicely with the aims expressed by Goldoni in, for example, his comments on an early reform play, *La putta onorata* (1749): "I offered my audience a model for imitation. Provided that one inspires honesty, is it not better to win over hearts with the attractions of virtue than with the ugliness of vice?"[6]

The success of this enterprise hinges on the presence of such realist devices as a preference for plausible explanations, a distaste for language laced with metaphors and other rhetorical devices, and a desire to use the theatre to reinforce general social truths. Without them, the spectator would find neither himself nor his neighbor on the stage, and comedy would lose the chief source of its moral didactic power: the pleasure of recognition.[7] But some interpretations take a different view of Goldoni's realism, concentrating less on its promotion of virtue than on the society it represents on stage. Bartolo Anglani makes one of the most forceful arguments of this kind; he views Goldoni's comedy as a theatre of failed bourgeois social therapy, ultimately unable to eradicate the

---

5 Johann Georg Sulzer, *Allgemeine Theorie der schönen Künste*, 2nd edn. (Leipzig, 1792; reprint, Hildesheim: Olms, 1994), vol. 1, p. 488.
6 *Mémoires de M. Goldoni*, in Goldoni, vol. 1, p. 256.
7 Mario Baratto has a compelling formulation of the didactic functions of Goldoni's reformed comedies: "At the end of the spectacle we are sent back to ourselves more enlightened and full of wonder; disposed, through an intellectual pleasure, to know, and thus with an increased capacity for change." *Tre studi sul teatro (Ruzante–Aretino–Goldoni)* (Venice: Neri Pozza, 1964), p. 216.

original social disorder it diagnoses and portrays.⁸ Although Anglani sometimes gives more weight to bourgeois matters than Goldoni's intentions or the evidence of the comedies will bear,⁹ his readings have been highly influential. Ted Emery, for example, bases much of his study of the intermezzos on Anglani's ideological foundations, in ways that strictly oppose theatrical and realistic impulses. For Emery, the conventional devices of comic theatre – or, to use Goldoni's oft-cited metaphor, *Il teatro* rather than *Il mondo* – only stand in the way of a fully developed realistic, social theatre.¹⁰

But for Goldoni it was not enough just to represent virtue on the stage – its presence had to be attractive. The realization of this aim required not a separation of the theatre from the world, but rather a fusion of the two. Such a union was achieved under the guiding hand of sentimentalism, a concept using realism for theatrical and aesthetic effect. Sentimentalism was a potent force in numerous areas of eighteenth-century thought, and following its migrations from novel into play and then into libretto can illuminate the aims and achievement of some of the most important and successful *opere buffe* of Mozart's Vienna.

OF SINCERITY AND ARTIFICE: RICHARDSON'S "PAMELA"

Like taste, reason, and nature, sentimentalism (and its cognate, sensibility) eludes most efforts to capture its meaning. One reason for this is etymological. Derived from the Latin *sentire*, sentimentalism in its many and varied uses embraced two opposing meanings of the root, a rational one (to perceive in the mind) and a

---

8 Bartolo Anglani, *Goldoni: il mercato, la scena, l'utopia* (Naples: Liguori, 1983), see especially pp. 79–82.
9 This is especially so in *Il teatro comico*, where the financial concerns of a number of parties are arguably sideshows to the main business of the play. Anglani, however, moves these monetary matters to center stage.
10 Emery, *Goldoni as Librettist*, pp. 5–6.

sensual one (to feel through the senses); in the eighteenth century the meaning drifted away from the intellectual toward the passionate.[11] Another complication comes from the breadth of the concept. Far more than a bourgeois phenomenon or a specific subgenre of comedy like the *comédie larmoyante*, sentimentalism is a central issue in disciplines ranging from moral philosophy and aesthetics to medicine and psychology.[12] Yet the word first brings to mind the literature of the eighteenth century, and here its presence was so strong that "Age of Sensibility" has been proposed as a banner around which to marshal works written roughly from the 1740s to the 1790s.[13] Although a single work obviously cannot speak for the entire corpus, Samuel Richardson's *Pamela* (1740) ranks among its most significant representatives, and its popularity and influence on Goldoni make it a good exemplum of the aims and devices of sentimental literature.

One of Richardson's most effective strategies in *Pamela* was to set it as a series of letters coming directly from Pamela herself. In one place only (Pamela's abduction) can the reader detect Richardson's presence, and there it is as an editor rather than an author. The rest of the book proceeds from the fiction that *Pamela* is

---

11 Jean H. Hagstrum, *Sex and Sensibility: Ideal and Erotic Love from Milton to Mozart* (Chicago: University of Chicago Press, 1980), p. 161. See also E. Erämetsä, "A Study of the Word 'Sentimental' and of Other Linguistic Characteristics of Eighteenth-Century Sentimentalism in England," Thesis, University of Helsinki, 1951.

12 In his introduction to a volume of essays entitled *Poets of Sensibility and the Sublime* (New York: Chelsea House Publishers, 1986), Harold Bloom rejects limiting the term to a "Victorian exaltation of middle-class morality [or] a modern celebration of proletarian, natural simplicity" (p. 8).

13 Northrop Frye, "Towards Defining an Age of Sensibility," anthologized in Bloom, *Poets of Sensibility and the Sublime*, p. 11. For an argument against Frye's application of the term, see Howard D. Weinbrot, "Northrop Frye and the Literature of Process Reconsidered," *Eighteenth-Century Studies* 24 (1990–91), 173–95. Frye's effort to find a satisfying designation for the literature of the time addresses the same kind of historiographical issues raised by Daniel Heartz concerning the music from 1730 to 1770 in "Opera and the Periodization of Eighteenth-Century Music," in International Musicological Society, *Report of the Tenth Congress, Ljubljana 1967* (Kassel: Bärenreiter, 1970), pp. 160–68.

less Richardson's creation than his discovery. This use of the epistolary mode collapses the distinction between the fictional characters and real reader, an effect Richardson exploited by having all of the major characters (and some of the minor ones, too) read Pamela's letters. This leaves the physical reader of the tale with the impression that he is only one of several observers of these events.

The use of the epistolary mode has other consequences for the structure and character of the tale, especially with regard to plot. Because it pretends to lack a conspicuous authorial voice that governs and arranges events, *Pamela* appears to take place in the present tense only, with a future as yet unimagined. Northrop Frye, in an influential essay, calls this "literature as process over product."[14] Samuel Johnson puts it less delicately: "Why, Sir, if you were to read Richardson for the story, your impatience would be so much fretted that you would hang yourself."[15] Following this Richardsonian model, works like Sterne's *Sentimental Journey* (1768) and Mackenzie's *Man of Feeling* (1771) show characters chancing from incident to incident, with much less weight given to rationally ordered events, and much more to the feelings these episodes evoke. Again, Johnson: "You must read [Richardson] for the sentiment, and consider the story as only giving occasion to the sentiment."[16]

The fragmented sentimental plot is intimately connected to the nature of its protagonist and can even be considered a kind of extension of the protagonist's psyche. The sentimental character practices a curious kind of heroism: he or she is not an active doer of deeds but is instead passive, a victim of a cruel society or world.[17] But if the external world is malevolent and flawed, the pro-

---

14 Frye, "Towards Defining an Age of Sensibility," pp. 12–13.
15 George Birkbeck Hill, ed., *Boswell's Life of Johnson* (Oxford: Clarendon Press, 1887), vol. 2, p. 175.
16 Ibid., p. 175. The relationship between plot and character is also discussed by Ann Jessie Van Sant, *Eighteenth-Century Sensibility and the Novel: The Senses in Social Context* (Cambridge: Cambridge University Press, 1993), pp. 117–19.
17 Janet M. Todd, *Sensibility: An Introduction* (London: Methuen, 1986), p. 3. The relationship of sensibility to sex is a topic for a different paper. In literature and on the spoken stage, sentimentalism was often seen as a means of civilizing the male, as it is in *Pamela*. Most sentimental types on the operatic stage, however, were female.

tagonist's internal, moral one approaches the heroic, revealing an almost unbounded optimism in the human capacity for altruism: "Sentimentality is a state of mind based on the assumption that one's own character is perfect, or as near perfection as necessary, or if certain grave faults seem to emerge, they must not be regarded as inherent."[18] As much in her swift and complete forgiveness of her wrongdoers as in her lengthy resistance to their assaults on her virtue, Pamela speaks nicely for this optimistic reading of human nature.

The sympathetic portrayal of the deeply feeling protagonist forces a reconception and refashioning of virtually every component of literary representation; this is as true of language as it is of plot and character. Like plot, language normally indicates rational activity. And, again like the sentimental plot, sentimental language abjures coherent speech to dramatize the emotional intensity of the protagonist, who is generally more interested in feeling for its own sake than for the object that inspires it. "Teach me, dear sir," Pamela says as she kisses Mr. B.'s hand, "teach me some other language, if there be any, that abounds with more grateful terms, that I may not thus be choaked with meanings, for which I can find no utterance."[19] This is a wonderfully representative passage – the heroine's keen emotional sensitivity paralyzes the mind, and almost the body, too; to suggest that madness is the ideal expression of sentimental passion barely overstates the issue.

At the same time, this moment in *Pamela* and others like it only *appear* to be devoid of artifice. The repetition of Pamela's command "teach me" calls to mind the rhetorical figure *conduplicatio* – a device using repetition of a phrase for emotional effect – and its use here reveals the fine line sentimentalism holds between realism and artifice. A realistic depiction of lower-class figures like Pamela required a simple style, and Richardson's success can be seen, ironically, in the criticism he received for the baseness of the novel's

---

18 Paul E. Parnell, "The Sentimental Mask," PMLA 78 (1963), 535.
19 *Pamela; or, Virtue Rewarded*, ed. Peter Sabor (New York: Penguin, 1980), pp. 390–91.

122 | Edmund J. Goehring

language. But verisimilitude in language was not enough for sentimentalism, whose aims were not just to instruct, but to persuade. (In *Pamela*, Richardson solves this problem by creating the fiction of Pamela's education under the guidance of her mistress. In a literally realistic depiction, Pamela would not have been able to read at all.)

One obvious function of this treatment of plot, character, and language is to conceal the artifice of the novel. The epistolary mode dissolves the boundaries between reader and author; the representation of lower classes and the reliance on unaffected language makes the protagonist's heroism more convincing. But these nods toward the verisimilar are also highly theatrical, and, what is more, self-consciously so. Clearly, Pamela is conscious of being a theatrical object; indeed, she deftly wields the spectacle of her life as a weapon in the defense of her virtue.[20] Nor does Richardson shy away from exposing the artifice of the work, otherwise he would have excised remarks like this, from Mrs. Davers: "Pr'ythee, child, walk before me to that glass: survey thyself, and come back to me, that I may see how finely thou canst act the theatrical part given thee."[21] Paradoxically, Richardson uses the artifice of *Pamela* precisely to break down the boundaries separating fictional character from reader. In this way, the book attempts to realize the quintessentially sentimental aim of using the devices of realism to awaken sympathy in the reader.

Sentimentalism's confounding of the world with the theatre has much in common with the pastoral mode, which seems to issue from the same impulse. Richardson's appropriation of the pastoral encompasses both ends of the mode, the nostalgic and the cynical. The nostalgic version is evident in the equation of virtue with the simplicity of the lower orders of society, yet this view is itself founded upon a cynical dissatisfaction with the higher strata of society. And the novel is as aware of its own pas-

---

20 Mary Hunter, "Rousseau, the Countess, and the Female Domain," in Cliff Eisen, ed., *Mozart Studies*, 2 (Oxford University Press, forthcoming 1997).
21 *Pamela*, p. 410.

toral nostalgia as it is of its theatricality, most notably in a long speech delivered by Mr. B. on the sixth day after his marriage to Pamela. Only one from Pamela's class will do as a wife, he argues, because wealth has spoiled all those from his own.[22] In other words, "the lower in social order you go, the more admirable mankind appears to be."[23] The point is less to give an accurate depiction of rural life than to open up a path for readers and their emotions to enter into the work.

The inherent theatricality of sentimental works left them open for ridicule and parody. Fielding's *Shamela* (1741) turns Pamela into a brazen opportunist; in another anti-sentimental work, Goethe's *Der Triumph der Empfindsamkeit* (1787), the protagonist discovers he has been in love not with a woman but with a dummy stuffed with sentimental novels. Mixed in with the chaff (Häckerling) at the bottom of this sack he finds, among other things, *La Nouvelle Héloïse* and *Die Leiden des jungen Werthers*. Still, to see sentimental works only as acts of authorial bad faith overlooks a fundamental epistemological question with which their authors wrestled: Was it possible to feel another's emotions? Not according to Adam Smith, who argued in his *Theory of Moral Sentiments* that the only possibility for creating an empathetic or sympathetic experience was for the beholder, using external signs as a guide, to recreate the emotional experience of the object.[24] This makes sympathy an imaginative experience, and therefore also an aesthetic one: "Our sympathy, like the work of art that moves us, takes place within the realm of fiction, mimesis, representation, and reproduction. If the success of a novel, play, or painting depends on acts of

---

22 Ibid., pp. 463–66.
23 R. F. Brissenden, *Virtue in Distress: Studies in the Novel of Sentiment from Richardson to Sade* (New York: Barnes and Noble, 1974), pp. 5–6. Michael Fried observes a similar process of breaking down the distance between object and beholder in pastoral painting, which creates the "fiction of the beholder's physical presence within the painting, by virtue of an almost magical recreation of the effect of nature itself." *Absorption and Theatricality: Painting and Beholder in the Age of Diderot* (Berkeley: University of California Press, 1979), p. 132.
24 Adam Smith, *The Theory of Moral Sentiments* (London, 1759; reprint, New York: Garland, 1971), p. 2.

sympathy, our experience of sympathy depends on an aesthetic experience."²⁵

But if the sentimental character cannot help but be an actor, a question still remains: What kind? In an essay relating sensibility to the theatre, Earl Wasserman identifies two reigning eighteenth-century theories. The naturalistic school takes its motto from the Horatian "Si vis me flere," and insists that the actor can create a convincing representation only if he shares the feelings of his character.²⁶ This theory invokes a Cartesian metaphor: the successful actor, rather than having a strong personality, is malleable, much like soft wax.²⁷ Diderot represents the other position, which holds that the actor "must render exactly the external signs of ideal feeling, but must himself be a disinterested onlooker having intellectual penetration but no sensibility."²⁸ In its insistence on the actor's detachment and coldness, Diderot's theory seems diametrically opposed to the Horatian. Yet neither suggests that acting is anything but an illusion, and each theory leads to the annihilation of personality: the one through the actor's getting lost in a part, the other through a chameleon-like behavior that arises from changing roles. Whatever the theory, realism is not an issue: even the "sincere" variety cannot be equated with realism, for "the sympathetic imagination . . . permits the actor to enter, not into the distinctive, but into the ideal forms of reality."²⁹ Acting is mimesis, reality filtered through the lens of the theatre.

The thespian dimensions of the sentimental protagonist set into relief a paradox of this character-type. On the one hand, a distinguishing trait of characters like Pamela is an almost maudlin hypersensitivity. A famous instance in Richardson is the episode at the pond with Mrs Jewkes, where Pamela throws back a carp she

---

25 David Marshall, *The Surprising Effects of Sympathy: Marivaux, Diderot, Rousseau, and Mary Shelley* (Chicago: University of Chicago Press, 1988), p. 21.
26 Earl R. Wasserman, "The Sympathetic Imagination in Eighteenth-Century Theories of Acting," *Journal of English and Germanic Philology* 46 (1947), 264–72. See also Carl Dahlhaus, "'Si vis me flere,'" *Die Musikforschung* 25 (1972), 51–52.
27 Wasserman, "The Sympathetic Imagination," p. 268.
28 Ibid., p. 272.   29 Ibid., p. 271.

caught because she could not separate her own misfortune from that of the fish. This is a sentimental move through and through, where the subject's feeling is disproportionate to the object that inspires it.[30] But the sentimental protagonist also has another side, often remarkably cold. Perhaps the best eighteenth-century representation of this double nature is Suzanne, the heroine of Diderot's *La Religieuse*, who moves from intensely passionate, even erotic, behavior to a stony distance. In *Pamela*, the heroine's coldness wears a slightly different guise, as "pertness" or "sauciness," terms given to Pamela by her adversaries. This particular manifestation of the double nature has comic potential, which will sometimes be exploited in the move from sentimental novel to sentimental opera.[31] Indeed, Pamela's quick, "saucy" retorts to challenges to her virtue set her in the tradition of the finest comic servants.

This overview of the aims and techniques of sentimentalism as exemplified in Richardson provides a foundation for understanding the nature of Goldoni's reform. By way of preface, it is important to note that sentimentalism's theatrical mask does not completely conceal realism in Goldoni's plays, but it does alter its significance. Like *Il mondo* and *Il teatro*, realism is a metaphor describing a theatrical experience that unites the verisimilar with the artificial. The intimate connection of the two is no less important in Goldoni than in Richardson, and it reveals the extent to which mimesis, rightly understood, still held a vital place in eighteenth-century

---

30 Many have observed the moral problem created by sensibility when imitation becomes an occasion solely for raising feelings. See, for example, Van Sant, *Eighteenth-Century Sensibility and the Novel*, p. 123. Another danger of sentimentalism is its clouding of the distinction between real and theatrical distress, between life and representation. For a discussion of this issue in relationship to Rousseau's antitheatrical prejudice, see Marshall, *The Surprising Effects of Sympathy*, ch. 5, "Rousseau and the State of Theater."
31 A stimulating discussion of this sentimental double nature in Mirandolina from Goldoni's *La locandiera* is found in Gerhard Regn, "Jenseits der 'commedia borghese': Komödienspiel, Karnevalisierung und moralische Lizenz in Goldonis 'Locandiera,'" *Germanisch-Romanische Monatsschrift*, n.s., vol. 44 (1994), pp. 324–44.

aesthetics. Imitation is nature beautified, which is another way of saying that the author has freedom to exercise imagination and genius in his depiction of the world.

FROM NOVEL TO PLAY: "PAMELA NUBILE"

Pamela nubile (1750) was not Goldoni's first reformed comedy,[32] but its proximity to Richardson's novel makes it a logical place to examine the transformation of the sentimental impulse from novel to play. Only the epistolary format was too unwieldy to make the move to the new genre, and the play makes but an occasional nod to Pamela's letter-writing. Most of the other traits of the sentimental novel, however, are present and conspicuous. Milord Bonfil, for example, is transformed from a brute into a paragon of sentimental sensitivity; furthermore, the fundamental passivity of the couple is emphasized in the resolution of the play, which is possible only by the lucky discovery of Pamela's noble lineage.[33] Also like Richardson, Goldoni spares no theatrical device in casting Pamela's virtue in the most heroic and flattering light, as in her speech in Act I, scene 6. Part rebuke against libertinism, part defense of honor, part plea for social egalitarianism ("Noble blood is an accident of fate; true greatness comes from noble actions"), the resulting soliloquy, among the longest in the play, is so effective that Bonfil is left literally dumbfounded, speech being returned to him only in the next scene.

Like Richardson's *Pamela*, Goldoni's reformed comedies are

---

32   Emery argues that *Pamela nubile* is not even a reform work at all; rather, it represents an Arcadian phase of Goldoni's output that runs against the reforming impulse. *Goldoni as Librettist*, pp. 124, 212.

33   This is a clumsy solution from the standpoint of realism, but necessary for a satisfying psychological conclusion. Emery, however, takes an opposing view of the denouement of *Pamela nubile*, arguing that "we can hardly call love the victor here, for passion triumphs in *Pamela* only by default: love is possible in the end only because reason allows it to be so" ("Goldoni's *Pamela* from Play to Libretto," *Italica* 64 [1987], 576). I would argue that love is indeed the victor here, that a conclusion *not* allowing the fulfillment of the couple's passion would be still more unsatisfactory.

beholden to the pastoral world in their nostalgic portrayal of the lower classes, and this means a change in the style of language. His oft-stated distaste for the elevated style stems in part from a desire to create a more natural representation of the simple heroism of gardeners, villagers, and foundlings. This is the reason he gives for using Venetian dialect to portray the gondoliers in *La putta onorata*. But Goldoni also rightly understood that elevated language was a central part of comic hyperbole. Indeed, this was an important tool in the commedia dell'arte, especially for the part of the lovers (*innamorati*), whose *zibaldoni*, or commonplace-books, provided a repository of *concetti* and rhetorical devices.[34] Goldoni did not object to the language of the commedia dell'arte because it was too low (with the obvious exception of vulgarity) but because it was too high, associated with an aristocratic conceit.[35]

In *Pamela nubile* the presence of sentimentality leads to a remaking of comedy, which is why it and similar plays should be numbered among reform works.[36] Not only did Goldoni relegate ridiculous characters to the side,[37] he even took the rather desperate measure of trying to improve the behavior of the comic actors of the spoken and musical stage. This is an important issue in *Il teatro comico*, and it shows Goldoni's affinity for the Horatian theory of acting: both actor and character should be held to the same high standards of morality. In any case, Goldoni was keenly aware of the extent of his reform, so much so that he proposed a different generic label for the *Pamela nubile*: "Following the definition of the French, the comedy *Pamela* is a *drame*."[38] What he means by *drame* and the French definition of it is explained earlier in the *Mémoires*, in his discussion of *La putta onorata*:

---

34 K. M. Lea, *Italian Popular Comedy: A Study in the Commedia dell'arte, 1560–1620, with Special Reference to the English Stage* (New York: Russell & Russell, 1962), vol. 1, pp. 104–5.

35 Regn, "Jenseits der 'commedia borghese,'" p. 334, equates Mirandolina's coquetry with aristocratic behavior.   36 See note 32, above.

37 He calls Ernold the character who "infinitely cheers the seriousnesss of the work." Goldoni, vol. 1, pp. 279–80.   38 Ibid., p. 280.

> When I speak of virtue, I do not mean that heroic virtue, touching through its misfortunes and tearful in its delivery. These works, which in French are given the title *Drames*, certainly have their merit; they are a type of theatrical representation between comedy and tragedy. This is an entertainment made more for tender hearts [*coeurs sensibles*] – the misfortunes of heroic tragedies interest us from a distance, but those of our kind ought to move us even more.
>
> Comedy, which is nothing other than an imitation of nature, does not deny itself virtuous and pathetic sentiments, provided that it's not stripped of those significant and amusing actions that form the fundamental core of its existence.[39]

It is hard to overemphasize the theatrical importance of this mixing of styles. Goldoni sought to make tragedy more effective and more touching; and he made this possible by attaching nobility of feeling and behavior to character-types who, unlike the heroes of tragedy, were close to the audience in status and experience.

OPERA BUFFA IN THE SENTIMENTAL MODE

Goldoni's sentimental comedies provided a widely imitated model for opera buffa librettos. The success of a work like *La Cecchina; ossia La buona figliuola*, set to music by Piccinni (1760), is measured not only in the number of productions generated but especially in the number of works that follow in this tradition: *La finta giardiniera* (Mozart/Petrosellini[?], 1775), *La vera costanza* (Haydn/Puttini, 1779), *La pastorella nobile* (Guglielmi/Zini, 1788), *La cifra* (Salieri/Da Ponte, 1789), *Nina, o sia La pazza per amore* (Paisiello/Lorenzi, 1789), and so on. Another sentimental opera, *Il disertore* (Bianchi/Benincasa, 1785), contains a preface with dramaturgical aims virtually identical to those articulated by Goldoni decades earlier. Like Goldoni, Benincasa draws inspiration for his conception of drama from France: "There it's called simply *Drame* and is indicated with the term *Pièces larmoyantes*. It aims to excite tender or terrifying affects with ordinary actions and characters

---

39 Ibid., p. 256.

who are not heroic but instead common."[40] But the opera most permeated with sentimentalism is Martín y Soler's and Da Ponte's *Una cosa rara* (1786), among the most successful operas of the Josephine decade.

Opera is inherently disposed to convincing representations of sentimental passion: music, a pre-verbal medium, persuasively conveys the emotional intensity central to its psychology, and opera, often a singer's rather than a composer's art, tends to conceal the author behind the work. But sentimental opera also highlighted its heroines with a specific subtype of aria, the "breathless" cavatina. "Ah pietade, mercede," the number marking Lilla's initial entry, is an exemplary musical expression of virtue in distress (Example 5.1). Its text displays the keenness of Lilla's sensibility through a collapse of language itself. She literally lacks the words to convey adequately the intensity of her emotion. Her grief is incoherent, of course (otherwise it would not be grief), but its pointedly physical manifestation, where it leads to a shutdown even of breathing, is typical of the physiology of sensibility.

This loss for words has a parallel in musical representation. But whereas Richardson needs hundreds of pages to sustain this emotional intensity, music takes the road of brevity. The absence of an introductory ritornello, the avoidance of periodic closure (the only perfect authentic cadence falls in the antepenultimate measure), the reliance on a single affect, and the ever-present eighth-note string figures generate emotional urgency and immediacy. These cavatinas seem designed to surprise, even astonish, their listeners by their compactness. This is music as "process over product," in other words; it abandons clearly articulated formal patterns that create a rationally ordered presence comprehending past, present, and future. In Martín as in Richardson, the sentimental type knows only the present.

"Ah pietade, mercede" may be exemplary in its portrayal of the sentimental heroine's distressed virtue, but it is not unique. It belongs, rather, to a subtype used to depict sentimental heroines

40 Preface to *Il disertore* (Venice, 1785), p. 8.

130 | Edmund J. Goehring

Example 5.1 Lilla, "Ah pietade, mercede" (No. 3) from *Una cosa rara*

Example 5.1 (cont.)

Lilla: Ah pity, mercy, help. I am so weary from fear, torment, and running that I am out of breath and scarcely have the energy to speak.

from Violante in *La finta giardiniera* to Rosina in *La vera costanza* (Example 5.2). In some of these other sentimental operas, so high-pitched is the protagonists' emotional sensitivity that they occasionally go mad, as does Violante in *La finta giardiniera* or Nina in Paisiello's opera; the latter – in a fine display of sentimental philanthropy – gives presents to the poor villagers who take care of her during her amnesia. To be sure, distress is not the only characteristic of operatic heroines of feeling: like Pamela, they, too, can reveal a double nature that has its "saucy" sides. In *Una cosa rara*, for example, Lilla accuses Ghita of plotting against her out of jealousy at Lilla's superior beauty: "From the day that they said I was more beautiful, you always looked upon me with spite" (I. 13). But even these comic episodes ultimately serve a serious purpose, as a yardstick by which to measure the virtue of the heroine. As with Goldoni in *Pamela nubile*, Martín and Da Ponte dedicate the devices of the theatre to portraying the most heroic sides of the sentimental protagonist. In *Una cosa rara*, the ethos of reformed comedy is evident in this melding of a common type (a villager) with heroic constancy and virtue. Although Ghita may be mocking Lilla when she calls her the phoenix of her sex (II. 3), the voice of the opera means this seriously, naming her "una cosa rara."

If "breathless" cavatinas like "Ah pietade" are reserved for special

Example 5.2a Barbarina, "Soccorretemi, Sorelle," from *La forza delle donne* (Anfossi / Bertati)

Example 5.2a (*cont.*)

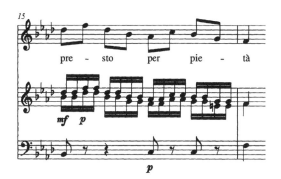

Barbarina: Help me, sisters. Quickly, quickly, for heaven's sake.

Example 5.2b Rosina, "Dove fuggo" (No. 12b) from *La vera costanza* (Haydn/Puttini)

Rosina: Where do I flee, where do I hide without help and without escort?

134 | Edmund J. Goehring

Example 5.2c Violante, "Crudeli, fermate" (No. 21) from *La finta giardiniera*

Example 5.2c (*cont.*)

Violante: Stop, cruel ones, oh God.

characters in special situations, the simplicity of their vocal and instrumental style has a much wider range in the repertory. In an essay appearing in this collection, Mary Hunter gives a persuasive account of the appeal of song style in *Una cosa rara*.[41] I would add that this style – not so much a middle point between the elevated and ridiculous as a typically Goldonian union of simple language with noble bearing – emanates from a sentimental and pastoral impulse. As in Richardson, all of the operatic sentimental types are or seem to be from the lower orders of society. Violante in *La finta giardiniera* is a slight exception, as she is aware of her aristocratic lineage from the start. Yet even her and Belfiore's madness in the second act takes the form of a dialogue reenacted between two pastoral types, Thyrsis and Cloris (Example 5.3). The duet typifies the wonderful complexity arising out of sentimentalism's union of nature and artifice, of the world and the theatre: though mad, and though acting out a scene, Violante is in some sense at her truest here, expressing in the bucolic idiom the thoroughly pastoral desire to escape from society to a place offering an uncomplicated life with her beloved.

---

41 The designation "song style" is from Dorothea Link, "The Da Ponte Operas of Martín y Soler" (PhD diss., University of Toronto, 1991).

Example 5.3 *La finta giardiniera* (II.17)

Sandrina: My Thyrsis, hear the sweet Sirens. With soothing enchantment they unloose their song.

This episode has the following setting: "A deserted and wild region of ancient, partly ruined aqueducts, among which there is an accessible dark cave."[42] These are all emblems of the sublime mode. At first glance, the tenderness and the civilizing character of sentimentalism seem to have little in common with the majesty of the sublime, but in its focus on the transcendental, its abandonment of reason for passion, and especially in its heroic aspirations, sensibility enjoys a "complex fusion" with the sublime mode.[43] It is important to recognize sentimentalism's relation to the sublime because it discourages facile equations of musical simplicity with sincerity and artifice with deceit. Opera has its own stylistic and linguistic idioms, and these do not always work well in a spoken setting. Witness, for example, Benincasa's dismay at having to include wretched language in the libretto to *Il disertore*: "I myself protest against certain words that please in music but that in writing are displeasing to good taste, and against the repetitions of so many other words that make up the impoverished, dilapidated dictionary of grand arias."[44] Here, opera buffa departs somewhat from Goldoni's reforms, since it can make allowance for the sympathetic portrayal of virtue in an elevated language.[45]

The appeal of works like *Una cosa rara* gives a measure of the

---

42 For a discussion of stage settings in opera buffa, see Mary Hunter, "Landscapes, Gardens, and Gothic Settings in the *Opere Buffe* of Mozart and his Italian Contemporaries," *CM* 51 (1993), 94–104.

43 Bloom, *Poets of Sensibility and the Sublime*, p. 8.

44 Preface, p. 10.

45 See Mary Hunter, "Some Representations of *Opera Seria* in *Opera Buffa*," *COJ* 3 (1991), 107, both for the importance of context and for the observation that the presence of opera seria within opera buffa is not an *a priori* cause for ridicule. An example of elevated musical language used to portray sentimental virtue is Eurilla's "Sola e mesta fra tormenti" from Salieri's *La cifra*. Of this aria and its introductory recitative, Salieri remarked that they were "pieces of great seriousness, but suitable for the character who sings them and the situation in which they are found, and above all because they were composed for a celebrated virtuoso who knew how to execute them with perfect sentiment and who had the greatest applause." Cited in Rudolph Angermüller, *Antonio Salieri: Sein Leben und seine weltlichen Werke unter besonderer Berücksichtigung seiner "großen" Opern*, Part III: Dokumente (Munich: Katzbichler, 1971), p. 54.

vitality of the sentimental tradition on the musical stage. It is both instructive and amusing to refer to an anecdote to illustrate the effect this kind of opera had upon its audiences. In the first run of Paisiello's *Nina* in Naples in 1789, it was reported that during Nina's romanza "Il mio ben quando verrà" men in the audience were weeping and cried out to Coltellini, "Rest assured, your lover will return!"[46] The opera had achieved its aims of moving the audience to the point of collapsing the wall separating the audience and the stage. In any case, the offspring of Goldoni's reform flourished, and so great was their success that some have argued that sentimental comedy eradicated more artificial traditions, like the commedia dell'arte, during the second half of the century.[47] Yet it is important to recall that artificial forms of comedy indeed survived alongside sentimental ones,[48] and the clearest image of the boundaries and limitations of operatic sentimentalism can be detected in Mozart's handling of the phenomenon.

"COSÌ FAN TUTTE LE COSE RARE": ANTI-SENTIMENTALISM IN THE MOZART-DA PONTE OPERAS

Mozart made a contribution to the sentimental opera, but not in a Da Ponte work: as suggested above, rather, in *La finta giardiniera*. In

---

46 Cited in Andrea Della Corte, *Paisiello* (Turin, 1922), p. 175. The literary example par excellence of this sentimental breaking down of the wall between the novel and reader is Diderot's *La Religieuse*, which started out as a practical joke.

47 Piero Weiss, "Carlo Goldoni, Librettist: The Early Years" (PhD diss., Columbia University, 1970), p. 100. See also Allardyce Nicoll, *The World of Harlequin: A Critical Study of the Commedia dell'arte* (Cambridge: Cambridge University Press, 1963), p. 189; and David Kimbell, *Italian Opera* (Cambridge: Cambridge University Press, 1991), p. 291.

48 In his *The Rakish Stage: Studies in English Drama, 1660–1800* (Carbondale: Southern Illinois University Press, 1983), Robert D. Hume cautions against the idea of a comedy of laughter struggling to reassert itself against a dominant tearful strain. Tracing this fallacy in part to Goldsmith's attack on sentimental comedy, Hume argues that Goldsmith's argument refers to, at best, a trend during a single season (p. 313 *passim*).

Violante one finds the defining gestures of the sentimental type: refinement of feeling that leads even to madness, a union of the pastoral and the elevated in her disguise as a gardener, even the "breathless" aria (see Example 5.2). The Da Ponte operas, however, all depart from this model, and in the forefront is *Così fan tutte*. This work offers a rebuttal not just of sentimentalism in general but of *Una cosa rara* in particular, which in fact was in the repertory during the 1789–90 season, having performances on 3 and 23 November 1789 and 2 and 24 January 1790, the last of these only two days before the premiere of *Così fan tutte*. Even the two titles vie with each other, offering competing claims about the proper nature of comedy: if Goldonian sentimental opera aims to champion the exceptional – "una cosa rara" – as an object worthy of imitation, comedy generally takes a more leveling view – "così fan tutte."[49] But the most conspicuous parody in Mozart's opera is Don Alfonso's cavatina "Vorrei dir" (Example 5.4). Virtually a direct quotation of Lilla's "Ah pietade, mercede" (see Example 5.1), it is, if anything, a more eloquent statement of sentimental distress, with its dismay at the cruelty of the world ("barbaro fato") and depiction of a passion so overwhelming that words become impossible: "Balbettando il labbro va;/Fuor la voce uscir non può." Musically, Mozart's parody shows stronger formal organization (mm. 9 and 14 have perfect-authentic cadences, and there is a double return at measure 20). Nonetheless, by beginning in *media res* and eliding its phrases, "Vorrei dir" creates the immediacy required of the portrayal of sentimental affliction.

Don Alfonso's cavatina destroys the naturalist, sentimental

---

49 Alan Tyson has suggested that *Così fan tutte* was Mozart's own title for *La scola degli amanti*, and that it was chosen at a very late stage in the genesis of the opera; see "On the Composition of Mozart's *Così fan tutte*," in *Mozart: Studies of the Autograph Scores* (Cambridge, MA: Harvard University Press, 1987), pp. 190, 197. More recently it has become clear that the libretto was originally to be set by Salieri; see Bruce Alan Brown and John A. Rice, "Salieri's *Così fan tutte*," *COJ* 8 (1996), 17–43. Perhaps the recent performances of *Una cosa rara* were one of the inspirations behind the last-minute change.

140 | Edmund J. Goehring

Example 5.4 "Vorrei dir" (No. 5) from *Così fan tutte*

theory of the Horatian school of acting. "Vorrei dir" seems to say that one need not feel emotion in order to touch; it is enough to mimic the gestures that represent feeling. Don Alfonso admits as much several scenes later, following the nostalgic "Soave sia il vento": "Non son cattivo comico," he says, and by "comico" he must mean not just comedian, or even actor, but creator.

Example 5.4 (cont.)

Countering the sentimental strategy of effacing the author to give the characters the appearance of autonomy and spontaneity, Don Alfonso exposes the theatricality of this illusion by wresting control of the stage. This is the reason for *Così fan tutte*'s artifice, for the symmetry of its organization: we are seeing everything through the contrivance of Don Alfonso. Were *Così fan tutte* a film,

142 | Edmund J. Goehring

Example 5.4 (cont.)

gran fa-ta - li - tà, dar di peg - gio non si può

Alfonso: I would like to tell you, but I don't have the heart. My lips are stuttering, I can't get the words out, they are stuck in my throat. What will you do? What will I do? O, what a great catastrophe. There could be nothing worse.

then Don Alfonso would be controlling the lens that presents the spectacle to us.[50]

To be sure, Don Alfonso's direction is often subtle and understated. *Così fan tutte* typically does not resort to the farce of an "Ah chi mi dice mai," for example, where the composer, through the agency of Don Giovanni and Leporello, surrounds Donna Elvira's oath of vengeance with ironic marginalia. The irony of "Come scoglio," on the other hand, resides less in its musical language (big vocal leaps and ornamentation by themselves are not necessarily tokens of ridicule) than in the context in which this style appears.[51] Unlike in *Pamela nubile*, where Milord is left stunned by the persuasiveness of Pamela's words, Fiordiligi is denied the exit her aria

50 This argument suggests that Don Alfonso's authority is not successfully usurped in the opera, indeed, that the voice of the opera and that of Don Alfonso are virtually identical. Although this is not a common view of the opera, a couple of readings have looked more favorably upon Don Alfonso. See, in particular, Cornelia Kritsch and Herbert Zeman, "Das Rätsel eines genialen Opernentwurfs – Da Pontes Libretto zu *Così fan tutte* und das literarische Umfeld des 18. Jahrhunderts," in *Die österreichische Literatur: ihr Profil an der Wende vom 18. zum 19. Jahrhundert (1750–1830)*, Part I (Graz: Akademische Druck- und Verlagsanstalt, 1979), pp. 359–60; and Bruce Alan Brown, *W. A. Mozart: "Così fan tutte"* (Cambridge: Cambridge University Press, 1995), pp. 82–85.
51 See Sergio Durante's essay elsewhere in the volume.

demands, and this fatally undermines her authority. The same procedure of placing passion at a distance – of moving the private into the public – also informs the climactic duet "Fra gli amplessi." In a different context, this seduction duet could be an unambiguously stirring moment for the audience. But the audience is not exactly watching a seduction duet: it is watching Don Alfonso and an enraged Guglielmo watch a seduction duet. Don Alfonso raises questions about the sentimental vision merely by holding it up for inspection, and he weakens the fourth wall of the theatre simply by showing us that it is there, by calling to the spectator's attention the theatricality of the dramatic activity.[52]

For this reason, *Così fan tutte* has been called an inhumane work, and Don Alfonso a heartless or diabolical scientist.[53] But the last vestige of sentimentalism to fall away from *Così fan tutte* is the *amanti*'s overblown confidence in the perfectibility of human nature, where everyone aspires to be a phoenix or at least a Penelope. Don Alfonso is the one, after all, who urges the soldiers to avoid the test of fidelity in the first place: "O pazzo desire! / Cercando scoprire / quel mal che trovato / meschini ci fa" (O mad desire, seeking to uncover that evil, which, when found, makes us wretched ["La mia Dorabella," 1. 1]), a statement bringing *Così fan tutte* into the orbit of works like Ariosto's *Orlando furioso*, several cantos of which place blame not on those who fail tests of fidelity, but on those who make them in the first place.[54] The soldiers figure this out, eventually, when they take back the sisters with these words: "Te lo credo, gioia bella, / Ma la prova io far non vo" (I believe it of you, my joy, but I do not want to make a test of it

---

52 This makes Don Alfonso a quintessentially comic protagonist along the lines of Baudelaire's "double man," in whom "there is not one single phenomenon of his double nature of which he is ignorant." "On the Essence of Laughter," p. 465.

53 Donald Mitchell calls him (along with Despina) "rather disagreeable" and "a little sly" ("The Truth about 'Così,'" in *A Tribute to Benjamin Britten on his Fiftieth Birthday*, ed. Anthony Gishford [London: Faber and Faber, 1963], p. 97). Intimations of a wicked, diabolical side come from, among others, Wolfgang Hildesheimer, *Mozart*; trans. Marion Faber (New York: Farrar, Straus, Giroux, 1981), pp. 289, 294.

54 On the relations of *Così fan tutte* to Ariosto, see Brown, *Così fan tutte*, pp. 60–70.

Edmund J. Goehring

[11.18]). This admission signals the downfall of the *amanti*'s sentimental/heroic vision. Don Alfonso's view, eschewing the rigid extremes of rationalism and sentimentalism, is intended to be reasonable and humane, first gently exposing then accepting human frailty. It is this recognition of human contingency that motivates *Così fan tutte*'s refutation of the sentimental tradition.

To say that *Così fan tutte*'s intentional artifice turns it away from realism, to say that the work cautions its audience about sympathetic responses at the same time that it encourages them, is to venture a definition of comedy itself.[55] And a look at the comic in *Così fan tutte* might reshape the understanding of the earlier Da Ponte operas. One appealing assessment of them is that they liberated comic opera from convention and fixed types, creating in their place a psychological realism hitherto unseen on the operatic stage.[56] But artifice, whether in the portrayal of the impossibly successful and impossibly damned libertine or in the sudden discovery that an adversary turns out to be one's long-lost and beloved mother, was positively inspirational for Mozart. Realistic readings, whether psychological or social, are in their own way sentimental, accepting the pretense of realism without acknowledging the theatrical devices used to create it. They are of limited utility even for truly sentimental works, and still less so for those that, like the Mozart-Da Ponte operas, move moments of private passion (upon which so much of the success of sentimental education hinges) into a public light.

A compelling illustration of the distance between Goldoni and Mozart-Da Ponte can be found in a comparison between their respective treatments of the Don Juan legend. Mozart and Da Ponte restore many of the improbabilities of the sub-literary traditions that Goldoni tried to eradicate. They also restored the elevated language that Goldoni rejected, for, as Stefan Kunze has

---

55 For these dimensions of comedy, see Christopher Herbert, *Trollope and Comic Pleasure* (Chicago: University of Chicago Press, 1987), pp. 23–26.
56 Cf. Paolo Gallarati's essay elsewhere in this volume.

persuasively argued, the incorporation of *seria* elements paradoxically increased the potential for farce and ridicule.[57] The Da Ponte operas take the range of tone afforded by Goldoni's reform, but jettison the moralizing dimension.

This is not to argue that comedy is not true, or that one does not find on stage some element of society. But, to paraphrase Don Alfonso in one of his many metatheatrical moments, comedy undeceives through deceiving, and the mirror it holds up to society, like those in a carnival, distorts for amusement and pleasure (and instruction), granting to the imagination a release from the quotidian. In his reform of comedy Goldoni proposed an ambitious program: to find in comedy a means for the sympathetic portrayal of passion. That the Mozart-Da Ponte operas treat passion with considerable ambiguity and irony reminds one of their distance from sentimentalism.

[57] Kunze, *Don Giovanni*, p. 55.

Part IV
Orientalism and Exoticism

[14]

Mozart in Turkey[1]

BENJAMIN PERL

Abstract: The essay analyses the Turkish mode in Mozart's output, discovering some unexpected examples, particularly Don Giovanni's aria 'Fin ch'han dal vino', whose uncommon sonority, obsessive rhythm and harmonic poverty evoke this *topos*. Don Giovanni may present Turkish features because his character coincides with eighteenth-century Western European views of the Turks as a threat to the established order and inclined to reckless sensuality. The romantic view of Don Giovanni as an ideal figure may also be connected with eighteenth-century thinking about 'orientals' as the representatives of utopia.

The Turkish mode, or mood, persists through Mozart's oeuvre. The list of works which prominently include this *topos* starts with the sketch for the ballet-music 'Le gelosie del seraglio' for '*Lucio Silla*' (1773)[2] and the inserted section in the last movement of his fifth violin concerto KV 219 (1779); after this it appears most expansively, of course, in *Die Entführung aus dem Serail* (1782), next comes the 'alla turca' movement from the piano sonata KV 331 (1783);[3] and its last appearance is in Monostatos's aria 'Alles fühlt der Liebe Freuden' from *Die Zauberflöte* (1791).[4]

The musicological literature has dealt extensively with the 'alla turca' style in eighteenth-century music in general,[5] as well as in Mozart in particular. Earlier writers concentrated on the use of percussion instruments representing the

---

[1] This article is based on a paper read at the annual meeting of the Mozart Society of America in Kansas City, November 1999.
[2] Walter Senn ('Mozarts Skizze der Ballettmusik zu *Le gelosie del seraglio*', *Acta Musicologica*, 33 [1961], 169–92) shows that six (of eight) pieces forming the sketch for the ballet music to 'Le gelosie del seraglio' were not original pieces by Mozart, but citations by memory from Starzer's ballet *Le cinque soltane*. None of these is the 'Turkish' piece later included in the violin concerto, but the originality of the ballet sketch, following the revelations of Senn, was doubtful enough for the NMA not to include it in the score of *Lucio Silla* but in the volume dedicated to doubtful and spurious compositions. It is curious to note that the first appearance of the 'Turkish' mode in Mozart's compositions may have been a conscious plagiarism from another composer.
[3] This sonata has long been dated from Mozart's visit to Paris in 1778. NMA editors Angermüller and Plath, referring also to Tyson's watermark researches, date it to about 1783, that is, after *Die Entführung*.
[4] Monostatos is certainly not Turkish, but the Turkish features of the aria are obvious, as is Mozart's tendency to amalgamate all extra-European features.
[5] The following is a list of some publications on the subject in the last century: Walter Preibisch, 'Quellenstudien zu Mozarts 'Entführung aus dem Serail', ein Beitrag zur Geschichte der Türkenoper', *Sammelbände der Internationalen Musikgesellschaft* 10 (Leipzig, 1908–9), 430–76; Bence Szabolcsi, 'Exoticisms in Mozart', *Music & Letters*, 37 (1956), 323–32; Miriam Karpilow Whaples, *Exoticism in Dramatic Music, 1600–1800*, Ph.D. diss., Indiana University (1958); Carl Signell, 'Mozart and the mehter', *Consort* (Annual Journal of the Dolmetsch Foundation), 24 (1967), 310–22. Kurt Reinhard, 'Mozarts Rezeption türkischer Musik', *Bericht über den internationalen musikwissenschaftlichen Kongress Berlin 1974*, ed. Helmut Kuhn und Peter Nitsche (Kassel, 1980), 518–23; Peter Gradenwitz, *Musik zwischen Orient und Okzident, eine Kulturgeschichte der Wechselbeziehungen* (Wilhelmshaven, 1977); Anke Schmitt, *Der Exotismus in der deutschen Oper zwischen Mozart und Spohr*, Hamburger Beiträge zur Musikwissenschaft 36, ed. Constantin Floros (Hamburg, 1988), 301–65; G. Joppig, 'Alla turca, Orientalismen in der europäischen Kunstmusik vom 18. bis zum 19. Jahrhundert',

continued on next page

Janissary orchestras: especially bass drum, cymbals and triangle, obligatory for every operatic representation of 'Turkish' music. Recently more attention has been paid to the purely musical means by which composers in this period portray extra-European, 'oriental' music, as they knew and heard, or just imagined it.[6]

Though the alla turca pieces mentioned above are far from being stylistically uniform, they have in common a marked difference from Mozart's 'non-orientalist' styles and *topoi*. In addition, Mozart tends not to integrate the alla turca *topos* smoothly into the movements in which it occurs, so that most instances appear abruptly or unexpectedly. Compare, for example, the last movements of violin concertos Nos. 3, 4 and 5 (KV 217, 218 and 219): each includes an inserted passage in different tempo, metre and mode, in folk-like character. In both Nos. 3 and 4 this passage is a gavotte in French style which is stylistically or gesturally continuous with the main part of the movement. In No. 5, however, the so-called 'Turkish' episode feels much more intrusive and altogether harsher. The A minor episode bursts in without preparation and sounds alien to everything preceding and following it, like something erupting from beneath. The score of this passage, however, nowhere designates it as 'Turkish', and, to be sure, it was not always identified as such: some writers associated it, justifiably, with the 'all'ongherese' style, which is prominent in a few Haydn compositions from the same period.[7] To ascribe quite different ethnicities to the same set of musical characteristics is, of course, entirely consistent with orientalist practice.

Another 'Turkish' moment, never designated as such but nevertheless quite striking in context, occurs in the first movement of the sonata KV 331. Hermann Abert already noted the coloristic resemblance between a passage in the last variation of the first movement, with its low-register chords imitating the cymbals, and the accompaniment of the major section in the alla turca movement.[8] But another likeness, no less significant, has been overlooked: the third (A minor) variation in the first movement has a curiously winding line, slightly chromatic, which gives it an orientalist tinge; moreover, the curious parallel-octave 'orchestration' of the repetitions of both parts of this variation, connects it with the clearly 'Turkish' major theme of the last movement;

---

continued from previous page
Europa und der Orient, 800–1900, ed. G. Sievernich and H. Budde (Gutersloh, 1989), 295–304; Thomas Betzwieser, *Exotismus und 'Türkenoper' in der französischen Musik des ancien Régime* (Laaber, 1993); R. M. Jäger, *Die türkische Kunstmusik und ihre handschriftlichen Quellen aus dem 19. Jahrhundert* Schriften zur Musikwissenschaft aus Münster (Eisenach, 1996); Mary Hunter, 'The "Alla Turca" Style in the late Eighteenth Century: Race and Gender in the Symphony and the Seraglio', in *The Exotic in Western Music*, ed. Jonathan Bellman (Boston, 1998), 43–73.

[6] Among the publications mentioned in the foregoing note, Reinhard, Szabolcsi and Hunter concentrate mainly on these aspects.

[7] See Wyzewa – St. Foix and Dénes Bartha, cited in the introduction to the NMA edition of the concerto: *W. A. Mozart, Neue Ausgabe sämtlicher Werke* (Kassel, 1955), V:14:i. A list of Haydn's works inspired by Hungarian folk music may be found in H. C. Robbins Landon, *Haydn: Chronicle and Works* (London, 1978) III, 280–1. The current designation of this Mozart concerto as 'Turkish' probably comes from the association of this passage with the identical section from 'Le gelosie del seraglio'.

[8] Hermann Abert, *W. A. Mozart* (Leipzig 1956), I, 511.

Ex. 1: Mozart, Sonata for Piano in A major, KV 331 (300i), first movement, Var. III.

nowhere else in Mozart, to my knowledge, is there a legato melody in octaves for the piano (see Ex. 1).

If we consider Mozart's recurring preoccupation with this style, and take into account that it may also appear in places where it is not explicitly designated as such, we should be prepared to make more discoveries of 'Turkish' pieces among Mozart's compositions. Such a discovery is one of the most famous arias in Mozart's operatic oeuvre, Don Giovanni's 'Fin ch'han dal vino'. This number is especially difficult to place in context and seems in many ways quite un-Mozartean. Much has been written about the stunning effect of this aria,[9] but I have long been struck primarily by its negative qualities: its crudity, its lack of refinement, the roughness of its sound, the monotony of its rhythm and its unsophisticated harmony. The text of this aria is anything but an outpouring of feeling. Don Giovanni is simply planning a feast: the catering, the music, and, most cynically, the outcome for him: 'la mia lista ... d'una decina voglio aumentar'. And yet, compared to his two other arias in the opera, the serenade sung to an anonymous (and even unseen) girl in an empty window ('Deh, vieni alla finestra') and his instructions to Masetto ('Metà di voi qua vadano'), this is

---

[9] E.g., Abert *W. A. Mozart*, II, 325, 'But even this fundamental power has a shrill and breathless quality, and it has something elemental and volcanic about it'. See also Joseph Kerman, 'Reading Don Giovanni', in *Don Giovanni, Myths of Seduction and Betrayal*, ed. Jonathan Miller (Baltimore, 1990), 117 ff.

Ex. 2: Mozart, *Don Giovanni*, 'Fin ch'han dal vino', bars 1–10.

musically a most personal uttering. Its very strangeness sheds some light on the dark recesses of Don Giovanni's soul.

The first thing that may strike the listener is the unison of high-pitched instruments in the orchestral introduction, presenting the main motif: flutes and oboes 'à 2' in unison with the first violins, producing a shrill sound, uncommon in Mozart. Secondly, the fast repeated notes in the middle range (second violins and violas, clarinets and bassoons, in the postlude even joined by horns) creating a noisy effect, again most untypical of Mozart's background sonorities (Ex. 2). As the music goes on, we may wonder at the obsessive repetition of the same rhythmic motif: the pattern ♩♫|♩♩ is there practically all the time. If we take into account some variants: ♩♫|♫♩, ♫♩|♩ ♪, ♫♩|♫, ♫♩|♫♫, ♫♩|♩, the pattern is repeated fifty-nine times in the course of the aria.[10] Our attention is caught next by the aria's harmonic crudities: endless alternation of I and V, mostly in root position, and the total absence of the

---

[10] Abert (*W. A. Mozart* [see n. 8], I, 361) cites Paisiello's aria for Don Peppe 'Sore mia bella' (*La vedova di bel genio* Act I scene 1) where this rhythm is prominent. He calls it 'The rhythm of unrestrained exhilaration'.

Ex. 2: cont'd.

subdominant (or its substitutes) all through the aria![11] There are recurring parallel octaves between the melodic line and the bass (bars 7–8, 15–16, 27–32, 55–56 etc.); there are many literal repetitions of motifs, not just twice but three (bars 27–32), four (bars 37–44), and even six times (bars 105–16), and not just in closing sections (which would be normal), but all through the aria. All these features combine to present an irresistible impression of roughness.

The problem is not to explain why Mozart took such pains to strip away all the refinements and delicacies of his style. This may well be justified by the dramatic context of the aria: the 'volcanic' quality of unrestrained sexual desire, the spontaneous explosion of Don Giovanni's innermost feelings, hidden otherwise behind the mask of the Spanish nobleman. Don Giovanni feels threatened by Donna Anna's and Don Ottavio's suspicions, pronounced in the foregoing quartet ('Non ti fidar, o misera'). He needs now to escape into a world of profligacy and noisy feasts, where he feels protected. Perhaps, already sensing approaching doom,

[11] The only hint of a subdominant function appears in bars 94–5: the unison notes Eb–G, leading back (through A) to the main theme.

he strives for total abandon. 'Fin ch'han dal vino' is certainly not joyful and merry, but maniacal, obsessive,[12] and aggressive.[13] The problem here is to associate this aria meaningfully with a *topos*, to put it in a resonant social and musical context in order to consider what category of utterance this is.[14]

We may think in the first place that our aria is a kind of *contredanse*. This dance actually appears a bit later in the opera, when the feast planned in this aria becomes a reality: it is one of the three dances performed simultaneously on stage in the first act finale (bars 449 ff). Wye Allanbrook reads the aria this way, calling the *contredanse* a 'new dance' and a 'dance of No-Man', bringing it thus into relation with Don Giovanni's anarchic character. Actually, though, it was the most popular dance of the upper middle class in Western Europe at Mozart's time, with a tradition of more than a hundred years. Allanbrook rightly perceives the additive construction of the aria, with no qualitative differentiation between consecutive phrases, and brilliantly connects this trait with Don Giovanni's list of conquests. Nevertheless, she shows no similarity between this unique mode of construction and the actual music of *contredanses*, including the many by Mozart himself. These show a quite normal rondeau form. Furthermore, I know no *contredanse* with the typical rhythmic pattern of 'Fin ch'han dal vino' nor with its breathless tempo. Thus there seems to be no real foundation for identifying the *contredanse* as the original *topos* of this aria, and we must look for it elsewhere.

The *topos* most suitable to this aria is in fact the 'Turkish mode', with which it shares $\frac{2}{4}$ time, rapid tempo, wild and orgiastic character, many repetitions of motifs, rudimentary harmony and fast repeated notes in middle-range accompaniment. In Pedrillo's and Osmin's 'Vivat Bacchus' and Monostatos's 'Alles fühlt der Liebe Freuden' – both explicitly alla turca pieces – we have also the high unison of woodwinds,[15] which, together with the middle-range repeated notes, create a shrill and tumultuous sonority (even in Monostatos's aria, where the dynamics are *pp*). The most general feature common to 'Fin ch'han dal vino' and most 'Turkish' pieces of Mozart is the lack of rhythmic and harmonic variety – a variety notably

---

[12] A similarity may indeed be observed between this aria and the restless and obsessive last movement of the piano sonata in A minor, KV 310, $\frac{2}{4}$, *Presto*.

[13] Kerman, 'Reading Don Giovanni' (see n. 9) discusses 'Fin ch'han dal vino' and anger. See below for more on this subject.

[14] 'For Mozart was in possession of something we may call an expressive vocabulary, a collection in music of what in the theory of rhetoric are called *topoi*, or topics for formal discourse. He held it in common with his audience, and used it in his operas with the skill of a master craftsman. This vocabulary, when captured and categorized, provides a tool for analysis which can mediate between the operas and our individual responses to them, supplying independent information about the expressive content of the arias and ensembles'. Wye Jamison Allanbrook, *Rhythmic Gesture in Mozart, Le nozze di Figaro and Don Giovanni* (Chicago, 1983), 2.

[15] This may be an imitation of the sound of the *zurna*, a high-pitched oboe-like wind instrument, which carried the melodic line in the Janissary orchestras. This refers us again to the third variation of KV 331.

Ex. 3a: Mozart, Concerto for Violin in A major, KV 219, third movement, bars 134–138.

Ex. 3b: Mozart, Sonata for Piano in A major, KV 331, third movement, bars 25–9.

Ex. 3c: Mozart, Sonata for Piano in A major, KV 331, third movement, bars 122–7.

Ex. 3d: Mozart, *Die Entführung aus dem Serail*, Overture, bars 1–4.

Ex. 3e: Mozart, *Die Entführung aus dem Serail*, No. 14, 'Vivat Bacchus' bars 1–3.

Ex. 3f: Mozart, *Die Entführung aus dem Serail*, No. 21b, Chor der Janitscharen, bars 21–4.

present in most of Mozart's non-Turkish music. This lack makes explicit the feeling of a 'primitive', less articulate musical culture.[16]

Let us add to these the principal motif of 'Fin ch'han dal vino', the rising and falling third, which has been recognised as a characteristic trait of 'Turkish' music by several commentators.[17] In Mozart's 'Turkish' output this trait is prominent in the major section of the 'alla turca' movement from the sonata KV 331, in the

---

[16] 'in the absence of specific signs of "Turkishness", "deficiency" and "incoherence" must take particular forms to function as markers of exoticism' (Hunter, 'The "Alla Turca" Style' [see n. 5], 49). As signs of deficiency she mentions later on 'lack of polyphony or harmony'. These are, as I have shown, prominent features of 'Fin ch'han dal vino'. The incoherence in our aria manifests itself by its lack of formal articulation. Her description of the final Scythian dance movement from Gluck's 'Iphigénie en Tauride' (*ibid.*, 51) as an example of 'deficiency' and 'incoherence' in the alla turca style could apply almost literally to 'Fin ch'han dal vino'.

[17] Szabolcsi, 'Exoticism, in Mozart' (see n. 5), finds this melodic feature in a Hungarian, march-like dance called 'Törökös' ('Turkish' in Hungarian) which appears in several sources from the eighteenth to the twentieth centuries.

Ex. 4a: Mozart, *Don Giovanni*, No. 7, 'Là ci darem la mano', bars 1–2.

Ex. 4b: Mozart, *Don Giovanni*, No. 17, 'Metà di voi qua vadano', bar 1.

principal theme of the overture to the 'Abduction' and in its second Janissary choir; if we include the up and down leaps of a fourth, we find it also, most pronouncedly, in 'Vivat Bacchus' and in the violin concerto (see Exx. 3a–f).[18] We may even go further: this rising and falling third may be called Don Giovanni's leitmotif: it appears clearly as head motif in 'Là ci darem la mano' and 'Metà di voi qua vadano' (see Exx. 4a–b).

Odd as it may sound, Don Giovanni's aria is in a sense more 'Turkish' than most compositions recognized under this label. Kurt Reinhard lists fourteen characteristics for the alla turca style,[19] of which ten may be found in 'Fin ch'han dal vino': duple metre, marked accents on strong beats, loudness, simple rhythmic patterns and repeated notes in the accompaniment, rudimentary harmony, doubling of the sung melodic line by octaves, thirds as melodic outline, short motifs, and multiple repetitions of motifs.[20] This is more than may be said about any other single overtly 'Turkish' composition by Mozart. To these we may add the 'heterophonic' effect of the ornaments added in some places in the doubling of the voice by the flute and the violins, for example bars 15, 27, 63 etc., and the sudden change to minor in bars 57–69. We may compare these 'Turkish' traits in 'Fin ch'han dal vino' with the most obviously 'Turkish' piece by Mozart, the 'alla turca' movement from the sonata KV 331, where we have the $\frac{2}{4}$ time, the drum-like ostinato in the bass, the repeated notes in the middle range, the ornamented melody built on thirds, with many repeats and sequences, the back-and-forth between parallel minor and major, the octave doublings in the major section and the relatively impoverished harmonic language, consisting mainly of alternations between I–V in root position. Both pieces as wholes manifest a striking voluntary impoverishment of musical means.

Let us move one step further into the field of pure speculation, considering the choice of tonality, B flat major, for 'Fin ch'han dal vino'. C. F. D. Schubart (1739–91) in his *Ideen zu einer Ästhetik der Tonkunst*,[21] an often-cited source about Janissary music in Mozart's time, says: 'F major and B flat major seem to be the

---

[18] This motif, though, is also a characteristic of gypsy music.
[19] Reinhard, 'Mozarts Rezeption türkischer Musik' (see n. 5).
[20] The typical rhythmic pattern of 'Fin ch'han dal vino' also appears in other 'alla turca' contexts: Gluck, *Iphigénie en Tauride*, Act I scene 6, chorus of the Scythian priests, 'Blut kann den göttlichen Zorn'; Haydn, *Lo speziale*, Act III no. 20, Volpino's aria 'Salamelica, Semprugna cara'; Mozart, *Die Zauberflöte*, Act II no. 13, Monostatos, aria 'Alles fühlt der Liebe Freuden'.
[21] C. F. D. Schubart, *Ideen zu einer Ästhetik der Tonkunst* (Vienna, 1806), 332.

favourite tonalities of the Turks, because in these the range of all their instruments coincides most precisely'. In Mozart's 'Turkish' output the tonality of A is prominent (see especially the violin concerto and the piano sonata).[22] Both of Beethoven's contributions to this style, the Turkish March from his incidental music to *The Ruins of Athens* and the strophe 'Froh wie deine Sonnen' from the 'Ode to Joy' are in B flat major. If we grant that the tuning of Janissary orchestras did not correspond exactly to Western instruments, we may assume that much of the Janissary music Mozart and Beethoven might have heard was in a tonality somewhere between A and B flat. This may explain why these tonalities occurred to them immediately when they wrote in this style.[23] Even Osmin's 'Erst geköpft, dann gehangen' which appears unexpectedly in A minor (appended to an aria in F major) may belong here. Mozart's own explanation of this unprepared modulation, in his famous letter to his father (26 September 1781) is as follows:

But as passions, whether violent or not, must never be expressed in such a way as to excite disgust, and as music even in the most terrible situations, must never offend the ear, but must please the hearer, or in other words must never cease to be *music*, I have gone from F (the key in which the aria is written) not into a remote key but into a related one, not, however into its nearest relative D minor, but into the more remote A minor.[24]

This explanation is not altogether convincing: it is not obvious why the tonality of A minor would be more expressive of anger in this context than D minor, solely because it is a bit more remote from F major than D minor. It may be a rationalization concealing the compulsion Mozart felt to use the tonality of A whenever he needed to show 'Turkishness', especially in its wild aspect. Actually, this excerpt recalls the eruptive A minor episode in the fifth violin concerto, and perhaps, again, the last movement of KV 310, which is of course in A minor too (see n. 12). Nevertheless, the key of A is otherwise absent from the 'Abduction'. The 'alla turca' pieces are written for the most part in C major, and one ('Ach, wie will ich triumphieren') in D major.

Another melodic detail in 'Fin ch'han dal vino' may lead us again on to the same track: the chromatic descent from C to G, to the words 'teco ancor quella cerca menar' (bars 21–4). This chromaticism is a curious feature in a melody governed otherwise by strict diatonism and broken chords (some hint of it appears three times later, to the words 'chi il minuetto ... la follia ... l'alemanna', bars 45–54). Chromaticism normally goes with heightened expression, mostly of pain or fear. Julian Rushton convincingly interprets these same notes as a death-motif, making its first appearance in the opera immediately after the death of the Commendatore, then twice transposed, first at the end of Donna Anna and Ottavio's duet where they swear revenge, and finally at Don Giovanni's descent into hell in the second

---

[22] We may add to this Gluck's overture to *La rencontre imprévue*, also in A major, also using the Turkish instrumentarium and showing other marked exotic musical characteristics.

[23] Let me add here, as a mere curiosity, that Mozart's 'alla turca' movement from the sonata KV 331 was incorporated, orchestrated by Auber, into a performance of *Don Giovanni* by the Paris Opéra in 1866 (Rudolph Angermüller, 'Pariser *Don Juan* – Rezensionen 1805–1866', in *Mozart-Studien*, ed. Manfred Hermann Schmid (Tutzing, 1998), 213.

[24] Emily Anderson, trans. and ed., *The Letters of Mozart & His Family* (London, 1938), 1144.

Ex. 5: Mozart, Violin Concerto No. 5, KV 219, third movement, bars 197–214.

finale.[25] This descending chromaticism is a prominent feature of some of Mozart's finest instrumental compositions of the same period: amongst others the C minor piano concerto KV 491 (first and last movements), the G minor quintet KV 516 (first movement), and above all in the A minor Rondo for piano KV 511.[26] All

---

[25] Julian Rushton, *W. A. Mozart: Don Giovanni* (Cambridge, 1981), 117–19. A similar interpretation may be found in Daniel Heartz, *Mozart's Operas* (Oxford, 1990), 181. Heartz, like Rushton, sees the symbolism of death in descending chromaticisms, but at the same time rising chromaticism is connected with sexual desire. He cites in this context the rising chromatic line of clarinets and bassoons in bars 107–10 of our aria.

[26] Later it appears again, most emphatically, in Pamina's 'Des Jämmers Mass ist voll', *Die Zauberflöte*, Act II, finale, bars 84–6.

these pieces have a quality of deep sorrow, even wailing, which bring them in direct relation to the examples in *Don Giovanni* quoted by Julian Rushton.

But does the chromatic motif in 'Fin ch'han dal vino', as conspicuous as it is, have anything to do with the mood just described? The words are not really significant and have no emotional impact. The fast tempo and the rhythmic shape suggest altogether different issues. It seems absurd to assume that Don Giovanni, in the midst of his preparation for the feast, is subconsciously haunted by guilty thoughts of imminent death. I would suggest that this motif in this aria points in a quite different direction: it functions as a kind of stylistic reference to the chromatic passage from the A minor section of the last movement of the fifth violin concerto (bars 204–12), which manifests the same fast tempo and fiercely agitated mood. This may be seen as another link between this aria and the Turkish *topos* (see Ex. 5).

This motif has yet another history within the opera, connected to its genre:[27] in the monumental sextet in Act II (from bar 61) it appears in a pattern of dotted notes, repeated over and over again by the violins. When sung by Donna Anna and Zerlina to the words 'che mai sarà?' (bars 125–7), this motif concisely expresses uneasiness, worry, underlying fear – but looked at with a certain (comic) irony, as if from outside. The culmination of this passage is Leporello's plea for mercy 'pietà, Signori' (bars 98–102) where the colour of the music is unmistakably 'oriental'. Leporello sings in the Phrygian mode, harmonized in a unique way (the Neapolitan chord figuring as an upward returning chord, above a tonic organ point) and the chromatic descent of the woodwinds in octaves, punctuating the sung phrases, reminds us again of the *zurna* (see Ex. 6). If we believe that Don Giovanni is related to Turkey in some way, then Leporello, his shadow or alter ego, should also be. It seems as if, believing himself about to die, Leporello falls back upon his musical mother tongue. This passage, then, combines very well with Rushton's death motif.

But why would Don Giovanni sing in Turkish style? He is a Spanish aristocrat and nothing in his story connects him in any way to Turkey. Yet a closer inspection reveals a connection. Since the Turkish siege on Vienna in 1689, the Turks were remembered as a very tangible threat to Western civilisation. Even though the relations between the Ottoman Empire and Europe had improved considerably during Maria Theresia's reign[28] the threatening image of the Turks was still alive in the minds of Mozart's contemporaries[29] and Joseph II was just about to wage war once more against the Turks.[30] If we keep in mind that the character of Don Giovanni has been interpreted as undermining established

---

[27] This motif has also a 'buffo' tradition in other Mozart operas: Figaro's 'e stravolto m'ho un nervo del piè', *Le nozze di Figaro*, Act II, finale. Further such examples may be found in the fragment 'L'oca del Cairo'.

[28] See C. M. Altar, 'W. A. Mozart im Lichte osmanisch-österreichischer Beziehungen', *Revue Belge de Musicologie*, 10 (1956), 138–48.

[29] Turks, and 'orientals' in general, from Montesquieu's *Persian Letters* on, were often said to represent both the enlightened rulers of utopian domains and cruel or threatening figures. In Mozart's *Entführung* we have both: Osmin versus Bassa Selim. See below.

[30] In 1788, joining the Russians.

Ex. 6: *Don Giovanni*, No. 19, Sextet, bars 96–101.

society,[31] it might not be beyond the pale to associate this figure with the malicious Turk.

But there is a more specific association: in the view of the eighteenth century, Turks were associated with sexual licentiousness,[32] their rulers thought to possess harems with hundreds of women, among whom they could choose at will for sexual enjoyment. In fact the women in Turkey enjoyed much more freedom, and had their say even in politics, but what concerns us here is how they were perceived by Mozart and his Western European contemporaries: nothing more remote from official Christian morality. Instead of incorporating the morals of his caste, the stiff manners of Spanish nobility, Don Giovanni creates a behavioral ethical code much closer to the 'Turkish': he keeps a successive harem, instead of the simultaneous one of the Turkish pasha. His rules are even stricter: every woman may fulfill her role

---

[31] Frits Noske, 'Don Giovanni: an Interpretation', in *The Signifier and the Signified: Studies in Mozart and Verdi* (The Hague, 1977), 86.

[32] Cf. Gradenwitz, *Musik zwischen Orient und Okzident* (see n. 5), 212–13; Thomas Bauman, *W. A. Mozart: Die Entführung aus dem Serail* (Cambridge, 1987), 273–4; and Hunter, 'The "Alla Turca" Style' (see n. 5), 56.

in the harem just once, and is then cast out. Yet she is symbolically 'kept' there: the harem-keeper being Leporello, Giovanni's Osmin, who holds the famous 'catalogo', a harem in book form, enclosing all his master's women.[33]

We have no unequivocal indication of Mozart's intention to create any link between Don Giovanni and the Turks. And yet a curious detail may point in this direction: when Leporello in his catalogue-aria presents the statistics about Don Giovanni's amorous achievements in different countries, he mentions, after Italy, Germany and France, 'in *Turchia* novantuna'. This detail becomes more significant if we compare Da Ponte's text to his model: Bertati's words for this aria are as follows:

> Dell'Italia, ed Allemagna
> Ve ne ho scritto cento, e tante.
> Della Francia, e della Spagna
> Ve ne sono non so quante[34]

[From Italy and Germany I've written a hundred or more; I have no idea how many from France and Spain].

Bertati mentions all countries found in Da Ponte, except Turkey. Thus it seems that the bewildering idea of mentioning Turkey among the countries where Don Giovanni made his conquests was Da Ponte's, or perhaps even Mozart's own (there is no direct testimony confirming it, but it is clear that the collaboration between the two in creating the libretto was close).[35] Even the number of Don Giovanni's conquests in Spain – the famous 'mille e tre' – may evoke oriental associations: perhaps it stems from '1001 Nights'.

Don Giovanni's 'Turkish' connection may be approached from another direction as well. Joseph Kerman's 'Reading Don Giovanni' presents a detailed and masterly analysis of 'Fin ch'han dal vino', stressing its violent musical qualities, lingering on its curious construction and the unusual relation between the stanzas of the poem and the sections of the aria.[36] Kerman, too, brings it into relation with Osmin's rage aria from the *Entführung*, especially with the A minor section 'Erst geköpft, dann gehangen' and with Figaro's cavatina 'Se vuol ballare', referring again mainly to the fast section 'L'arte schermendo'. The musical common denominator to all three of

---

[33] A hint, referring negatively to this association, may be found in Bernard Williams, 'Don Giovanni as an Idea', in Rushton, *W. A. Mozart: Don Giovanni*, 85: 'The catalogue, as Jean Massin said, is the negation of the harem'. I could not find the phrase in Massin's book, and Williams gives no precise reference. He obviously means that Don Giovanni's pursuits are concerned with the moment only, with immediate conquest, and not with long-lasting possession. But if that is true why is there a catalogue? The catalogue is clearly instituted by Don Giovanni himself, as it is mentioned not only in Leporello's aria but also in 'Fin ch'han dal vino'. If Don Giovanni feels the need to keep on record all the women he seduced, this must indicate some instinct of possession.
[34] *Don Giovanni, o sia il convitato di pietra*, libretto di Giovanni Bertati, musica di Gazzaniga, ed. S. Kunze, (Kassel and Basle, 1974). Cited in Alfred Einstein, *Mozart, his Character, his Work* (London, 1945), 437, and in John Platoff, 'Catalogue Arias and the "Catalogue Aria"', *Wolfgang Amadè Mozart: Essays on his Life and his Music*, ed. Stanley Sadie (Oxford, 1996), 304.
[35] Daniel Heartz gives several examples of Mozart's probable interference in the creation of Da Ponte's libretto of *Don Giovanni*. See Heartz, *Mozart's Operas* (Berkeley, 1990), 165–9.
[36] Kerman, 'Reading Don Giovanni,' (see n. 9).

these arias is the obsessive repetition of the same rhythmic pattern in a fast tempo – and Figaro's aria uses exactly the same pattern as Giovanni's. Dramatically, then, this pattern seems to represent uncontrolled anger 'associated with, about, at, or in sex'.[37] Osmin's fierce hatred against the Europeans is motivated by his rejection by Blonde, who turns him down because of her attachment to Pedrillo.[38] Figaro is enraged by jealousy because of the Count's advances to Susanna. Don Giovanni, though he never says so, is frustrated in all his amorous attempts from the beginning of the opera: his attempted rape of Donna Anna (probably) failed, and Elvira's intrusion has thwarted his seduction of Zerlina.

Let us add here a sentence from Mozart's famous letter on the composition of Osmin's rage-aria: 'Der Zorn des osmin wird dadurch in das Komische gebracht, weil die türkische Musik dabey angebracht ist'.[39] In other words: 'if you want him to sound angry, let him sing Turkish, and then it will sound really ridiculous'. Here we have an amalgamation of anger, Turkishness and ridicule. No wonder that in later situations when Mozart needed musical expression of extreme anger (which, seen from outside, is never devoid of ridicule) he would come back to the musical associations of the Turkish mode.[40]

The association of Don Giovanni's figure with the Turkish sphere, whether consciously intended by Mozart or not, would also confirm some impressions of this exceptional operatic hero. On the one hand he is the monster, the enemy not only of the established order, but alien to human feelings of sympathy: coldly planning his seductions, cruelly rejecting those women who, once possessed, claim his love and fidelity. In these qualities he may resemble the image of the ferocious Muslim Turk, who lacks all restraint and Christian humanity – a figure which most probably persisted in the imagination of Europeans in Mozart's time. Bauman cites Norman Daniel: 'The two most important aspects of Muhammad's life, Christians believed, were his sexual license and his use of force to establish his religion'.[41] On the other hand, Don Giovanni is the preacher of 'libertà', the representative of a new, utopian order of things, where he, as a kind of Nietzschean *Übermensch*, may experience his life to the full, unhampered by traditions and arbitrary rules. In

---

[37] *Ibid.*, 119.
[38] Nowhere in *Die Entführung* is Osmin referred to as a eunuch, but his position as harem-keeper and his irritable and malicious character may imply this. Montesquieu's fictional description of a eunuch's state of mind and behaviour strikingly resembles Osmin: 'I hoped that I would be delivered from attacks of love by the impossibility of satisfying them. Alas! The effects of passion were extinguished in me without extinguishing the cause, and far from being soothed, I found myself surrounded by objects which ceaselessly excited them ... The harem is like a little empire for me, and my only ambition, the only passion left to me, can be satisfied a little ... I voluntarily burden myself with the hate of all these women ...' *Lettres Persanes* (Paris, 1975), Lettre IX, 23–6.
[39] Mozart, *Letters* (see n. 24).
[40] Wye Allanbrook shows us that Mozart can express jealous anger by quite opposing means: In the Count's aria 'Vedrò mentr'io sospiro' in *Le nozze di Figaro* the protagonist's extreme anger is shown by extending the 'paradigmatic' two-bar phrases into three bars (to the words 'Tu non nascesti, audace') and adding a bar to repeat the words 'per ridere'. This is anger expressed by extension and lingering, as opposed to the model we examined, where it is expressed by rushing forward and mechanical repetition.
[41] Bauman, *W. A. Mozart: Die Entführung aus dem Serail* (see n. 32), 27.

Kierkegaard's words: 'This force in Don Juan, this omnipotence, this animation, only music can express, and I know no other predicate to describe it than this: it is exuberant Joy of life'.[42] This can be associated with the 'enlightened Orientals' of eighteenth-century literature and art, who may represent a utopian ideal, or a higher stage of humanity.[43] This ambiguity finds its correspondence in the Don's music: 'Fin ch'han dal vino' certainly presents a negative view of Don Giovanni's character, while in many other numbers where his role is prominent – the duet 'Là ci darem la mano', the hymn to liberty in the first act finale and the serenade with the mandoline – he gets some of Mozart's most attractive music. Thus Mozart achieves a high degree of identification on the part of the listener with this hero. Moreover, the scene of his downfall in the second finale has a claim as Mozart's highest achievement in staged musical tragedy. The death of a repellent and unworthy character would surely not be shown in such a sublime and deeply moving way.

This duality of Don Giovanni's character may be better understood if we compare him to other heroes from Mozart's mature operas. Kierkegaard sees him as the third and final step of evolution in the hierarchy of eroticism: from Cherubino through Papageno to Giovanni (Papageno having been invented later does not seem to undermine the theory). But having established the possibility of a 'Turkish' interpretation of Don Giovanni, I would like to draw another line of inter-relations between three operas, where Don Giovanni may be seen as a fusion of two character types, separate in the other two works: Bassa Selim and Osmin of the 'Abduction' becoming one in *Don Giovanni*, and splitting up again into Sarastro and Monostatos in *Die Zauberflöte*.

Bassa Selim has his harem of course, and in his endeavours to gain Konstanze's favours 'runs the gamut from persuasion to force'[44] (he threatens her with 'Martern aller Arten'). But in the end he emerges as the magnanimous ruler who deals out 'libertà' to his prisoners. His lack of a singing voice despite being one of the main characters of the plot remains a mystery. Maybe Mozart was not really sure what voice he should sing in: he could not sing in Sarastro's voice, being a Turkish despot kidnapping innocent Westerners. Moreover, Sarastro's music was not part of Mozart's musical vocabulary at this pre-Masonic stage of his career. On the other hand, Selim could not use Osmin's 'Turkish' idiom, being a Christian-born renegade, and, after all, an enlightened ruler. Osmin, on the other hand, has a very clear voice of his own: he has the fierce and angry side of Don Giovanni, without any of his attractive, immediately erotic qualities.

Giovanni, as we have seen, has both sides: the hellish, devouring, unrestrained one, which predominates, but in some places, shining through, the idealistic, utopian

---

[42] Søren Kierkegaard, *Either/Or*, trans. David F. Swenson and Lillian Marvin Swenson (New York, 1959), 100.
[43] The Persian Uzbek, in Montesquieu's *Lettres Persanes* (see n. 38), 169, describes the ideal government: 'I have often considered which would be the government which would most conform with reason. It has seemed to me that the most perfect would be that . . . which led men in a way which best suited their desires and inclinations.'
[44] Kerman, 'Reading Don Giovanni' (see n. 9), 110.

side. In addition to the hymn-like 'libertà'-chorus this aspect is tangible in a phrase he sings in the second finale: after having invited Elvira, ironically, to dine with him, he sings in praise of women and wine, 'sostegno e gloria dell'umanità'. The words seem to point to an ironic interpretation, but the melody, again, has a lofty tone, which is otherwise absent from Don Giovanni's music.[45] Again, as mentioned earlier, this idealistic quality may be sensed in his last scene, where it is difficult not to admire Don Giovanni's proud standing.

If we crystallize just these aspects of the Don Giovanni who speaks about 'umanità', we may discover them later on in the figure of Sarastro,[46] the full-fledged prophet of humanistic ideals. But Sarastro, too, has his Don Giovanni aspects, or rather, he goes back to the Bassa Selim model: 'Zur Liebe kann ich dich nicht zwingen . . .'[47] – I cannot force you to love (my position would not permit that, though perhaps I would wish to). This sentence disavows Sarastro's claim to have kidnapped Pamina to save her from the evil influence of her mother. Tamino, at least before his conversion to Sarastro's cult, seems to understand it this way: 'Die Absicht ist nur allzuklar!' (The intention is all too clear!). Later on, like Bassa Selim, Sarastro gives up Pamina and hands her over to Tamino. But in the first place he abandons her to Monostatos, his 'harem-guardian' (though what we see in the opera is only a one-woman harem).[48] And indeed, Pamina is subjected to the same kind of treatment as she would be in Bassa Selim's harem: seclusion and sexual harassment. Monostatos represents, of course, Sarastro's dark side,[49] in any sense of the term. He resembles Don Giovanni in his cold sexuality,[50] never expressing – or even pretending to express – love to Pamina. He is the Don Giovanni of 'Fin ch'han dal vino', rushing forward to fulfilment. Being black he is, in the terms of the drama, predestined to act this way, while Don Giovanni repudiates the codes of behavior of his class. Thus, Monostatos may figure as a one-sided, basically simple character, whereas Giovanni is more complex, retaining, even in Mozart's eyes, the privileges of his birth. Thus, that Monostatos's only aria is 'Turkish' ('Alles fühlt'), is justified not merely by his race, but by his dramatic persona. Except that here this music comes already 'as if from afar':[51] it is Mozart's farewell to Turkishness.

---

[45] It is, perhaps by mere coincidence, the same melody that Papageno sings in his 'suicide'-aria, to the words 'Schöne Mädchen, denkt an mich'.
[46] Something gets lost as well in this transformation: the ideals we hear of in the *Die Zauberflöte* are wisdom, virtue, perseverence, never 'libertà' in any meaning of the term. It sounds all more like submission: more spiritual, but also tamer than *Don Giovanni*.
[47] See Peter Branscombe, *W. A. Mozart, Die Zauberflöte* (Cambridge, 1991), 128.
[48] For all practical purposes, Bassa Selim's is a one-woman harem as well, since we see only Konstanze and Blonde. See Bauman, *W. A. Mozart: Die Entführung aus dem Serail*, 33.
[49] See Anthony Besch, 'A Director's Approach', in *W. A. Mozart: Die Zauberflöte*, ed. Branscombe, 198.
[50] See Abert, *W. A. Mozart* (see n. 8), II, 663–5.
[51] A general direction for the performance of the orchestra and the singer in the score of this aria (unique, as far as I know) says: 'Alles wird so piano gesungen und gespielt, als wenn die Musik in weiter Entfernung wäre' (Everything should be so quietly sung and played that it seems as if the music were in the distance).

Don Giovanni remains the only Mozartean figure where both voices, the demoniac and the idealistic, unite into one.[52] He is the lascivious Turk and the utopian Oriental at the same time.[53] The Mozart of *Don Giovanni* is already a Mason, fully mature, aware of his forces, sensing the unrestrained cravings of instinct and, at the same time, the tragic limitations of human existence. The Turkish 'other', loitering through Mozart's music, is nowhere better integrated into the composition than in *Don Giovanni*, but its weirdness is still perceptible in those passages of the opera where Mozart steps out of his 'style': in 'Fin ch'han dal vino' and in Leporello's orientalizing plea for mercy.

---

[52] 'The sense of freedom that he expresses does not have all the metaphysical resonances that existentialist writers found in it, but it does have a significance which goes beyond an individual personal characteristic . . .', Bernard Williams, 'Don Giovanni as an Idea', in *W. A. Mozart: Don Giovanni*, ed. Rushton, 90.

[53] Matthew Head's *Orientalism, Masquerade and Mozart's Turkish Music* (London, 2000) appeared after this article was in the publication process, and thus could not receive the attention it deserves. Head does not mention *Don Giovanni* in relation to the Turkish topic in Mozart's music, but in Ch. 4 he describes the popularity of Turkishness in late 18th-century Vienna as one manifestation of a general delight in masquerade, citing Pezzl's description of a carnival ball at the Redoutensaal with the blur of one music against another (p. 101). This brings to mind, of course, the first finale of *Don Giovanni*. However, in my interpretation Don Giovanni does not wear a Turkish 'mask', but is, rather, a 'Turk' disguised as Spanish nobleman, whose 'true' identity occasionally shines through.

[15]

ORIENTAL TYRANNY IN THE EXTREME WEST: REFLECTIONS ON *AMITI E ONTARIO* AND *LE GARE GENEROSE*

PIERPAOLO POLZONETTI

ABSTRACT

This is a study of eighteenth-century operatic representations of slavery in America, focusing primarily on two Italian comic works: Ranieri de' Calzabigi's libretto for Amiti e Ontario *(1772) and its adaptation,* Le gare generose, *or 'The Contests in Generosity' (1786), set by Giovanni Paisiello. Significant changes between the two are interpreted in relation to these works' original cultural and political contexts, reconstructed through the examination of contemporary dramatic, journalistic and other non-fictional literature. As an operatic theme, in the late eighteenth century, slavery challenges the long established assumption of the westward migration of progress and civilization.*

The geographical and political entity identifiable with the United States of America began to inspire operatic subjects during the second half of the eighteenth century, considerably later than did other non-European territories. South America, for example, had been providing material for opera plots and settings since the previous century, and in the course of the eighteenth century inspired countless *opere serie* and *balli eroici* predominantly based on Voltaire's *Alzire*, on the tragic story of Montezuma or on Columbus's enterprise.[1]

I have read different shorter versions of this article at the Annual Meeting of the American Musicological Society (Washington, D. C., 2005), at the Program of Liberal Studies of the University of Notre Dame and at the Biannual Meeting of the Society for Eighteenth-Century Music (Williamsburg, VA, 2006). I am grateful for the feedback I received from my colleagues on each of these occasions, especially from Anthony DelDonna and Steven Fallon. An expanded version of this article will appear as a chapter in my forthcoming book, *Italian Opera in the Age of the American Revolution*. The most recent research behind this article is partially sponsored by the American National Endowment for the Humanities.

1 For a preliminary study on eighteenth-century European operas based on South American subjects see Donatella Ferri, *L'America nei libretti italiani del settecento* (Rome: Bulzoni, 1992), and Enrique Alberto Arias, 'New Worlds to Conquer: Operatic Depictions of the Age of Discovery', *The Music Review* 54/1 (1993), 14–23 (mostly concerned with Columbus's discovery and Spanish colonization of South America). The Pacific islands started to attract the attention of European musicians later than South America and the Middle or Far East, but earlier than North America: see David Irving, 'The Pacific in the Minds and Music of Enlightenment Europe', *Eighteenth-Century Music* 2/2 (2005), 205–229. Ranieri de' Calzabigi contributed to this genre with his libretto *Cook o sia Gl'inglesi in Othaiti* (1785), discussed by Irving (223) and by Maria Irene Maffei, 'Alcune osservazioni sul Cook o sia Gl'inglesi in Othaiti', in *Ranieri Calzabigi tra Vienna e Napoli: atti del convegno di studi (Livorno, 23–24 settembre 1996)*, ed. Federico Marri and Francesco Paolo Russo (Lucca: Libreria Musicale Italiana, 1997), 209–238. On Africa and the Middle East see especially Timothy Taylor, 'Peopling the Stage: Opera, Otherness, and New Musical Representations in the Eighteenth Century', *Cultural Critique* 36 (1997), 65–88; Miriam Whaples, 'Early Exoticism Revisited', and Mary Hunter, 'The Alla Turca Style in the Late Eighteenth Century: Race and Gender in the Symphony and the Seraglio', both in *The Exotic in Western Music*, ed. Jonathan Bellman (Boston: Northeastern University Press, 1998), 3–25 and 43–73 respectively; for the Far East see Vom Takt, 'Chinoiserien in der Musik- und Tanzgeschichte bis 1800', *Festschrift Christoph-Hellmut Mahling zum 65. Geburtstag*, ed. Christoph-Hellmut Mahling and others (Tutzing: Hans Schneider, 1997), 1171–1186. A general overview of orientalism in opera (including the eighteenth century) is offered by Ralph Locke, 'Reflections on Orientalism in Opera and Musical Theater', *The Opera Quarterly* 10/1 (1993), 48–64. The only comprehensive study of representations of North American subjects in eighteenth-century Italian opera remains my 'Opera Buffa and the American Revolution'

If South American dethroned kings and defeated civilizations found their perfect theatrical locus of representation on the seria stage, which already favoured ancient history and mythology, North America provided fashionable subjects to the comic genre. This is not because North Americans were perceived as funnier than their Southern neighbours, but because the appeal of North American subjects, typical of the revolutionary era, was justified by the increasing interest of Europeans in alternative configurations of society; and so opera buffa was the logical home for these new subjects, considering the leaning of the genre towards the representation of contemporary socio-political reality. The introduction of American subjects in Italian comic opera coincides in fact with the first episodes of unrest in the English colonies against the British central government and with the first dissemination in Europe of American political ideas, immediately perceived in the entire Western world as the cutting-edge of Enlightened political thought. Although scarcely documented in historical and musicological accounts, opera buffa responded to the American Revolution with considerable promptness, resulting in a group of works reflecting the interest of the European public in the first great revolution of the century, a strong interest that manifested itself also in gazettes, pamphlets and other fictional and non-fictional genres of literature.[2] As early as 1768 the Italian *Gazzetta di Firenze* (which became *Notizie del mondo* later that year) informed its readers about the British military occupation of Boston in response to the recent American uprising against the Townshend Acts. The gazette added a pronouncement to the citizens of Boston. This document paraphrases Samuel Adams's inflammatory 'circular letter', stating the Bostonians' opposition to foreign laws and the principle of no taxation without representation ('che nessun uomo sarà governato da leggi straniere, né tassato che da sé medesimo, o dal suo Rappresentante legalmente e liberamente eletto').[3] By the end of the summer Niccolò Piccinni had set a comic libretto by Francesco Cerlone, *I napoletani in America*, which can be considered the first opera based on a North American subject. This *commedia per musica* represents an Italian woman of humble origins who becomes the governor of a remote province of North America, where she brings civilization and freedom, introduces appropriate clothing and food, and spreads enlightened philosophy among the natives (before her reforms they were living in a state of uncivilized and immoral savageness, which included nudity, horrible food and a tyrannical social organization). Starting with Piccinni's second Americanist opera, *L'americano* (Rome 1772), and during the whole decade, Native Americans started to be represented less as uncouth barbarians and more as free individuals living in a form of natural anarchy free from constricting socio-cultural norms.[4] At the same time American characters of European

---

(PhD dissertation, Cornell University, 2003), currently under revision. Relevant contributions to the theme of exoticism in eighteenth-century theatre (both spoken and musical) can be found in *Le arti della scena e l'esotismo in età moderna*, ed. Paolo Giovanai Maione and Francesco Cotticelli (Naples: Centro di Musica Antica Pietà de' Turchini, 2006). Additional literature will be cited later in this article.

2 In Italy a boom in the gazette industry coincided with the earliest stages of the American Revolution in the late 1760s. The newly founded *Gazzetta estera*, *Notizie del mondo*, *Gazzetta Universale* and other journals were generally published twice a week and disseminated in all the important urban centres of the peninsula. See Paola Urbani and Alfredo Donati, *I periodici dell' Ancien Régime e del periodo rivoluzionario nelle biblioteche italiane* (Rome: Biblioteca Casanatense, 1992); on the dissemination of news concerning the American Revolution see Franco Venturi, *The End of the Old Regime in Europe, 1768–1776: The First Crisis*, trans. Burr Litchfield (Princeton: Princeton University Press, 1989), 377–438.

3 *Gazzetta di Firenze* 2 (27 August 1768), 10–11; other news items published from February 1768 concerning the American uprising are documented and discussed by Venturi, *The End of the Old Regime in Europe*, 377–438.

4 Francesco Cerlone, *I napoletani in America: commedia per musica di Francesco Cerlone da rappresentarsi nel Teatro de' Fiorentini l'està di quest'anno 1768* (Naples: Flauto, 1768). The second Americanist opera by Piccinni is *L'americano, intermezzi per musica a Quattro voci da rappresentarsi nel teatro alla Valle degl'Illustrissimi Sig[nori] Capranica* (Rome: Lorenzo Corradi, 1772). On these two works see Pierpaolo Polzonetti, 'L'America nelle opere di Piccinni', in *Niccolò Piccinni musicista europeo*, ed. Alessandro Di Profio and Mariagrazia Melucci (Bari: Adda, 2004), 173–192. On *I napoletani* see also Francesco Cotticelli, 'Problemi della drammaturgia di Francesco Cerlone. Appunti sui drammi esotici' in *Le arti della scena e l'esotismo in età moderna*, 363–369. The term 'noble savage' is historically incorrect for the

descent – usually Quakers –made their entrance onto the buffa stage. The Quaker was taken as a champion of the American revolutionary elite, based on the assumption that Quakers had already established, since William Penn's foundation of Pennsylvania, an alternative model of society liberated from feudal (religious or political) hierarchies based on birth privileges of either class or gender. By the 1760s Voltaire had in fact already redirected his and his readers' attention from the English Quaker (about whom he wrote earlier in the century), who was typically portrayed as an extravagant sectarian, to the Pennsylvanian Quaker, now presented as an enlightened citizen of an egalitarian republic. In contemporary French literature (which means in mainstream and internationally disseminated European literature) the good American Quaker was often portrayed as a philosophical equivalent to the *bon sauvage* or good savage, but with a difference. In her seminal work *The Good Quaker in French Legend* Edith Philips in fact documents how during the decade preceding the French Revolution, when the Quaker fad was at its peak, Friends were praised as living proof that the 'return to a state of comparative simplicity' was possible 'without going back to barbarism'.[5]

Pennsylvania at first and soon the rest of the uprising American colonies were seen by many European intellectuals as the most admirable example of an advanced society that was about to put into practice what until then were unattained utopian ideals. The result was a revival of the symbolic opposition of Orient versus Occident. This dualistic spatio-temporal concept, prevalent at least since the Roman conquest of Greece, was conceptualized by Horace, Horosius, Polybius and Saint Augustine as a sign of the migration of human civilization from East to West, a migration of power and enlightenment that appeared to be following the natural course of sunlight. Harold Jantz has observed that 'the concept of the westward movement of civilization is about as old as the concept of golden-age primitivism and is at its point of origin closely related to it. The trend westward is simply the course of the sun as it moves towards its rest beyond the Pillars of Hercules and the ultimate bound of the Ocean Sea.'[6] The West was and still is a movable concept, not only in space, but also in time. It is interesting to observe that in Thomas More's *Utopia* (1516) we are told that the character Raphael Hythloday, who reports to More on his journey to Utopia, went to America with Amerigo Vespucci, but instead of going back to Europe with his commander, proceeded westwards towards India until he discovered the island of Utopia. By the same token, in Francis Bacon's *New Atlantis* (first published in 1627, one year after the author's death) the utopian and futuristic state of New Atlantis is located

---

eighteenth century (and also ideologically biased), as convincingly demonstrated by Ter Ellingson, *The Myth of the Noble Savage* (Berkeley, Los Angeles and London: University of California Press, 2001). Ellingson does not take into account primary or secondary Italian sources, which nevertheless confirm his argument. For this reason the more historically correct term *buon selvaggio* or *bon sauvage* is preferred in this article and is anglicized as 'good savage'.

5 Edith Philips, *The Good Quaker in French Legend* (Philadelphia: University of Pennsylvania Press, 1932), viii, 119–126. This still unsurpassed study of Quaker typology and mythology in non-Quaker literature considerably expands intuitions and observations by Gilbert Chinard, *L'Amérique et le rêve exotique dans la literature française au xviie et au xviiie siècle* (Paris: Librairie Hachette, 1913). For the dissemination of the Quaker legend in Italy see Stefania Buccini, *The Americas in Italian Literature and Culture: 1700–1825*, trans. Rosanna Giammarco (University Park: Pennsylvania State University Press, 1997), 107–117. On the conflation of the good-Quaker myth with the good-savage myth see Antonello Gerbi, *La disputa del nuovo mondo* (Milan: Adelphi, 2000), 821–823, and Conti, '*Amiti e Ontario*', 149. Voltaire, *Traité sur la Tolérance* (1760), the *Essay sur les Moeurs* (completed in 1765) and the *Dictionnaire Philosophique* (1765), together with Guillaume-Thomas Raynal, *Histoire philosophique et politique des établissements et du commerce des Européens dans les deux Indes*, 6 volumes (Geneva: Libraires Associés, 1775), are discussed in Philips, *The Good Quaker*, 96–113. Raynal praised American Enlightenment even more in his equally influential *La Revolution de l'Amérique* (London: Locker Davis, 1781). His positive account of Quakers was confirmed, reinforced and also widely disseminated by Hector Jean de Crèvecoeur, *Lettres d'un cultivateur américain écrites à W. S., ecuyer, depuis l'annee 1779, jusqu'à 1781* (Paris: Cuchet, 1784), and by Jean-Baptiste Mailhe, *Discours . . . sur la grandeur et l'importance de la révolution qui vient de s'opérer dans l'Amerique Septentrionale* (Toulouse: D. Desclassan, 1785). On the influence of French literature on opera buffa as practised in Austria (which is of primary importance in this article) see Bruce Alan Brown, 'Viennese Opera Buffa and the Legacy of French Theatre', in *Opera Buffa in Mozart's Vienna*, ed. Mary Hunter and James Webster (Cambridge: Cambridge University Press, 1997), 50–81.

6 Harold Jantz, 'The Myths about America: Origins and Extensions', *Jahrbuch für Amerikastudien* 7 (1962), 6–18.

west of Peru, from where the fictional narrator sailed for China and Japan. The governor of the New Atlantis refers to America as a less advanced old 'Atlantis', whose great civilization disappeared after a deluge that left only 'simple and savage people . . . not able to leave letters, arts, civility to their posterity'.[7] Bacon presents a diachronic teleological narrative that left its traces in a geopolitical atlas where, synchronically, fallen civilizations are located east of rising civilizations. This is important in order to understand why – after the ancient American cultures (represented in opera seria) had been wiped out from the New World and after the first major revolution presented the American English colonies as the avant-garde of the Enlightenment – the United States began to be universally viewed as the Extreme West (designated as America *tout court* in obvious disregard of non-revolutionary, hence non-advanced, countries on the same continent). At the same time, the classical geopolitical opposition was reasserted in the usual terms of Eastern obscurantism versus Western enlightenment and progress. Thus if the Muslim Middle East still represented a past civilization of harems, slaves and masters, Europe was now diagnosed by enlightened intellectuals as a decadent present at the brink of a crisis, and so America came to represent the Occident's brighter future – a hyper-Occident located in the westernmost part of the world, beyond which there was no need to fantasize about a 'further west'. What Abbé Ferdinando Galliani (one of Niccolò Piccinni's protectors) wrote in 1776 to Mme d'Épinay suffices to get a sense of how powerful the idea of westward cultural migration was during these years: 'the time has come of the total collapse of Europe and of transmigration to America. Everything is decaying here – religion, laws, arts, sciences – and everything will be rebuilt in America'.[8] Almost at the same time Abbé Raynal, in his best-selling history of America (1775), wrote of Pennsylvania: 'This Republic, without wars, without conquests, without effort became a spectacle for the whole universe . . . All nations rejoiced to see renewed the heroic times of antiquity, which the customs and laws of Europe had made to seem like a fable. They saw at last that people could be happy without masters and without priests.'[9]

The American Revolution reinvigorated the concept of the westward movement of enlightenment, but at the same time it challenged it, because the persistence of the legal condition of slavery (as typically practised by Oriental potentates) in the post-revolutionary decade was gradually perceived as a paradox that transcended the narrow contingency of colonial politics and economics.[10] The problem of

---

7 Thomas More, *Utopia*, trans. and ed. Robert E. Adams (New York: Norton, 1992), part one. Francis Bacon, *Selected Philosophical Works*, ed. and introduced by Rose-Mary Sargent (Indianapolis and Cambridge: Hackett, 1999), 241, 250–251. Bacon acknowledges More's *Utopia* as his model (259), but, interestingly, in More's island slavery plays an important role in the economy and social configuration of the Utopians, while it doesn't in the New Atlantis. I am grateful to Phillip Sloan for calling my attention to the relevance of Bacon's text.

8 Ferdinando Galliani, *Correspondance inédite de l'abbé Ferdinand Galiani, conseiller du roi, pendant les années 1765 à 1783* (Paris: Dentu, 1818), volume 2, 280. Quoted and translated by Antonio Pace, *Benjamin Franklin and Italy* (Philadelphia: The American Philosophical Society, 1958), 120–121, who also points out that 'Polybius may have been the first to observe that civilization has a way of following the sun, arising in the east and lowing toward the west. This idea of *ab oriente lux*, which subsequently fascinated thinkers from Machiavelli to Spengler ultimately assumed the proportions of a myth . . . While much study needs yet to be made on the evolution of this idea in Italy between the date of the discovery of America and the time of the European Enlightenment, it is certain that by the 1770s many Italians were convinced that civilization, after a final stand in Paris and London, was moving inexorably across the Atlantic.' Note that 'ab oriente lux' means 'light away from the East', while 'ex oriente lux' means 'light from the East'. For similar remarks see also Gerbi, *La disputa del nuovo mondo*, 343–346.

9 Guillaume-Thomas Raynal, *Histoire philosophique et politique*, quoted by Philips, *The Good Quaker*, 100.

10 The presence of slavery in North America had been the subject of vehement attacks in Italy since at least 1785, when Alberto Fortis published a series of articles on this subject in the *Nuovo giornale enciclopedico*, in which he casts serious doubts on the success of the Revolution beyond the achievement of independence, as documented by Piero Del Negro, *Il mito americano nella Venezia del settecento* (Padua: Liviana, 1986), 166–168, and by Carlo Mangio, 'Illuministi italiani e Rivoluzione Americana', in *Italia e America dal settecento all'età dell'imperialismo*, ed. Giorgio Spini and others (Padua: Marsilio, 1976), 39–66. Buccini, *The Americas in Italian Literature*, 115, documents the presence of abolitionist Italian journalism since 1769, namely in the *Gazzetta di Milano*, although in the late 1760s slavery – as I will show – was perceived as a vice of pre-revolutionary European colonialism that the revolution was going to eliminate.

ORIENTAL TYRANNY IN THE EXTREME WEST

ideologically linking America to the East on the basis of the presence of slavery involved the potential crisis of an entire *Weltanschauung*, according to which the world and its historical course were conceived in terms of a spatial revolution from east to west together with a political revolution from tyranny to democracy, from obscurantism to enlightenment, from slavery to freedom, and ultimately from past to future. The comic works that I shall discuss end happily, with freedom granted to slaves, albeit only to certain slaves, providing a rapid but imperfect solution to a problem that was destined to reach epic and epochal proportions.

During the years separating Raynal's impression of America as a 'Republic without wars and without masters' and Fortis's denunciation of slavery after the War of Independence, both the American nation and her image abroad went through a rapid transformation. This explains, at least in part, the striking differences among the works I am going to examine. While a Neapolitan play entitled *Pulcinella da Quacquero* (1770) presents slavery as an almost obsolete European feudal practice that the American Enlightenment is about to eradicate, Ranieri de' Calzabigi's comic libretto *Amiti e Ontario* (1772) represents the internal conflict of a Pennsylvanian Quaker who believes in equality and yet exploits Native American slaves on his farm. A later Neapolitan revision of *Amiti e Ontario*, Palomba and Paisiello's *Le gare generose*, or 'The Contests in Generosity' (1786), is no longer set in rural Pennsylvania, but in urban Boston, and this change of location reflects a recontextualization of slavery within the emerging modern economy based on capitalism and trade. A Viennese revision of *Le gare* undertaken six months later ennobles this new ideology by elevating the musical style of a crucial dramatic point in the opera. Changes in the perception and interpretation of slavery from *Amiti e Ontario* to the two versions of *Le gare generose* can be explained by looking at these works' original cultural and political contexts and the way they react to news and debates published in contemporary gazettes and legal memoirs.

It is not surprising that a cosmopolitan and fashionable intellectual like Ranieri de' Calzabigi was the first to introduce an American Quaker character and to address the issue of American slavery in North America in his *Amiti e Ontario*, a libretto set by Giuseppe Scarlatti (the score is unfortunately lost), written for a private performance in the country residence of the Austrian Princess of Auersperg.[11] Calzabigi's decision to write a libretto about Native Americans enslaved by a Pennsylvanian Quaker of English descent may seem peculiar to the modern observer, aware that other and different groups were in fact more deeply involved as victims and offenders of the slave trade. By choosing these particular stereotypes Calzabigi in all likelihood never intended to provide a realistic representation of American society, and preferred instead to stage American types charged with a familiar allegorical value brought into play in recent fictional and philosophical writings. Against the backdrop of these widely circulating cultural and literary models, Calzabigi needs only a few strokes of his pen to recall the analogy between the good-Quaker legend and the good-savage legend. In the first act of his libretto Amiti observes that the personality and ideas of Mr Dull, the Pennsylvanian Quaker, are kindred to her own sense of natural morality:

---

11 Ranieri de' Calzabigi, *Amiti e Ontario: dramma per musica* (Vienna: Giuseppe Kurtzboeck Stampatore Orientale di SMIRA, 1772); this libretto was later reprinted in Calzabigi, *Poesie* (Livorno: Stamperia dell'Enciclopedia, 1774), volume 1, 125–170 (the edition consulted). This text attracted the attention of several modern commentators owing to its eminent librettist. Although none of them focuses on the issue of slavery or discusses the literary and journalistic sources examined in the present article, I am nonetheless indebted to each of the following contributions: Luigi Chinatti, 'Calzabigi's Vision of an Enlightened America', *Comparative Literature Studies* 14/2 (1977), 135–142; Francesca Romana Conti, '*Amiti e Ontario* di Ranieri Calzabigi: l'esotismo 'borghese' di un intellettuale classicista', in *Opera e libretto*, volume 2, ed. Gianfranco Folena, Maria Teresa Muraro and Giovanni Morelli (Florence: Olschki, 1993), 127–156; Rosy Candiani, '*Amiti e Ontario* di Ranieri de' Calzabigi: il mito del buon selvaggio nella Vienna asburgica', in *Il teatro musicale italiano nel Sacro Romano Impero nei secoli XVII e XVIII*, ed. Alberto Colzani and others (Como: AMIS, 1999), 509–549; Francesco Paolo Russo, 'Una 'parodia' napoletana di *Amiti e Ontario*', in *Ranieri Calzabigi tra Vienna e Napoli*, 227–238.

Amiti:
... Di là da' mari	[...] beyond the seas
Ei nacque, è ver, ma sembra	he was born – that's true – but it is as if he had been
Educato fra noi. Le altrui sventure	educated among us. He sympathizes with other people's
Addolcisce, e compiange, odia l'orgoglio:	misfortunes and eases them, hates pride, despises luxury
Disprezza il fasto e la ragione ascolta:	and listens to reason;
L'ingiustizia ha in orrore;	injustice horrifies him;
E concorde col labbro ha sempre il core.[12]	and his mouth and heart are always in agreement.

The paradox of Calzabigi's libretto is that notwithstanding his natural morality and enlightened visions ('la ragione ascolta'), Mr Dull is a slaveholder, which means that his own acts are in blunt disagreement with his mouth and heart. The Quaker, and hence the white American enlightened elite that this character allegorically represents, is caught up in a conflict between ideology and interest that proved to be a powerful source of irony. On the one hand the business-oriented American society appeared as a modern, in fact almost futuristic, society, showing the possibility of a democratic alternative to the predetermined and rigid social hierarchies regulating the European ancien régime. On the other hand, by perpetuating slavery (already considered the most primitive form of tyranny), the same white American elite appeared not too dissimilar from Oriental potentates. This paradox is a source of tragic irony, rather than farce, whatever the immediate affect of Dull's name, considering that in opera buffa names are often chosen to give an immediate glimpse of the personality of the character. Although the name Dull seems to encourage a preconceived idea of the stupidity of this character, reflected in the inconsistency of his ideals with his actions, Mr Dull is far from being portrayed as the stereotypical old fool, as are Uberto in Federico's *La serva padrona*, Buonafede in Goldoni's *Il mondo della luna*, Don Tammaro in Lorenzi's *Socrate immaginario* and other gullible ageing guardian figures populating the world of opera buffa. The term *dull* seems to be used in two denotations that were also common in eighteenth-century English and that coincide with two stereotypical characteristics of the Quaker as presented in European literature of the time: 'phlegmatic' or 'slow in motion or action', and 'having the natural vivacity or cheerfulness blunted'. As we shall see, in the Neapolitan adaptation of *Amiti e Ontario*, *Le gare generose*, Mr Dull calls himself 'flemmatico', diagnosing in so doing his constitutional indolence or apathy.[13] A third connotation of the Quaker's name can be added when one considers that this opera was written for a German-speaking audience: 'Dull' sounds close enough to the German *dulden*, meaning 'to tolerate' and to the related *duldsam*, meaning 'tolerant', both of which anticipate Mr Dull's final act of forgiveness and mercy. This characterization emerges in the vaudeville finale, which concludes the opera with a triumphal declaration of Quaker ethics:

Io son giusto, umano, e schietto:	I am righteous, human and frank;
Amo il prossimo, e rispetto	I love my fellow man and I obey
E le leggi, e la virtù.	both laws and virtue.
Ma non giuro: vesto semplice:	But I never swear, I dress modestly,

---

12 Ranieri de' Calzabigi, *Amiti e Ontario*, Act 1 Scene 7, 146. Translations are mine unless otherwise indicated. In Nunziato Porta's comic libretto *L'americana in Olanda* (Venice: Fenzo, 1778), Act 1 Scene 10, 18, the American Quaker Naimur who is visiting Europe with the beautiful savage Zemira instructs her that 'tutti qui son scaltri, e maliziosi, / E con il labbro il cuor non corrisponde' (Everybody here (in Europe) is cunning and malicious / and the mouth is never in agreement with the heart), establishing in so doing a kinship between him and the Native American girl by pointing at what distinguishes them from Europeans.

13 'Dull, a., definitions 3a and 4', *The Oxford English Dictionary*, second edition, 1989. *OED Online*, Oxford University Press <http://dictionary.oed.com/cgi/ entry/50070704>, accessed 24 January 2007. Definition 3a is attested also in Benjamin Franklin's autobiography of 1788, and definition 4 in Sir Richard Steele's *The Tatler* (1709). Conti, '*Amiti e Ontario*', 135, also points out that in Calzabigi's libretto there is an 'ironic usage of self-explanatory personal names' and concludes that the name 'Dull' is 'prognostic of pedantic phlegm'.

ORIENTAL TYRANNY IN THE EXTREME WEST

non corteggio – non guerreggio:	I do not flirt, I do not wage war.
Non saluto; e do del tu:	I do not salute and I say 'thou'.
E per questo son ridicolo?	And for this I am ridiculous?
Oh miseria! O cecità.[14]	Oh misery! Oh blindness!

That Mr Dull finally and openly points out that it would be 'blindness' to consider him ridiculous is another clue in support of the fact that Calzabigi's *dramma giocoso* avoids farce. But there are more important reasons to interpret this opera as belonging to the subgenre of sentimental opera rather than slapstick musical comedy. Not only the seria parts of Amiti and Ontario, but also the part of Mr Dull (which, as an old guardian of young lovers, should be typically comic), present a consistently elevated style of language, albeit never to the point of being lofty. In line with the general sentimental tone of the opera, the paradoxical relationship between enlightened master and Native American slaves is problematized with tact rather than with pungent irony. One might object that in opera buffa parody or sarcasm is always skulking behind any manifestation of elevated style. Even when the style of the lines is not exaggeratedly grand, the composer first and the interpreter second can swing the rhetorical level in the direction of parody; therefore any interpretation of comic opera based exclusively on the libretto is destined to be partial and potentially erroneous.[15] We can assume, though, that this risk is fairly limited in *Amiti e Ontario*, considering Calzabigi's awareness of the interplay between text and other expressive operatic domains during his Viennese years (1761–1773), when in the so-called 'reformed operas' he and his collaborators reached more coherent artistic results by working in close partnership. If we are not dealing with a case of parody or comic irony, as his libretto indicates, then rather than demystifying a legend *Amiti e Ontario* reveals the same modern approach to myth shown in Calzabigi's *Orfeo ed Euridice*, set by Gluck ten years earlier. In both cases, mythological characters cease to be fixed and distant allegories and, once infused with human breath, engage in dialectical relationships with the archetypical associations that they embody, reaching out to contemporary reality. In *Amiti e Ontario* the noble savage, allegory of freedom, is enslaved by the Quaker, allegory of equality: both are dissociated from their characteristic mythological associations and strive to regain them on a different, more human dimension. Through a process of self-questioning the Quaker decides to grant freedom to his slaves, but reacquires their possession at a more human level: his slaves are not lost after all, since they decide to accept their master's invitation to become members of his own family and be subject to him not as slaves but as his own children.

This solution makes sense in the context of the early 1770s, when European intellectuals (together with many enlightened Americans) believed, or hoped, that America was about to put an end to slavery and convert former slaves into fellow citizens. At this time, slavery was still perceived as a remnant institution

---

14 Calzabigi, *Amiti e Ontario*, Act 2 Last Scene (9), 170.
15 A discussion of parody in opera buffa has proliferated especially in efforts to understand Mozart and Da Ponte's most controversial and ambiguous opera, *Così fan tutte*: see Dolores Jerde Keahey, '*Così fan tutte*: Parody or Irony?', in *Paul Pisk: Essays in His Honor*, ed. John Glowacki (Austin: College of Fine Arts, University of Texas Press, 1966), 116–130; Rodney Farnsworth, '*Così fan tutte* as Parody and Burlesque', *The Opera Quarterly* 6 (1988–1989), 50–68; Frits Noske, '*Così fan tutte*: Dramatic Irony', in *The Signifier and the Signified* (New York: Oxford University Press, 1990), 93–120. For a perspective beyond *Così fan tutte* see Andrew Steptoe, 'Parody: The Mozartean Method', in *The Mozart-Da Ponte Operas* (Oxford: Clarendon, 1988), 221–230, and the recent essay by Michele Calella, 'Entblößte Natur: transformierter Ernst in Mozarts *La finta giardiniera*', presented at the 2005 Mozart Conference in Salzburg (proceedings in print), which offers a useful comparative analysis of opera buffa and seria libretti and shows Mozart's musical and dramatic treatment of parody in *La finta giardiniera*. The essay also discusses German and French literature on parody not taken into account in the previous essays mentioned above. On the often disregarded power of the singer-actors to add or subtract meaning through their performance see Alessandra Campana, 'The Performance of Opera Buffa: *Le Nozze di Figaro* and the Act IV Finale', in *Pensieri per un maestro: studi in onore di Pierluigi Petrobelli*, ed. Stefano La Via and Roger Parker (Turin: EDT, 2002), 125–134. See also Jessica Waldoff, *Recognition in Mozart's Operas* (New York: Oxford University Press, 2006), 211–217.

from the 'East'; Calzabigi is one of the first to question the ability of the Americans to get rid of such an Oriental practice. The relevance of this context becomes clearer when *Amiti e Ontario* is set next to what I believe is one of its literary sources: *Pulcinella da Quacquero*, a 1770 comic play by Father Jerocades, a teacher in a Catholic college in the town of Sora, at that time part of the Kingdom of Naples.[16] In this comedy slavery is presented as an evil introduced and practised by corrupted Europeans, an evil which the more 'advanced' and more Western American Quakers are fighting against. The plot is simple: two European aristocrats enslave the children of a rich Quaker merchant from Pennsylvania. While the two aristocrats are duelling for possession of the American slaves, explaining to the perplexed servant Pulcinella that 'this is the knightly way to acquire power over people' ('ecco il modo di acquistare il dominio delle persone all'uso de' Cavalieri'), Pulcinella swiftly approaches the American girl and proposes marriage. At this point her father makes his entrance. Learning that his daughter has promised her hand to Pulcinella, he is ready to welcome him as his son-in-law upon his conversion to Quakerism and manages to persuade him by explaining that Quakers believe in perfect equality, that they do not believe in empty words and rituals but only in good deeds, and finally that since all human beings are children of God, they reject the ecclesiastical hierarchy. Easily persuaded, Pulcinella finally appears transformed into the typical Quaker: he greets everybody using the informal *tu* (thou) instead of the formal *voi* or *lei* (you), does not bow to the aristocrats and does not remove his Quaker hat in the presence of his former master, explaining to him, 'I'm a free man now: I have no master' ('Io son libero, non ho Signiò'). The other characters try to stop Pulcinella from following his new American family by reminding him that he will not see Naples again, which makes this most traditional Neapolitan *commedia dell'arte* figure hesitate until the Quaker removes his last-minute doubts by saying that 'Pennsylvania is worth a thousand Italies: Philadelphia is richer than Naples' ('La Pensilvania vale per mille Italie: Filadelfia è più ricca di Napoli').[17]

Not surprisingly, the play was censored by local authorities, but the ensuing trial, in which the author was accused of heresy and disrespect for the Church and the Kingdom of Naples, granted this text unexpected public resonance.[18] This can explain some subtle but inescapable similarities between *Amiti e Ontario* and *Pulcinella da Quacquero* in the general conception of the drama, outlined in a letter by Calzabigi, dated 22 August 1772, to his friend Paolo Frisi, a Milanese scientist who had been corresponding with Benjamin Franklin for about twenty years; the young enslaved pair of siblings in *Pulcinella* becomes a young enslaved pair of lovers who pretend to be siblings:

> I had already abandoned the Lyre four years ago when my duty towards a beautiful Lady persuaded me to take it up again. . . . I imagined a Quaker colonist living in a rural area of Pennsylvania, in North America. I gave him a sister-in-law and a niece [her daughter], and I imagined the sister-in-law as a widow. Amiti and Ontario, both savages, are enslaved to him for reasons of war,

---

16 (Father) Antonio Jerocades, *Pulcinella da Quacquero*, unpublished comedy for the Real Collegio Tuziano in Sora (Naples, 1770). A century ago F. De Simone Brower unearthed the manuscript text of this spoken intermezzo and meticulously reconstructed the whole episode concerning its repression in his 'Un intermezzo indiavolato', *Rendiconti della Reale Accademia dei Lincei. Classe di scienze morali, storiche e filologiche* 5/13 (June 1904), 345–365. The original manuscript has been removed from Naples National Library, folder XIV.B.5, containing most of the documentation on the legal and religious investigation in the case and on the ensuing public scandal. This latter is documented indirectly by an article on the *Mercurio d'Olanda* (June 1770). In his article Brower reproduces the unabridged manuscript copy he found in a legal memoir by Jerocades's defence attorney (Naples, Biblioteca Nazionale Braidense, XV. C. 42).

17 Jerocades, *Pulcinella*, Scene 9 and Scene 10 (final scene).

18 Brower, 'Un intermezzo indiavolato', 351–354. It is likely that Ranieri de' Calzabigi, at that time in Vienna, was informed about the scandal, at least via his connections with the Freemasons of Naples. Among them was the singer Antonia Bernasconi (protagonist of Gluck's *Alceste*): see Mariangela Donà, 'Dagli Archivi Milanesi: lettere di Ranieri de' Calzabigi e di Antonia Bernasconi', *Analecta musicologica* 14 (1974), 294–295. An episode of Masonic greeting to Signora Bernasconi occurred before one of her performances at the San Carlo theatre of Naples, and her presence in feminine lodges is reported by Harold Acton, *The Bourbons of Naples* (London: Methuen, 1956), 134, 151.

ORIENTAL TYRANNY IN THE EXTREME WEST

and they are lovers, but they are pretending to be brother and sister for their own good and so as not to appear suspicious. The Quaker would like to marry Amiti because he sees in her some inclination to passion. His sister-in-law wants Ontario, because he is a beautiful young man; and so does her daughter. To avoid this entanglement, the two [Native] Americans flee, but Amiti is caught, and Ontario goes back to share the destiny of his beloved. The Quaker decides what to do according to his principles: he forgives the two savages and adopts them as his own children.[19]

The differences between *Amiti e Ontario* and its possible model are no less evident. Most notably, in Calzabigi's text the Quaker is transformed from a victim of European slave-dealers to a slaveholder himself. That the libretto took such a different view of slavery from the play and in such a short time (from 1770 to 1772) can be explained on the basis of historical evidence that indicates that the comic stage was reacting very quickly to contemporary political events. In the Italian gazettes we find a relatively long period of silence on the state of affairs in America – from the autumn of 1768 to the spring of 1772 – following a period of intensive coverage during the first half of 1768; remarkably, no opera buffa based on American subjects was composed during these years of news blackout.

On March 1772, five months before Calzabigi's letter to Frisi, the Somerset case called new attention to the American colonies and inaugurated a new period of press coverage of America. Somerset was an American slave of African descent who ran away from his master during their sojourn in England. Shortly after his attempted escape he was captured and put in chains in the hold of a ship headed for Jamaica, where he was destined to be sold to a new master. Somerset, however, never left England: an appeal to the King's Bench against this abduction prevented Captain Knowles from sailing with the recaptured fugitive and immediately started a debate over the legitimacy of slavery in general, questioned now from a legal as well as moral standpoint. Two recently published monographs on this judicial affair, Alfred and Ruth Blumrosen's *Slave Nation* and Steven Wise's *Though the Heavens May Fall*, give unprecedented prominence to the Somerset case, the former pointing out that Lord Mansfield's deliberation 'would have monumental consequences in the American colonies, leading up to the American Revolution, the Civil War, and beyond'.[20] The *cause célèbre* was rapidly disseminated in the rest of Europe. Here, as an example, is how an Italian gazette, *Notizie del mondo*, recounted the news:

> Londra, 18 febbraio. Si è cominciata a trattare al Banco del Re la causa d'un Negro, il quale da un abitante della Giammaica si vuole obbligare a seguitarlo in detta Colonia. Il Sig. Davy, che parlò il primo per quest'infelice, prese il suo discorso dall'origine della schiavitù in Inghilterra. Fece vedere non esser questa stata tollerata, che ne' primi tempi; ma che a' giorni nostri nessuno può esser schiavo nella Gran Brettagna; che il potere di far degli schiavi è puramente locale, e dipendente dalle Leggi di alcuni luoghi; che l'assoluta necessità ha potuto autorizzare la schiavitù nelle Colonie, ma subito che uno Schiavo ha avuta la sorte di scendere in Inghilterra, l'aria che vi

---

19 Letter of Ranieri Calzabigi to Paolo Frisi, Vienna, 24 August 1772; the original text can be read in Donà, 'Dagli archivi milanesi', 294–295. Most probably Frisi was also a Freemason, and as such or as a scientist had been in contact with Benjamin Franklin since at least 1756: see Antonio Pace, *Benjamin Franklin and Italy*, 34–35, 82–83. Candiani, 'Amiti e Ontario', 515–516, supposes that the Princess might be either Maria Wilhelmine Countess von Neipperg, wife of Johann Adam Joseph Auersperg, or Maria Josepha Rosalie, the wife of Prince Joseph Anton Auersperg. The location of the first and only performance is no better identified than as 'Sleppe', as Calzabigi wrote to Frisi; Candiani hypothesizes that this is a bad spelling of Schleßen. I am grateful to James Webster for suggesting me that the location could be Schlesien, or Silesia. I believe Webster's intuition to be the correct one, since a lineage of the Princes von Auersperg were also Dukes of Schlesien, as one can see at <http://genealogy.euweb.cz/auersperg/auersperg5.html>, accessed 24 January 2010.

20 Alfred Blumrosen and Ruth Blumrosen, *Slave Nation: How Slavery United the Colonies and Sparked the American Revolution* (Naperville, IL: Sourcebooks, 2005); Steven M. Wise, *Though the Heavens May Fall: The Landmark Trial that Led to the End of Human Slavery* (Cambridge, MA: Da Capo, 2005). The quotation is from Blumrosen, *Slave Nation*, 1.

respira lo rende libero; che egli ha diritto di esser governato dalle leggi del Paese, e di vivere in esso sotto la loro protezione, come qualunque altro Cittadino; che in assicurando la libertà agli Schiavi, i quali passavano in Europa, si faceva uso dell'unico mezzo di impedire al loro padrone il condurveli; che se vi fossero stati soggetti alla schiavitù, si vedrebbero insensibilmente alcuni orgogliosi coloni, i quali hanno dei beni in Inghilterra, condur seco i loro schiavi per attaccarli alle loro carrozze, e calessi per fare affronto all'umanità. . . . I risultati della causa si attendono.

London, 18 February. The King's Bench has begun to address the cause of a negro who has been compelled to follow his kidnapper to Jamaica [the plaintiff's name was Somerset; the defendant was his master, Charles Stewart, a slave trader from Norfolk, Virginia, who delivered Somerset to Captain Knowles to be sold in Jamaica]. Mr Davy [William Davy was Somerset's attorney] spoke first in defence of this unhappy man, and started his speech by addressing the origins of slavery in England. He pointed out that slavery had been tolerated only at the beginning, but today nobody can possibly be a slave in Great Britain. The power of enslaving people is purely local, and depends on local laws of certain places. It is absolute necessity that can authorize slavery in the colonies, but as soon as slaves have chance to land in England, the air they breathe makes them free, and here they have the right to be governed and protected by English law like any other citizen. Mr Davy also pointed out that granting freedom to slaves travelling to Europe is the only means to discourage their masters to bring them here. This will avoid having arrogant colonists with possessions in England bringing slaves with them, attaching them to their carriages and cabriolets, so as to offend [the whole of] humankind. . . . We await the verdict.[21]

Judge Lord Mansfield delivered the verdict on 22 June, declaring that 'the state of slavery is of such a nature, that it is incapable of being introduced on any reasons, moral or political', and finally that 'whatever inconveniences, therefore, may follow from the decision, I cannot say this case is allowed or approved by the law of England; and therefore the black must be discharged'.[22] This verdict granted Somerset freedom, but more notably it also created a judicial precedent that led to the release of many other American slaves accompanying their masters in England. According to the Blumrosens the verdict caused in fact a chain reaction in the American colonies starting from the summer of 1772, when the news spread among the slaves, many of whom ran away; understandably, this alarmed the Southern landlords, igniting their quest for independence from a motherland that was putting in jeopardy one of the backbones of their productive system. As a result they made the perpetuation of slavery in America a precondition for their contribution first to the War of Independence and, thereafter, to the commonwealth of the newly founded Republic. As Steven Wise points out,

> the Somerset case was exceptional . . . not just because it provided a platform for airing the stirring issue of the legality of English slavery, but because it catalyzed what was, for late eighteenth-century London, an unusually prolonged and public struggle, one that echoed not just through cavernous Westminster Hall, but in the pages of monographs, newspapers and magazines, in extraordinary letters to the editor and in pubs and drawing rooms throughout England and the Americas. Everyone began talking about black slavery and the African slave trade, and they didn't stop until both had been abolished.[23]

Because of its public and global resonance, after the Somerset episode it became difficult to see slavery as an evil introduced and perpetuated by the European old regime. Nonetheless, there is not yet a perception of

---

21 *Notizie del mondo*, 10 March 1772. I have made corrections and added information in square brackets based on Blumrosen, *Slave Nation*.
22 *Howell's State Trials*, volumes 20, 82 (1771–1777), quoted in Blumrosen, *Slave Nation*, 11; see also Wise, *Though the Heavens May Fall*, 182.
23 Wise, *Though the Heavens May Fall*, xvi.

ORIENTAL TYRANNY IN THE EXTREME WEST

America as an entity entirely separated from England, and, in fact, *Amiti e Ontario* presents slavery as an internal paradox of English-American enlightened society (Mr Dull is designated as 'uomo inglese' while his American Quaker identity, as we have seen, was associated with enlightened trans-Atlantic ideals). Unlike Somerset's master, Mr Dull is tragically aware of the conflict between his Quaker and enlightened ethics and his role as a domestic tyrant. In Act 1 the Quaker disagrees with his Anglican sister-in-law Mrs Bubble, who opposes his intention to free his slaves, and offers to buy one from him to keep all for herself (not coincidentally the handsome Ontario). At this point the Quaker delivers the most powerful abolitionist speech to be found in Italian opera, in which he calls slavery an 'iniquitous Commerce of men who are also created by High Providence' and 'a commerce that is a sinful abuse and our eternal shame':

Mr Dull:	*Mr Dull*
Tu vuoi comprarlo, ed io	You want to buy him and I
Penso di farlo libero. L'iniquo	Think I should set him free. The iniquitous
Commercio che facciam per coltivare	Commerce of men that we practise for the
Il zucchero e il tabacco	farming of sugar and tobacco,
D'uomini come noi; creati anch'essi	of men like us, who are also created by High
Dall'Alta Provvidenza che nel mondo	Providence, which in the world moves and rules
Tutti muove e governa:	all of us, this commerce is a sinful abuse and
È un empio abuso, e nostra infamia eterna.	our eternal shame.
Miss Bubble: Ma non troppo diversi	*Miss Bubble*: But they are not too different from
Son costoro dai bruti.	animals.
Mr D.: E che ti sembra	*Mr D.*: And do you think
Che noi tutti siam Angeli! . . .	that we are all angels? . . .
Miss B.: Ma il diritto dell'armi	*Miss B.*: But Ontario and Amiti are condemned
Ontario ed Amiti a servitù condanna	to servitude by the law of war.
Mr D.: Un altro eccesso è questo	*Mr D.*: This is another excess
D'immensa ferocia. Oltre la guerra,	of great ferocity. Prolonging hate, the use of
Odio, forza, vendetta	force and vengeance after the war is over is a
Il protrarre è delitto.	crime.
. . .	. . .
Ascolta:	Listen:
Non son mercante d'uomini;	I am not a merchant of men;
Schiavi non ho.[24]	I do not hold slaves.

Towards the end of the second act Mr Dull has not yet freed his slaves. Now he appears alone, coming to grips, probably in an obbligato recitative, with his internal struggle. As Mr Dull hears noises from offstage, he fears a revolt of his black slaves and ponders the injustice of slavery, calling it 'an excessively inhuman traffic that is turning us into executioners and tyrants':

Sento rumori . . .	I hear noises . . .
Esser dovrebbe	it might be
De' neri schiavi miei qualche congiura.	some plot of my black slaves.
In servitù sì dura,	Oppressed under such a harsh servitude,
Sotto sferza crudel, qual maraviglia	and by the cruel whip, it is not surprising
Se meditan vendetta,	if they think of revenge,
Se bramano libertà; miseri! . . . e noi	if they are longing for freedom; wretched
Più miseri di loro! Abbiamo sconvolto	people! . . . and we are even more wretched than

---

24 Calzabigi, *Amiti e Ontario*, Act 1 Scene 3, 136.

Del giusto e dell'ingiusto	they! We have overturned every idea of
Tutte le idee. La natural difesa,	good and evil. Our natural protection,
La sicurezza; ecco, ci vuole in questo,	our need for security in dealing with this
D'un traffico inuman fino all'eccesso,	excessively inhuman traffic, are making
Carnefici e tiranni a un tempo istesso.[25]	of us executioners and tyrants at once.

This eloquent condemnation of slavery and the formidable analysis of the master's fear caused by the awareness of the injustice he perpetrates are among the ideologically progressive and clear-sighted aspects of this text. It is not to be excluded that in the back of Calzabigi's mind there was the desperate attempt to salvage the cherished idea of westward migration of enlightened civilization. If slavery started in the Orient and affected Europe first, and if it spread from Europe to America, it is only logical that, like a wave of flu, this social disease would end first in England and soon thereafter in America, granted that it did not become a chronic disease as in the Middle and Far East. The latter risk seems in fact to hover over the entire text. It is worth noticing that the way the whole crisis is resolved is by a sudden dramatic denouement and reversal, which resorts to power dynamics typical of pre-revolutionary Europe. If in 1772 slavery seemed to be about to end in an act of enlightened jurisdiction, Mr Dull does not change or reform the law but overrides it by freeing Amiti and Ontario in an act of mercy. The three concepts of tyranny, slavery and mercy are inextricably interrelated in pre-modern Western culture. In Slavoj Žižek's and Mladen Dolar's *Opera's Second Death*, Dolar discusses 'the logic of mercy' apropos of Mozart's *Idomeneo* and *La clemenza di Tito*, pointing out that only individuals whose position of power transcends human law (gods and tyrants) have the authority to grant mercy, which 'has to be understood . . . as an act beyond the law'.[26] Moreover, Dull's decision to grant freedom to his slaves is not entirely spontaneous: it is Amiti who persuades the old Quaker to grant mercy, during a long recitative and an aria ('Placato renderti') in which she no longer calls the Quaker 'padrone' (master); but 'padre' (or father):

Placato renderti	That you should calm your rage
No: non pretendo;	I dare not expect;
Padre, condannami;	Father, condemn me;
Non mi difendo:	I do not defend myself:
Ma non dividermi	but do not divide me,
Nel tuo rigore,	In your severity,
Da lui ch'è spasimo	from the one who is the desire
Di questo core;	of this heart of mine;
Da lui ch'è l'anima	from he who is the soul
Ch'io sento in sen.	that I feel in my bosom.

---

25 Calzabigi, *Amiti e Ontario*, Act 2 Scene 6, 161–162. Similarly in Act 2 Scene 9, 166, Dull explains to Miss Bubble and Miss Nab that 'it is not a crime when the servant seeks freedom' ('Non è delitto al servo / Cercar la libertà').

26 Mladen Dolar, 'The Logic of Mercy', in Slavoj Žižek and Mladen Dolar, *Opera's Second Death* (New York and London: Routledge, 2002), 20. Dolar's observations are inspired by Ivan Nagel, *Autonomy and Mercy: Reflections on Mozart's Operas*, trans. Marion Faber and Ivan Nagel (Cambridge, MA, and London: Harvard University Press, 1991); originally published as *Autonomie und Gnade: über Mozarts Opern* (München: C. Hanser, 1985). By contrast, Daniel Heartz uses exclusively the word 'clemency' (instead of 'mercy') and describes it as a 'virtue ardently espoused by the Enlightenment', maintaining that 'clemency' in Mozart's *Idomeneo*, *Die Zauberflöte* and *La clemenza di Tito* has to be understood as a reference to Masonic enlightened values: Heartz, 'La Clemenza di Sarastro: Masonic Benefice in the Last Operas', in *Mozart's Operas* (Berkeley, Los Angeles and London: University of California Press, 1990), 272–275. For Dolar, however, in *Die Zauberflöte* we have 'nothing else than mercy turned upside down' (82). See also Wilhelm Seidel, 'Seneca – Corneille – Mozart. Ideen- und Gattungsgeschichtliches zu *La clemenza di Tito*', in *Musik in Antike und Neuzeit*, edited by Michael von Albrecht and Werner Schubert (Frankfurt am Main, Bern and New York: Peter Lang, 1987), 109–128.

ORIENTAL TYRANNY IN THE EXTREME WEST

Se un fato barbaro	If a cruel destiny
Lo guida a morte;	leads him to death,
Padre, accompagnami	Father, let me be
Col mio consorte:	with my companion:
Le nostre ceneri	our ashes at least
Confondi almen.	shall be mingled.
(*S'inginocchia*).[27]	(*kneeling down*).

After this aria, Mr Dull gives orders to free Amiti and Ontario, the whole action being staged with simple, eloquent Metastasian gestures typical of heroic opera: Amiti kneels, her Master rises.

Dull: Vi libero: v'assolvo; e vi perdono.	*Dull*: I free you, I absolve you and I forgive you.
Bubble: Come!	*Bubble*: How?
Nab: Perché?	*Nab*: Why?
Dull:(*s'alza*)	*Dull*: (*rising*)
Non è delitto al servo	It is not a crime for the servant
Cercar la libertà.	to seek freedom.

In the end, Mr Dull accepts Amiti and Ontario as his own children, and restores in so doing the original hierarchy by converting his power from a public to a domestic sphere. And the final tutti celebrates the unity and harmony of the new enlarged family:

Regni l'amabile	Joyful and loving
Pace ridente:	peace shall rule:
Vera sorgente	true source
Della domestica	of domestic
Felicità.[28]	happiness.

This conclusion tends towards reconciliation and the re-establishment or re-formation of power relationships, albeit, as I have already suggested, at a morally higher level. At the same time Calzabigi reassures his audience of reformist aristocrats that the Quaker's mercy results in a redefinition of his authority and not in a loss of power. The centrality of the act of mercy itself shows the opera's alignment with the reformist attitude of a large part of the Austrian aristocracy, an audience accustomed to contemporary tragedy and heroic opera. Finally, the solution of the initial paradox – how to reconcile American Quakerism and slavery – is imperfectly reached in the end. After the opera several questions remain unanswered: what happens to the black slaves? From Mr Dull's speech one may infer that they are going to be freed, but that does not happen on stage, and if we trust this character's good intentions, are they going to be part of his family, like the Native Americans, or not? If not, why? Is the Quaker 'righteous, human and frank', as he claims to be in the vaudeville finale, or is he an opportunist who wants to preserve power in whatever form he is able to? By leaving these questions unanswered, Calzabigi throws seeds of doubt on the whole positivistic idea of westward progress. In the adaptation of *Amiti e Ontario* for the public theatres the plot would be reworked; the question is whether those changes provided any better or clearer solution to those problems.

---

27 Calzabigi, *Amiti e Ontario*, Act 2 Scene 9, 166.
28 Calzabigi, *Amiti e Ontario*, Act 2 Scene 9.

Mr Dull arrived in the Kingdom of Naples in 1786, in a remake of *Amiti e Ontario* entitled *Le gare generose* a libretto probably by Giuseppe Palomba set by Giovanni Paisiello. Textual cuts and substitutions, replacement of characters and alterations to the original plot were made in order to adapt the opera to the taste and expectation of the paying audience of one of the largest maritime cities in the world.[29] The venues and audiences for *Amiti e Ontario* and *Le gare generose* could not have been more dissimilar, and the most relevant difference is that while the former is a court opera, the latter is a public opera. Consequently Calzabigi's libretto was updated to serve a different practical and ideological function, while the work was performed in Naples with a different cast of singers and needed to establish a dialogue with a different kind of audience. It is for this reason that this opera displays a rhetorical level that is generally lower than its source, although the hyperboles or displacement typical of parody are absent.[30] From an ideological standpoint this is an important factor, because – as we shall see – it contributes to the dismantling of the logic of mercy, which determines a profound change to the overall message. As *Amiti* alters *Pulcinella da Quacquero*, similarly *Le gare* alters *Amiti* by replacing and/or redefining American myths and types, and it does so in a way that reflects both American reality as perceived before and after the Revolution and the European audience for which each opera is conceived. First of all the American landscape is different. *Amiti e Ontario*, produced in an aristocratic country residence, is set in a rural Pennsylvania where the relationship between the landlord and his slaves is inscribed within feudal paradigms; on the other hand, *Le gare* is set in a modern and urban Boston, and the agrarian pre-modern economy of its source is replaced by a capitalistic economy based on trade and money exchange, which also reflects the relationship between masters and slaves.[31] The table below summarizes the conversion of *dramatis personae* from *Amiti* to *Le gare*. In *Le gare* Mr Dull is no longer a Pennsylvanian Quaker, but a merchant from Boston with no religious connotations (even though he retains some of the basic stereotypical attributes of Quakerism, including the name). His slaves are no longer Native Americans, but middle-class Italians: Gelinda is the daughter of a French merchant who died in Naples, leaving her under the tutelage of a cruel relative who manages her finances.

---

29 (Giuseppe Palomba,) *Le gare generose: commedia per musica da rappresentarsi nel Teatro de' Fiorentini per prim'opera in quest'anno 1786, con licenza de' superiori* (Naples, 1786). A list of the many sources of this opera score is in Michael Robinson, *Giovanni Paisiello. A Thematic Catalogue of his Works*, 2 volumes (Stuyvesant, NY: Pendagon, 1991–1994), volume 1, 373–386. Francesco Paolo Russo, 'Una 'parodia' napoletana di *Amiti e Ontario*', reads *Le gare generose* as a parody of *Amiti* (a useful interpretation to understand the lower rhetorical level of the former). Like Robinson, Russo casts doubts on Palomba's authorship (the name of the librettist does not appear in the numerous librettos of this opera until 1800) and supposes a direct participation of Calzabigi in the Neapolitan libretto. Unfortunately, this interesting hypothesis is supported by no other evidence than the obvious similarities between the two texts. On the reception history of *Le gare generose* see Otto Michtner, *Das alte Burgtheater als Opernbühne. Von der Einführung des deutschen Singspiels (1778) bis zum Tod Kaiser Leopolds II (1792)* (Vienna: Böhlau, 1970), 404; and Christine Villinger, *Mi vuoi tu corbellar: Die Opere Buffe von Giovanni Paisiello. Analysen und Interpretationen* (Tutzing: Hans Schneider, 2000), 312–316. On *Le gare* see Mary Hunter, *The Culture of Opera Buffa in Mozart's Vienna: A Poetics of Entertainment* (Princeton: Princeton University Press, 1999), 310, for a useful and detailed plot summary; her 'Bourgeois Values in Opera Buffa in 1780s Vienna', in *Opera Buffa in Mozart's Vienna*, 170–185, provides the most useful insights on this opera (to which I shall return). For a historical account of the economy of Naples in the eighteenth century see Biagio Salvemini, 'The Arrogance of the Market: The Economy of the Kingdom between the Mediterranean and Europe', in *Naples in the Eighteenth Century: The Birth and Death of a National State*, ed. Girolamo Imbruglia (Cambridge: Cambridge University Pres, 2000), 44–69, which challenges the general assumption that the Kingdom of Naples' production system was agrarian and pre-modern (given the relative lack of manufacturing industry) by documenting the intense activity of international trading (primarily in food products). Obviously, the presence and interdependence of extensive agrarian producers and international traders of farmers' products makes the Neapolitan economy not dissimilar from the American one.

30 For this reason I disagree with Russo's interpretation of *Le gare* as parody of *Le gare* in his 'Una "parodia" napoletana di *Amiti e Ontario*'.

31 Hunter, 'Bourgeois Values'.

ORIENTAL TYRANNY IN THE EXTREME WEST

Calzabigi, *Amiti e Ontario*			(Palomba,) *Le gare generose*	
Mr Dull	Quaker, settler in rural Pennsylvania		Mr Dull ('primo buffo toscano') (bass)	Boston businessman
Mrs Bubble	Dull's sister-in-law, (of Anglican persuasion)		Miss Meri ('prima donna mezzo carattere') (alto)	Dull's niece
Mrs Nab	Mrs Bubble's daughter, Mr Dull's niece		Mrs Nab ('prima donna giocosa') (soprano)	Mr Dull's daughter
Amiti	young woman (*parte seria*)	Native American couple enslaved to Mr Dull for reasons of war	Gelinda, alias Deianina ('prima buffa assoluta') (soprano)	Italian couple, enslaved to Mr Dull for financial reasons
Ontario	young man (*parte seria*)		Bastiano Ammazzagatte, alias Bronton ('primo buffo napoletano') (bass)	
			Don Berlicco ('primo tenore mezzo carattere') (tenor)	Young Italian man
			Perillo ('altro primo mezzo carattere') (added in Turin and Milan, 1791)	Italian 'fashion freak', friend of Berlicco

Prior to the events occurring in the course of the opera's two acts, both set in Boston, Gelinda has escaped her evil relative, accompanied and supported by her lover Bastiano, a Neapolitan fellow 'di civile condizione', which means belonging to the middle classes. They have changed their names to Deianina and Bronton respectively and married in Cádiz – one of the major transatlantic ports – from where they have sailed for America after converting Gelinda's investments into a certified cheque (or *cambiale*), to be cashed in Halifax at the Bubble Bank ('Ragion Buble'). If Amiti and Ontario were enslaved for 'reasons of war', the Italian travellers Gelinda and Bastiano are enslaved for financial reasons resulting from two accidents, one more rocambolesque than the other. The first is that pirates assaulted and took their ship. However, a Bostonian vessel immediately attacked and burned the equipage (including Gelinda's cash) of what the American sailors believed was a buccaneer ship; they took all the crew members and travellers to be hanged in Boston according to the law, but while the pirates were immediately executed, Gelinda and Bastiano survived. This they owed to the richest man in Boston, Mr Dull, who was moved by Gelinda's supplications and, owing to his riches and power, managed to convert their death sentence into perpetual slavery and then acquired them from the captain of the ship as his personal servants. The second accident is more complex and less interesting, but dramatically equally important. We learn that Gelinda's relatives froze her assets after her disappearance, so that the Spanish banker was unable to issue the cheque to Halifax. Eventually, though, they would issue new valid cheques to the Spanish banker, allowing the transfer of Gelinda's investments to America once they learned of the cruelties perpetuated against Gelinda by her guardian in Naples. All of this information is given to the readers of the libretto in the *argomento*, or narrative preface to the opera (typical of Neapolitan productions), recounting the facts before the opera starts, providing the necessary information to understand the complex plot and the sudden denouements (such as why, in the end, Gelinda acquires the necessary financial means to buy back her freedom once the certified cheque becomes available to her).[32]

---

32 (Giuseppe Palomba,) *Le gare generose* (Naples, 1786), 1–3.

The 'de-Quakerization' of Mr Dull may reflect the new attention being paid to a predominantly secular business-oriented society. More likely, however, the loss of the master's Quaker identity could be related to the change in European public opinion concerning slavery in America. First, Quakers had regained their reputation as the strongest abolitionist group in America, which made their representation as slaveholders implausible. Abbé Raynal, in a public reply to the *Faculté de théologie* (1781), written to defend himself against the censorship of his *Philosophical and Political History of America* (in which he had previously praised the 'heretic' sect), admits that one of the few things Friends should be ashamed of is that they have been keeping slaves for a long time, 'but in 1769', he informs his readers, 'they abolished the evil. Now all the other colonies are imitating their tolerance.' A few years before, in 1777, François La Combe stated that 'In Pennsylvania Quakerism has made rapid progress and has become the admiration of all because of the generous liberty it has granted to the black slaves. A numerous, peaceful, laborious sect gives liberty to two hundred thousand blacks and makes them a society of brothers. What a lesson for monarchs!'.[33] Second, the Italian *Gazzetta Universale* tried to inhibit the increasing emigration to North America by propagandistic reports claming that 'the larger part of those who go to settle in Pennsylvania are sold as slaves and treated as animals'.[34] Third, and most importantly, as the Blumrosens document, in the discourse on slavery during the War of Independence and thereafter, the main concern became more economic than moral, focusing on issues of property and the value of labour.[35] Even Quaker abolitionism was deeply affected by this economic approach, which replaced or combined purely moral issues with financial considerations: the 1779 Quaker Yearly Meeting encouraged the Friends not only to free slaves but also to pay them for their past services, 'as a matter of justice' – they declared – 'and not of charity'.[36]

Mary Hunter, who focused on the Viennese version of *Le gare generose*, has already noticed that descriptions of financial transactions are pervasive in and essential to the plot, pointing out that '*Le gare generose* is . . . unusual in its positive attitude to trade and investment' and that 'financial competence and honesty' play a central role in this opera with these qualities being presented as 'hallmarks of virtue'.[37] If this is true for the Viennese version, in the Neapolitan version, the attitude towards the world of money exchange and business is more ambiguous. Here the traditional aristocratic mistrust of trade is not completely abandoned. When compared to that of the landlord Mr Dull of the more Arcadian rural Pennsylvania of Calzabigi, the psychological characterization of the merchant Mr Dull of Boston regresses to a lower comic level, resembling the less complex psychological characterization of *commedia dell'arte* masks. The

---

33 Raynal is quoted by Philips, *The Good Quaker*, 102; and so is La Combe, *Observations sur Londre* [sic] *et ses environs* (Paris, 1777). The year before, Vincenzo Martinelli also reported that in Pennsylvania Quakers were questioning the 'peculiar institution' in his *Istoria del governo d'Inghilterra e delle sue colonie in India e nell'America settentrionale* (Florence: Gaetano Cambiagi, 1776), 34, 36, 40. On these and similar reports see Venturi, *The End of the Old Regime*, 391–392, and Del Negro, *Il mito americano*, 246–247.

34 *Gazzetta Universale* 48 (14 June 1774), 226 (report written in London, 18 March). A year before *Le gare* was performed, a booklet by Benjamin Franklin was published in Italian translation: *Osservazione a chiunque desideri passare in America e Riflessioni circa i selvaggi dell'America Settentrionale del Dottor Franklin*, Italian trans. by Pietro Antoniutti (Padua: Conzatti, 1785); this book warned perspective immigrants that North America was not Eden, that the country needed hard workers and specialized artisans rather than adventurers and that new settlers were valued solely on the basis of their work and not for prestige based on family lineage.

35 Blumrosen, *Slave Nation*, especially 134–138, 159, 235.

36 Herrick, *White Servitude in Pennsylvania*, 83–84, documents the reimbursement of a Negro woman for her many years of unpaid work. On Quaker abolitionism see also Barbour and Frost, *The Quakers*, 145–149, and Jane E. Calvert, 'Dissenters in Our Own Country: Eighteenth-Century Quakerism and the Origins of American Civil Disobedience' (PhD dissertation, University of Chicago, 2003). Isaac Sharpless, *The Quakers in the Revolution*, volume 2 of *A History of Quaker Government in Pennsylvania* (Philadelphia: Leach, 1899), 137–138, 234–251 also brings a wealth of documentary evidence from the minutes of the American Quaker meetings to show how during the Revolutionary War the Society of Friends required its members to free all their slaves.

37 Hunter, 'Bourgeois Values', 170–173.

ORIENTAL TYRANNY IN THE EXTREME WEST

Bostonian character is not too different from the Pantalone-derived tutor figure of the most stereotypical buffa plots, combined with the contradictory and multifaceted nature typical of buffa characterizations of American Quakers.

Mr Dull is not the only character to become funnier (and therefore to have his status lowered). With good reason, Hunter also writes apropos of the Viennese version of this opera that 'for much of the libretto, the characters and the action seem to follow the commedia-dell-arte-derived plot archetype of the *innamorati* escaping the clutches of the lustful guardian'.[38] In fact, in the Neapolitan version, the enslaved couple is even less serious than in the Viennese one, resembling more a couple of cunning servants (buffa parts) than a couple of *innamorati* (typically seria parts). Accordingly, Mr Dull's dispensation of freedom in the Neapolitan version is no longer to be cunningly extorted and therefore is presented more as a mistake than as a deliberate act of mercy.

Gelinda uses her aria 'Deh Padron' to seduce Mr Dull just as the servant Serpina fools the old Uberto in Pergolesi's *La serva padrona*, which Paisiello had reset successfully in 1781. In the simple recitative preceding the aria (present in both the Neapolitan and Viennese versions), Gelinda, like Amiti, informs Mr Dull that she is already married to Bastiano; but unlike the naive savage girl, she embarks on a report on her and her husband's financial troubles (a story that a stockbroker might find more moving than the average spectator). During this recitative Mr Dull is hardly moved to pity, in fact he tends towards rage, asking about her debts ('ma i debiti?'), to which Gelinda answers that she could pay them off if the Bostonians had not burned a ship containing her money and other valuables and if she had a chance to cash a bill of exchange worth 3,000 guineas in Halifax. Mr Dull is just about to explode as Gelinda reveals that she and Bastiano are not siblings, but wife and husband: 'Tu maritata?' asks Dull in shock and disbelief, 'Che sento! ... dunque... maritata già sei!' ('Married? What do I hear! So you are already married!').[39] After this recitative Gelinda's ensuing aria serves the purpose of calming her master down and extorting mercy from him:

Deh Padron, non mi guardate	Please, oh master, do not look at me
Con quel viso brutto brutto,	with that scary scary face,
Ch'io son tenera, e mi fate	because I am so tender that you make
Quasi gelida restar.	me almost freeze with fear.
Vo' baciarvi quella mano,	I want to kiss that hand,
Che ogni misero accarezza,	which pets every poor creature.
Quella man, ch'è solo avvezza	That hand which is used only
Gl'altri falli a perdonar.	to forgive others' faults.
(Il mio pianto par lo mova,	[aside] (It seems that my weeping is moving
Vacillar lo veggo già.)	him, I can see that he is already yielding.)
Perdonatemi, signore,	Forgive me, sir,
Riflettete a' casi miei	consider my condition
All'eccesso del dolore,	of unbearable suffering,
Alla mia fatalità.	consider my misfortune.
Ah d'un guardo omai pietoso	May heaven alleviate my fate
La mia sorte il Ciel consoli,	with your finally merciful eyes,
Goda il core almen riposo	may the heart find at least
Nella mia cattività.[40]	some peace in my captivity.

---

38 Hunter, 'Bourgeois Values', 173–175.
39 (Palomba,) *Le gare generose* (Naples, 1786), Act 2 Scene 13, 56–57; same as in (Palomba,) *Le gare generose* (Vienna, 1786), Act 2 Scene 12, 55–57.
40 (Palomba,) *Le gare generose* (Naples, 1786), Act 2 Scene 13, 57–58.

Example 1 Paisiello, Gelinda's aria 'Deh Padron', Neapolitan version of *Le gare generose*, bars 1–12 (manuscript score A-*Wn*, 17807)

This piece is a quiet and monotonous through-composed aria, pervaded (almost uninterruptedly) by a circular hypnotic figuration played mostly by the second violins *con sordino* (see Example 1).[41] This pattern, usually a gesture of emotional uneasiness, acquires here a subtle mechanical quality, with the first violin staccato quaver *ticks* on the upbeats inserted as a gear in the rhythmic mechanism regulated by the inexorable

---

41 For this example I used a Genoa copy that reflects the Neapolitan original: Paisiello, *Le gare generose*, manuscript score in 2 volumes, I-Gl, 5b. 29/30 -L8 3/4. I compared it with A-Wn, 17807, to which I will return. This number has been removed from the autograph score, I-Nc, Rari 3.2.14/15, as pointed out by Robinson, *Giovanni Paisiello*, 378.

pizzicato quaver *tocks* in the bass. Gelinda, through a fragmented vocal line and her baby talk ('brutto brutto'), exposes her vulnerability and docility, but it soon becomes clear that it is rather a passive-aggressive dissimulation in order seductively to soften Mr Dull's temper. In fact, in the two lines of aside, she appears pleased with herself for being able to trick the old man. Similarly, in both Pergolesi's and Paisiello's versions of *La serva padrona*, Serpina sings an aria ('A Serpina penserete') alternating between a Largo in duple meter, in which she moves the old master to compassion, and an Allegro section (triple meter in Pergolesi), in which she merrily and derisively observes that little by little Uberto is yielding to her tears.[42] After Gelinda's aria, when Mr Dull announces his intention to free her and her husband, we cannot help laughing at his stupid generosity.

Several months after the Neapolitan premiere, *Le gare generose* was readapted for the Burgtheater in Vienna, most probably by Lorenzo Da Ponte, who made several changes that restored some of the original seriousness of Calzabigi's *Amiti e Ontario*.[43] For the Viennese production, Bastiano's part was translated, as customary, from Neapolitan to standard Italian; in addition, Carl Ditters von Dittersdorf wrote a new setting for Meri's 'Così destino e voglio', while Gelinda had two arias replaced. One is her buffa aria 'Or vedete in che imbarazzi', replaced by a sentimental aria, 'Infelice, sventurata'; the other is 'Deh Padron', replaced by 'Perché volgi altrove il guardo' and preceded by a new accompanied recitative following (not replacing) the previous simple recitative.[44] Most of the changes were intended to give more prominence to Gelinda, a role well suited to the singer Nancy Storace, whose role in *Le gare generose* Count Zinzendorf described as 'grand' in his diary entry.[45] The prominent status of buffa stars in late eighteenth-century Vienna was often what generated many of the revisions, including the composition of substitute arias, but the replacements were also the product of changing aesthetic and ideological trends. As a case in point, one should consider that when in April 1787 Nancy Storace moved to London, she chose for her English debut to interpret the role of Gelinda again, although she did not use the Viennese version that was already tailored for her role, but a new, extensively revised version of *Le gare* under the title *Gli schiavi per amore*, in which Anglo-American characters were cautiously replaced by French ones, and the whole opera was no longer set in revolutionary Boston, but in royalist Canada.[46]

---

42 Reinhard Strohm, *Die Italianische Oper im 18. Jahrhundert* (Wilhelmshaven: Heinrichshofen, 1979), 138, rightly observes that 'A Serpina penserete', in the second intermezzo, 'is not a sentimental aria, but rather an aria that is supposed to drive Uberto to sentimentality'.

43 (Lorenzo Da Ponte (ed.), after (Palomba,)) *Le gare generose: commedia per musica in due atti da rappresentarsi al teatro di corte l'anno 1786* (Vienna: Giuseppe Nob. de Kurzbek [, 1786]), Act 2 Scene 12, 57–58. There is no certainty that Da Ponte made the revisions, but it is likely given his official position, at the time, as Poet of Viennese Imperial Theatres.

44 Robinson, *Giovanni Paisiello*, 378–379, records several other minor changes, such as the transposition of a couple of numbers. Of the four scores reflecting the Viennese performance, and labelled as 'variant 2' by Robinson, I have used US-Wc, M1500 P23 G3. In the first page of the manuscript one can read 'Rappresentata nel Teatro di Corte a Vienna l'Anno 1786'. Although housed in the Austrian National Library, A-Wn, 17807 (like other four sources) maintains the part of Bastiano in Neapolitan idiom and therefore reflects the Neapolitan premiere (Robinson, *Giovanni Paisiello*, 377–378). This is because copies of Neapolitan operas were usually made in Naples and sent abroad, where more or less extensive revisions were made. The revised copies probably left with the singers, while the unrevised original from Naples was left behind. It is worth pointing out that one of Dittersdorf's first compositions for the theatre was a two-act musical farce entitled *Il viaggiatore americano in Joannesberg*, premiered in Johannisberg on 1 May 1771 (the literary and musical sources are unfortunately lost), according to the catalogue in Margaret Grave and Jay Lane, 'Dittersdorf, Carl Ditters von', *Grove Music Online*, ed. Laura Macy, <http://www.grovemusic.com>, accessed 29 October 2006.

45 Dorothea Link, *The National Court Theatre in Mozart's Vienna: Sources and Documents 1783–1792* (New York: Oxford University Press, 1998), 278: Zinzendorf wrote, 'Au Theater. Le gare generose [jolie musique de Paisiello]. La Storace en esclave Gelinda a un grand rôle, dont elle s'acquitte bien'.

46 Nancy Storace reached the peak of her career in Vienna, starting in April 1783 as the Countess in Salieri's *La scola de' gelosi* and playing thereafter many other important and very different roles in more than twenty, mostly buffa operas. During

A good example of how revisions were informed by local trends is the Viennese replacement of Gelinda's 'Deh Padron' with 'Perché volgi altrove il guardo'. The new aria avoids ambiguity or dissimulation and does not present the stylistic concoction of Paisiello's replaced buffa aria, featuring instead a consistently earnest rhetorical mode. The choice of the aria form, a rondò aria, is significant in itself: this two-tempo aria form is emblematic in operatic aesthetics in late eighteenth-century Vienna, where it became popular, being characterized by earnestness of expression and an elevated stylistic level.[47] The rondò can be seen as a prototype of the Romantic grand multi-tempo aria, anticipating both its form and function: the accompanied recitative preceding the rondò corresponding to the scena, the first tempo of the rondò to the adagio and the faster second tempo to the cabaletta.

The text of the Viennese rondò aria shows also that the librettist was aware of Calzabigi's original aria for Amiti and wished to restore its dramatic function. Like Amiti, Gelinda shifts from the formal *voi* to the informal *tu* and calls Mr Dull 'amico' ('friend' – as Quakers were called and called each other) and 'father' rather than 'master', asking him for a redefinition of his role from tyrant to *paterfamilias*.

[Larghetto]

Perché volgi altrove il guardo,	Why are you turning your eyes away
E non odi il pianto mio?	and do not listen to my weeping?
In chi mai sperar poss'io	Who else could I rely on
Se tu sei crudele ancor?	if even you are cruel to me?
Tu che sai della mia sorte	At least you, who understand
Quanto è barbaro il tenor,	how awful is the nature of my fate,
non mi dare ahimè la morte	do not bring me death
Cogli sdegni, e col rigor.	by being disdainful and harsh.
Padre, amico, o caro oggetto	Father, friend, dear source
Di speranza, e di timor;	of hope and fear,
Ah non regge al fiero aspetto,	Ah, before such a fierce look
Già si perde il mio valor.	my courage fails and weakens.

---

the years 1785 and 1786 her roles included Susanna in Mozart's *Le nozze di Figaro*, Ofelia in Salieri's *La grotta di Trofonio*, Eleonora in his *Prima la musica poi le parole*, Angelica in Martin y Soler's *Il burbero di buon cuore*, Lilla in *Una cosa rara*, Rosina in Paisiello's *Il Barbiere di Siviglia* and Serpina in Paisiello's new version of *La serva padrona*. See Dorothea Link, *Arias for Nancy Storace: Mozart's First Susanna* (Middleton, WI: A-R Editions, 2002), xiv-xvi. The libretto of the English version of *Le gare generose* is *Gli schiavi per amore: A New Comic Opera in Two Acts as Performed at the King's Theatre in the Hay-Market; the Music by the Celebrated Signor Paisiello Under the Direction of Mr Storace* (London, 1787). A later Italian production of *Le gare generose* under the latter title does not specify where in the world the action takes place: *Gli schiavi per amore: dramma giocoso per musica da rappresentarsi nel Teatro di S. A. A. il Signor di Carignano nell'autunno dell'anno 1791* (Turin: Derossi, 1791); in this case the characters' names do not change and the references to America are kept intact in the text (as in Gelinda's recount of her story and travels in Act 2 Scene 13, 47–48).

47 Don Neville, 'The 'Rondò' in Mozart's Late Operas', *Mozart Jahrbuch* 1994, 141, writes that the rondò 'always identifies with a sincerity of expression' and 'a moment of truth'. On rondò aria form see Stefano Arteaga, *Le rivoluzioni del teatro musicale italiano dalla sua origine al presente* (Venice: Palese, 1785). Among the modern studies of this aria form see Helga Lüning, 'Die Rondò-Arie im späten 18. Jahrhundert: dramatischer Gehalt und musikalischer Bau', *Hamburger Jahrbuch für Musikwissenschaft* 5 (1981), 219–246; John A. Rice, 'Emperor and Impresario: Leopold II and the Transformation of Viennese Musical Theater, 1790–92' (PhD dissertation, University of California, Berkeley, 1987), 92–110; James Webster, 'The Analysis of Mozart's Arias', in *Mozart Studies*, ed. Cliff Eisen (Oxford: Clarendon, 1991), 108, 149–151, 170–174.

ORIENTAL TYRANNY IN THE EXTREME WEST

[Allegro]
Che più resta o numi ingrati	O cruel gods, of what other cruelties
Alla vostra crudeltà?	could you be capable?
Dite, amanti sventurati	Tell me, unfortunate lovers,
S'io son degna di pietà.[48]	if I don't deserve some mercy.

The particular treatment of form in this piece (see Table 1, outlining the formal plan of the aria) could not accommodate better its dramatic function. The syntactical units of the text are coherently matched to different structural units in the music, and the orchestra's accompanying patterns do not contradict, but rather underscore the concepts and emotions expressed by the character. This total lack of displacement or mismatch among the textual and musical signifiers prevents ambiguity and in final analysis avoids comedy (which is not always the case in Mozart's own rondò arias).[49] The key moment of the aria, when Gelinda calls her master 'father' and 'friend' (see Example 2), is supported by an accompanying pattern that at first glance may resemble Paisiello's pervading figuration in 'Deh Padron'. Its zigzag, more geometrically defined melodic contour and staccato phrasing, however, do not confer the hypnotic quality of Paisiello's smooth legato and arc-shaped figuration. Further, the accompaniment figuration is not inserted as a gear in a rhythmically uninterrupted mechanism (absent here are Paisiello's pizzicato bass notes and the staccato upbeat strokes in the violins). Rather, this segment appears as an isolated and relatively short moment, inserted in an aria that articulates different sections using different accompaniment patterns – each one appropriate to the meaning of the text. In contrast, Paisiello's never-changing orchestral accompaniment appears like a hypnotic pendulum, seductive rather than persuasive, indifferent to the concepts expressed by the singing character. The shift to the faster tempo in the Viennese aria, typical of the rondò form, is used to bring the emotional temperature to a boiling point, as happens in nineteenth-century cabalettas. The persuasive power of the rondò aria form, granted by its potential for dramatic and musical intensification and implemented by an excellent performer like Nancy Storace, certainly persuaded not only Gelinda's on-stage addressee (Mr Dull) but also the Viennese audience. To them Mr Dull's act of mercy did not appear to be sneakily extorted (as it did in Naples), but fairly conceded. 'Perché volgi', in fact, redefines not only Gelinda's direct addressee but also her role; her more serious characterization gives new coherence even to the second and last act of mercy (Act 2, last scene). Inspired by the generosity of her former master and present 'friend', having regained her financial security, Gelinda decides to save the character Berlicco from jail (where he is headed, having defrauded Mr Dull of a considerable sum of money destined for investments in the European market). The meaning of her final act of generosity goes beyond the usual dispensation of happiness and forgiveness in the last-act finale and signifies that not only has she regained her lost freedom, but also that she has acquired a position of brotherly equality with Mr Dull (by means of the acquisition of financial independence), which entitles her too to perform the dispensation of mercy:

Ah Signor, se generoso	Ah, Sir, since you have been generous
Meco foste, anch'io tal sono;	with me, now I will do the same;
A Berlicco io già perdono,	I forgive Berlicco,
Al suo debito sto avante,	I will clear his debt,
E in riscatto anche il contante	and I will ensure that he will also
Per dover rimborserà.[50]	reimburse the cash he owes you.

---

48 This is a replacement aria in the Viennese production of *Le gare generose* (1786), (Da Ponte after Palomba,) *Le gare generose* (Vienna (, 1786)), Act 2 Scene 12, 57–58.
49 For a discussion of the independence of various operatic parameters in opera buffa (or 'multivalence') in Mozart's set pieces see James Webster, 'Mozart's Operas and the Myth of Musical Unity', *Cambridge Opera Journal* 2/2 (1990), 198.
50 (Da Ponte after Palomba,) *Le gare generose* (Vienna: Kurzbek (, 1786)), Act 2, last scene, 68.

Table 1 Outline of the rondò aria 'Perché volgi', substitute aria in *Le gare generose* (Vienna, 1786), replacing the original 'Deh padron' (Naples, 1786)

LARGHETTO 2/4

Form:	M¹		E	T	M¹		E		T	
Bars	1-10 (intr.1)	11-15	17-21	22-	25-	30	31-	36	37	42-	46-	49	50-	55	57	58-	65
Thematic material — orchestra	a				b						c; (a+b)+c					d	closing material
Thematic material — voice		1	2	2' fragmented			3		1	2	x fragmented		2''	4			
Text		A¹⁻²	A³⁻⁴	B¹	B²		B²⁻³		A¹⁻²	A³⁻⁴	C¹		C²	C³⁻⁴		C⁴	
Tonal plan: G major	I				V/V		V		I				V/V	V			

ALLEGRO 4/4

Form:	M²	T	E		(m¹)		(e)	M²	T		C
Bars	66-	70-	75- intens.	77-	83	84-	88-	91-	95-99	100-	104-	109-127
Thematic material — orchestra	5				e			f	b		5	closing material
Thematic material — voice		light coloratura		4'		2	4'	x fragm		5		light coloratura
Text	D¹⁻²	D³⁻⁴		C³⁻⁴		A³⁻⁴		C¹	C¹⁻²	D¹⁻²	D³⁻⁴	D¹...⁴
Tonal plan	I		IV			ii- V		i	V	I		

M¹ = main theme of the first tempo
M² = main theme of the second tempo
E = Episodes, or contrasting sections
T = transition
C = Closing section

ORIENTAL TYRANNY IN THE EXTREME WEST

Example 2 Anonymous (possibly Dittersdorf), Gelinda's aria 'Perché vogli altrove il guardo?', Viennese pasticcio version of *Le gare generose*, bars 1–24 (manuscript score US-Wc, M1500 P23 G3)

The financial security that is a guarantee of freedom in America now blesses the social microcosm on stage and the final tutti rejoices in everyone's ability to be equally generous. In *Amiti e Ontario*, the act of mercy, as we have seen, converts the initial power relationship of master/servant into an equally bonding and hierarchically structured (albeit morally higher and more human) relationship of father/daughter, which duplicates at a sublimated level gender and social roles (the father figure as allegory of the ruling male, hence – at the highest hierarchical level – the King; the daughter as allegory of the subjected woman, hence the faithful subject). In *Le gare generose*, instead, the daughter cuts herself loose from the father figure, leaves her master's house and – what is truly revolutionary – acquires the power to grant mercy herself, but chooses to extend the power to others by freeing them rather than punishing or subjecting them. The Viennese version of the opera, by elevating the tone of the drama and of the music, presents this not as a victory snatched by a shrewd servant, but as a well deserved and almost heroic achievement by an honourable middle-class woman.

Because the Viennese production of *Le gare* dates from only months after the Neapolitan premiere, the changes were more likely determined by the different local aesthetic and political orientation than by any particular development in the political situation in America or Europe. The aesthetics of Viennese opera buffa during these years is deeply affected by a trend towards the sentimental and the *mezzo carattere* modes,

Example 2   *continued*

as well as towards a more thoughtful, almost philosophical function for this genre.[51] The politics of Viennese opera buffa in the mid-1780s, as Hunter has pointed out, need to be understood in the context of the recent alliance of the court and the bank, of aristocracy and commerce, and the ensuing pride of the middle classes in quintessential bourgeois values such as honest entrepreneurship. These differences explain the uplifting of rhetorical level in the Viennese version of *Le gare generose*, an opera that, as we have seen, is centred on financial transactions and represents the business-oriented middle classes.[52] It is also important to add and to stress that this pride in honest, generous and free commerce was perceived at the time as one of the virtues of the new American nation. As Gordon Wood maintains, honest and free commerce was one of the highest values in post-colonial America. Eighteenth-century comedies about American Quakers are indeed centred on similar honest, generous transactions, such as L. F. Faur's *Le Veur anglais*, or Chamfort's *La jeune indienne*, played in Vienna under the title *Die Quäkerin*.[53] Compared to these different plays revolving

---

51 This trend is engagingly discussed by Edmund Goehring, *Three Modes of Perception in Mozart: The Philosophical, Pastoral, and Comic in 'Così fan tutte'* (Cambridge: Cambridge University Press, 2004). See also Stefano Castelvecchi, 'Sentimental Opera: The Emergence of a Genre, 1760–1790' (PhD dissertation, University of Chicago, 1996).

52 Hunter, 'Bourgeois Values', 166–167, 170.

53 On the emphasis that the new American nation put on business see Wood, *The Radicalism of the American Revolution* (New York: Vintage, 1991), 325–346. On *Le vrai anglais* see Philips, *The Good Quaker*, 129–130; the play was premiered in November 1786 at the Théâtre Italien, and the show included a ballet of Quakers. Another domestic drama based on

ORIENTAL TYRANNY IN THE EXTREME WEST

Example 2 *continued*

around the theme of Quaker generosity, the situation in *Le gare generose* is complicated by the issue of slavery and the usage of financial resources to trade human freedom. There is little attempt in the opera to provide a unilateral perspective; if money buys the two Italian travellers Gelinda and Bastiano as slaves, money also buys their freedom. In this particular opera, the view of America as a plutocratic democracy, in which freedom can be negotiated through monetary transactions, explains the representation of slavery as a condition determined not by ethnicity, but by social status, the latter determined by finances and not by rights of birth.

Moreover, many of the open questions in *Amiti e Ontario* are still unanswered in *Le gare*. Most notably they concern slaves of African descent, who are represented in these two operas together with Native American and Italian slaves. In *Le gare* Bastiano, Gelinda's husband, appears tied to a black slave and – significantly – the Italian slave is 'deprived of his own clothes' and therefore (since we can assume that he is

North American subjects in which money plays an important role is Sébastien-Roch-Nicolas Chamfort, *La jeune Indienne*, reprinted with an introduction by Gilbert Chinard (Princeton: Princeton University Press, 1946). Chinard indicates as a proto-source of this story Richard Ligon's *True and Exact History of the Island of Barbadoes* (1657), containing the story of Inkle and Yariko. *Yariko* was performed in Vienna in the early 1770s. Elaine R. Sisman, 'Haydn's Theater Symphonies', *Journal of the American Musicological Society* 43/2 (1990), 332–333, hypothesizes that Haydn's Symphony No. 49 in F minor (1768) was written expressly for *Die Quäker*, or *Die junge Indianerin*, on the basis that in a Viennese source its title is 'Il Quakuo [sic!] di bell'humore [sic]' (The good-humoured (or good-natured) Quaker).

Example 2 *continued*

not naked) probably dressed in the same fashion as the slave of African descent.[54] Though the two men appear similarly dressed, there is no hint of equality; like the mute part of Vespone in *La serva padrona*, Bastiano's companion does not utter a word, nor a single note. Black slaves are denied the most powerful operatic resource of expression: the singing voice. And in *Amiti e Ontario* only noises of black slaves are heard from off stage: here the Africans in America are denied not only the operatic voice, but also a presence on stage. In both cases Mr Dull does not free them in the end. Even Gelinda, once she acquires the power to dispense mercy, does not do anything to change the condition of the innocent slaves, preferring instead to free her deceitful countryman Don Berlicco.

At the time when *Le gare generose* was still playing around Europe, Benjamin Franklin, the most widely read and highly respected American thinker in Europe, was serving as the president of the Pennsylvania Society for the Abolition of Slavery. With his usual formidable ability to combine common sense and ideals, he expressed the need to provide previously enslaved people with the necessary skills to exercise freedom and maintain it with dignity:

> Slavery is such an atrocious debasement of human nature that its very extirpation, if not performed with solicitous care, may sometimes open a source of serious evils. . . . To instruct, to

---

54 (Da Ponte after Palomba,) *Le gare generose* (Vienna: Kurzbek (, 1786)), Act 2 Scene 3, 41: 'Bastiano spogliato dell'abito proprio e incatenato con un Africano' (Bastiano, deprived of his own clothes and chained to an African).

advise, to qualify those who have been restored to freedom, for the exercise and enjoyment of civil liberty, to promote in them habits of industry, to furnish them with employment suited to their age, sex, talents, and other circumstances, and to procure their children an education calculated for their future situation in life; these are the great outlines of the annexed plan.[55]

As we all know, it took much longer than a last-act buffa finale to carry out Franklin's plan, and it is still not clear whether there has ever been a happy ending. To late eighteenth-century people the future looked brighter because present institutions seemed to be under the constant pressure of radical impending reforms. This emerges from the tone of journalistic accounts about revolutionary events in America, a country that was still a new world and in rapid transformation. The way the operas examined in this article reflect those journalistic accounts is oblique, because actual political events or situations are never directly represented in eighteenth-century opera buffa, notwithstanding the important role contemporary reality played in shaping its dramatic subjects. And yet metaphorical transpositions often result in a remarkably lucid analysis of contemporary reality.[56] In *Amiti e Ontario* that happens by means of a necessary mediation of stereotypes and myths (the good Quaker and the good savage) that were able to stimulate a debate over slavery and freedom framed within familiar cultural and philosophical paradigms. In *Le gare generose* those stereotypes are not entirely abandoned, but they are radically modified in order to produce a more up-to-date image of America, a country that to European gazette readers of the mid-1780s was no longer an Arcadian garden, a projection of a European utopian dream, but rather a modern revolutionary society in which skills in trading and business replaced power structures based on birthrights and congenital privileges (determined by cast and gender). The main question asked by the operas' authors seems to be whether capitalism was actually able to produce a better or more just social system. The Eurocentric *Weltanschauung* linking Asia (or the East) to the past (agrarian economy and tyranny), Europe to the present (mixed economy and reformed absolutism) and America to the future (free trade and democracy) is still a powerful paradigm for *Le gare*. As represented in this opera, the presence of slavery in America does not invert the natural and cosmic movement of Earth's history because American slavery is of a very different kind from the one practised in Oriental harems: unlike in Mozart's *Die Entführung aus dem Serail*, in Paisiello's *Le gare* there is no need for an abduction, since in Boston freedom can be acquired by monetary transactions. But the fact that people could be enslaved for debts or remain in slavery for not being able to pay them off carries the symbolic movement westward to the dangerous point where extreme West seems to collide with the extreme East, as if Columbus's idea of reaching Asia through a transatlantic journey by virtue of the rotundity of Earth was not so foolish after all.

---

55 Benjamin Franklin, 'A Plan for Improving the Condition of Free Blacks', Philadelphia, 26 October 1789, quoted in Blumrosen, *Slave Nation*, 253.
56 I have already adopted this research and interpretative methodology in my article 'Mesmerizing Adultery: *Così fan tutte* and the Kornman Scandal', *Cambridge Opera Journal* 14/3 (2002), 263–296. For the use of metaphors (sometimes derived from highly conventional domestic drama) during a more turbulent revolutionary era see George Taylor, *The French Revolution and the London Stage, 1789–1805* (Cambridge and New York: Cambridge University Press, 2000). The theoretical framework for this kind of hermeneutics is akin to Frederic Jameson, *The Political Unconscious: Narrative as a Socially Symbolic Art* (Ithaca, NY: Cornell University Press, 1981).

Part V
Opera and Politics

[16]

On the Freedom of the Theatre and Censorship: the *Adrien* Controversy (1792)

Elizabeth C. Bartlet
Duke University, USA

Résumé : En 1792, première application de la loi de 1791 sur la censure, la Commune de Paris interdit la représentation d'*Adrien* à l'Académie Royale de Musique. Pourquoi a-t-elle adopté cette ligne de conduite, comment a-t-elle géré ce défi lancé à l'Assemblée ? Les réponses montrent les positions politiques antagoniques de la période, dont la seule base commune est la foi en le pouvoir du théâtre comme instrument d'éducation morale et patriotique.

Abstract: In 1792 the Commune de Paris forbade the performance of Adrien at the Académie Royale de Musique. This is the first major challenge to the censorship law of 1791. Why did the Commune follow this course of action, how did they get away with challenging the Assemblée? The answers show conflicting political positions of the time, whose only common ground was the belief in theatre's importance as an instrument for moral and patriotic education.

> La mission des Censeurs est de faire la guerre à la raison, à la liberté; sans talens & sans génie, leur devoir est d'énerver le génie & les talens; ce sont des Eunuques qui n'ont plus qu'un seul plaisir : celui de faire d'autres Eunuques.[1]

Thus wrote one disappointed young playwright in 1789. Marie-Joseph Chénier (brother of the poet, André Chénier) had just seen the performance of his *tragédie*, *Charles IX, ou l'école des rois*, blocked for political reasons: the portrayal of an evil king, a wicked cleric and bad governance on stage could be interpreted as an attack on the institutions of the monarchy and church. Chénier protested that such was not his intention and defended his play as moral, since it drew the audience's attention to serious themes (abuse of power, intolerance, corruption) and so contributed to public instruction, which should, according to him, be theatre's function.[2] In this he followed, though with greater vehemence, the French aesthetic position of the late *ancien régime*, as seen in the definitions in the *Encyclopédie*. Common to all is an assessment of desired audience reaction as well as a description of the aspects proper to each form. Thus, *tragédie* is the «représentation d'une action héroïque dont l'objet est d'exciter la terreur & la compassion... Les poëtes dramatiques dignes d'écrire pour le théâtre, ont toujours regardé l'obligation d'inspirer la haine du vice, & l'amour de vertu, comme la première obligation de leur art.» *Comédie* , too, through exaggeration and ridicule, seeks to teach the spectators: «elle peint le vice qu'elle rend méprisable, comme la tragédie rend le crime odieux.» [3]

In the same pamphlet quoted above, *De la liberté du théâtre en France*, Chénier also pleaded for the abolition of censorship.[4] In this he joined ranks with a number of authors during the 1780s hostile to the practice; Beaumarchais, who had to fight hard for *Le mariage de Figaro*

(1784), is the most famous example. But, whereas Beaumarchais succeeded by lining up powerful allies at court and conducting a clever campaign to arouse public interest, just five years later Chénier had an additional avenue open to him. He appealed to the newly formed Assemblée Nationale:

> Vous tous, Législateurs élus par le Souverain, Citoyens de toutes professions; vous tous que nous avons chargés de rendre à la France les droits qu'on avoit usurpés sur elle; ces droits qui sont à tous les hommes...; parcourez un moment cet écrit... Vous sentirez combien la liberté du Théâtre est à désirer pour l'utilité publique... Dans un pays libre, tout ce qui n'est pas expressément défendu par les loix, est permis de droit.[5]

The last sentence is a clear reference to article V of the Declaration of the Rights of Man and Citizen («Tout ce qui n'est pas défendu par la loi ne peut être empêché»), then being debated and shortly thereafter enacted. Chénier argued too that censorship was contrary to freedom of thought and speech, addressed in article XI («La libre communication des pensées et des opinions est un des droits les plus précieux de l'homme; tout citoyen peut donc parler, écrire, imprimer librement; sauf à répondre de l'abus de cette liberté dans les cas déterminés par la loi»). In 1789 the Assemblée did not take up the subject of censorship, as Chénier had wished, but they did lift the interdiction of *Charles IX*. Its 4 November première at the Comédie Française was the young author's first dramatic triumph and, given its history, assured him a place among the leaders in the fight for authors' rights. The following year the Société des Auteurs dramatiques (founded by Beaumarchais) presented a petition to the Assemblée in which they requested legislation to give them control over their works, to break the monopoly of the Comédie Française and to encourage competition among theatres. Here «liberty of the theatre» meant the abolition of long-held privileges of a few institutions and the introduction of safeguards for all authors.[6] Strangely, the censorship issue did not come up again in the petition itself. The Assemblée turned the matter over to the Comité de Constitution -an indication that they took seriously the argument about the possible extension of fundamental rights in this case.

On 13 January 1791 Isaac Le Chapelier, in the Comité's name, presented their report. At the outset he affirmed that the issue «tient réellement aux principes de la liberté & de la propriété publiques; elle doit être décidée par ces principes».[7] What followed was very favourable not only to the authors' petition but also to Chénier's pamphlet (Le Chapelier's choice of phrases in many places confirms that he was addressing both directly). He, too, echoed the Declaration of the Rights of Man: «Les auteurs dramatiques devoient, autant & plus que tous les écrivains, être libres dans le choix de ceux qui représentent leurs ouvrages & dans l'expression de leur pensée»,[8] and Chénier's position that a free theatre would turn away from ridiculous, often indecent farce (standard fare on the boulevards) to worthier subjects and become excellent schools for citizenship:

> Les amis de l'ordre public & des moeurs, qui le sont toujours des principes & de la liberté... ne doivent former qu'un souhait : ...c'est que par-tout les spectacles donnent quelque chose à apprendre, & que toutes les pièces fassent désormais gagner la patrie, en formant de meilleurs citoyens. Espérons qu'un règlement sage dirigera cette partie de l'éducation publique; car c'en sera une alors.[9]

In order to fulfill the function of the citizens' 'school', theatres had to be free, he argued. The abolition of the privileges at the Comédie Française (and by extension the Opéra), the protection of authors' rights, the freedom for actors to perform whatever they wished without legal or ecclesiastical controls -all followed logically. Le Chapelier reluctantly allowed to maintain public order -«il peut être quelquefois nécessaire d'employer la force publique pour calmer des gens qui cherchent à mettre le trouble»- but, except for a limited presence at potentially tumultuous performances, authorities should not, according to him, interfere. During the same session, he proposed a law establishing the liberty of the theatres. Among its provisions was the explicit suppression of censorship:

> VI. Les entrepreneurs ou les membres des différens théâtres seront, à raison de leur état, sous l'inspection des municipalités. Ils ne recevront des ordres que des officiers municipaux, qui ne pourront arrêter ni défendre la représentation d'une pièce, sauf la responsabilité des auteurs & des comédiens.[10]

In the ensuing debate only Robespierre saw a danger in the wording:

> L'opinion publique est seule juge de ce qui est conforme au bien. Je ne veux donc pas que par une disposition vague on donne à un officier municipal le droit d'adopter ou de rejeter tout ce qui pourrait lui plaire ou lui déplaire; par là on favorise les intérêts particuliers et non les mœurs publiques.

Le Chapelier assured him that the Comité agreed completely that municipal officers should not have that power and that they felt that article VI could not be misinterpreted. It and the rest of the bill passed without amendment.[11] A year later Robespierre was proved right, although the result in the specific case would not have displeased him: the Commune de Paris forbade the performance of *Adrien* (an opera by Etienne Nicolas Méhul to a libretto by François Benoît Hoffman) on the eve of its première at the Académie Royale de Musique (the Opéra). Since this was the first major challenge to the censorship section of the 1791 law, it merits a closer look than it has received heretofore. Why did the Commune follow this course of action, and how did they get away with challenging the Assemblée's authority? The answers will reveal conflicting political positions of the time, whose only common ground was the belief in theatre's importance as an instrument for moral and patriotic education.

* * *

Up till now many scholars have seen in the banning of *Adrien* evidence of the growing anti-*monarchical* sentiments in Paris at that time.[12] Since Louis XVI was to lose his throne five months later, it was a natural assumption, but a careful reading of contemporary sources does not bear it out entirely. After the king had accepted the Constitution on 14 September 1791, there was a strong pro-royalist movement. Theatrical works given during the autumn and winter reflected his new popularity. While it had begun to wane in the spring, Louis was seldom directly criticized. The same cannot be said of the king's brothers, the comte de Provence and the comte d'Artois, who were by now *émigrés*. In French eyes, they were seen as collaborating with the enemy, Austria. During the winter Emperor Leopold II fuelled the antagonism with his declarations critical of the French Assemblée Nationale's actions. When he concluded a mutual defence treaty with Prussia on 7 February 1792, France considered it, with reason, an action threatening to her. Within the country, several groups, among them the Girondins who momentarily controlled the government, saw war as inevitable, and some even considered it desirable and necessary to consolidate the new distribution of power.[13] The growing hostility towards Austria in the early part of 1792 (leading to the declaration of war on 20 April) had unfortunate consequences for Queen Marie-Antoinette, Louis' wife and sister of Francis II (Leopold's successor as Emperor on 1 March 1792). Never truly popular among the people, she was suspected of collusion with the enemy. The radical press were quick to publicize whatever actions of hers could be interpreted as favouring Austria.

Adrien, too, was a victim of this campaign. Based in part on a libretto by Metastasio portraying an emperor's act of clemency, its origin lent itself to unfortunate interpretations. As Austrian court poet, Metastasio often made explicit flattering parallels between the Roman emperor of classical history and the Holy Roman Emperor, the ruler of Austria, in his own day. The potential glorification of the enemy was more than the patriotic French could tolerate. Days before the planned première (6 March) they attacked *Adrien*, not as a *royalist* work, but as an *imperialist* one. Combining fact with wild flights of imagination and involving the queen for good measure, the leftist *Annales patriotiques* informed its readers that the court sponsored the work, and as part of the triumphal march, the captives were forced to pull Adrien's chariot. Noting that Marie-Antoinette planned to attend the première, the journalist added in an editorial comment: «il faut espérer que les spectateurs ne lui donneront pas lieu de croire que les Parisiens soient de si-tôt près à s'atteler au char de l'empereur son frère».[14] While in the 1770s and 1780s the court frequently solicited operas directly or indirectly (and the queen's patronage of Gluck, Sacchini and Grétry was important for their careers [15]), there is no evidence for any royal pressure on the Opéra in the early 1790s after the institution no longer was under the control of the *maison du Roi* (the city was now its legal supervisor, and, as we shall see below, this had important consequences). The description of the triumphal march was certainly inaccurate, for, as Hoffman had bragged earlier in a letter to his brother-in-law, in it was «un char traîné par des chevaux réels, dont chacun coûte cent louis et les vaut»[16], and this accords with the specifications in the manuscript and printed libretti.[17]

Nevertheless, the public's interest was piqued, and the radical press took up the fight. Representative of the most extreme position, Antoine Joseph Gorsas, editor of *Le courrier des LXXXIII départemens*, was one of the most persistent critics.[18] By 3 March he had obtained a copy of the printed libretto, promising to allow his readers to judge for themselves, although, as he warned, «il soit difficile de juger ailleurs que sur la scène de ces sortes d'ouvrages où l'appareil & la musique elle-même peuvent prêter à des allusions».[19] The press was reporting rumours, but the unfavourable publicity alarmed the Opéra administration, who had, after all, invested heavily in the production at a time when their theatre was in dire financial straits.[20] The previous month other theatres, notably the Vaudeville, had been the scene of violent demonstrations caused by political differences,[21] and they were anxious to avoid similar problems at their theatre. They postponed the première of *Adrien*, and in an open letter the librettist, Hoffman, sought to justify his work against false charges that it «contient des opinions contraires au nouvel ordre des choses». Expressing amazement that an opera, «genre d'Ouvrage le plus frivole de la Littérature», could arouse controversy and perhaps result in public demonstrations, he went on to point out that his work was written before 1789 and to describe it as «une intrigue d'Amour, peu de Scènes, des Danses, du Spectacle».[22] The only lines capable of a political interpretation were, by a fortunate coincidence, constitutional, he argued. Hoffman had in mind here Adrien's first speech on the duties of a ruler (to his followers):

Ce n'est point moi que vous servez;
C'est Rome, Rome seule à qui vous vous devez.
Au faîte des grandeurs je saurai reconnaître
Que je suis votre Chef et non pas votre maître.
Respectons, vous le trône, et moi la liberté.
Empereur et sujets, ce saint nom nous rassemble.
Réunis par l'honneur nous servirons ensemble
Pour la gloire de Rome et sa prospérité.

(act 1, scene 3)

Indeed, the sentiments expressed here accord well with the current French political position (after all, the country was still a monarchy by the 3 September 1791 Constitution). The librettist went on to stress his repugnance for mixing extended references to fashionable political and social trends with literature, and to justify his position further, he announced that the published libretto would be available to the public at the Opéra from the next day on.[23]

The première's delay and Hoffman's actions did not quell the rumours. The Opéra administration did their best to prove their patriotism and lobby influential journalists, such as by their personnel's installation of a trophy to Liberty in a local café «aux sons de la plus brillante musique & aux applaudissemens d'un grand concours de patriotes», as even Gorsas reported.[24] But the librettist's intransigent tone in his letter and his stubbornness about making any changes whatsoever did not serve his cause well. Those who supported *Adrien* earlier urged him to make revisions. The relatively moderate *Chronique de Paris*, though emphasizing that Hoffman himself was beyond suspicion (for he had not, in fact, made contemporary allusions), wrote that some might intentionally misinterpret him and Méhul: «nous croyons d'ailleurs les auteurs de cet ouvrage trop bons citoyens & trop prudens pour ne pas retrancher des mots auxquels les contre-révolutionnaires donneroient un autre sens que celui qu'ils leur ont attaché».[25] The advice went unheeded. Hoffman was reluctant to alter his text -an action which might be seen as an admission of guilt. His opponents renewed their attack. Again they emphasized the 'imperial' theme of *Adrien*. The Opéra's postponement of the work was interpreted, not as waiting for the negative furore to abate, but as showing respect for the recent death of Emperor Leopold: according to Gorsas, «Il n'est pas probable que lorsque l'un des Césars est sur le *lit de mort*, on nous représente le successeur de Trajan sur *un char triomphal* ».[26] Whatever the librettist's intentions, *Adrien* had become a focal point for political controversy. On 12 March 1792 the Commune of Paris, on the recommendation of Pierre Manuel, its *procureur* [27], strongly supported by Jérôme Petion de Villeneuve, the mayor [28], stepped in and forbade its performance scheduled for the following day:

MUNICIPALITE DE PARIS
Du 12 mars 1792, l'an 4ᵉ de la Liberté

Sur le compte rendu par les administrateurs au département des Etablissemens publics, de l'intention où ils seroient de faire jouer l'opéra d'*Adrien*.

Le corps municipal, après avoir entendu le Procureur de la Commune;

Considérant qu'on a répandu sur cet ouvrage les impressions les plus défavorables;

Que sa représentation pourroit être le prétexte d'un rassemblement et des troubles qu'on voudroit occasionner, soit par des applications relatives aux circonstances actuelles, soit par tout autre motif;

Considérant qu'il est de la sagesse de la municipalité de prévenir toute sorte d'excès, pour ne pas se trouver dans la dure nécessité de les réprimer;

20 Music, History, Democracy

> Arrête que l'opéra d'*Adrien* ne sera pas joué tant que ce spectacle sera à la charge de la municipalité.
>
> Signé: Boucher Saint-Saveur,
> *doyen d'âge, président*
> De Joli, *secrétaire-greffier.* [29]

Note that the council cited the potential for riots, and on this point they were certainly right. With the advance publicity given the opera and several unfortunate scenes at theatres in the capital the previous month, in which some spectators were killed or injured in the mêlée, *Adrien*'s première would surely have been the excuse for a violent demonstration. While the 1791 law gave the municipality the right to keep order in theatres during performances, the council went much further here in claiming an extension of it to prevent troubles by controlling repertory. The central government through the Ministre de l'Intérieur had indirectly criticized the city authorities earlier for their handling of the February incidents.[30] In their response, the mayor and other members of the Commune sought to justify their actions saying that the law was not strong enough:

> Nous pensons que, pour réprimer efficacement les agitateurs du peuple, de simples mesures de police seroient très-insuffisantes, que les agitations de toute espèce qui tourmentent sans cesse le peuple *tiennent à de bien plus grandes causes*... Nous veillerons sans relâche au maintien de l'ordre et de la tranquillité publique, et qu'avec *le courage de la liberté* et du saint amour de la patrie, nous dénoncerons aux tribunaux tous ceux qui pourroient la troubler.[31]

The implication of their assertion that they would bring to justice not only those who *had* troubled the public peace, but also those who *could* trouble it was not lost on the federal executive of the Assemblée Nationale. It shifted the responsibility from the demonstrators who had taken illegal actions to authors who had directly or indirectly 'caused' them. In their reply to the city, the federal executive, acting through the administrators of the Seine department, were quick to point out the limits of municipal powers; cutting through vague generalities, they reminded the council of the 1791 law's protection from censorship:

> On sait avec quel funeste habilité l'esprit de parti saisit toute espèce d'occasion de faire des applications propres à exciter du tumulte. Que la censure préalable des pièces de théâtre, moyen que la loi n'autorise point, et que la liberté ne sauroit approuver, à quelque degré de rigueur que cette censure fut portée, seroit encore un moyen impuissant de prévenir de pareils désordres. Les seules mesures de prévoyance qui soient à la disposition des magistrats, pour maintenir la police des spectacles, se bornent donc à faire trouver, au besoin, des forces suffisantes pour contenir et livrer aux tribunaux ceux qui excitent des émeutes.[32]

In spite of the executive's clarity, two weeks later the Commune defied their explicit instructions in banning *Adrien*.

The 12 March city decree did not go unchallenged. The Opéra administration remonstrated with Mayor Petion.[33] After all, the preparations for *Adrien* were costly, and the financial state of the theatre, already precarious, could hardly withstand the loss. They denied the city's right to forbid the opera by rescheduling the première for 15 March and immediately delaying it, publicizing as the cause the convenient illness of two of the leading singers. They hoped that, by keeping the controversy alive, they would gain support for their position.[34] Hoffman cited article VI of the 13 January 1791 law on the liberty of theatres in *Adrien*'s defence, condemning the Commune's actions as illegal.[35] Others supported him. The arch-conservative *Journal royaliste* took up the same theme and ironically pointed out that the Commune, who professed to be ardent defenders of the Constitution, instead violated it.[36] Taking his inspiration from Hoffman's description of his work in his first open letter [37], the author of *Les sabats jacobites*, François Marchant (who remained a royalist even after the declaration of the Republic), wrote a poem in its honour, accusing Manuel of being a republican (and by implication against the current Constitution) and dismissing the imputation of imperialism:

> Un char brillant, deux superbes coursiers,
> Jeux et combats d'un peuple de guerriers,
> Tableaux divins, musique enchanteresse,
> Ballets charmans qu'eût embelli Vestris,
> Et ces plaisirs qu'idolâtroit la Grèce
> Et que l'amour appella dans Paris,
> Tout s'y trouvoit. Un public idolâtre
> De nouveautés, et qui croit que les loix
> Doivent toujours protéger le théâtre,
> Veut d'Adrien voir chanter les exploits.
> Mais Manuel, qui n'aime point les Rois
> Et qui de plus ne veut pas qu'on les aime,
> Doit encor moins aimer les Empereurs.
> Or Adrien ceignoit le diadême,
> Même il étoit jaloux du rang suprême,
> Et détestoit les dénonciateurs.
> Ce Prince enfin, qu'en tous lieux on renomme,
> Si l'on en croit les antiques auteurs,
> Déplaisoit fort aux Manuels de Rome.[38]

Note, too, that like Hoffman and the *Encyclopédistes* (now considered literary conservatives), he claimed opera was a genre designed to delight the eye and ear -not a vehicle for politics.

On the other hand, some of *Adrien*'s opponents, such as Collin, evoked the Declaration of the Rights of Man, implying that Hoffman's position contravened articles IV-V and X, arguing that individual liberty could not be invoked to harm others, take action against the greater good of society or trouble public peace.[39] Others hostile to the librettist had to allow that legally he had grounds, but challenged his interpretation.[40]

Resistance did not end: it increased. Gorsas and others praised the Commune for suppressing the «imperial menace» and preventing bloodshed. Labelling with derision one character a *modéré* (the enemies of the Jacobins), the editor of *Le courrier des LXXXIII départemens* asked rhetorically:

> *Où est le danger* de représenter sur la scène un tyran qui fait la guerre à un peuple qui *combat* pour sa liberté, & auquel il ne daigne donner la paix qu'après avoir attelé à son char ? Où est le danger, dans les circonstances actuelles, d'ouïr Flaminius (le modéré de cet opéra), chanter ces vers:
>
> > Règne, César & que ton front auguste
> > S'accoutûme au laurier sacré...
> > Arbitre souverain de Rome souveraine

> Fais voler tes décrets au bout de l'univers,
> Et que le monde, orgueilleux de ses FERS,
> Bénisse la main qui l'enchaîne...
> Le Ciel, d'un œil jaloux,
> Voit le monde en tes FERS & Rome à tes GENOUX.[41]

Now even moderate editors, who had supported *Adrien* earlier, began to have second thoughts. The editor of the *Chronique de Paris* published several letters critical of Hoffman and advised that, although the librettist's intentions were not suspect, the work should be withdrawn [42] -a course of action echoed by his *confrère*, Levacher de Charnois: «Que doit faire M. Hoffman ? A notre avis, il doit gémir de l'injustice qu'il éprouve, mais sacrifier absolument son amour-propre à la tranquillité publique, qui n'est déjà que trop troublée».[43] And the extreme left stressed that Commune was right not to allow «le char d'*Adrien* [de] rouler sur les cadavres des citoyens françois».[44]

An appeal for public peace was insufficient in itself. The supporters of the Commune's actions sought official justification. The 1791 law did not give it; it was necessary to look elsewhere. The conclusion of the interdiction provided a starting-point. The Opéra at this time had been placed under municipal control (instead of that of the court *surintendant des spectacles*, the official who oversaw it during the late *ancien régime*); the city was responsible ultimately for the theatre's debts. In this capacity, the Commune had the right to forbid *Adrien*, the leftist *Le patriote françois* emphasized:

> Nous observons à M. Hoffman que si la municipalité, comme municipalité, ne peut pas défendre de jouer une pièce; la municipalité, comme chargée de l'*entreprise*, et de l'administration de l'opéra, a le droit d'accepter, de refuser ou de suspendre toute pièce qui peut nuire, de quelque manière que ce soit, aux intérêts du spectacle. La municipalité pouvoit rejetter la pièce de M. Hoffmann comme médiocre, à plus forte raison, elle a pu la suspendre comme dangereuse.[45]

This was the argument that finally gained the Commune's cause, for financially dependent on the city for a subsidy, the Opéra could not break away. In vain, Hoffman tried to counter that by approving the theatre administration's acceptance of the work and permitting rehearsals, the city had *de facto* granted acceptance and therefore had a legal obligation either to allow the première of *Adrien* or to give the authors an indemnity.[46] His opposition only left him open to the charge of being a bad citizen, willing to be the tool of a plot against public order.[47] By the end of March the *Adrien* debate disappeared from the newspapers and from public attention.

***

The *Adrien* episode is a remarkable illustration of the concerns of French society in the capital in the winter of 1792. The unpopularity of Marie-Antoinette is a recurrent theme (in the numerous references to the two horses which the public believed she gave, or did not give, the theatre depending on the side chosen).[48] In part, this was a reflection of French attitudes towards her native country, Austria, and *Adrien*, seen as a glorification of imperial dignity, was the victim of pre-war fever. Although the right saw in opposition to the opera a republican bias (and subsequent events verify these suspicions), Louis XVI was not himself criticized openly by their opponents. While the librettist and some of his supporters tried to argue at first for the traditional view of opera as primarily entertainment, they and conservatives in general pointed out at length how *Adrien* supported the view of monarchy and its role in government guaranteed under the Constitution and Bill of Rights.[49] Radicals stressed that in their interpretation of the latter, the good of society superceded the interest of individuals (a theme to be developed at length in other contexts during the Terror). In the end, the assumption common to both sides of the debate was that opera, like spoken theatre, was now a vehicle for political and social philosophies and a means by which the public could be 'educated' and influenced. All believed that lyric theatre was important; not merely entertainment for the eyes and ears, it could affect profoundly men's lives. The war of words over *Adrien* was carried on not just in newspapers specializing in cultural affairs (such as the *Journal des théâtres*) or in those with substantial sections devoted to theatre (such as the *Journal de Paris*), but as well in those which generally ignored plays and operas (*Le courrier des LXXXIII départemens,* and *Le patriote françois*).[50] This attitude to opera remained a factor throughout the Revolution; it was no longer considered the «genre d'Ouvrage le plus frivole de la Littérature», as Hoffman alleged following *ancien régime* precedents, appropriate for literary or musical debate, but nothing more.

The city's victory over central authorities by default was significant in several respects. The Commune successfully challenged executive orders, and the Assemblée failed to check this encroachment on their laws.[51] It is a brief, but important, example of breakdown in political control at upper levels that was shortly to lead to the crisis of 10 August 1792 and the abolition of the monarchy.[52] More specifically, the case of *Adrien* meant the effective reintroduction of censorship (although it was not necessarily called by that name; «surveillance» was a favourite substitute).[53] It set an important legal precedent. The original distinction of municipal administration of a theatre as a requisite for municipal power over its repertory was ignored; instead, its new 'right' to prevent performances they deemed *potentially* harmful to public peace was exercised. Less than a year later, the Commune forbade Laya's *L'ami des lois*, an anti-Jacobin play performed at the Théâtre Français (not under municipal aegis). The argument used was very similar to that part of their decree for *Adrien* rebutted earlier:

> Le conseil général, d'après les réclamations qui lui ont été faites contre la pièce intitulée l'*Ami des lois*, dans laquelle des journalistes malveillants ont fait des rapprochements dangereux...
> Considérant qu'il est de son devoir de prévenir par tous les moyens qui sont en son pouvoir les désordres que l'esprit de faction cherche à exciter;
> Considérant que, dans tous les temps, la police a eu le droit d'arrêter de semblables ouvrages, qu'elle usa notamment de ce droit pour l'opéra d'*Adrien*...
> Arrête que la représentation de la pièce intitulée l'*Ami des lois* sera suspendue...[54]

Now, however, the example of *Adrien* provided in itself a justification.

In opposing the council's decision, the author accepted the legality of the *Adrien* interdiction (and with it the Commune's right to censure riot-causing theatrical works), but argued that the situation for *L'ami des lois* was different, for its performance had not caused demonstrations:

> Le Conseil-général avoit arreté cet Opéra; & que ce qui fut alors un acte de patriotisme, n'est ici qu'acte de tyrannie; que d'ailleurs, son refus de jouer *Adrien*, avoit précédé la

représentation: qu'ici, c'est après quatre épreuves paisibles, qu'elle ose suspendre *l'Ami des Loix*.[55]

Although the council's decision was challenged, they won again.

Scholars have long recognized the *L'ami des lois* controversy as a landmark in the history of censorship in France.[56] Most have passed over *Adrien* very quickly; no modern writer has seen in it the legal precedence acknowledged by contemporaries.[57] For the Revolution, opera was not a frivolous form: it was the equal in importance as a 'school' for the citizen as any type of theatre. Perhaps sensitive to the criticism of *Adrien*, Hoffman and Méhul proved their patriotic intentions in other operas. Significantly, both chose to extol love of country and promote its defence in works with subjects drawn from Classical history to be interpreted allegorically -the traditional operatic approach- rather than presenting current events and taking political sides in one of the debates of the day, as some of their *confrères* were doing. The moral of Hoffman's *Callias, ou nature et patrie* (a one-act opera, music by Grétry, première 3ᵉ jour complémentaire an II -19 September 1794), a rare example of a *tragédie* at the Opéra-Comique, is the necessity of bravery and self-sacrifice to save one's country from foreign oppressors.[58] In Méhul's *Horatius Coclès* (a one-act opera, libretto by Antoine Vincent Arnault, première Opéra, 30 pluviôse an II -18 February 1794), the heroism of Horace defending the bridge and the defiance of Mutius Scevola in the enemy camp are combined. As the librettist later recalled, his intention was «de choisir dans l'histoire un sujet analogue à la position où la France se trouvait avec l'Europe coalisée contre elle, ce qui... me fournirait l'occasion de louer, dans le patriotisme d'un ancien peuple, celui qui animait les armées françaises».[59] He succeeded, for the parallels were readily grasped by all critics and the audience. It was one of the few works of the an II repertory to be revived.[60] Méhul also contributed to the government-sponsored *fêtes*; his most famous song, *Le chant du départ* (to a text by M. J. Chénier), had its première at that celebrating the taking of Ostende (16 messidor an II -4 July 1794) and soon was second only to the *Marseillaise* in popularity.[61]

In addition, the *Adrien* episode had consequences for morale at the Opéra itself. The charge of being unpatriotic was a serious one. The administration reconsidered their entire repertory with the result that no new operas were given in 1792 (and some already in rehearsals, such as Pierre Candeille's *Ladislas*, were never performed). After the 10 August crisis and the declaration of the Republic on 21 September they increased their performances of patriotic songs in *tableau patriotique* setting: François Joseph Gossec's *Offrande à la Liberté* includes his arrangements of *Veillons au salut de l'empire* and the *Marseillaise* (the first fully scored version, which quickly became accepted as the standard one).[62] The Opéra administration remained very sensitive to any criticism of civic behaviour: an anonymous letter complaining of their neglect to remove fleur-de-lys decorations was taken seriously indeed.[63] The following year newly written patriotic works (beginning with Gossec's *Le triomphe de la République, ou le camp de Grand-Pré*) dominated the repertory.[64]

Neither the Opéra administration nor the authors abandoned *Adrien* definitively. On 16 prairial an VII (4 June 1799) Méhul's second setting of the libretto (reusing some of the original music substantially revised) had its première at this theatre, renamed the Théâtre de la République et des Arts. A critical and popular success, it was banned after the fourth performance, again for political reasons, both similar to, and different from, those in 1792. This second crisis tells us much about the situation surrounding the 30 prairial an VII *coup* d'état (18 June 1799), which in turn prepared the terrain for Napoleon Bonaparte's assumption of power 19 brumaire an VII (10 November 1799). But that is another subject.[65] What the history of *Adrien* in 1792 and 1799 tells us is that the dearly held position that theatre must not only passively conform to Revolutionary tenets, but also actively teach patriotic lessons prevented the most significant French opéra of the decade from entering the repertory.

---

1. Marie-Joseph Blaise de Chénier, *De la liberté du théâtre en France* ([Paris], 1789), pp. 8-9.

2. Ibid., pp. 4-5 : «L'influence du Théâtre sur les mœurs n'a pas besoin d'être prouvée, puisqu'elle est indispensable... Mais dans une belle pièce de Théâtre, le plaisir amène le spectateur à l'instruction sans qu'il s'en aperçoive, ou qu'il y puisse résister... Un livre dispersé dans les Cabinets parvient à faire lentement une multitude d'impressions différentes, mais isolées, mais presque toujours exemptes d'enthousiasme. La sensation que fait éprouver à deux mille personnes rassemblées au Théâtre François, la représentation d'un excellent ouvrage dramatique, est rapide, ardente, unanime», and p. 30: «Le Théâtre est ... un moyen d'instruction publique. L'instruction publique est importante pour tous les Citoyens.» Interestingly, the mayor of Paris, Jean Sylvain Bailly, who was responsible for blocking *Charles IX*, assumed the same power of theatre (compared to the written word, such as the press) and came to the conclusion shared by many of his predecessors and contemporaries, namely that, therefore, theatre should be more strictly controlled. Reflecting on the *Charles IX* crisis in 1791, he wrote: «Je crois que la liberté de la presse est la base de la liberté publique; mais il n'en est pas de même du théâtre. Je crois qu'on doit exclure du spectacle, où beaucoup d'hommes se rassemblent et s'électrisent mutuellement, tout ce qui peut tendre à corrompre les mœurs ou l'esprit du gouvernement. Le spectacle est une partie de l'enseignement public, qui ne doit pas être laissé à tout le monde, et que l'Administration doit surveiller. Il est aisé de donner à la censure théâtrale une forme qui en exclue l'arbitraire, et qui la rende toujours juste. Ce n'est point une atteinte à la liberté des uns: c'est respect pour la liberté et la sûreté morale des autres». *Mémoires*, 3 vols. (Paris: Baudouin, 1804), 2:283. As well as an appreciation that people behave differently *en masse* than as individuals, the late eighteenth-century French intellectual élite still tacitly assumed that the literate (in a society where most were not) were more rational, and the illiterate, more emotional and therefore less controlled and potentially dangerous.

3. Denis Diderot, et al., eds. *Encyclopédie, ou dictionnaire raisonné des sciences, des arts et des métiers, par une société de gens de lettres, mise en ordre et publié par M. Diderot, et quant à la partie mathématique, par M. d'Alembert*, 35 vols. (Paris: Briasson [and others], 1751-80; reprint ed., Stuttgart: Friedrich Frommann, 1966), s.v. «Tragédie» by Diderot, «Comédie» by Louis de Jaucourt.

4. He defended this position publicly in letters to the editor of several papers and in speeches; see, in particular, the speech he gave on 5 July 1789, «Dénonciation des inquisiteurs de la pensée», *Œuvres*, ed. Antoine Vincent Arnault, D. Ch. Robert, Pierre Marie Michel Lepeintre-Desroches, and Pierre Claude François Daunou, 8 vols. (Paris: Guillaume, 1823-27), 4:388-429, in which he drew unflattering parallels between censors and inquisitors as tormentors of the human race.

5. *De la liberté*, pp. 30-31.

6. The petition and address to the Assemblée were written by Jean François de la Harpe; both of them are published in: *Adresse des Auteurs dramatiques à l'Assemblée, prononcée par M. de la Harpe, dans la séance du mardi soir 24 août* ([Paris, 1790]). Beaumarchais and Chénier were among the signatories. See also *Discours sur la liberté du théâtre; prononcé par M. de la Harpe le 17 décembre 1790, à la Société des Amis de la Constitution* (Paris: Imprimerie Nationale, 1790).

7. *Rapport fait par M. Le Chapelier; au nom du Comité de Constitution, sur la pétition des auteurs dramatiques, dans la séance du jeudi 13 janvier 1791, avec le décret rendu dans cette séance* (Paris: Imprimerie Nationale, 1791), p. 3. It was also published in abbreviated form in the *Gazette nationale, ou le moniteur universel* (Paris), 15 January 1791, reprint edition, 7:116-18.

8. *Rapport*, p. 5.

9. Ibid., p. 10. See also p. 9: «Il faut que les spectacles épurent les mœurs, donnent des leçons de civisme, qu'ils soient une école de patriotisme, de vertu... C'est à la liberté que nous devrons cette perfection du théâtre, tandis que nous perdrions à jamais l'espoir de trouver dans nos amusemens une grande école nationale, si ce spectacle étoit un lieu privilégié et si l'imagination des auteurs étoit soumise au despotisme.»

10. Ibid., p. 23.

11. *Moniteur universel*, 15 January 1791, reprint ed., 7:118-20.

12. Victor Hallays-Dabot, *Histoire de la censure théâtrale en France* (Paris: E. Dentu), p. 169; Arthur Pougin, *Méhul: sa vie, son génie, son caractère* (Paris: Fischbacher, 1889; reprint ed., Geneva: Minkoff, 1973), pp. 159-60; Ernst Jauffret, *Le théâtre révolutionnaire* (Paris: Furne & Jouvet, 1869), pp. 166-69; Henri Welschinger, *Le théâtre de la Révolution, 1789-1799, avec documents inédits* (Paris: Charavay frères, 1880), p. 99.

13. Georges Lefebvre, *The French Revolution*, trans. Elizabeth Moss Evanson, John Hall Steward and James Friguglietti, 2 vols. (London: Routledge & Kegan Paul, New York: Columbia University Press, 1962-64), vol. 1, chap. 12.

14. *Annales patriotiques et littéraires de France et affaires politiques de l'Europe* (Paris), 2 March 1792, p. 277. This and many of the documents cited in what follows are transcribed in M. Elizabeth C. Bartlet, «Etienne Nicolas Méhul and Opera during the French Revolution, Consulate, and Empire: a Source, Archival, and Stylistic Study» (Ph.D. dissertation, University of Chicago, 1982), appx. 2, nos. 1-25, 73, pp. 1497-1514, 1553-56.

15. Adolphe Jullien, *La cour et l'opéra sous Louis XVI: Marie-Antoinette et Sacchini; Salieri; Favart et Gluck d'après des documents inédits conservés aux archives de l'état et à l'Opéra* (Paris: Didier, 1878), and M. Elizabeth C. Bartlet, «Grétry, Marie-Antoinette and La rosière de Salency», *Proceedings of the Royal Musical Association*, 111 (1984-85), 92-120.

16. Letter of 27 February 1792, transcribed in Paul Jacquinet, *François Hoffman: sa vie, ses œuvres* (Nancy: impr. Berger-Levrault, 1878), p. 45. See also the public statement of Levacher de Charnois, *Journal de théâtres*, 23 March 1792, p. 45.

17. «Adrien, empereur de Rome, opéra en trois actes», Paris, Archives Nationales, AJ[13] 1023, and *Adrien, empereur de Rome, opéra en trois actes, représenté pour la première fois sur le théâtre de l'Académie Royale de Musique le mars 1792* (Paris: impr. P. de Lormel, 1792).

18. Gorsas, who had been imprisoned in the Bastille for writing pamphlets that could corrupt (politically) his students, participated in the 20 June 1792 manifestation and the invasion of the Tuileries 10 August following, which led to the collapse of the monarchy. In addition, as a member of the Assemblée, he defended the September massacres as necessary for the sake of the country -the position of the extreme left. He became secretary of the Convention Nationale (the Assemblée's successor) in January 1793, but shifted to a position closer to that of the Girondins and attacked Marat. As a result, like them, he was arrested and later guillotined 7 October 1793.

19. *Le courrier des LXXXIII départemens* (Paris), 3 March 1792, p. 41. Gorsas' views are representative of the radical press, and since he conducted the most vigorous campaign against *Adrien*, he will be used as example.

20. As, with mixed feelings due to his inherent conservative position in literary taste, Hoffman wrote his brother-in-law, Louis Arnauld de Praneuf, 27 February 1792: «Cet ouvrage est attendu avec impatience pour la magnificence avec laquelle on sait qu'il doit être donné. Nous avons dans cet opéra tout ce qui peut piquer la grosse curiosité du vulgaire : des danses de tout genre, des combats, une marche triomphale qui passe sur un pont, un pont qui s'écroule dans un combat et qui renverse tous les combattants dans la fleuve, un char trainé par des chevaux réels, dont chacun coûte cent louis et les vaut, une montagne singulière, taillée à pic, de laquelle une armée descend d'une manière périlleuse et pittoresque, toutes les décorations neuves et riches, tous les habits neufs, costumes romains, parthes et syriens; 120 comparses sans compter tous les chœurs et toute la danse de l'Opéra, enfin c'est une vraie lanterne magique, digne en tout du mauvais goût du siècle et de la décadence de la littérature, aussi, mon cher frère, il est à parier que mon *Adrien* aura un très-brillant et très-honteux succès». Transcribed by Jacquinet, *François Hoffman*, pp. 45-46.

21. See the summary in the *Chronique de Paris*, 27 February 1792, pp. 230-32.

22. This description accords well with the private one he wrote his brother-in-law; see note 20 above. Hoffman was referring to the traditional French view of opera; see the definition in the *Encyclopédie* : according to Diderot, it is «espèce de poëme dramatique fait pour être mis en musique, & chanté sur le théâtre avec la symphonie, &

toutes sortes de décorations en machines & en habits. La Bruyère [un librettiste] dit que l'*opéra* doit tenir l'esprit, les oreilles & les yeux dans une espèce d'enchantement». Enchanting the eye and ear, entertaining not educating (in contrast to spoken theatre), was the main end of this theatrical art, and partly for this reason irregularities in dramatic structure could be tolerated here (while condemned in the *tragédie* and *comédie*).

23. Letter of 1 or 2 March 1792, *Journal de Paris*, 3 March 1792, supplement p. 2. Hoffman kept his word, since the printed libretto was available to Gorsas on 3 March (as noted above).

24. *Le courrier des LXXXIII départemens*, 4 March 1792, p. 57.

25. 9 March 1792, p. 274.

26. *Le courrier des LXXXIII départemens*, 12 March 1792, p. 188. Leopold died 1 March 1792, but the news took several days to reach Paris. See also the article of 13 March 1792, pp. 202-03 : «L'*Académie* royale de musique est en pleurs: l'opéra d'Adrien est renvoyé aux calendes. -Quand il s'est agi de la tranquillité publique, on ne s'est pas occupé, si cet opéra pouvoit la troubler... Mais le tyran du Nord meurt, *peste* ! les convenances !... l'étiquette !»

27. Manuel, who had been imprisoned in the Bastille, was an ardent Jacobin. Like Gorsas (see note 18), he participated in the days of 20 June and 10 August 1792. Staunchly anti-royalist even before then, he was profoundly affected by the September massacres, which he criticized publicly, unlike other Jacobins. This and his continued support of Mirabeau, though disgraced, marked the turning-point in his political career. In 1792 he argued for due judicial process for Louis XVI and when that initiative failed, voted for his imprisonment and exile, rather than death. Ironically this fervent republican before being republican was acceptable was guillotined 14 November 1793 for wanting to save the king.

28. Petion, also a member of the Assemblée Nationale, supported extremist positions. In 1791 he was responsible for bringing the king and his family back from Varennes after their ill-fated attempt to escape and argued that Louis XVI should be dethroned. An ally of Robespierre until the September massacres, he was revolted by what he saw as evidence of barbarism and in the king's trial voted for death but with a stay of execution. In 1793 he shifted to a position closer to the Girondins. A warrant was issued for his arrest with them 2 June 1793, but he succeeded in fleeing. A year later he died under mysterious circumstances.

29. *Journal de Paris*, 15 March 1792; quoted in Pougin, *Méhul*, p. 162.

30. Letter of 25 February 1792, published in the *Journal de Paris*, 26 February 1792, and other newspapers.

31. Letter of 27 February 1792, published in *Le patriote françois* (Paris), 1 March 1792, pp. 244-45. Although the Commune strongly defended the Constitution and did not criticize the king (who, after all, had a place in French government guaranteed by it), their emphasis on «la souveraineté du peuple françois» aligned them closely with radicals, from whose ranks a few months later leading republicans would come. Note that they chose to have this letter published in a strongly leftist paper, who in a footnote highly praised their actions.

32. Letter of 1 March 1792, published in the *Mercure universel* (Paris), 5 March 1792, pp. 72-73.

33. Among other things pointing out that they had hired the horses, not received them from the queen. *Les sabats jacobites*, n° 63 (Paris, 1792), pp. 200-01.

34. Hoffman's letter, *Chronique de Paris*, 16 March 1792, pp. 302-03.

35. Ibid. He developed this argument at greater length in a *mémoire* submitted to Petion. Although it was unpublished at the time and the original manuscript does not appear to have survived, Hoffman later included it in his *Œuvres*. While in general we must be sceptical of justifications published long after changes in regime, in this case the author's position accords well with that he took publicly through his letters to newspapers in 1792. «Mémoire adressé à Monsieur le maire de Paris par l'auteur de l'opéra d'Adrien» *Œuvres*, ed. L. Castel, 10 vols. (Paris, Lefebvre, 1829), 3:1-9.

36. 18 March 1792, p. 7.

37. *Journal de Paris*, 3 March 1792, supplement p. 2.

38. N° 63 (Paris, 1792), pp. 199-201. Although *Adrien*'s opponents were careful not to attack it as a royalist work, in their counterattack its supporters argued that the former were veiled republicans; see, for example, the conservative, Levacher de Charnois, *Journal des théâtres* (Paris), 23 March 1792, p. 45 (see note 43).

39. Collin, letter to the editor, *Chronique de Paris*, 17 March 1792, p. 306.

40. See, for example, the dramatist Philippe Fabre d'Eglantine in his open letter to Collin, ibid., 19 March 1792, p. 314. Fabre d'Eglantine was an ardent Jacobin; he is credited with devising the names of the months for the Revolutionary calendar, which he certainly promoted. A supporter of Danton, he was arrested with him and his followers and guillotined 16 germinal an II (5 April 1794).

41. 19 March 1792, pp. 299-300. See also his articles of 13 March, pp. 202-03; 14 March, pp. 218-19; and 21 March, pp. 324-25, and Collin's letter, cited above.

42. The letters of Collin and Fabre d'Eglantine cited above and the editor's note, 18 March 1792, p. 312. Some extremists did not even allow Hoffman this concession (see, for example, Gorsas, *Le courrier des LXXXIII départemens*, 19 March 1792, pp. 299-300). Others including Fabre d'Eglantine accused him of bad faith -a charge that earned him a sarcastic reply from the librettist in *Affiches, annonces et avis divers, ou journal général de France* (Paris), 21 March 1792, pp. 1153-54.

43. *Journal des théâtres*, 23 March 1792. Levacher de Charnois, son-in-law of the famous actor Préville, was the most intelligent of theatre critics in Paris; he also undertook significant research on costumes. A moderate and supporter of the monarchy, he spoke out strongly against leftist demonstrations in theatres, branding them savagery. After 10 August 1792 he was arrested and perished 2 September 1792 during the prison massacres.

44. For example, *Le patriote françois* (Paris), 17 March 1792, p. 308.

45. Ibid. Others quickly took up this argument, often quoting or paraphrasing *Le patriote françois*; for example, the *Chronique de Paris*, 18 March 1792, p. 312; Fabre d'Eglantine, ibid., 19 March, p. 314; Gorsas, *Le courrier des LXXXIII départemens*, 19 March, pp. 299-300, and 21 March, pp. 324-25.

46. Open letter, *Affiches, annonces et avis divers*, 19 March 1792, p. 1122.

47. *Le patriote françois*, quoted with approval in *Le courrier des LXXXIII départemens*, 21 March 1792, pp. 324-25.

48. Louis Marie Prudhomme, a republican before the declaration of the Republic, gave another example in *Adrien*'s air (act 3, scene 6):

O Rome!, ô ma patrie !
Révoque une sévère loi;
Obéis sans rougir à la fille d'un roi :
Celle qui fait l'ornement de l'Asie
Est digne de régner sur César et sur toi.

This indirect compliment to the queen, who though a foreigner, was worthy to rule over France, was, he maintained, commissioned and paid for by the court. *Révolutions de Paris dédiées à la nation et au district des Petits-Augustins* (Paris), 24 March 1792, p. 542. There is no evidence that his assumption was accurate. Rather, these lines are typical of a late *ancien régime* tradition starting with Gluck's «Chantez, célébrez votre reine» (*Iphigénie en Aulide*, opening of the second-act *divertissement*, 1774), in recognition of Marie-Antoinette's active role as patron of the Opéra. When Hoffman wrote the libretto in 1788, such lines would not have stood out as unusual in the least, but four years later they were an incitement to the patriotic left.

49. See Levacher de Charnois, *Journal des théâtres* (Paris), 23 March 1792, p. 45 : «La cour ne connoissoit point Adrien; la reine n'avoit point fait présent des chevaux, qui avoient été achetés d'un maquignon dont l'administration avoit la quittance. L'ouvrage avoit été commencé avant la révolution, à laquelle il n'a aucun rapport; enfin, si parmi les braillards qui hurloient *haro* sur la pièce il s'en étoit trouvé quelques-uns d'instruits, ils auroient su qu'*Adrien* fut un des monarques les plus populaires de l'univers connu, et qu'il étoit impossible de mettre des maximes aristocratiques dans la bouche d'un prince, qui pensoit et disoit souvent, *que l'empire n'étoit pas à lui, mais au peuple*. Mais les tyrans imbéciles qui nous persécutent, n'ont pas besoin de connoître l'histoire, et ils croient qu'ils en savent toujours assez quand ils savent que, non seulement ils veulent une chose, mais encore qu'ils sont en force suffisante pour la vouloir. Ils crièrent donc, en menaçant, qu'ils ne vouloient pas que l'on jouât Adrien, *opéra aristocratique* », and the *Journal encyclopédique ou universel* (Bouillon), 10 May 1792, pp. 132-36 : «Nous demandons s'il est possible de tracer un caractère plus grand, plus magnanime & plus digne d'être admiré d'une Nation *libre & éclairée*. Si les mots *soumis, sujets* &c., ont blessé quelques particuliers, c'est qu'ils n'ont pas senti, qu'être soumis à un homme du caractère d'*Adrien*, ce n'est qu'être soumis aux loix dont il est le premier organe. Quand on s'explique, comme le fait *Adrien*, on peut tout dire, tout interpréter en sa faveur.

Pourquoi ne prouvons-nous pas à nos voisins & à ceux qui n'aiment pas notre nouvel ordre de choses, que la liberté, que nous avons tant ambitionnée, est surtout pour le génie, pour les talens, pour les artistes ? Si le génie est encore circonscrit dans des bornes étroites; s'il ne peut disposer de tous les mots de la langue, s'il ne peut donner à chaque tableau la phisionomie antique qui lui est propre, s'il est soumis enfin à une censure d'autant plus tyrannique, qu'elle ne marche qu'avec le bruit, les vociférations & les menaces, le génie sera donc esclave en France, & bientôt tout le monde ne tardera pas à l'être. Où seront donc l'énergie, le courage & cette noble fierté qui doivent être l'attitude d'un Peuple libre, si son patriotisme s'allarme d'un *Opéra nouveau* ?... Encore il n'y a dans cet opéra, que six vers tout au plus qu'on ait improuvés. Il faudra donc dorénavant nous priver des ressources de l'histoire, des oppositions & des fortes leçons qu'elle offre aux rois & aux peuples; ou, si nous traitons quelque sujet de l'antiquité, il faudra trembler d'y mettre un seul vers, un seul mot qui puisse exciter les cris de certaines gens, plus cautuleux, plus minutieux que vraiment Patriotes !... Est-ce ainsi qu'on verra les lettres fleurir sous le règne de la liberté, comme on les a vues s'accroître sous le règne de ceux qu'on appelle aujourd'hui des despotes ! Est-ce ainsi qu'on encouragera les artistes & qu'on sçaura les fixer parmi nous ? Que dirons-nous si, à l'exemple de quelques-uns de nos grands peintres & sculpteurs, nos habiles musiciens alloient chercher un sol où ils fussent libres de faire briller leurs talens sur quelque sujet que ce fût !... Car il est bien douloureux pour un artiste, comme M. *Méhul*, d'avoir employé plus d'une année à faire une partition (on prétend que c'est un chef-d'œuvre de musique) qui se trouve aujourd'hui perdue pour lui... François, mettez donc aussi votre gloire à vous montrer autant admirateurs des talens que l'étoient ces rois, l'objet de votre haine !... Encouragez-les donc sous quelque forme qu'ils se présentent, ces talens; & soyez assez fiers pour penser que six vers d'un *Opéra nouveau* ne porteront jamais d'atteinte à cette Constitution que vous avez élevée, & à cette liberté que vous chérissez tant, & qui doit s'étendre à tout; car ce ne seroit pas la peine de réformer un abus pour en créer un autre plus monstrueux, plus abusif & plus tyrannique».

50. In fact, Levacher de Charnois at first shied away from entering the controversy, insisting that his paper only reviewed works after their premières, but that because publicity in all the papers had so aroused interest, even in the provinces, he was forced, he claimed, to bow to the wishes of his subscribers. *Journal des théâtres*, 23 March 1792, p. 45.

51. Some conservatives noted the dangerous precedent at the time. The *Journal royaliste*, for example, decried the result: «Voilà la constitution encore une fois violée, aux yeux même de l'assemblée législative. Elle l'est d'ailleurs d'un bout du Royaume à l'autre; c'est quand le peuple est souverain, tout le monde est maître; et nous ne connoissons pas de plus terrible esclavage». 18 March 1792, p. 7.

52. Lefebvre, *The French Revolution*, vol. 1, chaps. 12-13.

53. Prudhomme, one of the most severe of *Adrien*'s critics, argued that it should be given: «Car si cette année un magistrat patriote prend sur lui d'empêcher la représentation d'une tragédie ou un opéra aristocratique; un municipal aristocrate, l'année suivante, se permettra de s'opposer à la représentation d'un drame patriotique, & celui-ci aura tout autant de motifs que l'autre pour justifier sa conduite... Un peuple n'est pas long-temps libre quand ses représentans ou ses magistrats composent & entrent en accommodement avec les loix qu'il a faites & qu'ils ont jurées de maintenir. Il n'est point de circonstance où l'on puisse modifier ou restreindre la liberté des opinions». *Révolutions de Paris*, pp. 540-45. He was the only one of the hostile side to see any risk to supporting the council's actions.

54. Decree of 11 January 1793, printed in the *Moniteur universel*, 14 January 1793, reprint edition, 15:119; quoted in Hallays-Dabot, *Histoire de la censure théâtrale*, p. 174.

55. Jean Louis Laya, *Discours qui devoit être prononcé par le citoyen Laya, auteur de l'Ami des loix à la barre de la Convention* (Paris: impr. N. H. Nyon, 1793), pp. 2-3.

56. Hallays-Dabot, *Histoire de la censure théâtrale*, pp. 171-76. Marvin Carlson, *The Theatre of the French Revolution* (Ithaca, N. Y.: Cornell University Press, 1966), pp. 143-47. Henri Quentin [pseud. Paul d'Estrée], *Le théâtre sous la Terreur (théâtre de peur) 1793-1794, d'après les publications récentes et d'après les documents révolutionnaires du temps imprimés ou inédits* (Paris: Emil-Paul frères, 1913), passim.

57. Not even the composer's principal biographer, Pougin, realized its significance; his discussion of the 1792 *Adrien* ends with the council's interdiction and part of Hoffman's *mémoire*. *Méhul*, pp. 162-66. Adelaïde de Place's recent treatment of the affair quotes from the *Journal des théâtres*, the *Chronique de Paris* and Hoffman's statements (allowing the vivid rhetoric of the debate to speak for itself, but without making the positions and

30 Music, History, Democracy

issues clear), but again ignores the legal implications. *La vie musicale en France au temps de la Révolution* (Paris: Fayard, 1989), pp. 97-100.

58. For an examination of this opera, hitherto thought lost, see Bartlet, «Patriotism at the Opéra-Comique during the Revolution: Grétry's 'Callias, ou nature et patrie'», *Atti del 14e convegno della Società Internazionale di Musicologia, Bologna, il 24 agosto - il 1 settembre 1987* (Bologna: Università di Bologna, 1989).

59. Antoine Vincent Arnault, *Souvenirs d'un sexagénaire*, 4 vols. (Paris: Duféy, 1833), 2:70; cited in Pougin, *Méhul*, pp. 87-88.

60. Bartlet, «E. N. Méhul and Opéra», pp. 320-37.

61. See Constant Pierre, *Les hymnes et chansons de la Révolution: aperçu général et catalogue* (Paris: Imprimerie Nationale, 1904) and Bartlet, «*La victoire en chantant* : the Contribution of the Chanson and *Hymne* to the Spirit of the French Revolution», paper read in the series the French Revolution: Bicentennial Program International Lecture Series, University of California, Los Angeles, 10 May 1989.

62. See Bartlet, ed., *Art and Revolution: the Paris Opéra's Contribution to Fêtes and Tableaux Patriotiques during the 1790s*, Recent Researches in the Music of the Classical Period (Madison: A-R Editions, 1991).

63. «Registres de l'Opéra», *F-Po* AD 6 [*olim* 102] [committee meeting minutes, 8 Sept. -*recte* Oct. 1792].

64. On the use of patriotic song at the Opéra, see Bartlet, «Revolutionschanson und Hymne im Repertoire der Pariser Oper, 1793-94», *Die Französische Revolution als Bruch des gesellschaftlichen Bewusstseins: Vorlagen und Diskussionen der internationalen Arbeitstagung am Zentrum fr interdisziplinûre Forschung der Universität Bielefeld, 28. Mai -1. Juni 1985*, ed. Reinhart Koselleck and Rolf Reichardt (Munich: R. Oldenbourg, 1988), pp. 479-507. For an overview of state-theatre relations, see Bartlet, «From *Académie Royale de Musique* to *Opéra National* : the Republican 'Regeneration' of an Institution», paper read at the conference entitled 'The French Revolution, a Bicentennial Celebration: Representations and Reality, a Multi-disciplinary Symposium', Michigan State University, 20 April 1989 (publication forthcoming), and for an examination of certain Revolutionary symbols, see Bartlet, «The New Repertory of the Opéra during the Reign of Terror: Revolutionary Rhetoric and Operatic Consequences», paper read at the International Conference on Music and Society during the Period of the French Revolution, University of Cardiff, Wales, 8 July 1989.

65. On the second version of *Adrien* and its problems, see Bartlet, «E. N. Méhul and Opera», pp. 407-70, and appx. 2, nos. 26-72, pp. 1514-53.

[17]

SONGS TO SHAPE A GERMAN NATION: HILLER'S COMIC OPERAS AND THE PUBLIC SPHERE

ESTELLE JOUBERT

ABSTRACT

In this article I assert that our modern understanding of the singspiel as a genre has been shaped not by eighteenth-century principles but rather by nineteenth-century notions of 'romantic' German opera. In contrast to a later through-composed ideal, Johann Adam Hiller's comic operas, often viewed as the prototype of the German comic genre, were designed precisely in order that the songs might easily be detached from the spoken dialogue, disseminated outside of the public opera house and sung by audiences in various other contexts. The express purpose of these songs, as articulated by librettist Christian Felix Weisse, was to promote communal singing in social circles across Germany. The genre was thus designed for circulation within what Habermas describes as the public sphere: a conceptual space between the State and the private home in which texts, ideas and musical works were circulated and debated.

Composed in what was called the German Volkston *(in the manner of the* Volk*), Hiller's melodies are recorded as being sung and played throughout the streets and parks of major German cities and became so popular that they became known as folksongs. This idea of the* Volk *as a collective entity and of the* Volkston, *however, was rooted in a deeper sense of the public as nation. Inspired by* Le devin du village *and J. J. Rousseau's writings on politics, language and the fine arts, Weisse and Hiller's operas employ the pastoral mode, in which idealized peasants sing in the manner of a folksong. The idyllic simplicity of these early German-language comic operas appealed to a diversified German audience by affirming their roots, the public use of their language and their morally upright character as a nation. Thus comic opera as a genre was circulated within the public sphere with the intention of transcending the boundaries of social class to unite the German nation in song.*

The ideal of the through-composed romantic German opera has long occupied a place of prominence in histories of European opera and indeed within the broader German historical tradition itself. Indicative of the substantial influence of this ideal is its role as yardstick against which other operatic genres and traditions

---

An earlier version of this paper was presented at a panel entitled 'Public Sphere and Literary Form' at the Annual Meeting of the American Society for Eighteenth-Century Studies, Las Vegas, 31 March to 3 April 2005. Support for my research was generously provided by the Social Sciences and Humanities Research Council of Canada and the Clarendon and Scatcherd Funds at the University of Oxford. I am very grateful to Gudula Schütz and Laurenz Lütteken for allowing me to use their electronic database 'Musikalisches Schrifttum im Diskurs der Aufklärung' (Music Literature in the Discourse of the Enlightenment) based at the Herzog August Bibliothek in Wolfenbüttel, now published as *Die Musik in den Zeitschriften des 18. Jahrhunderts,* ed. Laurenz Lütteken (Kassel: Bärenreiter, 2004). Also, my thanks to the librarians at the Stadtbibliothek in Leipzig for their kind assistance in locating and allowing me access to rare source material. Finally, I would like to express my gratitude to Reinhard Strohm, who commented extensively on several drafts of this article, to Emanuele Senici and Barbara Eichner for their invaluable comments and suggestions and to Mario Brandhorst for providing me with fascinating insights into the nuances of the eighteenth-century German language.

have historically been discussed and defined.¹ Notable in this regard is our modern understanding of singspiel: an eighteenth-century German comic operatic genre distinguished by its mixture of spoken dialogue and song.² Within late nineteenth- and early twentieth-century histories of opera, the singspiel is viewed as a generic prototype, the seed from which a long lineage of German operas emerged. Commencing with Johann Adam Hiller's *Die Jagd* (1770), which is characterized by its spoken dialogue and song, this evolutionary narrative continues through operas such as Carl von Dittersdorf's *Doktor und Apotheker* (1786) and Carl Maria von Weber's *Der Freischütz* (1821), which feature increased participation between composer and librettist, and finally culminates in the crowning achievement of Richard Wagner's *Die Meistersinger* (1868).³ In fact, some authors believe that Wagner himself established this pattern in operatic history, as he is said to have envisaged an operatic season featuring the development of German comic opera as a genre.⁴

Viewed within the political and ideological contexts from which they emerged, it becomes increasingly apparent that these histories are based on nationalistic motivations rather than any explicit generic similarities among the operas. As Jörg Krämer remarks, 'in Wagner's construction of history, [Hiller's] *Die Jagd* thus gained a pioneering status as the beginning of a specifically German comic opera, which consequently determined the assessment of the work up until the time of nationalist socialist Germany'.⁵ While the ideological underpinnings of this tradition of scholarship gradually faded, a value judgment of the singspiel as a lesser predecessor of a more fully developed through-composed ideal remained prevalent in early and mid-twentieth-century scholarship. The author of the entry on singspiel in the 1954 *New Grove Dictionary of Music and Musicians* claims that

> Nowadays ... the singspiel has fallen into a well merited oblivion; for the German operas of Mozart, Beethoven, and Weber, though containing spoken dialogue, are musically too highly organized to be considered typical.... In any case, the singspiel was not well suited to the romantic aspirations of 19th-century Germany. Yet Mozart had shown how it could be transformed, and in

---

1 The predominance of through-composed romantic German opera, particularly the Wagnerian music drama, and its central place in the German historical tradition have resulted in the marginalization of most other operatic genres. For a discussion of the effect of the Wagnerian model on the history of opera, particularly Italian opera, see Lorenzo Bianconi and Giorgio Pestelli, *Opera Production and Its Resources*, trans. Lydia G. Cochrane (London: Chicago University Press, 1998), i–xvi, and Elvidio Surian, 'Musical Historiography and Histories of Italian Opera', *Current Musicology* 36 (1983), 167–175.

2 Prior to the mid-nineteenth century, the terms *Oper* and *Singspiel* were used interchangeably by composers and critics to denote an opera. Hiller referred to his operas as *komische Opern* and not *Singspiele*; see Thomas Bauman, 'The Eighteenth Century: Comic Opera', in *The Oxford History of Opera*, ed. Roger Parker (Oxford: Oxford University Press, 1994), 67. For a discussion of the changing meaning of singspiel throughout the eighteenth century see Alfred A. Neumann, 'The Changing Concept of the Singspiel', in *Studies in German Literature*, ed. Carl Hammer, Jr, (Baton Rouge: Louisiana State University Press, 1963), 63–71.

3 For early histories of German comic opera see Robert Eitner, 'Die deutsche komische Oper', *Monatshefte für Musik-Geschichte* 92/2 (1892), 37–92, and Ludwig Schiedermaier, *Die Deutsche Oper: Grundzüge ihres Werdens und Wesens* (Leipzig: Quelle & Meyer, 1930).

4 Included in Wagner's planned series were Hiller's *Die Jagd*, Dittersdorf's *Doktor und Apotheker*, Lortzing's *Zar und Zimmermann* and, finally, Wagner's own *Die Meistersinger*. This series is referred to in the Introduction to Georg R. Kruse, *Die Jagd: Komische Oper in drei Aufzügen von J. A. Hiller* (Leipzig: Reclam, 1904); Bernard Naylor, 'Albert Lortzing', *Proceedings of the Royal Musical Association* 58 (1931–1932), 5; and Jörg Krämer, *Deutschsprachiges Musiktheater im späten 18. Jahrhundert: Typologie, Dramaturgie und Anthropologie einer populären Gattung*, 2 volumes (Tübingen: Max Niemeyer, 1998), volume 1, 130–131.

5 Krämer, *Deutschsprachiges Musiktheater*, volume 1, 130. One of the most extensive works excavating 'Germanness' in Hiller's operas under this regime is Gerhard Sander's 1943 dissertation (Berlin), published as *Das Deutschtum im Singspiel J. A. Hillers* (Würzburg: K. Triltsch, 1943).

so doing had laid the foundations for later German opera – for Beethoven, for Weber, and through them for Wagner.[6]

More recent scholarship pertaining to the singspiel is much more nuanced, including a number of fruitful studies of the repertory and of Hiller's comic operas. Thomas Bauman has contributed a landmark study on German-language opera of the period, Jörg Krämer's more recent investigation of the repertory features a subtle account converging around *Die Jagd*, and John Warrack's history of German opera from its inception to Wagner skilfully situates Hiller's comic operas within a broader context.[7] These represent considerable new research, giving accounts of performance history (particularly the involvement of travelling troupes) and musical and poetic features of the genre, as well as investigating the aesthetic milieu of Hiller's operas. And yet within these studies devoted to a particular repertory, and indeed within generic histories that are narrowly construed, it is difficult to contextualize and elucidate the seemingly incidental nature of Hiller's songs within librettist Christian Felix Weisse's spoken drama.

It is important to recognize that the separation of dialogue and song – the integral element on which our modern definition of the genre hinges – was initially highlighted in order to distinguish a selection of eighteenth-century comic works from their nineteenth-century counterparts. In short, eighteenth-century singspiel was defined by not yet having achieved the through-composed ideal that was sought after almost a century later. In effect, the predominance of the nineteenth-century German operatic ideal has significantly (mis)shaped our understanding of eighteenth-century German comic opera as a genre. For it is precisely the flexibility of the singspiel as a genre, allowing for the detachment of songs from their dramatic context and their subsequent mass dissemination, that contributed to the immense popularity of one of its first collaborative efforts during the 1760s and 1770s: that of librettist Weisse and composer Hiller.

In effect, then, one of the most important aspects of the singspiel which has thus far been overlooked is the tremendous facility with which the genre was spread throughout the public sphere: a conceptual space between the State and the private home in which texts, ideas and musical works were circulated, discourse flourished and institutions such as the public opera house were founded.[8] Ironically, it was this facility that allowed it to play a central role in the initial stirrings of a German national consciousness that early historians attempted to trace. Hiller's songs, separated from their dramatic context, travelled via oral transmission and in print throughout German-speaking Europe,[9] and Hiller gained popularity as 'the favourite German

---

6 'Singspiel', in *The New Grove Dictionary of Music and Musicians*, fifth edition, ed. Eric Blom (London: Macmillan, 1954), volume 6, 815 and 818.

7 Thomas Bauman, *North German Opera in the Age of Goethe* (Cambridge: Cambridge University Press, 1985); Krämer, *Deutschsprachiges Musiktheater*, 130–201; John Warrack, *German Opera: From the Beginnings to Wagner* (Cambridge: Cambridge University Press, 2001).

8 The public sphere is typically viewed as a conceptual space in which public opinion is voiced, and the public is generally viewed as an educated and literate group of individuals combining to form arguably one of the most powerful cultural forces during the eighteenth century (for a discussion of the social makeup of the public, see note 32 below). Since the public was first and foremost a reading public, the primary means of communication in the public sphere was through printed materials: periodicals, newspapers, novels and so forth. The public sphere also included institutions such as coffeehouses, salons, museums and, in the case of music, the public concert hall and opera house. For literature on the rise of the public sphere see Jürgen Habermas, *The Structural Transformation of the Public Sphere: An Inquiry into a Category of Bourgeois Society* (Cambridge: Polity, 1989), 14–56; Timothy C. W. Blanning, *The Culture of Power and the Power of Culture: Old Regime Europe, 1660–1789* (Oxford: Oxford University Press, 2002), 103–181; and James van Horn Melton, *The Rise of the Public in Enlightenment Europe* (Cambridge: Cambridge University Press, 2001). Further see Anthony J. La Vopa, 'Conceiving a Public: Ideas and Society in Eighteenth-Century Europe', *Journal of Modern History* 64/1 (1992), 79–116.

9 The issues of music printing and dissemination are central to my argument. The songs from Hiller's comic operas were printed (in piano-vocal score only) by Breitkopf very shortly after the premiere of each opera. The firm, having made substantial improvements to movable type in 1754, was one of the leading music publishers in German-speaking Europe. For a discussion of Breitkopf's improvements see Anik Devriès-Lesure, 'Technological Aspects', in *Music*

composer', one who wrote for the German people and in the manner of the German people. Separated from the context of the drama, his songs became known not as opera songs but as folksongs. Although it is impossible to know how many copies of his music were sold, or to whom, to say nothing of the exact scope of oral transmission, it is clear that the generic features of eighteenth-century comic opera were designed to circulate within the public sphere and thus allowed it subsequently to play an essential role in constructing a German national identity. In this article I shall examine Hiller's comic operas as a genre, their suitability for use within the Enlightenment public sphere and their role in shaping the early formation of a German national consciousness.

GERMAN COMIC OPERA AND THE PUBLIC SPHERE

Mid-eighteenth-century German comic opera as a literary and musical genre exhibits unique attributes that facilitate circulation within the public sphere: the overall structure of spoken dialogue and detachable songs, poetic features of individual song forms and their melodic simplicity enable widespread dissemination. In fact, the genre selected by Weisse and Hiller reflects their aim of promoting the singing of the lied in particular groups of German society. Although these songs were initially performed in a public theatre, Weisse's 1778 preface to his *Komische Opern* indicates that they were intended for use outside their dramatic context:

> Doch der besondere Zweck, den ich mir dabey vorsetzte, war, das kleine gesellschaftliche Lied unter uns einzuführen . . . Kein Mittel aber kann kräftiger seyn, den Gesang allgemeiner zu machen, als die komische Oper. Gefällt bey der Vorstellung ein Liedchen, so kann man darauf rechnen, daß es bald von dem ganzen Publikum gesungen wird. Meine Erwartung hat mich auch hierin nicht getäuscht, und ich darf mich kühn auf diejenigen Örter berufen, wo diese komischen Opern gespielt worden. Alle Gesänge, die bey der Vorstellung gefielen, waren bald in aller Munde, machten einen Theil des gesellschaftlichen Vergnügens aus, und giengen so gar zu dem gemeinen Volke über. Man hörte sie auf den Gassen, in den Wirthshäusern und auf den Hauptwachen, in der Stadt und auf dem Lande, von Bürger- und Bauernvolk singen.[10]

> Yet the particular purpose which I myself had in mind [for comic opera] was to introduce among us the little social song . . . No medium can, however, be more powerful in making song more universal than comic opera. Once a song has been deemed pleasant in performance, one can count on the fact that soon it will be sung by the entire public. My expectation has not disappointed me, and I can boldly point to all the places where these comic operas are being performed. All the songs which were well liked in performance were soon sung by all, at first bringing enjoyment to social gatherings, and then even going over to the ordinary *Volk*. One heard them in the lanes, in taverns and at the guard station, in the city and in the countryside, sung by burgher and farmer alike.

Evidently the presence of detachable songs and their melodic suitability for public consumption was a driving force behind Weisse and Hiller's comic operas. Although collections of opera arias for domestic use

---

Publishing in Europe 1600–1900 (Berlin: Berliner Wissenschafts-Verlag, 2005), 70–71. For studies of the issue of music dissemination during the eighteenth century see Sarah Adams, 'International Dissemination of Printed Music during the Second Half of the Eighteenth-Century', in *The Dissemination of Music: Studies in the History of Music Publishing*, ed. Hans Lenneberg (New York: Gordon and Breach, 1994), 21–43; Klaus Hortschansky, 'The Musician as Music Dealer in the Second Half of the Eighteenth Century', in *The Social Status of the Professional Musician from the Middle Ages to the Nineteenth Century*, ed. Walter Salmen (New York: Pendragon, 1983), 189–218; and, most recently, Stephen Zohn, 'Telemann in the Marketplace', *Journal of the American Musicological Society* 58/3 (2005), 761–764, to mention only a few.

10 Christian Felix Weisse, *Komische Opern* (Carlsruhe: C. G. Schmieder, 1778), volume 3, 2v–3r. All translations are my own.

SONGS TO SHAPE A GERMAN NATION

were not unheard of during the eighteenth century,[11] the distinguishing feature of Weisse and Hiller's songs is their stated intention to be communally singable.[12] Importantly, Weisse and Hiller were relatively uninterested in producing a through-composed, fully staged music drama; their interest lay, rather, in creating operatic songs in order that they might be sung by an amateur audience outside the theatre.

The poetic form of Hiller's songs also plays a critical role in allowing the genre to circulate within a public sphere. The song types include simple through-composed songs, numerous strophic songs and, among strophic songs, usually one *Romanze*[13] per opera. The *Romanze*, a strophic form, is of particular interest, since it is essentially self-reflexive:[14] a character in the drama tells an ancient tale, usually a thinly disguised microversion of the drama. For instance, in *Die Liebe auf dem Lande* (1767) Lieschen, the female protagonist, tells of an evil nobleman who comes with his horse in an effort to lure away a young peasant girl with his riches. Because of her moral character traits and perspicacity, the girl outsmarts the nobleman and escapes. Although Lieschen sings this 'ancient tale' to her lover Hännschen as though it has nothing to do with herself, the audience is well aware that this is not the case. Thus once the *Romanze* has been detached and is sung outside the theatre, it is possible to know the basic plot and moral of the story without having attended the performance.

---

11 For an excellent account of opera arrangements for domestic use see Thomas Christensen, 'Public Music in Private Spaces: Piano-Vocal Scores and the Domestication of Opera', in *Music and the Cultures of Print*, ed. Kate van Orden (Chicago: Chicago University Press, 2000), 67–93. See also Klaus Hortschansky, 'Formen populärer Musikrezeption im Deutschland des 18. Jahrhunderts', in *Bühnenklänge. Festschrift für Sieghardt Döring zum 65. Geburtstag*, ed. Thomas Betzwieser and others (Munich: Ricordi, 2005), 457–469. For a localized study of the domestication of Italianate operatic genres (primarily the Italianate cantata) by adding song-like comic arias and the association of the Enlightenment lied with a so-called German national style see Ann Le Bar, 'The Domestication of Vocal Music in Enlightenment Hamburg', *Journal of Musicological Research* 19/2 (2000), 97–134. While collections of lieder composed for domestic use formed an essential part of Enlightenment music cultivation, and Hiller's songs were in fact musically very similar to the song collections of his contemporaries within the genre of opera, Hiller and Weisse's incorporation of the lied as one of the main song-types sung outside the theatre just as it was on stage seems to be an endeavour preceded only by the works of J. C. Standfuss.

12 This aim of communal singing was articulated in both the second and third editions of Weisse's *Komische Opern* (1777 and 1778). Hiller concedes in his autobiography that this was not his initial intention in composing comic opera. For Schiebeler's *Lisuart und Dariolette* (1767), he was interested in composing more challenging Italianate and da capo arias for the singers. The theatrical impresario Heinrich Gottfried Koch, however, disagreed, and suggested instead that he fashion light and simple songs in order that everyone in the audience could sing along; see Johann Adam Hiller, *Mein Leben: Autobiographie, Briefe und Nekrologe*, ed. Mark Lehmstedt (Leipzig: Lehmstedt, 2004), 24. Hiller seems to have taken this advice seriously, since in the Preface to his very next opera, *Lottchen am Hofe* (1767), he states first of all that 'Ausführliche Arien, Arien mit Da Capo, mit öfterer Wiederholung des Textes, mit langen melismatischen Ausdehnungen und Figuren finden diesmal die Liebhaber nicht' (Enthusiasts will not this time find detailed arias, da capo arias with frequent repetitions of the text and long melismatic prolongations and ornaments); see Johann Adam Hiller, *Lottchen am Hofe* (Leipzig: Breitkopf & Härtel, 1769). Thus the aim of including short songs for everyone to sing, rather than Italianate arias for virtuosos, seems to have been established by Hiller, Weisse and Koch relatively early on in their collaboration. It should be noted, however, that Weisse's articulation of this ideal of furthering communal singing in the preface to the 1777 and 1778 editions of his *Komische Opern* was of course self-serving in that it fuelled the (already established) popularity and tremendous commercial value of the songs; they sold a great number of copies of the piano-vocal scores of the operas (for statistics see notes 19 and 20 below).

13 The seminal study of the operatic *Romanze* is Daniel Heartz, 'The Beginnings of the Operatic Romance: Rousseau, Sedaine, and Monsigny', *Eighteenth-Century Studies* 15/2 (1981–1982), 149–178.

14 For the idea of self-reflexivity in opera see Carolyn Abbate, *Unsung Voices: Opera and Musical Narrative in the Nineteenth Century* (Princeton: Princeton University Press, 1991), 63–118. For comments on self-reflexivity in opéra comique see David Charlton, 'The Romance and Its Cognates: Narrative, Irony and *Vraisemblance* in Early *Opéra Comique*', in *Die Opéra comique und ihr Einfluß auf das europäische Musiktheater im 19. Jahrhundert*, ed. Herbert Schneider and Nicole Wild (Hildesheim: Georg Olms, 1997), 74.

Strophic songs such as the *Romanze* are perhaps best suited for public singing, since once the melody is mastered, it can easily be repeated with subsequent verses of text. In the context of the staged production, however, Weisse indicates that strophic songs were by no means performed in their entirety. Rather, the director (in Leipzig, Heinrich Gottfried Koch) was entrusted with the decision as to how many stanzas were appropriate; frequently one stanza would suffice:

> [Ich habe] oft die Lieder in mehr Strophen verfertiget, als sie auf dem Theater brauchen gesungen zu werden. Hier ist oft Eine genug, und die Direktoren thun wohl, wenn sie sich hierinn nach den Umständen richten. Das Lied hält immer die Handlung auf: denn oft ist eine bloße Empfindung ausgedrückt, und die Melodie muß vorzüglich schön seyn, wenn man sie zu wiederholten malen hören soll.[15]

> [I have] often composed the songs in more strophes than necessary for sung performance in the theatre. Here, often one is enough, and the director does well to adjust according to the circumstances. The song always slows down the plot, since frequently a single emotion is expressed, and the melody must be exquisitely beautiful if one is to hear it repeated several times.

The practice of omitting many of the song stanzas during a staged performance while publishing songs with all the stanzas reinforces the central purpose of communal singing for this genre. In order to facilitate rapid dissemination and communal singing by members of the public, pamphlets containing all of the stanzas to the song texts were distributed to audience members at performances. These pocket-sized prints, on thin, relatively inexpensive paper, only occasionally contain information such as the date of the performance, the name of the publisher or printer, or the print run.[16]

Publication data and contemporary reviews also indicate that Hiller's piano-vocal editions of these operas were extremely popular. According to Arthur Loesser, *Lottchen am Hofe* and *Die Liebe auf dem Lande* went through four print runs totalling 2,750 copies within fifteen years,[17] and according to Hermann Hase *Die Jagd* underwent three print runs in the five years following its first performance, totalling more than 4,000 exemplars and earning Hiller 1,383 Reichsthaler.[18] Reviews of the piano-vocal editions in various journals were extremely positive and included brief descriptions of the arias as well as advertisements for the next available opera in this format. Judging from numerous reviews of the scores[19] advertised for a price of 1 Reichsthal 12 groschen,[20] it is almost certain that the songs were widely distributed and used by members of the public. Copies of the librettos were sold at semi-annual book fairs in Leipzig and Frankfurt[21] and were

---

15 Weisse, *Komische Opern*, volume 3, 3r.
16 Several of these pamphlets survive in the Stadtbibliothek Leipzig – Musikbibliothek: *Arien und Gesänge aus der Comische Oper: Lottchen, oder Das Bauermägdchen am Hofe* (shelfmark B69); *Arien und Gesänge aus der Comischen Oper: Die Liebe auf dem Lande* (shelfmark B85); *Arien und Gesänge zur komischen Oper die Jagd* (shelfmark PT1462); *Arien und Gesänge zur comischen Oper: Der Aerndtekranz* (shelfmark PT213). It is unclear whether these pamphlets were distributed free or sold to the audience (thereby contributing to the commercial aspects of Hiller and Weisse's project), since there is no indication of price.
17 Arthur Loesser, *Men, Women and Pianos: A Social History* (New York: Dover, 1990), 153–154.
18 Hermann Hase, 'Johann Adam Hiller und die Breitkopfs', *Zeitschrift für Musikwissenschaft* 2 (1919), 1–22. Cited in Krämer, *Deutschsprachiges Musiktheater*, volume 1, 130.
19 Johann Friedrich Agricola, 'Lottchen am Hofe, Die Liebe auf dem Lande', *Allgemeine Deutsche Bibliothek* 13/1 (1770), 84–90; Anonymous, 'Arien und Gesänge aus der comische Oper: Lottchen, oder das Bauermädgen am Hofe', *Wöchentliche Nachrichten und Anmerkungen* 1/48 (1767), 376–377; Anonymous, 'Die Jagd, Der Aerndtekranz', *Allgemeine Deutsche Bibliothek* 17/2 (1772), 564–568; Anonymous, 'Leipzig', *Unterhaltungen* 5/4 (1768), 368–370; Anonymous, 'Leipzig', *Unterhaltungen* 4/1 (1767), 650–651.
20 *Lottchen am Hofe* was advertised for this price, as was *Lisuart und Dariolette*.
21 Anonymous, 'Leipzig' (1768), 368.

available in local bookshops. In fact, Weisse's librettos were pirated, printed and sold before he had a chance to publish them himself.[22]

Finally, in addition to the detachable nature of the songs and the accessibility of the song types used, the melodies themselves were easy to sing and to recall. One reviewer praises Hiller's operas for their lack of da capo arias and Italianate style:

> Von der Musik des Hrn. Hillers können wir nichts als gutes sagen; sie hat uns zu allen Empfindungen hingerissen, die sie verlangt und Kenner haben uns versichert, daß sie noch mehr Verdienste, ein vortreffliches unterstützendes und neues Accompagnement, schöne Wendungen und charakteristische Züge in der Melodie, und eine reine Harmonie hätte. Von den Rasereyen des italiänischen Theaters haben wir nichts bemerkt, keine einzige Arie hatte einmal ein Dacapo.[23]
>
> Regarding the music of Herr Hiller, we can make nothing but positive comments; it has enraptured us with all the affects that are called upon, and the connoisseurs have assured us that it has still more merits: a splendid new supporting accompaniment, beautiful turns of phrase and characteristic features in the melody and a pure harmony. Of the recklessness of Italian theatre we have not noticed anything; not a single aria contains a da capo.

Hiller's melodies were known for their simplicity. J. F. Reichardt notes in his extensive publication on German comic opera, 'the song is such that I can sing along the second time round'.[24] Moreover, Weisse's Preface to the comic operas indicates that Hiller's melodies were specifically designed for public singing and not for virtuoso singers on stage: 'uns lag mehr daran, von einer fröhlichen Gesellschaft, als von Virtuosen gesungen zu werden'[25] (for us, it was more important that our songs be sung by a merry society than by a virtuoso). In essence, generic structural features of German comic opera – the detachment of songs from the spoken dialogue, various song types and a simple melodic style – are indicative of a deliberate design for ease of dissemination and communal singing by the public. Inextricably bound to the public sphere, however, is the question of audience: who constituted the public and why was it important for them to sing?

QUESTIONS OF AUDIENCE

In a lengthy Preface to the *Komische Opern* explicitly stating his intended social function for the lied, Weisse at the same time reveals his intended audience for these songs. His description of the *gesellschaftliches Lied*[26] used in particular sociable spaces such as *Gesellschaften*, salons, reading societies and similar gatherings gives a reasonably clear idea of the kind of audience present. This initial audience Weisse aptly refers to as *Publikum*,[27] and so his concept of *Publikum* is first of all an educated and reading public. Although Habermas describes the public as substantially bourgeois,[28] more recent political historians have revised his essentially

---

22 See Krämer, *Deutschsprachiges Musiktheater*, volume 1, 131–132.
23 Anonymous, 'Vermischte Nachrichten, die schönen Künste betreffend', *Unterhaltungen* 5/4 (1768), 368–70.
24 Johann Friedrich Reichardt, *Über die deutsche comische Oper* (Hamburg: Carl Ernst Bohn, 1774), reprinted in *Schriften zur Musik, Facsimilia* 2 (Munich: Emil Katzbichler, 1974), 11.
25 Weisse, *Komische Opern*, volume 3, 3r–3v.
26 The early repertory of the *Gesellschaftslieder* as social songs sung by the educated public is documented in Hoffmann von Fallersleben's 1860 *Die deutschen Gesellschaftslieder des 16. und 17. Jahrhunderts*, 2 volumes (reprinted Hildesheim: Georg Olms, 1966). For a discussion of the *Gesellschaftslied* and Salieri's contribution to the genre see Rudolph Angermüller, 'Salieris Gesellschaftsmusik', in *Studien zur italienisch-deutschen Musikgeschichte (Analecta Musicologica* 17), ed. Friedrich Lippmann (Cologne: Volk, 1976), 146–193.
27 Weisse, *Komische Opern*, volume 3, 2v.
28 Habermas states that 'the authorities addressed their promulgations to "the" public, that is, in principle to all subjects. Usually they did not reach the "common man" in this way, but at best the "educated classes". Along with the apparatus of the modern state, a new stratum of "bourgeois" people arose which occupied a central position within the "public".'

Table 1 Reconstruction of Weisse's description of audiences and dissemination processes of the opera songs, taken from the 1778 preface to his *Komische Opern*

Sphere 1	Sphere 2	Sphere 3
• Public opera performance	• Society meetings	• Singing of songs on streets, in parks and in workplaces
• Spoken dialogue and songs	• Communal singing of songs	
• Paid admission	• Open to members of 'public'	
• 'Public' audience	• Song texts, piano-vocal scores and librettos available	• Oral transmission of songs
• Song text distributed		
• Public theatre as space	• Semi-private spaces	• Singing *Volk* as particpatory audience
		• Open-air spaces and work spaces

Marxist view of the rising bourgeoisie and now describe the public as 'socially heterogeneous and politically multi-directional',[29] thereby consisting of both aristocracy and bourgeoisie.[30] This, however, is not the only audience for which Weisse intended his opera songs. He subsequently claims that 'these songs first bring pleasure in social gatherings, and then they even go over into the ordinary *Volk*'.[31] Although his process of diffusion is described in several stages or spheres, the audiences in the several spheres are not necessarily mutually exclusive.

Using Weisse's vivid description of the circulation of the opera songs, it is possible to reconstruct the process as in Table 1. The first and second spheres of operatic distribution are ones with a specific target audience: the literate public (of varying social strata) who had the financial means of purchasing cultural commodities and who met within already established spaces of sociability. These spaces vary from meetings in private homes to discussions in numerous *Gesellschaften* and reading societies. Various types of texts were used in these contexts, and one might presume that the song texts handed out at performances would resurface in these settings. But although piano-vocal scores were used in domestic spaces, the practice of

---

He goes further to clarify that the 'bourgeois' were not burghers in the traditional sense (craftsman and shopkeepers), but that the bourgeoisie (merchants, bankers, entrepreneurs) were from the outset a reading public. Habermas, *The Structural Transformation*, 22–23.

29 Blanning, *The Culture of Power*, 15. For a discussion of the revisions made to Habermas's view see Blanning, *The Culture of Power*, 8–15, and Melton, *The Rise of the Public*, 12. For an eighteenth-century perspective on the use of the term 'public', especially with reference to Kant's famous essay 'What is Enlightenment?', see John Christian Laursen, 'The Subversive Kant: The Vocabulary of "Public" and ' "Publicity" ', in *What is Enlightenment? Eighteenth-Century Answers and Twentieth-Century Questions*, ed. James Schmidt (Berkeley: University of California Press, 1996), 253–269.

30 It is important to note that the public cannot be understood as being synonymous with the middle class. Political historians such as Blanning describe the public sphere as a 'neutral vessel, carrying a diversity of social groups and ideologies'. Regarding public concerts during the eighteenth century he notes that often 'it was not the middle classes who took the initiative in organizing concerts but the nobility ... Moreover, it was aristocrats just as much as bourgeois who were the beneficiaries of this new cultural space, for they now had the opportunity to emancipate themselves from both the hegemony previously exercised by the court and the isolation of their rural estates.' Blanning, *The Culture of Power*, 15 and 170. Regarding Hiller and Weisse's comic operas, Friedrich Rochlitz, too, notes the mixture of social class when referring to the 'public': 'Weit beliebter und allgemein bekannt sind Hillers Operetten; auch sind sie von weit mehr Einfluss auf die Bildung des *gemischten Publikums* für Musik, und auf die Erweckung der Liebhaberey am Gesange bey demselben gewesen.' (Hiller's operas were widely loved and universally known; they were also of far greater influence in the cultivation of music for the *mixed public*, and for the awakening of the fondness for singing for the same [public].) Rochlitz, 'Zum Andenken Johann Adam Hillers', in Hiller, *Mein Leben*, 151.

31 Weisse, *Komische Opern*, volume 3, 3r.

SONGS TO SHAPE A GERMAN NATION

reading (books) aloud and playing for a small audience in reading rooms (semi-private spaces) should not be underestimated. Evidence exists of music rooms being part of reading and lending libraries.[32] Importantly, members of the public sphere were individuals who had the financial means to attend comic opera performances and to purchase and read literary and musical texts, and who had access to a keyboard instrument and a basic training in music. The success of opera dissemination within this sphere was dependent on a group of individuals that were able to cultivate themselves, take leisure time and enjoy leisure activities.

Extending his final sphere far beyond this limited concept of 'public', Weisse claims that his opera songs were so popular that they even 'went over to the ordinary *Volk*. One heard them in the lanes, in taverns and at the guard station, in the city and in the countryside, sung by burgher and farmer alike'. Thus Weisse's final sphere of dissemination is characterized by widespread circulation and includes a large group of individuals – the ordinary or common *Volk*. Taken literally, Weisse, in this particular instance, is referring to the lower classes or rural peasants. The inclusion of this final sphere allows him to claim that just about everyone is singing these songs; in effect, it serves to complete his image of widespread participation and enables him to speak of a collective audience that includes both burgher and farmer, singing in the city and in the countryside. Within this seemingly idealized image of an all-encompassing audience singing opera songs, Weisse's claim invites an important question: did rural peasants actually sing these songs?

Even though it is impossible to reconstruct the scope of circulation, particularly through oral transmission, it is possible to glean some evidence regarding various arenas in which these songs were sung or played and whether rural peasants might have sung them. Another account of the widespread diffusion of Weisse and Hiller's opera songs in everyday spaces is found in a 1772 review in the *Allgemeine Deutsche Bibliothek*:

> Die Arien aus diesen beyden Operetten, werden hier bey uns so gut als die aus irgend einer Oper in Wälsch=land, in allen Straßen gesungen, oder bald mit diesen bald mit jenen Instrumenten gespielet.[33]
>
> Die Romanze S. 49. Als ich auf meiner Bleiche u.[s.w.], in Berlin wenigstens, die Hälfte der Einwohner auswendig, sie wird in allen Straßen, auf allen Spatziergängen auf allen Wasserfahrten, auf allen Paraden gesungen und gespielt.[34]
>
> The arias from both of these operettas [*Die Jagd* and *Der Aerndtekranz*] are as popular with us as those of any opera in Italy, are sung in all the streets or are soon being played with this or that instrument.
>
> The *Romanze* on page 49, 'Als ich auf neiner Bleiche' etc. – in Berlin, at least, half of the residents know it by heart, and it is being sung and played in all the streets, on all walkabouts and boat trips, on all parades.

In view of the open-air spaces mentioned by the reviewer above, it appears that for the most part these songs were heard in bourgeois spaces of leisure or popular entertainment. Buskers playing on the streets were considered professional musicians earning a living in rapidly growing urban centres, and walkabouts, boat trips and parades were open-air entertainments closely associated with eighteenth-century pleasure gardens and fairgrounds. It begins to appear more likely that this audience overlaps with the audiences attending the staged performance and singing in societies than with rural peasant farmers.

In fact, urban contexts noted by reviewers could provide a clue as to the motivation behind Weisse's inclusion of the ordinary *Volk*. Rapidly growing urbanization during the mid- to late eighteenth century contributed to an increase in rural sentimentalization – a sense of loss of an idyllic past in response to urban

---

32 Reinhard Wittmann, 'Was There a Reading Revolution at the End of the Eighteenth Century?', in *A History of Reading in the West*, ed. Guglielmo Cavallo and Roger Chartier (Cambridge: Polity, 1999), 308.
33 Anonymous, 'Die Jagd, Der Aerndtekranz', 565.
34 Anonymous, 'Die Jagd, Der Aerndtekranz', 566.

individuality and isolation. Bourgeois constructions of the idealized peasant and of the *Volk* as a collective community were widespread in German literature, painting and opera during the 1760s.[35] The notion of a folksong, too, was constructed for and by the bourgeoisie as they yearned for the former simple lifestyle in rural areas. Collections of folksongs published and sold were not authentic folksongs heard in rural areas; rather, they were constructions by and for an ever-increasing urban middle class, appealing to the memory of a lost Arcadia.[36]

Similarly, during the height of their popularity in the 1770s and 1780s Weisse and Hiller's songs became known not as opera songs but as folksongs. In his autobiography Weisse describes the success of *Lottchen am Hofe* and *Die Liebe auf dem Lande*: 'the composition of these pieces from the splendid Hiller was so catchy and easily comprehensible that the songs of both of these operas soon became folksongs'.[37] In places as far away as South Germany and Switzerland Hiller's songs were described as folksongs. Schwab remarks that these songs of Hiller did indeed find their way across the walls of Leipzig and across distant borders. Jean B. Laborde wrote down the song 'Ohne Lieb und ohne Wein' in 1780 as a supposed Strassbourg folksong; in Erk-Böhme's 'Liederhort' this same song exists, with a different text and musical variants, as a folksong from Hesse-Darmstadt. These songs were even encountered by a travelling Saxon in remote Switzerland.[38]

Finally, in his retrospective account describing the tremendous popularity of their opera songs, Weisse connects the idea of the folksong with that of the *Volk*, this time, however, not only the ordinary *Volk*, but the *Volk* as a collective entity:[39]

> Weißens Lieder waren ihrem Inhalte und ihrer Faßlichkeit nach, wie Hillers Melodien, für Leute von einer mittlern Bildung geeignet, und deren ist die größere Anzahl. Hiller sagte einmal bey Erscheinung der Schulzischen Volkslieder: 'Jetzt werden Volkslieder herausgegeben, welche das Volk nicht kennen lernt, nicht singt und nicht singen kann. Weiße und ich haben nicht mit diesem Titel geprahlt, aber unsere Lieder sind wirklich von der Nation, dem Volke der Deutschen gesungen worden.' Und er hatte Recht. In wie viel geselligen Zirkeln, wo man vorher nicht ans Singen gedacht hatte, wurden die Lieder der Weißischen Operetten gesungen, wenn diese an einem Orte gegeben worden waren. Die Lieder: Ohne Lieb' und ohne Wein u.[s.w.] Schön sind Rosen und Jesmin u.[s.w.] Die Felder sind nun alle leer u.[s.w.] Schön ist das Feld zur Frühlingszeit u.[s.w.] Was noch jung und artig ist u. nebst mehreren andern – wer konnte sie nicht vor einigen zwanzig Jahren auswendig, und wer sang sie nicht?[40]

---

35 For a discussion of the idealization of the peasant in literature and painting as it relates to music see Tilman Seebass, 'Idyllic Arcadia and Italian Musical Reality: Experience of German Writers and Artists (1770–1835)', *Imago Musicae* 7 (1990), 149–188.

36 Perhaps the best known collection is *Des Knaben Wunderhorn*, compiled during the early nineteenth century by Clemens Brentano and Ludwig Achim von Arnim. Eighteenth-century collections of songs in the manner of the *Volk* include J. A. P. Schulz's tremendously popular *Lieder im Volkston* (Berlin: G. J. Decker, 1782) and numerous collections by J. F. Reichardt.

37 'Die Compositionen dieser Stücke von dem vortrefflichen Hiller war so einschmeichelnd und faßlich, daß die Gesänge dieser beyden Operetten sehr bald zu Volksliedern wurden'; Christian Felix Weisse, *Christian Felix Weissens Selbstbiographie, herausgegeben von dessen Sohne Christian Ernst Weisse und dessen Schwiegersohne Samuel Gottlob Frisch, mit Zusätzen von dem Letztern* (Leipzig: Georg Voss, 1806), 104.

38 Heinrich W. Schwab, *Sangbarkeit, Popularität und Kunstlied* (Regensburg: Gustav Bosse, 1965), 100.

39 The concept of a *Volk* is notoriously difficult to define. As David Gramit notes, 'the identity of the *Volk* was by no means self-evident – did it refer to all the people of a nation, or to the common, unspoilt people, or to the ignorant in need of the cultivation that *Volkslieder or Lieder im Volkston* might provide?'; see David Gramit, *Cultivating Music: The Aspirations, Interests, and Limits of German Musical Culture, 1770–1848* (Berkeley: University of California Press, 2002), 65. In this instance the opaqueness of the definition works to Weisse's advantage; it enables him to speak of a collective audience in which individuals of all backgrounds could stand united.

40 Weisse, *Selbstbiographie*, 325–326.

SONGS TO SHAPE A GERMAN NATION

Depending on their content and comprehensibility, Weisse's songs, like Hiller's melodies, were suitable for people of a moderate cultivation, which are the largest in number. Hiller once said upon the occasion of the new publication of Schulz's *Volkslieder*: 'Now folksongs are being published which the *Volk* does not get to know, does not sing and cannot sing. Weisse and I did not boast of such a title, but our songs really were sung by the nation, by the German *Volk*.' And he was right. In how many social circles, where previously one would never even have thought about singing, were the songs of the Weisse operettas sung. The songs 'Ohne Lieb' und ohne Wein [etc.]', 'Schön sind Rosen und Jesmin [etc.]', 'Die Felder sind nun alle leer [etc.]', 'Schön ist das Feld zur Frühlingszeit [etc.]', 'Was noch jung und artig ist [etc.]', among many others – who did not know them by heart some twenty years ago, and who did not sing them?

From this it is evident that Weisse's audience comprises an emerging bourgeoisie, singing these songs within their social circles. Simultaneously, however, the notion of the *Volk* and the German nation carries a universal appeal in which seemingly everyone is singing these *Lieder im Volkston* (songs in the manner of the *Volk*). Thus there appears to be a discrepancy between Weisse's actual audience and his ideal audience. In fact, the ideal of a *Volk* – a seemingly indistinguishable and faceless mass of individuals – served as a construct in which individuals of various classes and educational backgrounds could be united.[41] Weisse's invocation of the *Volk* – a collective entity in which burgher and farmer could ideally sing side by side – forms a part of a larger Enlightenment ideal of universal brotherhood. Even though the peasant farmer may or may not actually have joined the burgher in singing these songs, within the articulated ideal of a German *Volk* they certainly stood united.

NEGOTIATING THE PASTORAL

Strangely absent from Weisse and Hiller's Enlightenment ideal of uniting the German people in song is the aristocracy; within the dramatic context of the operas, however, they do play a role. Displayed through the lens of the pastoral mode, the corruptness and artificiality of the courts typically form the backdrop within which pastoral inserts reveal the idyllic surroundings and virtues of the idealized peasant.[42] The very use of the pastoral mode to construct a favourable image of the *Volk*, a concept which Weisse and Hiller borrowed from Jean-Jacques Rousseau's *Le devin du village* and writings concerning politics and the fine arts,[43] is in itself an ideological statement. While pastoral operas previously featured nymphs and shepherds, typically thinly veiled representations of ruling families and the aristocracy, the pastoral mode in Hiller's operas serves to amplify the merits of the rural peasant. Moreover, these peasants sing songs in the manner of the *Volk*. This melodic simplicity, emulating a folksong, was Hiller's hallmark, and the basis of his popularity. Within the pastoral mode, however, this melodic style necessarily exists in opposition to the highly ornamented Italian opera seria style, court culture and the aristocracy. The presence of the pastoral mode effectively

---

41 For a discussion of the *Volkston* as cultural construct and Enlightenment ideology see Margaret M. Stoljar, *Poetry and Song in Late Eighteenth-Century Germany* (Kent: Croom Helm, 1985), 149.

42 Weisse and Hiller's operas are not explicitly pastoral operas in the sense of a drama set in Arcadia containing nymphs and shepherds. Instead they are in the pastoral mode, containing isolated instances or 'insets' of the pastoral. For a description see 'Pastoral Insets' in Andrew V. Ettin, *Literature and the Pastoral* (New Haven: Yale University Press, 1984), 75–95. Typically these pastoral insets are 'suspended' in contemporary society; the tension between these two spheres results in irony. For a description of pastoral suspension see Paul Alpers, *What is Pastoral?* (Chicago: Chicago University Press, 1996), 68.

43 Hiller published a collection of writings concerned with morality, politics and the fine arts which was not a direct translation of Rousseau's works but, in accordance with established eighteenth-century practice, was Hiller's translation and interpretation of Rousseau's thinking; see J. A. Hiller, *J. J. Rousseau: Auserlesene Gedanken über verschiedene Gegenstände aus der Moral, der Politik, und den schönen Wissenschaften* (Danzig: Daniel Ludwig Wedel, 1764).

amplifies the virtues of the idealized German peasant but also serves to construct an ideological connection between this peasant and the essential (morally upright) character of the German *Volk*. Consider, for example, the portrayal of the female protagonist Lottchen as a quintessentially virtuous peasant girl.

The opening scene in *Lottchen am Hofe* (1767) is set in the countryside with farmers' huts in the background. Lottchen, a young farm girl, is spinning thread and singing about the joys of daily work while her lover Gürke picks cherries. Soon the audience is made aware of Astolph (the local Duke), his present unhappiness with his chosen partner Emile and his intention to pursue Lottchen instead. The two worlds converge for the first time (in Act 1 Scene 4) when Astolph sees Lottchen singing merrily in the fields; he approaches her regarding marriage.

Astolph: Ist es möglich, mein schönes Kind, daß man in dieser Dunkelheit so heiter, so zufrieden sein kann?
Lottchen: Diese Dunkelheit? Warum Dunkelheit? Die Sonne scheint bey uns so heiter, als an irgend einem Ort: keine hohe Mauern verschließen uns den Tag, und wenn es ja jene Gebüsche thun, so sind es bloß willkomme Schatten, die uns vor den Strahlen der Sonne beschützen.
Astolph: Ich meine die Niedrigkeit deines Standes, mein liebes Kind.
Lottchen: O nicht doch! diese Niedrigkeit verbirgt uns vor allen fremden Sorgen. Weder Neid noch Mißgunst schleicht sich in unser friedsames Thal, unsere Sorgen sind unsre Arbeit. Diese erhält uns gesund, und wenn man gesund ist, ist man immer froh.
Astolph: Aber was habt ihr denn hier für Freuden?
Lottchen: Was für Freuden? Wenn wir mit unserer Arbeit fertig sind, so haben wir deren unzählige.

Astolph: Is it possible, my beautiful child, that one can be so cheerful, so content in this darkness?
Lottchen: This darkness? Why darkness? The sun shines as brightly here for us as it does in any other place. No high walls shut out the day from us, and if these shrubs do so, they just make welcome shadows that protect us from the rays of the sun.
Astolph: I mean the lowliness of your social class, my dear child.
Lottchen: Oh, but no! this lowliness protects us from all foreign cares. Neither envy nor misfortune creeps into our peaceful valley; our cares are our work. It keeps us healthy, and when one is healthy, then one is always happy.
Astolph: But what sort of pleasures do you have here?
Lottchen: What pleasures? When we're finished with our work, then we have innumerable possibilities.

Rather than continuing the discussion in spoken dialogue, Lottchen responds in song, singing about the delights of living in the rustic countryside (see Figure 1).

Bald pflück ich mir Rosen zu Kränzen;
Bald laden zu lüsternen Tänzen
In bunten fröhlichen Reihn
Mich meine Gespielinnen ein.
Bald singen wir zärtliche Lieder:
Es singet das Echo sie wieder,
Und was im Scherze dieß sprach,
Das schwatzen im Scherze wir nach.

Bald hüpf' ich durch blühende Wiesen,
Die Bäche geschwäßig durchfließen,
Zum Hayn, wo Zephyr mir rauscht
Und wo mich mein Schäfer belauscht
Und bin ich des Lachens nun müde,

Then will I pick roses for wreaths
Then I will be summoned for pleasurable dances
In colourful bright rows
By my [female] companions
We'll then sing tender songs
That will be sung by the Echo again
And that which it [the Echo] says in jest,
We'll repeat with jest once again.

Then I'll be hopping through blossoming meadows
Through which the bubbling streams flow
To the grove, where Zephyr rustles around me
And where my shepherd listens in on me
And once I am tired of laughing

Figure 1 Lottchen's song 'Bald pflück ich mir Rosen zu Kränzen' from J. A. Hiller, *Lottchen am Hofe*, Act 1 Scene 4 (1768 piano-vocal edition, exemplar in the Stadtbibliothek Leipzig – Musikbibliothek, 4 III 74, pages 24–25). Used with permission

So wiegen mich Unschuld und Friede Then innocence and peace
In Schlaf, der schmeichelnd und leicht Will lull me to sleep, which disappears
Früh mit Auroren entweicht. gentle and light, early with Aurora.

The intersection of Lottchen's and Astolph's spheres in this scene embodies the central pastoral opposition: the simplicity and purity of the peasantry in opposition to the complexities and artificiality of court life. Lottchen's simple folk melody – a lilting tune in 6/8, set syllabically and free of excessive ornamentation – is most obviously interpreted as portraying her rural simplicity. While accurate in essence, this realist reading is arguably a one-dimensional view of the collaborative musico-dramatic forces at work, both in this specific scene, and more broadly, in these operas.

In the case of Lottchen, her naivety and rural simplicity are evident in her manner of speech and comprehension in conversation with Astolph. Certainly, when confronted with the metaphor of 'darkness' for her social position, Lottchen is unable to think or to respond in terms of literary metaphor. However, as soon as she speaks through song there is an abrupt change in her literary ability.[44] The poetic language of her song invokes imagery and mythological references far beyond the education of a peasant girl: Zephyr, the god of the gentle west wind; Echo, from the tale of Echo and Narcissus; and Aurora, goddess of the dawn. Lottchen's song embodies numerous pastoral themes. She belongs, for instance, to a larger community who meet one another for the purpose of singing songs, playing games and dancing. Their songs are conceived and sung in a natural landscape; moreover, this natural landscape participates by echoing back their music. Love is a central theme in her song. Her lover is referred to as a shepherd; she meets him in idyllic pastures. This landscape also serves as a habitat for numerous classical mythological gods – she and her community dwell in their presence. At the end of each day she is completely content; her basic sustenance comes from nature alone.

Yet it seems unreasonable within the context of the opera for a peasant girl to be singing of her experiences with classical mythological figures and meeting her shepherd in an idyllic landscape. Accordingly, the scene is not just a straightforward 'realistic' depiction of Lottchen as a naive and simple farm girl. While her folk-like melody speaks of a naive and idyllic simplicity, combined with the text and within the context of the scene the overall musico-dramatic effect is complex. In fact, it appears that there is irony at work: it is not Lottchen but Astolph who is 'living in darkness', figuratively speaking. While demonstrating the innocence and simplicity of peasant characters, the use of the pastoral mode simultaneously contends for the moral superiority of the rural folk.

The natural singing style for which Hiller was renowned is one that is associated primarily with morally upright peasant character types such as Lottchen. In discussing his choices of character types, Weisse indicates that it is far more natural to have peasants sing a simple and agreeable song than the grotesque *commedia dell'arte* characters of Italian opera buffa:

> Sie suchten nicht, wie die meisten Italienischen durch Possenreißereyen und groteske Carrikaturen lautes Lachen zu erregen, sondern stellten in Ausführung einer artigen Fabel, meistentheils auf dem Lande lebende Personen auf, in deren Munde der Gesang eines kleinen, leichten Liedchens der Natur ziemlich angemessen war. Diese Chansons waren von so faßlicher und singbarer Melodie daß sie von dem Publico sehr geschwind behalten und nachgesungen wurden und das gesellschaftliche Leben erheiterten.[45]

> They did not seek, like most Italians, to create laughter through buffoonery and grotesque caricatures. Instead, they presented a pleasant tale consisting mostly of rural persons in whose mouths a small, light song sounded quite natural. These songs had melodies that were so easily grasped and so easily sung that the public swiftly retained them; they were repeated and provided entertainment in social circles.

Weisse thus connects the simple songs sung by the moral peasants in the opera,[46] noting that their style (in the manner of the *Volk*) was simple and pleasant so that the public could sing them, with benefits to the community as a whole.

---

44 This sudden change in literary ability of a character of a lower social class, signalling knowledge beyond her socially expected abilities and to be understood with reference to the pastoral mode, occurs later in the character of Despina in Mozart's *Così fan tutte*; see Edmund J. Goehring, 'Despina, Cupid and the Pastoral Mode of *Così fan tutte*', *Cambridge Opera Journal* 7/2 (1995), 107–133.

45 Weisse, *Selbstbiographie*, 103.

46 The issue of song forms and musical styles associated with particular character types is relatively consistent for the virtuous peasant, but for noble characters such as the king or local duke, it is much more varied. For a discussion of the reception of Italian aria forms, particularly the da capo aria in Hiller's singspiels, see Estelle Joubert, 'Public Perception and Compositional Response: The Changing Role of the Da Capo Aria in Hiller's Singspiele', forthcoming in *Musica e Storia*.

SONGS TO SHAPE A GERMAN NATION

The ideological implications of a literate audience singing songs in the manner of idealized German rural peasants are inextricably bound to the idea of a German *Volk*. A duality exists within the character of the idealized peasants. On the one hand, they exemplify ancient shepherd-poets, singing 'folksongs' with and to one another. On the other, they are generic representatives of the German *Volk*. Characters named 'the honest Michel', Töffel, Hännschen, Lieschen or Lottchen are at once members of an anonymous and faceless mass of individuals comprising the *Volk* and intimately known examples of the German *Jedermann* (everyman). Thus there was a strong connection between the portrayal of morally upright peasant character types in the operas and the German people.

Moreover, in capturing this *Volkston*, Hiller was perceived to have also captured the collective essence of the German people while affirming the moral superiority of the working classes and bourgeoisie. This connection between Hiller's ability to write in the manner of the *Volk* and its subsequent connection with the German people is evident in Schubart's discussion of the composer's success:

> Hiller... der Lieblingscomponist der Deutschen. So sehr Hiller den welschen Gesang studierte; so studierte er doch noch weit mehr den deutschen, daher schneiden seine Gesänge so tief in unser Herz ein, dass sie durch ganz Deutschland allgemein geworden sind. Welcher Handwerksbursche, welcher gemeine Soldat, welches Mädchen singt nicht von ihm die Lieder: 'Als ich auf meine Bleiche u.s.w.' Ohne Lieb und ohne Wein u.s.w., und verschiedene andre? Im *Volkstone* hat Hiller noch niemand erreicht. Er ist der erste, der nach Standfuss komische Opern in deutsche Sprache auf die Bühne gebracht hat. Sein *lustiger Schuster* – seine *Jagd*; sein *Dorfbarbier*; sein *Erndtekranz*, und mehrere andere Opern, haben allgemeine Sensation in Deutschland hervorgebracht. Es gibt kein Theater unter uns, wo sie nicht mehr als einmal aufgeführt worden wären.[47]

> Hiller... the favourite composer of the Germans. As intently as Hiller studied Italian song, he studied German song even more so. Hence his songs cut so deeply into our hearts that they became universal in all of Germany. Which journeyman, which ordinary soldier, which girl does not sing his songs 'Als ich auf meiner Bleiche etc.', 'Ohne Liebe und ohne Wein etc.' and various others? In capturing the *Volkston* Hiller has not been equalled. He is the first since Standfuss to bring the comic opera in German onto the stage. His *lustiger Schuster*, his *Jagd*, his *Dorfbarbier*, his *Erndtekranz* and many other operas created a universal sensation in Germany. There is no theatre among us where they were not performed more than once.

In effect, when composing *volkstümliche Lieder* (songs in the manner of the *Volk*) Hiller's ideal audience was that of a united German people finding their identity in German song. Even though the operas did not incorporate folksongs, by virtue of being in the style of folksongs they were perceived as intended for all Germans; the idea of the *Volk* had become synonymous with that of a nation. Hiller's opera songs were crafted to resonate with the ideals of the German bourgeoisie. To reciprocate, it was this same public, soon viewed as a nation, that judged the songs worthy of embodying a German national identity.[48]

AFFIRMING THE GERMAN NATION: HILLER'S SONGS AND THE GERMAN NATIONAL IDENTITY

> I write as a citizen of the world who serves no prince... From now on all my ties are dissolved. The public is now everything to me – my preoccupation, my sovereign and my friend. Henceforth I belong to it alone, I wish to place myself before this tribunal and no other. It is the only thing I fear

---

47 Christian Friedrich Daniel Schubart, *Ideen zu einer Ästhetik der Tonkunst* (Vienna: J. V. Degen, 1806; reprinted Hildesheim: Georg Olms, 1969), 106–107.
48 For an excellent study pertaining to a German national identity in music, highlighting also the crucial role of the public sphere, see Celia Applegate, *Bach in Berlin* (Ithaca: Cornell University Press, 2005).

and respect. A feeling of greatness comes over me with the idea that the only fetter I wear is the verdict of the world – and that the only throne I shall appeal to is the human soul.[49]

The rise of the public as a cultural entity serving as the single most important patron and audience for which poets and composers write was an essential aspect not only of Schiller's but also of Weisse's and Hiller's social, cultural and artistic milieu. This idea of the public as a collective entity judging the merits of works of art, however, soon gained nationalistic import: with respect to Weisse and Hiller, it was not just the public but also the German nation that assessed the merits of their opera songs. The concept of the nation as arbiter of taste is evident already in 1774, when Reichardt describes the tremendous popularity of Hiller's *Romanze* 'Als ich auf meiner Bleiche' from *Die Jagd* as a collective national pronouncement:

> The entire German nation has already decided that [the song] is completely as songs of this type ought to be. For every man, from highest to the lowest, sings and plays it and whistles it, and I might almost say drums it, so widely is it used in every possible way throughout Germany.[50]

Reichardt speaks of the German nation as a single unified cultural concept, possessing the ultimate authority and ability to judge whether or not a song is worthwhile. Moreover, reference is made to a range of social status – from highest to lowest – representing the Enlightenment ideal of a nation uninhibited by social or educational barriers, and this nation is united by one of Hiller's most popular songs; every man is said to have sung or whistled it.

Not only was the nation viewed as the ultimate arbiter of taste: for Hiller, national fame and acclamation were seen as the most worthy achievements for a composer.

> Von dieser Seite betrachtet, halte ich Herr H. in der Musik ... für das, was Gellert in der Poesie war; und auch dasselbe Schicksal, dieselbe Belohnung, hat H. H., die Gellert hatte: denn er ist der Lieblingscomponist seiner Nation, so wie ihr Gellert der Lieblingsdichter war. Welche Belohnung! Nicht Geld und Titel der Großen, ja selbst das würdige Lob des Kenners, belohnen so angenehm, als die Stimme einer ganzen Nation.[51]

> From this perspective, I hold Herr H[iller] to be that in music which Gellert was in poetry; and also, H[err] H[iller] had the same destiny, the same reward, that Gellert had: for he is the favourite composer of his nation, just as Gellert was the nation's favourite poet. What a reward! Not the money and title of the great, not even the worthy praise of the connoisseur, is as pleasing a reward as the voice of an entire nation.

Former values of wealth and title esteemed by court culture seemingly faded as the bourgeoisie began not only to assert themselves within the public sphere but also began to sense the collective force of a German national consciousness. As readers and listeners across a geographic area were able to read the same journals and newspapers, and play and sing from the same Hiller piano-vocal score, such a collective force was strengthened. For some, reading and singing the opera songs would have been sufficient, while for others the opportunity to express one's view in public debates, both in social gatherings and in print (which was then disseminated across a wide geographic area), was a novel but empowering experience. Even though the political features of a nation state were nowhere yet in sight, a sense of 'imagined community' – to use Benedict Anderson's term[52] – was greatly facilitated by the workings of the public sphere.

---

49 Blanning, *The Culture of Power*, 211 (Schiller, in 1784, cited in Helmuth Kiesel and Paul Münch, *Gesellschaft und Literatur im 18. Jahrhundert* (Munich: Beck, 1977), 78).

50 Reichardt, *Über die deutsche comische Oper*, 60: 'Die ganze deutsche Nation hat schon darüber entschieden, daß es [das Lied] völlig so ist, wie Lieder von der Art seyn müssen. Denn jeder mann, vom hohen bis zum niedrigsten, singt und spielt es und pfeift es, und fast sollte ich sagen und trommelt es, so sehr wird es in ganz Deutschland auf alle nur mögliche Art gebraucht.'

51 Reichardt, *Über die deutsche comische Oper*, 23.

52 Benedict R. Anderson, *Imagined Communities: Reflections on the Origin and Spread of Nationalism*, revised edition (London: Verso, 1991).

SONGS TO SHAPE A GERMAN NATION

Without the political features of a nation state in place, the unifying element within this emerging sense of national community was overwhelmingly that of the German language. Johann Christoph Adelung defined 'nation' as 'the native inhabitants of a country in so far as they have a common origin and speak a common language, whether they constitute a single state or are divided into several'.[53] Johann Gottlieb Fichte is famous for furthering the notion of language defining the boundaries of a national community, having claimed that 'wherever a separate language can be found, there is also a separate nation which has the right to manage its affairs and rule itself'.[54] Both Rousseau and Herder produced their famous essays on the origins of language,[55] investigating the ontological connections between linguistic community (particularly with regard to spoken language) and national identity. Herder's thought on language, however, is not limited to discussions of the origins of human sounds; rather, his writings, more broadly conceived, are concerned with the use of the German language by the German public.[56] Mid-century discussions of the use and merits of the German language by the public and particularly within German courts were often reactions against the preoccupation with French fashion, culture, literature and, of course, the use of the French language in polite society. Johann Christoph Gottsched, a fervent defender and reformer of the German language, complained that German princes could hardly speak their own language.[57]

Within eighteenth-century musical discourse, the ultimate display of a nation's language and musical taste is of course in opera. Debates concerning the supremacy of French and Italian opera are well documented throughout the century[58] but occurred alongside ongoing struggles to legitimize the idea of a German-language opera. Mid-century reformers such as Gottsched strongly agitated against opera as a genre, although Gottsched sought to cultivate a German theatrical tradition and translated French tragedies into the German language.[59] Johann Adolph Scheibe, on the other hand, was much more sympathetic towards opera as a genre and wrote his *Thusnelde* (1749) to demonstrate good operatic taste, though his opera libretto was never set to music. Prior to Hiller, attempts at a German-language opera had met with only limited success.[60] From this point of view it is not difficult to see why Hiller was hailed as the German nation's favourite composer in 1774: he provided the nation with opera songs both in the style of the *Volk* and in the language of the German people. Weisse and Hiller's use of the language in their operas was viewed as proof of its worthiness:

> Es ist noch nicht lange, daß wir eigentlich comische Opern haben. Dem Herrn Weiße in Leipzig, ist unser Theater dieses Geschenk vorzüglich schuldig. Er hat es versucht, ob unsre Sprache dazu fähig wäre, und wir haben gefunden, daß sie es sey, wenn ein großes Genie sie bearbeitet.[61]

---

53 Blanning, *The Culture of Power*, 17.
54 Peter Burke, *Languages and Communities in Early Modern Europe* (Cambridge: Cambridge University Press, 2004), 164.
55 *On the Origin of Language. Jean-Jacques Rousseau: Essay on the Origin of Languages. Johann Gottfried Herder: Essay on the Origin of Language*, trans. John H. Moran and Alexander Gode (London: Chicago University Press, 1966).
56 For a discussion of the public use of the German language in both Herder's and Kant's philosophy see Anthony J. La Vopa, 'Herder's Publikum: Language, Print and Sociability in Eighteenth-Century Germany', *Eighteenth-Century Studies* 29/1 (1996), 5–24.
57 Eric A. Blackall, *The Emergence of German as a Literary Language, 1700–75* (Cambridge: Cambridge University Press, 1959), 117.
58 The initial and perhaps best known debate on the merits of the French and Italian languages as suitable for opera was the Querelle des Bouffons in Paris during the 1750s.
59 For a discussion of early German theatre, including original German librettos but primarily translations of French tragedies by Racine, Corneille and Destouches, see Johann Christoph Gottsched, *Die deutsche Schaubühne nach den Regeln und Exempeln der Alten*, 6 volumes (Leipzig: Bernhard Christoph Breitkopf, 1741–1745).
60 Johann Georg Standfuss's *Der Teufel ist los*, performed in Leipzig in 1752 by the Koch company, represents one of the first successes of the comic genre in the German language.
61 L. M. N., 'Schreiben über die comische Oper, aus dem Hannöverischen Magazin 56tes Stück', *Wöchentliche Nachrichten und Anmerkungen* 3/12 (1769), 93.

It has not been long that we have actually had comic opera. Herr Weisse in Leipzig is responsible for this gift to our theatre. He was the one to try whether our language was capable and worthy of the task, and we have found that it is worthy when a great genius works with it.

'Es ist für einen patriotischen Deutschen eine allzu angenehme Sache, den deutschen Gesang sich bisweilen der Schaubühne bemächtigen zu sehen, von welcher ihn bisher der italiänische gänzlich verdrungen zu haben schien; wir sind daher auf alles aufmerksam, was die Ehre der deutschen Sprache zu retten die Absicht zu haben scheint, und uns immer noch mehr Gutes in der Folge verspricht, wenn Dichter und Componisten ohne Stolz und Eigensinn einander die Arbeit erleichtern, und in gewissen Stücken einer dem andern mehr zu Gefallen thun werden.[62]

For a patriotic German it is a very pleasant affair to see German song occasionally take hold of the theatre; until now it seems to have been entirely suppressed by Italian song. Hence we pay attention to everything that seems to have the intention of saving the honour of the German language and promises us still more good as a result, when poets and composers, without being proud or obstinate, make one another's work easier, and in certain respects do more for the benefit of others.

Weisse and Hiller's comic operas thus affirmed one of the defining features – language – that assisted in the formation of national identity during the mid- to late eighteenth century.

Finally, these German-language comic operas did not simply affirm an emerging national consciousness; the genre was seen as actively edifying and cultivating the German people. They functioned as part of an already existing project to educate the bourgeois public. Gellert produced morally edifying poetry for bourgeois domestic use, Lessing had stated already in 1769 that the theatre should be viewed as a school and Schiller delivered his famous statement on theatre as a moral institution in 1784. In the Schillerian spirit, Weisse remarks on the universal beauty and good of singing as part of the education of a nation:

Daß es aber Gewinn für die Bildung einer Nation ist, wenn das Singen anständiger, feiner, die Empfindungen für das Schöne und Gute belebender Lieder allgemeiner wird, bedarf keines Wortes zum Beweise.[63]

No word of proof is needed that it is profitable for the education of a nation when the singing of these songs, which are respectable and fine and enlivening of the sentiments for the beautiful and the good, becomes more universal.

In cultivating communal singing of German songs by various members of the public, comic opera as a genre was a unique contribution to the furthering of national ideology. The very limitations of a novel, poem or stage play – that they are being performed by individuals – are overcome by comic opera with its potential to unite the community in song. Indeed, the image of uniting a nation in communal song is one that lasted well into the nineteenth century, including the famous choral finale of Beethoven's Ninth Symphony, based on Schiller's *An die Freude*. Early historians' placing of Hiller at the beginnings of the history of German comic opera shows that they recognized the nationalistic impact of his opera songs. It is, however, only by affirming the essential defining feature of the genre – spoken dialogue interspersed with simple songs – that the importance of German comic opera comes fully alive.

---

62 Anonymous. Arien und Gesänge aus der comische Oper: Lottchen, oder das Bauermädgen am Hofe', 376.
63 Weisse, *Selbstbiographie*, 326.

Part VI
Mozart and His Viennese Contemporaries

[18]

Mozart's Fee for *Così fan tutte*

DEXTER EDGE

ACCORDING to one of his more heart-rending letters to Michael Puchberg, Mozart expected to receive 200 ducats from the directorate of the Viennese court theatres for composing *Così fan tutte*. This amount, equivalent to 900 gulden, would have been twice the usual fee paid for a newly composed opera at that time. Mozart's statement to Puchberg has long been accepted at face value, because the theatrical financial records for the season in which *Così fan tutte* had its première have been thought to be lost. Recently, however, an entry in a little-known theatrical ledger has come to light which shows that, in late February 1790, Mozart was paid 450 gulden for composing *Così fan tutte*, half of what he had claimed to expect. In attempting to account for the discrepancy between the documented payment and Mozart's expectation, this essay will investigate all fees and gifts received by composers and librettists for operas commissioned by the Viennese Nationaltheater from the founding of the German *Singspiel* in 1778 until the end of the theatrical season 1791–2. This investigation will not only help to suggest an explanation for the discrepancy, it will also illuminate the wider context in which Mozart's Viennese operas were commissioned, and will put into perspective the fees he was paid for them.

Almost nothing is known of the circumstances surrounding the composition of *Così fan tutte*. The notion that Emperor Joseph II suggested the subject himself, based on a contemporary incident in Viennese high society, has been traced to an account published in 1837[1] and must be considered questionable unless further evidence turns up to substantiate it. Mozart's early biographer Niemetschek speaks merely of a commission 'it was not in [Mozart's] power to turn down', seeming to imply that the commission came from the emperor.[2]

The opera is first mentioned in Mozart's correspondence in a letter to Puchberg written in late December 1789, in which Mozart offers his expected fee as security for a loan:

> Most worthy friend and brother Mason,
> Do not be shocked by the content of this letter. Only to you, my best friend, have I the courage to reveal myself with complete trust, because you know all about me and my circumstances. Next month I am to receive (according to

---

[1] See Rudolph Angermüller, 'Anmerkungen zu "Così fan tutte"', *Österreichische Musikzeitschrift*, 37 (1982), 379–86 (p. 382). The story is told in Friedrich Heinse's *Reise- und Lebens-Skizzen nebst dramaturgischen Blättern* (Leipzig, 1837).

[2] Franz Niemetschek, *W. A. Mozart's Leben nach Originalquellen beschrieben von Franz Niemetschek: Facsimiledruck der ersten Ausgabe, mit den Lesarten und Zusätzen der zweiten vom Jahre 1808 und Einleitung von Dr. Ernst Rychnovsky* (Prague, n.d.), 29. 'Es stand nicht in seiner Gewalt, den Auftrag abzulehnen . . .'. Niemetschek's discussion of *Così fan tutte* was taken over by Nissen with only minor changes of wording.

the present arrangement) 200 ducats from the directorate for my opera; if you can and will give me 400 gulden until then, you will lift your friend out of the greatest embarrassment, and I give you my word of honour that you will have your money back at the appointed time, in cash and in full, with all my thanks. . . . I ask you once again, extricate me from my fatal situation just this once; when I get the money for the opera, you shall most certainly have your 400 gulden back again.

At the end of the same letter, Mozart invites Puchberg to his apartment for a private performance.

I invite you (but only you alone) to a little opera rehearsal at my apartment on Thursday at 10 in the morning. I'm inviting only you and *Haydn*. I will tell you in person about Salieri's cabals, all of which, however, have already come to naught . . .[3]

In the event, Puchberg sent 300 gulden, but a further 100 gulden he sent in January probably represented the balance of the 400 Mozart had originally requested.

During the reign of Emperor Joseph II, the standard payment to composers for operas commissioned by the Nationaltheater was 100 ducats (equal, after 1 February 1786, to 450 gulden); but this sum was occasionally doubled or even tripled, depending upon the reception of the opera, the fame of the composer, or the whim of the emperor. Paisiello, for example, received 300 ducats, triple the normal fee, for his opera *Il rè Teodoro in Venezia*, which received its world première in Vienna on 23 August 1784. Salieri was paid a double fee of 200 ducats in the season 1785-6 for his *La grotta di Trofonio*, and again in the season 1787-8 for his *Axur, rè d'Ormus*. In early January 1790, shortly before the première of *Così fan tutte*, and shortly after the première of his own opera *La cifra* on 11 December 1789, Salieri was yet again paid 200 ducats (900 gulden); this time, however, the honorarium was intended as compensation not just for the new opera, but also for the composer's revisions to his *Il pastor fido*, which had been poorly received the previous season.[4] In light of the exceptional fees paid to Paisiello and Salieri, it is quite possible that

---

[3] 'Verehrungswürdigster Freund und Ordensbruder! Erschrecken Sie nicht über den Inhalt dieses Briefes; - nur bei Ihnen - mein Bester, da Sie mich und meine Umstände ganz kennen, habe ich das Herz mich ganz vertrauensvoll zu entdecken - künftigen Monat bekomme ich von der Direction (nach ietziger Einrichtung) 200 Ducaten für meine Oper; - können und wollen Sie mir 400 fl. bis dahin geben, so ziehen Sie Ihren Freund aus der größten Verlegenheit und ich gebe Ihnen mein Ehrenwort, daß Sie das Geld zur bestimmten Zeit baar und richtig mit allem Dank zurück haben sollen. . . . Ich bitte Sie nochmals reißen Sie mich nur diesmal aus meiner fatalen Lage, wie ich das Geld für die Oper erhalte, so sollen Sie die 400 fl. ganz gewiß wieder zurück haben. . . . Donnerstag . . . lade ich Sie (aber nur Sie allein) um 10 Uhr Vormittag zu mir ein, zu einer Kleinen Oper = Probe; - nur Sie und *Haydn* lade ich dazu. - Mündlich werde ich Ihnen Cabalen von Salieri erzählen, die aber alle schon zu Wasser geworden sind . . .'. Wilhelm A. Bauer and Otto Erich Deutsch, *Mozart: Briefe und Aufzeichnungen. Gesamtausgabe, herausgegeben von der Internationalen Stiftung Mozarteum Salzburg*, 7 vols. (Kassel, 1962-75), iv, 99-100. The letter, which is not dated, was probably written on 29 December 1789. The autograph is lost.

[4] Salieri's payment for composing *La cifra* and revising *Il pastor fido* is recorded in the same source as Mozart's fee for *Così fan tutte* (see below, note 8). *Il pastor fido* was premièred on 11 February 1789 and performed a total of three times before the end of the season, apparently with little success. It was not performed the following season until 18 October 1789, presumably with extensive revisions. The revisions seem not to have helped; the opera was performed only twice more, on 26 October and 1 November, apparently with no greater success than in the preceding season.

Mozart had likewise been promised a double fee for *Così fan tutte*, although no evidence of such a promise is known to survive.

Così fan tutte was premièred on 26 January 1790 and given four more times in the following two and a half weeks. The last of these performances took place on 11 February. On 13 February the theatre closed owing to the illness of Emperor Joseph II. On 20 February the emperor died, and the theatre remained closed until 11 April, the Sunday after Easter. *Così fan tutte* returned to the stage on 6 June 1790 and received a total of five additional performances in June, July and August.[5]

Apart from hints in Mozart's letters and in the autobiography of the librettist Lorenzo da Ponte, little is known about how operas were commissioned or otherwise selected for performance during Joseph's reign. On the other hand, quite complete records survive of payments to composers and librettists for commissioned operas, and of payments or reimbursements to middlemen for opera scores purchased elsewhere. Most of these payments are recorded in a series of theatrical account books (*Rechnungsbücher*) preserved in the court archives. These books – which are essentially annual or semi-annual financial reports – give a categorized and itemized account of the total income and expenses for each theatrical season.[6] Sources of income include ticket sales and subscriptions, the sale of librettos, the lease of the animal-baiting arena (*Hetzamphitheater*) and rent collected from two apartment houses belonging to the theatres. Total proceeds from ticket sales for entire seasons are recorded, but daily box-office receipts unfortunately are not. Expenses include, among other things, the salaries of the administration, actors, singers, orchestral players, music copyists, prompters, costumers, scene painters and watchmen; the costs of advertising and pensions; and the costs of repairing, heating and lighting the theatres themselves. The general rubric 'Extra Expenses' (*Extra Ausgaben*) encompasses several subcategories, including 'Rewards, Gifts, and Gratuities' (*Belohnungen, Geschenke, und Gnadengaben*), which lists special gifts and non-contractual compensation to composers, librettists, performers and theatrical employees; 'Compositions and Translations' (*Compositionen und Übersetzungen*), where the word 'Composition' refers to the writing of

---

[5] The emperor's death did not deprive Mozart's opera of more than two or three performances. According to theatrical regulations, operas were not allowed in the court theatres during Lent. In 1790 Lent began on 17 February (Ash Wednesday) and no operas would have been permitted until the week after Easter in any event.

[6] Vienna, Haus-, Hof- und Staatsarchiv, Generalintendanz der Hoftheater, Sonderreihe 11-34. Rechnungen der k. k. Theatralhofdirektion (hereafter abbreviated HHStA, Hoftheater, SR). Vols. 11-17 are semi-annual reports for the theatrical seasons 1776-7 to 1780-1; volumes for the second half of the season 1778-9 and the first half of the season 1779-80 are missing. Vols. 18-34 are annual reports for the seasons 1781-2 to 1801-2; volumes for the seasons 1789-90, 1790-1, 1792-3, 1795-6, 1797-8 and 1800-1 are missing. Until 1787, the theatrical season was reckoned from Holy Saturday (the day before Easter) to Good Friday the following year. Thus, for example, the report for the season 1785-6 (HHStA, Hoftheater, SR 22) is entitled 'Neunzehente, und zwanzigste kai[serliche] könig[liche] Theatral Hof = Directions = Cassa halbjährige Rechnung über Empfang und Ausgab pro Anno theatrali 1785 Id est vom 26ten: Mart[is] 1785. bis inclusive 14ten: Aprilis. 1786.' 26 March 1785 was the Saturday before Easter, and 14 April 1786 was Good Friday. In 1788 and 1789, on the other hand, the theatrical seasons ended on the last Friday in February. In 1794-5 the theatrical year was shifted to run from 1 August to 31 July. The new system begins with vol. 29; consequently, vol. 28 covers the short season 8 March 1794 to 31 July 1794.

librettos and plays; and 'Music and Copying Charges' (*Musique und Copiatur Spesen*), which lists all payments to composers, music copyists and supplementary and substitute musicians. The names of persons receiving payment and the titles of commissioned works are given, but payments are not dated. The account books refer to receipts (*Quittungen*) for payments to various employees and contractors, but these receipts apparently do not survive.

These account books are well known, although their significance for the history of musical life in Vienna has yet to be fully realized; they offer ample material for an as yet unwritten study of the organization and day-to-day management of the theatres. Among the items recorded in the books are payments to Mozart, his librettists and miscellaneous other persons for *Die Entführung aus dem Serail*, *Le nozze di Figaro* and *Don Giovanni*.[7]

Unfortunately, the annual account book for the season 1789–90 is lost. But two volumes of weekly ledgers covering this and several subsequent seasons do survive.[8] In contrast to the *Rechnungsbücher*, these ledgers were used for keeping daily accounts. Their physical layout is consistent throughout: each pair of facing pages records the income and expenses for a single week. Left-hand pages list the daily receipts from ticket sales for operas and plays, as well as the income from court-sponsored balls and payments received for subscription seats and boxes. Right-hand pages list weekly expenses, which are broken down into essentially the same categories as in the *Rechnungsbücher*. Weeks are reckoned from Saturday to the following Friday.

In the first few months covered by the ledger, entries on left-hand pages note only the date of the performance, the type of work performed (opera or play) and the gross receipts; titles are omitted. As it happens, the first opera for which a title is recorded is *Le nozze di Figaro*, for the performance on 24 October 1789. In spite of the missing titles, it is a simple matter to match receipts with operas, since the programmes of the theatres are well documented from other sources. Judging from ticket sales, both *Così fan tutte* and the revival of *Figaro* were hits; the première

---

[7] Most of these payments are transcribed in Otto Erich Deutsch, *Mozart: Die Dokumente seines Lebens*, Neue Mozart Ausgabe, Serie X, Supplement, Werkgruppe 34 (Kassel, 1961), 179, 240 and 276. Deutsch unaccountably omitted a payment of 52 gulden 30 kreuzer to Jean Huber de Camp for '3.mal gestellte kleinen Ballet zur Opera *le nozze di Figaro*'. This payment is recorded on the same page of HHStA, Hoftheater, SR 23, as Mozart's fee for the music.

[8] Vienna, Österreichische Nationalbibliothek (A-Wn), Theatersammlung, M 4000; no original title; later title, in pencil, 'Kassabuch der beiden Hoftheater 1789–1796, usw. Burgtheater 1789–1796 Kärntnertor theater, 16.11.1791–1796', 2 vols. The first volume covers the period 26 February 1789 to 30 July 1794, the second volume the period 1 August 1794 to 9 March 1797. These volumes, although known to Viennese theatre historians, have been overlooked by musicologists. They are cited in the bibliography to Otto Michtner, *Das alte Burgtheater als Opernbühne von der Einführung des deutschen Singspiels (1778) bis zum Tod Kaiser Leopolds II. (1792)*, Theatergeschichte Österreichs, 3/i (Vienna, 1970), and in Franz Hadamowsky, *Die Wiener Hoftheater (Staatstheater) 1776–1966: Verzeichnis der aufgeführten Stücke mit Bestandsnachweis und täglichem Spielplan*, i: *1776–1810*, Veröffentlichungen der Österreichischen Nationalbibliothek, Erste Reihe, Veröffentlichungen der Theatersammlung, 4 (Vienna, 1966), 153. Neither author mentions the fee for *Così fan tutte*. Note that the ledgers discussed here supply not only the missing information for the season 1789–90, but also for the seasons 1790–1, 1792–3 and 1795–6, for which Hoftheater *Rechnungsbücher* are also missing. My thanks to Evan Baker for directing my attention to these ledgers.

of *Così* took in more money – 553 gulden 19 kreuzer – than any other opera performance that season, surpassing its closest rival, the premiere of Salieri's *La cifra*, by almost 70 gulden (see Figure 1).[9] While this success cannot have endeared Mozart to Salieri, it may be taken as an indication of the continuing popularity of Mozart's music with the Viennese public during the last few years of his life.

As mentioned earlier, the theatre closed on 13 February 1790 owing to the illness of Joseph II and remained closed for almost two months following his death a week later. During the period of closure, few entries were made in the weekly ledger. But the following items were recorded as 'Extra Expenses' in the week of 20–26 February (see Figure 2):

Extra Ausgaben

Musiq[ue] Spesen

dem Kober Ignaz Instrumentstim[m]er .... ,,	3.58
dem Grebner Leopold für extra dienste .... ,,	6.--
dem Klingler Instrum[m]entstimer [*sic*] .... ,,	10.46
dem Mozart Wolfgang, für Componirung der Musi[que] zur Opera / Così fan Tutte .... ,,	450.--

Translation

Extra Expenses

Music Charges

To Ignaz Kober, instrument tuner .... ,,	3.50
to Leopold Grebner for extra services .... ,,	6.--
to Klingler, instrument tuner .... ,,	10.46
to Wolfgang Mozart for composing the music to the opera Così fan Tutte .... ,,	450.--[10]

All payments are reckoned in gulden and kreuzer. No other payment in the weekly ledgers mentions Mozart by name.

Apparently Mozart was paid only half as much as he had expected, and a month later than he had indicated to Puchberg. In attempting to explain this discrepancy, it may be instructive to consider both the standard fees paid for operas commissioned by the Nationaltheater and the supplementary gifts and rewards that composers, librettists and performers occasionally received. First, however, a brief digression on Austrian currency will prove helpful.

---

[9] See my forthcoming study 'Mozart Reception in Vienna, 1787–1791', which is based in part on a comparative analysis of the gate receipts from operas given in the court theatres during this period. The receipts from the première of *La cifra* were 485 gulden 21 kreuzer.

[10] The figure of 450 gulden is cited without reference by Rudolph Angermüller in ' "Seine Fehler waren, daß er das Geld nicht zu dirrigieren wuste": Mozarts finanzielle Verhältnisse', *Collectanea Mozartiana* (Tutzing, 1988), 35. Angermüller was told of the payment by the late Peter Riethus, an employee of the Österreichische Nationalbibliothek (personal communication from Dr Angermüller). Riethus should be credited with the discovery.

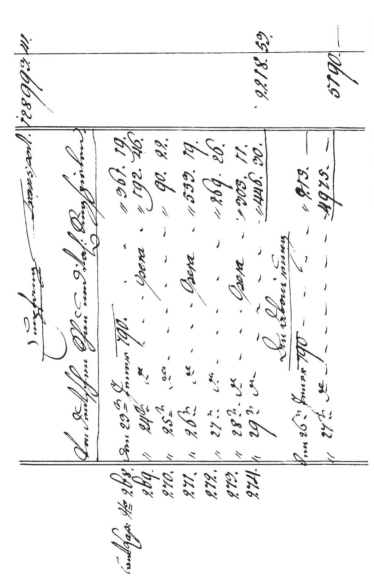

Figure 1. Box-office receipts from the Burgtheater for the week 23–29 January 1790 (A-Wn, Theatersammlung, M 4000).

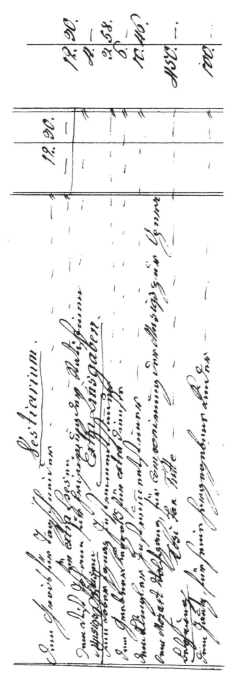

Figure 2. Mozart's fee for *Così fan tutte*, as entered in the weekly ledger of the Burgtheater in the week 20–26 February 1790 (A-Wn, Theatersammlung, M 4000).

The basic unit of money in Austria at the end of the eighteenth century was the gulden (also known as the florin, and hence abbreviated 'fl.' or 'f.'). The gulden was a standard unit into which the multitude of coins in circulation in various parts of the Habsburg empire could be converted, or against which they could be compared. According to an agreement signed by Bavaria and Austria in 1753 regulating the coining of money (the so-called *Münzkonvention*), the value of one taler was fixed at precisely two gulden or 120 kreuzer; thus one gulden was worth 60 kreuzer. The gulden itself had a kind of shadow existence; the only coin in circulation in Austria with a value of one gulden was more often called a half taler. Paper money, on the other hand, was printed in gulden denominations. Coins commonly in circulation included the taler, the half taler, various denominations of kreuzer (including coins of 30, 20, ten and, oddly, seven kreuzer) and various types of ducat.[11] It is often stated without qualification in the musicological literature that one ducat was worth four and a half gulden, but this was actually not true of any type of ducat until 1786. Three types of ducat appear in court payment records in the second half of the eighteenth century: imperial ducats (*kaiserliche Dukaten*), Kremnitz ducats (*Kremnitzer Dukaten*, so called because they were minted in Kremnitz, Hungary) and ordinary ducats (*Ordinari Dukaten*). Each type of ducat had a slightly different value based on the quality of gold from which it was made. From the beginning of the period considered here until September 1783, the respective values of the three types were 258 kreuzer per Kremnitz ducat, 256 kreuzer per imperial ducat and 254 kreuzer per ordinary ducat. Thus, until 1783, an imperial ducat was worth 4 gulden 16 kreuzer, or 14 kreuzer less than four and a half gulden.

From 15 September 1783 these values were slightly modified, and between then and 31 January 1786 the respective values were 262 kreuzer per Kremnitz ducat, 260 kreuzer per imperial ducat and 258 kreuzer per ordinary ducat. On 12 January 1786 Emperor Joseph II issued a proclamation fixing the value of both the imperial and the Kremnitz ducat at 270 Kreuzer, or four and a half gulden, to take effect on 1 February 1786.[12]

I have digressed into the history of Austrian currency because composers of operas and *Singspiele* seem always to have been paid in ducats, although payments were usually entered in the financial records in terms of gulden and kreuzer. The changing rates have obscured the consistency of the theatres' policy in paying for commissioned operas. In the season 1782–3, for example, Mozart was paid 426 gulden 40 kreuzer for *Die*

---

[11] Kreuzer was normally abbreviated 'kr.' or 'xr.' ('Kreuz' is the German word for 'cross' or 'x'). The standard reference on Austrian coins issued before the Second World War is Viktor Miller zu Aichholz, August Loehr and Eduard Holzmair, *Österreichische Münzprägungen, 1519–1938* (Vienna, 1948). See also Günther Probszt, *Österreichische Münz- und Geldgeschichte: Von den Anfängen bis 1918* (2nd edn, Vienna, 1983).

[12] Acts relating to Austrian currency values are transcribed in Siegfried Becher, *Das österreichische Münzwesen vom Jahre 1524 bis 1838 in historischer, statistischer und legislativer Hinsicht*, 2 vols. (Vienna, 1838). For the acts referred to here, see especially ii, 327–9, a table of currency values from 1 August 1779; 333–4, patent of 1 September 1783; and 336–7, patent of 12 January 1786.

Entführung aus dem Serail, an amount equivalent to 100 imperial ducats reckoned at 256 kreuzer per ducat. In February 1790, however, he received 450 gulden for *Così fan tutte*, an amount likewise equivalent to 100 ducats, but reckoned at 270 kreuzer per ducat, the rate prevailing at that time. Fractional gulden amounts recorded in the account books often turn out to be simply whole numbers of ducats; in the season 1778-9, for example, Ignaz Umlauf received 152 gulden 24 kreuzer for composing *Die Apotheke*, an amount equivalent to 36 ordinary ducats reckoned at 254 kreuzer per ducat.

The theatrical account books provide detailed information on the sources and costs of the music for almost every new operatic production in the court theatres between 1778 and 1792, including commissioned works, Viennese premières of works first produced elsewhere and revivals of works produced previously in Vienna. Table 1 lists the fees paid to composers and librettists for works having their world premières in Vienna; these works can be assumed to have been commissioned by the directors of the theatres or by the emperor himself.

A number of conclusions can be drawn from this table. On average, payments to composers for new German *Singspiele* were lower than payments for new Italian operas. With few exceptions, payments for *Singspiele* fluctuated between 36 and 75 ducats. Salieri was the first composer to receive as much as 100 ducats for his *Singspiel Der Rauchfangkehrer* in the season 1781-2.[13] The following season, Mozart received the same amount for *Die Entführung aus dem Serail*, and a few years later Dittersdorf received 100 ducats for each of three new German works, *Betrug durch Aberglauben*, *Die Liebe im Narrenhaus* and the enormously popular *Doktor und Apotheker*.

On the other hand, the standard fee for a commissioned Italian opera was 100 ducats throughout the period. Admittedly, the first two Italian operas listed in Table 1 are exceptions to this rule: Joseph Bartha received only 75 ducats for his ill-fated *Il mercato di Malmantile*, which closed after only three performances in 1784, whereas Paisiello received 300 ducats for his smash-hit *Il rè Teodoro* the following season. Otherwise, exceptional payments for new Italian operas were rare before 1792. In addition to Paisiello's work, the only operas between 1778 and the end of the season 1791-2 that fetched fees greater than 100 ducats were Salieri's *La grotta di Trofonio* and *Axur, rè d'Ormus*, both of which brought the composer 200 ducats, and Cimarosa's *Il matrimonio segreto*, probably the most popular Italian opera in Vienna at the end of the century, for which the composer received 300 ducats.[14] Thus, of the 26 commissioned Italian operas for which payment records are known, only four brought fees of more than 100 ducats. Some of those bringing merely

---

[13] Salieri's payment was actually recorded in the financial report for the following season.

[14] Salieri's payment of 200 ducats for *La cifra* is not counted here as an exceptional fee, since it was also intended, in part, as compensation for his revisions to *Il pastor fido*. Because so little is known about the process by which operas were commissioned, it is difficult to say whether extraordinary fees like those paid to Salieri, Paisiello and Cimarosa were fixed before the première (and thus predicated upon the composer's previous success), or if such fees were determined after the première, on the basis of the new opera's reception or the emperor's good opinion of it. Mozart's letter to Puchberg cited at the beginning of this article implies that the fee was discussed before the première.

TABLE 1

FEES TO COMPOSERS AND LIBRETTISTS
FOR OPERAS AND *SINGSPIELE* HAVING WORLD PREMIÈRES IN VIENNA
1778–92

Note: Although entries in the theatrical accounts are usually in gulden and kreuzer, composers' fees are converted here into ducats at the prevailing rate, as discussed in the text. Sources for the table are: the account books for the seasons 1777–8 to 1788–9 (HHStA, Hoftheater, SR 13–25; volumes for the second half of the season 1778–9 and the first half of 1779–80 are missing); the weekly ledger for the seasons 1789–90 and 1790–1 (A-Wn, Theatersammlung, M 4000); and the account book for the season 1791–2 (HHStA, Hoftheater, SR 26).

* indicates that the composer or librettist received an additional gift from the funds of the court theatre for the work in question. That gift is recorded in Table 2.

KD = imperial ducats (kaiserliche Dukaten)
OD = ordinary ducats
fl. = gulden

season	work	composer	composer's fee	librettist	librettist's fee
1777–8	*Die Bergknappen*	Ignaz Umlauf	—[a]	Joseph Weidmann	24 KD
1778–9	*Diesmal hat der Mann den Willen*	Carlo D'Ordonez	24 KD	Johann Friedrich Schmidt	one third of 250 fl.

Table 1 (cont.)

Year	Title	Composer	Fee	Librettist	Extra
	Die Apotheke	Umlauf	36 OD	Johann Jakob Engel, adapted by Joh. Fr. Schmidt	one third of 250 fl.
	Die Kinder der Natur	Franz Aspelmayr	36 OD	Joh. Fr. Schmidt, adapted by Johann Joseph Kurz	—
	Da ist nicht gut zu rathen	Joseph Bartha	36 OD	Stephanie d. J.	24 KD
	Frühling und Liebe	Maximilian Ulbrich	36 OD	Joh. Fr. Schmidt	one third of 250 fl.
1779–80	Die schöne Schusterin	Umlauf	—[b]	Reworking by Stephanie d. J. of French original	—[c]
1780–1	Der adelige Taglöhner	Bartha	—	Joseph Weidmann	part of 150 fl.[d]
	Was erhält die Männer treu?	Martin Ruprecht	72 KD	Ludwig Zehnmark	100 fl.
	Claudine von Villa Bella	Ignaz von Beecke	50 KD	Goethe	—
1781–2	Adrast und Isidore	Franz Adam Mitscha	36 OD	Christoph Friedrich Bretzner	—
	Der Rauchfangkehrer	Antonio Salieri	100 KD[e]	Leopold von Auenbrugger	—
	Das Irrlicht	Umlauf	75 KD	Adapted from Bretzner by Stephanie d. J.	—
1782–3	Der blaue Schmetterling	Maximilian Ulbrich	50 KD[f]	Maximilian Ulbrich	—
	Die Entführung aus dem Serail	Mozart	100 KD	Bretzner, adapted by Stephanie d. J.	100 fl. (to Stephanie)

Table 1 (cont.)

Year	Title	Composer	Payment	Librettist	Additional
	Welches ist die beste Nation	Umlauf	33 KD	Cornelius Hermann von Ayrenhoff	—
	Rose	Johann Mederitsch	75 KD	M. von Schönborn, adapted by Stephanie d. J.	—
1783–4	Die betrogene Arglist	Joseph Weigl	30 KD	F. L. Schmidel	—
	Il mercato di Malmantile	Joseph Bartha	75 KD	Goldoni, adapted by Francesco Bussani	8 Kremnitz ducats
1784–5	Il rè Teodoro in Venezia	Paisiello	300 KD	Casti	—
	Il marito indolente	Giacomo Rust	100 KD	Mazzolà	Included in da Ponte's yearly salary of 600 fl.
	Il ricco d'un giorno	Salieri	100 KD	Lorenzo da Ponte	200 fl.
	Die glücklichen Jägers	Umlauf	75 Kremnitz ducats	Stephanie d. J.	130 fl. (30 KD)
1785–6	L'incontro inaspettato	Vincenzo Righini	100 KD	Nunziato Porta	130 fl. (30 KD)
	Gli sposi malcontenti	Stephen Storace	100 KD	Gaetano Brunati	—
	La grotta di Trofonio	Salieri	200 KD	Casti	100 fl.
	Die Dorfhändel	Ruprecht	36 KD	Weidmann	—
	Die Dorfdeputirten	Franz Teyber	36 KD	Gottlob Ephraim Heermann	
	Il burbero di buon cuore	Martín y Soler	100 KD	da Ponte	(100 fl.)[h]
	Der Schauspieldirektor	Mozart	50 KD	Stephanie d. J.	100 KD?[i]
	Prima la musica, e poi le parole	Salieri	100 KD	Casti	—

Table 1 (cont.)

Year	Title	Composer	Fee	Librettist	Fee
	Il finto cieco	Gazzaniga	100 KD	da Ponte	(see note h)
1786–7	Le nozze di Figaro	Mozart	100 KD	da Ponte	(200 fl?)j
	Doktor und Apotheker	Dittersdorf*	100 KD	Stephanie d. J.	200 fl.
	Il Demogorgone	Righini	100 KD	da Ponte	(200 fl?)
	Betrug durch Aberglauben	Dittersdorf	100 KD	Ferdinand Eberl	—
	Una cosa rara	Martín y Soler*	100 KD	da Ponte	(200 fl?)
	Der Ring der Liebe	Umlauf	75 KD	Weidmann	100 fl.
	Gli equivoci	Stephen Storace	100 KD	da Ponte	(200 fl?)
	Il Democrito corretto	Dittersdorf	100 KD	Brunati	30 KD
1787–8	Die Liebe im Narrenhaus	Dittersdorf	100 KD	Stephanie d. J.	225 fl.
	Das wütende Heer	Ruprecht	75 KD	Ruprecht, after an original by Bretzner	—
	Il Bertoldo	Piticchio	100 KD	da Ponte, based on Brunati	200 fl.
	L'arbore di Diana	Martín y Soler*	100 KD	da Ponte*	200 fl.
	Im Finstern ist nicht gut tappen	Johann Schenk	50 KD	Leopold Hiesberger	100 fl.
	Die Illumination	Paul Kürzinger	50 KD	Johann Groß	100 fl.
	Axur, rè d'Ormus	Salieri	200 KD	da Ponte*	(see Table 2)
1788–9	Don Giovanni^k	Mozart	50 KD	da Ponte	100 fl.
	Il talismano	Salieri	100 KD	da Ponte	—
	Il pazzo per forza	Weigl	100 KD	Mazzolà	—
	Il pastor fido	Salieri	100 KD	Guarini, adapted by da Ponte	—
1789–90	La cifra	Salieri	200 KD^l	da Ponte	—
	Così fan tutte	Mozart	100 KD	da Ponte	—

Table 1 (cont.)

1790–1	*La caffettiera bizzarra*	Weigl	100 KD	da Ponte	200 fl.
1791–2	*Ariadne und Bachus* (melodrama)	Maria Theresia Paradies	50 KD	Riedinger	—
	Il trionfo d'amore	Pierre Dutillieu	—	Mazzolà	200 fl.
	Il matrimonio segreto	Cimarosa	300 KD	Bertati	—

a Oddly, no payment to Umlauf for *Die Bergknappen* has yet been found in the theatrical accounts. Umlauf was promoted from viola player to kapellmeister, and the promotion itself may have been his reward. He also received 128 fl. (30 KD) the following season for 'einige zu liefernde musikalische Stücke', but this payment seems unlikely to have been connected with *Die Bergknappen*. It is possible that the emperor rewarded the composer for the *Singspiel* out of his own pocket.
b Payment is probably recorded in the missing account book for the first half of the season 1779–80.
c The adaptation may have been treated as part of Stephanie's obligation as a salaried employee, or payment for it may have been recorded in the missing account book.
d The 150 fl. was intended as compensation both for this libretto and for the play *Mißbrauch der Gewalt*.
e Payment is recorded in the account book for the season 1782–3 (HHStA, Hoftheater, SR 19).
f The payments of 50 ducats was intended as compensation for both the music and the text.
g Payments to both Umlauf and Stephanie d. J. for this *Singspiel* are recorded in the account book for the season 1785–6 (HHStA, Hoftheater, SR 22).
h Da Ponte was paid 100 fl. 'for writing one Italian opera beyond his contractual obligation' ('für eine über seine Schuldigkeit vermög seines Contracts componirte italienische Opera', HHStA, Hoftheater, SR 22, item 176). Since da Ponte wrote only two librettos in this season, it is clear that his contractual obligation was one libretto per season (cf. the payment to da Ponte in the season 1786–7).
i According to a report in the *Brünner Zeitung* (no. 15, 21 February 1786), Stephanie d. J. received a gift of 100 ducats for writing *Der Schauspieldirektor*. There is no known record of this gift in the court archives.
j In addition to his regular salary, da Ponte was paid 600 fl. for writing three librettos over his contractual obligation. As demonstrated in note h, his obligation was one libretto per season. Since he produced four librettos in the season 1786–7, he was in effect paid 200 fl. each for three of the four.
k *Don Giovanni* was commissioned by and received its world première in Prague. Although Mozart and da Ponte collaborated on revisions and additions to the opera for its Viennese première, it was unprecedented for them to have received special payment (equal to half the usual fee for a newly commissioned work) for doing so. This is the only instance in the period under consideration of a composer or librettist being paid a fee by the Nationaltheater for an opera that had its world première outside Vienna. In 1784, Sarti received the box-office receipts from a performance in the Burgtheater of his *Fra i due litiganti*, which had its world première in Milan in 1782 (see Table 2). But Sarti received no fee from the court theatres for the opera, and the receipts were a special reward for its popularity.
l For this opera and revisions to *Il pastor fido*.

standard fees included such hits as Martín y Soler's *Una cosa rara* and *L'arbore di Diana*, and Mozart's *Le nozze di Figaro*. As will be seen, however, Martín y Soler reaped additional rewards for his two operas, whereas Mozart, as far as we know, did not receive anything extra for *Figaro*.

Payments to librettists appear more haphazard than those to composers. But most of the gaps in the column 'Librettist's Fee' in Table 1 can be explained. Some librettists, such as da Ponte and Stephanie the Younger, were salaried theatrical employees who received special compensation only for librettos beyond their contractual obligation.[15] Librettists from the minor nobility, such as Leopold von Auenbrugger and Cornelius von Ayrenhoff, would have considered accepting payment of any kind inappropriate to their station.[16] Librettos by 'foreign' authors such as Goethe or Bretzner were simply appropriated without compensation, since they were not protected by copyright.

It is also evident from Table 1 that the number of commissioned works varied widely from season to season. The rate of commissions was high from 1785 to 1788, when German and Italian opera companies were operating concurrently: nine new operas were commissioned in the season 1785-6, eight in 1786-7 and seven in 1787-8. The number of commissions fell dramatically in the following three seasons, owing to the disbanding of the German company and to general economic retrenchments necessitated by the Turkish war. Only three newly commissioned works were premièred in 1788-9, only two (including *Così fan tutte*) in 1789-90, and only one in 1790-1, the first theatrical season under the reign of Emperor Leopold II.

Fees were not the only means by which a composer, librettist, playwright or performer could be compensated; he or she might also receive a lump sum as a special gift, or be given the box-office receipts from a particular performance. In fact, until 1789, it was the policy of the Nationaltheater to reward authors of some new German plays with the box-office receipts from the third performances of those plays. Not all new plays were rewarded in this way, and the criteria by which works were selected for such a reward are not clear. In 1782 Emperor Joseph II proclaimed that the best translations into German of plays by such authors as Corneille, Racine and Voltaire should be rewarded with 50 ducats *and* the box-office receipts of the third performance.[17] In the *Allgemeiner Theater Allmanach von Jahr 1782*, third box-office receipts were referred to as 'prizes'; five plays premièred in 1781 were listed as

---

[15] Johann Gottlieb Stephanie was known as Stephanie the Younger (Stephanie der Jüngere, abbreviated Stephanie d. J.) in order to distinguish him from his half-brother Christian Gottlob Stephanie (Stephanie der Ältere), who was also employed by the Viennese court theatres.

[16] An author from the nobility had the option of donating the proceeds to charity: von Ayrenhoff, for example, donated to a local orphanage the box-office receipts of 264 gulden 25 kreuzer from the third (and last) performance on 22 January 1780 of his play *Alte Liebe rostet wohl!* (HHStA, Hoftheater, SR 15). On the policy of rewarding the author of a new German play with the box-office receipts from the third performance, see below.

[17] See point 3 of 'Punkten für die Theatral-Direction', 8 February 1782, in Rudolf Payer von Thurn, *Joseph II. als Theaterdirektor: Ungedruckte Briefe und Aktenstücke aus den Kinderjahren des Burgtheaters* (Vienna, 1920), 28.

having been accorded this honour.[18] However, financial records show that as early as the season 1777–8 almost all authors of new German plays received third box-office receipts, apparently in lieu of any other cash fee, and apparently regardless of the success of the play. In fact, several works rewarded in this way closed after the third performance. The practice of giving such rewards was halted upon the reorganization of the theatrical administration in 1789. The rewarding of box-office receipts was invariably recorded in the theatrical account books as an expenditure; there is no indication that such rewards were ever omitted from normal accounting.[19]

Composers, singers and actors were occasionally given box-office receipts as well, although there was no established policy of doing so. In fact, such rewards were rare, and apparently given at the whim of the emperor for works or performances he thought particularly meritorious.[20] As with playwrights, all such rewards seem to have been recorded as expenditures in the theatrical accounts. Between 1778 and 1792, box-office receipts were given seven times to actors, four times to composers, once to the four principal singers in the Viennese production of Paisiello's *Il barbiere di Siviglia*, and once to Klara Rothe, a member of the German *Singspiel*, to help her out of her 'disrupted circumstances'.[21] All 13 of these rewards are listed in Table 2. No librettist was rewarded with box-office receipts during the period, nor did Mozart ever receive a reward of this type.

Also listed in Table 2 are special cash gifts paid out of theatrical funds to composers, librettists and performers. These gifts, given at the command of the emperor, were normally treated as regular expenditures in the theatrical accounts. Such gifts were relatively rare; only 12 are recorded in the accounts between 1778 and 1792, six in the final season of that period. Of the 12, four went to performers in concerts or entr'actes, two to singers, two to actors, two to da Ponte (for the librettos to *Axur, rè d'Ormus* and *L'arbore di Diana*, for the latter of which he had also received a standard fee of 200 fl.), one to Cosimo Morelli and his dancers, and one to Martín y Soler for composing *Una cosa rara*.[22] No such gift to Mozart is recorded in any of the surviving theatrical records.

---

[18] *Allgemeiner Theater Allmanach von Jahr 1782* (Vienna, 1782), 144.

[19] Payments of third box-office receipts ('3te: Einnahme') are usually, but not invariably, recorded under the rubric 'Compositions and Translations'.

[20] A typical entry reads 'To Karl von Dittersdorf, the receipts from the opera *Doktor und Apotheker* on 10 February 1787, commanded according to the most high provision of His Majesty. Under No. 122 . . . 687.17' ('Dem Dittersdorf v: Karl, die auf allerhöchste Anschaffung Sr Mait: anbefohlene Einnahme der Opera *der Doktor und der Apodecker*, von 10ten: Hornung [1]787. sub N^o:122 . . . 687.17'; HHStA, Hoftheater, SR 23, p. 52).

[21] The story is reported by F. Kasimir Kunz in *Allmanach der kais. königl. National = Schaubühne in Wien auf das Jahr 1789* (Vienna, n.d.): 'Die Theatraldirektion stellte Seiner Majestät dem Kaiser die zerrütteten Umstände der Madame Rothe vor, und bat, der Sängerin aus ihrer Verlegenheit zu helfen, die Einnahme einer Oper zu bewilligen. Der gnädigste Monarch genehmigte die Bitte, und Madame Rothe sah sich wenigstens auf eine Zeit in einer besseren Lage' (p. 118). Rothe was given the receipts of 535 gulden 5 kreuzer from the performances in the Kärntnertortheater on 13 January 1788 of the two *Singspiele Die drey Pächter* and *Der Faßbinder*. The payment is recorded as item 123 in HHStA, Hoftheater, SR 24.

[22] In the *Brünner Zeitung* of 12 January 1787, it is reported that the emperor gave Martín a golden box as well as a sum of money: 'The new Italian opera *La cosa rara*, set to music by the

TABLE 2

GIFTS AND BOX-OFFICE RECEIPTS PAID OUT OF THEATRICAL ACCOUNTS TO COMPOSERS, LIBRETTISTS AND PERFORMERS, 1778–92

Note: This table includes gifts to composers, librettists and performers. Not included are: gifts of third box-office receipts to playwrights; fees for guest roles (although these were often quite generous); gifts to entrepreneurs of non-court theatres for free performances (*Freykomödie*) held at the command of the court during special court festivities; payments to composers or librettists for revisions or numbers inserted into operas by other composers; severance pay; or gifts intended to help cover the costs of illness or burial of theatrical employees. Members of the theatrical staff often received gratuities for services performed during the year (Stephanie the Younger frequently received such a gift at the end of a season), and composers, directors and librettists occasionally received lump sums for miscellaneous services rendered during the theatrical year. Gifts of these types are also excluded from this table. Sources are as in Table 1. Amounts are given in gulden and kreuzer, with ducat equivalents where appropriate; thus 333.05 stands for 333 gulden 5 kreuzer.

Bth = Burgtheater
Kth = Kärntnertortheater
KD = imperial ducats (kaiserliche Dukaten)

season	recipient	type	amount
1778–9	Martin Ruprecht, singer, *Die Bergknappen*	Gift	100.—

Table 2 (cont.)

1779–80	Joseph Lange and wife Aloisia, for performing in *Der Hausfreund*[a]	Receipts, 4th performance, 8 June 1778	333.05	
	Franz Brockman, actor, *Hamlet*	Receipts, 2nd performance, 5 Dec. 1779	504.11	
1780–1	None known			
1781–2	'The young people' who performed in an academy for the Grand Duke of Russia, 25 Dec. 1781	Gift	1177.36[b]	(276 KD)
1782–3	Maria Adamberger, actress, *Der Fähndrich*	Half of the receipts, 3rd performance, 30 Sept. 1782	355.48	
	Joseph Lange, actor, *Der Fähndrich*	ditto	355.48	
	N. Klinger, actor, *Der falsche Spieler*	One third of the receipts, 3rd performance, 12 Sept. 1782	69.15	
1783–4	Bussani, Benucci, Mandini and Storace, singers, *Il barbiere di Siviglia*	Receipts, 2nd performance, 15 Aug. 1783	614.58	
	N. Hutwalker, actor, *Der unglückliche Heyrath*	Receipts, 3rd performance, 10 Jan. 1784	434.29	
	Stephanie d. Ä., actor, *Kleopatra und Antonius*	Receipts, 3rd performance, 27 Dec. 1783	324.50	
1784–5	Paisiello, composer, oratorio, *La passione di nostro Signor Gesu Cristo*	Receipts, performance 30 May 1784 (Whit Sunday)	656.54	
	Sarti, composer, *Fra i due litiganti*[c]	Receipts, performance 2 May 1784?[d]	490.33	
1785–6	Giovannina Nani, singer	'ein extra angeschaffte Remuneration'	58.—	
1786–7	Dittersdorf, composer, *Doktor und Apotheker*	Receipts of performance in Kth, 10 Feb. 1787	687.17	

Table 2 (cont.)

Year	Recipient	Occasion	Amount (fl.)	(KD)
	Martín y Soler, composer, *Una cosa rara*	Special gift beyond the regular fee of 450 fl.[e]		(100 KD)
1787–8	Da Ponte, librettist, *L'arbore di Diana*	Gift	450.—	
	Da Ponte, librettist, *Axur, rè d'Ormus*	Gift	400.—	
	Martín y Soler, composer, *L'arbore di Diana*	Receipts of 5th performance, 27 Oct. 1787[f]	400.—	
	Klara Rothe, member of the German Singspiel	Receipts of performance of *Die drey Pächter* and *Der Faßbinder*, 13 Jan. 1788	565.37	
			535.05	
1788–9	Christiane Friederike Weidner, actress, for 40 years' service	Receipts of performance of *Emilia Galotti*, 7 Feb. 1788	579.56	
1789–90	None known			
1790–1	None known			
1791–2	Franz Rettich, actor	Gift	200.—	(12 KD)
	Doppler, actor	Gift	54.—	(18 KD)
	Cosimo Morelli, ballet-master, and his dancers	Gift, for two *pas de deux* danced in Bth, 9 April 1791	81.—	
	The Petrides brothers, Waldhornists	Gift for a Waldhorn duet performed in Bth, 11 Nov. 1791[g]	90.—	(20 KD)
	Zeno Menzel, violinist	A *douceur* (gratuity) for a violin concerto performed at Laxenburg	54.—	(12 KD)
	'Franz Vicario', flautist[h]	Gift, for concert on the 'flauto dolce', 14 Jan. 1792	108.—	(24 KD)

Table 2 (cont.)

[a] Two plays were performed on this date, *Der Hausfreund* and *Der Sklavenhändler von Smyrna*, but 8 June was the fourth performance of *Der Hausfreund* in particular.

[b] Equal to 276 imperial ducats, the largest gift in the period under consideration. Payment was actually made to Johann Leger and Kaspar Dombay, members of the administrative staff, who were charged with distributing the gifts to the performers. According to a report in the *Preßburger Zeitung* (no. 4, 12 January 1782), the concert included a quartet by Joseph Haydn performed by Luigi Tomasini, Franz Aspelmayr, Joseph Weigl and Thaddäus Huber. Haydn received 'an enamelled golden box set with brilliants', and the members of the quartet each received a golden snuff-box (see Marianne Pandi and Fritz Schmidt, 'Musik zur Zeit Haydns und Beethovens in der Preßburger Zeitung', *Haydn Yearbook*, 8 (1971), 165–265 (p. 182), and Eugene Hartzell's English translation, *ibid*., 267–93 (p. 274)). The concert occurred on the day after Mozart's celebrated musical duel with Clementi. It is not clear whether or not the sum of 276 ducats includes the costs of the golden box and the snuff-boxes.

[c] This opera, which was extremely popular in Vienna, was not commissioned by the Viennese court theatre; it was premièred at La Scala in Milan on 14 September 1782. It was first performed in Vienna on 28 May 1783. Sarti received no fee from the Viennese theatrical administration for the opera; the box-office receipts, which were given to Sarti at the command of the emperor, were a reward for the popularity of the opera or for the emperor's good opinion of it.

[d] *Fra i due litiganti* was not performed in the Nationaltheater on 2 May; according to Hadamowsky, the play *Geschwind, ehe es jemand erfährt* was performed on that date. The date in the payment book (HHStA, Hoftheater, SR 21) may be incorrect. Sarti's opera was performed on 2 June 1784; perhaps this was the date meant.

[e] The *Brünner Zeitung* reported that the emperor gave Martín a golden box as well as a sum of money (no. 4, 12 January 1787, p. 30).

[f] The performance was a special one, put on for Martín's benefit in the Kärntnertortheater.

[g] *Hamlet* was performed in the Burgtheater on this date, and the horn duet was probably an entr'acte. The Kärntnertortheater had been closed since February 1788 and remained closed until 16 November 1791 (with the exception of one performance on 17 July 1791); thus it is highly unlikely the horn duet was performed there.

[h] See Mary Sue Morrow, *Concert Life in Haydn's Vienna* (Stuyvesant, 1989), 279, for the text of the programme to this concert, where the name is given as Francesco Vicaro von Navara.

If the weekly ledger gives a complete picture of the theatrical accounts for the season 1789-90 – and there is no reason to assume it does not – then Mozart received neither the box-office receipts from a performance of *Così fan tutte* nor a special monetary gift from the funds of the theatres. Could Joseph II have given Mozart a gift out of his own pocket? Although characterized by Mozart as a 'tightwad',[23] the emperor is known to have given such cash gifts on other occasions. In March 1783 he sent 25 ducats to the box-office before Mozart's academy in the Burgtheater.[24] In February 1786 he furnished 1,000 ducats from his own discretionary funds to be divided between Mozart, Salieri, the theatrical company and the orchestra as compensation and reward for the composition and performance of *Der Schauspieldirektor* and *Prima la musica, e poi le parole* in the Orangerie at Schönbrunn.[25] In June 1786 the *Brünner Zeitung* reported that the emperor was so impressed with the singing of the soprano Brigida Banti that he sent her a gift of 100 ducats while her academy was still in progress:

> Recently, the singer Madame Banti, who is travelling to Warsaw and from there to St Petersburg, gave a musical academy in Vienna. Her voice is one of the most charming and moving, and is so melodious that it can scarcely be compared. She also received unanimous acclaim, and it is said that the monarch had a present of 100 ducats sent to her while she was still singing.[26]

An anecdote published in the Viennese newspaper *Rapport von Wien* in 1789 further testifies to the emperor's characteristic generosity:

> [A few years ago] the emperor was dining with several members of the nobility at his country palace Schönbrunn; by chance, a band of miners came by and made music in the garden; the emperor sent them 100 ducats. A lady expressed her astonishment that he would give so much money for some symphonies that resembled an inflammation of the bowels; the monarch answered:

Spanish kapellmeister Martini, has received quite extraordinary acclaim on account of the prevailing Spanish flavour, which is new here [i.e. in Vienna]. The monarch therefore condescended to present the aforementioned with a precious golden box and a sum of money.' ('Die von dem Spanischen Kapellmeister Martini in Musik gesetzte neue wälsche Oper, *la cosa rara* betitelt, erhält wegen des darin herrschenden und allhier neuen Spanischen Geschmacks ganz außerordentlichen Beifall. Der Monarch hat denselben dafür mit einer kostbaren goldnen Dose, und einer Summe Gelds zu beschenken geruht'; *Brünner Zeitung*, no. 4, 12 January 1787, p. 30). It is not certain whether both the golden box and the sum of money are subsumed under the payment listed in the theatrical accounts.

[23] 'Der kayser ist ohnehin knicker' ('anyway, the emperor is a tightwad'; *Mozart: Briefe*, iii, 201, letter from Wolfgang to Leopold, 10 April 1782).

[24] *Ibid.*, 261, letter from Wolfgang to Leopold, 29 March 1783.

[25] Regarding this payment, see the transcription of Joseph's letter to Count Orsini-Rosenberg of 7 February 1786 in Deutsch, *Mozart: Die Dokumente seines Lebens*, 230. According to the *Brünner Zeitung* (no. 15, 21 February 1786, p. 118), Stephanie the Younger received a reward of 100 ducats for writing *Der Schauspieldirektor*. Stephanie's reward is not mentioned in Joseph's letter to Rosenberg.

[26] 'Neulich hat sich zu Wien die nach Warschau und von dort nach Petersburg reisende Sängerin, Madame Banti, in einer musikalischen Akademie hören lassen. Ihre Stimme ist eine der reizendsten und rührendsten, und so melodisch, daß man kaum ein Beispiel hat. Auch erhielt sie einen ungetheilten Beifall, und es heißt, daß ihr der Monarch noch während des Singens ein Geschenk von 100 Dukaten abreichen ließ' (*Brünner Zeitung*, no. 52, 30 June 1786, p. 413). No record of this present has been found. The concert is probably that reported by Count Zinzendorf in his diary on 15 June 1786; see Mary Sue Morrow, *Concert Life in Haydn's Vienna: Aspects of a Developing Musical and Social Institution* (Stuyvesant, 1989), 263.

Princess! In such manner many hundreds of thousands go out of my purse each year and yet I'm called – stingy.²⁷

Unfortunately this personal generosity is difficult to document. Yet even though the mass of surviving archival material has yet to be thoroughly sifted by music historians, it is clear that Joseph II occasionally gave undocumented gifts to musicians from his own discretionary funds.²⁸

I know of only one instance in which a composer or librettist was compensated for an opera commissioned by the Nationaltheater with a gift from the emperor's pocket rather than from the theatrical funds. On 1 December 1784 Joseph instructed Count Orsini-Rosenberg to give a snuff-box (apparently full of ducats) and two additional rolls of ducats to the poet Giovanni Battista Casti, partly as a reward for his libretto to the opera *Il rè Teodoro in Venezia*:

> You are to hand over to the Abbate Casti in my name the enclosed snuff-box (of 105 ducats) along with the 2 rolls of ducats for *Il rè Teodoro* and the poem *Tartaro*.²⁹

Shortly after the première of the opera in August, Casti had turned down a payment of 100 ducats. Why he did so remains obscure, but his decision may have been motivated by theatrical politics. The emperor may have given the reward privately for the sake of discretion.³⁰

While a similar private gift from the emperor for the composition of *Così fan tutte* cannot be ruled out, such a gift must be regarded as highly unlikely in this case. Joseph was desperately ill at the time of the première, and almost certainly attended neither a rehearsal nor a performance of the opera. Even if Mozart had received a verbal promise of a special reward – whether double fee, cash gift or the box-office receipts from one of the performances – the promise may simply have been forgotten in the confusion surrounding Joseph's death and the accession of

---

²⁷ 'Wir erinnern uns . . . eines Vorfalles, der . . . ein Paar Jahre alt ist. . . . Der Kaiser saß mit mehreren Herrschaften auf seinem Lustschlosse Schönbrunn an der Tafel; von ungefähr kam eine Bande Bergknappen und musizirte im Garten; der Kaiser schickte ihnen 100 Dukaten – eine Dame äußerte ihre Verwunderung, das Er für einige gedärmentzündungsähnliche Simphonien so viel Geld hergebe; der Monarch antwortete: Fürstin! auf solche Art gehen des Jahres viele Hunderttausende aus meinem Beutel, und doch nennt man mich – geizig' (*Rapport von Wien*, XXXXIII Stück, 25 February 1789, p. 663).

²⁸ In discussing such gifts given by the emperor, H. C. Robbins Landon has pointed to payment records for the jewellery given to Princess Elisabeth Wilhelmine of Württemberg on the occasion of her marriage to Archduke Franz in January 1788. Landon suggests that such records might include information about gifts to musicians; see *Mozart: The Golden Years, 1781–1791* (New York, 1989), 191 and note 28. The source cited by Landon – Vienna, HHStA, Oberstkämmereramt, Sonderreihe, vols. 8–10, Geheime Kammerzahlamt, 'Vorschreib Buch auf Kostgelder, Anschaffungen, Präsenten, Kanzleÿ Aufgaben' (title from volume for 1788–91) – covers certain miscellaneous expenses for the years 1781–91, but contains nothing directly concerning gifts to musicians; it should be mentioned, however, that some pages appear to have been removed from the volumes (as, for example, from vol. 10, where pp. 89–98 are missing, and appear to have been cut out). These records appear to record the cost of snuff-boxes and similar items made to be given as gifts, but the recipients of the gifts are not named.

²⁹ 'Beygeschlossene Tabatiere (von 105 #) nebst den 2 Rouleaux Ducaten werden Sie dem Abbate Casti für den Re Teodoro und das Poema Tartaro als ein Geschenk in meinem Namen übergeben.' Transcribed in Payer von Thurn, *Joseph II. als Theaterdirektor*, 59. The symbol '#' was frequently used to refer to ducats.

³⁰ Letter from Joseph II to Rosenberg, dated 29 August 1784, six days after the première on 23 August (*ibid.*, 53). No payment to Casti for the libretto is recorded in the theatrical accounts.

his brother Leopold to the throne, or the promise may not have been honoured for some other reason.

There is no further mention of the fee for *Così fan tutte* in Mozart's letters, either to Puchberg or to anyone else. In a letter dated 20 January 1790, Mozart invited Puchberg to the first instrumental rehearsal of the opera, which was to be held in the theatre on the following day, and asked Puchberg for 100 gulden – in fact, these 100 gulden probably represented the remainder of the 400 Mozart had originally requested at the end of December.[31] On 20 February – that is, the day the emperor died and the beginning of the week in which Mozart was paid for the opera – Puchberg sent a further 25 gulden in response to Mozart's plea for money to pay an obligation 'that cannot be put off'.[32] Around the end of March or beginning of April, Mozart's letters to Puchberg began to refer to the composer's intention to petition the new emperor, Leopold II, for a position as second kapellmeister. No surviving Mozart letter dated after the première of the opera refers in any way to the fee for *Così fan tutte*, even by implication.

To summarize: Mozart claimed he was going to receive 900 gulden for composing *Così fan tutte*, yet only a payment of 450 gulden is documented. Potential explanations of the discrepancy are of two types: those that assume that Mozart actually received 900 gulden, and that the payment in the theatrical ledger represents only part of it; and those that assume that the 450 gulden recorded in the ledger is all that Mozart received, and that the explanation of the discrepancy lies elsewhere.

If we assume that Mozart actually received 900 gulden, then the 'missing' 450 gulden might be explained in two ways: it could have been paid out of the budget of some division of the imperial bureaucracy other than the court theatres, or it could have come out of the emperor's private purse. As has been pointed out, the confirmation or refutation of the first possibility would require a more thoroughgoing investigation of surviving court financial records and correspondence than has yet been undertaken. But preliminary research has turned up few promising leads; furthermore, since almost every known gift or extraordinary fee for a commissioned opera is accounted for in the theatrical records,[33] there is little reason to think that new payments will turn up elsewhere. If, however, Joseph II gave Mozart a gift out of his own pocket, and if no itemized accounting of the emperor's expenditures survives, then we shall never know about the gift. While the possibility of such a gift cannot be

---

[31] See *Mozart: Briefe*, iv, 102, letter of 20 January 1790. Mozart writes: 'Dearest friend! They forgot to deliver your recent so generous letter to me at the proper time, consequently I too could not answer sooner. I am deeply moved by your friendship and kindness; if you can and will still entrust the 100 gulden to me, I will be most obliged.' ('Liebster Freund! – Ihr letzteres so gütiges Billet hat man vergessen mir zu gehörigen Zeit einzuhändigen, folglich konnte ich auch nicht eher darauf antworten – Ich bin ganz gerührt von Ihrer Freundschaft und Güte; können und wollen Sie die 100 fl. mir noch anvertrauen, so verbinden Sie mich recht sehr –'.) In saying 'still entrust the 100 gulden' Mozart seems to be referring to the previous loan of 300 gulden.

[32] *Ibid.*, 103, letter of 20 February 1790: 'weil es eine Sache betrifft, die sich nicht verschieben läßt'.

[33] Exceptions are Casti's gift for the libretto of *Il rè Teodoro*, which was commissioned by the Nationaltheater, and payments to composers, librettists and performers for *Der Schauspieldirektor* and *Prima la musica, e poi le parole*, works commissioned privately by the emperor.

ruled out, there is no evidence to support it, and there are several good reasons to doubt it. For one thing, the emperor was mortally ill at the time of the première of *Così fan tutte* and obviously had other things on his mind.

If, on the other hand, it is assumed that Mozart actually received only 450 gulden, then one might think that he intentionally misrepresented his expectation in order to persuade Puchberg to lend him money, or that he was engaged in wishful thinking based on vague or perhaps misinterpreted discussions with the theatrical administration. No attempt will be made here to second-guess Mozart's motives; suffice it to say that no evidence suggests that he was lying or deluding himself. And a perfectly logical explanation of the discrepancy between the amount stated in the letter and the payment recorded in the ledger can be found without resorting to amateur psychoanalysis.

Let us assume that Mozart was promised 900 gulden for composing a new opera. We have seen that such rewards were bestowed on successful composers of commissioned operas, albeit infrequently. Mozart, whose operas before *Così fan tutte* had been well received, and who had composed, apparently without compensation, a number of arias for insertion into operas by other composers, was perhaps overdue to receive such a reward.[34] Emperor Joseph II was, by and large, favourably disposed toward Mozart; he had, after all, given Mozart a sinecure as court chamber composer. If, by any chance, further evidence should turn up to support the legend that the emperor himself proposed the subject for *Così*, it would be all the more likely that the opera was earmarked for special reward.

Yet the financial drain of the war against the Turks, as well as Joseph's preoccupation with that war and his own declining health, had led to retrenchments in the theatre, and at one point had threatened to lead to the disbanding of the Italian opera. A number of large budgetary cuts had already been made by the time of the première of *Così fan tutte*: the German *Singspiel* had been dissolved, the number of operatic commissions drastically reduced, and the policy of giving playwrights third box-office receipts stopped. On the other hand, Joseph had always been inclined to support local artists over foreigners, and there is no reason to believe that an extra outlay of 450 gulden for *Così* would have put an undue strain on the theatrical budget.

However, the emperor's death could not have come at a worse time for Mozart. Joseph almost certainly did not attend any performance or rehearsal of *Così fan tutte*. When he died on 20 February 1790, Mozart had apparently yet to be paid; payment was entered in the theatrical ledger in the week following the emperor's death. Any additional gift or payment to Mozart would have to have been made at the command of the emperor.[35] With Joseph dead, court chamberlain Count Orsini-

---

[34] Oddly, Mozart seems to have received no payment for the arias and ensembles he composed for insertion in operas by other composers, although other composers of such pieces were paid, at least occasionally.

[35] We know only that Mozart was paid in the week beginning 20 February, the day the emperor died. Since the exact date of payment within that week is not recorded, it is possible, strictly speaking,

Rosenberg, who was perhaps less favourably disposed toward Mozart than the emperor had been, may have been reluctant to honour purely verbal commitments of which there was no written record. And perhaps Salieri's 'cabals' – if such existed – did not, after all, 'come to naught'; the extra 450 gulden Salieri received for revising his opera *Il pastor fido* and an additional 450 gulden he received in May 1790 for 'modifications to various operas' seem particularly suspicious in this regard.[36]

Although it cannot be proved, evidence suggests that Mozart was a victim of circumstance. If an unwritten promise of 900 gulden had in fact been made, that promise may simply have evaporated upon the emperor's death. What impact this financial setback may have had on Mozart's precarious financial circumstances awaits further investigation.[37]

University of Southern California

---

that the fee was paid on 20 February. Thus, theoretically, the dying emperor could have made some last-minute pronouncement concerning Mozart, but this seems extremely unlikely.

[36] In the week of 1–7 May 1790, Salieri received 450 gulden 'for modifications beyond his obligation made over several years to various operas' ('dem Salieri Anton, für die durch einige Jahre ausser seiner Schuldigkeit gemachte Abänderungen bei verschiedenen Opern . . . 450.--'; in A-Wn, M 4000).

[37] Julia Moore, in her article 'Mozart in the Market-Place', *Journal of the Royal Musical Association*, 114 (1989), 18–42, gives a table of Mozart's income during his years in Vienna (Table 3, p. 21). That table can now be corrected to show a documented income of 1500 fl. in 1789 (800 fl. salary and 700 fl. for the String Quartet K.575) and 1385 fl. in 1790 (800 fl. salary, 450 fl. for *Così fan tutte* and 135 fl. for a performance before the elector in Mainz).

[19]

How original was Mozart?
Evidence from *opera buffa*

John Platoff

1   Gianantonio Zuliani, Garden scene from Carlo Goldoni, *Arcadia in Brentà* (Venice: Zatta, 1790)

It is precisely in the nature of genius that it seems inexplicable. We find Mozart's solutions astonishing in part because we cannot begin to see how they were arrived at—the path is smooth, all traces of struggle have vanished.[1] But our inability to understand Mozart's thinking is not as total as it might appear; and the fact that we cannot explain completely should not prevent us from attempting partial explanations, partial understandings, of his compositional thought processes.

In the case of Mozart's *opere buffe* the task is made far easier by what can be learned from the operas of his time. These works, whether by Salieri, Paisiello, Martin y Soler or some lesser composer, depended at every level on dramatic and musical conventions for their focus and logic. Flexible and unwritten rules governed their plots and disposition of characters, their length, the number and arrangement of musical pieces, and aspects of key structure, as well as the typical poetic and musical features appropriate to arias for particular characters. Mozart could no more stand outside these conventions than a brilliant Hollywood director of today (among whom, admittedly, it is hard to see a Mozart) can ignore the commercial realities of modern film-making. Instead Mozart and his librettist Da Ponte made the most of the typical procedures and structures of which *opera buffa* was constructed, at times relying on them literally, at other times altering, subverting or transcending them in original ways. By identifying as precisely as possible what the applicable conventions were for any particular operatic number or situation, we begin to be able to divine Mozart's thoughts as he worked within or around their constraints.

Mozart's own letters reveal that he was very attentive to what his operatic contemporaries in Vienna were writing—what worked and what did not. So it should not be surprising that much of the time he accepted and worked within the norms of *opera buffa*, his protestations of originality notwithstanding.[2] Donna Anna's final aria from *Don Giovanni*, 'Non mi dir', illustrates Mozart's straightforward adoption of some of these norms. Some writers have been uncomfortable either with the style of the piece or with its placement; Wye Allanbrook, for example, called it both 'a chilling affair' and 'the most intrusive aria of the opera'. In Hermann Abert's view, the scene 'is dramatically one of the weaknesses of the opera . . . probably included to allow more time for the setting of the final scene'. Edward J. Dent went so far as to say that the scene 'has no reason whatever for its existence' beyond providing Donna Anna with an aria, while Julian Rushton felt compelled to defend its dramatic importance from such attacks.[3]

Yet 'Non mi dir' is a rondò, a fact that explains the style, form and placement of the piece. The rondò, a showpiece aria in two tempos, in each part of which the main theme returns at least once, was a fixture in late 18th-century Italian opera.[4] One such aria was invariably provided for the leading soprano, above all if she were portraying a *parte seria* such as Donna Anna. What has not been previously recognized is that in Viennese opera in the 1780s, the rondò was routinely placed just before the Act 2 finale. (This is the case in more than half the *opere buffe* written for Vienna in that decade.[5]) So however we may choose to read 'Non mi dir' for what it says about Donna Anna, the location of the aria and its musical style—two sections in contrasting tempos, the second full of elaborate coloratura—reflect Mozart's and Da Ponte's adherence to a conventional procedure in Viennese opera.

By contrast 'La vendetta', Dr Bartolo's revenge aria from *Figaro*, illustrates Mozart's ability to combine or subvert stylistic conventions to make a dramatic point.

Bartolo's status as a secondary comic character calls for a *buffa* aria, an overtly comic piece that builds towards a climax of rapid patter declamation (like, for example, Figaro's 'Aprite un po' quegl'occhi').[6] But while 'La vendetta' largely fulfils these expectations at later points, its opening music is that of a grand aria in the *seria* style: a D major Allegro in common time, a full woodwind contingent to which trumpets and drums are added, and the noble stride of the 'exalted march'.[7] To an 18th-century audience, Bartolo would clearly have been singing music that was above his station, and its inappropriateness is confirmed later in the aria when he descends to the rapid babble of quaver triplets. This opening, with its temporary grasping at the noble style, depicts Bartolo's own visions of grandeur which the rest of the aria unceremoniously deflates. By employing a recognizable set of stylistic features 'inappropriately' Mozart pokes fun at his character, revealing the distance between Bartolo's view of himself and his actual status.[8]

A more self-conscious, 'intertextual' use of a conventional type may be observed in Don Alfonso's brief aria early in *Così fan tutte*, 'Vorrei dir, e cor non ho', which is perhaps the first representation of the underlying irony that pervades the opera. The tiny piece (only 38 bars) presents an agitated man barely able to stammer out to Fiordiligi and Dorabella his alarming news that Guglielmo and Ferrando must go off to war. All its musical elements underscore this agitation—the minor key, the rapid tempo, the rushing offbeat accompaniment pattern in the upper strings and the broken, fragmented phrases of the vocal line (ex.1). Later the mood is heightened by intense chromatic suspensions (as in bars 15 and 27). Yet the piece gains in richness because of its ironic stance: the audience, unlike the sisters, knows that Alfonso is merely feigning alarm, that his news is part of an elaborate game. To us this is a comic situation, whose humour is only intensified by the truly dark and painful character of the music. We understand that Alfonso is throwing himself fully into his role.

Mozart's Viennese audience would have understood something more: that Alfonso was displaying and parodying a stereotypical agitation, one they would have recognized from its non-ironic use in other operas. In Da Ponte's and Martin y Soler's *Una cosa rara* (1786), perhaps the most beloved *opera buffa* of the decade, the first entrance of the heroine is made with precisely the same expression of alarm (ex.2). The same key, tempo and metre, accompaniment pattern and breathless vocal phrases used by Alfonso express Lilla's dismay and calls for help. Here, however, they are to be taken seriously.

Ex.1 *Così fan tutte*, Act 1 scene iii: aria, 'Vorrei dir, e cor non ho', bars 1–9

My claim is not that Mozart's Alfonso was making fun of poor Lilla. Instead, and more broadly, Mozart took a conventional set of stylistic features that had an understood meaning and, by using it in an ironic context, heightened the expressive power of the irony.

At times, as I have suggested, Mozart embraced rather than challenged a given set of conventions; particularly in a less important number, such as a chorus, he might simply write an entertaining number that fulfils conventional expectations in a straightforward and unambitious way. This may be seen in a comparison of some peasant choruses by Mozart with those of his contemporaries (exx.3–6). Such pieces rely on the 6/8 metre,

2 Martin y Soler, *Una cosa rara*, Act 1 scene iv: aria, 'Ah pietà de mercede soccorso', opening

Ex.2 Martin y Soler, *Una cosa rara*, Act 1 scene iv: aria, 'Ah pietà de mercede soccorso', bars 1–8

Ex.3 *Le nozze di Figaro*, Act 1 scene viii: chorus, 'Giovanni lieti', bars 9–16

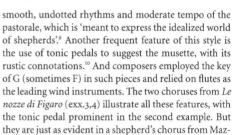

smooth, undotted rhythms and moderate tempo of the pastorale, which is 'meant to express the idealized world of shepherds'.[9] Another frequent feature of this style is the use of tonic pedals to suggest the musette, with its rustic connotations.[10] And composers employed the key of G (sometimes F) in such pieces and relied on flutes as the leading wind instruments. The two choruses from *Le nozze di Figaro* (exx.3,4) illustrate all these features, with the tonic pedal prominent in the second example. But they are just as evident in a shepherd's chorus from Maz-

3 Joseph Weigl, *Il pazzo per forza*, Act 1 scene vi: solo and chorus, 'Pecorelle, pascolate', bars 7–19

Ex.4 *Le nozze di Figaro*, Act 3 scene xi: chorus, 'Ricevete, o padroncina', bars 9–17

Ex.5 Joseph Weigl, *Il pazzo per forza*, Act 1, scene vii: solo and chorus, 'Pecorelle, pascolate', bars 12–20

zolà's and Weigl's *Il pazzo per forza* (1788) (ex.5) or a chorus of gondoliers from Casti's and Paisiello's *Il re Teodoro in Venezia* (1784) (ex.6), suggesting that everyone understood how groups of peasants or simple townspeople 'should' sound and presented them in stereotypical fashion without a great deal of thought.

We may contrast these choruses, in which Mozart adopted the typical approach without demur, to two more complex examples in which he strove for originality. Both of them arise from a desire to give the dramatic situation a more effective and realistic musical setting. Moreover, both produce their effects by rejecting or transforming conventional musical procedures.

The *opera buffa* duet typically functions dramatically to create or confirm a common emotional state in the two characters who sing it. Most often this state is love, but it may also be friendship, the profession of a common goal, or even mutual anger, as when two lovers quarrel. Not surprisingly, duets are constructed in a way that suggests this common emotional state in the music. Nearly all duets move from an initial dialogue, with the two singers alternating, to passages of simultaneous, largely homophonic singing in which they communicate their shared feelings.[11] This progression is generally repeated, so that a duet consists of dialogue, a 'tutti' passage for the two singers together, then more dialogue (either to new text or to the initial text repeated) and a closing tutti more extended and elaborate than the first.[12] Closing with a tutti passage both confirms the parallel feelings of the characters and provides an appropriately full musical climax for the duet.

Ex.6 Paisiello, *Il re Teodoro in Venezia*, Act 2 scene viii: chorus, 'Chi brama viver lieto', bars 24–38

For the most part librettists wrote duet texts with a final stanza to be sung by both characters together, making the composition of the closing tutti quite straightforward; but the need for this tutti was so powerful, and so clearly understood, that it was provided for even when the characters sang different words at the end of the duet. This was accomplished by writing their lines to rhyme and to fit together rhythmically. Here for instance are the two couplets at the end of 'Via resti servita', the duet of argument between Marcellina and Susanna in Act 1 of *Figaro*:

MARCELLINA:	*Per bacco, precipito*	I'll fly into a rage
	Se ancor resto qua.	If I stay here any longer.
SUSANNA:	*Sibilla decrepita,*	Decrepit old witch,
	Da rider mi fa.	She makes me laugh.

Not only do these two couplets share a final rhyme, but the first line of each is *sdrucciolo*, with two unaccented syllables following the final strong syllable. They are the only two *sdrucciolo* lines in the duet, and were clearly paired this way by design. The lack of dramatic parallelism—Marcellina expresses her anger to herself, while Susanna is triumphantly dismissive of her rival—does not prevent the couplets from being poetically parallel.

But whether two singers shared a final stanza or sang complementary lines, composers closed duets with a lengthy final tutti that relied on parallel, homophonic singing. At its most appropriate, as in love duets, this passage stressed the emotional union of the two characters (see for example the closing 6/8 section of 'Là ci darem la mano' from *Don Giovanni*). When the characters expressed disagreement or conflict, the musical parallelism may have been a bit less fitting but it occurred nonetheless. The final tutti of a duet from *Una cosa rara* is given in ex.7. The comic lovers Ghita and Tita have been arguing, chiefly by calling each other names: 'assassino', 'malandrina' and so on. Their final shared angry couplet may be translated as 'He/she wants to be my ruin, and wants to drive me crazy'. After trading a short phrase back and forth, with Ghita singing Tita's melody in inversion, the two sing the rest of the passage in homophony, concluding with a number of repeated cadential phrases. While they are by no means 'in harmony' dramatically, one might claim that the music still reflects their common emotion—mutual rage.

With this discussion as background we may consider one of Da Ponte's and Mozart's most original creations: the duet 'Crudel perchè' between Susanna and Count Almaviva in Act 3 of *Figaro*. The unusual psychological relationship depicted by the text is matched by an unusual musical setting; it is hard to avoid the conclusion that Mozart chose such a setting in light of the dramatic situation of the duet. The situation, of course,

Ex.7 Martin y Soler, *Una cosa rara*, Act 1 scene vi: duet, 'Un briccone senza core', bars 132-61

is that Susanna raises the Count's hopes by falsely promising to meet him in the garden by night. Their final couplets reflect none of the typical feelings:

COUNT:	*Mi sento dal contento*	In contentment I feel
	Pieno di gioia il cor.	My heart full of joy.
SUSANNA:	*Scusatemi se mento,*	Forgive my deception,
	Voi che intendete amor.	You who understand love.

This is neither the joy of united lovers, the agreement of friends, nor the mutual anger of two quarrelling characters. Da Ponte instead presents two dissociated emotional states—the Count expressing joyful anticipation while Susanna in an aside apologizes for her deception. The lack of any congruence between the feelings of the two is virtually unique in an *opera buffa* duet.

Musically the duet follows the usual formal pattern, with dialogue leading to a central tutti, then a repetition of most of the dialogue and a lengthier closing tutti. But the musical treatment of the tuttis is not at all typical: it depicts the dissociation between the two characters, while also (especially in the final tutti) addressing the need for a musical culmination to the duet. A comparison of the two passages appears in ex.8. The Count's vocal line presents the music he sings both in bars 28-36, the first tutti passage, and 53-61, the initial bars of the second tutti. Susanna's music for the two passages is given separately on the top two staves.

The initial tutti emphasizes the lack of connection between Susanna and the Count. The latter expresses his happiness in a pair of lyrical two-bar phrases, continuing to the cadence by repeating the opening bar of the first phrase. Susanna does not even sing for four bars, and when she enters, her one-bar patter phrases contrast

Ex.8 *Le nozze di Figaro*, Act 3 scene ii: duet, 'Crudel, perchè finora', bars 28–36, 53–61

Ex.9 *Le nozze i Figaro*, Act 3 scene ii: duet, 'Crudel, perchè finora', bars 61–9

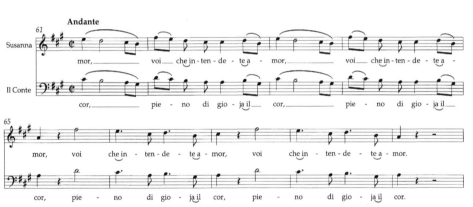

sharply with the Count's lyricism. Only for the last five beats of the eight-bar tutti do the two characters sing homophonically. (By comparison, in the preceding example from *Una cosa rara* the singers always sing the same sort of material, whether it be longer phrases, passages of detached syllables or rapid patter.)

In the closing tutti a greater musical richness prevails, which is fitting for the end of the duet but diminishes the sense of separation between the characters. While Susanna's line is virtually identical in its latter four bars to the previous tutti, its beginning replaces silence with a two-bar phrase (bars 54–6) that imitates the Count's first phrase. This suggests a greater connection between them, but that may not be the prime purpose for the addition. For Mozart has taken other steps to make the closing tutti more full, in particular adding pairs of flutes, bassoons and horns to support the vocal and string lines. (The initial tutti employed no woodwinds beyond a single flute in bars 32–4 and two flutes in bar 35.) Moreover, the closing tutti extends far beyond the eight bars of the first, continuing with nine bars of purely parallel singing for Susanna and the Count supported by the full orchestra (ex.9). In this closing passage musical considerations have superseded dramatic ones, and the conventional parallel writing that might be seen as contradicting Mozart's previous message serves to provide an effective end to the duet. It might be argued that having made his psychological point in the initial tutti passage, Mozart could have been less concerned if the point were weakened in the closing tutti. Despite its conventional ending the duet represents a striking instance of Mozart's ability to transcend typical musical procedures to make a particular dramatic point.[13]

To ignore or rework a set of conventions in a particular instance obviously represents an important compositional choice, whether conscious or not. And in Mozart's operas this choice seems to be made consistently for dramatic rather than musical reasons. Mozart frequently wrote magnificent music in his operas without having to break free of convention; his rejections of conventional approaches instead serve the goal of greater dramatic or psychological realism. Nowhere is this more forcefully demonstrated than in a particular setting of a thoroughly hackneyed situation—the revelation scene.

The surprise revelation or discovery of a character occurs over and over in *opera buffa*. And whether someone is exposed from a hiding place, or a disguised character reveals his true identity, or someone believed to be dead reappears, or the wrong character turns up in the right place—no matter the variation played on the theme—the sequel is inevitably a comic scene of stunned reaction from the other characters. Examples abound, in the operas of Mozart and his contemporaries alike. In the Act 2 sextet of *Don Giovanni* Leporello pleads for his life and reveals that he is not the Don, merely disguised in his cloak. In *Una cosa rara* the heroine Lilla emerges from a closet: this momentarily suggests that she has been dallying with the Prince of Spain, except that Lilla is followed from the closet (to everyone's shock) by Corrado, the Prince's elderly minister whose presence proves her innocence. In Livigni and Cimarosa's *Giannina e Bernardone* (1781; Vienna, 1784), the jealous Bernardone locks his wife Giannina out of the house, upon which she threatens to throw herself into the well, but instead drops in a large stone. When Bernardone rushes out to save her, she slips quietly into the house. Moments later, with the entire cast in an uproar of grief and confusion at Giannina's presumed death, she puts her head out the window and

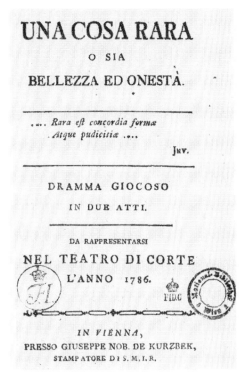

4 Martin y Soler, *Una cosa rara*, libretto (Vienna, 1786), title-page

asks, in effect, 'What's all the fuss? I'm trying to sleep!' And in the trio from Act 1 of *Figaro*, the Count unexpectedly discovers the hidden Cherubino while recounting how he earlier discovered the hidden Cherubino—an especially witty example of the genre.

Surely the most famous use of this plot device in 18th-century opera occurs later in *Figaro*, during the Act 2 finale when Susanna emerges from the closet instead of Cherubino. The Count, of course, is stunned; but what makes the scene particularly funny is that the Countess, the beneficiary of Susanna's quick thinking, is as taken aback by it as her husband. Mozart's musical handling of the scene reflects his determination to transcend the normal, somewhat undramatic procedure for setting revelation scenes. His original and exquisite solution can only be understood by examining the way such scenes are traditionally set to music.

The usual musical setting separates the revelation

Ex.10 Cimarosa, *Giannina e Bernardone*, Act 1 finale: 'Qui non c'è, neppure in casa', bars 340–61

scene into two discrete parts with quite different music. In the first part the character reveals him- or herself in a brief solo; in the second, the others react in astonishment, often in a self-contained musical movement, the shock tutti.[14] This arrangement undermines any sense of dramatic realism, since the surprised reaction must wait until the revealed character finishes singing his solo, long after the moment of actual revelation. Giannina's surprise reappearance in *Giannina e Bernardone* is typical (ex.10). The preceding passage of energetic activity comes to a halt so that Giannina can reveal herself in 16 sprightly bars in G. Only when she has finished, on a half-cadence, do the other characters express their surprise, in a Largo movement in E♭ (the third modulation by means of a deceptive cadence underscores their shock). Leporello's moment of confession in the *Don Giovanni* sextet has the same dramatic difficulty. He also takes 16 bars to reveal himself, whining somewhat piteously in G minor (bars 98–114). It is not until after he has asked for mercy four times that the others finally react (again with a deceptive cadence and shift to E♭). The striking change of key and texture at their entrance is musically effective, but it contradicts the fact that Leporello's presence has already been obvious for as much as a minute.

But in the closet scene from the *Figaro* finale Mozart achieves a musical setting that does not sacrifice realism: it presents Susanna's little speech without letting it upstage the shocked reaction of the Count and Countess. This is accomplished in two ways. First, Da Ponte and Mozart employ the simple expedient of giving the Count and Countess an initial reaction to Susanna's appearance *before* she announces herself (see the text of the scene below). Each of them simply exclaims 'Susanna!' in accompanied-recitative fashion, as part of the four-bar passage that links the first movement of the finale to the second (bars 122–5). As a result their silence in the succeeding 20 bars is comprehensible rather than inexplicable: having seen Susanna where they expected Cherubino, they are trying to figure out how this could possibly be, instead of (as in the typical revelation scene) waiting an unnatural length of time to voice their surprise.

COUNT & COUNTESS:	*Susanna!*	Susanna!
SUSANNA:	*Signore!*	My lord!
	Cos'è quel stupore?	Why this astonishment?
	Il brando prendete,	You've drawn your sword
	Il paggio uccidete,	To kill the page;
	Quel paggio malnato	Here you see
	Vedetelo qua.	that rascal.
COUNT: (aside)	*Che scuola! la testa Girando mi va.*	What do I see? My head is spinning.
COUNTESS: (aside)	*Che storia è mai questa! Susanna v'è là?*	What can have happened? Susanna in there?
SUSANNA: (aside)	*Confusa han la testa, Non san come va.*	They're both baffled And can't understand.
COUNT:	*Sei sola?*	Are you alone?
SUSANNA:	*Guardate Qui ascoso sarà.*	Look and see Who can be hidden there.
COUNT:	*Guardiamo, guardiamo, Qui ascoso sarà.*	Let's see, let's see Who is hidden there.

The second part of Mozart's original solution is the unique conception of the 3/8 Molto andante movement (bars 126–66), which effectively combines Susanna's solo with the shock tutti that would ordinarily follow it in a separate movement.[15] The Andante is an ABA form that works at two levels of musical stasis. In its first 20 bars Susanna presents herself to the Count in an elegant minuet, clearly mocking him both in her words and with the grave irony of a dance step appropriate to his noble station.[16] But this passage also typifies the shock tutti: it is slow and quiet, moving in two-bar phrases that initially are completely detached and separated by rests. These phrases go nowhere harmonically and melodically, their melodic pattern D–E♭–C–D sounding above a I–V, V–I progression (ex.11). Thus the quiet, static music of this passage already serves to convey the astonishment of the Count and Countess, though they have yet to voice it in words.

Ex.11 *Le nozze di Figaro*, Act 2 finale: 'Esci omai, garzon malnato', bars 126–9

The music that follows in bars 145–55 is even more static: the suspended animation of this brief passage represents the centre, the true shock tutti of this scene. The minuet disappears, and the only harmonic motion is an alternation between I and VII, attenuated by the tonic pedal and the smoothly descending scales in the

Ex.12 *Le nozze di Figaro*, Act 2 finale: 'Esci omai, garzon malnato', bars 145–51

first violins and first bassoon (ex.12). These scales also weaken the sense of the 3/8 metre, by moving through each even-numbered downbeat without a break while arriving on an unaccented low note on each odd-numbered one. The second violin's slurred two-bar units group into bars of I–VII harmony, offsetting the two-bar phrases of the Count and Countess that group into VII–I patterns. And floating above the other lines are Susanna's murmured triplets, which further weaken the clarity of the metre. In her solo the minuet dominated; here it has vanished into the mist.

Only with the descent of the bass to G and then F in bars 154–5 are the characters and the audience released from this moment of dreamlike confusion. The Count pulls himself together enough to inquire further, and Susanna bids him search the closet. Her ironic minuet appropriately returns during this dialogue, which soon gives way to the following Allegro movement.

This scene from the Act 2 finale of *Figaro* represents an ingenious effort by Mozart to avoid the standard musical clichés used in setting revelation scenes and to find a more dramatically convincing alternative. The key element is that the expression of shock by the Count and Countess is not unnaturally delayed; instead it is integrated realistically into the scene by the static music of the minuet, along with Susanna's mocking of the Count. While the use of a shock tutti is utterly conventional, Mozart's creation within it of a deeper level of suspended animation is brilliant and original.

In this case, as in the other instances discussed above, we can understand what Mozart was thinking about only by knowing the typical way such scenes were set to music, both by Mozart and by his contemporaries. An awareness of conventional procedures enables us to recognize both the conventional and the unconventional in Mozart's operatic music. As our comprehension of the conventions in this repertory becomes further refined, we should be able to talk more confidently about Mozart's compositional intentions. We can look forward as well to the new questions this approach will generate. Among them will certainly be a more systematic examination of Mozart's relationship to operatic conventions. To put it simply: when was Mozart conventional and when original, and why?

John Platoff is Associate Professor of Music at Trinity College in Hartford, Connecticut. His book Mozart and the opera buffa *in Vienna is in preparation.*

[1] The enormous interest in Beethoven's sketches clearly arises from our great desire to find those traces, to illuminate somewhat the mysterious thought processes that led to the brilliant result.

[2] In a letter to his father dated 10 February 1784 Mozart wrote 'I guarantee that in all the operas which are to be performed until mine is finished [*L'oca del Cairo*, which was never completed], not a single idea will resemble one of mine.' *The Letters of Mozart and his Family*, ed. E. Anderson, rev. S. Sadie and F. Smart (London, 1985), p.867. In many other letters Mozart refers to operas he had heard or scores and librettos he had acquired.

[3] W. J. Allanbrook, *Rhythmic Gesture in Mozart: 'Le nozze di Figaro' and 'Don Giovanni'* (Chicago, 1983), pp.229, 369-70 n.20; H. Abert, *Mozart's 'Don Giovanni'*, trans. P. Gellhorn (London, 1976), p.119; E. J. Dent, *Mozart's Operas* (London, 2/1947), p.171; J. Rushton, *W. A. Mozart: 'Don Giovanni'*, Cambridge Opera Handbooks (Cambridge, 1981), pp.102-3

[4] See D. Heartz, 'Mozart and his Italian Contemporaries: La clemenza di Tito', *Mozart-Jahrbuch* (1978-9), pp.281-3.

[5] In *Figaro* the rondò is the Countess's 'Dove sono'; initially Mozart also intended a rondò for Susanna immediately preceding the last-act finale, before replacing it with 'Deh vieni, non tardar'.

[6] For more on the *buffa* aria see J. Platoff, 'The buffa aria in Mozart's Vienna', *Cambridge Opera Journal*, ii (1990), pp.99-120.

[7] The term 'exalted march' is used by Allanbrook, *Rhythmic Gesture*, p.19 and *passim*, to describe the solemn *alla breve* style of utterances by noble characters. Daniel Heartz has pointed out the close relationship between the opening of this aria and the opening of King Theodore's first aria from Casti's and Paisiello's *Il re Teodoro in Venezia* (1784), a connection that underscores the inappropriateness of this music for Bartolo. See Heartz, *Mozart's Operas*, ed. T. Bauman (Berkeley, 1990), p.128.

[8] Many of the points in this paragraph are also made by M. F. Robinson, 'Mozart and the Opera Buffa Tradition', in T. Carter, *W. A. Mozart: 'Le nozze di Figaro'*, Cambridge Opera Handbooks (Cambridge, 1987), p.27.

[9] Allanbrook, *Rhythmic Gesture*, p.43, after Heinrich Christoph Koch, *Musikalisches Lexikon* (Frankfurt am Main, 1802), s.v. 'Pastorale'. See also D. Heartz, 'The Creation of the Buffo Finale in Italian Opera', *PRMA*, civ (1977-8), p.69.

[10] Allanbrook, *Rhythmic Gesture*, pp.52-5. For her discussions of the two Mozart choruses, see pp.92-3, 148-9.

[11] Hans Engel discusses this 'duet principle' in 'Die Finali der Mozartschen Opern', *Mozart-Jahrbuch* (1954), pp.115ff.

[12] The exceptions to this pattern are duets in which the characters sing together throughout, as for example 'Al fato dan legge' from *Così fan tutte*.

[13] While it is beyond the scope of this article, a great deal might also be said about the passages in which the Count asks Susanna, 'Will you come? You won't fail me?' and her 'Yes' and 'No' answers get confused. These passages, which Mozart created by reusing and rearranging bits of Da Ponte's text, have been cited as a psychologically acute depiction of Susanna's discomfort with her deception.

This duet is not entirely unique in the Viennese repertory. Salieri attempted something similar, though less complex psychologically, in a duet for Lisotta and Sandrino, 'Un abbraccio idolo mio', in his and Da Ponte's *La cifra* (1789).

[14] See J. Platoff, 'Musical and Dramatic Structure in the Opera Buffa Finale', *Journal of Musicology*, vii (1989), pp.219-22.

[15] Some of the following discussion is drawn from J. Platoff, *Music and Drama in the 'opera buffa' Finale: Mozart and his Contemporaries in Vienna, 1781-1790* (diss., U. of Pennsylvania, 1984), pp.69-71, 306-12.

[16] Among the many writers who have made this point see especially Allanbrook, *Rhythmic Gesture*, pp.123-4.

[20]
Salieri's *Così fan tutte*

BRUCE ALAN BROWN and JOHN A. RICE

The several contradictory, and even apologetic, explanations that were put forward concerning the origins of Mozart's *Così fan tutte, ossia La scola degli amanti* in the years following its première in 1790 reflect both the dearth of hard information concerning the commission to Mozart, and the unease with which the post-Josephinian era greeted this most unsettling of comic operas. One of the composer's first biographers, Franz Xaver Němetschek, wrote:

> In the year 1789 in the month of December Mozart wrote the Italian comic opera *Così fan tutte*, or 'The School for Lovers'; people are universally amazed that this great genius could condescend to waste his heavenly sweet melodies on such a miserable and clumsy text. It was not in his power to refuse the commission, and the text was given expressly to him.[1]

Constanze Mozart's second husband, Georg Nikolaus von Nissen, repeated Němetschek's assertion in his biography of the composer,[2] and in 1837 the theatre critic Friedrich Heinse sketched in further details, claiming that

> ... Mozart was in fact expressly commissioned by Joseph II to compose precisely this libretto. According to a rumour, an incident that had actually happened at that time in Vienna between two officers and their lovers, which was similar to the plot of the libretto, offered the emperor the occasion of honouring his court poet Guemara [*sic*.; Heinse confuses Da Ponte with one of his successors, Giovanni de Gamerra] with the commission to make this piece of gossip into a *Drama giocoso da mettersi in musica*.[3]

This seems unlikely. The attention that the emperor devoted to opera declined markedly in the final two years of his life, as his health failed, and his military campaign against the Turks absorbed what little of his energies remained.

---

[1] See Němetschek, *Lebensbeschreibung des k. k. Kapellmeisters Wolfgang Amadeus Mozart, aus Originalquellen* (Prague, 1808; rpt. Leipzig, 1978), 43: 'In dem Jahre 1789 im Monat December schrieb Mozart das italienische komische Singspiel, Così fan tutte, oder die Schule der Liebenden; man wundert sich allgemein, wie der große Geist sich herablassen konnte, an ein so elendes Machwerk von Text seine himmlisch süßen Melodien zu verschwenden. Es stand nicht in seiner Gewalt, den Auftrag abzulehnen, und der Text ward ihm ausdrücklich aufgetragen.' (All translations are those of the authors unless otherwise noted.) The overly precise date of December 1789 perhaps reflects Němetschek's awareness of the earliest mention of the opera by Mozart himself, an entry in his thematic catalogue ('Verzeichnüß aller meiner Werke') during that month for the rejected aria 'Rivolgete a lui lo sguardo' for Guilelmo.

[2] Georg Nikolaus von Nissen, *Anhang zu W. A. Mozarts Biographie, nach Originalbriefen, Sammlungen alles über ihn Geschriebenen, mit vielen neuen Beylagen, Steindrücken, Musikblättern und einem Facsimile*, ed. Constanze Mozart Nissen (Leipzig, 1828; rpt. Hildesheim, 1964), 92–3.

[3] Friedrich Heinse, *Reise- und Lebens-Skizzen nebst dramaturgischen Blättern. 1. Teil* (Leipzig, 1837), 183ff., quoted in Kurt Kramer, 'Da Pontes "Così fan tutte"', *Nachrichten der Akademie der Wissenschaften in Göttingen*, 1. Philologisch-historische Klasse, Jhrg. 1973, No. 1 (Göttingen, 1973), 1–27 (4): '... Mozart nämlich von Joseph II. ausdrücklich mit der Composition gerade dieses Librettos beauftragt worden ist. Einem Gerücht nach hätte eine zwischen zwei Offizieren und deren Geliebten damals in Wien wirklich vorgefallene, dem Intreccio des Textbuches ähnliche Stadtgeschichte dem Kaiser Veranlassung geboten, seinen Hofpoeten Guemara mit der Kommission zu beehren, aus dieser Klatscherei ein Drama giocoso da mettersi in musica zu machen.'

Furthermore, the emperor's opinion as of 1788 was that Mozart's music was 'too difficult for the voice'.⁴

We are not on any firmer ground with respect to Da Ponte's own accounts of the opera's genesis. In his *Extract from the Life of Lorenzo da Ponte* (a preliminary version of his memoirs), published in 1819, the poet included what is clearly a fabricated letter in which Mozart, reporting to his collaborator on the triumphant première of *Don Giovanni* in Prague, asks him to '*Prepare another opera for your friend Mozart*'. Da Ponte adds:

> I was so happy of the opportunity, that although I had on hand at that time [October 1787] two other dramas, nevertheless I did not neglect my favourite Mozart, and in less than three months I gave a tragicomic drama, entitled Assur, king of Ormus, to Salieri, ... an heroicomic to Martini, called L'Arbore di Diana, and a comic opera to Mozart, with the title of La scola degli Amanti, which was represented in Vienna, in Prague, in Dresden, and for several years in Paris, with unbounded applause.⁵

His claims with regard to the opera's success in Dresden and Paris are exaggerated, to say the least. And not only is the sequence of works here wrong (*L'arbore di Diana* had in fact preceded *Don Giovanni*), but this explanation is also at variance with the one Da Ponte offers in his Italian *Memorie*. There *La scola degli amanti* – Da Ponte's preferred title for *Così* – is said to have resulted from his liaison with the singer Adriana Ferrarese del Bene – the first Fiordiligi, who had only arrived in Vienna in the latter part of 1788:

> ... to my misfortune, there arrived [in Vienna] a singer, who without having any great claims to beauty, delighted me first of all by her voice; later, as she showed great propensity towards me, I ended by falling in love with her. ... For her I wrote *Il pastor fido* and *La cifra* with music by Salieri, two operas that marked no epoch in the annals of his musical glory, though they were in many parts very beautiful; and *La scola degli amanti*, with music by Mozart, a drama which holds third place among the sisters born of that most celebrated father of harmony.⁶

In neither account does Da Ponte offer any words on the actual content of the libretto. This stands in contrast to the relative abundance of self-serving analysis and anecdotal detail concerning *Le nozze di Figaro*, *Don Giovanni*, and many other of his libretti, in both the *Extract* and the *Memorie*.

The literary saturation of the libretto of *Così fan tutte* is so pronounced as to make Heinse's notion of an origin in a Viennese *Stadtgeschichte*, and Da Ponte's claims regarding his muse Ferrarese, almost beside the point. A text that draws as heavily as does *Così* upon mythology (via Ovid and Boccaccio) and Renaissance pastoral and epic poetry (by Sannazaro and Ariosto) would not seem especially congenial to

---

⁴ Letter of 16 May 1788 to Count Franz Orsini-Rosenberg, quoted in Rudolf Payer von Thurn, *Joseph II. als Theaterdirektor* (Vienna and Leipzig, 1920), 75.
⁵ Da Ponte, *An Extract from the Life of Lorenzo da Ponte, with the History of Several Dramas Written by Him, and among others, Il Figaro, Il Don Giovanni, & La scola degli amanti: Set to Music by Mozart* (New York, 1819), 19–20.
⁶ Da Ponte, *Memorie*, ed. Cesare Pagnini (Milan, 1960), 135: 'Per mia disgrazia capitò una cantante, che, senza avere gran pregio di bellezza, mi dilettò pria col suo canto; indi, mostrando gran propensione per me, finii coll'innamorarmene. ... Scrissi per lei *Il pastor fido* e *La cifra* con musica di Salieri, drammi che non formaron epoca nelle glorie musicali di quello, sebbene in varie parti bellissime; e *La scola degli amanti*, con musica di Mozart, dramma che tiene il terzo loco tra le sorelle nate da quel celeberrimo padre dell'armonia.'

Mozart, who had once declared that a comic opera was no place for anything 'learned'.[7] But in Vienna at this time there was another composer of opera buffa – Antonio Salieri – who, by virtue of his keen literary interests, was a more logical recipient of a text such as *Così fan tutte*. Evidence that he was in fact intimately involved in the genesis of what would become Mozart's final opera buffa has long lain close at hand, though without attracting the attention it deserved.

1

One eyewitness to the creation of *Così fan tutte* was the young composer Joseph Eybler, who helped coach the temperamental leading ladies while Mozart hastily finished the scoring.[8] Another witness was none other than Constanze Mozart. During the summer of 1829 the music publisher Vincent Novello and his wife Mary, both ardent lovers of Mozart's music, travelled to Salzburg to offer assistance to the composer's elderly and indigent sister; while there, and in Vienna, they interviewed Mozart's widow and as many others as they could find who had known Mozart, with the intention of writing a biography based on the materials gathered. Although the Novellos' plan for a Mozart biography was never realised, their surviving travel diaries represent an important source of information about Mozart and his circle.[9] Constanze Nissen (or 'Constance de Nissen Veuve Mozart', as she signed her name into their autograph album),[10] resident in Salzburg since 1820, spoke with the

---

[7] Letter of 16 June 1781 to Leopold Mozart, in *Mozart: Briefe und Aufzeichnungen*, ed. Wilhelm A. Bauer, Otto Erich Deutsch and Joseph Heinz Eibl, 7 vols. (Kassel, 1962–75), III, 132. Prominent among explorations of *Così*'s literary content are Ernst Gombrich, '*Così fan tutte* (Procris Included)', *Journal of the Warburg and Courtauld Institutes*, 17 (1954), 372–4; the discussion of the opera in Charles Rosen's *The Classical Style* (New York, 1971), 314–17; the above-cited article by Kurt Kramer; Andrew Steptoe, 'The Sources of *Così fan tutte*: A Reappraisal', *Music & Letters*, 62 (1981), 281–94 (later incorporated into Chapter 6 of *The Mozart-Da Ponte Operas: The Cultural and Musical Background to Le nozze di Figaro, Don Giovanni, and Così fan tutte* [Oxford, 1988]); Daniela Goldin, *La vera fenice: Librettisti e libretti tra Sette e Ottocento* (Turin, 1985), 116–29; Chapters 13 and 14 of Daniel Heartz, *Mozart's Operas*, ed., with contributing essays, by Thomas Bauman (Berkeley and Los Angeles, 1990); and the as yet unpublished study by Elizabeth M. Dunstan, 'Da Ponte and Ariosto'. See also Bruce Alan Brown, *W. A. Mozart: Così fan tutte* (Cambridge, 1995), 57–81.

[8] Friedrich Rochlitz, '*Nachschrift* zur Recension von *Eyblers Requiem*', *Allgemeine musikalische Zeitung*, 28: 21 (24 May 1826), cols. 337–40 (338–9): 'Denn als Mozart die Oper *Così fan tutte* schrieb, und mit dem Instrumentiren noch nicht fertig war, gleichwohl die Zeit drängte: so ersuchte er mich, die Gesang-proben zu halten und besonders die beyden Sängerinnen, Ferarese und Villeneuve, einzustudiren; wo ich Gelegenheit vollauf fand, das Theaterleben, mit seinen Unruhen, Kabalen u. dgl. m. kennen zu lernen . . .' (For when Mozart was writing the opera *Così fan tutte*, and was not yet finished with the scoring, and time was short, he asked me to conduct the vocal rehearsals, and particularly to coach the singers Ferarese und Villeneuve, whereby I had more than enough opportunity to become acquainted with life in the theatre, and with its disturbances, cabals, and so forth . . .).

[9] Vincent and Mary Novello, *A Mozart Pilgrimage. Being the Travel Diaries of Vincent & Mary Novello in the Year 1829*, ed. Rosemary Hughes and Nerina Medici di Marignano (London, 1955).

[10] See Pamela Weston, 'Vincent Novello's Autograph Album: Inventory and Commentary', in *Music & Letters*, 75 (1994), 365–80 (367). Weston notes (374) that Constanze Mozart Nissen conversed with the Novellos mainly in French.

Novellos on several occasions during their stay from 12 to 17 July. Many of her statements, as paraphrased by the Novellos, can be verified by other sources; others have the ring of truth.

Among the many subjects upon which the Novellos' conversations with the widow Mozart touched was Salieri's attitude towards Mozart, which prompted Constanze to speak of *Così fan tutte*. Mary Novello paraphrased Constanze's remarks as follows: 'July 15th. Salieri's enmity arose from Mozart's setting the *Così fan tutte* which he had originally commenced and given up as unworthy [of] musical invention.'[11] The 'of' here was supplied editorially, when the Novellos' diaries were finally published in 1955, and probably reflects the many opprobrious comments that have been levelled against the opera's libretto from Mozart's time onward. But Vincent Novello's more ample paraphrase of Constanze's comments tends to confirm that Salieri's dissatisfaction was with his own efforts, not his collaborator's:

Salieri first tried to set this opera but failed, and the great success of Mozart in accomplishing what he could make nothing of is supposed to have excited his envy and hatred, and have been the first origin of his enmity and malice towards Mozart ...

Neither Mozart's nor Salieri's biographers have taken much notice of Constanze's declaration, despite its resonance with Mozart's mention of 'Salieri's cabals, which however have all come to naught', in a letter inviting his Masonic brother Michael Puchberg to a rehearsal of *Così*.[12] This scholarly scepticism may be due partly to the fact that – if one believes Mozart – Salieri began to act maliciously towards Mozart as early as 1783 (the episode surrounding the replacement arias that Mozart wrote for Anfossi's *Il curioso indiscreto*)[13] and partly because physical evidence supporting Constanze's statement has been lacking. But such evidence has recently come to light in the form of a musical manuscript in Salieri's hand that records his attempt to set the libretto that Da Ponte entitled *La scola degli amanti* but that later, as set by Mozart, came to be known as *Così fan tutte*.

The card catalogue of the Musiksammlung in the Österreichische Nationalbibliothek in Vienna documents the library's extensive collection of Salieri's music manuscripts, including many autographs. Under the subheading 'Terzette' is a card that records the text incipits of two such pieces: 'È la fede delle femine' (*sic*) and 'La mia Dorabella', with the further annotation 'Così fan tutte'.[14] The manuscript to which this card refers, S.m. 4531, is in Salieri's hand throughout. That it has failed to

---

[11] Novello, *A Mozart Pilgrimage*, 127.
[12] H. C. Robbins Landon, for instance, quotes without comment the remarks of Mary Novello, along with other statements on the origins of *Così fan tutte*, in *Mozart: The Golden Years, 1781–1791* (London and New York, 1989), 174. Mozart's invitation to Puchberg, from the end of December 1789, is worded as follows: 'Donnerstag aber lade ich Sie (aber nur Sie allein) um 10 Uhr Vormittag zu mir ein, zu einer kleinen Oper=Probe; – nur Sie und *Haydn* lade ich dazu. – Mündlich werde ich Ihnen Cabalen von Salieri erzählen, die aber alle schon zu Wasser geworden sind –' (*Mozart: Briefe*, IV, 100).
[13] See Mozart's letter to his father of 2 July 1783, in *Mozart: Briefe*, III, 276–7.
[14] The manuscript was transferred to the Musiksammlung from the former Hofkapelle in 1929, at which time it was given a standard library binding. The authors are grateful to Dr Rita Steblin of Vienna for checking the accuracy of our transcription of the catalogue card, and for supplying information on the library's acquisition of the manuscript.

Plate 1. The first page of 'È la fede delle femmine' from the autograph of Antonio Salieri's *Così fan tutte* (A-Wn, S.m. 4531)

attract the attention of Mozart scholars is not surprising; but that students of Salieri's music have not noticed it calls for some explanation. Those who have browsed through the catalogue of the Musiksammlung's holdings of Salieri's operatic music have naturally focused on completed works, not the many individual numbers, or collections of these, which are catalogued separately. Only Rudolph Angermüller has attempted to list Salieri's complete secular vocal works. His list includes several terzetti in the archive of the Gesellschaft der Musikfreunde, the other great repository of Salieri's autograph manuscripts,[15] but not 'È la fede delle fem[m]ine' or 'La mia Dorabella'. Nor do these numbers appear in his list of 'Varia', which includes some fragments and beginnings of operas that were never brought to completion.

S.m. 4531 consists of eight oblong folios, with Salieri's signature – 'd'Ant. Salieri' – at the upper right of folio 1^r (see Plate 1).[16] The terzetti are bound in reverse order, compared to that in Mozart's *Così*. 'È la fede delle fem[m]ine' is written on folios 1^r to 4^r, and 'La mia Dorabella' occupies folios 5^r to 8^v; on folio 4^v (the back of the leaf on which 'È la fede' concludes) there is a short recitative beginning

---

[15] Rudolph Angermüller, *Antonio Salieri: Sein Leben und seine weltlichen Werke unter besonderer Berücksichtigung seiner 'großen' Opern*, 3 vols. (Munich, 1971–4), vol. I.

[16] This same form of signature is to be found on other of Salieri's autograph scores, particularly those of detached or miscellaneous pieces – e.g., the aria 'Sento l'amico speme' from the disorderly collection of numbers from the composer's *Semiramide* (Munich, 1782; A-Wn, Mus. Hs. 16605). The full score of *La locandiera* (Vienna, 1773; A-Wn, Mus. Hs. 16179) is also signed by Salieri in this fashion.

Ex. 1 Antonio Salieri, 'È la fede delle femmine' (transcription, in short score)

'Terminiamo una volta' and, after the recitative, the instructions 'segue subito – È la fede delle femine' (see Plate 3, below). Reinforcing this instruction is another note in Salieri's hand at the top of folio 1^r: 'NB. Si canti prima il Recit° ch'è scritto nell' [cancelled:] altra facciata [added later:] ultima facciata'. At present, the first four folios comprise a bifolium flanked by two loose sheets; whether the latter originally formed another bifolium is impossible to say without dismantling the modern

Ex. 1 (cont'd)

binding. The torso of 'La mia Dorabella' fills two nested bifolia. 'È la fede' is complete, and in full score, with an accompaniment of strings, oboes, bassoons and horns in D. For 'La mia Dorabella' only the vocal parts have been entered, up to bar 65, at the end of folio 8^v, at which point the manuscript breaks off; presumably

Ex. 1 (cont'd)

this is all that survives of what was once a complete draft. There are marginal indications for an orchestra of strings, oboes and horns in B♭, but Salieri wrote out only the first two bars of the first violin part, and less than a bar of the bass (b. 51).

Salieri composed the two numbers on at least two different kinds of paper, one of which Mozart is known also to have used. 'La mia Dorabella' is on paper showing a watermark that Alan Tyson designated as no. 100 in his catalogue of watermarks in Mozart's autograph scores; this was the second of the two types of paper used by Mozart for most of *Così fan tutte*, and in several other works composed from 1789 until shortly before his death.[17] Salieri used the same paper also in parts of the autograph score of *La cifra*, first performed on 11 December 1789 (A-Wn, Mus. Hs. 16514). The appearance of Watermark no. 100 in the autograph score of Salieri's terzetti does not in itself pinpoint the date of their composition, but suggests that their origin was roughly contemporary to *La cifra* and to Mozart's *Così*.

Mozart completed *Così* shortly before its première on 26 January 1790; in his thematic catalogue he dated the opera 'im Jenner'. His entry from December 1789 describing the aria 'Rivolgete a lui lo sguardo' as having originally been 'meant for the opera *Così fan tutte*, for Benucci', is clearly from a late stage of the compositional process – by which time the definitive title of the opera had already been decided upon. It is unlikely that Salieri would have begun composing *La scola degli amanti* after the completion of *La cifra* (premièred on 11 December 1789), because by then Mozart was certainly far along with his setting of the libretto. Assuming that Salieri was busy with *La cifra* at least from the beginning of November until the première, and that Da Ponte did in fact write his libretto with Ferrarese in mind, Salieri probably began and then broke off the composition of *La scola degli amanti* sometime between his mistress's Viennese début (13 October 1788) and early November 1789. As shall be seen presently, the period during which Salieri worked on the project may actually have been considerably shorter than this.

There are good reasons for supposing that Da Ponte might have intended the libretto of *La scola degli amanti* for Salieri rather than for Mozart. Foremost among them is the close accord between the nature of the text and Salieri's literary knowledge and interests. In his memoirs, the librettist describes Salieri as 'cultivated, and learned, though a composer, and extremely enamoured of literati'.[18] Such erudition, unusual in a composer, was the result of a careful programme of training (supervised by Salieri's mentor Florian Gassmann), which included instruction in Latin and in Italian poetry; the young Salieri was also in frequent contact with the

---

[17] The paper of watermark no. 100 corresponds to 'Type II' in Tyson's analysis of paper-types used in *Così*, in *Mozart: Studies of the Autograph Scores* (Cambridge, Mass., and London, 1987), 180–3. The first completed and dated work that Mozart wrote on this paper was the aria 'Schon lacht der holde Frühling', K. 580 (17 September 1789). See Alan Tyson, *Dokumentation der autographen Überlieferung: Wasserzeichen-Katalog*, in Mozart, *Neue Ausgabe sämtlicher Werke*, X: 33/2 (Kassel, 1992), 47–8. Surviving examples of this paper among Mozart's autographs are all ruled with twelve staves, whereas the score of Salieri's piece has only ten; as Tyson suggests elsewhere (227), Mozart may have maintained a stock of unruled paper, portions of which he took to a music shop for ruling from time to time.

[18] Da Ponte, *Memorie*, 91: 'colto, dotto, sebbene maestro di cappella, ed amantissimo de' letterati'.

imperial poet Metastasio and other Italian librettists resident in Vienna. Among Salieri's Italian operas – both serious and comic – works derived from or parodying higher forms of literature figure prominently. His 1789 setting of *Il pastor fido*, Da Ponte's operatic adaptation of Guarini's pastoral epic, has already been mentioned. Salieri's first work for the stage, *Le donne letterate* of 1770, was also overtly literary in content, with a cast that included choruses of 'Letterati' and scholars in doctoral robes. The work's librettist, Giovanni Gastone Boccherini, collaborated with Salieri two years later to produce *La secchia rapita* (The stolen bucket), after a 'poema eroicomico' by the late Renaissance writer Alessandro Tassoni. Boccherini's libretto, like its model, mocked the style of epics by poets such as Homer and Ariosto; extending this parody in a more musical direction, Boccherini also included humorous imitations of favourite Metastasian arias. Several other libretti offered to Salieri fairly bristle with literary references – Da Ponte's *Il ricco d'un giorno* (1784), for instance, with its 'sentenza' quoted from Cato (I.2), and Giambattista Casti's *Prima la musica e poi le parole* (1786), which alludes to two characters from Ariosto's *Orlando furioso* (in Scene 5).

This much is suggestive of a composer eager to associate himself with libretti of some literary ostentation, in a genre where this was not always expected. In the realm of serious opera, too, Salieri was anxious that posterity regard him as well versed in the higher genres of literature, which librettists regularly mined for source material. As he did with many of his operatic works, late in life Salieri read through and annotated his autograph score to *Armida* (1771, on a libretto by Marco Coltellini), explaining his compositional goals and methods:

Already at that [young] age I had acquired the habit, in setting to music poetry taken from history or from some other source, of reading the poem or story from which the poet had drawn his subject during the entire time I was composing. Reading those cantos of Tasso's *Gerusalemme liberata* that involve Rinaldo on the island of Armida gave me the idea of composing a sort of pantomime for the overture of this opera, as a preface [antisoggetto] . . .[19]

One supposes that in embarking on a setting of *La scola degli amanti* Salieri read (or reread) that other great Renaissance epic, *Orlando furioso*, which was one of the principal sources for Da Ponte's libretto.

Another feature of Da Ponte's libretto that points to Salieri is its original title, *La scola degli amanti*. Da Ponte never departed from calling the opera by this title, even when referring, many years later, to Mozart's setting. Da Ponte may have intended not only the libretto's original title (with its distinctive spelling 'scola') but also several aspects of the plot as references to the opera with which Joseph's comic troupe introduced itself in 1783: Salieri's *La scola de' gelosi*, on a text by Da Ponte's

---

[19] A-Wn, Mus. Hs. 16517: 'Già d'allora [i.e., 'in fresca età'] pigliai il costume, mettendo in musica poesia tirata dalla storia o d'altra fonte, di legger, per tutto il tempo che componevo, il Poema e la storia da cui il Poeta avea tirato il suo soggetto. La lettura dei Canti nella Gerusalemme liberata del Tasso che riguardano Rinaldo nell'Isola d'Armida, mi han fatto venir l'idea di compor per sinfonia di quest'opera una specie di Pantomima, come un antisoggetto.'

friend and mentor Caterino Mazzolà.[20] In this opera, the attempts of the amorous Count to seduce the middle-class Ernestina inflame the jealousy of both his wife the Countess and Ernestina's husband Blasio. The lieutenant, the teacher of this school, advises Blasio and the Countess to make their spouses jealous. He is a man of experience, playing a role analogous to that of Don Alfonso in *La scola degli amanti*. Like Alfonso, he coveys his knowledge of women in the form of a maxim:

> Chi vuol nella femmina
> Trovar fedeltà,
> La lasci padrona
> Di sua libertà.

(He who wishes to find fidelity in a woman should allow her to remain mistress of her liberty.)

The lieutenant's maxim appears – always in G major and accompanied by two horns – at the beginning and end of his aria 'Chi vuol nella femmina', and again, quoted by the servant Lumaca, in the finale of Act II.

Don Alfonso gives a similarly epigrammatic lesson on the fidelity of women in the opening scene of *La scola degli amanti*, in the terzetto 'È la fede delle femmine', which takes its first quatrain (with one crucial alteration in the first line) from an aria in Metastasio's *Demetrio* of 1731 (III.3):

> È fede degli amanti
> Come l'araba fenice:
> Che vi sia, ciascun lo dice;
> Dove sia, nessun lo sa.

(The faith of lovers is like the Arabian phoenix; everyone says it exists, but no one knows where to find it.)

Although the phoenix-metaphor (or simile) was ubiquitous in Classical and Italian literature – appearing, for example, in the frame to a tale in *Orlando furioso* upon which Da Ponte drew in composing *La scola degli amanti*, both Goldoni and Da Ponte had earlier quoted or paraphrased this specific Metastasian version, with the expectation that their audiences would recognise it.[21] Salieri had shown himself partial to Metastasian quotation and parody earlier in his career as well, with *La secchia rapita* of 1772. Even in the single German *Singspiel* he wrote for Joseph's Nationaltheater, *Der Rauchfangkehrer* of 1781, Salieri managed to create opportunities for settings of Metastasian verses from both *Attilio Regolo* and *Didone*

---

[20] Mazzolà's and Salieri's opera had first been performed in Venice during Carnival 1779. French 'école' plays (i.e., with this word in their titles) far outnumber Italian 'scuola' (or 'scola') libretti. When Da Ponte wrote *La scola degli amanti* only a handful of such operas had been performed; see Claudio Sartori, *I libretti italiani a stampa dalle origini al 1800*, 7 vols (Cuneo, 1990–94), V, 160–6. These works included, as it happens, an opera entitled *La scola degli amanti* by Giuseppe Palombo which, with music by Giacomo Tritto, was given in Naples in 1783 and in Palermo in 1784.

[21] Goldoni quoted the quatrain in *La scuola moderna* of 1748; see Heartz, *Mozart's Operas*, 229. Da Ponte's earliest use of this maxim was in his first libretto for Vienna – and for Salieri, *Il ricco d'un giorno* of 1784 (II.9, Giacinto to Emilia): 'Siete savissima,/Ciascun lo dice,/Siete l'arabica/Rara Fenice.'

abbandonata.²² (One assumes that Salieri's suggestion lay behind his librettist Joseph Leopold Auenbrugger's ploy of making the title character an Italian chimneysweep, singing teacher, and former student of Metastasio's 'caro gemello', the castrato Farinelli).²³ Mozart knew and respected Metastasio's works (as is clear from the correspondence surrounding *Idomeneo*), but there is no example in his comic operas, prior to *Così fan tutte*, of overt quotation or parody of his aria texts, as there is in Salieri's œuvre.

If the libretto for *La scola degli amanti* shows affinities to texts previously set by Salieri, and to the title of one of them in particular, in its final form as *Così fan tutte* it also contains pointed references, both textual and musical, to his own and Mozart's earlier opera *Le nozze di Figaro*. The most obvious of these references is the motto of the title, taken from the lines 'Così fan tutte le belle,/Non c'è alcuna novità' which Basilio sings in No. 7 of *Figaro*, commenting on Count Almaviva's discovery of Cherubino in Susanna's chambers. Evidence from Mozart's autograph score of *Così* suggests that the opera's 'lesson' (No. 30), which ends with the words 'Così fan tutte' sung by Alfonso to a deceptive cadence and repeated by the officers to an emphatic full cadence, was incorporated into *La scola degli amanti* late in the compositional process, perhaps at Mozart's suggestion.²⁴ We cannot know, given the fragmentary nature of Salieri's setting, whether the libretto already contained these words at the time he received it. But Mozart gave the motto great prominence by using it as a frame for his opera's Overture; it was also probably also Mozart who chose the motto as the opera's primary title, moving Da Ponte's original title to a subsidiary position. The poster for the opera's first performance advertised it as 'COSI FAN TUTTE,/O SIA:/LA SCOLA DEGLI AMANTI' (the alternative title in letters smaller than those of the main title). With this change Mozart (presumably) obscured the libretto's references to *La scola de' gelosi* and put his personal stamp on the libretto with a title recalling one of his own operas rather than one of Salieri's.

2

The Nationalbibliothek manuscript suggests that Salieri started *La scola degli amanti* at the beginning, as was his usual practice. Salieri recorded in an autobiographical sketch how he went about the composition of his first comic opera, *Le donne letterate*, in 1769. Having first developed a tonal plan for the entire opera, he writes,

I felt an irresistible urge to set to music the opera's *introduzione* [the ensemble, often multipartite, with which opere buffe of the period generally opened]. I tried to imagine as vividly as possible the personalities of the characters and the situations in which they found themselves, and right away I found an orchestral motif that seemed to me to carry and unify the piece's vocal line, which was fragmentary on account of the text. I now imagined myself in the parterre, hearing my ideas being performed; they seemed in character; I tried them

---

[22] The pieces in question are the aria 'Se più felice oggetto' from the first-named opera, and the recitative 'Basta, vinceste: eccoti il foglio' and aria 'Ah non lasciarmi, no' from the second.
[23] See Volkmar Braunbehrens, *Maligned Master: The Real Story of Antonio Salieri*, trans. Eveline L. Kanes (New York, 1992), 75, 273.
[24] See Tyson, *Mozart: Studies of the Autograph Scores*, 190, 197.

again, and since I was satisfied with them, I continued further. So, in half an hour, a sketch of the *introduzione* was down on paper. Who was happier than I!²⁵

Twenty years later, in embarking upon *La scola degli amanti*, Salieri was confronted not with an *introduzione* per se, but with a libretto beginning with three terzetti in rapid succession (assuming that the third already existed prior to Mozart's involvement in the project). But as these numbers were all small in scale, and for the same three characters, together with their intervening recitatives they can be considered as a modified *introduzione*. The two terzetti of S.m. 4531 are in keys a third apart ('La mia Dorabella' in B♭, 'È la fede' in D); in Mozart's later setting all three pieces are related by thirds, descending through the opera's tonic triad, G–E–C. Salieri composed the numbers' vocal framework first; this is evident even in the completed piece, from the differing shades of inks used, and also from the absence of instrumental parts in two bars (25a and 27a) that Salieri cancelled while revising his initial draft. Such a procedure seems also to be implied in the account of composing the *introduzione* for *Le donne letterate*: first the vocal line, then an orchestral motif to 'carry and unify' it. Salieri's biographer Ignaz von Mosel is even more explicit in describing the way he had composed *Axur* 'scene by scene, as Da Ponte brought them to him, sometimes with just the vocal part and bass, and sent them to the copyist so that the singers might learn them without delay.'²⁶ When Emperor Joseph, unaware of this procedure, wished to hear something of the work-in-progress, the original manuscripts were fetched from the copyist and found to contain 'just the vocal parts'; 'the other staves (apart from a few ritornelli, or here and there an indication of the accompaniment) for the instruments had been left empty'.²⁷

The present binding of S.m. 4531 has obliterated any physical clues as to the order in which Salieri sketched the two terzetti. But the one he proceeded to finish was that most likely to arouse his literary interests: the second terzetto, with the quotation from Metastasio. This is not the only literary reference in the terzetto as set by Salieri. At the midpoint in the piece, Ferrando and Guilemo again try to defend their beloveds' honour, but can only partly utter their names – 'Dorabel...'/ 'Fiordili...' – before the philosopher cuts them off with a return of his original

---

[25] See Ignaz von Mosel, *ueber das Leben und die Werke des Anton Salieri* (Vienna, 1827), 32: '... befiel mich ein unwiderstehliches Verlangen, die Introduction der Oper in Musik zu setzen. Ich suchte mir daher den Character und die Situation der Personen recht lebhaft vor Augen zu stellen, und plötzlich fand ich eine Bewegung des Orchesters, die mir den, dem Texte nach zerstückten Gesang des Tonstückes angemessen zu tragen und zu verbinden schien. Ich versetzte mich nun im Geiste in das Parterre, hörte meine Ideen ausführen; sie schienen mir characteristisch; ich schrieb sie auf, prüfte sie nochmal, und da ich damit zufrieden war, fuhr ich wieder fort. So stand in einer halben Stunde der Entwurf der Introduction auf dem Notenblatte. Wer war vergnügter als ich!' Salieri's account is discussed and quoted at greater length by Heartz in *Mozart's Operas*, 139, 154–5.

[26] Mosel, *Salieri*, 130: 'schrieb er Scene für Scene, wie Da Ponte sie ihm brachte, einstweilen blos die Singstimmen mit dem Basse, und schickte sie zum Copisten, damit die Sänger sie unverzüglich einstudieren konnten.'

[27] Mosel, *Salieri*, 130: 'Diese [the musicians] bemerketen bald, daß in den eingelangten Notenblättern blos die Singstimmen vorhanden, die übrigen Linien aber (einige Ritornelle, oder hier und dort eine Andeutung des Accompagnements ausgenommen) für die Instrumente leer gelassen waren.'

melody. This is a comic echo of the dismemberment of the original Fiordiligi's name in Canto 42 of Ariosto's *Orlando furioso*, as her dying husband Brandimarte tells his friend Orlando:

> ... fa che ti raccordi
> di me ne l'orazion tue grate a Dio;
> né men ti raccomando la mia Fiordi...–
> Ma dir non poté: – ... ligi –, e qui finio.

(... endeavour to remember me in your prayers to God; no less do I recommend to you my Fiordi ... – but he could not say – ... ligi –, and here he ended.)

As Ariosto's Fiordiligi had done with respect to her husband, in Da Ponte's libretto Fiordiligi sets off to join her fiancé on the battlefield – with the difference that she betrays him before even managing to depart. In the definitive version of the opera the game with Fiordiligi's name occurs not here, but shortly before the dénouement, where the effect is both more noticeable and more comical. As Guilelmo asks the whereabouts of the fiancée who has just betrayed him, there is this exchange:

> FERRANDO: Chi? la tua Fiordiligi?
> GUILELMO: La mia Fior... fior di diavolo, che strozzi
> Lei prima e dopo me!

(FERRANDO: Who? your Fiordiligi [literally: lily-flower]?/GUILELMO: My Fior ... fior di diavoli [devil-flower], may she be strangled first, and then me!)[28]

The Ariostan allusion in 'È la fede' was probably an idea originating with the composer, rather than something already present in Da Ponte's draft libretto, since the men's exclamations 'Dorabel...'/'Fiordili...' clumsily disrupt the prevailing *ottonario* metre. In both Ariosto's epic and in Da Ponte's final text to *Così*, the fragmentation of Fiordiligi's name is fit comfortably within *endecasillabo* verses.

The point of this reference to the original Fiordiligi, wherever it occurred, was to bring to the spectators' attention Da Ponte's considerable debt to Ariosto, in terms of his opera's themes, its characters' names, even actual locutions (e.g., in Fiordiligi's first aria, 'Come scoglio immoto resta', and in Guilelmo's aria 'Donne mie, la fate a tanti').[29] Not only Fiordiligi's name, but also Dorabella's derives from *Orlando furioso*. Dorabella, writes Elizabeth Dunstan, is 'a composite name deriving from the two ladies who frame the story in Canto 28. Rodomonte is in love with one after the other: his fiancée Doralice betrays him for Mandricardo and Isabella

---

[28] Confirmation that this allusion was consciously intended can be found in a much later poem (*c*. 1821) by Da Ponte, a *capitolo* addressed to the American consul in Florence. Depicting the recitation of his students of Italian literature, Da Ponte describes Ariosto in terms that recall Brandimarte's dying utterance:

> Pianger vedreste giovani e vecchioni
> al pianto di Francesco e d'Ugolino[,]
> fremer con Monti, rider con Goldoni;
> a mente declamar *Mirra* o il *Mattino*;
> e al suon celeste del cantor di Fiordi –
> ligi gridar: – Per Dio, questo è divino! – ...

(Personal communication from Elizabeth M. Dunstan, 6 July 1994.)

[29] As Dunstan has pointed out (see n. 7), Fiordiligi's aria derives from a passage in 44: 61, Guilelmo's from the opening of Canto 28.

Plate 2. The first page of 'La mia Dorabella' from the autograph of Antonio Salieri's *Così fan tutte* (A-Wn, S.m. 4531)

escapes his embraces by cleverly contrived suicide.'[30] There is striking confirmation of this in Salieri's aborted setting, as twice within his draft of 'È la fede' Salieri slips and writes 'Doralice' instead of Dorabella (see bars 26 and 28, in Ex. 1, above).

The manuscript of Salieri's attempted setting of *La scola degli amanti* is also illuminating with regard to the heroes' names. In examining both Mozart's autograph score to *Così fan tutte* and the libretto printed for the first production, Alan Tyson noticed that Ferrando's fellow officer is in fact never called Guglielmo, but rather 'Guilelmo' (or 'Guillelmo').[31] This Latinate form persists in several early libretti and published scores, only gradually giving way to the more usual spelling 'Guglielmo'. The marginal indications for both terzetti in S.m. 4531 unambiguously give 'Guilelmo', confirming Tyson's suspicions that this was what Da Ponte intended. Salieri seems to have had second thoughts as to Ferrando's name, however, crossing it out on the first page of 'È la fede' and replacing it with 'Feramondo' – the name of the protagonist in Da Ponte's and Martín y Soler's *Il burbero di buon cuore* (after Goldoni), an opera already in the repertory of the Viennese troupe. In view of Salieri's habits with regard to his manuscripts, we must entertain the possibility that he made this change many years later, perhaps in a vain attempt to disguise the work's relation to Mozart's opera.

Turning now to the draft of 'La mia Dorabella' (see Plate 2 and Ex. 2), we are confronted with a piece in a much earlier stage of the compositional process, with

---

[30] Dunstan, 'Da Ponte and Ariosto', 8.
[31] See Tyson, *Mozart: Studies of the Autograph Scores*, 185–6.

32   Bruce Alan Brown and John A. Rice

Ex. 2 Antonio Salieri, 'La mia Dorabella' (transcription, in short score)

many corrections plainly visible – even in the two-bar violin flourish at the beginning. Motivic resemblances are few; presumably, more would have been supplied by the orchestral material. The voices have only just come together for the

Ex. 2 (cont'd)

first time as the manuscript breaks off. Essentially all of the text has been used up by this point, and little can have followed but cadential perorations.

Plate 3. The recitative 'Terminiamo una volta' from the autograph of Antonio Salieri's *Così fan tutte* (A-Wn, S.m. 4531)

The recitative on folio 4^v was written after No. 2 ('È la fede') had been at least drafted, if not necessarily orchestrated. Its text is shorter and quite different from that set by Mozart, not least in being for Alfonso alone:

> Terminiamo una volta
> O amici queste ciarle.
> Che ognun di voi la fedeltade vanti
> Della sua cara amata,
> Trovo naturalissimo:
> Ma per me rimarrò sempre
> Nel dire ostinatissimo:

(Friends, let us stop this chattering once and for all; I find it only natural that each of you vaunts the fidelity of his dear beloved; but as for me, I will always remain obstinate in saying:)

The last line sets up the Metastasian quotation even more directly than in the final version. But technically, this text is unimpressive: witness the rather facile rhyme 'naturalissimo'/'ostinatissimo', and the superfluous syllable that spoils the *settenario* metre of the penultimate line.[32] Other differences of literary style and dramaturgy will occupy us shortly. Salieri's setting of these words is unremarkable, except in the way it connects harmonically to the preceding and following numbers (see Plate 3).

[32] The word 'sempre' was possibly added by Salieri; without it, the line is a proper *settenario tronco*.

The opening E-major chord is rudely effective in 'terminating' the B♭-major disputes of No. 1, though the abruptness of the transition is mitigated by the melodic half-step across the gap in Alfonso's line. The third-relation into No. 2 is mild by comparison (with two common tones), functioning much as does the colon that spans the syntactical gap between the two texts.

3

Salieri's decision to leave *La scola degli amanti* incomplete is uncharacteristic. When he broke off the composition of *L'isola capricciosa* in 1779 because of the death of the impresario who had commissioned it, the opera lay unfinished until 1793, when Salieri completed it; the work was presented two years later as *Il mondo alla rovescia*.[33] In 1780 he began a setting of Metastasio's *Semiramide* for Naples but left the score uncompleted when, fearing that he might fall out of favour with his patron, Emperor Joseph, he asked to be excused from his contract and hurried back to Vienna. But two years later when he was commissioned to write an opera seria for Munich, he took the opportunity to finish and present *Semiramide*.[34] Salieri's tendency eventually to salvage projects that he had put aside stands in contrast to Mozart's several operatic false-starts, which during the 1780s included *L'oca del Cairo*, *Lo sposo deluso* and a setting of a German translation of Goldoni's *Il servitore di due padroni*.[35]

The Novellos' records of Constanze Nissen's comments do not suggest that Salieri found Da Ponte's libretto to *La scola degli amanti* wanting in any respect. His decision to abandon *La scola degli amanti* probably had less to do with the quality of the libretto than with his state of mind in 1788 and 1789 – years marked by artistic indecisiveness, a low level of creative energy, and varying degrees of dependence on earlier music. The first months of 1788 had represented a peak in Salieri's career. In January *Axur re d'Ormus* (by Da Ponte, after Beaumarchais) was performed for the first time in celebration of the marriage of Archduke (and later Emperor) Francis and Elizabeth of Württemberg. *Axur* became Joseph's favourite opera, performed often during the next two years; it was probably no accident that within a few weeks of the première Salieri attained the most prestigious musical position in Vienna, that of Hofkapellmeister. Joseph's intervention was doubly necessary for this appointment, because in order to make it he also had to pension off the current occupant of the post, the aged Giuseppe Bonno. Normally the Hofkapellmeister held this position for life, but for the sake of his protégé Salieri, Joseph overruled tradition.

Salieri's twin achievements of 1788 were followed by several disappointments. One of these was the souring of the composer's almost brotherly friendship with Da Ponte early in 1789, on account of disputes connected with the librettist's pasticcio *L'ape musicale*. Performed for the benefit of the participating singers during late February

---

[33] Mosel, *Salieri*, 66–7, 144.
[34] Ibid., 67–9, 74.
[35] Whether Mozart actually began setting this text we do not know; certainly the preparation of the libretto was well under way by the time he abandoned the project. See his letter of 5 February 1783 to his father, in *Mozart: Briefe*, III, 255.

and early March, this unusual work included an array of arias and ensembles (changed each night) from operas recently performed by the troupe, integrated into a plot that was, as Da Ponte describes it, 'a rather witty and agreeable satire of the public, of the impresari, of the singers, the poets, the composers, finally of myself'. The manner in which Da Ponte put the work together was a sure recipe for trouble:

> Having composed this opera without the aid of a composer, and chosen for it those singers who, on account of their talents, had a right to the munificence of the public and of the sovereign, all the others who saw themselves excluded became enraged, as much at my mistress, for whom I had imagined this spectacle, as at me. The worst offended of all was the good maestro Salieri, a man whom I loved and esteemed both out of gratitude and inclination, with whom I passed many learnedly happy hours, and who for six years in a row ... had been more my brother than my friend. His excessive affection for la Cavalieri (let us name her), a woman who had enough merit not to need to raise herself by means of intrigues, and my equally immoderate affection for la Ferraresi (let us name her too), was the sorry motive for breaking a bond of friendship that should have lasted unto death ...[36]

The rage of these two must have been all the greater on account of the considerable sums earned by Da Ponte and his mistress in benefit performances of the pasticcio on the 4th and 6th of March, respectively. Here then are two factors directly relevant to the genesis of the opera that became *Così fan tutte*: the two friends' shared literary recreations ('molte ore dottamente felici'), and Da Ponte's favouring of his mistress over Salieri's candidate for leading roles.[37] It is difficult to imagine their collaboration on *La scola degli amanti* surviving such a rupture, and even more difficult to imagine it being initiated after this time. Of necessity *maestro di cappella* Salieri and theatre-poet Da Ponte continued to deal with each other in the Burgtheater, but the only work of theirs to reach the stage subsequent to the Cavalieri debacle, the above-mentioned *La cifra*, was an adaptation.[38] Da Ponte's resentment was such that he named Salieri as his 'primary enemy' in a memorandum he wrote following his dismissal by Emperor Leopold in 1791, including in his indictment the fact that Salieri had 'made sing in the capacity of prima donna la Cavalieri, whom I had proposed to dismiss'. In the same memorandum, Louise Villeneuve – the first Dorabella – is called the 'third minister' of Da Ponte's

---

[36] Da Ponte, *Memorie*, 136: 'Avendo io composto quell'opera senza soccorso di compositore, e presivi quelli tra cantanti, che aveano un diritto alla munificenza del pubblico e del sovrano per i loro talenti, tutti gli altri, ch'esclusi vidersi, divenner furenti tanto contra la mia amica, per cui io avea immaginato quello spettacolo, che contra me. Quegli, che sopra tutti si risentì fu il bravo maestro Salieri; un uomo ch'io amai e stimai e per gratitudine e per inclinazione, con cui passai molte ore dottamente felici, e che per sei anni continui ... era stato, più che amico, fratello mio. Il suo troppo affetto per la Cavallieri (nominiamola), donna che aveva abbastanza di merito per non aver bisogno d'alzarsi per via d'intrighi, e il mio, parimente soverchio, per la Ferraresi (nominiam anche questa), fu il dolente motivo di rompere un nodo d'amicizia, che dovea durar colla vita ...'.

[37] Franziska Kavalier, known by the stage-name Catarina Cavalieri, had created the role of Constanze in Mozart's *Die Entführung aus dem Serail*.

[38] In December 1790, a time when Da Ponte was still trying to ingratiate himself with the theatrical direction, he claimed to be collaborating with Salieri on an opera to be called *Il filarmonico*, but no trace of such a work remains; see Vienna, Staatsarchiv, Vertrauliche Akten, Karton 40, Nr. 2 ('Cose dell' Ab. da Ponte'), 'Memoria da me presentata alla Direzione il mese di Xbre dell'anno 1790', fol. 23^v.

destruction, her motivation also being exclusion from Da Ponte's lucrative pasticcio.[39]

Of the four operas completed by Salieri during the last two years of Joseph's reign, only three reached the stage, and two of these, *Il talismano* and *La cifra*, were based on earlier works. Only *Il pastor fido* was a setting of a newly written libretto, but even for this opera Salieri borrowed the overture, from *Prima la musica e poi le parole*. Salieri's other opera from this period, *Cublai, gran kan de' Tartari* (begun in Paris in 1786, and presumably intended for performance following his return to Vienna the following year), was never given, probably because it could be interpreted as a satire of the Russian imperial court.[40] That a composer as well connected as Salieri, at the height of his career, should complete an opera that went unperformed is extraordinary. In composing *Cublai*, Salieri would seem temporarily to have lost his judgement as to what was or was not acceptable to the administration of the Burgtheater. His sense of the public's taste seems also to have faltered around this time, for *Il pastor fido* failed to please the Viennese. Salieri withdrew it after a few performances, revised it and presented it again; but again it failed.[41]

In both *Il talismano* and *La cifra* Salieri did something he had rarely done before: he presented old music as if it were new. Three of Salieri's older opere buffe for Vienna had been revived during the 1780s.[42] But Salieri did not pretend that these were new works, and he did not receive a separate fee for any of them, as far as we know.[43] Salieri presented *Il talismano* and *La cifra* as new works, and received the fee normally paid to composers for new operas, in spite of the fact that both are based on earlier scores. *Il talismano* has its origins in a collaborative setting (for Milan, in 1779) of a libretto by Goldoni, in which Salieri had set Act I and Giacomo Rust Acts II and III. Da Ponte, preparing Goldoni's libretto for Salieri in 1788, made very few changes in Act I, probably because this allowed Salieri to reuse his old music. *La cifra* is a reworking and expansion of *La dama pastorella*, which had been performed for the first and apparently the only time in Rome during Carnival 1780. In composing *La cifra* Salieri reached back also to *Der Rauchfangkehrer*, from which

---

[39] 'Cose dell' Ab. da Ponte', fol. 19ʳ: 'Per far cantare la Cavalieri da prima Donna, ch'io aveva proposto di pensionare'. Regarding 'La Willeneuve', Da Ponte states (fol. 19ᵛ): 'Costei dimenticò tutte le beneficenze e cortesie della mia amicizia perchè non l'ho fatta entrare nell' *Ape musicale*' (She forgot all my friendly favours and courtesies because I did not include her in *L'ape musicale*). This document is quoted also by Otto Michtner, in 'Der Fall Abbé Da Ponte', *Mitteilungen des Österreichischen Staatsarchivs*, 19 (1966), 170–209 (199).

[40] See Braunbehrens, *Maligned Master*, 158–60.

[41] *Il pastor fido* was performed three times in February 1789, then three more times in October and November. That Salieri revised the opera is known from payment records cited by Dexter Edge in 'Mozart's Fee for *Così fan tutte*', *Journal of the Royal Musical Association*, 116 (1991), 211–35 (212, n. 4).

[42] *La locandiera* (first performed 1773) was restaged in 1782, and for the inauguration of Joseph's new buffo troupe in 1783 Salieri refurbished *La scola de' gelosi* with several new arias; *La fiera di Venezia* (1772) was revived in 1785.

[43] See Edge, 'Mozart's Fee for *Così fan tutte*', 222. However, the fee of 450 gulden that Salieri received in May 1790, 'for modifications beyond his obligation made over several years to various operas', may have been intended as remuneration for the changes that he made in his earlier operas in preparation for their performance by Joseph's troupe; see Edge, 235.

he took the overture (though with a different second theme), and to an earlier pastoral opera, *L'amore innocente* (1770), which provided the concertante aria 'Non vo già che vi suonino'.

This increasing tendency of Salieri's – reminiscent of his mentor Gluck – to plunder his own works is ironic, in view of an earlier episode involving Emperor Joseph. When Salieri returned to Vienna in 1780 after his Italian sojourn, Joseph ordered him to compose a Singspiel for his German troupe. Salieri suggested a translation of one of the operas he had written in Italy. ' "No translation", answered the monarch, smiling, "an original Singspiel!" '[44] Eight years later Joseph was in no position to make such distinctions. He was absent from Vienna for much of 1788, leading his army against the Turks, and seriously ill besides. Under these circumstances, he had no patience for the excessive (as he thought) salary demands of his Italian singers, and in July he wrote to theatre director Rosenberg of his plans to dismiss the troupe.[45] Rosenberg and Da Ponte (among others) persuaded him to reconsider, and the troupe stayed; but the emperor henceforth displayed little interest in opera. All this must have contributed to an operatic environment in which Salieri was not encouraged to do his best. His attempt to set *La scola degli amanti* was probably affected by this climate, but the experience of failure on this project may also have aggravated Salieri's self-doubt, particularly as it coincided with the loss of an important and creative friendship with Da Ponte.

4

Salieri's misfortune was Mozart's good luck. As Da Ponte wrote many years later, 'Mozart must have been pleased with [my verses], because after the first and second of my dramas, he was happy to have the third'.[46] Indeed, Mozart, in precarious financial condition, must have welcomed the chance to set the libretto, whether or not he was the first to whom Da Ponte offered it.[47] Leopold Mozart's prediction with regard to *Le nozze di Figaro* – namely, that it would cost his son 'much running back and forth, and arguing, until he gets the libretto so arranged as he wishes for his purpose' – can probably be applied to *Così* as well.[48] Comparison of Salieri's setting of *La scola degli amanti* – incomplete though it is – to Mozart's reveals several changes in the final form of the libretto, many of them for the better. In addition to the aforementioned postponement of the game with Fiordiligi's name, there are notable differences in the versions for Salieri and for Mozart of the first recitative text. The latter (given below) is not only longer but also more theatrical, in ways that point to Mozart's active involvement in its drafting.

[44] See Mosel, *Salieri*, 72.
[45] Payer von Thurn, *Joseph II. als Theaterdirektor*, 81.
[46] Da Ponte, *Extract*, 32.
[47] Da Ponte could not offer his text to Martín y Soler, another favourite collaborator, as the latter was by this time established at the Russian court in St Petersburg.
[48] Letter (to his daughter) of 11 November 1785, in *Mozart: Briefe*, III, 444: 'das wird ihm eben vieles Lauffen und disputieren kosten, bis er das Buch so eingerichtet bekommt, wie ers zu seiner Absicht zu haben wünschet...'; quoted and translated in Heartz, *Mozart's Operas*, 136.

Fer.:	Fuor la spada! Scegliete Qual di noi più vi piace.	Draw your sword! And choose whichever of us you prefer.
Alf.:	Io son uomo di pace, E duelli non fo, se non a mensa.	I'm a peaceable man, and don't fight duels, except at table.
Fer.:	O battervi, o dir subito Perchè d'infedeltà le nostre amanti Sospettate capaci!	Either fight, or say at once why you think our lovers are capable of infidelity!
Alf.:	Cara semplicità, quanto mi piaci!	Sweet simplicity, how delightful you are!
Fer.:	Cessate di scherzar, o giuro al cielo! . . .	Stop joking, or I swear, by heaven! . . .
Alf.:	Ed io, giuro alla terra, Non scherzo, amici miei. Solo saper vorrei Che razza d'animali Son queste vostre belle, Se han come tutti noi carne, ossa e pelle, Se mangian come noi, se veston gonne? Alfin, se dee, se donne son . . .	And I swear by the earth, my friends, that I'm not joking. I only wish to know what kind of creatures are these beauties of yours, if they are of flesh, bones and skin, like us, if they eat as we do, if they wear skirts, in the end, if they're goddesses, or women . . .
{Fer.:	Son donne,	They're women,
{Gui.:	Ma . . . son tali . . . son tali . . .	but . . . such . . . such women . . .
Alf.:	E in donne pretendete Di trovar fedeltà? Quanto mi piaci mai, semplicità!	And in women you would expect to find fidelity? How delightful you ever are, simplicity!

All three singers now participate, instead of just Alfonso, and this last character is more sharply delineated, with humour that helps prepare the 'scherzando' delivery of the number that follows (his disclaimer 'Non scherzo, amici miei' notwithstanding). The threatened swordplay at the beginning (shrugged off by Alfonso) has spilt over from the opening terzetto, and is comically reminiscent of the very real duel between the Commendatore and Don Giovanni, at the same point in the action in that opera. Near the end of the recitative the officers sing *a due* – a parodistic idea more likely to have come from the composer than the librettist. In between there are pointed oppositions of 'cielo' and 'terra', 'dee' and 'donne' – dualities that will constantly be invoked throughout the rest of the opera. The line concerning 'carne, ossa e pelle' is closely paraphrased from a tale in Boccaccio's *Decameron* (II. 9) that is an ancestor to this opera's plot; while it is hardly likely that this was Mozart's suggestion, Da Ponte may well have added the line in response to a request for some preparation for the Metastasian quotation in the following number. Also carefully planted are Alfonso's two exclamations of delight at the officers' 'semplicità', with a symmetrical exchange of clauses that hints at the many textual and musical exchanges to come.[49] In short: the features most characteristic of Da Ponte's collaborations with Mozart became part of this text only after Salieri's abandonment of the project.

---

[49] See especially the duets Nos. 4 and 7, in both of which the participants trade off in singing difficult *passaggi* against a long sustained note.

Ex. 3 Mozart, *Così fan tutte*, 'La mia Dorabella', Ferrando's first statement

In contrast to this recitative, in the first two terzetti Salieri and Mozart set essentially the same texts. Of course, it is hardly fair to compare a finished composition with a mere vocal skeleton (as in No. 1), or even two finished pieces (as with No. 2), when one composer has had the opportunity to polish his work during rehearsals and performances, and the other has not. But even if we confine our comparison to those aspects that are complete in both composers' pieces, several notable differences in approach emerge. While both Salieri's and Mozart's melodies for 'La mia Dorabella' initially feature dotted rhythms (Mozart's being assimilated into the prevailing triplets of the accompaniment), Salieri drops his after Ferrando's first phrase; see Examples 2 (above) and 3. Mozart's more persistent dotted rhythms, together with the sing-song melodic profile, suggest the taunting attitude of the officers towards Alfonso, as well as their own rivalry. In the latter respect it is an advantage that Mozart's Guilelmo sings a version of the same melody (with its second half in the dominant), whereas Salieri's sings completely new material. And with canny dramatic calculation, Mozart has Alfonso start his first line with different material, but end it with the same sort of triplet phrase with which both officers had cadenced – in effect, preaching reconciliation with his melody as well as with his words ('Ma tali litigi/finiscano qua').

Salieri's first terzetto is conceived on a smaller scale than Mozart's, lacking the substantial opening ritornello that Mozart used to introduce the characters and set the scene.[50] Salieri is also more sparing in his repetitions of text phrases, relying rather more on fermatas for emphasis. Mozart repeats text throughout, either in melodic sequences (e.g., 'O fuori la spada'), or in antecedent/consequent phrases. An interesting point of comparison is the text beginning 'Sul vivo mi tocca'. Salieri sets the officers' complaint homophonically, as Alfonso repeats his previous lines, illustrating how the officers have ceased to listen to their friend. Mozart conveys the same situation by interlarding the characters' lines. Even after all three are singing together, Mozart staggers the declamation so as to render the text at least somewhat comprehensible (see Ex. 4).

In Salieri's setting of 'È la fede delle femmine', Alfonso's amiable, bounding tune in 6/8 seems as elusive as the Arabian phoenix of which he sings. His melody, the periodicity of which is nicely disrupted in order to emphasise the repeated question 'dove sia?', bears a resemblance to that of an aria in Martín's *Il burbero di buon cuore*,

---

[50] This was Mozart's normal procedure at the beginning of an opera buffa, and also later in the drama, when introducing characters in a set piece; see James Webster, 'The Analysis of Mozart's Arias', in Cliff Eisen, ed., *Mozart Studies* (Oxford, 1991), 101–99 (124–5).

Ex. 4 Mozart, *Così fan tutte*, No. 1, bb. 39–47

Ex. 5 Martín y Soler, *Il burbero di buon cuore*, 'Son trent'anni ch'io porto livrea' (beginning of vocal line)

though probably unintentionally; see Examples 1 (above) and 5. The violins bear the main burden of conveying the officers' irritation, at their entrance in bar 11, with dotted figures that nervously decorate the vocal lines. Mozart, in contrast, sets the Metastasian axiom in an offhand manner, more declamatory than sung, and in cut time. A major difference is the inseparability of vocal and instrumental parts in Mozart's setting. As Alfonso repeats 'Che vi sia ciascun lo dice', his motif echoes in the first violin, flute and bassoon during his rests, and even after he has moved on to his next line, 'dove sia', anthropomorphically illustrating the sense of his words (see Ex. 6). During the reprise of this material Mozart never actually combines the officers' voices with Alfonso's, as had Salieri (at the end), but he does have the former repeatedly interpolate their beloveds' names into the latter's dismissal of the 'phoenix' of womanly fidelity. The men's anger spills over into the ensuing recititative without the impediment of a ritornello – in contrast to Salieri's setting, with its four-bar postlude. It is indeed unfortunate that Salieri's manuscript breaks off just before this key recitative, since one would like to know whether the text already included the opening lines of the definitive version:

FERRANDO: Scioccherie di poeti!
GUILELMO: Scempiagini di vecchi!

(FERRANDO: Poetic nonsense!/GUILELMO: Old men's foolishness!)

Ex. 6 Mozart, *Così fan tutte*, No. 2, bb. 5–13 (short score)

which bear so directly on how these characters, and the audience, are to take this quotation from Metastasio.

5

Fragmentary though it is, Salieri's attempted setting of *La scola degli amanti* sheds light on a difficult time in Salieri's career, and allows us to dispel some of the more fanciful notions concerning the manner by which Mozart came to set this text. The successful 1789 revival of *Le nozze di Figaro* may indeed have spurred the theatrical direction to request a new opera from Mozart, but the libretto that was offered him was hardly new itself. The knowledge that he was not the original recipient of the libretto lends support to Tyson's theory concerning the change of main title from *La scola degli amanti* to *Così fan tutte*, and suggests that other resonances with *Le nozze di Figaro* were likewise added at Mozart's insistence. This new information fits into a larger context of rivalry between these two composers, which includes also the recent discovery that the commission for the Prague coronation opera for Leopold II, *La clemenza di Tito*, was initially offered to Salieri, who reluctantly refused it.[51] Finally, Salieri's score affords a touchstone by which to gauge Mozart's specific musical and dramaturgical choices – a reminder that the seemingly perfect balance of wit and sonic delight in this scene was not preordained, but the result of careful calculation.

Whether or not Mozart knew Salieri's music for the first scene of the opera (as we have seen, it is conceivable that copyists had already begun to provide parts for the singers), he must certainly have been aware that his colleague had commenced a setting. Da Ponte might have preferred to keep silent about having previously offered his libretto to another composer, one imagines, in order to spare Mozart's feelings. But news of Mozart's work on *Figaro* had travelled as far as Paris long before his score was complete, and we must suppose that Salieri's setting of *La scola*

---

[51] See John A. Rice, *W. A. Mozart: La clemenza di Tito* (Cambridge, 1991), 7, 45.

degli amanti was no secret either.⁵² (Indeed, Constanze Mozart had learnt of it, at some point.) Before any composer began serious work on the score for the Burgtheater, the approval of the director, Count Rosenberg (or the emperor), would have been necessary – as Mozart himself informed his father in 1781,⁵³ and as Salieri discovered through bitter experience, in the case of *Cublai, gran kan de' Tartari*.

In lending credence to Da Ponte's account of his break with Salieri – an account supported by the librettist's personal papers, we are compelled to doubt his claims of having received a request for a new opera in October of 1787 from his 'friend Mozart', and of having speedily rewarded this 'favourite' with a new libretto called *La scola degli amanti*. To some extent, this picture of amicability was a construction of a later period, and an attempt to paper over a messy beginning to an opera made famous by Da Ponte's composer of second choice. Much remains uncertain in this story: the degree to which Mozart was aware of Da Ponte's dealings with Salieri on this project, the extent of other changes in the libretto, and the nature of Salieri's – and of Villeneuve's – cabals. But more than anything else, one would like to know the reaction of the composer who demonstrably *had* been Da Ponte's 'favourite' and 'friend', Salieri, as he heard, in the theatre, Mozart's music – to what should have been his opera.⁵⁴

---

⁵² See Heartz, *Mozart's Operas*, 138.

⁵³ Letter of 16 June 1781: '. . . denn wenn ich wirklich schon ein buch hätte, so würde ich doch noch keine feder ansetzen, weil der graf Rosenberg nicht hier ist – wenn der auf die letzt das Buch nicht gut fände, so hätte ich die Ehre gehabt umsonst zu schreiben' (. . . for even if I actually had a libretto already, I wouldn't set pen to paper yet, since Count Rosenberg isn't here – if in the end he didn't approve of the libretto, I would have had the honour of writing [an opera] in vain); *Mozart: Briefe*, III, 132.

⁵⁴ Part of John Rice's research for this article was made possible by a fellowship from the Alexander von Humboldt-Stiftung.

[21]

Die Zauberflöte, Masonic Opera, and Other Fairy Tales*

David J. Buch
Cedar Falls, Iowa

THE TERM 'MASONIC OPERA' is often applied to Mozart's *Die Zauberflöte* to indicate pervasive Masonic content in the form of a hidden coherent allegory with a complex representation of the order's symbols and initiation rituals. This view has been influential in musicology and other scholarly writing,[1] but a review of the primary sources reveals that it is speculative, with no compelling evidence to support its broad claims. Moreover, some evidence suggests that the 'Masonic opera' theory is an unlikely interpretation. Allegory and symbolism function somewhat differently in opera at this time and no eighteenth-century singspiel is known to have communicated its meaning so indirectly, leaving essential and ubiquitous content to be deciphered by a small group possessing the code.

The historical context for the opera, fairy-tale singspiel or *Märchenoper*, has been explored only superficially; not a single scholarly study in the twentieth century has been devoted to this operatic tradition. Some modern writers have even derisively dismissed this aspect as unworthy of consideration. A review of fairy-tale opera will reveal that most musical and dramatic elements in *Die Zauberflöte* are present in previous operas with no demonstrable Masonic content. These works situate *Die Zauberflöte* in an accurate theatrical context and provide much needed perspective on the question of Masonic symbolism. While the notion of a complex, coherent Masonic allegory does not withstand scrutiny, a few passages in the libretto appear to have been drawn from Masonic sources. Here I will suggest a plausible explanation for the presence of this material and review the reasons that one should not assume a more prevalent use of symbolic reference to Freemasonry.

It might seem odd that some 210 years after the premiere of *Die Zauberflöte* scholars continue to debate the most basic level of the opera's content. Unfortunately, distor-

---

* An earlier version of this article was given as a paper at the annual meeting of the American Society for Eighteenth-century Studies, Notre Dame, IN, 2 April 1998. I wish to thank Michel Noiray, John Rice and Peter Branscombe for their comments and suggestions.
1. For example, see James Stevens CURL, *The Art and Architecture of Freemasonry: An Introductory Study*, Woodstock, N.Y., 1993, 135-68, and Magnus OLAUSSON, 'Freemasonry, Occultism and the Picturesque Garden towards the End of the Eighteenth Century', in: *Art History*, 8 (1985), 413-33. These authors base their arguments on the assumption that the decoration and imagery in *Die Zauberflöte* are almost entirely Masonic.

tion in early Mozart biographies, particularly in regard to Die Zauberflöte, still influences modern scholarship. The lack of documentation about the commission and genesis of the opera was (and remains) problematic. The composer's deification in the pantheon of German 'masters' following his death, and his subsequent association with burgeoning German national identity, led to hagiography. When the holes in Mozart's biography needed plugging, rumor and imagination filled the gaps. High-minded commentators in the late eighteenth-century generally disapproved of the popularly styled Die Zauberflöte.[2] By the nineteenth century the prevailing idea of a 'genius's work of art' required serious and coherent 'masterpieces'. Thus many read into the libretto a sophistication and profundity to match their regard for Mozart's music, and allegorical interpretations of the libretto served this aim. Ignorance of concurrent repertory allowed for a myth of singularity and autonomy, both for the opera and for its composer. A variety of interpretations still thrives in this vacuum, unhampered by the contradictions that would be raised by an examination of the theatrical context.

Masonic Opera

Paul Nettl, the first modern scholar to advance a detailed scheme of the symbolic content of the libretto and score of Die Zauberflöte, asserted that the opera contains a pervasive allegorical subtext depicting various Masonic rituals and symbols.[3] Jacques Chailley expanded this view, finding indications of Masonic symbolism in almost every scene and musical number, and suggesting that these form a coherent whole.[4] Yet neither Nettl nor Chailley demonstrated a narrative allegory; rather they suggested a symbolic complex of language, image, and music without a discernable linear plot.

A number of scholars appear to have accepted the general thrust of the Masonic reading. For example, Julian Rushton in The New Grove Dictionary of Opera[5] writes that while 'different significations' of the opera coexist simultaneously, the libretto is basically an allegory, intended by the librettist, Emanuel Schikaneder, and Mozart as a 'coded

---

2. Examples are given in Otto Erich DEUTSCH, "Mozart: Die Dokumente seines Lebens", in: Neue Ausgabe sämtlicher Werke [NMA] Serie 10, Werkgruppe 34 (Kassel, 1961), including a 1791 review in the Musikalisches Wochenblatt (page 358) and comments of Karl von Zinzendorf (page 360). Also see the deprecatory review (1793) discussed in Manfred SCHULER, 'Eine zeitgenössische Kritik an der "Zauberflöte"', Mitteilungen der Internationalen Stiftung Mozarteum, 39/1-4 (1991), 125-31.
3. See Paul NETTL, Mozart und die königliche Kunst. Die freimaurerischen Grundlagen des <Zauberflöte>, Berlin, 1932; '<Sethos> und die freimaurerische Grundlage der <Zauberflöte>', Bericht über die musikwissenschaftliche Tagung der Interntionalen Stiftung Mozarteum in Salzburg, Leipzig, 1932, 142-9; 'Die königliche Kunst. Die Freimaurerie und Freimaurermusik', in: W. A. Mozart, Frankfurt a. M, 1955, 145-54; 'Masonry and the Magic Flute', in: Opera News, 20/17 (1956), 8-10; and Musik und Freimaurerei, Esslingen, 1956, trans., Mozart and Masonry, New York, 1957.
4. Jacques CHAILLEY, La Flûte enchantée: Opéra maçonnique. Essai d'explication du livret et de la musique, Paris, 1968, 2/1983; English trans. Herbert Weinstock, 1972. Also see CHAILLEY's, "Die Symbolik in der Zauberflöte", in: Mozart-Jahrbuch 1967, 100-10; and "La Flûte enchantée, opera maçonnique", in: L'Avant-scène Opéra, 1 (1976), 82-9.
5. Julian RUSHTON, "Die Zauberflöte", in: NGroveDO, ed. Stanley SADIE, 4 vols. (London and New York, 1992), IV 1215-18, and "Mozart", in: NGroveDO, III, 489-503.

representation of Freemasonry.' Rushton asserts that the composer made a significant contribution in this regard: 'Mozart transformed the Singspiel into an allegory of his own quasi-religious commitment to Freemasonry'. In another article in the same dictionary, Cecil Hill describes *Die Zauberflöte* as representing but one example of Masonic opera, suggesting that others existed in the eighteenth century.[6] But the author provides no evidence to support this assertion. All these claims are presented as facts rather than as speculation.

Both Nettl and Chailley base their theory on the wording of a few dialogues in the libretto and the presence of Egyptian and Masonic images on the frontispiece of the opera's original libretto. The dialogues do have similarities to Masonic writings, specifically the pseudo-Egyption French novel *Sethos* by Jean Terrasson[7] and Ignaz von Born's essay, *Über die Mysterien der Ägyptier* (1784).[8] The strongest similarity to Terrasson's material is found in act 2, scene 1, the dialogue and aria with chorus (n°. 11 in Mozart's autograph score), "O Isis und Osiris," which bears a resemblance to Hymn 1 in Book 1 and the hymn in Book 3. Let us compare these texts, first Schikaneder's act 2, scene 1:

Zweiter Aufzug
Erste Auftritt

Das Theater ist ein Palmenwald;
Alle Bäume sind silberartig, die Blätter von Gold, 18 Sitze von Blättern. Auf einem jeden Sitze steht eine Pyramide und ein großes, schwarzes Horn mit Gold gefaßt. In der Mitte die größte Pyramide, auch die größten Bäume.

Sarasto nebst anderen Priestern kommen in feierlichen Schritten, jeder mit einem Palmenzweige in der Hand. Ein Marsch mit blasenden Instrumenten begleitet den Zug.
[Nr. 9. Marsch der Priester]

[*Sarasto, Sprecher, Priester*].
Sarasto (*nach einer Pause*). Ihr, in dem Weisheitstempel eingeweihten Diener der großen Göttin Osiris und Isis! Mit reiner Seele erklär ich euch, daß unsere heutige Versammlung eine der wichtigsten unserer Zeit ist. Tamino, ein Königssohn, zwanzig Jahre seines Alters, wandelt an der nördlichen Pforte unseres Tempels und seufzet mit tugendvollem Herzen nach einem Gegenstande, den wir

---

6. In "Masonic Music", in: *NGroveD*, ed. Stanley SADIE, London and New York, 1980, II, 755, Cecil Hill writes of 'masonic operas' and accepts Chailley's speculations apparently without regard to the objections raised by scholars, most notably Peter Branscombe's critical review in *Music & Letters*, 53 (1972), 434-36, Jean-Victor HOCQUARD, *La Flûte enchantée*, Paris, 1979, 246-48, and Jay MACPHERSON, "The Magic Flute and Viennese Opinion", *Man and Nature/L'Homme et la Nature*, 6 (1987), 161-72. Macpherson argues that Masonic allegories are inconsistent with the contemporary context. John MOREHEN, "Masonic Instrumental Music of the Eighteenth Century: A Survey", in: *The Music Review*, 42 (1981), 215-24, characterizes Chailley's interpretation as 'contentious', and Robert WANGERMÉE, "Quelques mystères de 'La Flûte enchantée'", in: *Revue Belge de Musicologie*, 34/35 (1980/81), 147-63, cites the lack of a documented tradition of initiation mysteries on the stage.
7. Abbé Jean TERRASSON, *Sethos, histoire ou vie tirée des monuments, anecdotes de l'ancienne Égypte d'un manuscrit grec*. 3 vols., Paris, 1731, Amsterdam, 1732, German trans., Mathias Claudius, 1777. These passages are given in full in Peter BRANSCOMBE, *W. A. Mozart: Die Zauberflöte*, Cambridge Opera Handbooks, Cambridge, 1991, 10-18, 222-23.
8. Ignaz VON BORN, "Über die Mysterien der Ägyptier", in: *Journal für Freimaurer*, Vienna, 1784. Again, these are given in Branscombe, 20-25.

alle mit Mühe und Fleiß erringen müssen. Kurz, dieser Jüngling will seinen nächtlichen Schleier von sich reißen und ins Heiligtum des größten Lichtes blicken. Diesen Tugenhaften zu bewachen, ihm freundschaftlich die Hand zu bieten, sei heute seine unsrer wichtigsten Pflichten.
Erster Priester (*steht auf*). Er besitzt Tugend?
Sarasto. Tugend!
Zweiter Priester. Auch Verschwiegenheit?
Sarasto. Verschwiegenheit!
Dritter Priester. Ist wohltätig?
Sarasto. Wohltätig! – Haltet ihr ihn für würdig, so folgt meinem Beispiele. (*Sie blasen dreimal in die Hörner.*) Gerührt über die Einigkeit eurer Herzen, dankt Sarastro euch im Namen der Menschheit. Mag immer das Vorurteil seinen Tadel über uns Eingeweihte auslassen! Weisheit und Vernunft zerstückt es gleich dem Spinnengewebe. Unsere Säulen erschüttern sie nie. Jedoch das böse Vorurteil soll schwinden und es wird schwinden, sobald Tamino selbst die Größe unserer schweren Kunst besitzen wird. – Pamina, das sanfte, tugendhafte Mädchen, haben die Götter dem holden Jüngling bestimmt; dies ist der Grundstein, warum ich sie der stolzen Mutter entriß. Das Weib dünkt sich groß zu sein, hofft durch Blendwerk und Aberglauben das Volk zu berücken und unsern festen Tempelbau zu zerstören. Allein, das soll sie nicht. Tamino, der holde Jüngling selbst, soll ihn mit uns befestigen und als Eingeweihter der Tugend Lohn, dem Laster aber Strafe sein. (*Der dreimalige Akkord mit den Hörnern wird von allen wiederholt.*)
Sprecher (*steht auf*). Großer Sarastro, deine weisheitsvollen Reden erkennen und bewundern wir; allein wird Tamino auch die harten Prüfungen, so seiner warten, bekämpfen? Verzeih, daß ich so frei bin, dir meinen Zweifel zu eröffnen! Mich bangt es um den Jüngling. Wenn nun, im Schmerz dahingesunken, sein Geist sich verließe und er dem harten Kampf unterläge. Er ist Prinz.
Sarastro. Noch mehr – er ist Mensch!
Sprecher. Wenn er nun aber in seiner frühen Jugend leblos erblaßte?
Sarastro. Dann ist er Osiris und Isis gegeben und wird der Götter Freuden früher fühlen als wir. (*Der dreimaliger Akkord wird wiederholt.*) Man führe Tamino mit seinem Reisegefährten in den Vorhof des Tempels ein. (*Zum Sprecher, der vor ihm niederkniet.*) Und du, Freund, den die Götter durch uns zum Verteidiger der Wahrheit bestimmten. – vollziehe dein heiliges Amt und lehre durch deine Weisheit beide, was Pflicht der Menschheit sei, lehre sie die Macht der Götter erkennen. (*Sprecher geht mit einem Priester ab, alle Priester stellen sich mit ihren Palmenzweigen zusammen.*)
[Nr. 10. Arie mit Chor]
Sarastro. O Isis und Osiris, schenket
    Der Weisheit Geist dem neuen Paar!
    Die ihr der Wandrer Schritte lenket,
    Stärkt mit Geduld sie in Gefahr.
Chor. Stärkt mit Geduld sie in Gefahr.
Sarastro. Laßt sie der Prüfung Früchte sehen;
    Doch sollten sie zu Graben gehen,
    So lohnt der Tugend kühnen Lauf,
    Nehmt sie in euren Wohnsitz auf.
Chor. Nehmt sie in euren Wohnsitz auf.

    (*Sarastro geht voraus, dann alle ihm nach ab.*)[9]

---

9. In his letter of 8-9 October, 1791, addressed to his wife Constanze, Mozart referred to this merely as the 'solemn scene.' He was describing an evening at the theatre with a man he held in low esteem. This man [the name was cancelled later] 'zeugten über *alles* recht sehr ihren beifall, aber Er, der allwissende, zeigte so sehr den *bayern*, daß ich nicht bleiben konnte, oder ich hätte ihn einen Esel heissen müssen; - Unglücklseeligerweise war ich eben drinnen als der 2:te Ackt anfieng, folglich bey der feyerlichen Scene. – er belachte alles; anfangs hatte ich gedult genug ihn auf einige Reden aufmerksam machen zu viel- ich heiss ihn *Papageno*, und gieng fort – ich glaube aber nicht daß es der dalk verstanden hat.' Mozart made no mention of any kind of allegory or Masonic content here, despite repeated attempts by modern writers to interpret his words as doing so.

Here are the two hymns from Claudius's translation of *Sethos*:

<u>Book I, stanza 4</u>:
Horus, Gott der durch die Weisheit erworbenen Verschwiegenheit,
Der du die unschuldige schwache Kindheit
Jedes Dinges auf dem Wege zu seiner Reise gänglest;
Erhalte einem Prinzen, der noch Kind, dein Blut, dein Ebenbild ist,
Einen Beystand, den dir selbst in seinem Alter
Deine Mutter Isis geleistet hat.

<u>In the middle of Book III</u>:
O Isis, grosse Göttin der Egypter, gieb deinen Geist dem neuen Diener, der so viel Gefahren und Beschwerlichkeit überstanden hat, um vor dir zu erscheinen. Mache ihn auch sieghaft in den Proben seiner Seele, und lehre sein Herz deine Gesetze, damit er würdig werde, zu deinen Genheimnissen zugelassen zu werden.

Schikaneder seems to have loosely paraphrased Terrasson's text for his scene. There are differences: Sarastro addresses Isis and Osiris, while the first hymn is directed to Horus, who is never even mentioned in *Die Zauberflöte*. Nor is Osiris mentioned in the hymns. Words like *Isis, Weisheit, Verschwiegenheit, Prinz*, and *Göttin der Egypter* do occur in both texts, but these do not demonstrate that Schikaneder intended any allegorical meaning in using them. At the most one can safely say that Schikaneder likely drew upon *Sethos* in creating his own text.

The second example of a text derived from Terrasson is from the finale of act 2, scene 28, the scene for the two men in black armor. Here the wording is perhaps less similar than that in the previous example, but the meaning seems closer:

Die schwarzgeharnischten Männer.
Der, welcher wandert diese Straße voll Beschwerden,
Wird rein durch Feuer, Wasser, Luft und Erden;
Wenn er des Todes Schrecken überwinden kann,
Schwingt er sich aus der Erde Himmel an.
Erleuchtet wird er dann im stande sein,
Sich den Mysterien der Isis ganz zu weihn.

Terrasson's text (translated by Claudius) is as follows:

Wer diesen Weg allein geht, und ohne hinter sich zu sehen, der wird gereiniget werden durch das Feuer, das Wasser und durch die Luft; und wenn er das Schrecken des Todes überwinden kann, wird er aus dem Schooss der Erde wieder herausgehen, und das Licht wieder sehen, und er wird das Recht haben, seine Seele zu der Offenbarung der Geheimnisse der grossen Göttin Isis gefasst zu machen!

Both texts concern wandering through the elements (fire, water, air, and earth) to be purified, overcoming the fear of death in the process. While it is plausible that this was Schikaneder's source for the duet, there is no justification to interpret it in a broader allegorical context. Moreover, this was not the only time Schikaneder referred to the elements. At least two other librettos, with no known allegorical content, use similar language. In his libretto to *Der Höllenberg* (premiere, 23 November, 1795),[10] the quintet in act 2, scene 7 begins with an invocation by the magician Harmonesus to his four spirits:

> Hervor aus dem Dunkel ihr sichtbaren Geister,
> Entreißt euch der ewig euch denkenden Kluft;
> Zeigt euch diesem Manne ihr mächtigen Geister,
> Durch Wasser und Feuer, und Erde und Luft!

The ideas of wandering and the power of the elements are also invoked by two priests in Schikaneder's *Babylons Piramiden* (premiere, 25 October 1797), in the act 2 finale: "Hier im Feuer, wandelt er; Hier am Wasser, wandelt sie."[11] The elements are also part of title of his singspiel *Das Labyrinth, oder Der Kampf mit den Elementen* (premiere, 12 June 1798), which, as the sequel to *Die Zauberflöte*, has numerous textual similarities with *Die Zauberflöte*.

Commentators have suggested that Schikaneder drew upon Ignaz von Born's essay when creating the scene with the Speaker (act 2, scene 6) and Sarastro's aria in act 2, scene 12 (n°. 16 in Mozart's autograph score), texts that extol friendship and brotherhood while warning against superstition. The final chorus praises wisdom, beauty and strength. Here the similarities are so vague that they need not be connected to Born's text at all. The wording in the libretto seems more like an invocation of popular cant and the platitudes praised in Masonic and other liberal ideologies rather than a specific citation with an allegorical meaning. The other textual similarity is even more tenuous. Ignaz von Born briefly cites Plutarch's story of Prince Horus being saved from a serpent that his evil uncle's mistress set against him. While this may have inspired Schikaneder to write the opening scene where Tamino is saved by the three ladies from a deadly serpent, it is not a parallel situation: there is no indication that the evil Queen in *Die Zauberflöte* sent the serpent to kill Tamino. Thus if Born's passage was the inspiration for the *introduzione* of the opera, it is not a part of any allegory found in 'Über die Mysterien der Ägyptier'.

Schikaneder's use of Egyptian lore and platitudes in these passages does not prove that he intended a broad allegory, and the few references in the libretto do not prove a Masonic subtext. The frontispiece of the opera's libretto, in which the printer Ignaz Alberti, a Freemason, presents Egyptian iconography, certainly brings Freemasonry to mind. But this imagery is also consistent with the Egyptian setting of the fairy tale. Many of the same Egyptian symbols are found in engravings of opera scenes from Schikaneder's singspiel *Babilons Piramiden* (Wiednertheater, 1797),[12] an opera that evokes Assyrian and Babylonian

---

10. *Der Höllenberg. / Eine / heroisch=komische Oper / in zween Aufzügen / von / Emanuel Schikaneder. Die Musik von Herrn J. Wölfl, / Kapellmeister. / Altona,/ gedruckt mit Bollmerschen Schriften / Grüne=Straße. n°.138*. This songbook is found in Vienna, Gesellschaft der Musikfreunde., Signatur 6847 Tb. The quoted text is found on p. 26.

11. A Viennese libretto survives in Mannheim, Reiß-Museum, shelfmark N 5: *Babilons / Piramiden. / Eine grosse / heroisch-komische Oper/ in zwey Aufzügen. / Verfaßt / von / Emanuel Schikaneder. / Wien. / gedruckt mit Jahnischen Schriften, 1800*. Once again the number three has a magical association (see below).

12. Twelve engravings are found in the piano-vocal score: *Babilons Piramiden / Eine grosse herroisch=komische*

occult practices with locutions remarkably similar to that in *Die Zauberflöte*, but without any apparent allegorical Masonic content. Alberti's engravings prove neither an intentional Masonic subtext in the opera nor Mozart's participation in creating an allegory.

Two of the most widely read recent discussions of Masonry and *Die Zauberflöte* come to quite different conclusions about the allegory of this putative 'Masonic opera.' For H. C. Robbins Landon *Die Zauberflöte* is 'the first Masonic opera;'[13] the intent of Mozart and Schikaneder was 'to protect Masonry' from hostile attacks and attempts to abolish it (pp. 134-35). 'Mozart and Schikaneder risked a long shot — to save the Craft by an allegorical opera, *The Magic Flute* (p. 60). Landon boldly asserts that the opera's creators were presenting a Masonic ritual on the stage: "But Mozart and Schikaneder intended to show more than just the Masonry of the St John ceremony; they also represented that of the higher degree" (p. 127). His evidence for this statement rests on two suppositions (p. 129). The first is the following sentence: "At the words 'fire, water, air and earth' the holy tetragrammaton *JHVH* was presumably shown." One cannot base an interpretation on an image one merely 'presumes' was shown. The other statement of proof is: "The Thirtieth Scene in act 2 [...] is symbolic of the 30° in the Scottish Rite, the 'Degree of Revenge' [...]." This coincidence of the number thirty sounds a bit more convincing, as "the sacrifice of our vengeance" (unserer Rache Opfer) is mentioned at the end of the scene. But here the Queen, her three ladies, and Monostatos are furtively attempting to usurp the leadership of the temple by force. Revenge is just one of many themes and images in the scene. Act 2, scene 8, with the famous aria for the Queen of the Night ("Der Hölle Rache"), stresses revenge much more than scene 30.

Landon's assertions are based less on original scholarship than on a re-interpretation of secondary literature, especially Chailley. A critical examination of Landon's account reveals a number of fallacies: the half truth, circular reasoning, illicit process, faulty generalization, faulty analogy, etc. Statements like "one symbol after another derived from the Craft. The symbolic figure three dominates the entire work [. . .]" (p. 127) create the impression of a logical argument, but these claims are just more unsubstantiated assertions. The images on the title page are again offered as proof of a consistent system of Masonic symbols, as is the numerical interpretation of the three-fold accord.[14] But even at face value Landon's general thesis is unsound, for how could an opera "save" or "protect" Masonry if the creators put the message into a code that only initiates could understand?

Oper / von Emanuel Schikaneder / in Musik gesezt / der Erste Aufzug / von Hr. Iohann Gallus / der Zweyte Aufzug / von Hr. Peter Winter..., Vienna 1797. A copy is preserved in the Musiksammlung of the Österreichische Nationalbibliothek in Vienna [henceforth A-Wn], shelfmark MS 50.011.

13. H.C. ROBBINS LANDON, *1791. Mozart's Last Year*, London: Thames and Hudson, 1988, p. 131 and p. 135. Landon's arguments are presented in the chapter, "The Magic Flute" on pp. 122-47, and specifically the section "The message" (pp. 127-37) is the heart of the argument. For his information on Freemasonry, Landon relies almost exclusively on information concerning Masonry on the British Isles from Robert F. Gould, *The History of Freemasonry*, 3 vols., Edinburgh, n.d. [1886].

14. Landon asserts that the dotted 'three-times-three chords' derive from the practice of French Lodges.

The account by Volkmar Braunbehrens comes to a very different conclusion concerning the function of Masonry in the opera: 'Against the background of Viennese Freemasonry, *Die Zauberflöte*'s initiates appear not as monolithic bloc but as a group full of contradictions, without any claim to infallibility.'[15] 'The Masonic message of this opera is not one of confidence in Sarastro's limited wisdom' (p. 265).

What are we to make of this variability in interpretation if not to say that one can interpret this kind of evidence to support as many different and contradictory allegories as scholars can devise? This variability reveals an essential aspect in the nature of the evidence—that the presence of material that recalls aspects of Masonry cannot lead to any conclusion about the intent of the composer or the librettist. It can only lead to speculation.

Historical perspective sheds light on the Masonic allegory theory. Emil Karl Blümml has shown that the earliest interpretations of the libretto were political.[16] The two Masonic accounts that surfaced in the first decade after the opera's premiere were anecdotal, and had no connection to Mozart, Schikaneder, or even Vienna. Both asserted a political context for the Masonic content. The purely 'Masonic allegory' theory only gained precedence in the twentieth century, when it emerged from a number of varied interpretations that the opera had accrued.

The first specific Masonic reading of the libretto seems to be unknown in the secondary literature. It is an anonymous account found in the *Hamburgischer Briefträger* 15 November, 1794 (1795 issue):

> Müssen doch auch einmal ein Wort von der Geschichte der *Zauberflöte* sagen. Es ist bekannt: das von jeher das Freymaurer-Wesen den neugierigen Frauenzimmern ein Stachel im Auge gewesen ist, die bis jetzt alle Mühe angewandt haben das Geheimniß derselben zu erforschen. Wie thöricht ihre Begriffe davon sind zeigt die Königen der Nacht. In einem nicht freydenkenden Lande schienen nemlich einer gewissen Fürstinn die Maurer gefährliche Leute zu seyn, und sie bewirkte, weil sie nicht in die Weisheit der Loge eindringen konnte, daß solche aufgehoben wurde. Der Verfasser der Zauberflöte, Meister des Stuhls, suchte sich dadurch zu rächen, daß er diese Geschichte in eine Oper einkleidete, und so die Mauerey, welches auch bey jener Fürstinn geschehen seyn soll, siegen ließ. *Relata refero* (oder ich erzählte von Hören sagen.)[17]

Here we find the basic elements of both the political and the Masonic interpretations in a far-fetched and clearly imaginary account where the Master of a Lodge (Ignaz von

---

15. Volkmar BRAUNBEHRENS, *Mozart in Vienna*, trans., Timothy Bell (orig. German edn., Munich, 1980); New York: Grove Wiedenfeld, 1986: 264.
16. Emil Karl BLÜMML reviewed a number of these in "Ausdeutungen der 'Zauberflöte'", in: *Mozart-Jahrbuch*, 1 (1923), 111-46.
17. Page 25: "Now we must also say a word about the story of *The Magic Flute*. It is well known that Freemasonry always has been a thorn in the side of curious women, who until now have spared no effort to find out its secrets. The Queen of the Night shows just how foolish their notions of it are. You see a certain princess of a land where freethinking was not allowed saw the Masons as a danger. Because she could not penetrate the wise teaching of the Lodge, she tried to abolish it. The author of *The Magic Flute*, the Master of the Lodge, sought to avenge this through couching the story within an opera, so that Masonry would triumph, which also happened with [in the land of] that princess. *Relata refero* (or so I have heard)." The remark concerning curious women may be a reference to Carlo Goldoni's play *Le donne curiose* (1753), which also targets Freemasons.

Born?) writes a libretto about some princess (presumably Maria Theresia of Austria), represented by the Queen of the Night.

The Masonic interpretation seems to have been restricted to northern German commentators. The east Prussian Ludwig von Batzko wrote an 'Allegorie aus der Zauberflöte' in 1794,[18] interpreting the opera as a political allegory of light versus darkness and superstition versus enlightenment. Without naming Freemasonry he wrote that some 'scenes obliquely allude to the ceremonies of certain orders; even the uninitiated will know this, provided they are acquainted with mysteries of the ancient culture'.[19] Like the Hamburg account, this commentary is a personal, subjective view from an individual with no connection to the opera or its creators. But unlike the Hamburg interpretation, it contains nothing that is clearly false, and it offers insight both into how individuals understood theatrical allegory at the time and a more plausible view of possible symbolic content (see below).

The first Viennese assertion of a 'glorification of the Masonic element' came from Leopold von Sonnleithner in 1857, 66 years after the premiere of the opera; it was actually printed in 1919.[20] Sonnleithner, who knew contemporaries of Mozart, does not assert that his evidence comes from any source contemporary with the opera. Rather it is his own theory that suggests that Schikaneder introduced the Masonic element at the end of act 1 in order to differentiate his opera from Joachim Perinet's contemporary singspiel, *Kaspar der Fagottist oder Die Zauberzither*.

New interpretations have proliferated in the twentieth century, including Rosicrucian mysticism,[21] alchemy,[22] numerology,[23] Gnosticism,[24] or even a fully worked-out numerical code of hidden messages based on Cabalistic *gematria*.[25] Explaining the hidden meanings of *Die Zauberflöte* became a dominant theme in Mozart studies. Each of these modern writers cites peripheral conditions and conjunctions of similar events to posit a central cause for the writing of the opera. Association is causation in all of these interpretations, whose authors assert a 'true' interpretation of the opera's supposed secrets that often

---

18. *Journal des Luxus und der Moden*, 9, Weimar, 19 April 1794, 366-71.
19. Ibid., 371: "daß manche Szenen Anspielungen auf gewisse Orden sind, selbst ohne Erklärung wissen. die nicht Mitglieder des Ordens sind, werden sie auch zum Teil selbst deuten können, dafern sie einige Kenntnis von den Mysterien der Alten haben". Also see Johann Jakob Engel's letter (1792) in Deutsch, *Dokumente*, 389.
20. Leopold von Sonnleithner, "Über die Zauberflöte", in: *Mozarteums Mitteilungen* 1/1-2 (Salzburg, 1919-1920).
21. Nicolas Till, *Mozart and the Enlightenment: Truth, Virtue and Beauty in Mozart's Operas*, London, 1992, 294-313, asserts with certitude a Cabalistic, numerological, and Rosicrucian nature in *Die Zauberflöte*, complete with 'coded secrets': 'The elaborate symbolism of the opera is a sure indication that *Die Zauberflöte* carries within it a Rosicrucian programme' (page 298).
22. Siegfried Morenz, "Alchemie und Zauberflöte", in: *Mozart Jahrbuch 1971/72* (1973), 173-81.
23. I. Grattan-Guinness, "Counting the Notes: Numerology in the Works of Mozart, especially *Die Zauberflöte*", in: *Annals of Science*, 49 (1992), 201-32.
24. Romolo Perrotta, "Gnostiche 'Ethos'" im Textbuch der 'Zauberflöte', in: *Mozart Jahrbuch 1997*, 45-67.
25. Hans-Josef Irmen, *Mozart. Mirglied geheimer Gesellschaften* ([Mechernich], 1988).

contradicts the claims of other interpretations, and the symbols keep changing according to the interpretation. While the most diplomatic manner of dealing with these different readings is to say that they 'coexist simultaneously', one can hardly concede equal weight to contradictory interpretations. If this were so then Mozart and his librettist were superhuman mystic-scientists, intent upon offering their audience the most arcane and complex operatic riddle ever created in a mere matter of a few months.

Allegory in the late Eighteenth Century

The rule of the commonplace states that unless there is some compelling reason to believe otherwise, an event or person adheres to the normative conditions of the time in question. Applying the rule of the commonplace, one should find examples of contemporary singspiels with similar cryptic programs in Vienna. Yet none of Schikaneder's other operas have complicated hidden subtexts. Nor do fairy-tale singspiels by other librettists. Eighteenth-century singspiels were not vehicles for concealing recondite philosophies and secret rituals. Like other Viennese fairy-tale singspiels, Die Zauberflöte was a product of the popular theatre. Mozart and Schikaneder never mentioned Freemasonry in regard to Die Zauberflöte in any surviving source; Mozart called it a 'teutsche Oper' and Schikaneder called it a 'große Oper'.[26]

Of course eighteenth-century comedies and court operas sometimes contained symbolic content and allegory. But the nature of these subtexts and their evidentiary basis differ fundamentally from the Masonic reading of Die Zauberflöte, whose elaborate and coded representation seems highly unusual for late eighteenth century Vienna. The creators of theatrical allegories at the time intended the symbolic content to be easily recognized and not remain hidden. The allegory would be a coherent narrative, not a complex of discontinuous abstract symbols. Additionally, the symbolic material either had a direct connection to royal patronage or evoked a theme with broadly popular interest to the audience. For example, Carlo Gozzi's *fiabe teatrali* included polemics on the pretensions of the literary reform of Carlo Goldoni, criticizing the Venetian Enlightenment and its theatrical paper war. Symbolic content is also found in French fair plays and related Italian-style comedies; but the purpose in this case was satire, ridiculing a familiar target that the audience would easily recognize. Moreover, the evidence for Gozzi's ideological substratum is a contemporary witness, the author's brother Gasparo, who publicly explained the symbolic content of Gozzi's first play, *L'amore delle tre melarance*.[27] No such evidence exists for the arcane representation of an elaborate network of Masonic rituals and symbols in Die Zauberflöte.

---

26. In his preface to *Der Spiegel von Arkadien*, Vienna: Joseph Ochß, 1795, Schikaneder asserted that his sole aim was to write for a general audience rather than for intellectuals: "Ich schreibe fürs Vergnügen des Publikums, gebe mich für keinen Gelehrten aus. Ich bin Schauspieler – bin Direkteur – und arbeite für meine Kaße". [I write for the pleasure of the public, I do not claim to be a scholar. I am an actor – a director – and I work for my box-office.] The preface is reproduced in *Maske und Kothurn*, 1 (1955), 359-60.

Another kind of symbolism is found in court opera, which often employed mythological allegory for the edification of its royal patrons. Pietro Metastasio's *Alcide al Bivio* (Vienna 1760), a *festa teatrale* for the wedding of Joseph II to Isabella of Bourbon-Parma (with music by Johann Adolf Hasse), contains such an allegory, directed at the young Joseph. Once again, Metastasio intended the allegory to be recognized, and this genre has a long and demonstrable tradition that is entirely different than the sui generis Masonic interpretation posited for *Die Zauberflöte*.

Not only is there no compelling evidence for a hidden Masonic subtext, but one contemporary witness speaks against it. In the biography by Georg Nissen (written with Mozart's widow Constanze), we find a clear statement that Mozart did not intend a hidden allegory:

> Was war denn die Absicht des Dichters gewesen? Eine Parodie, eine Apotheose des Freymaurer-Ordens. Symbolisch: der Kampf der Weisheit mit der Thorheit—der Tugend mit dem Laster—dem Licht mit der Finsterniss [...] Ruft die Kindheit zurück, wenn Ihr die Zauberflöte verstehen wollt [...] nur als Unerklärbares die Kinderseele entzückend berauscht. Wahrlich, der Gewinn ist nicht erheblich, zu ergründen, wie und warum die Fabel in dem Kinde entstanden: das Mährchen nur und der Glaube daran kann das Mährchen belohnen. So glaubt zwey kurze Stunden, oder entsagt dem Genusse des holden Wahnes.
>
> Mozart hat es zuversichtlich nicht anders gemeint. Er hat nicht [...] in thöriger Weisheit die Tiefe gesucht [...] allem Vermögen des Kindes gebeut er [...] Hört nur die Ouvertüre, wie ernst es ihm war, wie dem holden Kinde im Glauben an die Zauberwelt die erste Ahnung eines Göttlichen in feyerlichen und so kindlich süssen Weisen erwacht![28]

Masonic interpretations of *Die Zauberflöte* too often exclude the literary background, the theatrical tradition, and the musical conventions that contributed to the character of this singspiel and others like it. These operas do not fit into any mixture of the heroic, comic, and pastoral categories.[29] Something essential is missing in these generic formula-

---

27. *La Gazzetta veneta* 103, 27 January 1761. For further details, see Carlo Gozzi, *Five Tales for the Theatre*, ed. and transl. by Albert BERMEL and Ted EMERY, Chicago and London, 1989, 185, and Ted EMERY, "Autobiographer as Critic: The Structure and 'Utility' of Gozzi's Useless Memoirs", in: *Italian Quarterly*, 154 (1983), 43-9.

28. Georg Nikolaus NISSEN, *Anhang zu W. A. Mozarts Biographie, nach Originalbriefen, Sammlungen alles über ihn Geschriebenen, mit vielen neuen Beylagen, Steindrücken, Musikblättern und einem Facsimile* (1828; R. Hildesheim, 1964), 112-14: "What was the intention of the poet? A parody, an apotheosis of the Masonic order, a symbolic struggle of wisdom and folly, virtue and vice, light with darkness. If you want to understand Die Zauberflöte recall childhood [...] only the inexplicable things will delightfully enthrall the soul of the child. Truly there is little advantage in fathoming how and why the fable arises in childhood. Only a fairy tale itself and the belief in it will justify the story. So be a believer for two hours or renounce the pleasure of charming illusion.

Mozart certainly intended nothing else. He did not [...] probe into the depths of foolish wisdom [...] He commands all the faculties of the child [...] Listen to the overture—how serious it was to him. Like a good child who believes in the magical world, these solemn and so childlike and sweet melodies awaken the first inkling of the divine."

29. A few modern discussions suggest some kind of mixed genre, e.g., James L. JACKSON, "Palella, Antonio", in: NGO, II, 831, who generically describes *Die Zauberflöte* as sub-species of *opera buffa* that he calls "'magic' opera". Mixed genres were discussed in eighteenth-century commentary, and fairy-tale singspiels like Schikaneder's *Der Stein der Weisen* (1790) sometimes bore the generic appellation 'heroisch-komische Oper'.

tions, both in regard to music and libretto. The explanation resides in fairy tales and the supernatural operas of the period.

Fairy Tales

In allegorical interpretations of *Die Zauberflöte* the fairy-tale element is posited merely as a superficial pretext for the symbolic representation of a Viennese secret society and its rituals. In *Mozart The Dramatist*, Brigid Brophy refers to the 'neutral or nonsensical (the 'fairy-tale') façade presented to outsiders—to cloak an utterance in code'.[30] This dismissive attitude toward fairy tales is apparent from the seventeenth century through the first half of the twentieth century.[31] French classicists derided the marvelous and the supernatural as vulgar and childish, associating them with low genres. Critiques during the Enlightenment savaged genres with supernatural content, including serious and comic opera. The values of these 'progressive' critics in the eighteenth century have often been adopted uncritically by modern scholars.

The notion that the Enlightenment banished superstition and the supernatural from the stage in favor of more natural and rational representations[32] results from accepting the ideological polemics of Enlightenment thinkers like Diderot, Grimm, and Rousseau.[33] In fact the supernatural enjoyed continued popularity on the stage as the challenge to religion and aristocratic authority increased. Writers like Jean-François Marmontel, Louis de Cahusac, and Carlo Gozzi pressed popular fantastic narratives into service, sometimes for their own ideological aims. As the fantastic was being challenged in the religious and political life of the period, it came to be reconstructed in the theatre where it fulfills a number of diverse functions. The new 'marvelous' of the eighteenth century treats certain 'exotic' cultures, derived from 'oriental' tales, as well as the indistinct agrarian past of

---

30. Brigid BROPHY, *Mozart The Dramatist: The Value of his Operas to Him, his Age and to Us* (New York, 1968/1988), 143.
31. The long tradition of disdain for fantastic and marvelous elements in opera begins with the polemics of Boileau and other classicists. A similar disdain is apparent in Claude PALISCA, *Baroque Music*, 3rd ed., New York, 1991, 141-2. Here the author judges the marvelous in Roman and Venetian opera as 'bauble', dismissing it from discussion or analysis. Likewise, Graham Sadler's articles in: *NGO* and his 'Rameau', *The New Grove French Baroque Masters*, New York, 1986, 262, delegates Rameau's *Zoroastre* to a lower status simply because it "makes excessive use of the supernatural".
32. See M. Elizabeth BARTLET, "Pièce à machines", in: *NGO*, III, 1008, who notes the "virtual disappearance of magic and gods as prime movers in the action" of opera in the late eighteenth century. Similarly, Daniel HEARTZ, "Les Lumières: Voltaire and Metastasio; Goldoni, Favart and Diderot", in: *International Musicological Society: Report of the Twelfth Congress Berkeley, 1977*, Kassel, 1981, 237, states that "Opéra comique inherited from the Théâtre de la Foire a certain amount of magic or mythological content, but the 'merveilleux' receded as the new type of libretto took shape, in favor of common everyday settings and plots".
33. Rousseau's polemics were integrated in historical writing and became accepted as fact by writers like Charles BURNEY, whose discussion of opera in: *A General History of Music*, London 1789, ed. Frank MERCER, New York, 1935, 555, "The Progress of the Music of Drama", is at times a literal translation from Jean-Jacques Rousseau's *Dictionnaire* [Paris, 1768], mod. ed. in: *Œuvres complètes* v, Écrits sur la musique, la langue et le théâtre, ed. Bernard GAGNEBIN, Marcel RAYMOND et alii, Paris, 1995.

indigenous European fairy tales. Here magic, superstition, and spirit rule once again, after being banished from the real world, that is to say, a reality verified only through natural science. This is one of the important roles of Freemasonry, which tells us much about the context of *Die Zauberflöte* and the libretto's apparent contradiction between fairy-tale fantasy and enlightened reason. Rather than a recondite subtext, Schikaneder probably intended the occasional Masonic reference in the text to evoke popular sentiment (see conclusions). This tension between reason and fantasy is one of the characteristic forces in the marvelous of the eighteenth century, and it informs most theoretical discussions of the topic. It lurks in the theatrical works themselves, where critiques of reason, of magical thinking, and proposed reconciliation of these two seemingly opposing spheres are frequently present in some form.

All theatrical productions require the suspension of disbelief to some degree. Audiences willingly participate in illusion and sacrifice the reality principle because fantasy allows for a safe distance from which to broach topics that would be disturbing if presented in a more explicit manner. In the repressive society of the eighteenth century the more controversial the topic, the greater need to distance it from everyday life when presenting it on the stage.

Fairy tales too often have been classified as children's literature, women's narratives, and folk material, products not of artistic genius but expressions of less sophisticated or even 'primitive' writers. This has been unfortunate. It is also true of oriental literature, which has been viewed as exotic and primitive, with consequences for reception comparable to that of the European fairy tale.

Fairy-tale Opera

Fairy-tale operas and plays have a long history, both in Viennese and other European theatres. Exotic oriental fairy tales, probably taken from the collections of Straparola and Basile, were used in seventeenth-century commedia dell'arte plays. Beginning c. 1697, the rage for *contes de fées* by Charles Perrault and his contemporaries, along with the French translations of *contes orientaux* in the early eighteenth century, inspired numerous musical comedies at the 'petit' theatres of Paris, and even large-scale operas and ballets at L'Académie royale. German operas and comedies also used this material, usually in adaptations from French sources. English and Italian writers did much the same, for example, Carlo Gozzi's *fiabe teatrali*.

Vienna's comic theatre repertory had a remarkable penchant for the marvelous, staging supernatural *Maschinenkomödien*, a term that refers to the stage machinery that facilitated the spectacular illusions in these productions. References to the numerous supernatural comedies are documented in Viennese periodicals. By the late 1770s, the term *Märchen* was used to describe fairy-tale singspiels. Johann Friedrich Schmidt adapted Carlo Gozzi's *Turandot* as *Hermannide, oder die Rätsel*, referring to the genre as 'ein altfränkisches Märchen' in five acts; it was performed at Vienna's Burgtheater on 25 Oct. 1777. In the preface to his *Das wütende Heer, oder Das Mägden im Thurme*, Christoph Friedrich Bretzner describes the singspiel as an example of Märchen. Graf von Spaur designated his Egyptian fairy-tale singspiel, *Der Schiffbruch*, as 'ein Mährchen' in four acts. Wenzel Müller refers to fairy-tale operas as 'Maschinenkomödie, Feenmärchen,' and 'Zauber Komödie' in his chronicle 'Kaiser=Königlich privil: Theater in der Leopoldstadt in Wien' [1781-1830],[34] and in his diary from 1781-1789.[35] The term is also used in various periodicals, for example, *Das Wienerblättchen*, *Die Wiener Zeitung*, and the *Kritisches Theater-Journal von Wien*. Karl Friedrich Hensler called his *Philibert und Kaspar im Reiche der Phantasey oder Weiber sind getreuer als Männer*, a 'Feenmärchen mit Maschinen, Flugwerken, und lustigen Charakteren' (Theater in der Leopoldstadt, 20 Jan. 1785). Friedrich Spengler's *Der Zauberdrachen oder Etwas für den Fasching* was designated as a 'Feenmärchen mit Maschinen und Gesänge[n] und Chören' (Theater auf der Wieden, January 1792).[36] Complete scores for fairy-tale operas of the period have survived. These operas were performed both in the Burgtheater and on other Viennese stages.[37]

Emanuel Schikaneder assumed the management of the Theater auf der Wieden in 1789 and soon produced his first fairy-tale opera based on Christoph Martin Wieland's epic tale, Paul Wranitzky's *Oberon, König der Elfen* (7 Nov. 1789). New *Märchenopern* were mounted at least three times a season. On 22 April 1790 Schikaneder staged his own musical 'Zauberkomödie', *Die schöne Isländerin oder Der Mufti von Samarkanda*, followed in September by his heroic-comic opera, *Der Stein der Weisen*. Schikaneder then mounted his 'Lust- und Zauberspiel', *Der wohltätige Derwisch oder Die Schellenkappe* less than half a year after *Der Stein der Weisen*. *Ludwig Herzog von Steiermark oder Sarmäts Feuerbär*, a Schauspiel 'nach einem alten Volksmärchen bearbeitet', credited to Eleonore Schikaneder, was staged the following August. One month later *Die Zauberflöte* had its premiere. It was the fourth in Schikaneder's series of fairy-tale productions based on texts associated with Wieland.

Analysis of the manuscript copies of the librettos of *Der Stein der Weisen* and *Der wohltätige Derwisch* in Berlin, Frankfurt, and Hamburg reveals a consistent approach on Schikaneder's part. He takes the general outline of one story from the fairy-tale collection *Dschinnistan*,[38] and appends elements from other stories in the collection. For *Der*

---

34. Wiener Stadt- und Landesbibliothek, [henceforth A-Wst], shelfmark Ja 51926.
35. A-Wst, shelfmark Ja 40426.
36. A poster for the sixth performance of the opera on 3 Feb. 1792 survives in Vienna's Gesellschaft der Musikfreunde.
37. These include André-Ernest-Modeste Grétry's *Zémire et Azor* (both the French original and several German adaptations), *Der Ring der Liebe [oder] Zemirens und Azors Ehestand*, a singspiel in three acts by Paul Weidmann, music by Ignaz Umlauf, Kärntnertortheater, 3 Oct. 1786, Bretzner's *Das wütende Heer, oder Das Mädgen im Thurme*, music by Joseph Martin Ruprecht, Kärntnertortheater, 1 June 1787, *Kaspar der Fagottist, oder Die Zauberzither*, a singspiel in three acts by Joachim Perinet, music by Wenzel Müller, Theater in der Leopoldstadt, 8 June 1791, *Das Irrlicht, oder Endlich fand er sie*, a heroisch-komisches Singspiel in two acts (based on *Der Irrwisch* by Christoph Friedrich Breztner), music by Ignaz Umlauf, Burgtheater, 17 Jan. 1782, and *Was erhält die Männer treu? oder Das Räthsel*, a romantische Oper in two acts, by Ludwig Zehnmark, music by Ruprecht, Burgtheater, 30 Mar. 1780.

Die Zauberflöte, Masonic Opera, and Other Fairy Tales

Stein der Weisen he relied mostly on Wieland's first story, 'Nadir und Nadine'. For *Der wohltätige Derwisch* he used Friedrich Hildebrand von Einsiedel's 'Die Prinzessin mit der langen Nase'. He would proceed similarly with *Die Zauberflöte*, using Jakob August Liebeskind's 'Lulu oder die Zauberflöte' as a model. All of these librettos exploit marvelous devices such as mysterious voices, oracles, spirits, magical spells and scenes with magical implements. Sages with supernatural powers make pronouncements, and initiations and trials are central to the plots. Some elements that modern writers often designate as Masonic in *Die Zauberflöte* appear in these fairy tales without such meaning. A trial of fire and water is mentioned in 'Der Stein der Weisen', one of Wieland's fairy tales in *Dschinnistan* that contains several Egyptian references (there is little or no relationship to Schikaneder's opera of the same name). Also depicted here is an exclusively male ritual. In 'Der Druid' an enlightened group of older males instruct a headstrong youth. Egyptian symbols also appear in this story. In 'Der Palast der Wahrheit' the hero is warned against 'women's falsehood'. In 'Der Zweikampf' the hero is required to make a vow to renounce associating with women. This is the same misogynistic tone that we find in *Die Zauberflöte*; it is more consistent with the exotic orientalism than with Freemasonry. 'Trials of silence', a common motif in fairy tales, were a familiar plot device on the stage, as demonstrated by the many Orpheus operas. In archetypal commedia dell'arte plots like *Il pozzo*[39] a magician requires the young hero to remain silent before his beloved as an initiatory trial of his virtue. Schikaneder used the admonition again in his 1797 singspiel, *Babilons Piramiden* (act 1, scene 3). As was the case in Mozart's opera, a wise elder cautions 'silence' to a hopeful (but in this case, corrupt) aspirant to the throne who comes to an ancient Babilonian temple. The point here is evoking ancient occult practice and not specifically Freemasonry.

Die Zauberflöte contains some of the motifs most frequently found in fairy tales. These include magic instruments and objects that have the power to change the hero's life, sagacious magicians, severe tests and trials, secret orders of initiates, temples, a pair of contrasting comrades on a mutual quest, and young couples, generally a prince and a princess.[40] The matching male and female forms of characters' names are typical (Nadir

---

38. *Dschinnistan, oder Auserlesene Feen- und Geistermärchen*, (Winterthur 1786, 1787, 1789), ed. Gerhard SEIDEL (Berlin, 1968). For details see my 'Fairy-Tale Literature and Die Zauberflöte', Acta Musicologica, 64 (1992), 30-49.
39. *Il pozzo* is found in Rome, Biblioteca Corsiniana, Ms. 45 G. 5 and 6, 'Raccolta di scenari più scelti d'istrioni divisi in due volumi', 1, 25, and in Rome, Biblioteca Casanatense, F. IV, 12-13, now codices 1211, 1212. 'Della scena de Soggetti comici et tragici di B(asilio) L(ocatelli) R(omano)' in two parts (1618 and 1622), nº. 6. Carlo Gozzi also used this motive in his 'tragicomic' tale *Il corvo* (1761). Other examples include Louis de Cahusac's 1743 fairy-tale comedy *Zénéide* (based on Antoine Hamilton's fairy tale, 'Zéneyde'), and the *dramma giocoso* by Caterino Mazzolà, *Rübenzahl, o sia il vero amore* (Dresden, 1789). In Wieland's fairy tale 'Die klugen Knaben', published in *Dschinnistan*, drei Knaben command the hero to be 'steadfast, patient and silent'.
40. For details, see Stith THOMPSON, *Motif Index of Folk Literature*, Bloomington, IN, 1955, 6 vols., and Idem, *The Types of Folktale: A Classification and Bibliography. Antti Aarne's Verzeichnis der Märchentypen*. Translated and Enlarged by Stith Thompson, Helsinki, 1961.

and Nadine, Mandolino and Mandolina, Papageno and Papagena, Tamino and Pamina). Plots often have heroes captured and then liberated. Humor is a common element, as are admonishing tales of drunkenness, lying, and exaggeration (Papageno's vices). Cowardice and talkativeness are punished by the loss of speech (Papageno's punishment). There are similar moralizing *Reden* in all of Schikaneder's fairy-tale singspiels, delivered in the cant of the current day. One should not be surprised if these speeches were pilfered from a variety of sources, including Masonic literature.

Mystics, dervishes, alchemy, temples, and Gnosticism are also common elements in fairy tales and fairy-tale operas of this period; they need not imply an allegory or a Masonic influence. Chailley asserts that armored men ('geharnischte Männer') are unusual characters, and that they allude to the clanking of armor in the Masonic initiation ritual. But 'geharnischte Männer' are found in Schikaneder's earlier works like *Ludwig Herzog von Steiermark oder Sarmäts Feuerbär* and *Der Stein der Weisen*. Chailley also includes the comic characters and sequences in his symbolic scheme. But this material is standard Schikaneder comedy, drawn from years of experience on the stage. There is little change from one singspiel to the other in this regard: Schikaneder's own rustic character is a constant. His wife is either a dominatrix or a young beauty.

A number of musical aspects of *Die Zauberflöte*, often characterized as Masonic, are apparent in Schikaneder's earlier non-Masonic singspiels. These include 'enchanted' wind music, trombones, ensembles of spirits, unearthly choruses, the use of the 'magic' solo flute, extensive and vividly pictorial instrumental writing, 'stage-machine' music, and the march for magic pantomime scenes. Chailley claims that Papageno's bells are an elemental symbol of the earth in the Masonic allegory. Yet Mandolino's (Schikaneder's comic character) magic bells in *Der wohltätige Derwisch*, attached to his enchanted fool's cap, were clearly the inspiration for Papageno's bells in *Die Zauberflöte*. (Other similar musical features include the Queen of the Night's scene with recitative and a B flat coloratura aria, bearing a strong resemblance to the appearance of Astromonte in act 1 of *Der Stein der Weisen*.) Chailley characterizes the arias for Sarastro in his Masonic scheme, claiming that the aria with chorus, 'O Isis und Osiris' is analogous to a prayer in the 'ceremony that opens the [Masonic] proceedings'. But Franz Xaver Gerl's character in *Der wohltätige Derwisch*, antedating Mozart's music for Sarastro by a half a year, was given similar sermonizing texts and a hymn-like musical style. The vocal music of these operas was tailored to the capabilities of the singers in the Wiednertheater, not to an abstract allegorical scheme.

Masonic Elements in *Die Zauberflöte*

If there was no acknowledged 'Masonic Opera' in the period, might there be enough demonstrable elements of Freemasonry in the libretto and score to warrant the appellation today? Peter Branscombe has observed that 'it is difficult to sift the sources in such a

---

41. BRANSCOMBE, p. 21.

way that no doubt is left as to the origins of specific details in the libretto of the opera.'[41] The evidence suggests that most of the putative 'Masonic' elements in Die Zauberflöte are ambiguous and not indisputably Masonic. Many of these elements are found in earlier stage works based on fairy tales.

Nettl and Chailley assert that the number three clearly designates Masonry. But the number three has symbolic meaning in a variety of older occult traditions (especially Egyptian) as well as in Christian mysticism. All of these supernatural associations predate Freemasonry. One finds the symbolic number three in theatrical fairy tales dating back at least to Lesage and d'Orneval's opéra comique Roger de Sicile, surnommé le roi sans chagrin, with music by Jean-Claude Gilliers (Foire St. Laurent, 28 July 1731).[42] The plot concerns King Roger, reputed to be the most joyful man in the world. But Roger has a terrible secret. Years ago he sent his ambassador to bring back his future bride from Castille. The ambassador, a cabalist and a magician-philosopher, fell in love with the princess on the trip back to Sicily. Throwing himself at her, she slapped him three times to rebuff his advance. He seized her and blew upon her three times, casting a spell on her. Every time her husband approaches she becomes ill. For three years this enchantment has persisted. Later Arlequin finds the statue of a giant with a saber that protects a magic elixir. A cartouche shows a rebus with three hands, three heads, and three suns. Beneath it is a sign explaining that the elixir in the bottle will cure the princess of the magician's spell. Only the honorable husband of a virtuous wife who has been married for three years will be able to take the bottle without fear of the giant that protects it. All others will be beheaded by the saber when they try to seize the bottle. Arlequin helps to retrieve the elixir and explains that the three hands represent the three slaps that the princess gave to the magician, the three heads are the decapitations, and the three suns are the three years duration of the enchantment.

A trio of supernatural beings is a common element in 'marvelous' opera, for example the Three Fates and the Three Furies. Some examples of the number three in fairy-tale singspiels include the three fairies that appear in Ludwig Zehnmark's Was erhält

---

42. Published in Alain-René LESAGE and D'ORNEVAL, Le Théâtre de la Foire ou l'Opéra-Comique... aux foires de S. Germain et S. Laurent. 10 vols., Paris 1721-37. Reprint in 2 volumes, Geneva, 1968, 1, [vii], vol. 9, 1737. [Émile CAMPARDON, Les Spectacles des foires... depuis 1595 jusqu'à 1791, 2 vols., Paris 1877, R. Geneva, 1970, 1, 267, gives the name Jacques-Philippe Dorneval, but I know of no source that corroborates this name.] This comic opera is based on the fairy tale 'Hormoz et Bedreddin Lolo', from François Pétis de la Croix, Les mille et un jours. Contes persans traduits en françois par M Pétis de la Croix, Paris, 1710-12, 5 vols. Published in modern edition (Paris, 1848), and more recently as Les mille et un jours. Contes Persans, texte établi, avec une introduction, des notices, une bibliographie, des jugements et une chronologie par Paul Sebag, Paris [c. 1980].
43. The libretto (Vienna: Logenmeister, 1780) is preserved in: A-Wn, shelfmark 629.128 B.Th, and in Vienna, Österreichisches Theatermuseum, Bibliothek, shelfmark Mus., 647.433-AM TB, and in the Library of Congress [henceforth Wc], shelfmark Schatz 9161. A manuscript score of Was erhält die Männer treu, ein Originalsingspiel is in A-Wn, shelfmark Mus. Hs. 16519. Ruprecht originally sang the role of Passerdo, the comic servant. He also composed music for Der blinde Ehemann, produced at Schikaneder's Wiednertheater in 1794. The card catalogue of A-Wn differentiates Stefan Ruprecht from Josef Martin while the NGO does not.

die Männer treu? a romantische Oper with music by Joseph Martin [or Stefan] Ruprecht, Burgtheater, 30 March [or 1 May] 1780.[43] Three magic lightning bolts strike in Christian August Vulpius's 'Egyptian' fairy-tale singspiel Der Schleyer (1786).[44]

Schikaneder used the occult association with the number three in numerous operas without apparent Masonic content. In Der Stein der Wiesen, Schikaneder's fairy-tale singspiel from one year before Die Zauberflöte, three thunderbolts accompany the magical appearance of the evil sorcerer Eutifronte (act 1, scenes 11-12). A magic drum must be struck three times in order to conjure an army of Turkish warriors in the fairy-tale singspiel that directly preceded Die Zauberflöte, Der wohltätige Derwisch (early 1791). In Schikaneder's singspiel Babilons Piramiden (1797) the number again has a magical association: Three knocks open a door to an ancient building used for Babilonian prophesy (act 1, scene 1); three leaves from a tree are required to consult an oracle (act 1, scene 2); a three-fold roll of thunder confirms the oracle (act 1, scene 2); three wise men of Assyria intercede to save Babylon; and finally, three glances of a sword open the Babylonian book of laws (act 2, scene 25). In all of these cases the number three suggests an occult or magical association and does not signify Freemasonry.

Another element presumed to be Masonic in Die Zauberflöte is the so-called 'trial' scenes in act 2, said to be thinly veiled representations of the Masonic initiation ritual. But there is nothing in these trial scenes that duplicate the Masonic ritual; walking through fire and water was never a part of Masonic initiation, much less an initiation for both a man and a woman simultaneously. While the scene may have been inspired by Masonic initiation, there is nothing here to suggest an intentional "Masonic' allegory of any kind was being communicated to the audience.

Many kinds of trials are common in fairy tales and in fairy-tale opera, where virtue, fidelity, friendship, and true love are proved through the testing of a youth or a young couple. Among the earliest staged fairy tales is the aptly titled Les Epreuves des fées, an opéra comique by Louis Fuzelier (Foire de St. Laurent, 28 July 1732).[45] The young initiate Finfinette undergoes a series of trials for induction into the 'ordre de féerie', beginning in act 3 at Merlin's magic cavern. To save the life of her beloved Alamir, Finfinette transforms him into a rock. She then tricks her nemesis, the evil fairy Papillone, and she changes Amalir back to his natural form. She proceeds with her trials, which are accompanied by music, a processional march similar in function to the one in Die Zauberflöte.

---

44. Music by Ernst Wilhelm WOLF (lost), produced at Weimar's Herzogliches Komödienhaus. Three librettos were published:
   1) C. A. Vulpius, Opern, Bayreuth and Leipzig: 1790, Wc, shelfmark Schatz 11084a.
   2) Gesänge aus dem Singspiele: Der Schleyer, Hamburg: Johann Matthias Michaelsen 1788, Wc, shelfmark Schatz 11084.
   3) Bayreuth and Leipzig: J.A. Lübecks Erben 1789. A copy is preserved in the Yale University's School of Music Library.

45. Manuscript in the Bibliothèque nationale de France [henceforth F-Pn], shelfmark f.f. 9337, fols. 115-50.

Young couples undergo initiatory trials in *Les Fées*, a comedy by Michel Procope Coltelli (called Procope-Coutaux) and Jean-Antoine Romagnesi, with music by Jean-Joseph Mouret[46] (Théâtre-Italien, 14 July 1736).[47] Other examples include *Les Ages ou la fée du Loreau*, a comedy by Anne-Claude-Philippe de Tubières Grimoard de Pestels de Lévis, comte de Caylus (Château de Morville, 20 Sept. 1739),[48] and *L'Oracle*, a comedy by Germaine-François Poullain de Saint-Foix, with music by Nicolas Ragot de Grandval, Théâtre-Français, 17 Apr. 1740.[49] In *La Belle Arsène*, a *comédie-féerie* by Charles-Simon Favart with music by Pierre-Alexandre Monsigny (Théâtre-Italien, 6 Nov. 1773[50]) the fairy Aline contrives a painful trial for the vain Arsène. The title character of *Fleur d'épine*, an 'opéra comique mêlée d'ariettes' by Claude-Henri Fusée de Voisenon,[51] is subjected to a trial that tests her steadfastness in the face of danger. She also withstands the improper advances of an undesirable suitor. This is done to prepare her for marriage to her intended prince, Tarare. Together they learn the lessons of delayed gratification and sacrifice, necessary virtues for beneficent monarchs.

Rameau's and Cahusac's *Zaïs* is an adaptation of a middle-Eastern fairy tale as a *pastorale-héroïque* (L'Académie royale, 29 Feb. 1748).[52] Zaïs, a genie of the air, falls in love with the shepherdess Zélide. The couple endures a trial where Zaïs abandons his supernatural power and immortality by renouncing his magic ring in order to be united with the virtuous Zélide (the king of the genies later restores his power and grants Zélide immortality after the couple proves their virtue). Rameau's most ambitious *tragédie en musique* was another collaboration with Cahusac, *Zoroastre* (L'Académie royale, 5 Dec. 1749, rev. 19 Jan. 1756).[53] Cahusac's 'Persian story'[54] concerns the magician Zoroastre, who by 1749

---

46. The music consists of a divertissement and vaudeville at the end, all of which is found in: J.-J. MOURET, *Sixième Recueil des divertissements du Nouveau Théâtre Italien*, Paris: author, s.d., 263-74. F-Pn, Acq. 7927, film R. 7197.
47. For details, see the *extrait* in *Mercure de France*, Aug. 1736, 1882ff. A print survives, *Les Fées, comédie en trois actes, par Messieurs Romagnesi & C*; [Procope Coutoceux] (s.l., s.n., s.d.), F-Pn, Musique, ThB 4023.
48. Manuscripts are preserved in the Bibl. de l'Arsenal 2748, fols. 1-16, along with another copy on fols. 17-44. Also a manuscript in F-Pn, f.f. 24343.
49. Paris: Prault fils, 1740, copy in F-Pn, 8° Yth 13088, and a later print, Paris: Prault fils, 1764, F Pn, Mus. Th.B 486B.
50. The *livret* was first printed in 1772. The music survives in a printed *partition*, Paris: Houbaut 1775, without overture, and printed parts, Paris: Houbaut, s.d.
51. Based on a satirical *conte de fées* by Antoine Hamilton, with music by Marie-Emmanuelle Bayon, Théâtre-Italien, 19 or 22 August 1776. The *livret* was published, Paris: Duchesne, 1777, with melodies appended at the end. Score edition, *Fleur d'Épine: Comédie en deux actes*, Paris: Huguet, [c. 1776], F-Pn, Musique, Rés. F.358, and H. 954. A collection, *Airs detachés de Fleur d'épine*, survives in F-Pn, Musique, Y. 552.
52. Published in reduced score, Paris: Delormel, s.d.
53. A reduced score was published c. 1749, Paris: Veuve Boivin, s.d. For a modern edition of the 1749 version, see *Zoroastre (version 1749)*, in: *Opera Omnia Rameau*, série iv/19 [RCT 62A], ed. Graham Sadler, Paris, 1999. For an edition of the 1756 revision see *Zoroastre. Tragédie Lyrique de L. de Cahusac. Resitution par Françoise Gervais*, Paris, 1964.
54. For a synopsis of both, see NGO, III, 1244-46. Like *Die Zauberflöte*, this opera has been read as a Masonic allegory, owing the fact that Cahusac was a Freemason and the story is set in Egypt. As in the case of Mozart's opera, there is no compelling evidence for this interpretation, which is purely speculative.

was already a familiar figure in the French musical stage.⁵⁵ The fairy-tale theme of trial and initiation is especially emphasized in the 1756 revision. Amélite has been abducted and imprisoned in order to undergo a trial to determine her virtue. Zoroastre is also tested to see if he will keep his faith in face of the impending loss of Amélite. Rameau's *Acante et Céphise, ou La Sympathie*, a *pastorale-héroïque* in three acts on a text by Jean-François Marmontel (L'Académie royale, 19 Nov. 1751),⁵⁶ is yet another pastoral fairy story about the testing of a young couple. Johann Christian Bach's *tragédie lyrique, Amadis de Gaule* (L'Académie royale, 14 Dec. 1779)⁵⁷ includes a short pantomime trial scene for the hero and his beloved Oriane at the conclusion of the opera. Amadis overcomes a series of obstacles leading to the 'Air pour le moment ou Amadis passe sous l'arc de loyaux amans', an elegant and solemn march for wind ensemble.

Urbélise et Lanval ou la Journée aux aventures is a three-act 'comédie-féerie ornée de musique et de chant' by Antoine-Jean Bourlin (called Dumaniant), with music by [?] Dupré (Théâtre des Variétés [Palais-Royale], 30 Apr. 1788).⁵⁸ On the day of her birth Destiny said that if Urbélise ever yielded to love, she would be in danger of losing her attractions and powers. The one who touches her heart must be unalterably faithful, for even one slight indiscretion or a chance word will bring her the greatest misfortune. The knight Lanval declares his love for her and his willingness to undergo any trial to win her. She tells him he must prove his fidelity, never uttering her name to anyone and never being unfaithful in word or deed. Her fate is in his hands, and they will be separated forever if he fails. He swears to meet these conditions, and succeeds.⁵⁹

Egyptian fairy-tale operas have a number of elements in common with *Die Zauberflöte*. Because Egyptian elements were absorbed into Masonry, they could be interpreted as Masonic; but that interpretation is speculative.⁶⁰ *Der Schiffbruch*, 'ein Mährchen' in four

---

55. Zoroastre is a character in *Les Forces de l'amour et de la magie*, a 'divertissment comique en trois intermèdes', by Maurice Vondrebeck and Charles Alard (St. Germain, 3 Feb. 1678), the oldest printed fair play. Zoroastre is also a character in *Sémiramis* by Destouches, 4 Dec. 1718, in *Pirame et Thisbé* by Rebel & Francœur (17 Oct. 1726), and in the 1732 ballet, *Les Génies ou les caractères de l'amour*, by Fleury de Lyon, music by Mlle. Duval, L'Académie royale, 18 Oct. 1736.
56. Printed score (Paris: Boivin, Le Clerc, s.d.), copies in F-Pn, X. 856, H. 709. A modern edition will appear in the *Opera omnia*, série IV/21, edited by Robert FAJON and Sylvie BOUISSOU.
57. The music was published in a score edition (Paris: Sieber, s.d.). The *livret* by Alphonse-Denis-Marie de Vismes du Valgay was based on Quinault's text for the opera by Lully.
58. The *livret* (Paris: Gattey 1788) is preserved in F-Pn, Imprimés, 8° 12653/54: "L'ouverture, les entre-actes & les airs de danse de M. Dupré, maître de musique du Th. du Palais-Royale". Michel Noiray, in a private communication, has evidence of an earlier premiere at the Théâtre des Variétés, 28 April, 1787.
59. The comic element occurs in the typical exchanges with the Arlequin character whose *lazzi* include a hanging scene at the scaffold. Other standard elements include a beautiful young fairy disguised as an old woman. There is also a scene where the hero falls in love with an image in a small portrait.
60. Richard ENGLÄNDER, *Johann Gottlieb Naumann als Opernkomponist (1741-1801)*, Leipzig, 1922, 167-68, 326-28, 337-59, has suggested that *Osiride*, a *dramma per musica* in two acts by Caterino Mazzolà, with music by Johann Gottlieb Naumann, Kleines Kurfürstliches Theater, 27 Oct. 1781, is a direct Masonic precursor of *Die Zauberflöte*. But unlike Schikaneder's singspiel, this is an Italian court opera, occasioned by the wedding of Prince Anton, the duke of Saxony, and Princess Caroline of Sardinia. The allegory here clearly reflects the nuptial circumstance. Engländer also suggests that Lorenzo da

acts by Graf von Spaur, was first performed in Königsberg in 1778, with music by Nikolaus Mühle (lost).[61] This Egyptian fairy-tale opera borrows elements from the commedia dell'arte,[62] Greek tragedy, and the biblical account of Joseph. The solemn scenes with priests in the temple predate a similar episode in the second act of *Die Zauberflöte* by over thirteen years. The plot concerns two brothers, the Egyptian King Malsora and his brother Makon, a wise magician who has been unjustly banished by his brother. Masora must successfully pass a trial of his virtue and be freed from the guilt of his crime against Makon. Makon in turn must restrain himself as his brother endures the trial. He tells Malsora that his daughter Selma has agreed to be punished for her father's crime against the gods. Selma has been imprisoned by the Furies in a rocky abyss, banished from humanity just as Makon was banished by Malsora. Through this trial Malsora sees the error of his ways, enduring his hardships with dignity and honor.

The most ambitious Parisian musical setting of a fairy-tale is *Alcindor*, an 'opéra-féerie' in three acts for the Royal Academy, on a text by Marc-Antoine-Jacques Rochon de Chabannes, with music by Nicolas Dezède (17 Apr. 1788).[63] Alcindor, king of the Island of Gold, only desires the glory of war. His genie-protector, Almovars, wants to make him more responsive to the happiness of his people, and so he subjects Alcindor to rigorous trials that test his virtue and teach him wisdom. There are several mysterious ceremonial scenes in a solemn temple and a dark grotto.

Like *Die Zauberflöte*, Christian August Vulpius's singspiel *Der Schleyer*, with music by Ernst Wilhelm Wolf (Weimar, Herzogliches Komödienhaus, 1786), has initiatory trials for both the noble and the comic couples, and magic implements. Christoph Friedrich Bretzner's three-act 'Operette', *Der Irrwisch, oder Endlich fand er sie* (also titled *Das Irrlicht*), was one of the most popular fairy-tale singspiel texts of the late eighteenth century.[64] The libretto includes an elaborate trial scene with maidens at the temple with a prophetic fire on the altar.

Ponte participated in the writing of the libretto and that Mozart knew the opera. Both suggestions are entirely speculative. The opera shares a number of elements with *Die Zauberflöte*, including moralizing speeches on enlightened rule, and a scene with a portrait given to the hero, causing him to fall in love with the beautiful image of a woman. The lovers are subjected to a trial of their virtue and the earth opens up and swallows the villains at the end. There is a scene for Ferdinando and Bodino in a dark subterranean area with unseen voices that promise that Ferdinando can rescue his beloved. All of this is couched in an archetypal Manichean struggle, with light and fire symbolizing good.

61. A libretto survives from the 1778 Frankfurt production, Frankfurt: Andreäische Schriften, 1778, with music by Franz Hugo, Freihern von Kerpen (lost).
62. Particularly the 'naufrage' plot, where a magician causes a shipwreck.
63. The *livret* was published, Paris: Delormel 1787, and Paris: Ballard 1787. The manuscript score and parts are in Paris, Bibliothèque-Musée de l'Opéra, shelfmark A. 319 (I-III), Mat. 18 [6 (parts); the dance music is found in the same library's *Recueil d'airs de ballet*, vol. 26.
64. Musical settings include 1) Friedrich Preu, Leipzig, Theater am Rannstädter Tor, 1779 (a manuscript score survives in Hamburg's Staats- und Universitätsbibliothek Carl-von-Ossietzky, and the libretto was printed (Leipzig: Carl Friedrich Schneider, 1779, and Leipzig: C. F. Schneider, 1788), 2) O. F. Holly, Breslau, 1779 (lost), 3) Otto Carl Erdmann, Freiherr von Kospoth, Berlin, Döbbelin's Theater, 2 Oct. 1780, 4) Nikolaus K. Mühle (in four acts, Königsberg, 1780, lost), 5) Christian Ludwig Dieter (Stuttgart, Kleines Theater,

The three direct predecessors of Die Zauberflöte at the Theater auf der Wieden all employ initiatory elements in their fairy-tale plots. Like Die Zauberflöte, Oberon, König der Elfen (7 Nov. 1789)[65] includes an initiatory trial for the lovers (Hüon and Amande, performed by the original Tamino and Pamina, Benedikt Schack and Anna Gottlieb). In Der Stein der Weisen (11 Sep. 1790) a young couple (Nadir and Nadine) are tested in order to merit the possession of the greatest of all magic implements, the philosopher's stone. In Der wohltätige Derwisch (early 1791) a prince named Sofrano must learn to withstand the seductive powers of an evil fairy-princess in order to learn the virtue of self-control and merit the inheritance from his father, a wise magician-king. In his fairy-tale singspiels that followed Die Zauberflöte Schikaneder regularly employed initiatory trials as a dramatic plot device.

August von Kotzebue's libretto Der Spiegelritter (Frankfurt, Nationaltheater, 11 Sept. 1791, with music by Ignaz Walter), also based on Dschinnistan, stresses the battle between good magic and evil sorcery. Again a prince undergoes trials by being offered food and wine on a magically set table (a device found in at least as far back as Shakespeare's The Tempest) by the evil dwarfs and beautiful maidens of the enchantress Milmi, who make seductive proposals.[66] The music includes prayers of thanks to heavenly powers that recall similar texts for Sarastro and his priests.[67]

The smaller details of the putative Masonic scheme are no less problematic. Chailley believes that the padlock, placed on Papageno's mouth as punishment, is a Masonic symbol borrowed from the female initiation ritual.[68] But Schikaneder used the padlock in approximately the same place in the first act of Der Stein der Weisen, where the woodsman Lubano (Schikaneder's role) places a padlock on the door of his cabin to imprison his unfaithful wife. Mozart even employs the music from Der Stein der Weisen's padlock episode in his first Quintet of Die Zauberflöte, when the padlock has been removed from Papageno's mouth (see Example 1).

The 'Masonic Overture'

Both Nettl and Chailley have asserted that the three flats in the key of E flat and the repeated chords at the beginning of Mozart's overture were intended to suggest Masonry's numerological symbolism. But no contemporary commentator on keys ever

---

23 Sept. 1782, 6) The musical numbers were revised and the work was retitled Das Irrlicht by Gottlieb Stephanie. Ignaz Umlauf provided music for a Viennese production, Burgtheater, 17 Jan. 1782.

65. The three-act romantisch-komische Oper by Karl Ludwig Giesecke was based on the more elaborate libretto by F. S. Seyler, who based her libretto, Hüon und Amande, Schleswig, 1788, on Wieland's epic poem.

66. Four prattling ladies have an ensemble scene with the comic companion, as in Die Zauberflöte. In the finale of act 3 Milmi sings a coloratura passage swearing vengeance ('Fluch über Dich! den bitterlichsten Fluch!... hört mein wüthendes Geschrei') that recalls the Queen of the Night's second aria.

67. Although it is not a fairy-tale opera, Karl Friedrich Hensler's Das Sonnenfest der Braminen, Leopoldstadttheater, 9 Sept. 1790, with music by Wenzel Müller, may have also inspired Schikaneder to include similar 'feierlich' choral numbers.

68. CHAILLEY, 1972, 111-12.

Example 1

designated this key as Masonic.[69] For C. F. D. Schubart (c. 1784), three flats represented the trinity; thus it had a Christian association.[70] The combination of winds (particularly the trombones[71]) and low-pitched strings do create a special timbre that suggests an exotic and otherworldly affect. This timbre permeates a number of different scenes in the opera. Mozart used a similar timbre in his *Requiem;* here the instrumentation suggests Christian solemnity. At least one earlier fairy-tale opera at the Wiednertheater, *Der Stein der Weisen*, has similar orchestration in the solemn finale of the second act, with trombones, trumpets, horns and low strings. This is a traditional instrumentation for episodes in the *merveilleux* style of many different types of opera. Gluck was particularly adept at employing these timbres in supernatural scenes.

The form of Mozart's overture recalls an old tradition, the French overture, which is suggestive of the source of operatic *merveilleux*, Lully's *tragédies en musique*. Quinault's operas had experienced a revival over the last fifteen years, and *Roland, Atys, Armide,*

---

69. See Rita STEBLIN, *A History of Key Characteristics in the Eighteenth and Early Nineteenth Centuries*, Ann Arbor, 1983.
70. Christian Friedrich Daniel SCHUBART, *Ideen zu einer Ästhetik der Tonkunst* [c. 1784-85], Vienna, 1806/Leipzig: Wolkenwanderer-Verlag, 1924, 261-62. Also see Jean-François LESUEUR, *Exposé d'une musique*, Paris: Vve. Hérissant, 1787.
71. Mozart's use of the basset horn is also supposed to suggest Freemasonry. But the composer employed the instrument in operas that have no Masonic content. For example, Mozart used a pair of basset horns in the insertion aria for Adriana Gabrieli ('la Ferrarese') in the revival of *La nozze di Figaro*, Vienna, July 1789, K. 577: 'Al desio, di chi t'adora,' and a solo basset horn in the aria 'Non più di fiori' from *La clemenza di Tito*, Prague, 1791. Schikaneder and Johann Baptist Henneberg recycled the latter aria (with a new German text) in their 1793 Wiednertheater singspiel, *Die Waldmänner*.

and *Amadis* were set to contemporary music in abridged *livrets* for the Paris stage. The opening chords of the overture in *Die Zauberflöte* are an invocation of sorts, an 'annonce', as the French called such instrumental segments in their operas. The initial wind and string 'Accords' serve as a kind of motto as well, as found in the introduction to Pamina's address to Sarastro in the first finale, 'Herr, ich bin zwar Verbrecherin', and 'der dreimalige Accord' in act 2, scenes 1 and 19.

The overture starts with material that recalls a celebrated Viennese supernatural court opera, Traetta's *Armida*, performed as late as 1780 in Vienna (see Example 2). The allegro as well as the slow introduction uses melodic material similar to *Die Zauberflöte*. Rather than a reference to a putative 'Masonic' musical style, these are references to a traditional aspect of the *merveilleux* in opera. Giuseppe Gazzaniga's opera seria, *La Circe* (D. Perelli, Venice, S Benedetto, 20 May 1786) has a similar opening, suggesting that this music may have had an association with marvelous operas with a powerful sorceress as an antagonist (see Example 3).[72] Operas without supernatural references also have similar opening chords, for example, Cimarosa's *Il matrimonio segreto* (Burgtheater, Feb. 1792). The use of three-fold chords in opera is an old tradition, without Masonic meaning. Gluck has a chord repeated three times to signal an otherworldly force in the ballet *Sémiramis* (Vienna, 1765), at the conclusion of *Telemaco, ossia l'isola di Circe* (Vienna, 1765),[73] and in *Iphigénie en Tauride* (1774, performed in a German translation at Vienna's Burgtheater in 1781).

Example 2

Traetta, *Armida*, "Sinfonia."

---

72. An almost identical motive is used to begin the overture to Ignaz Walter's *Des Teufels Lustschloss* (1801), also in E flat and also treated with counterpoint.
73. Christoph Willibald GLUCK, *Telemaco, ossia l'isola di Circe* in *Christoph Willibald Gluck: Sämtliche Werke*, gen. ed. Rudolf GERBER, Kassel, i/2, ed. Karl Geiringer, 1972.

Example 3

Gazzaniga, *La Circe*, Overture

The melodic and textural aspects of the contrapuntal allegro section hardly suggest Masonry. The main melody is a cliché used by numerous composers of that time, not just by Clementi in his 'allegro con brio' movement from the B flat sonata, Op. 24, n°. 2.[74] The motive suggests the idea of flight and exhibits Mozart's compositional virtuosity in a contrapuntal opening that is rare in contemporary opera overtures. French overtures with fast contrapuntal movements and intermittent sections of wind music recall Rameau's overtures, especially the overture to *Zoroastre*. The contrapuntal texture here suggests the learned style of church music, a frequent reference in supernatural operas. The key of E flat had been associated with the infernal realm by composers from Lully to Gluck.

Conclusions

Having demonstrated that elements often said to be Masonic were already at hand without Masonic meaning in earlier supernatural opera, one might re-evaluate the reasons for and against assuming that Schikaneder or Mozart deployed these elements as Masonic references in *Die Zauberflöte*. The fact that Mozart and Schikaneder were both Freemasons (although there is no evidence that Schikaneder was ever involved with a Viennese lodge) does not constitute a reason as such. Other Viennese librettists and composers were Freemasons and there is no evidence of them including Masonic references in their operas. One composer, Paul Wranitzky, whose Masonic credentials equaled those of Mozart, even composed the music for the earlier fairy-tale opera at the Wiednertheater in 1789, *Oberon, König der Elfen*. Like *Die Zauberflöte*, the text of *Oberon* was based on the writing of Christoph Martin Wieland. Schikaneder's theatre poet, Karl Ludwig Giesecke, adapted the text from an earlier libretto. While Giesecke was also a Freemason and a member of Mozart's lodge there is nothing in the opera to suggest Freemasonry. Nor was Giesecke ever known to have produced a 'Masonic' text among the numerous pieces he wrote for Schikaneder. Schikaneder's own libretto for *Der Stein der Weisen*, with a hint of alchemy in its title, seems even more suitable for the Masonic treatment, and Mozart was even involved in some of the music for this opera.

---

74. Otto JAHN, *W. A. Mozart*, Leipzig 1859, repr. Hildesheim, 1976, iv, 612, cites another similar theme from J. H. Collo's cantata, *Lazarus' Auferstehung*, Leipzig, 1779.

But again, there is nothing here to suggest Freemasonry as a broad subtext. Fairy-tale elements are the basis for this libretto, just as there are for *Die Zauberflöte*.

Another frequently cited reason for assuming Masonic references in *Die Zauberflöte* is that Schikaneder paraphrased a few passages from Jean Terrasson and perhaps from Ignaz von Born. It is far more likely that he used these texts because they offered convenient jargon suggesting arcane, occult wisdom, rather than to create a hidden level of meaning. Ludwig von Batzko's statement that 'scenes obliquely allude to the ceremonies of certain orders; even the uninitiated will understand provided they are acquainted with mysteries of the ancient culture' is accurate when seen in this light. Schikaneder probably intended that these scenes (for example, act 2, scene 1) should suggest authentic occult ceremonies, including but not limited to those used in Freemasonry. But one cannot conclude from this that he intended a broader allegory or one that was specifically Masonic. The only plausible reason to interpret other elements in the opera as casual, fragmentary references to Freemasonry is that Schikaneder and Mozart may have wanted to include something familiar for members of the audience aware of Masonic practices. This was, after all, Schikaneder's stated aim: to insure a successful box office.[75] (Creating a network of hidden references would not further this aim.) The problem with this explanation is that not many members of the audience would be familiar with the minute details of Masonic ritual. But many would be entertained by vague allusions to occult ceremony and wisdom. Indeed, no contemporary account of *Die Zauberflöte* in Vienna even mentions Freemasonry or suggests allegory of any kind.

Assuming a complex of hidden Masonic references also contradicts what we know of Schikaneder's approach to writing librettos. Throughout his career Schikaneder had to address charges of literary ineptitude and a lack of sophistication. His librettos contain few literary allusions and occasional awkwardness in poetry, language and plot.[76] *Die*

---

75. Schikaneder's intentions were stated several times and in different contexts. The best example is cited in note 26. Another example is found in a verse he added to his aria 'Ein Weib ist das herrlichste Ding auf der Welt' from his comic opera, *Der dumme Gärtner aus dem Gebürge, zweiter Theil, oder Die verdeckten Sachen* (1789):

   Ich bin wohl der glücklichste Mann von der Welt,
   Wenn stets unser Schauspiel den Gönnern gefällt,
   Ich suchte von jeher durch stetes Bemüh'n,
   Den Beyfall des Publikums an mich zu zieh'n,
   Ich danke dafür mit dem wärmsten Gefühl,
   Ihn stets zu verdienen, sey einzig mein Ziel...

   This *envoi* is found in *Text der Arien des dummen Gärtners aus dem Geburge oder die zween Anton...*, Vienna: Matthias Ludwig in der Singerstrasse Nro. 928: 1790, copy in Vienna, Österreichisches Theatermuseum, Bibliothek, shelfmark 698.427-A Ths. 200b.

76. Ignaz von SEYFRIED, "Commentar zur Erzählung: Johan Schenk, von J. P. Lyser, in Nr. 27 u. s. des 11ten Bandes der neuen Zeitschrift für Musik," *Neue Zeitschrift für Musik* xii, Jan-June 1840, Leipzig: Robert Friese, n° 45, 2 June 1840, 179-80, described Schikaneder as a practical, instinctive and unsophisticated librettist: 'Schikaneder [...] war und blieb im strengsten Wortsinn Naturalist; [...] sah er sich stets nur auf sich selbst beschränkt; [...] Jenen gänzlichen Mangel literarischer Kenntnisse ersetzte aber, wenigstens theilweise, ein offener Kopf, praktische Erfahrung, richtiger Tact, gesunder Menschenverstand,

Zauberflöte is no exception, and it is consistent with his other librettos, which do not contain symbolic material to be decoded. Thus Schikaneder's evocations of occult ceremony, cant, and platitudes used by Freemasons was more likely to be perceived on the "surface" of the performance rather than as a key to some deeper meaning.

In summary the evidence suggests that it is unlikely that Schikaneder and Mozart intended a pervasive Masonic allegory, although a few fragmentary elements in the libretto may obliquely refer to Freemasonry. This is not to say that the Craft played an insignificant role in Mozart's and Schikaneder's circle, that it ought to be ignored when discussing the intellectual background of the opera, or even that the librettist and composer of *Die Zauberflöte* never associated Freemasonry with their project in some way. But the evidence presented above challenges the equalizing of the indisputable fairy-tale elements with interpretations that are purely speculative and based on flimsy evidence at best. While one would not argue for an end to speculation based on peripheral sources, one must separate speculation from fact, and apply a more rigorous standard of evidence in advocating a theory. The fairy-tale singspiels that directly preceded *Die Zauberflöte* in the Wiednertheater establish the context of Mozart's opera and reveal the importance of fairy tales and the theatrical 'marvelous' in its libretto and score.

Mutterwitz, Bühnenroutine, und eine, obschon regel= und zwangslos ausschweifende, aber nichts destoweniger fruchtbare Phantasie; wodurch es denn auch erklärbar wird, weshalb die vorzüglichsten Componisten jener Epoch seine poetischen Ausgeburten nicht verschmähten, bei der elenden Verselei und dem erbärmlichen Reimgeklingel gutmüthig die Augen zudrückten, und dagegen an den reichen Situationswechsel, an die stets wohlberechneten, musikalisch=effectvollen Momente sich hielten.' Although Seyfried's second- and third-hand accounts are often unreliable, in this instance he is speaking from first-hand knowledge. He had been composing music for Schikaneder's productions (and librettos) since 1797 and he became a music director at the Theater auf der Wieden and then at the Theater an der Wien. His contact with Schikaneder in exactly the same collaborative role as that of Mozart makes this assessment more credible than those based on second-hand reports and rumor.

Part VII
Opera Seria

[22]

The Venetian Role in the Transformation of Italian Opera Seria During the 1790s

Marita P. McClymonds

While opera seria in Italy during most of the century had remained impervious to innovations initiated outside its borders, the fact remains that the genre did change, and change radically, between 1785 and 1800. So marked is the difference that the term opera seria no longer seems appropriate. How did this happen so quickly and with such apparent uniformity?[1]

Theaters in four cities appear to have functioned as the principal trend-setters in Italy during the last two decades of the century: Naples, Milan, Florence, and Venice. From them new librettos regularly emanated, and through them most successful librettos from domestic and foreign theaters were introduced to the Italian circuit.

Operas produced at these four centers in the 1780s fell into five categories, listed here in order of frequency; 1) newly-composed works on pre-existing but revised libretto; 2) revivals of previously-composed works revised to suit the local theater; 3) works for which both the text and the music were new; 4) composite works, known as *pasticci*, based on a revised libretto with music borrowed from several previously-composed works; 5) faithful reproductions of previously-composed works.

So strong was the tradition to revise operas and librettos for local requirements that the honor of a revival faithful to the composer's original score or the librettist's original text was seldom accorded. Even with new librettos, theaters mounting subsequent productions were more likely to order a new setting than to import the original. Furthermore, if successful, the

---

[1] This study would have been impossible without the help of such monumental bibliographical tools as Claudio Sartori's *Primo Tentativo di catalogo unico dei libretti italiani a stampa fino all'anno 1800*, (Milano: URFM, 1980), photocopy; *The New Grove Dictionary of Music and Musicians*; Oscar Sonneck, *Catalogue of Opera Librettos Printed before 1800*, 2 vols. (Washington: Government Printing Office, 1914); Ugo Sesini, *Catalogo della Biblioteca del Liceo Musicale di Bologna*, Vol. 5, *Libretti d'opera in musica* (Bologna: Azzoguidi, 1943); Franz Stieger, *Opernlexikon*, 6 vols. (Tutzing: Schneider, 1980); Taddeo Wiel, *I teatri musicali veneziani del Settecento* (Venezia: Visintini, 1897); Felice de Filippis and R. Arnese, *Cronache del Teatro di S. Carlo (1737–1960)* (Napoli: Politica Popolare, 1961); Giuseppe Pavan, *Saggio di cronistoria teatrale fiorentina: serie cronologica delle opere rappresentate al Teatro degli Immobili in Via della Pergola nei secoli xvii e xviii* (Milano: G. Ricordi, ca. 1900); Carlo Gatti, *Il Teatro alla Scala nella storia e nell'arte (1778–1963), cronologia completa degli spettacoli e dei concerti*, Giampiero Tintori, editor (Milano: Ricordi, 1964); and the Albert Schatz Collection of Librettos in *US-Wcm*, microfilm. I am indebted to the libraries whose sigla appear here for their generosity in providing access to their collections of librettos and music manuscripts. Research in Europe was made possible through a fellowship from the American Council of Learned Societies, 1984–85, and a Sesquicentennial Associateship through the Center for Advanced Studies, University of Virginia, 1985–86.

libretto was likely to circulate in several distinct versions written for subsequent productions, sometimes under different titles.²

The number of serious operas mounted in each city remained remarkably stable throughout the last twenty years of the century. Milan produced about two dozen per decade, and the other three about twice that number. The 1790s saw a slight increase everywhere except in Venice, where the number virtually doubled, almost as if, after preoccupying themselves with comic opera for several decades, Venetians began to view opera seria as a novelty to be cultivated.

The formal aspects of the repertory during the early 1780s offer few indications of the radical changes to come. The traditional format of alternating recitative and exit aria still prevails. The average libretto has three acts and thirteen to sixteen arias, perhaps one or two cavatinas, which are arias without a subsequent exit, and rarely one or more choruses. The third act is quite short and has one to three arias. The first two acts end with an ensemble—one is always a duet for the principal couple and the other a trio or occasionally a quartet, which may contain some minimal action. The last act usually ends with a construction that requires some solo participation on the part of the principals in addition to the traditional tutti Coro.³ A Venetian libretto nearly always has an additional duet or other ensemble in the third act, a practice that did not become common in Naples until after 1785 and was never established in Milan.

Each center had its own preferences regarding the selection of existing librettos for new settings. All theaters depended on Metastasian texts for the heart of the season along with a sprinkling of reworked librettos by others writing before mid-century—namely Zeno, Salvi, Silvani, Pizzi, Roccaforte, and Piovene. The number of new operas produced depended on the availability of a talented librettist, while the equally rare revival was likely to be a work by Gluck or a particularly successful setting of a new libretto.

All four centers imported from Vienna or St. Petersburg some French-inspired librettos based on mythological subjects with their attending machine spectacle, multiple choruses frequently combined with soloists and ballet, and scene complexes, which are scenes containing more than one musical number without an attending exit. A scene complex may contain no more than a couple of choruses. It may also freely combine recitative, cavatinas, short ensembles, ballet, and chorus into units that extend over more than one scene, meaning that it involves an increase or decrease in personnel. The scene complex stands at odds with Italian practice, which dictated that exits must follow all ensembles and most arias and that choruses and ensembles must be kept to a minimum. Furthermore, composers frequently set scene complexes in combinations of obbligato, accompagnato and measured recitative, whereas in Italian opera of the 1780s orchestrally-accompanied recitative was still invariably reserved for emotional solo scenes and seldom accompanied action.

---

² For the history of one such set of related librettos, see McClymonds, "Haydn and His Contemporaries: *Armida abbandonata*" in *Haydn Kongress Wien 1982*, Eva Badura-Skoda, editor (München: Henle, 1986), pp. 325–32.

³ This may take the form of a short ensemble preceding the Coro, of which Metastasio's *Antigono* of 1744 carries about the earliest example. It may take the form of a group of short solo comments sandwiched between two statements of the Coro, as Metastasio used to conclude his *Il trionfo di Clelia* of 1762, or there may be a rondo finale in which several solo, duo or trio sections alternate with the tutti, a form taking its inspiration from the French *vaudeville*.

Only Naples and Florence mounted a Gluckian revival, that of *Alceste* in 1785 and 1786 respectively. Wiel records a Venetian revival in 1783 of Bertoni's setting of Calzabigi's *Orfeo*, which Florence mounted the following year, and both theaters produced Tarchi's new setting of Coltellini's *Ifigenia in Tauride* as revised for Milan in 1784. Milan and Naples also ordered new settings of Coltellini's librettos. Schuster on a visit from Dresden set his *Amore e Psiche* for Naples in 1780, and Milan, in 1789, produced Campobasso's setting of his Russian libretto *Antigona*, written for Traetta in 1772. In addition Naples produced several totally new operas on Greek subjects involving deities including Paisiello's *Fedra* of 1788 on Salvioni's translation of Quinault.[4] The only one to achieve any success in the North was Sertor's *Enea e Lavinia* of 1785, which was written for Guglielmi, newly-resettled in Naples at the culmination of an international career. *Enea* is among the first of many operas to incorporate a ghostly appearance. Venice imported Guglielmi's *Enea* in 1788, and Milan followed in 1789 with a revised version, in which a new scena and aria for Lavinia replaces the scene complex in which Dido's ghost appears, and the number of acts are reduced by providing a quick closing following the trio that originally concluded Act II.[5]

The wide-spread though infrequent productions of French-inspired operas in Italy during the 1780s by no means insured the adoption of their distinctive characteristics into opera seria, where these, along with Verazi's formal innovations introduced in the opening season of La Scala, 1778–79, appear only sporadically and in very modest proportions in opera seria before 1786. Indeed, Verazi's controversial operas left no traces in the Milanese repertory other than the modest incorporation of chorus and ballet within operas produced from 1780 to 1784.[6] The operatic innovations in Ferdinando Moretti's early librettos for Milan are modest indeed. In 1783, *Idalide* can boast only of an exotic Peruvian setting with an earthquake, and *Ademira*, an introductory antiphonal chorus, a chorus with central solo section, and, more significantly, a short duo cavatina with an interruption by a third character. Moretti reverses the construction in *Il conte di Saldagna* for Milan in 1787, where an aria has interruptions by

---

[4] Ranieri de' Calzabigi and Christoph Willibald Gluck, *Alceste* (Napoli, 1785), libretto in *I-Nc*; (Firenze: Albizziniana, 1786), libretto in *I-Fc*; Wiel, *I teatri* ... p. 371; Conte de Salvioli, Calzabigi and Ferdinando Bertoni, *Aristo e Temira, ed Orfeo ed Euridice* (Firenze, 1784), libretto in *I-Bc*; Marco Coltellini and Angelo Tarchi, *Ifigenia in Tauride* (Venezia: Fenzo, 1786), libretto in *US-Wcm*; (Firenze, 1786), libretto in *I-Fc*; Coltellini and Carlo Monza, *Ifigenia in Tauride* (Milano: Bianchi, 1784), libretto in *US-Wcm*. All of the *Ifigenia* librettos cited have been quite wrongly attributed to Benedetto Pasqualigo. Coltellini and Joseph Schuster, *Amore e Psiche* (Napoli: Flauto, 1780), in *I-Nc*; Coltellini and Vincenzo Campobasso, *Antigona* (Milano: Bianchi, 1789), in *US-Wcm*, which also holds a copy of Traetta's score of 1772; Abate Salvioni and Giovanni Paisiello, *Fedra* (Napoli: Flauto, 1788), in *US-Wcm*.

[5] Gaetano Sertor and Pietro Guglielmi, *Enea e Lavinia* (Napoli: Flauto, 1785), in *US-Wcm*, (Venezia: Fenzo, 1788) and (Milano: Bianchi, 1789) in *I-Bc*. Vincenzo de Stefano has also been credited with this libretto.

[6] For detailed discussions of Mattia Verazi's innovations see: McClymonds, "Mattia Verazi and the Opera at Mannheim, Stuttgart and Ludwigsburg," in *Studies in Music from the University of Western Ontario* 7-2 (1982), pp. 99–136; and McClymonds, "Verazi's controversial *drammi in azione* as realized in the music of Salieri, Anfossi, Alessandri and Mortellari for the opening of La Scala, 1778–1789," in *Scritti in memoria di Claudio Sartori*, edited by François Lesure and Mariangela Donà, 43–87. Strumenti della ricerca musicale, 3. Lucca: Libreria Musicale Italiana Editrice, 1997.

two others. A Verazi legacy, such constructions will become regular operatic components in the 1790s.[7]

Venetian librettos in the early 1780s, like those for Milan and Florence, are still conservative for the most part, but unlike in Milan, they do show indications of Verazi's influence. In 1780, Bianchi's *Demetrio*, a rare opera with only two acts, has a quartet within Act II and concludes with a big action ensemble finale extending over two scenes. The same year, Anfossi, who had set one of Verazi's librettos for La Scala, composed for *Nitteti* a duet interrupted by a third person who then leaves, and an ensemble finale occupies the entire final scene.[8]

Hereafter either new or newly-set librettos by the Venetian librettist Gaetano Sertor cautiously incorporated innovations destined to become standard in the 1790s. New settings of Bianchi's two operas on Sertor's texts for Naples in 1781, *Arbace* (Borghi) and *Zemira* (Anfossi), were ordered for Venice in 1782. Anfossi's setting of *Zemira* in two acts begins with a storm and a trio, and there are two duets and a trio in addition to a quartet finale, which incorporates some action. Bianchi's *Piramo e Tisbe* of 1783 has an ensemble finale that begins as a duet and becomes a trio. Giordani's *Osmane* of 1784 has multiple cavatinas (four long ones for solo and one duo), an aria interrupted by the sounds of battle, another where the character offers some concluding comments in recitative before exiting, and a dynamic trio that dispenses with the traditional static quatrain for each character by moving directly into short solos and comments.[9]

Besides the innovations to be found in Sertor's librettos, Sarti's *Attalo re di Bitinia* of 1783 has two internal action ensembles (a quartet within Act II and a duet within Act III), and Act II concludes with an aria based on three strophes of poetry replete with instructions for stage actions—another Verazi legacy.[10] None of these modest inroads into Italian operatic conventions begin to compare with French-inspired revivals of Bertoni's *Orfeo* or Tarchi's *Ifigenia in Tauride*, but their significance must not be underestimated, because they, like Moretti's innovations, occur within the context of Italian opera seria itself rather than within an anomalous foreign import. Furthermore, all the departures from traditional formal practices observed above will become regular options for librettists in the 1790s.

---

[7] After Moretti wrote his first operas, *Idalide* (Sarti) and *Ademira* (Tarchi), for performance in Milan in 1783–84, he produced nine more librettos mainly for Milan with settings by Tarchi or Zingarelli. His *Castore e Polluce*, set by Sarti for St. Petersburg in 1786, earned him an invitation to that city where between 1788 and 1791 he provided a number of works for Cimarosa. Ferdinando Moretti and Giuseppe Sarti, *Idalide* (Milano: Bianchi, 1783), in *I-Bc*; Moretti and Angelo Tarchi, *Ademira* (Milano: Bianchi, 1784), in *I-Bc*; Moretti and Sarti, *Castore e Polluce* (St. Petersburg, 1786), manuscript scores in *US-Wcm, F-Pn, I-Nc* and *Mc*; Moretti and Tarchi, *Il conte di Saldagna* (Milano: Bianchi, 1787), in *US-Wcm, I-Bc* and *Mc*.

[8] Metastasio and Francesco Bianchi, *Demetrio* (Venezia: Fenzo, 1780), in *US-Wcm*. Metastasio and Pasquale Anfossi, *Nitteti* (Venezia: Fenzo, 1780), in *US-Wcm*.

[9] Sertor and Bianchi, librettos for both *Arbace* and *Zemira*, (Napoli: Flauto, 1781), in *I-Nc*; librettos for both Sertor and Anfossi, *Zemira*, and Sertor and Giovanni Battista Borghi, *Arbace* (Venezia: Fenzo, 1782), in *US-Wcm*. Sertor and Bianchi's *Piramo e Tisbe* (Venezia: Fenzo, 1783), in *US-Wcm*, is based on Coltellini's tragic intermezzo for Johann Hasse (Vienna: Ghelen, 1768), in *GB-Lbl*, but with a happy ending appended. Sertor and Giuseppe Giordani, *Osmane* (Venezia: Fenzo, 1784), in *US-Wcm*.

[10] Antonio Salvi and Sarti, *Attalo re di Bitinia* (Venezia: Fenzo, 1783), in *US-Wcm*.

Two works performed during Carnival, 1786, proved pivotal for Italian opera seria: Pietro Giovannini's *La vendetta di Nino ossia La morte di Semiramide*, which Prati set for Florence, and Giuseppe Foppa's *Alonso e Cora*, which Bianchi set for Venice. Based on Voltaire's *Semiramis*, *Nino* treated the forbidden topics of inadvertent incest and matricide. Here, in total disregard for the rules of sensibility, the vengeful ghost of the king presides over his guilty wife's murder at the hands of their son, not offstage, as in Voltaire's version, but before the horrified audience. This opera initiated a trend towards the depicting of death on stage and led to a rash of both "vendetta" and "morte" operas.[11]

Alonso e Cora, the first opera from the pen of a second innovative Venetian librettist, Giuseppe Foppa, has a Peruvian plot based on stories of Marmontel and others. Components soon to become standard are the extensive opening chorus with solos and duos, the multiple cavatinas of one, two, and three strophes, and the scene complexes incorporating cavatina, ensemble, chorus and dance that conclude Acts I and III. In combination they succeeded in challenging the most persistent of all eighteenth-century conventions, the exit aria, here reduced from the usual fourteen or fifteen to only eleven.[12]

In 1787, Moretti responded with an even more radical work for Milan, *Il conte di Saldagna*. The setting is not the traditional Greek or Roman one, but medieval Spain. The central characters are not the traditional betrothed couple, but are secretly married. Choruses occur singly, assert themselves within scenes as characters, alternate with solo voices, follow ensembles and combine with dance, and each act closes with a divertimento-like scene complex incorporating elaborate pantomime ballets, a Verazi legacy replacing the traditional ballets between the acts. The finale is, if possible, even more shocking than that of *Nino*. It

---

[11] Abate Pietro Giovannini and Alessio Prati, *La vendetta di Nino ossia La morte di Semiramide* (Firenze, 1786), in *I-Bc*. Moretti has frequently been credited with this libretto, but Robert L. Weaver in a letter to me dated 12 November 1987, states, "the *Gazzetta universale*, p. 224, and *Gazetta toscana*, p. 53, have notices that correct the *Indice dei spettacoli teatrali*, which assigns the text to Ferdinando Moretti, by stating that the true author of the poetry is Abate Pietro Giovannini [...]". Moretti's libretto on this subject, entitled *Semiramide*, which has been wrongly attributed to Metastasio, was produced in Milan with music by Mortellari the previous year (Milano, 1785, in *US-Wcm*). The author himself chose a somewhat revised version of this text for publication in the four-volume *Opere drammatiche di Ferdinando Moretti* (St. Petersburg, 1796, in *I-Vgc*). (See also R.-Aloys Mooser, *Annales de la Musique et des Musiciens en Russie au XVIIme Siècle: Tome II L'époque glorieuse de Catherine II (1762–1796)*, Genève, Mont-Blanc 1951, pp. 499–502.) Though Moretti's approved version as published in Russia and the Florentine version share a common plot plan (inherited from Voltaire), they are otherwise totally different, not even sharing the same cast of characters, as John Rice was first to point out. Furthermore, in the Milanese version, Moretti avoids the need for a vengeful matricide by establishing the queen as a remorseful accomplice not directly responsible for her husband's murder. Thus, by killing his father's actual murderer, offstage, Arsace could be happily reconciled with his mother. Antonio Sografi's reworking of Giovannini's version began with Act I for Sebastiano Nasolini (Padova 1790, in *I-Vcg*), and was completed for Giovanni Battista Borgi (Milano, 1790, in *US-Wcm*). Even Sografi modified the ending so that the parricide is accidental. The version Venice imported (Venezia, 1791, in *US-Wcm*), though it attributes all of the music to Prati, is a three-act version of the Paduan composite, which retains the original matricide. Beginning with the Paduan composite, Sografi's reworkings are entitled *La morte di Semiramide*, though he is credited only in librettos of the complete reworking for Borghi in Milan and thereafter.

[12] Giuseppe Foppa and Bianchi, *Alonso e Cora* (Venezia, 1786), in *US-Wcm*.

begins with a dance of celebration for the publicized marriage. While the chorus sings of joy, the hero is handed a poisoned glass. Dying, he interrupts their song, and they join with the principals in a short final ensemble as he expires.

In applying French-inspired elements to plots based on human affairs rather than ancient mythological subject matter, Foppa's *Alonso* and Moretti's *Il conte di Saldagna* of a year later both took a giant step beyond Coltellini's and Calzabigi's French-inspired operas, as well as beyond Verazi's La Scala operas of the late 1770s and Paisiello's *Fedra* still to come in 1788. Paisiello's enormously successful *Pirro*, produced in both Naples and Venice in 1787, provided yet further strong impetus for change. Paisiello had just returned to Naples after nearly ten years in Russia and Vienna. *Pirro* was the work of Gamerra, who had provided three new operas for Salieri in Vienna in the mid-70s and had most recently done a successful opera *Erifile*, which Bianchi first set for Florence in 1779.[13] Undoubtedly *Pirro*, which was based on a historical subject traditional in opera seria, was largely responsible for establishing a legitimate place within the genre for the two most powerful formal constructions in comic opera—the multisectional, action ensemble finale spread over several scenes of increasing personnel (see Example 1A and 1B) and its modest counterpart at the opening of the opera, the Introduzione.

Indirectly Paisiello also encouraged the incorporation of scene complexes within opera seria through a setting of Metastasio's *Nitteti* for St. Petersburg in 1777, which Florence revived in 1788. Mid-Act II, scenes 11-14, of this opera, a great scene complex encompassing several scenes combines an antiphonal chorus, a cavatina of two strophes, an action ensemble with chorus, an exit aria of three strophes, and a final chorus (see Example 2.). Thereafter, Milan engaged Bianchi, and Venice hired Bertoni to write new settings of *Nitteti* incorporating the Russian innovations for performances in 1789.[14]

The importation of *Pirro* to Venice in 1787 marks yet another historical milestone. After years when the San Benedetto was the only Venetian theater producing opera seria, it was the San Samuele that first imported *Pirro* and followed the next year with Guglielmi's *Enea e Lavinia*, in which Dido's ghost scene remains intact.[15] Two faithful revivals imported from Naples in successive years constituted an unprecedented and audacious initiation. Furthermore, the San Samuele produced more serious operas than did the San Benedetto that year. Thereafter the number of opera seria done in Venice each year doubled, and the rate continued unabated even after La Fenice took over opera seria production from the San Samuele in 1793.

In the last years of the decade, operas containing the formal departures already discussed as well as more recent innovations became increasingly numerous. Foppa continued to provide operas for Venice based on exotic subjects that incorporated chorus, ballet and scene complexes. *Calto*, based on Britanni's *Poemi d'Ossian*, in 1788, also reinforced the trend towards ghost scenes and established the practice of featuring duets for other than the principal couple. These were frequently for two characters of the same sex, here taking the form of an

---

[13] Giovanni de Gamerra and Paisiello, *Pirro* (Napoli: Flauto, 1787), in *I-Bc*; Gamerra and Bianchi, *Erifile* (Firenze: Risaliti, 1779), in *I-Bc*.

[14] Metastasio and Paisiello, *Nitetti* [sic] (St. Pietroburgo: Academia delle Scienze, 1777), in *US-Wcm*; *Nitteti* (Firenze: Albizziniana, 1788), in *I-Bc*; Bianchi, *Nitteti* (Milano: Bianchi, 1789); and Bertoni, *Nitteti* (Venezia: Fenzo, 1789), both in *US-Wcm*.

[15] Gamerra and Paisiello, *Pirro* (Venezia: Fenzo, 1787) and Sertor and Guglielmi, *Enea e Lavinia* (Venezia: Fenzo, 1788), both in *I-Bc*.

aria for Corimba with interruptions by Duntalmo. By 1789 the scene complex had become a regular component in Venetian operas, and four of the five operas employing them that year used ballet and chorus. The season included Gamerra's *Arsace*, Bertoni's setting of Paisiello's *Nitteti* as revised for St. Petersburg, Metastasio's *Ipermestra*, which had acquired a scene complex including a battle, Foppa's move from the exotic to the magical with a *Rinaldo*, and the first Venetian "morte" opera, Sertor's *La morte di Cesare*, in which Caesar is discretely murdered offstage.[16]

For Carnival, 1790, a third Venetian librettist, Antonio Sografi, in his *Gli Argonauti in Colco ossia La conquista del vello d'oro* set by the veteran Gazzaniga,[17] took the final step towards ensuring the demise of the exit aria as well as the eradication of strict delineations not only between recitative and formally set pieces whether arias, choruses, marches or ensembles, but also among individual elements functioning within those pieces. Within Sografi's ensembles can be found a free, dramatic interplay between the textural options of solo, ensemble and chorus without regard for the traditional formal procedures present even within the relatively free constructions of the multisectional action ensemble finale with its succession of textural climaxes. Central to the new style was the use of the chorus as a freely-participating character rather than as an unyielding and unwieldy block of music interacting with smaller forces only on the most formal of terms. The current practice of realizing whole scenes in various styles of accompanied recitative had undoubtedly encouraged the proliferation of short lyrical expressions in the form of cavatinas, short ensembles and choruses within scenes most likely to be selected for obbligato treatment. Sografi's fluid interpenetration of textures is no more than a logical extension of this practice.

Sografi's free constructions give his librettos an unmistakably new look, and their swift adoption together with other innovations already established led to a totally new style in opera librettos after 1795. The differences are easiest understood when compared with previous constructions incorporating chorus. Coltellini's *Ifigenia in Tauride,* Act I, scene 6 (see Example 3) has an opening chorus with soloists and a subsequent scene complex of recitative, solo cavatina, choral cavatina and final closing chorus and dance. In the opening chorus with soloists, each tutti, solo, and duo is marked off in clearly-defined formal blocks, with the chorus finally acting as a refrain. Similarly in the subsequent scene complex, the cavatinas are equally distinct from the recitative and from each other. Compare this with the final scene from the first act of Sografi's *La morte di Semiramide* for Milan in 1791 (see Example 4) which opens with a dance rather than a chorus. The subsequent chorus with soloists has become an emotional expression bursting forth from the recitative with no effort at symmetry—first a duplet for two, a duplet for a third, two quatrains for a fourth finalized with a duplet for chorus and a move back into recitative. Suddenly Nino's ghost appears. Such a scene would normally have been realized in obbligato style, but here Sografi has provided text for a sort of action trio with chorus serving as one of the members. Continuing on, the chorus introduces an equally informal closing duettino, unorthodox as much for its shortness and lack of initial quatrains for the principals as for its choral interjection. Finally, compare this dynamic ending

---

[16] Foppa and Bianchi, *Calto* (Venezia: Fenzo, 1788), in *US-Wcm*; Gamerra and Guglielmi, *Arsace*; Metastasio and Astaritta, *Ipermestra*; Sertor and Bianchi, *La morte di Cesare*; and Foppa and Guglielmi, *Rinaldo* (Venezia: Fenzo, 1789), in *US-Wcm*.

[17] Sografi and Giuseppe Gazzaniga, *Gli Argonauti in Colco ossia la conquista del vello d'oro* (Venezia: Fenzo, 1789), in *US-Wcm*.

with the final trio for *Pirro* (see Example 1B). In sum, Sografi's constructions simply defy the application of traditional descriptive labels.

Sografi's new style spread quickly. Characteristic of the close connections between the four cities, Milan produced a libretto by Sografi, a reworking of Giovannini's *La morte di Semiramide*, in 1791. In 1792 Nasolini composed for Florence a new version of *Calliroe* on a libretto wrongly attributed to Verazi, which bears Sografi's unmistakable stamp. Even Verazi had not dealt so freely with the chorus and ballet as here. Finally in 1793, Naples mounted a collaboration between Sografi and Piccinni, newly-returned from Paris—another mythological piece entitled *Ercole al Termedonte*, which is remarkable for the scant amount of simple recitative remaining and the extensive program music provided for action. Meanwhile there was a proliferation of new Venetian librettists following in Sografi's footsteps, whose works served to assist in the spread of the new style. Bianchi's setting of Botturini's *Seleuco* for Carnival, 1792, in which both scene complexes encompass a change of personnel, was imported to Bologna the same year, and Nasolini's setting of the Venetian librettist Rossi's *Le feste d'Iside* was first produced in Florence in 1794 and then exported to Venice for the 1795 season.[18]

Nor had Sertor ceded the innovative edge to his younger colleagues though he never really adopted their free constructions. His contribution lay in his continued efforts to cut the number of exit arias both by replacing them with aria-length cavatinas of two and three quatrains, as he does in his *Zenobia* and *Aspasia* for Carnival, 1790, and with multiple ensembles, some even functioning as cavatinas, as in his *Angelica e Medoro* of 1791.[19]

By 1792 chorus and dance had become so commonplace within Venetian opera that the libretto for Foppa's *Aci e Galatea* makes no mention of ballets as entr'actes, a situation that continues until 1796, when they begin to reappear in librettos for operas not containing ballets. The regular appearance of some kind of musical number at the beginning of the opera and the scene complex as an alternative to the ensemble at the close of an act also dates from 1792. In Milan, where the ballet never became a standard component, the regular incorporation of scene complexes and chorus in opera dates from the production of Borghi's setting of Sografi's *La morte di Semiramide* in 1791.[20]

Never before 1793 had there been a year without older, more conservative works interspersed among the new ones. Venetians saw Sertor's *Tarara*, based on Beaumarchais's one attempt at an opera libretto, Giotti's modern drama *Ines de Castro*, Foppa's *Tito e Berenice* and two operas by Sografi, *Pietro il Grande* and *Apelle*. This was also the year of Foppa's experiment with the melodrama *Dorval e Virginia*. Among this astonishing group of new works, Zingarelli's recent setting of Gamerra's *Pirro* must have seemed positively old-fashioned. Of this group, only Foppa's opera lacks scene complexes. All the others have several, and both of Sografi's

---

[18] Compare Verazi and Alessandri, *Calliroe* (Milano: Bianchi, 1779) and Sografi and Sabastiano Nasolini, *Calliroe* (Firenze: Albizziniana, 1792), in *US-Wcm*. Sografi and Niccolò Piccinni, *Ercole al Termedonte* (Napoli: Flauto, 1793), in *US-Wcm*. Mattia Botturini and Bianchi, *Seleuco, re di Siria* (Venezia: Fenzo, 1791), in *US-Wcm*; (Bologna: Sassi, 1792), in *I-Bc*. Gaetano Rossi and Nasolini, *Le feste d'Iside* (Firenze: Albizziniana, 1794) and (Venezia: Fenzo, 1795), in *I-Bc*.

[19] Sertor and Anfossi, *Zenobia in Palmira* (Venezia: Fenzo, 1789); Sertor and Giordani, *Aspasia* (Venezia: Fenzo, 1790); and Sertor and Bertoni, *Angelica e Medoro* (Venezia: Fenzo, 1791), in *I-Bc*.

[20] Foppa and Bianchi, *Aci e Galatea* (Venezia: Fenzo, 1792) and Sografi and Borghi, *La morte di Semiramide* (Milano: Bianchi, 1791), in *I-Bc*, *US-Wcm*.

open with them. All have multiple cavatinas, and several have multiple ensembles, including trios and quartets placed within acts, some of which contain action or expand in personnel. In addition *Apelle* contains four-strophe arias, among the first of their kind. As the number of arias diminish, those remaining become more weighty. Rossi's *Feste d'Iside* of 1794 is the first opera to contain multiple arias with interruptions, which are thereafter adopted as common practice, and after 1795 nearly every opera has at least one four-, five- and even six-strophe aria sometimes with action and/or interruptions. Finally, in his reworking of the old libretto *Merope* of 1796, Mattia Botturini carried Sografi's innovations to a logical conclusion, combining the concept of the action ensemble with Sografi's constructions of freely-alternating textures to build enormous freely-constructed action pieces with chorus encompassing a change of personnel (see Example 5).[21]

One aspect of the Verazi/Giovannini/Moretti legacy is yet to be discussed, that of the unhappy ending, and of murder, suicide and death both on and off stage. The rules governing the handling of such events in the theater had developed during the formative years of seventeenth-century French classical tragedy, and thereafter passed on not only to eighteenth-century opera in France, but also in Italy through the Arcadian literary reform movement.[22] Like the exit aria, these rules proved to be among the aspects of operatic tradition most difficult to overcome. While it is true that Venice kept Giovannini's ending when *La morte di Semiramide* was produced there in 1791, Sografi's less objectionable version for Milan, in which Arsace inadvertently stabs his mother when she steps between him and his intended victim, traveled far more widely throughout Italy, and even Florence retrenched in hiring Foppa to write for the 1790 season a version of *Hamlet* in which no one dies.[23]

Nevertheless, efforts to restore the option of death and tragedy to the operatic stage persisted. In 1792, Marinelli's *Medea*[24] shows the betrayed sorceress murdering her children before the eyes of their faithless father, and then flying off in her carriage as her palace is destroyed in a rain of fire. Similarly, the abandoned Circe has a final scene reminiscent of Metastasio's Dido where she finally throws herself into the sea. In the following year, Sertor's *Tarara* emphasizes the cruelty of the tyrant during a scene in which a slave is brutally murdered, thus justifying the tyrant's own death later on at the hands of another. Finally in 1794, Count Alessandro Pepoli, a Venetian poet and writer, wrote a version of *Virginia*, which ends with a scene in which a father murders his own daughter by order of a tyrant who is then murdered by her betrothed. In a previous version, which Tarchi set for Florence in 1785, the father

---

[21] Sertor and Bianchi, *Tarara o sia La virtù premiata*; Foppa and Tarchi, *Dorval e Virginia* (Venezia: Fenzo, 1792), in *US-Wcm*. Cosimo Giotti and Giordani, *Ines de Castro*; Foppa and Nasolini, *Tito e Berenice*; Sografi and Giuseppe Rossi, *Pietro il Grande ossia Il trionfo dell'innocenza*; Sografi and Zingarelli, *Apelle* (Venezia: Fenzo, 1793), in *US-Wcm*. Gaetano Rossi and Nasolini, *Le feste d'Iside* (Venezia: Fenzo, 1795), in *I-Bc*. Botturini and Nasolini, *Merope* (Venezia: Fenzo, 1796), in *US-Wcm*.

[22] For a more detailed discussion of this subject, see McClymonds, "*La morte di Semiramide ossia La vendetta di Nino* and the restoration of death and tragedy to the Italian operatic stage in the 1780s and 90s," paper read at the meeting of the International Musicological Society, Bologna, 1987.

[23] Foppa and Luigi Caruso, *L'Amleto* (Firenze: Albizziniana, 1790), in *I-Bc*.

[24] Anonymous and Gaetano Marinelli, *La vendetta di Medea* (Venezia: Fenzo, 1791) in *I-Vcg*. Domenico Perelli and Ferdinando Paër, *Circe* (Venezia: Fenzo, 1792), and Alessandro Pepoli and Felice Alessandri, *Virginia* (Venezia: Fenzo, 1794), in *US-Wcm*. Anonymous and Tarchi, *Virginia* (Firenze: Albizziniana, 1785), in *I-Bc*.

appears onstage carrying his dead daughter and predicting the downfall of the tyrant—an unsatisfactory ending though less shocking to the sensibilities of the audience than Pepoli's two staged murders.

Still the equivocation concerning murder of other than villains continued. Suicide had always been viewed as less objectionable. In Botturini's *Merope* of 1796 the villain is killed onstage, but the hero of Calzabigi's *Elfrida* imported from Naples the same year, is murdered offstage, and his wife learns of his death in the last scene. Later the same year Foppa produced yet another Shakespearian adaptation, *Giulietta e Romeo*, in which Romeo stabs himself onstage, after which Giulietta commits suicide offstage and then reappears to die in the finale. Finally, what could have been more appropriate than to have the disappearance of the Metastasian libretto from the Venetian stage marked in 1796 with his most violent drama, *Issipile*, in which the villain desists only when his mother is threatened with death and even then unrepentant throws himself into the sea.[25]

In 1797, the number of tragic endings and the amount of staged carnage suddenly increased greatly in Venice, all within the context of the newly-fashionable modern tragedy and under the aegis of the newly-formed Citizen's Republic. In Botturini's *Bianca de' Rossi*, based on a contemporary tragedy peopled with ordinary folk by Pier Antonio Meneghelli, the grieving Bianca buries herself in her dead husband's tomb. When the sealing stone is raised, she is found dead. In Botturini's *Zaira*, having killed Zaira in fit of jealous rage, her grief-stricken lover kills himself as well. Sografi's ending to *Gli Orazi e i Curiazi* is particularly shocking because Orazia is not only killed but thrown down the stairs by an enraged brother who remains defiant and remorseless.[26]

Equally shocking is the calloused treatment of deposed tyrants. In *La morte di Mitridate* of 1797, Mitridate has already taken poison offstage when he hears the victory shouts, stabs himself and falls. His death is hardly noticed as the triumphant people and Mitridate's traitorous son Farnace celebrate their new liberty. Similarly, in Sertor's *La morte di Cesare*, the ending is changed so that the murder takes place onstage, and the opera closes as the conspirators celebrate their triumph over tyranny.[27]

When produced in other centers such endings tended to be tempered. The Milanese were very much slower to depict death onstage. In fact, there were no staged deaths after Erifile's suicide in Moretti's *Ifigenia in Aulide* of 1788 until Bajazet's vengeful murder of Rossane in Calvi's *La Rossana* of 1795. In Naples staged deaths never really caught on at all in the eighteenth century. Only the unhappy queen in *La morte di Semiramide* of 1795 is actually murdered onstage in the final quartet.[28] Sografi's *Gli Orazi* for Cimarosa in 1796 was based on a libretto that Sernicola had done for Naples the previous year, but, rather than being brutally

---

[25] Calzabigi and Paisiello, *Elfrida* (Napoli: Flauto, 1792), in *I-Bc*; (Venezia: Valvasense, 1796), in *US-Wcm*. Foppa and Niccolò Zingarelli, *Giulietta e Romeo* (Venezia: Valvasense, 1796), in *I-Vcg*. Metastasio and Marinelli, *Issipile* (Venezia: Valvasense, 1796), in *US-Wcm*.

[26] Botturini and Vittorio Trento, *Bianca de' Rossi*; Botturini and Nasolini, *Zaira* (Venezia: Fenzo, 1797); and Sografi and Domenico Cimarosa, *Gli Orazi e i Curiazi* (Venezia: Valvasense, 1796), in *US-Wcm*.

[27] Sografi and Zingarelli, *La morte di Mitridate* (Venezia: Valvasense, 1797), in *US-Wcm*; Sertor and Bianchi, *La morte di Cesare* (Venezia: Valvasense, 1797), in *I-Vcg*.

[28] Calvi and Paër, *La Rossana* (Milano: Bianchi, 1795), in *US-Wcm*. In Sografi and Guglielmi, *La morte di Cleopatra* (Napoli: Flauto, 1796), in *I-Bc,* and (Napoli: Flautina, 1798), in *US-Wcm* and *I-Bc,*

murdered, in Sernicola's ending, Orazia is reconciled with her brother. Milan used Sografi's version in 1798 but with a modified ending in which Orazia is killed during an argument, after which her brother hides his face in remorse.[29]

Venetian formal innovations met with much less resistance in other theaters than did staged death and murder. Although their innovations quickly reached the other three centers, they did not catch on immediately. This was particularly true in Naples, where opera remained relatively conservative after 1794, when Gamerra went to Vienna and Calzabigi retired. The latter, like Sertor, never learned to write the new fluid forms, so that his new operas for Paisiello, *Elfrida* of 1792 and *Elvira* of 1794, are still constructed of familiar identifiable forms as is Sertor's *Tarara* of 1793. Nevertheless his flexible use of cavatinas and ensembles enabled him to cut the exit arias in *Elfrida* to only four, and to none at all in his last opera *Elvira*.[30]

New librettos from Venice in the early 1790s suffered the most revisions. In Giotti's *Ines de Castro* of 1793 as Andreozzi reset it for Florence later the same year, the introductory chorus and trio became a simple duet for two men. When De Sanctis revised it for Bianchi in Naples the following year, the same introduction became a simple quartet. In both cases the action in Giotti's ensemble finale of two scenes became recitative with a simple concluding trio. The consequences of reducing a three-act opera to two acts, (a practice that never caught on in Venice), is nowhere more apparent than here. In both Naples and Florence, all the innovative elements in the last two acts disappear in favor of a speedy climax and conclusion. Giotti's long aria for Ines with interjections by the queen and her accomplice, who are forcing her to drink poison, becomes a simple aria or cavatina. All the choruses disappear, replaced with straightforward recitative, arias and ensembles. Gone also is Giotti's action-packed, freely-constructed scene complex of obbligato recitative, arioso, and chorus. Similar kinds of changes were made in Sografi's *Apelle* of 1793 when reproduced in Milan in 1796.[31]

Nevertheless, by 1796, the differences in formal characteristics between the major centers were clearly diminishing. Foppa's *Giulietta e Romeo*, which originated in Milan in 1796, was performed unchanged in Venice the same year and in Florence in 1799.[32] There was still no such instance between Venice and Naples by the end of the century, though at least some of Sografi's fluid constructions remained in Guglielmi's setting of *La morte di Cleopatra* for Naples in 1796.

In any event, there can be no doubt that Venetian librettists had reestablished their ascendency in the realm of serious opera early in the last decade, and by the turn of the century had totally negated most of the old rules. Most significant of all, within less than a decade the sacrosanct

---

both the queen and Anthony die in the finale, but these are suicides, and Anthony has already stabbed himself when he appears on stage.

[29] Carlo Sernicola and Zingarelli, *Gli Orazi* (Napoli: Flauto, 1795), in *I-Nc*. Sografi and Cimarosa, *Gli Orazi e i Curiazi* (Milano: Bianchi, 1798), in *I-Mc*.

[30] Calzabigi and Paisiello, *Elfrida* (Napoli: Flauto, 1792), in *I-Nc*; *Elvira* (Napoli: Flauto, 1794), in *US-Wcm*.

[31] Giotti and Andreozzi, *Ines de Castro* (Firenze: Albizziniana, 1793), in *US-Wcm*; Luigi de Sanctis and Bianchi, *Ines de Castro* (Napoli: Flauto, 1794), in *I-Nc*; Sografi and Zingarelli, *Apelle* (Venezia, 1793), in *US-Wcm* and *I-Vcg*; Sografi and Giacomo Tritto, *Apelle e Campaspe* (Milano: Bianchi, 1796), in *US-Wcm* and *I-Mc*.

[32] Foppa and Zingarelli, *Giulietta e Romeo* (Milano: Bianchi, 1796), in *US-Wcm* and *I-Mc*; (Venezia: Valvasense, 1796), in *I-Vcg*; and (Firenze: Albizziniana, 1798), in *I-Fc*.

exit aria and the contrived happy ending along with all the idealistic classical formalism and gallant niceties of eighteenth-century opera seria had given way to more fluid and dramatic constructions better suited to the stark realism of revolutionary Europe, as expressed in staged contemporary tragedy. In transforming opera seria, the Venetian librettists had created a new kind of serious opera imbued with new life and new direction.

EXAMPLES

Example 1A. De Gamerra and Paisiello, *Pirro* (Napoli, 1787). Act II, Finale, pp. 36–9.

PIRRO
ATTO SECONDO
SCENA X.
Tutti.

36
Uli. Non aftringermi, o Pirro,
 Di moſtrarti qual ſono. A me d'intorno
Vedi la Grecia, e queſta
D' adempiré or t' impone
Le tue promeſſe, e 'l tuo dovere. Eſangue
Poliſſena qui cada, ed a Climene
Dell' ara ſacra al piè t' uniſca Imene.
Cli. (Che ſia!)
Dar. (Palpita il core!)
Ele. (Io taccio, e fremo!)
Pol. (Affannoſa, ed incerta io mi confondo!)
Pir. Alla Grecia, ed a te così riſpondo.
Di tanti Re l' aſſenſo in me depoſe

(a) *Avanzandoſi verſo Uliſſe con impeto, e diſprezzo, allorchè ſolo ſi è avvicinato a Pirro.*
(b) *Ad Uliſſe, dopo che queſto gli ha ordinato di uccider Poliſſena ſul ſepolcro di Achille.*
(c) *Ritornando al fianco di Poliſſena più affettuoſa.*
(d) *A Pʼ Uliſſe nell' atto che vuole impadronirſi di Poliſſena. In conſeguenza dei ſentimenti di Pirro, tutti gli Attori animeranno il quadro coi colori della propria paſſione.*

37
Il primo imper, finchè il Monarca d' Argo
Lungi è da Troja. In Ilio
Dunque Pirro ſol regna. Poliſſena
Fra le diviſe ſpoglie
A me ſortì. Di lei
Arbitro io ſon. Chi mel contraſta? Noto
Io mi credea che foſſe
Omai Pirro alla Grecia. Ei non diſcende
Dal ſovrano poter, nè i proprj dritti
Cede al ſuon di minacce, e men lo ſcuote
Il temerario aſpetto
Di violenza, o d' inſulto. Ognun rammenti,
Che Pirro uſo a dar leggi,
Tollerarle non ſa. Rieda Climene
Agli Atridi, ſe vuol; e Poliſſena,
Ancor vel dico, io voglio.
Ch' oggi d' Epiro aſcenda meco al ſoglio.
Uli. Coſì tu parli? Ah, Pirro,
 Non ripigli la Grecia
Contro la Grecia l' armi. A tanta guerra
Poliſſena è vil prezzo.
Pir. Arminſi i Greci.
Furo ad Achille ingrati;
Lo ſiano a Pirro. Ma ſan già per prova
Quanto tremendo ſia
De' Pelidi il furore... A che mi arreſto?
In garrir teco, troppo,
Troppo finor mi degradai. La mano,
Cara, mi porgi, e al Tempio
Ti affretta al fianco mio.
Uli.)
Cli.) a 3. (Smanio!)
Ele.)
Dar. (Che mai ſarà?)
Pir. Seguimi...
Pol. Oh Dio!

38
 D' un' infelice oppreſſa
 Tronca gli odiati giorni,
 E in mezzo a voi ritorni
 La pace, e l' amiſtà.
Pir. D' un odio ingiuſto in preda
 Laſciarti io non potrei;
 Ah troppo degna ſei
 D' amore, e di pietà.
Dar. Se penſo al ſuo deſtino,
 L' alma ſtraziar mi ſento;
 Ma il mio rival contento
 Non men gelar mi fa.
Pol. ⎧ Abbandonata all' ire
 ⎨ D' un' implacabil ſorte,
 ⎩ L' aſpetto della morte
 Per me terror non ha.
Pir. ⎫ a 3 Per involarti all' ire
 ⎬ D' un' implacabil ſorte,
 ⎭ Sfidar la ſteſſa morte
 Dolce per me ſarà.
Dar. Abbandonata all' ire
 D' un' implacabil ſorte,
 Nè in braccio della morte
 Vederla il cor non ſa.
Uli. Finchè v' è tempo ancora,
 Cedi a un miglior configlio
Dar. Pirro, più cauto, e ſaggio
 Ti renda il tuo periglio.
Pir. Del grande Achille il figlio
 I folli ſenſi aborre
 Di timida viltà.
Pol. Signor, ſoſpendi.
Pir. E' vano.
Pol. Ah no, la voſtra pace
 Non turbi un' infelice.
Pir. Di che ſon io capace,
 La Grecia apprenderà.
Uli. Dunque, che più s' aſpetta?
 Per la comun vendetta
 Ah più non v' arreſtate;
 Mora colei... (a)
39 *Pir.* Che oſate?
Uli. ⎫
Pir. ⎬ ⎧ In ſen divampa il cor.
Dar. ⎨ a6 ⎨ In ſeno incerto è il cor.
Cli. ⎩ ⎩
Pol. ⎫ In ſen mi trema il cor.
Ele. ⎭
Uli. All' armi... (b)
Pir. All' armi: (c)
Pol. Ceſſino (d)
 Signor gli ſdegni, e immergimi
 Il nudo acciaro in petto.
 L' ultimo colpo aſpetto, (e)
 E palpitar non ſo.
Uli. Greci, vibratevi... (f)

(a) *Verſo i Greci, che ſtanno in punto di lanciarſi contro di Poliſſena.*
(b) *Ai Greci ſnudando la ſpada.*
(c) *Sfodera la ſpada.*
(d) *Frapponendoſi ſmanioſa.*
(e) *S' inginocchia.*
(f) *Mentre Uliſſe ſeguito dai Greci vuole ermata mano impadronirſi di Poliſſena, Pirro corre loro incontro furioſamente. Poliſſena in queſto ſorge, e ſi abbandona nelle braccia d' Eleno. Darete è nella maſſima agitazione, e Climene pende confuſa nell' incertezza; quando entra in mezzo al tumulto.*

Example 1B. Conclusion, *Pirro*, Act II, Finale, pp. 40–41; Act III, Final Trio, pp. 44–5.

40
SCENA XI.
Calcante accompagnato dai Sagrificatori, dai Sacerdoti, e detti.

Cal. Olà. Fermatevi. (a)
Pir. ⎧ Nell'alma stupida
Uli. ⎪ L'ardir mancò.
Dar. ⎬ a6 Confusa, e stupida
Ele. ⎪ L'alma restò.
Cli. ⎪ Perchè una misera
Pol. ⎩ Morir non può.
Cal. Parlò l'Oracolo,
O Grecia, ascoltralo:
O Pirro vendichi
Nel sangue Iliaco
Lo scempio barbaro
Del Genitor;
O dalle ceneri
Sorgerà Troja,
Cogli' esterminio
Del vincitor. (b)
Pir. ⎧ Ah che non so risolvere;
⎨ Un improvviso fulmine
⎩ Su questo cor piombò.
Dar. ⎧ Che mai saprà risolvere;
Uli. a6 ⎨ Un improvviso fulmine
Cli. ⎩ Sul di lui cor piombò.

(a) *Tutti alla presenza del Sommo Sacerdote formano un quadro esprimente la sorpresa, e il rispetto.*
(b) *In un aspetto invasato impone a Pirro d' uccidere Polissena. Indi si arretra fra i Sacerdoti, ed i Sagrificatori lanciando su di Pirro delle occhiate fulminanti, rimanendo sempre a vista.*

41
Ele. ⎧ Ah che non sa risolvere;
Pol. ⎨ Un improvviso fulmine
⎩ Su questo cor piombò.
Pir. Dunque...
Dar. ⎧
Uli. a4 ⎨ E' deciso.
Cli. ⎪
Ele. ⎩
Pir. Io deggio...
Dar. ⎧
Uli. a4 ⎨ Vibrare il colpo.
Cli. ⎪
Ele. ⎩
Pir. ⎫ a2 (Oh Dei!)
Pol. ⎭
Pir. ⎧ Ah nel fatal cimento
⎨ Inorridir mi sento,
⎩ E cede il mio valor.
Pol. ⎧ In sì fatal momento
⎨ Tremare io non mi sento,
⎩ Nè langue in petto il cor.
Dar. ⎧ In sì fatal momento
Ele. a6 ⎨ Per lei tremar mi sento,
⎩ E langue in petto il cor.
Uli. ⎧ In sì fatal cimento
Cli. ⎩ Smania per mio contento,
Fine dell' Atto Secondo.

(a) *Calcante afferra per un braccio la vittima, che subito circondata resta dai Sagrificatori, e dai Sacerdoti; indi tutti si ritirano da parti opposte confusamente.*

44
ATTO TERZO.
SCENA II.

Tomba mi guida, e su di quella spiri
Polissena, o Signor.... Come? sospiri?
Pir. Oh momento! oh dovere! oh Grecia! oh padre!
Oh vendetta! oh destin!
Pol. Darete, il pianto
Rasciuga per pietà.
Dar. No, che non posso
Soffrir l'orrido aspetto
Della tua sorte.
Pir. (Il cor s'agghiaccia in petto!)
Pol. (Ah se si tarda ancora,
Vacillar può la mia costanza.) Vieni;
Il colpo vibra, e tronca
I giorni miei funesti;
Sbigottirmi non so.... perchè t'arresti?
Pir. Incerto, pentito,
Crudele, pietoso,
Ardisco, non oso,
Oh Dei! che farò.
Dar. Confuso, dolente,
M'affanno, sospiro;
E in tanto martiro
S'io viva non so.
Pol. Afflitta, e spogliata
Di speme, e d'aita,
Quest'alma smarrita
Resister non può.
Pir. Ma intorno del padre
Mi suonano i gridi.
Dar. Agghiaccio!...
Pol. M'uccidi...
Pir. ⎧ Fra il padre, e l'amante,
⎨ Sì oppresso, e tremante,
⎪ Voi ditelo, o Numi,
⎩ Chi mai si trovò.
Dar. ⎰ a3 In faccia all'amante,

45
Sì oppresso, e tremante,
Voi ditelo, o Numi,
Chi mai si trovò.
Pol. ⎧ Un'anima amante
⎨ Sì oppressa, e costante,
⎪ Voi ditelo, o Numi,
⎩ Se mai si trovò.
Pir. Vedi...ahimè!...forse m'inganno? (a)
Pol. Chi mai giunge?
Dar. Oh vista!.... oh affanno!
Pol.)
Dar. ⎬ a 3 (Ah cominciò a palpitar!)
Pir.)
Dar. ⎫
Pir. ⎭ a2 Tu ti turbi, e tremi....
Pol. Oh Dio!
Dar. ⎫
Pir. ⎬ a2. Oh momento!
Pol. Io vado...
Pir. ⎫
Dar. ⎬ a 3. Addio.
Pol. ⎭
) Oh giorno terribile!
) Destino implacabile!
) a3 Un duolo insoffribile
) E questo per me.

(a) *Avvicinandosi lentamente Calcante fra i Sacerdoti, scortato dai Greci, e accompagnato da tutti gli Attori.*

Example 2. Metastasio and Paisiello, *La Nitteti* (Firenze, 1788). Act II, scenes 11–14, pp. 31–5.

LA NITTETI
ATTO SECONDO.

SCENA XI.

Magnifico Tempio d'Iside; in mezzo il Simulacro della Dea. S'apre la Scena con un'allegra danza di giovani, e donzelle, che adornano di fiori l'Idolo, e il Tempio. In tanto s'avanza di fondo al Santuario una proceffione di Sacerdoti della Dea, preceduti da due Vergini, che portano il Fuoco facro per porlo full'Ara, e fi canta il feguente Coro.

Coro di Sacerdoti.
Ungi da quefte foglie
Occhio profanator;
Solo a fanciulli, e vergini
Ifide il vel difcioglie,
Che afconde il fuo fplendor:

Alla fine del Coro efce il Popolo dal Tempio, ed entrano di fondo le Vergini della Dea conducendo Beroe all'Altare.

Coro di Vergini, e Sacerdoti.
Vergine bella e pura,
Al Nume che t'accoglie
Muovi tremando il piè.
Ifide invoca, e giura
Pari alle bianche fpoglie,
Candore eterno, e fè.

Alcune delle Vergini cuopron Beroe d'un candido Velo.

Coro di Vergini.
Sai, che fi fcioglie in breve
In torbida onda impura
Falda di bianca neve,
Se afcofa al Sol non è.

Coro di Sacerdoti.
Ifide invoca, e giura
Candore eterno, e fè,

Ber. Alma luce del Ciel, vita del mondo
Accogli Ifide bella i voti miei:
La pace che io perdei
Fa' che ritrovi in te. Tutto confacro
Al tuo Nume, al tuo culto; ah ti perdona
Un' innocente amor, che non t'afcondo,
Ch' eftinguer fe poteffi io non vorrei:
Alma luce del Ciel vita del mondo,
Afcolta Ifide bella i voti miei.
   A te confacro il cuore,
   Tu fai ch'è puro, e fai
   Che nol macchiò giammai
   Quefto innocente ardor.
   Se reo divien, fe mai
   Le mie promeffe obliò,
   Fiamma dal Ciel funefta
   Piombi.... (*prendendo di mano a una delle Vergini la facra tazza del giuramento folenne.*)

SCENA XII.

Sammete furiofo con feguito di armati, e detti. S'avanza all'Altare, trattiene Beroe dal giuramento, gettando la tazza a terra, e togliendole il facro Velo dal capo.

Sammete.
T' arrefta, oh Dio!
Tu fai ch' è mio quel cor.
Coro di Vergini, e Sacerdoti.
Stelle! che audacia è quefta.
Sammete.
Sieguimi.....

Beroe.
Oh Dio! che fai?
Tutto il Coro.
Qual pena il Ciel t'apprefta
Empio profanator.
Beroe.
A quefto eccefso, ingrato.....
Sammete.
Mancava ogn' altra fpeme;
E perdere il fuo bene
E' troppo il gran dolor.
Tutto il Coro.
E' il Tempio profanato?
Beroe.
Il genitore oppreffo?...
Sammete.
Ah non afcolto adefso
Che un difperato amor.
traendola feco a forza, efce dal Tempio co' fuoi feguaci.
Tutto il Coro.
O fcellerato eccefso!
O giorno di terror.

SCENA XIII.

Amafi entrando dalla parte oppofta con guardie le Vergini, e i Sacerdoti gli vanno incontro.

Coro.
Ah corri Signore,
Ah vendica il Tempio,
Che un perfido un empio
Profana cofì.
Amafi.
Chi dunque?
Coro.
Il tuo figlio.
Amafi.
Oh atroce ferita!
Coro.
I Numi non teme;
Non cura la vita.
Amafi.
E Beroe?.....
Coro.
E' rapita.
Amafi.
E l' empio?
Coro.
Fuggì.
Amafi con tutto il Coro.
Oh Ciel quanta fpeme
Diftrugge un fol dì.
Amafi.
Figlio ingrato ah dove andrai
Dove lafci un padre afflitto?
All' orror del tuo delitto
Ah chi mai t' involerà?

Infelice! il folo oggetto
Fofti ognor de' voti miei!
Come, oh Dio! l' orror tu fei
Della mia cadente età.
Ma pera l' indegno
Si vendichi il trono
Più Padre non fono
Son giudice, e Re. *parte furiofo tolle*
Tutto il Coro. (*guardie.*
Di grazia, e perdono
Più degno non è.

Example 3. Coltellini and Traetta, *Ifigenia in Tauride* (Milano, 1768). Act I, scene 6, pp. 11–15.

IFIGENIA
IN TAURIDE
ATTO PRIMO
SCENA VI.

Tempio magnifico superbamente adornato. Trono da una parte su cui ascende fralle guardie Toante. Coro di Ministre, che conduce dal fondo del Teatro Oreste all' Altare, su del quale è il simulacro di Pallade. Mentre si canta il Coro ballando, si accende il fuoco sacro, si corona la vittima, e si fanno le libazioni.

Toante con guardie, Oreste colle Ministre del Tempio, poi Ifigenia, Dori, e popolo.

CORO.

Oh, come presto a sera,
 Misero giovanetto,
 Giunse tua fresca età.
Barbara morte, e fiera
 Il crudo ferro ha stretto,
 E impietosir non sa.
Dor. Qual struggerassi in pianto
 La Greca Verginella,
 Quando la rea novella
 Del tuo morir saprà.

Tutti.

Oh come presto a sera
Giunse tua fresca età.
A 6

Dor. Grave di morte i rai
 Il genitore amato
 Di dolorosi lai
 Il Cielo assorderà.

Tutti.

Barbara morte, e fiera
Impietosir non sa.
(Al gran voler del fato
If. e Dor. Piega la fronte, e taci.
(Giovane sventurato
(Quanta pietà mi fa.

Tutti.

Barbara morte, e fiera
Impietosir non sa.
If. Or dell' onda lustrale
La vittima s'asperge; il Nume adori,
 Alcune delle ministre spargono
 Oreste d' acqua lustrale.
E nel colpo fatal costanza implori.
Dor. Piegati umile all' ara.
 Conduce Oreste all' ara.
Or. Ah! sì ravviso
 Guardando con sorpresa il simulacro.
Vindice irata Dea; fu tuo consiglio
L' Oracolo bugiardo,
Che mi trasse ingannato all' empie sponde.
Or ti sazia, crudel; vibrami in seno
L' infuocate saette, e col mio sangue,
E l' ara, e il tempio istesso,
Che di sangue macchiai, si lavi adesso...
Ahimè! Chi mi soccorre? Ecco discuopre

La Gorgone fatal: dove m' ascondo?
Ecco il regno di morte, ecco l' abisso
Mi s' apre sotto i piè... Ma quale, oh Dei,
Turba d' orride larve ancora in questa
Mi persegue, e spaventa ombra funesta?
Lasciatemi, crudeli. Ah, chi m' invola
All' orribile aspetto, alla mia pena;
Chi compiange il mio stato, e chi mi svena?

Oh Dio, dov' è la morte?
In così fiera sorte
Il differirla a un misero
E' troppa crudeltà.
 Cade abbandonato fralle guardie:
If. (Morir mi sento.)
Toa. Or da compire il rito
 Qual pietà ti trattiene?
If. Oh Dio! Non vedi
 Avanzandosi verso il trono.
In che stato è la vittima? Le labbra
Gonfie di calda spuma, il volto asperso
Di livido pallor; stravolto il guardo,
E le membra tremanti
Agitata, e convulsa?
Dor. E non udisti
Come insultò la Dea?
Toa. Che importa a' Numi,
Che delirj, e s' affanni
Purchè si sveni il reo?
If. Signor, t' inganni.
Non è quel che li placa
Delle vittime il sangue; è la costanza
In chi l' ha da versar; l' anima invitta,
Che nel colpo fatal, perchè al Ciel piace,
Piega la fronte, adora il cenno, e tace.

Toa. Dunque...
If. Nel chiuso fonte
Sacro alla Dea convien purgarla, e al rito
Prepararla di nuovo. In quello stato
Se una vittima accetta offrir pretendi,
Contamini l' Altare, e il Nume offendi.

CORO.

Ah, si purghi quell' ostia macchiata
Se gradito il suo sangue non è.
Plachin l' ira di Pallade armata
Nuovi pegni d' amore, e di fè.

Toa. Dunque il fatal decreto
E d' un Nume, e d' un Re vuoi che dipenda
Dall' arbitrio d' un Reo?
If. Dal rito immondo
Dunque offesa la Dea, vuoi, che il suo sdegno
Tutto sopra di noi cader si veda?
Toa. (Donna infedel, t' appagherò.) Si ceda.
 Scendendo furioso dal trono.
Dello straniero indegno
L' empio sangue a versar pochi momenti
Giacchè si chiede, accorderò; ma senti.
Se la vittima impura
Non gradisce la Diva, al Trono offeso,
Alla mia sicurezza, al furor mio
Oggi si svenerà; pentita allora
La tua folle pietà vedrà che in vano
Non si delude un Re. *parte infuriato.*
If. e Dor. (Mostro inumano!)
If. Alle vicine stanze
Quel misero si scorga; e voi frattanto
 Alcune delle Ministre vanno
 a prendere Oreste.
Ver.

Ministre amiche, in lieto coro al Nume
Rinnovate le preci, e i balli usati
A placarlo intrecciate. Ah, santa Dea,
Se in Ciel son giunti i nostri falli a segno
Di provocarti a sdegno, e, s' hai desio
D' estinguerlo col sangue, eccoti il mio.

CORO DE MINISTRI DEL TEMPIO,
E DEL POPOLO.

Temuta Pallade
Figlia di Giove
Dea del saper,
Rivolgi altrove
L' asta terribile
Del tuo poter.

Si rappresentano ballando le diverse cerimonie
preparatorie del sacrificio.

FINE DELL' ATTO PRIMO.

Example 4. Sografi and Borghi, *La morte di Semiramide* (Milano, 1791). Act I, scene 10, pp. 26–30.

LA MORTE DI SEMIRAMIDE
ATTO PRIMO
SCENA X

Atrio magnifico contiguo alla Reggia di Semiramide con veduta del Mausoleo di Nino ec.
Trono da una parte.
Breve Danza, che durerà fino a tanto che viene in Scena Semiramide.
Semiramide. Azema. Arsace. Assur. Mitrane. Oroe. Magi. Grandi. Damigelle. Guerrieri. Guardie. Popolo.

Sem. Magi, Popolo, Prenci,
E' questo il punto in cui decisa io sono
Di nominar il Successore al Trono.
Della vostra obbedienza
Semiramide ognora
Ebbe non dubbie prove, e sol le resta
Di riportar quest'ultima, che chiede
Prova più grande della vostra fede.
Sì, vogl'io lusingarmi,
Che la mia scelta rispettar vorrete;
E perchè vieppiù siate
A sostenerla intesi,
Bramo, che innanzi a me tutti giuriate.

Azema. Mitrane, dirimpetto a Semiramide.

Regina, a te giuriamo
Omaggio, e fedeltà.
Ass. Alla tua scelta io bramo *con sarcasmo.*
Ogni felicità.
Ars. Per l'immortal suo nome *al Popolo.*
Glorioso in guerra, e in pace,
Popoli, giura Arsace
La scelta rispettar.

poi rivolgendosi a Semiramide.

Sin dai prim'anni miei,
Regina, io t'adorai,
E non potrà giammai
Quest'anima cangiar.

Coro.

Regina, a te giuriamo
Omaggio, e fedeltà.
Sem. Ebben, aifin sia noto,
Che quello a cui vogl'io
Lo scettro ed il cor mio
In tal punto donar, per cui tra poco
Vedrassi accesa d'Imeneo la face,
Magi, Popoli, Prenci, è il grande Arsace.
scende dal trono.
Az. Arsace!
Oroe (Eterni Dei!)
Ass. (Tel dissi.) *ad Azema.*

Ars. Come!
Io Regina!
Sem. Tu stesso. Tanto dono
E' ben dovuto a chi serbommi in Trono.
Ardiam.

Si oscura improvvisamente la Scena e cade un fulmine.

Cieli! Che sento!
Ars. Ass. Sem. Qual m'assale terrore!
Ars. S'apre la Tomba.
Sem. E' desso.

Tutti.

Ah quanto orrore!
Esce l'Ombra di Nino, la quale si rivolge minacciosa contro Semiramide.
Tutti fuorchè Semiramide.

Questa è l'Ombra del Re estinto...
Piange... freme...
Ars. Eterni Dei!
Sem. Deh sospendi
Ai pianti miei
Il tuo sdegno, il tuo furor.

Tutti supplichevoli seguendo, e circondando l'Ombra

Coro.

Deh t'arrendi
Al suo dolor.

L'Ombra facendo un gesto negativo s'addrizza di nuovo a Semiramide la quale si aggira atterrita per la Scena.
Sem. Dove son? Dove m'ascondo?
L'Ombra s'avvia verso il sepolcro.
Sem. Seguirò là i passi tuoi...
L'Ombra glielo impedisce.
Sì nel baratro profondo.
L'Ombra rientra, e la Scena si rischiara.
Ars. Qual prodigio!
Tutti smarriti e in grande costernazione.
Che terror!
La Scena rimane per poco in silenzio.
Sem. (Sconfigliata, che fo! Così mi lascio
In tal punto avvilir!) Popolo, Prenci,
Seguitemi, venite. Il Ciel sdegnato
E' d'uopo di placar. Ei, lo vedrete,
Implacabil non è. Meco venite.
Io vi farò d'esempio:
Discacciate il timor. Al Tempio.

Tutti

Al Tempio.
Sem. Minaccia il Ciel sdegnato *al Popolo.*
Ars. Tuona dall'alte sfere *ai suoi Guer.*
Sem. ⎧ Ma al pianto alle preghiere
Ars. a2 ⎨
       ⎩ Placato il Ciel sarà.

Tutto il Popolo.

Andiamo.
Sem. ⎫
Ars. a2 ⎬ Ah sì, si placherà.
       ⎭ Il Cielo irato

Tutti partono seguendo Semiramide.

Example 5. Botturini and Nasolini, *Merope* (Venezia, 1796). Act II, scenes 18–19, pp. 36–8.

MEROPE
ATTO SECONDO.

SCENA XVIII.

Nearco e seguaci di Polifonte, indi Merope, indi Ismene e Donzelle da un lato, Polidoro e seguaci di Merope dall'altro che tornano.

Mer. Figlio, ove sei?
　　Ah lo ricerco invano ... Il Ciel mi tese
　　Al par del mio Tiranno
　　Scellerata e crudel ... Ma dite, amici,
　　Ismene, Polidoro:
　　Il mio Timante ov'è?..(a)D'affanno io moro.
　　Figlio, senti ... Oh istante!.. Oh pena!..
　　　　Veggo il ferro, che lo svena ...
　　　　Veggo il sangue ... Veggo l' Ombra
　　　　Che mi viene a funestar.
　　Deh m'aspetta,
　　Ombra diletta,
　　Che di Lete il varco estremo
　　Teco bramo anch'io passar.
　　E tu reggi a tanto affanno,
　　　　Nè ti spezzi, o cor materno?
　　　　Furie, uscite dall'inferno
　　　　La mia morte ad affrettar.
　　　　　　　　　　　　　(*vuol partire.*

Ism. Polid. Donz. e seguci di Mer.
　　Ferma, ascolta.
Mer.　　　　Che bramate?

Ism. Polid. Donz., e seguaci di Mer.
　　La tua pace, la tua vita.
　　　　　　　　　　　　　Mer.

(a) *Ognuno fa cenno di non saper, dove sia.*

Mer. Alme fide, se m'amate,
　　Deh lasciatemi spirar.
　　　(*odesi strepito ne' vicini appartamenti.*

Ism. Polid. Donz. e seguaci di Mer.

　　Quali grida!... Qual rumore!...

SCENA XIX.

Timante, e varj seguaci di Merope preceduti da Adrasto, e detti.

Ism. Polid. Adr. Donz. e seguaci.

　　Calma il duol, serena il ciglio
　　Vedi salvo il caro Figlio
　　Al tuo seno ritornar.
Mer. Ah che miro! Il Figlio!... Vieni:
　　La tua madre, o Figlio, abbraccia.
　　　　(*Tim. e Mer. s'abbracciano.*
　　Dal tuo sen, dalle tue braccia
　　Non mi posso, oh Dio, staccar.
　　　　Vicina al Figlio amato
　　　　Ritrovo alfin la calma:
　　　　Un tenero diletto
　　　　Tutto m'innonda il petto;
　　　　E dagli Dei quest'alma
　　　　Di più bramar non sa.

Ism. Polid. Adr. Don. e saguaci di Mer.

　　Trionfa, esulta. Il Figlio
　　Il nostro Re sarà.
Tim. Oh giorno!... Oh Madre!... Il Figlio
　　Ognor t'adorerà.
　　　　Ma contro il Barbaro,
　　　　Che lo perseguita:
　　　　Contro que' perfidi,
　　　(*accennando Nearco ed i seguaci di Polifonte.*
　　　　Ch'io veggo fremere,
　　　　Chi mai mio Figlio
　　　　Difenderà?

Ism. Polid. Adr. Donz. e seguaci di Mer.

　　Si mostri al Popolo.
　　Ognun combattere
　　Per lui saprà.

[23]

MAYR, ROSSINI, AND THE DEVELOPMENT OF THE OPERA SERIA DUET: SOME PRELIMINARY CONCLUSIONS

Scott L. Balthazar

In his *Ammaestramenti* of 1841, Carlo Ritorni discussed changes in the treatment of the duet between the eras he termed « Metastasian » and « Rossinian »:

I duetti, de' quali Metastasio fece ogni due opere, diventarono frequenti [...]. I libretti metastasiani, che si andavan riproducendo con novelle musiche, come può vedersi nell'edizioni di que' tempi, venner abbreviati; accorciati i recitativi, alcune arie ommesse, altre accresciute di strofe, di riprese; quelli e queste decomposti, per fare duetti ed altri canti a più voci.[1]

As always, Ritorni's comments give a welcome contemporary account of an important stylistic development. Yet at the same time, the thoroughness with which he summed up our present knowledge of this topic is disquieting. For our inability to elaborate significantly on his thumbnail sketch reflects an unfortunate inattention to one of the most crucial periods in the history of the duet.

This apparent lack of scholarly interest might be attributed to a number of factors, among them the subordinate status of the eighteenth-century duet with respect to the

---

[1] C. Ritorni, *Ammaestramenti alla composizione d'ogni poema e d'ogni opera appartenente alla musica*, Milano, Luigi di Giacomo Pirola 1841, pp. 32-33.

aria, the seemingly irreconcilable structural diversity of duets written during the period 1790-1810, and the inaccessibility of reliable sources.² For whatever reasons, however, our limited knowledge of this transitional period has severely hindered our understanding of the later development of the Rossinian duet. More than fifteen years after Philip Gossett identified its characteristic four-movement form, we still have very little idea of how it evolved and cannot assess Rossini's particular contribution to its genesis.³

The ostensible dissimilarity between the musico-dramatic structure of the Romantic duet and its eighteenth-century predecessors has even led one Verdian scholar to doubt that a generative relationship exists between the earlier and later types.⁴ In a recently published discussion of Verdi's

---

² In contrast, the literature on late eighteenth - and early nineteenth-century arias is extensive. Several of the most important discussions are found in F. LIPPMANN, *Vincenzo Bellini und die italienische Opera seria seiner Zeit: Studien über Libretto, Arienform und Melodik*, « Analecta musicologica », VI, 1969, translated and revised as *Vincenzo Bellini e l'opera seria del suo tempo. Studi sul libretto, la forma delle arie e la melodia*, in M. R. ADAMO and F. LIPPMANN, *Vincenzo Bellini*, Torino, ERI 1981; S. DÖHRING, *Formgeschichte der Opernarie vom Ausgang des achtzehnten bis zur Mitte des neunzehnten Jahrhunderts*, Marburg 1975, pp. 105-130; and D. HEARTZ, *Mozart and his Italian Contemporaries: 'La clemenza di Tito'*, « Mozart-Jahrbuch », 1978-79, pp. 281-283 and ID., *Mozarts 'Titus' und die italienische Oper um 1800*, « Hamburger Jahrbuch für Musikwissenschaft », V, 1981, pp. 255-266.

³ P. GOSSETT, *Verdi Ghislanzoni, and 'Aida': the Uses of Convention*, « Critical Inquiry », I, 1974-75, pp. 291-334.

⁴ For example, whereas the Metastasian lyric duet tends to formalize dramatic positions already established in the preceding recitative, the nineteenth-century duet, particularly after 1830, plays a more integral role in the development of the drama, exposing, intensifying, or redirecting old conflicts, and in some cases even generating new ones. It presents conflicts of increasing severity and tenacity, which contrast with the less venomous and usually temporary querrels between lovers in Metastasio's duets. The large-scale textual returns that characterize the eighteenth-century duet are absent from its design. And the long-standing reliance of Rossini's followers on a relatively conventionalized four-movement structure contrasts the varied practice of eighteenth-century composers. I have discussed the development of the Italian duet during the first half of the nineteenth century in my Ph. D. dissertation *Evolving Conventions in Italian Serious Opera: Scene Structure in the Works of Rossini, Bellini, Donizetti, and Verdi, 1810-1850*, University of Pennsylvania 1985, pp. 87-161 and 331-505, and article *The 'primo Ottocento' Duet and*

THE DEVELOPMENT OF THE OPERA SERIA DUET

adherence to conventional scene structures, Harold Powers has argued that « the Grand Duet of Italian Romantic opera seems to me essentially an Ottocento invention; it is its most characteristic form, and it has no eighteenth-century prototypes, as does the aria scene, or for that matter, the central Finale ».[5] David Lawton has also dissociated the Romantic duet from earlier examples of its genre, suggesting that « the solo *aria* or *cavatina* provided a model from which the forms even of ensemble pieces were ultimately derived ». Although others have avoided such direct assertions, their analytical approaches in describing the duet rest on the same basic premises. Specifically, Julian Budden and David R. B. Kimbell have described the Rossinian duet in terms of the conventions of the nineteenth-century aria, as if the aria were its source.[6] Gossett has approached the problem even more cautiously, emphasizing our inadequate understanding of the context in which Rossini worked. He treats the form of the duet independently both from the contemporary aria and from its duet ancestors. Rather than address the issue of historical development, he focuses on the impact of immediate musical and dramatic concerns – the need to « perfect an approach to the ensemble which offered characters opportunity for lyrical expression while focusing on their dramatic confrontation and interaction ».[7]

Contemporary theoretical writings shed no more light on the process of stylistic transition, although they do help to differentiate the eighteenth- and nineteenth-century types. The critics Carlo Gervasoni and Alexandre Choron,

---

the Transformation of the Rossinian Code, forthcoming in the « Journal of Musicology ».

[5] H. S. POWERS, *'La solita forma' and 'The Uses of Convention'*, « Acta musicologica », LIX, 1987, p. 75.

[6] D. LAWTON, *Tonality and Drama in Verdi's Early Operas*, Ph. D. dissertation, University of California, Berkeley 1973, p. 1; J. BUDDEN, *The Operas of Verdi*, I, *From 'Oberto' to 'Rigoletto'*, London, Cassell 1973, pp. 17-18; D. R. B. KIMBELL, *Verdi in the Age of Italian Romanticism*, Cambridge, Cambridge University Press 1981, pp. 72-73.

[7] P. GOSSETT, *Verdi, Ghislanzoni, and 'Aida'* cit., pp. 300-301.

writing during the first decade of the nineteenth century, described a form in two sections (see *Appendix*, descriptions A and B). The first section consists of dialogue, which often takes the form of parallel solo statements either in the same key or in different ones, depending on the respective ranges of the voices.[8] The second section involves simultaneous singing in thirds and sixths, or at least more rapid interchange between the singers than would occur in the first section.

Two mid-century writers, Ritorni and Abramo Basevi, outlined the more complex Rossinian form (see *Appendix*, descriptions E and F). Ritorni provided by far the more detailed description of its four sections: an opening movement centering on parallel statements; a lyrical slow movement; a middle movement of declamatory dialogue; and a cabaletta of simultaneous singing. By 1859 this « solita forma de' duetti » was so well known that Basevi could bring it to mind simply by naming its movements.

Unfortunately, theorists whose writings were published in the early 1830s, and who might well have illuminated the transition between the late eighteenth- and early nineteenth-century models when they discussed other aspects of operatic design, failed to treat the structure of the duet in any detail. Bonifazio Asioli and Niccola Tacchinardi, for

---

[8] C. Ritorni, (*Ammaestramenti* cit., pp. 43-44) also regarded the alternation of solo statements as a species of dialogue: « Talor anco si mantiene la quantità del metro nella poesia e nella musica, e la parola passa da interlocutore a interlocutore per quantità ineguali, continuando eguale nelle sue metriche parti il complessivo dialogar cantato. Ma ciocché forma il particolare carattere, per esempio, del duetto è il rispondersi l'uno coll'altro in eguale misura di parole, il ché succede nelle seguenti maniere: Sentimenti diversi in quantità eguale e in tempo successivo: Sentimenti diversi, in egual quantità, contemporaneamente: sentimenti eguali contemporaneamente a più voci. Queste tre maniere poi si possono duplicare dal musicografo, facendo musica eguale a ciò che in poesia è diverso, e viceversa. Vuolsi anche notar il vezzo nella poesia, d'un più stretto rispondersi, or mercè le stesse desinenze o rime, or maggiormente in fare colla risposta la parodia, variando chi risponde ciò solamente che nelle sue circostanze diverso diviene o contrario, e nel restante rimanendo eguale la forma del sentimento ».

example, touched on numerous related topics (see *Appendix*, descriptions C and D). However, perhaps partly because of the variable structure of the turn-of-the-century duet, neither author addressed the issue of form directly. Asioli advised his students to seek out examples on their own, citing the works of composers ranging from Paisiello to Bellini. Significantly, he justified his omission in terms of the comparable « tessiture » of ensembles and arias, but not their forms. Similarly, conventionalized form was not mentioned specifically by Tacchinardi as one of the « difetti » of duets during the period in question. His silence on this issue contrasts sharply with Ritorni's disdain a decade later toward the « sazievole uniformità » of operas composed « tutte di parti d'una determinata struttura ».[9]

In short, we are left on our own to trace the development of the duet through a particularly complex period in its history. In the remainder of my brief essay I will address two aspects of this topic. I intend, first, to suggest that genetic connections do exist between eighteenth- and nineteenth-century duets; and, second, to examine the final stage of the transformation that led to the Ottocento duet, using pieces written by Simone Mayr from the beginning of his operatic career to 1813, the year of Rossini's first international success, *Tancredi*.

Elements of the Rossinian structure can be found in the texts of duets as early as Metastasio's opere serie. Timante and Dircea's *La destra ti chiedo* from Act II of *Demofoonte*, first performed in 1733, illustrates the most typical form employed in these pieces:

Section 1	*Timante*	La destra ti chiedo,
Interaction		Mio dolce sostegno,
		Per ultimo pegno
		D'amore e di fè.

---

[9] *Ivi*, p. 55.

	Dircea	Ah! questo fu il segno Del nostro contento; Ma sento che adesso L'istesso non è.
	Timante	Mia vita, ben mio!
	Dircea	Addio, sposo amato.
Section 2	*A 2*	Che barbaro addio!
Reflection		Che fato crudel!
Section 3		Che attendono i re
Reflection		Dagli astri funesti, Se i premii son questi D'un'alma fede?

Like many of Metastasio's duets, this one opens with two complete solo stanzas followed by the first part of a third stanza divided into dialogue. The poetic form of this interactive section resembles the initial movement of the Rossinian duet, although the latter usually expands the dialogue to at least a full stanza. In our example a reflective aside of two lines sung *a 2* completes the third stanza, creating a second section that functions like one of Rossini's slow second movements. More abstract reflection frequently takes place in a final complete stanza, Section 3, which may be either divided into solo statements followed by lines sung together or shared in its entirety, as in the duet for Timante and Dircea.[10] Rossini's early cabalettas also focus on simultaneous singing in many cases, either with or without the parallel solos, and often provide a more detached assessment of the situation.[11]

---

[10] For an example of the former approach, see the duet *Se mai turbo il tuo riposo* for Cleofide and Poro from *Alessandro nell'Indie*, Act I. Marita P. McClymonds has also discussed the form of the eighteenth-century duet text; see her *Niccolò Jommelli, the Last Years, 1769-1774*, Ann Arbor, Michigan, UMI 1980, pp. 248-253.

[11] For an example of the fully simultaneous approach see the cabaletta « Sì, tu sol, crudel, tu sei » from the duet *Lasciami, non t'ascolto* (*Tancredi*, Act II); for an example in which the first part of the cabaletta text is

THE DEVELOPMENT OF THE OPERA SERIA DUET

Thus, as early as the 1730s, the Metastasian duet already contained the rudiments of three of the four movements that make up the Rossinian model. It also follows a dramatic principle essential to the later design. That is, it progresses from expository interactive conflict in the first section to summarizing reflective asides in the second and third sections. In Rossini's duets an additional dialogue separates the two reflective passages and divides the musical number into two complete phases of interaction and reflection, the first consisting of the opening movement and slow movement, the second of the dialogue middle movement and cabaletta.[12] Because the Metastasian duet lacks the second dialogue, its two reflective sections function together to complete a single dramatic motion initiated by the opening interactive statements and dialogue.

Other studies have shown that eighteenth-century composers devised a number of musical forms for setting these three-part texts. Many of them involve the recapitulation of primary musical themes at the highest structural level, a non-Rossinian trait.[13] However, after 1770 one sometimes sees numbers that are through-composed at that level. For example, Mozart's duets from *Mitridate, Lucio Silla, Idomeneo* and *La clemenza di Tito* — all of which have texts that at least approximate the Metastasian design — avoid

---

performed as parallel statements (though not divided as such in the libretto) while the second half is performed simultaneously, see the cabaletta « Quell'alma perfida » from the duet *Perché mai, destin crudele* (*Elisabetta, regina d'Inghilterra*, Act I). The Metastasian three-section text may also have undergone other lines of development. In some cases the transformation may have involved both the insertion of a reflective stanza immediately following the opening solo stanzas and the elimination of one of the concluding reflective passages.

[12] I have discussed this aspect of the Rossinian duet at length in *Evolving Conventions* cit., pp. 87-104, and *The 'primo Ottocento' Duet* cit.

[13] For a useful summary discussion of earlier duets in *da capo al segno, dal segno*, and A B A' C form, see M. McClymonds, *Niccolò Jommelli* cit., pp. 248-253. See also R. Wiesend, *Zum Ensemble in der Opera seria*, « Analecta Musicologica », XXV, 1987 (*Johan Adolf Hasse und die Musik seiner Zeit*), pp. 187-222.

long-range cyclical return. Of course, none of them has the four separate movements of the later duet. Mozart instead chose either single slow tempos or slow-fast settings that change tempos between the first and second reflective sections.[14] Yet within a given tempo, he distinguished the various sections of the text through changes in theme, texture, and style of text-setting much as Rossini would years later.

Cimarosa's favorite treatment of the duet in the 1780s, which has been described by Friedrich Lippmann, resembles even more closely the nineteenth-century approach.[15] It includes all four sections of text and musical texture, although it incorporates them into a two-tempo, slow-fast design. The opening movement contains parallel statements and a first passage of simultaneous reflection; the second movement comprises dialogue and a concluding lyrical passage sung *a 2*, often with a cabaletta-like repetition of the principal theme. This setting of the four-section text in two tempos has the advantage of emphasizing the organization of the drama in two phases of interaction and reflection by articulating the division between them and by joining their constituent sections in single movements. One of Mozart's duets (*D'Eliso in sen m'attenti* for Giunia and Cecilio, *Lucio Silla*, Act I) also follows a varied version of this format. It combines the initial solo statements, first dialogue, first reflective section, and medial dialogue in an opening slow movement and sets the final reflective passage as the closing Allegro.

Even this all-too-brief re-examination of the duets of Metastasio, Mozart, and Cimarosa in light of later practice

---

[14] See, for example, *S'io non moro a questi accenti* for Ilia and Idamante (Un poco più Andante-Allegretto; *Idomeneo*, Act II) and *Ah perdona al primo affetto* for Servilia and Annio (Andante; *La clemenza di Tito*, Act I).

[15] F. LIPPMANN, *Über Cimarosas Opere serie*, « Analecta musicologica », XXI, 1982, *Colloquium: Die stilistische Entwicklung der italienischen Musik zwischen 1770 und 1830 und ihre Beziehungen zum Norden*, p. 42.

substantially narrows the perceived gap between the eighteenth- and nineteenth-century approaches. The development of the Rossinian duet from the type written by Cimarosa required primarily that the four musico-dramatic sections be separated and elaborated as independent movements. As I have argued elsewhere, this process of structural articulation was still ongoing in Rossini's Neapolitan operas. And, in fact, it would continue throughout the first half of the nineteenth century.[16]

The duets that Mayr wrote before 1813 show that the ultimate stage in defining the « solita forma » was begun well before Rossini made that design a cliché of Ottocento opera. Charles Brauner, in his dissertation on Bellini and the aesthetics of opera seria, has noted that Mayr was writing four-movement duets as early as *Ginevra di Scozia* in 1801.[17] And an even earlier example occurs in Telemaco and Mentore's *Giura, che i passi miei* (*Telemaco*, 1797), although its third movement sets *versi sciolti* instead of *versi lirici*. Brauner, however, failed to indicate precisely the extent to which Mayr anticipated later practice. One of Mayr's duets that resembles the Rossinian model is Zamoro

---

[16] S. BALTHAZAR, *Evolving Conventions*, cit., pp. 87-161 and 331-505, and ID., *The 'primo Ottocento' Duet*, cit. A few of Rossini's earliest duets even borrow Cimarosa's design, grouping two pairs of textual and musical subsections into an initial slow movement and a concluding fast movement. One example is Tancredi and Argirio's *Ah se de' mali miei* (*Tancredi*, Act II). There Rossini connects two solo stanzas in C major, a quatrain of modulatory dialogue (« Odiarti! ... Ah! son sì misero »), and two lines of simultaneous reflection in Eblat (« L'indegna odiar dovrei ») in a single opening Andante. Similarly a second Allegro movement unites a medial *parlante* dialogue created out of a stanza designated for both characters in the libretto (« Ecco le trombe ») with the concluding cabaletta in C (« Il vivo lampo »). These less innovative numbers occur alongside the four-movement duets that would predominate in Rossini's later operas.

[17] C. BRAUNER, *Vincenzo Bellini and the Aesthetics of Opera Seria in the First Third of the Nineteenth Century*, Ph.D.dissertation, Yale University 1972, p. 220.

and Idalide's *Ah, per chi serbai finora* from Act I of *Gli Americani* (1806):

Movement 1

Zamoro	Ah, per chi serbai finora Il mio cor gli affetti miei! Tutto, o ciel, sofferto avrei, Mai si nera infedeltà.
Idalide	A te sol serbai fin'ora Il mio cor gli affetti miei: Il mio bene, ognor tu sei, No, tradirti il cor non sa.
Zamoro	Ma in quel tempio! ...
Idalide	Te adorava.
Zamoro	Su quell'ara? ...
Idalide	Mi svenava.
Zamoro	Ma giuravi ...
Idalide	E il cor mentia.
Zamoro	Dunque? ...
Idalide	Ingiusto!
Zamoro	M'ami?
Idalide	E il chiedi?
Zamoro	M'ami ancor? ...
Idalide	Sei l'alma mia.
Zamoro	Sempre mia! ...
Idalide	Fedel morrò.

Movement 2

A 2	Come mai quel caro aspetto Mi seduce il cor nel petto! Dolce incanto mi rapisce, E d'amor languir mi fa.

Movement 3

Idalide	Vanne basta ...
Zamoro	Un'altro istante ...
Idalide	Notte scende. Và, se m'ami.

386

THE DEVELOPMENT OF THE OPERA SERIA DUET

Zamoro	Vado, si ... ma pria ...
Idalide	Che brami?
Zamoro	Di venir! prometti all'antro.
Idalide	Ciel! ...
Zamoro	Vacilli! ...
Idalide	Sé, verrò.

Movement 4

Zamoro	(Alla fin sarò contento.
	Vendicarmi alfin potrò.)
	Deh tu affretta il bel momento,
	E mai più ti lascierò.
Idalide	(Ah per me non v'è contento.
	Pace più sperar non so.)
	Tu trionfi in tal momento;
	Al destino io cederò.

As in Rossini's duets, a conflict is elaborated in two phases of interaction and reflection. In the first of these phases Idalide proclaims her fidelity to Zamoro and together they summarize their feelings (movements 1 and 2); in the second she urges his departure and again joins him in assessing the situation (movements 3 and 4). The four musical movements are clearly articulated with changes of tempo and, in some cases, with metrical shifts. Zamoro and Idalide's opening movement (Allegro moderato, C) incorporates parallel lyric solos followed by more declamatory dialogue. The slow movement (*Come mai quel caro aspetto*, Andantino larghetto, 2/4) is an extended *cantabile* sung primarily in thirds. Like Rossini's *tempi di mezzo*, Mayr's medial dialogue (*Vanne basta*, Moderato, C) mixes lyric, *parlante*, and declamatory styles of text setting. The final movement (*Alla fin sarò contento*, Con più moto, C) has the simultaneous singing and lively personality of the later cabaletta.

Within its individual movements this duet displays even more detailed affinities with the Rossinian model. For example, in the first movement Mayr treated Idalide and

Zamoro's opening statements as Rossini would have, dividing each of their quatrains into separate halves and repeating the third and fourth lines.[18] Thus each solo melody consists of three distinct sections, the first setting lines 1-2, the second lines 3-4, and the third reiterating the last two lines. In Zamoro's opening exclamation the first two lines are sung as short melodic fragments punctuated irregularly with orchestral interjections, anticipating the style of the « open melodies » that Rossini often wrote to begin similar solos.[19] Like Rossini, Mayr articulated the end of this section with a half cadence and an instrumental interlude and continued in the second section with a more continuous melodic line. A third section of closing phrases completes the melody. The tonal relationship of the two solos in this opening movement – the first modulates from tonic to dominant, the second begins and ends in the tonic – is one used in later duets. And Mayr's organization of the ensuing dialogue (beginning at « Ma in quel tempio ») corresponds to Rossini's practice of starting the final transition of the *tempo d'attacco* in *parlante* style, but then switching to more recitative-like music to signal the end of the movement.

Yet in this duet, as in others written by Mayr in what would become the « solita forma », one also sees a number of traits that recall earlier practice. For example, although the opening solos for Idalide and Zamoro begin with versions of the same melody, they diverge in their second and third sections. Mayr's tendency toward dissimilar statements differs from Rossini's usual pratice of giving the characters almost exactly the same material. And it echoes

---

[18] I have discussed the multi-partite solos of Rossini's opening movements in *Evolving Conventions*, cit., pp. 136-140, and *Rossini and the Development of the Mid-Century Lyric Form*, « Journal of the American Musicological Society », XLI, 1988, pp. 102-125.

[19] Lippmann has discussed the distinction between Rossini's « open » and « closed » melodic styles in *Per un'esegesi dello stile rossiniano*, « Nuova rivista musicale italiana », II, 1968, pp. 817-825, and Id., *Vincenzo Bellini und die italienische Opera Seria seiner Zeit* cit., pp. 154-169.

THE DEVELOPMENT OF THE OPERA SERIA DUET

the earlier method – described by Gervasoni and heard occasionally in Mozart's duets – of writing related but contrasting themes that convey the sense of separate emotional positions.[20] Mayr also set the slow movement of the Idalide-Zamoro duet in the tonic key, a holdover from the tonal stasis of some earlier duets. Idalide and Zamoro's *più mosso* lacks the repetition of the principal theme that would become a signature of the nineteenth-century cabaletta.[21] Finally, in several of Mayr's four-movement duets, thought not in this one, an offstage event – the sound of trumpets, for example – signals the end of the medial dialogue and motivates the final reflective passage, instead of occurring immediately after the slow movement to restore the dramatic pace as it would in later numbers.[22] This decisive musical articulation of the concluding dramatic section recalls Mozart's two-movement duets, in which the change of tempo often serves to mark the same point.

Thus even the duets of Mayr that closely approximate the Rossinian model show clear ties to their eighteenth-century heritage. This stylistc continuity is even more apparent in numbers which embrace the four-section text in two phases of interaction and reflection, but which fail to articulate each section with music. Some of these duets set the medial dialogue and final reflective passage as a single concluding fast movement, so that the piece as a whole follows a three-tempo, fast-slow-fast format.[23] Others link all four sections in a single tempo, and omit any notational indication of separate movements.

---

[20] See, for example, *S'io non moro a questi accenti*, cited above, fn. 14.

[21] Some of Rossini's duet cabalettas still lack this repeat as late as *Zelmira*. See, for example, Ilo and Polidoro's « Tu accresci il mio coraggio » from their duet *In estasi di gioia* (*Zelmira*, Act II).

[22] Compare, for example, the middle movements « Vado ... T'arresta ... Io deggio » from Ginevra and Ariodante's duet *Per pietà! deh! non lasciarmi* (Mayr, *Ginevra di Scozia*, Act II) and « Ecco le trombe » from Tancredi and Argirio's duet *Ah se de' mali miei* (Rossini, *Tancredi*, Act II).

[23] See, for example, Antinoo and Adrasto's concluding Allegro « Dammi, o padre, un altro amplesso » from their duet *Figlio mio ... Segui. Non posso* (I

SCOTT L. BALTHAZAR

The duet for Adelaide and Vandomo from Act I of Mayr's *Adelaide di Guesclino* (1799) illustrates this latter approach. The dramatic and poetic organization of its text resembles the Rossinian design:[24]

Section 1

Vandomo   Vado. Fra l'armi ancora
Ti porterò nel cor.
Dimmi: il mio cor t'adora,
E torno vincitor.

Adelaide   Vanne. Fra l'armi ancora
Ti seguirà il mio cor.
Salvami chi m'adora
E torna vincitor.

Section 2

A 2   Quale angoscioso palpito!
Dei! che di me lui sarà?
Oppressa, incerta l'anima
Fra dubbi suoi si stà.

Section 3

Vandomo   Vado; crudel! ma guardami.
Adelaide   Parti: Quei di conservami ...
Vandomo   Prosegui ...
Adelaide   Al campo. Addio.

Section 4

A 2   No, che non v'ha del mio
Più tormentato cor.

As in Rossini's duets, the four sections are delineated by changes in the textural relationship of the voices, orchestra-

---

misteri eleusini, Act I). Many of Rossini's duets also follow this plan. One is Amenaide and Tancredi's Allegro « Dunque? Addio - Lasciar mi puoi? » from the duet *Lasciami, non t'ascolto* (*Tancredi*, Act II).

[24] Rossini occasionally wrote duets like this one, in which the third and fourth movements share the same poetic stanza. See « Ecco le trombe », cited above, fn. 22.

tion, and accompaniment. However, other important articulative contrasts are lacking. All four sections are sung in the same Allegro tempo, none is set off by notation in the score, and each concluding cadence is elided with the beginning of the next section. Mayr further obscured the beginning of the first reflective section (« Quale angoscioso palpito ») by delaying both the start of simultaneous singing and the arrival of the contrasting key of D-flat major until the third line. Moreover, he set the entire reflective stanza, including its passage of simultaneous singing, in a declamatory vocal style that blends with the following dialogue.

In some of these single-tempo duets, unity is further enhanced, and even clearer ties maintained with earlier models, through the recapitulation of musical themes from section to section, a technique that is facilitated by the uniform tempo. However, whereas earlier composers recapitulated primary vocal themes, Mayr generally brought back secondary *parlante* transitions to integrate his designs. For example, the duet *Si cadrò: ma il suo diletto* for Vandomo and Adelaide in Act II of *Adelaide* uses varied versions of the same instrumental theme for both of the initial parallel statements, for the medial dialogue, and for the transition between presentations of the principal melody in the cabaletta. The practice of connecting the third and fourth sections with thematic return was particularly characteristic of Mayr, and it would remain important for Rossini as well.[25]

Alongside these four-section duets, which anticipate the Rossinian form to a considerable exent, Mayr also continued to write pieces that recall designs from earlier periods. Rather than immediately supplant traditional arrangements with more experimental structures, he incorporated all of the available alternatives into an expanding spectrum of

---

[25] See Elcia and Oxsiride's « Ah! qual suon! ... già d'Israele » from the duet *Ah! se puoi così lasciarmi* (*Mosè*, Act I).

organizational possibilities. Well after he had tested the Rossinian model in *Telemaco* and *Ginevra di Scozia*, Mayr wrote several lyrical duets in one movement that function like arias for two characters, providing reaction to a given situation and minimizing interaction and conflict. Some of these numbers even follow the outdated *da capo* form used in the middle of the century.[26] Other, more dynamic duets adapt the traditional Metastasian three-section text to the two-movement slow-fast format preferred by Cimarosa.[27] Even more frequently these traditional duets simplify the Metastasian text by eliminating one of the reflective passages that had followed the opening statements and dialogue. Mayr tended to set both of the remaining sections in a single tempo, differentiating them only in theme and texture.[28]

Finally, it would be tempting to assume that the four-movement form represented a culmination of the efforts of Mayr and his librettists to write duets of greater dramatic

---

[26] For example the «duettino» *Alfin risorgere* from Act I of *Il ritorno d'Ulisse* (1809) includes 1) an opening lyric section, in which parallel stanzas for the two characters are performed simultaneously; 2) a contrasting section of dialogue; and 3) an almost exact recapitulation of the opening section, followed by a long coda. The reprise of the first two stanzas is written out in the libretto.

[27] One example is the duet *Non palpitar, mia vita* for Creusa and Giasone from *Medea in Corinto*, in which the opening slow movement includes a solo stanza for each character and a third stanza divided into four lines of dialogue and two lines of simultaneous reflection. Mayr set the final reflective stanza *a due* as a cabaletta and provided the full reprise of the principal theme that later became standard. A predecessor for this two-movement arrangement of the three-section text is found in *S'io non moro a questi accenti*, cited above, fn. 14.

[28] In duets of this sort the text is shortened in one of two ways: 1) the final reflective section is omitted, so that the text includes two solo stanzas and one stanza divided into dialogue and simultaneous reflection (Adelaide and Nemours, *Ti lascio, mia vita*, from Act I of *Adelaide di Guesclino*); or 2) the first reflective section is replaced with dialogue, so that the parallel statements are followed by a full stanza of dialogue and one or more full stanzas of reflection (Penelope and Plistene, *Scostati. Il mio cordoglio*, from Act I of *Il ritorno d'Ulisse*).

This type of piece represents Mayr's treatment of the two-movement model described by Gervasoni and Choron. A prototype for this form can be found in Ilia and Idamante's replacement duet *Spiegarti non poss'io* (*Idomeneo*, Act II).

and musical complexity. However, evidence to the contrary is provided by several numbers from *Raùl di Créqui* (1810), *La rosa bianca e la rosa rossa* (1813) and *Tamerlano* (also 1813). They constitute an incipient attempt to further enlarge the duet by inserting additional phases of interaction and reflection in either the first or the third movement. For example, in the duet *Tu vivi ... Tu m'ami* for Adele and Raùl (*Raùl di Créqui*, Act II) the middle movement is divided into four dramatic and poetic sub-sections:

Movement 3

Coro	Olà ...
Adele/Raùl	Che inciampo!
Coro	Tu sei prigione.
Adele/Raùl	Ah! siam traditi!
Raùl	Chi mai l'impone?
Coro	Chi ti salvò.
Adele/Raùl	Qual mai di gioie, e pene
	Crudel vicenda è questa!
	Ahi! che da te, mio bene,
	Dividermi non so.
Adele	Spietati!
Raùl	Addio ...
Adele	T'arresta ...
A 2	Che smania! Oh dio! che orror!

Movement 4

A 2	Ahi! che fatal momento!
	Che fiero estremo addio!
	In cento parti, e cento
	Spezzar mi sento – il cor.

It begins with declamatory dialogue accompanied first by fully-scored martial flourishes as the chorus of guards enters, then by string tremolos moving to a half cadence to prepare the next sub-section. There the characters reflect in thirds on the threatening situation (beginning « Qual mai di gioie, e pene »). The next two brief sub-sections, the first consisting of exclamations accompanied by orchestral interjections (« Spietati! Addio ... T'arresta »), the second again presenting reflective thirds (« Che smania »), unfold over a dominant pedal that prepares the final movement (« Ahi! che fatal momento »). Although, to my knowledge, the logical step of elaborating these sub-sections as independent movements was never taken, such interpolations may eventually have led to the dramatic and musical freedoms observed in kinetic movements written by later composers.

My essay has left unanswered many significant questions regarding the precise chronology of Mayr's exploration of different structural options, the possibility of personal ro regional influences, and the priority of textual or musical factors in the development of various aspects of the design of the duet. Mereover, only a more comprehensive examination of the music of Mayr's contemporaries will allow us to judge whether he broke new ground of merely participated in a broader process of stylistic transformation.

However, the evidence presented here does indicate, contrary to the prevailing assumptions of Ottocento scholars, that the Rossinian duet in fact constitutes an outgrowth of its Metastasian predecessors. We have found many of its essential textual and musical elements in the duets of Metastasio, Mozart, and Cimarosa. Thus the « solita forma » represents a further stage – albeit an extremely consequential one – in a long developmental process extending well back into the eighteenth century. Mayr's duets contributed to this process; and some of them anticipated the nineteenth-century design with great precision. Yet these innovative pieces served as only one of many structural options for Mayr. Some of his alternatives reveal the stylistic continuity inherent in the genesis of the Rossinian approach by illustrating intermediate stages of development.

Others betray an impulse to expand the duet structure even beyond the four-movement layout that would eventually become the norm.

These observations allow us to re-evaluate Rossini's role in the development of the duet. He now seems to have pioneered few if any of the essential features of the nineteenth-century model. Rather, he narrowed the range of structural options by choosing most often a design that incorporates four fully developed movements. The variety of forms available to his predecessors also suggests that Rossini's many two- and three-tempo duets should be viewed not as deviations from a single archetype but rather as vestiges of the earlier range of possibilities. Perhaps most importantly, we can conclude that further efforts at tracing the roots of the Rossinian duet must be directed toward its Metastasian heritage.

Appendix

SOME DESCRIPTION OF THE ITALIAN DUET 1800-59

A) CARLO GERVASONI, *La scuola della musica in 3 parti divisa*, Piacenza, N. Orcesi 1800, pp. 518-59.

Nella Musica Teatrale il Duetto è un pezzo che il Compositore trattar dee per lo più a vicenda, e come precisamente lo richiede il vero sentimento della data Poesia. L'unità della melodia, e la perfetta distribuzione di questa fra le due Parti, sia il più importante oggetto di questa Composizione. Queste due Parti però non si debbono già equalmente disporre nel loro giro di Canto, ma diasi a ciascuna delle due quel carattere che sia meglio capace di dipingere lo stato dell'animo suo. Imperciocché rade volte succede che la situazione dei due Attori sia perfettamente d'accordo, onde debbano essi esprimere i loro sentimenti in egual modo. Quindi è che costumasi d'ordinario un Canto alternativo, per far intendere le due Parti separatamente, non meno che per dare a ciascheduna la più propria espressione. Accade finalmente nella conclusione del Duetto Teatrale di dovere riunire due sentimenti unanimi, o il vivo e rapido abbattimento di due sentimenti opposti. In questi casi le diverse commozioni dell'animo agitato scorrono da ambe le Parti in una sola volta, né lasciano luogo al dialogo. Di qui nasce poi la necessità di rinvenire un Canto che sia suscettibile d'un progresso per terze o per seste; e disporlo siffattamente, che da una parte si possa sentire il pieno suo effetto, senza smarrire dall'altra il sentimento.

B) ALEXANDRE CHORON, *Principes de composition des écoles d'Italie*, Paris [1808], book 3, p. 16.

Le duo, le trio, le quatuor, ne sont en quelque sorte que des airs à plusieurs parties, et principalement, lorsqu'ils sont dialogués. Il y a cette différence néanmoins que dans ce cas, qui est le plus ordinaire, la seconde partie répéte ce qu'à dit la première, soit dans le même ton, soit dans un autre selon le rapport des voix, ce qui oblige à plus de précision, et laisse surtout moins de place pour les instruments. Tous ces morceaux sont composés de deux parties; la première est dialoguée, et le dialogue doit être disposé de telle manière que le chant se suive d'une partie à l'autre, comme si une seule partie chantoit, en faisant néanmoins sentir le dialogue; la seconde partie qui est d'un mouvement plus animé fait ensemble et termine le morceau.

C) NICCOLA TACCHINARDI, *Dell'opera in musica sul teatro italiano e de' suoi difetti*, Firenze, G. Berni 1833^2, pp. 75-76.

La prima donna dovrà avere obbligatamente tre duetti, e per lo più due col musico, ed uno col Tenore. Questi ancora hanno il suo posto fisso. Spesso ne viene omesso uno, e sarà naturalmente quello di riuscita meno gradevole al Pubblico, o per cagione di troppa figurata fatica; ma il compositore tre ne deve scrivere, ed il Poeta deve, in qualunque soggetto, trovare tre situazioni per duetto, anche se il fatto richiedesse che due non si dovessero vedere che verso la fine dell'opera [...]. Al Tenore le viene assegnata quasi sempre [...] un duetto alla metà dell'atto primo, ed uno al cominciar dell'atto secondo. [...] L'obbligata situazione e sempre simile de' pezzi vocali, cagiona la somiglianza fra loro. Nei duetti dell'atto primo, lo stesso metro, lo stesso punto di scena, le stesse cadenze, la somiglianza ne' cantabili, e quella delle (così dette) cabalette, che par sempre di sentire lo stesso pezzo in tutte le opere.

D) BONIFAZIO ASIOLI, *Il maestro di composizione, ossia seguito del Trattato d'armonia, opera postuma*, Milano Ricordi, 1832², book 3, p. 44.

L'ordine metodico vorrebbe che qui si progredisse cogli esemplari del Duetto, Terzetto, Quartetto, Quintetto, Sestetto, e Finale; ma siccome la tessitura della composizione è sostanzialmente sempre la stessa, e parmi di averla fatta conoscere con bastante chiarezza nell'Aria precedente, così tralascierò di presentarli. Avverto peraltro che in questi pezzi s'incontrano degli affetti e dei caratteri affatto contrarj, i quali forzano il Compositore ad accordare insieme, o separatamente, le cantilene affettuose colle iraconde, le patetiche colle sdegnose, ecc., il quale accordo ben combinato fra le parti, produce quel contrasto che mirabilmente concorre ad imprimere un carattere di originalità e di unità di pensiero, a tutta la composizione. Vegga adunque il Giovine studioso i grandi esemplari di Paesiello, di Cimarosa, di Mayr, di Paer, di Rossini, di Bellini, ec., e ritenga che senza l'indefesso e attento studio di questi capi d'Opera, non potrà mai formarsi uno stile suo proprio, raffinare il buon gusto, dare i giusti slanci alla sua fantasia, conoscer l'uso degl'immensi mezzi che ha in mano, e condur bene la sua composizione.

E) Carlo Ritorni, *Ammaestramenti alla composizione d'ogni poema e d'ogni opera appartenente alla musica*, Milano, Luigi di Giacomo Pirola, 1841, pp. 44 and 49.

Un duetto, verbigrazia, comincierà da due strofe pari di quantità, nelle quali, con proposta e risposta, si dice un libero sentimento, tanto più degli altri importante nel senso poetico, quanto meno complicato nell'accompagnamento musicale, qualunque sia il tempo d'arte, che piaccia al maestro applicarci, e del quale non è qui luogo a parlare. Verrà talora dopo l'adagio, in cui si risponderanno perfettamente co' sentimenti e desinenze loro i versi de' due contendenti. Terrà dietro un dialogo di canto dissimulato aguisa de' recitativi. Finalmente nella cabaletta si combineranno a cantar assieme forse le stesse parole. Il coro interviene in questi *pezzi* dialoganti non altrimenti che nei monologici. [...] Il Metastasio non compose mai duetti che per donna e musico d'amoroso argomento. In questi legami non arrestossi la musica moderna, e ne fece gustare fra due voci diverse, e due personaggi del medesimo sesso; e piacquero assaissimo duetti di marziale argomento, contenenti non amorosi accordamenti ma opposte più gravi contenzioni.

F) Abramo Basevi, *Studio sulle opere di Giuseppe Verdi*, Firenze 1859, p. 191.

Oltreché si mostra con questo pezzo, che non manca l'effetto ancora quando altri si allontani dalla solita forma de' duetti, cioè da quella che vuole un *tempo d'attacco*, l'*adagio*, il *tempo di mezzo*, e la *Cabaletta*.

[24]

"La clemenza di Tito" and Other Two-Act Reductions of the Late 18th Century

BY SERGIO DURANTE (PADUA)

The starting point of my research has been the consideration of Mozart's "La clemenza di Tito", K. 621, within the context of the theatrical tradition most closely related to it; rather than establishing a comparison with works belonging to altogether distinct genres or with the prehistory of settings of the same libretto[1], I compared this opera in the first place with the contemporary reductions of original libretti by Pietro Metastasio, with particular reference to reductions in two acts.

The production of a Metastasian text was fairly common throughout the last decades of the century. Also the structural reduction in two acts was not rare and allows us comparison with at least 12 Metastasian subjects set by composers such as Domenico Cimarosa, Luigi Cherubini, Ferdinando Giuseppe Bertoni, Pasquale Anfossi, Luigi Caruso, Gaetano Andreozzi, Gennaro Astaritta, Peter Winter, Angelo Tarchi, Francesco Ceracchini, and Giovanni Paisiello (see Table 1: p. 740).

As we shall see, the comparison with productions of the same kind shows that the general shape and details of the Mazzolà-Mozart[2] revision present traits of distinguished originality, both in some of the aspects where Mazzolà (and/or Mozart) departed from the original and in some of those which they decided to maintain; furthermore, such originality seems to represent an attempt at merging into the new "Tito" two contemporary but distinct tastes: that for Metastasian texts (considered mainly as a literary product) and, on the other hand, that for stylistically advanced or "renovated" opera seria of the late eighties.

The broader frame for an analysis of the 1791 Prague production can be provided through a survey on the productions of Metastasian subjects in the period between 1780 and 1795. The results can be summarized as follows (Table 2: p. 741)[3]:

1. 227 Metastasian "drammi" were produced in Europe in the 16 years considered; the peak was reached with 22 productions three years before Mozart composed "La clemenza di Tito".
2. The production of Metastasian "drammi per musica" was both regular and common during this period; it probably represented for the impresari a safe choice because of the reputation of the author (a fact that is especially true for

---

[1] An excellent example of this method is Helga Lühning's Titus-Vertonungen im 18. Jahrhundert. Untersuchungen zur Tradition der Opera seria von Hasse bis Mozart, Laaber 1983. (Analecta Musicologica. 20.) It is clear, nevertheless, that this kind of research is based on the underlying assumption that the process of imitation between composers was following a pattern which belongs more to the history of literature. In other words, while it is an historical fact that Pietro Metastasio referred back to Jean Baptiste Racine, the same has yet to be demonstrated in the case of "La clemenza di Tito" between, say, Mozart and Christoph Willibald Gluck or Johann Adolf Hasse.

[2] I will refer to Caterino Mazzolà and Mozart as co-authors of the revision because, although we know that Mazzolà provided the revision of the text, we assume that Mozart had a part in the choice of set-pieces and consequent structural alterations. This complex problem is addressed in my dissertation, Mozart and the Idea of 'vera opera': A Study of "La clemenza di Tito", Phil. Diss. Harvard University, in progress.

[3] Further analysis of the Metastasian fortune in the late 18th century is presented in the thesis quoted in footnote 2 and concerns the different interest in Metastasio's subjects in different operatic centres and the variance of alterations.

Italian theatres, where the literary appreciation of the text provided a firm basis for success).
3. When presented within a regular season these "drammi" would usually be the prima opera (that is, the least important) when the seconda opera was a new one (with respect to both libretto and music); but there are notable exceptions to this rule: Metastasian subjects were also used as major events especially in fair-seasons or for particular celebrations: Cimarosa's "Olimpiade" (the most frequently performed among two-act reductions) was composed for the opening of a new theatre, Mozart's "La clemenza di Tito" for the coronation festivities of 1791.
4. Most of the composers of Mozart's generation were working at some time on a Metastasian subject; a few of these productions, though, including some of the two-act reductions, were "pasticci" for which either a librettist or a music director is perhaps to be considered responsible.
5. The choice of Metastasian subjects was selective; of the 26 original "drammi per musica", only five or six were more or less regularly performed within the 16 years considered (Table 3: p. 741).
6. Most of the 22 "drammi" performed during this period (1780–1795) had at least one two-act reduction (12).

Before touching upon these revisions, I would like to call attention to a couple of circumstances which should be kept in mind in relation to the Prague production of 1791: (1) although "La clemenza di Tito" was a "coronation" opera, its production should not be understood as a "Court" enterprise. It was, rather, the production of a private impresario who had to exploit the opera both for the celebrative purpose and for the whole period of the festivities. In other words, the opera had to pursue two parallel but distinct goals. (2) According to H. C. Robbins Landon[4] another opera seria was given during the celebrations for the crowning of Emperor Leopold on Monday, August 29, that is, Giovanni Paisiello's "Pirro", on a libretto by Giovanni de Gamerra. This work, which was premièred in Naples in 1787, was referred to by its composer as the first opera seria in which "finali" were introduced — a novelty which was indeed perceived as such (and won great acclaim), also on the occasion of the Milan performance in the winter of 1791 with music by Nicola Antonio Zingarelli[5].

The alterations imposed on pre-existing libretti can be categorized according to different perspectives: From the point of view of the text, these alterations could be classed as: (1) lexical, (2) metrical, (3) narrative, and (4) dramaturgical. But, if we consider the opera as a theatrical production, other perspectives are as much or even more important. The modification of visual aspects, for instance, is often a main concern in Metastasian revisions. Last but not least, we must consider the choice and configuration of musical structures as the means through which the "musical" dramaturgy as a whole is established. Of course, the distinction of these levels is no more than a useful

---

[4] H. C. Robbins Landon, 1791: Mozart's Last Year, New York 1988, p. 105.

[5] Paisiello mentioned the circumstance in his autobiographical sketch; the relevant passage is given in: Giovanni Paisiello: A Thematic Catalogue of His Works, ed. by Michael F. Robinson and Ulrike Hofmann, vol. 1, New York 1991, p. 396. A report on the Milan performance of December 26, 1791 is found in the Gazzetta enciclopedica di Milano of December 27: "Questo pubblico milanese è rimasto soddisfattissimo del nuovo dramma Pirro re d'Epiro [...] del Sig. Tenente de Gamerra [...] piaque moltissimo l'introdotta novità di terminare gli atti con dei finali pieni di moto e di azione" published in: Achille Maccapani, Luigi Marchesi, il sopranista pentito di Inzago (1754–1829), Inzago 1989, pp. 33–34.

abstraction. It is clear, for instance, that the Quintetto con coro which concludes Act I of "La clemenza di Tito" embodies many of the afore mentioned alterations: (1) metrical, (2) narrative, (3) dramaturgical, (4) visual, and (5) musical. It is of importance for a correct understanding of "La clemenza di Tito" to know which features belong to a tradition (or at least can be considered common) and which ones are to some degree original. Although all these different phenomena deserve detailed investigation, I will limit myself to a summary of the most relevant findings.

Let us consider first the elements which are more frequently found throughout the repertory, taking as a point of departure the general characteristics of the "drammi per musica" by Pietro Metastasio. These "drammi" are based on a relatively complex narrative structure in that the main plot is expanded (or, from the Metastasian point of view, strenghthened) through parallel plots developed by secondary characters. From a dramatic point of view, these have the function of repeating and reverberating in varied form the main moral theses of the drama. For instance, in "La clemenza di Tito" the episode of the exchanged mantles — eliminated by Mazzolà — had the function of presenting Sesto's dilemma between friendship and passion in yet another guise: Not only is he torn because of his love for Tito, but his conspiracy is also in conflict with Annio's friendship. These expansions or "spirals" of the main plot produced an abundance of situations proper for the deployment of the lyric element conveyed by the arias. Whether the need for numerous aria insertions was the cause or the consequence of a certain theatrical taste is of course a chicken-and-egg question. The fact is in any case that, with very few exceptions, the Metastasian revisions of the late 18th century, be they in two or three acts, show a substantial simplification and concentration of the plot around the main story (i. e., that of the principal characters). This is indeed a general and rather well-known trend, attested by Denis Diderot among others, which affected the structure of new works and the revision of old ones alike[6]. A similar example is the removal of the episode of Osmida's rescue in most contemporary productions of "Didone". In this respect, then, Mazzolà's major cut in the second act reflects a common practice[7]. What is perhaps less common is that the cut is performed in such a way that it does not need functional replacement — that is, new scenes or fragments of scenes which become necessary elsewhere in this repertory in order to restore proper narrative links[8]. This could be so rephrased: While some of the original events of the plot are omitted, there is no anticipation or delay with respect to the original sequence. Because the original narration is concentrated but not re-shuffled, no insertion of scenes newly-written

---

[6] On this subject see Daniel Heartz, From Garrick to Gluck: the Reform of Theatre and Opera in the Mid-eighteenth Century, in: Proceedings of the Royal Musical Association 94 (London 1967/68), pp. 11–127.

[7] A different matter is, of course, how skilfully the cut was made and what were its consequences in the dramatic mechanism. This is a subject which needs individual consideration for each different example.

[8] An example is Gaetano Andreozzi's Act II, Scene 13 of "Catone in Utica" (Reggio 1788), between Cesare, Fulvio, and Marzia. In the original version the scene ended with the exit of Marzia. Cesare remained on stage for the following confrontation with Arbace. Andreozzi inserted instead an exit aria for Cesare (the poetic structure resembles that of a rondo); therefore a new short scene had to be inserted for the characters remaining on stage (Marzia and Fulvio) while the long confrontation between Cesare and Arbace had to be replaced with a new short monologue for the latter character. In this case, the alteration had been obtained not only through abbreviation but involving also a considerable deviation from the original; the variant involved writing two basically new scenes and determined a double problem, from the point of view of the traditional theatrical mechanism: At the end of their scene, Marzia and Fulvio leave the stage before the entry of Arbace, who declaims only six verses of recitative before he himself leaves as the scene changes.

by the reviser is needed[9]. This calls our attention to the special faithfulness of Mazzolà to the original: The insertion of new verses (or the modification of old ones) is kept to a minimum and shows — in comparison with the work of other librettists — a clear conservative attitude as far as the language of the text is concerned.

This quasi-philological attitude also comes to the fore where Mazzolà inserts set pieces (or parts thereof), the text of which is based on, or refers to, elements of recitative sections omitted[10]. An extreme example is represented by the two additional verses by Mazzolà to Metastasio's aria "Parto, ma tu ben mio". The two "new" verses are in fact derived from a recitative otherwise entirely omitted (Act I, Scene 4), a monologue for Sesto. While eliminated, its essential element is recovered by Mazzolà scenes later as the ending lines of the afore-mentioned aria[11]. Even closer to Metastasio are the ensembles, the texts of which always consist of a rearrangement of verses taken from the original text (be it recitative or set pieces), a process found elsewhere in the repertoire but never applied so extensively and systematically[12].

In any case, Mazzolà's respect for the language and dramatic mechanism of Metastasio (as far as it is maintained), should not be taken as a plain conservative attitude. It runs parallel with the most unprejudiced approach to the structural disposition and the function of musical forms that can be found in the repertoire, features for which Mozart must be held especially responsible.

Decidedly far from the Metastasian taste was, for instance, the systematic replacement of lyrical or reflective arias with texts in which the soloist interacts with the other character(s) on stage. This also was not an invention by Mazzolà, but once again he seems to give a very radical application of the principle. It is remarkable that none of the arias in "La clemenza di Tito" (with the conspicuous exception of Vitellia's rondò "Non più di fiori") are sung alone on stage. All of them are indeed addressed to another character and represent a follow-up to the action of the recitative[13]. This means that the Metastasian concept according to which the set piece must be a lyrical expansion and an arrest of the action is reversed, in that action-time is "modulated" through all available

---

[9] It should be mentioned that Otto Jahn quoted erroneously in his book (part IV, p. 573, footnote 45) a scene that he attributed to Mazzolà but that in fact does not belong to the original tradition of the opera; also this intriguing problem is dealt with in the dissertation quoted in footnote 2.

[10] The Duettino "Deh prendi un dolce amplesso" amplifies and derives from the image of tender friendship which was lost with the cut of the previous recitative ("Impaziente anch'io / son che alla nostra antica, / E tenera amicizia aggiunga il sangue / Un vincolo novello").

[11] Note how the meaning of these two verses can be substantially different if one considers the Metastasian origin of this element. While on one side it could be considered as simple filler, the fact that Mazzolà chose to restore exactly this element indicates that the power of beauty was reputed relevant or even essential in order to explain Sesto's behaviour. Compare Metastasio (I, 4): "[...] Oh sovrumano / Poter della beltà! Voi che dal cielo / Tal dono aveste, ah non prendete esempio / Dalla Tiranna mia [...]", and Mazzolà (I, 9) verses 9—10: "Ah qual poter, oh Dei! / Donaste alla beltà".

[12] In order to have an idea of the ways in which other revisers would depart from the original, I will list some of the procedures more frequently found in the contemporary repertoire which are not used by Mazzolà: (1) alteration of recitative by addition of new verses, and creation of new scenes (often in conjunction with a new set piece); (2) alteration of the narrative order; (3) substitution of original arias with arias from other Metastasian libretti; (4) insertion of ensembles not derived from original verses (either recitative or set pieces); (5) narrative contractions, i. e., the grouping of the contents of many original scenes in one long scene (involving entries and exits) set in recitative style.

[13] The omitted arias are: I, 4 ("Opprimete i contumaci"); I, 7 ("Te solo amai"); I, 13 ("Quando sarà quel dì"); II, 5 ("Almen se non poss'io"); II, 7 ("Fra stupido e pensoso"); II, 16 ("Tremo fra dubbj miei"); and III, 11 ("Getta il nocchier talora" in the place of "Non più di fiori").

Sergio Durante: "La clemenza di Tito"

musical tools: recitatives, arias (of various formal patterns), and ensembles (also presented in different formal guises).

Coming finally to the central problem of the reduction in two acts, it must be pointed out that also in this case the particular solution of Mozart and Mazzolà can be seen as a re-interpretation of pre-existing procedures in a radical synthesis. Almost all the reductions pre-dating "La clemenza di Tito" maintained the first act virtually unchanged, while concentrating the contents of act II and III in a new second act. I was able to trace only one production before "La clemenza di Tito" in which the original Act II is divided, Anfossi's "Issipile" performed in London in 1784. Anfossi's quartet at the end of Act I might have provided a model. Mozart, however, goes a few steps further[14] with his complex ensemble and coro articulated in four scenes.

Mozart's arrangement of the first finale is a crucial point in many respects, which could be summarized thus:
1. The traditional arrangement in which Act I was left untouched (and which Mozart himself had adopted for "Il re pastore"), while abbreviating the opera as a whole, maintained one of the original act endings (the one between Act I and II); more important, it did not alter the functional units of the drama consisting in the aristotelean categories of exposition, peripeteia and catastrophe[15]. The only difference was, that the catastrophe-section would follow without interruption (except for the scene change).
2. The traditional arrangement presented a major disadvantage in that the size and the narrative pace of the two acts would be rather different, ranging from the "normal" Act I to a long and eventful Act II; the idea of dividing Act II, combined with the long cut of the mantle episode, restores a more balanced narrative pace throughout.

The Mozartean solution had further consequences because, while reestablishing the narrative balance, it achieved a parallel and substantial feat: the transformation of a section originally designed as a part of the peripeteia into a final part involving five characters and the chorus (a case of unseen action made visible)[16]. This was a suitable solution for a kind of dramatic structure that Mozart had never tried before, a finale serio: It absorbed from the peripeteia-function of the scenes, used the climactic element of general confusion, also characteristic of the buffa tradition, but transposed it from a low to a high style of serious opera using the verses of its most elegant poet.

The imposing character of the first-act Finale (whose visual impact is not second to the musical one) should not dim the fact that the use of musical forms in "La clemenza di Tito" is strongly innovative throughout the opera. The exceedingly high number of ensembles has been noted already; one should add that the position chosen for the set

---

[14] Three years after 1791 an "Antigono" adopting a similar solution was hailed in Florence as an "opera novissima". See Robert Lamar and Norma Weaver, A chronology of Florentine Theatre 1757–1800, vol. 2 (forthcoming).

[15] Note that these categories are recognized by Pietro Metastasio in his theoretical treatise on the theatre, the Estratto dell'Arte Poetica di Aristotele. The categories themselves, nevertheless, should be taken as general functions rather than strictly observed rules. While the character of these functions is rather clear, the outer limits of these functional sections is often debatable.

[16] What is meant by this is that a "fact" which was only alluded to (or conveyed by Tycoscopy) in the original version is actually brought on stage in the revision. One early example of this process, inclining to the spectacular taste of French Tragédie lyrique, is found in the second act of the "Nitteti" set by Giovanni Paisiello for St. Petersburg in 1777.

pieces is also of importance: The idea of placing as the first set piece of an opera a duet ("Come ti piace imponi") or beginning a scene with a terzetto ("Quello di Tito è il volto") is remarkably new.

Such a composite attitude, at the same time conservative towards the language of the text and entirely unprejudiced as to the articulation of musical dramaturgy, clarifies the strategies of Mozart and Mazzolà in the difficult task of creating a "true opera" over the ashes of an old "dramma per musica". Absorbing and using in an original synthesis a number of techniques and tools already in existence, they produced what can be safely considered not only the most advanced Metastasian revision of their time, but, more importantly from their point of view, a stage work which could compete in the same season and even overcome the recent ambitious experiments of Paisiello and of his librettist de Gamerra.

Diskussion

Pierluigi Petrobelli: You mentioned en passant "Il re pastore". Of course "Re pastore" is before. It is a typical example of three-act Metastasio reduced to two acts. It dates from 1775 — in fact, before, from 1767, which means it precedes the period of time you considered. But I would like to call your attention to the fact, that a two-act version of Metastasio's "Re pastore" was first performed in Venice, the summer of 1769. And more important was the occasion: for a private visit to Venice of Emperor Joseph II. Does this fact — and of course Mozart's "Il re pastore" was written for Salzburg between March and April 1775 for the visit of yet another son of Maria Theresia, Maximilian — can it be, then, that for the third son of Maria Theresia "La clemenza di Tito" was performed, with similar things in mind? Contrary to this hypothesis, may I call your and Ciliberti's attention to the time of origin of the composition of "La clemenza di Tito"? I do not actually want to go into that. I just want to call attention again to the fact that Caterino Mazzolà was not a Prague but a Dresden court poet. Only in the contract of Guardasoni that Tomislav Volek published in the Mozart-Jahrbuch 1959 is it clearly said that "Opera is to be new. When, if in the case that the new opera cannot be performed, then we go back to old Tito". The other thing is that all this incredible intellectual activity that is behind all the facts that you have presented in your paper — and I agree entirely with what you have said — should have taken less than two weeks, including travel from Vienna to Prague.

Sergio Durante: I am sure Helga Lühning has something to say on this subject. She has written extensively on the possibility that Mazzolà could work not only within two weeks, but also within a wider span of time on this project.

Helga Lühning: Mazzolà was at Vienna and not at Dresden at this time.

Sergio Durante: I do not remember exactly when he arrived in Vienna, but it was towards the end of May possibly.

Helga Lühning: April.

Sergio Durante: Right. So, I think that this kind of revision would mean that they would have to have a very clear idea of what they wanted to do, and of course Mozart had demonstrated on other occasions that he knew what he wanted from his librettists. But also sometimes I think that Helga Lühning's studies prove that the amount of time available was sufficient for this kind of endeavour.

Helga Lühning: Die Reduktion auf zwei Akte bei „Il pastore" ist ein anderer Fall. „Il re pastore" verkörpert ein Ausnahmestück von Metastasio, es ist fast schon eine andere Gattung, daher lag eine Reduktion nahe. „Titus" hingegen ist ein typisches Metastasianisches Drama. Darum denke ich, daß die Reduktion auf zwei Akte bei „Il re pastore" nahelag. Bei „Titus" ist das nicht der Fall. Hier taucht ein Problem auf, daß es nämlich durch die Reduzierung zur Störung des empfindlichen Gleichgewichts zwischen der Kaiser-Handlung und der Intrige kommt, daß nämlich die Intrige in den Vordergrund kommen könnte, und der Kaiser zur Nebenhandlung wird. Diese Gefahr würde durch die Kürzung (wie bei Mazzolà) noch größer.

Sergio Durante: "La clemenza di Tito"

Zur Frage nach dem Warum: Die Begründung ergibt sich aus der Musik. Durch die Kürzung war es möglich, den Brand des Kapitols an das Ende des ersten Aktes zu stellen. Dadurch wurde eine Teilung der Handlung erreicht, und das Quintett fungiert als eine Art Finale. Die Musik begründet also die Änderung, die Mazzolà vorgenommen hat, Mozart war daran beteiligt.

Sergio Durante: I have constantly used the name of Mazzolà because, of course, we do not have direct documentation of Mozart's participation, but it is clear that he did participate. It is true that librettists were handling the texts, but it is also true at this stage of the history of opera that composers were also increasingly making decisions, because one could not really plan the quintet with the Coro without having it be guided by the composer.

Friedrich Lippmann: Ganz so „modern" wie einige italienische Zeitgenossen sind Mazzolà und Mozart freilich doch nicht. Gemessen an den großen Szenenblöcken, den neuartigen „arie con coro" und anderen aus der Oper „Pirro" (1787), „Elfrida" und der „Giuochi d'Agrigento" (beide 1792) von Paisiello, oder von „Gli Orazi e i Curiazi" (1796) von Cimarosa hat der Mozartsche „Titus" noch eher einen traditionellen Zuschnitt.

Sergio Durante: I agree with you one hundred percent, but the fact remains that they had to work with this text, and within the limits of this text. I believe we have to understand they were making an effort to assert themselves. Of course "Elfrida" is another thing. It was written only one year after "La clemenza di Tito", but it was also a new libretto, so modernity must be understood in another dimension.

Table 1

Reductions in two acts of Metastasian subjects 1780–1795

year	title	city	composer
1780	Demetrio	Venice	Bianchi
1784	Issipile	London	Anfossi
1784	Olimpiade	Vicenza	Cimarosa
1784	Olimpiade	Lucca	Cimarosa
1784	Olimpiade	Modena	Borghi
1784	Alessandro nell'Indie	Mantua	Cherubini
1785	Artaserse	Brescia	Bertoni
1785	Olimpiade	Florence	Borghi
1786	Didone	Florence	"diversi"
1786	Alessandro nell'Indie	Florence	"varj maestri"
1787	Alessandro nell'Indie	Rome	Caruso
1787	Alessandro nell'Indie	Bologna	Bianchi
1788	Alessandro nell'Indie	Leghorn	Cherubini
1788	Artaserse	Rome	Anfossi
1788	Antigono	Rome	Caruso
1788	Catone in Utica	Reggio	Andreozzi
1788	Didone	Naples	Anfossi
1788	Olimpiade	Milan	Cimarosa
1788	Olimpiade	London	Cimarosa
1788	Nitteti	Piacenza	"diversi"
1789	Ipermestra	Venice	Astaritta
1789	Olimpiade	London	Cimarosa
1790	Artaserse	Reggio	Tarchi
1790	Olimpiade	Bologna	Cimarosa
1790	Olimpiade	Padua	Cimarosa
1790	Olimpiade	Venice	Cimarosa
1791	Catone in Utica	Venice	Winter
1791	La clemenza di Tito	Prague	Mozart
1792	Artaserse	Florence	"diversi"
1792	Didone	Madrid	Sarti-Paisiello
1792	Olimpiade	Florence	"diversi"
1793	Temistocle	Florence	"diversi"
1794	Antigono	Florence	Cerracchini
1794	Didone	Naples	Paisiello
1794	Olimpiade	Vicenza	Cimarosa
1795	Didone	Florence	Paisiello
1795	Olimpiade	Modena	Cimarosa

total 37 productions, 12 titles, 14 composers

Table 2

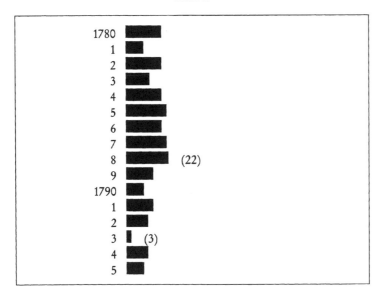

Table 3

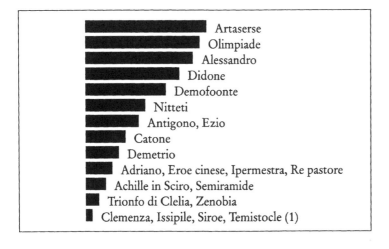

[25]

The Absent Mother in Opera Seria

MARTHA FELDMAN

OPERA SERIA WAS FOUNDED on the myth of the good king. As a prototypical tale aimed at legitimizing the prevailing political ideology of absolutism, the myth of the good king crystallized various propositions about the divinely ordained nature of the world and the role of the male monarch as a virtuous engine of its control. The king was the prime mover on earth, politically and morally, in a cosmic order that cascaded downwards from God through him to the different social orders below.

Such at least was the message codified, disseminated, and naturalized through the narratives of the classic Metastasian libretto, whose propositions—so it told the listener—were *not* up for review. This was an ironic message in the context of most eighteenth-century Italian theaters, since even as the myth (and its many variants) aimed to foreordain and foreclose its viewers' outlook on the world, in so doing it seems also to have freed them to listen when and as they pleased. Far from watching myths play out on the stage with the constant vigilance of modernist viewers, Italian spectators of Metastasian opera rarely gave their undivided attention.[1] It appears, then, that audiences' attentions were as anarchic, erratic, and unpredictable as the operas' narratives were axiomatic, inert, and repetitive—that, indeed, these two conditions were inherently linked.

In this sense, life in the opera house was hardly coextensive with the drama seen onstage, since the often tumultuous manner in which *opere serie* were experienced was at odds with the messages the works bore. These divided realities provide a useful caution that neither the domain of audience experience nor that of political narrative can be overlooked without loss to an analysis of the phenomenon of opera seria as a whole. Indeed it seems clear (as I have argued elsewhere) that discontinuous lis-

---

I am grateful to participants at the conference Representations of Gender and Sexuality in Opera (State University of New York at Stony Brook, September 1995) and to members of the study group on "The Anthropology of Music in Mediterranean Cultures" who attended the meeting Music as Representation of Gender in Mediterranean Cultures (Venice, Fondazione Levi, 9–11 June 1998) for ideas shared with me when I presented different versions of this essay in oral form. Special thanks are due to Lorenzo Bianconi, Philip Gossett, Mary Ann Smart, Martin Stokes, and the anonymous reviewers of this essay.

tening was possible only because endless, insuperable patriarchy was a foregone conclusion.[2]

Or so it was meant to be: other signs in Italian theater life, as we will see, betrayed deep ruptures in the field of patriarchal relations that ruled the old regime. To glimpse them, we should first recall the semiotics of space in the standard public theaters of eighteenth-century Italy, where a monarchical loge often formed the focal point for various rows of boxes, each looped around it in a semicircle, like embroidered lengths of ribbon. The classic example of such a theater was the Teatro San Carlo of Naples, built by the Bourbon king Carlo III in 1737; figure 1 shows its original architecture as it survives today.

Along the lower tiers in theaters like the San Carlo, boxes were typically owned by a noble family, with family constellations reproducing the patriarchal order articulated by the grand loge of the monarch. This same pattern repeated itself at various levels of the social order, from sovereign to nobles and on down, each box corresponding to that of the monarch and forming yet another microcosm of his family. The boxes of families higher in social station were normally situated in lower tiers of the hall and vice versa (although there were exceptions to this rule).[3] Families at higher social levels (the nobility and some wealthy civilians) generally owned their boxes, or (at minimum) leased them annually. All in all, the principal *unit* of theatrical viewing was the family; and the principal figure of power and authority within the family unit was of course the husband.

But the institution of marriage was in a peculiar state of crisis in eighteenth-century Italy, and many, if not most, husbands would not have been found in their family boxes. In the newly consolidated bourgeois public sphere, men of station were frequently drawn away by demands outside the domestic realm—by their traffic in commodities, their political engagements, and the new commerce in opinion and ideas.[4] Marriages had to respond to new economic pressures, new spheres of public exchange, and hence new patterns of existence, whose duties were largely inconsistent with the old courtly practices of baroque theatergoing. At the same time, older social forms remained strenuously in place, as if to ensure that aristocratic wives be accommodated with all the niceties of old courtly etiquette. For these and other reasons, a general state of disjunction between marital form and its content was inevitable. Indeed, if anything, the impulse to endow bourgeois marital form with courtly accoutrements seems to have increased as the content of marriage was depleted. In this respect, at least, the patriarchal order articulated by the visual arrangement of the hall was in practice drained of much of its message. Marriage, moreover, was only the most visible among a complex of family crises in *settecento* Italy: with the crisis of marriage came a crisis of motherhood, a generalized condition of doubt over whether the new public fantasy, which had begun

Figure 1. Naples, Teatro San Carlo, view of the back and sides of the theater gallery, showing the royal box. Photo from Franco Mancini, *Il Teatro di San Carlo, 1737–1987,* vol. 1 (Naples: Electa Napoli, 1987), 101. Reproduced with kind permission of the publisher.

to idealize the domestic sphere, was actually being realized by the contemporary habits of the aristocratic mother.

At the same time, over the course of the eighteenth century, the Italian opera libretto had its own strange history of managing some of these crises within its particular generic and representational parameters. When opera seria was first codified within the hallowed halls of the Arcadian Academy at the turn of the century, its most prominent practitioner, Apostolo Zeno, showed no special aversion to representing mothers onstage. Zeno's *Griselda* (1701), *Merope* (1712), and *Andromaca* (1724), for instance, all represented mothers—and valorous, protective ones at that. Yet once the genre was codified by Pietro Metastasio in the 1720s and 1730s, a canonical repertory of libretti came into being (to be set again and again throughout the century) in which almost nobody had a mother, and almost nobody seemed to notice.[5] It was only rather late in the century that mothers sometimes began to reappear, and when they did, they were most often shown in a terrible guise.

The figure of the mother will emerge as my theme toward the end of this essay. But it is not possible to understand the ambivalent and changing position of these operatic mothers without first understanding something of the quintessential father figure as structurally embodied in the divine king. As a generative figure, the father preceded even the mother in the minds of early-modern Europeans. To see how this was so, let me turn to what might be regarded as an archetype of the opera seria myth, Metastasio's *Artaserse*, to ask how the sovereign functioned as a pervasive engine of motherless kinship within the operatic imaginary.

2

The story of *Artaserse* typifies the Metastasian plot structure in oscillating continually between the demands of public duty and private desire. At the heart of this oscillation lies a tension that can only be subdued by resolving the fate of love interests, a process that tests and ultimately affirms the monarch's authority to decide affinal relations. Since the reigning monarch, King Serse, is mysteriously murdered offstage at the opera's outset, his son, prince Artaserse, becomes the immediate heir to the throne, at the same time as he is embroiled in one of the plot's two love interests: he loves a noblewoman named Semira, while his sister, the princess Mandane, loves Semira's brother Arbace. A symmetrical alliance involving a direct exchange of the young lovers between the two families seems destined early on, but for most of the opera the exchange exists only *in potentia*. Accession into the royal family by the brother-sister pair Arbace and Semira is confounded by an obstacle to their marriage imposed by their own father, the secret murderer (we later learn) of King Serse, who had acted to defend his son Arbace's honor against doubts about his worthiness as a suitor for Mandane's hand.

Details of the story need not concern us here. Rather, it is important to realize that within the context of a complex social order, the plot poses a specific problem of the *paterfamilias:* how can absolute loyalty to each consanguineal and symbolic father be maintained—and with it, loyalty to the practical and ideological exigencies of the father relation more broadly—in the face of demands that contradict and even negate one another? How can Arbace stand true to his father (who, for strategic reasons, has ended up framing him as the murderer) and yet also stand true to his murdered king and to his prince—also a friend and soon-to-be (fatherly) king? How can the princess Mandane be loyal to her beloved Arbace—who was soon to be her spouse and thus the head of her family—and yet also remain loyal to her murdered father (if, as she fears, Arbace is indeed his murderer)? How, in short, can the social order reproduce itself in the face of ineluctable conflicts, which always arise from attempts to resolve competing genealogical paradigms?

The liminal figure in this conundrum is not the one occupying the pinnacle of the hierarchy—namely, Artaserse—but his subject and friend, Arbace. Once the scent of guilt descends upon him early in Act I, his exoneration, and the devastating trials of conflicted loyalty he undergoes, become the keys to a general pacification of everyone in the realm, principals and onlookers alike: through Arbace's exoneration, the way is cleared for the two marriages, and the opera can end with the populace singing praises to king Artaserse. Analogues to Arbace's fate can be found in numerous other Metastasian plots (for example, Megacles in *L'Olimpiade,* or Ezio in the opera *Ezio,* to name two)—plots in which a beleaguered novice proves to be upwardly mobile through his virtuous nature, and thereby also to be an ideal object of identification for the new bourgeois viewing subject. Throughout the story, Arbace braves his wrenching dilemmas precisely so that he may establish his credentials as a worthy initiate into manhood and hence (beyond the reach of the plot) as a candidate for paternity, and moreover for the paternity of royal offspring. All the principal players undergo their own trials by fire, the women included; but because Arbace's trials rage fiercest, he experiences the most dramatic rite of passage, one that can be completed only once virtue triumphs by paying tribute simultaneously to multiple father figures. This is consistent with other Metastasian plots, in which females can, and usually do, inhabit a liminal role involving moral evolution, but are never the opera's leading moral figure. The prima donna was normally *suddita seconda* as far as sovereignty went—a partner in realizing the succession of the dynasty, yet in no sense a unilateral, much less equal, body.

In the midst of these trials, conflicts are mediated through an ethical hierarchy with obligations that point ever upward from lovers, friends, counselors, and confidantes, to fathers, brothers, and sisters, and finally to kings. As a rule, kings trump kin and kin trump nonblood relations in resolving conflict. Accordingly, the moral prerogatives postulated through this scalar movement also place public concerns above private ones, with the king at the apex of the earthly order as public representative of wider social interests. Larger clan relations are thought to bind king and kin, as well as other alliances, to help ensure the perpetuity of the patriarchy.

The king alone among all figures occupies at once the two categories of sacred and profane. In accordance with long-standing Western tradition (as described most famously by Ernst Kantorowicz), he is human with respect to person but divine and eternal with respect to office. This was not so much true in a legal sense (as it had been in medieval English and French traditions) as it was a matter of general consciousness, albeit one that was gradually being undermined, notwithstanding the tenacity of ideological tradition.[6] Accordingly, the direct link of the king to the sacred is instantiated in Metastasio's *Artaserse* through a host of symbols. When Artaserse attains the crown, he bestows sublime love on the people in exchange for their earthly loyalty (Act III, scene 11). In the midst of the rite he is to drink from a "sacred cup" by which he imbibes the eternal polity into the king's body and consolidates his connection to the sacred.[7] Mediating the two realms, his double position between sacred and profane is seen to function as an aid to securing new affinal relations, new princely offspring, and thus the general harmony and durability of the kingship.

At the same time the king works as an earthly link to the sacred *through* his subjects, and principally (again) through the heroic young male. Well into Act III, this link is affirmed in the major twist of the plot, when Arbace's sword becomes the divine rod of iron that breaks the back of his father's duplicitous accomplice, who has been conspiring to rouse the people against the king. Eventually the incident proves decisive in resolving dilemmas of alliance, but its immediate function is to offer proof that divine providence shines on the new reign.

3

In this respect, Arbace's liminal role is relevant not merely to him but also to others. More precisely, it is not just transformative *of* him but transforming *for* others, who depend for their own enlightenment on his extraordinary capacity to realize subjectively, through honorable action, the virtue immanent in the body social. Yet the enlightenment of those others—and specifically of eighteenth-century viewers—could not be achieved simply by altering certain objective facts of life depicted onstage. It depended on the effects of a communicative process to which human passions were fundamental. This is something audience members came to know by the very manner in which Arbace's intervention against insurrection was made known to them: rather than Arbace's heroism being shown onstage, his actions are reported by Mandane, whose account reveals the medium of passion to have been critical to the pacification of the populace (and, implicitly, to Arbace's subsequent moral ascent). A key feature of her account is that at the brink of his final upward resolution Arbace preserved the populace from unrest not with reason but with impassioned oratory: "On some with threats he wrought, on some with prayers; oft changed his looks from placid to severe" (III, 13). Arbace's fervor is finally the instrument that restores order to the kingdom and joins him to the royal family through his love for the princess. Occurring at the very moment when the polity is most threatened, passion becomes the kingdom's warrant against doom.

In this respect the magical effects of passion that Mandane recounts can be seen as a narrative token of the force that drives opera seria—the emotion collected and poured forth in singing and hearing arias. In the face of that lyric force, storytelling became relatively insignificant as an immediate agent in affecting most listeners, except perhaps when audiences were constrained to listen in a sovereign's presence. And even then, I would insist, following the plot did not mean acknowledging that the myth of the good king was *true*. Rather, it was proof positive of its power as myth, an affirmation that the medium of the message was effective, and that myths deserved to be legitimating because in some sense they were successful in objectifying certain subjective needs and conditions. It was for this reason that the person of the monarch (to recall Norbert Elias) was repeatedly made sovereign through the imitation of his behavior by his subjects.[8] By extending a condition of his bodily person, his subjects also extended his controls and benefits—of luxury, abundance, and virtue—into the body politic. Everyone collectively thereby became the monarch, who was dissolved into the new sovereign of the people.[9] When the king was present, performances demonstrated simultaneously to him and to his subjects the efficacy of the propositions at hand; when he was absent, performances iterated kingly force by virtue of reenactment.

The process of generating passions, magically linked to the sovereign's moral and spiritual condition, made sovereignty more than a mere site of power and charisma. It rendered sovereignty centerless, invisible, and pervasive—internalized by the sovereign's subjects. Consequently the sovereign's physical presence became all but unnecessary and the immortality of his spirit was ineffably demonstrated.[10]

If anything, the operatic plot contributed to this invisibility by dispersing propositions and symbolic currencies so thoroughly as virtually to absolve audiences of any requirement to evaluate events on stage for evidence of verifiable realities. That work was sooner done by genres that operated dramaturgically on more narrative terms. Narrative was necessarily minimized in a genre whose truth claims were decided in advance. Opera seria in its classic form asserts a social order that exists naturally, inevitably, and endlessly. As it progresses, it merely turns the pages of eternal time, its outcome preordained and its messages and denouements hardly susceptible to validation by earthly mortals. The characters in an opera seria therefore need not be situated in *real* histories of family, place, or time. They are abstract actors of a transcendental truth, divine messengers of absolutist metaphysics. Like Athena, they spring without origins from the head of Zeus—literally, for the Father is so engendering that mothers typically could be dispensed with altogether.

In this sense, seria's moral lessons had limits. They reminded people how to show deference to the king and other superiors, especially fathers. They could demonstrate how to court future spouses, how to treat brothers, how to identify and resolve conflicts between family and state. One thing they did not teach—or taught only by negation—was how to view mothers.

4

Mothers would have given centerless kingship a knowable core. Far from grounding itself in realistic polities and genealogies, opera seria thrived on roaming representations of kinship and power in which omnipresence was all—father, bishop, king, general; dynasty, oligarchy, principality, or papal state. As such, the claims of opera seria broke down within a material world of effects and of things. Its taken-for-granted nature depended on highly saturated and pliable signs—the divine king, noblesse oblige, the magnanimous prince, the royal crown, the divine sword, the altar and sun, the sacred cup. Enormously pliant, opera seria sounded the absolutist order in a general way while numerous changes were rung on the messages it was understood to express.[11]

In its classic form, the messages of opera seria were inscrutable precisely because they were transmitted in mystifying ways. Seria could more easily articulate such generalized messages by (paradoxically) disarticulating the *process* by which a viewer might test such truths, the modes that might lead viewers either to certify or to spurn them. Thus perspectival illusions could disregard the exigencies of human form; audiences could ignore the genders that inhabited characters on the stage; and kinship structures could circumvent the realities of human generation. Far from "promoters" and "producers" using material evidence and narrated stories to prove its propositions to listeners[12]—"the king is omnipotent and magnanimous," "princes are valiant lovers," "subjects must imitate codes of honor similar to those of their royal superiors," and so forth—those propositions could better be ratified through the illogical magicalities of operatic staging.

The high points of opera seria therefore occur when the critical junctures of plot—moral transformations and political turns—coincide with extra-

ABSENT MOTHER IN OPERA SERIA 37

ordinary outpourings of feeling. The emotional effect Mandane's rhetoric attributes to Arbace resembles the effects that seria itself enacted on its listeners by means of lyric expression. Arias by turn articulated and resolved conflicts, not through rational deliberation but through expressions of moral outrage, demands for justice, and outpourings of love that were concentrated effusively at the ends of scenes. Arias dissolved narrative into lyric magic, as recitative culminated repeatedly in outbursts of unfathomable, mystically empowered song.

This special role of song was defined as well through spatial location. Sharply demarcated musically, arias were performed at the forestage or *proscenio,* that border zone between stage and house typically flanked by proscenium boxes, which helped transcend the more everyday operations of plot and action. Lyric moments thus inhabited a liminal space where normal time and action were suspended, where feeling annihilated reason, and where the passion collected in the recitative could be unleashed at the scene's end. In this way, arias epitomized the myriad formal disjunctions that caught the attention of eighteenth-century writers on opera seria—between reciting and singing, story and song, opera and ballet, character and gender. To outsiders, it often seemed as if all of opera seria's forms had astounding license to disjoin other forms—indeed, to shake outer form loose from meaning altogether.[13]

5

So too, we might say, the lives of couples who watched from their boxes. For just as arias and the emotions they conjured up were disjunct from the narrative flow, the lived content of aristocratic marriages had largely been rent from its representation. Indeed by the eighteenth century, the institution of marriage in Italy had been laboring in a state of extraordinary tension for some time. Although wives now moved freely and frequently throughout the expanding public sphere, marriages within the Italian aristocracy were still typically arranged by parents.[14] Future husbands were often little known, if at all, to the females who were to wed them, a situation that was intensified by the fact that girls were often educated in convents and thus prevented from making acquaintance with men in the outside world, much less from knowing anything about marriage.

In reality, a marriage market that had long been depressed in Italy gave the lie to the idealized model of family, central to representations of eighteenth-century Italy. Too little capital was available for marriage. Many women ended up as spinsters or nuns, many men did not marry, and many women lived out most of their lives as widows, never able to remarry.[15] As the aristocracy experienced growing uncertainty, fiscal and social, financial expedients dictating the bottom line increasingly governed choices of husbands. At the same time, an expanding public sphere created new family conditions that often took husbands away for business and public life while wives kept up social appearances on the promenades, in carriage rides, at the theater, and in daily visits to church, where they continued to play their role as vessels of virtue by upholding religious practices for aristocratic (and, in some official symbolic sense, Italian) society as a whole. By the turn of the eighteenth century, the contradictions of early-modern married life had finally been stretched to their tolerable limit through the exploitation of a compensatory arrangement, which provided aristocratic wives with surrogates for husbands who were preoccupied with business affairs and who traditionally kept separate mistresses.

Enter the *cicisbeo,* an extreme manifestation of late courtly society. Roughly defined, the *cicisbeo* (often called synonymously the *cavaliere servente*) was a male escort in Italian noble society who fulfilled a wife's perceived needs for company, intimacy, and above all public partnership.[16] While extremely little is known of them, it seems that *cicisbei* could be either married or single, and were typically drawn from the noble class, possibly at times chosen by common accord between husband and wife. They often entered long-term relationships with a single married woman—relationships that in some cases lasted for decades—although *cicisbei* could also be engaged on an occasional or short-term basis. Those who assumed long-term positions took part in numerous activities, some of which, in centuries past, had had little or no existence in couples' lives and others of which had formerly been reserved for spouses: taking the wives they served on visits and outings to public theaters and cafes; attending morning toilet, when a wife was dressed and groomed by her maids, and thence to church; and helping to serve her at mealtimes.[17] Some of these activities were immortalized in Pietro Longhi's characteristic (if somewhat sardonic) portrayals from the mid-eighteenth century (see figure 2).[18] So widespread was the fashion of nonspousal escort that some women complained that they were forced to endure the *cicisbeo* over the company of husbands they preferred.[19] Yet as Charles De Brosses remarked, "it would have been a kind of dishonor had one not been publicly ascribed to her"[20]—and thus it happened that the order of marriage was disordered through a social rule.[21]

It seems unlikely that *cicisbeismo* met with immediate acceptance once the practice got underway, even in those parts of Italy where it evidently proliferated; nor that its place in society was ever safe from censure. The only extended scholarly publication on the phenomenon to date, Luigi Valmaggi's anecdotal monograph of 1927, traces a gradual but partial endorsement in moralist literature, starting from the outraged tirade of Carlo Maria Maggi in the late seventeenth century to an apologia by Paolo Mattia Doria near the mid-eighteenth century, followed by mounting resis-

Figure 2. *La dichiarazione,* copy after Pietro Longhi, oil on canvas (ca. 1750); Venice, Museo Correr. Reproduced with permission.

tance and renewed invective as the century wore on.[22] Maggi claimed in his "Ritiramenti per le dame" that far from being innocent, the practice (still novel in his time) was a sin against God, an *invitation* to sin given the best of intentions, and an assault on women's religious work, which gave women generally a bad example.[23] The principled grounds of objection were resolutely religious. But already by the second decade of the eighteenth century Giandomenico Barile, in his *Moderne conversazioni giudicate nel tribunale della coscienza* (Rome, 1716), was willing to mollify his global critique with a revealing, if limited, justification: exchanges between women and their *cicisbei* should not be silenced for being evil or scandalous so long as they took place between persons distinguished by nobility of birth and integrity of habits.[24] For Barile, birthright was enough to excuse an otherwise repugnant practice. Within a short time, it seems, the phenomenon could be characterized not as illicit, but as a form of "noble servitude" and the *cicisbeo* assumed the status of an honored escort—even in cases wherein a larger theological critique endured.[25] Thus by the time Doria published his *Dialogo* in 1741,[26] the ground had been laid for a justification by class that situated the *cicisbeo* equivocally at the endpoint of a quasi-feudal tradition while also trying to distance him from it: courtly manners were preferable (so Doria's argument went) to the old feudal modes of so-called honor—the "barbarous and dissolute" way of living previously in use in Italy, which allowed duels, violence, and abuses of various kinds to be admired, even though they were more suited to bandits than men of virtue. Doria went on to deny charges linking escorts to sex and to rehabilitate the practice by aligning it with models of Platonic love.[27]

This discourse in defense of the *cicisbeo* played to a surprising extent upon sentimental nostalgia for the dying tradition of chivalric service linked to an old feudal world, even as the *cicisbeo* was being repositioned on new terrain: not the hilltops and castles of the lord's estate, but the urban salon and the public theater; and not the more stable subjective ground of masculine valor but the increasingly precarious one of servility in swishy lace and ribbons. The seemingly feminized nature of servitude, widely attached to *cicisbei*, stirred up tensions throughout the century. The anonymous author of the "Reflessioni filosofiche e politiche sul genio e carattere de' cavalieri detti serventi" portrayed the *cicisbeo* as "the shadow of the body of the woman served, whom he never leaves wherever he goes."[28] Another account, this one by Joseph Baretti, a transalpine Italian who lived most of his years in London, detailed the elaborate rituals of servitude as they were played out in daily church-going in order to underscore how extravagantly the *cicisbeo* shadowed and foreshadowed his lady's every move.[29] Arriving for morning services at ten or eleven, the woman was ushered through the church portal by her faithful escort, who preceded her so as to raise the curtain at the entrance door. He bathed his finger in the holy water and came to place it on her, she responding with a little bow. After mass she would stay seated for several moments, then genuflect, make the sign of the cross, recite a short prayer, and give the book from which she had read to a domestic or to the *cicisbeo*. She would then take her fan, rise, make the sign of the cross again, bow to the main altar, and exit preceded by her *cicisbeo*, who would again present her with holy water, raise the curtain to exit, and extend a hand for the return home.

Even though many fashionable circles considered it essential that women not be seen in public without a male escort (and, conversely, it had become unseemly in the same circles for husbands to be seen performing marital tasks in public),[30] these extreme avatars of servitude could not fail to be problematically aligned with the old world of courtly etiquette and the subordinated character of the female sex. Thus while the *cicisbeo* must have helped make good use of male surplus in the marriage market by relieving husbands of marital chores, he was also victimized by his ambiguous status. Adorning and subjugating himself to the woman he accompanied, he became simultaneously (if insidiously) assimilated to her sex. In the later decades of the eighteenth century this assimilation was the most common target of moralists' barbs; the *cicisbeo* became a bird in flight, a fop, fatuous, vain—so coquettish as to be barely male.

As a figure uncertain in deed and in kind, moreover, he came to symbolize sexual ambiguity in its most depraved state and, worse, to flaunt his embodiment of it in a kind of vulgar spectacle. One moralist summarized this objection by comparing the spectacle of *ciscisbeismo* to a "national disease" in which all Italy had become the "*stage or theater* of a bordello."[31] But the objection was voiced in the face of the *cicisbeo*'s relatively unmarked incorporation into marital arrangements, in which he clearly took part precisely because of the performances he could provide: extravagant displays of honor, feints of spousehood that so thoroughly imitated its ideal form as to surpass the limitations of the real—compensations for absence, in short, through an exaggerated show of presence.

In the end, his ambiguity and his utility both derived inseparably (and ironically) from the spectacle he made of normativity, a spectacle that betrayed itself through its intemperate excess.[32] In truth, of course, he represented "norms" that were far more contested and less "normative" than his behavior could suggest. In this respect, the *cicisbeo* was not so different from the castrato, another member of a caste of deviants who—abstracted as the perfect male (most typically the prince or noble hero)—was called upon to represent a mythical patriarchy in a mythical homeland.

Like the castrato, the *cicisbeo* gave a command performance each evening at the theater, where he accompanied his "woman" to her family box. There, in the standard practice of eighteenth-century theater, the inner hall staged the audience as much as the *palcoscenico* staged the opera, each box curtained, framed, and flickering with its own candlelight.[33] Across the panorama of such little "theaters," the *cicisbeo* and his lady sat boxed like marionettes, and it was here that he appeared stereotypically—and ever more dubiously—as the supreme gallant.

Most striking in the invective that rained down on the practice of *cicisbeismo* later in the eighteenth century was the way it had come to signal ever-deepening social ills. Now seen as a corrupt proxy of the good husband, the *cicisbeo* became ruinous to the souls of women, a defiler of womanhood, wifedom, and motherhood. Under the sway of the *cicisbeo*, wives were thought to rebel against husbands and even lose their natural love for their own children. In time the *cicisbeo* became an icon of antiaristocratic discontent, attacked along with the vanities of aristocratic women.[34]

Not surprisingly, a sharp decline in the practice coincided in the last decades of the century with the period when the aristocracy was at its most vulnerable, and when its censure became inseparable from the larger moral project of reconstructing the family, a project in which literati such as Vittorio Alfieri played a clamorous role.[35] In this prerevolutionary imaginary, "true" love—of hearth and home—had been ravaged by the falsehoods of aristocratic dissimulation, of which the *cicisbeo* was simply the most glaring manifestation. But worst of all, *cicisbei* were ruinous to the ethical core of the nation, which was beginning to be understood—partly under the influence of prerevolutionary France—as "a family writ large."[36] In the new morality etched by reformers, religious and revolutionary alike, mothers were to be the moral educators of their children; and in this work *all* women, aristocratic and plebeian, would be created equal.[37]

6

Although this was the rhetoric of the French Revolution, it was one that had currency throughout most of western Europe by the 1780s and especially the 1790s. The discourses of the family that surrounded the Revolution bring out the implications of the absent mother and the king-as-father in a blaze of clarity. As Lynn Hunt argues, French society moved in the later eighteenth century from imagining its rulers as fathers to condemning the fathers of the ancien régime with near-pathological fear.[38] Within the imaginary collective of the ancien régime, virtually all princes and ladies had served as fantasy parents.[39] By the latter half of the century, however, such fantasies had come to be regarded as dangerous daydreams, phantasms of adolescence. Simultaneous with this new attitude, French culture was experiencing a shattering ambivalence about the role of fathers, figurative and real. Since the magical nature of kingship was inseparable from the axiomatic nature of fatherhood, parental authority generally—especially, though not only, paternal—had to be reevaluated.[40] Deference, as taught to the king's subjects and the father's children alike, could no longer be granted automatically. Each person was now in principle a contracting social being, responsible for his or her moral relations with the larger world.

The watchmen of the people's newfound liberty were to be the brothers of the republic—in a Freudian sense, children of the fallen father—banded together to ensure fraternal rights at any cost: "fraternité ou mort." The central drama of the Revolution was therefore the killing of the king, an act effected notionally on 21 September 1792 when kingship was legally abolished (and with it the very word, still regarded by many as what one deputy called "a talisman whose magical force can serve to stupefy").[41] To ensure that *both* the king's bodies were exterminated, however, only an execution framed in the regal terms of ritual sacrifice would do. Louis's last words on the scaffold augured the utility of his own death in precisely sacrificial terms, bidding that his blood be "useful to the French" and a way of "appeasing God's anger." A great crowd stood witness to the event, dipping their spikes and kerchiefs in the blood after the dripping head was hoisted aloft by the executioner. Soon afterwards, the radical weekly *Révolutions de Paris* claimed that the blood of Louis Capet had cleansed the French of a thirteen-hundred-year stigma, while depicting Liberty as a voracious pagan goddess whom one cannot "make auspicious . . . except by offering in sacrifice the life of a great culprit."[42]

Note that the "brothers" never denied the king's magical status: on the contrary, they set out to "devour" and thus encompass and transform him into and through themselves. As Hunt points out, following the historian David P. Jordan, the announcement in the *Journal des hommes libres* the day after the execution cast the event as pivotal not so much in the remaking of the French political system as in the remaking of French systems of belief: "Today people are at last convinced that a king is only a man; and that no man is above the laws."[43] By killing the king, the brothers depleted his magic and he became ordinary. Once dead, the king's head and body were quickly thrown into a grave and covered with a double layer of quicklime to aid its rapid decomposition. The space previously occupied by the king now marked a "sacred void" that would be filled by the collective body of individual citizens, equal in their rights, whom his death had helped to create.

How sisters would figure in this new body of citizens is a problem for others to take up; but it is telling that mothers too had failed the French symbolically and had to be held to account for fathers' failures. Central to the dramatization of this charge was, of course, the figure of Marie Antoinette. In 1793 the queen was indicted for a variety of sexual crimes, presaged in the popular realm by representations of her in pornographic and moralizing literature that had been flooding Parisian bookstalls through the 1780s and early 90s (see Figure 3). The litany of charges was exhaustive: adultery, homosexuality, sodomy, bestiality, incest. The queen's body bore an unbearable polysemy, a polysemy identified in her ability to dissemble. Hence a second set of charges accused her of "having taught the king to dissimulate—that is, how to promise one thing in public and plan another in the shadows of the court."[44] Her sexualized body was a mask. A malleable symbol, it was aristocratic and feminine, like the body of the courtier (or, in Italy, like the body of the *cicisbeo* and the castrato), and therefore meretricious; but it was also monstrous because part male and yet castrating.[45] The sacred void that loomed with the destruction, symbolic and literal, of the king and queen left only one measurable space for women when all was said and done, a space of pure monumentality. Women would be the Nation, Freedom, Reason, Virtue, the Statue of Liberty bearing her torch—an infinitely imitable figure because unreal.

Figure 3. Marie Antoinette in sexual embrace with a man and a woman; engraving from *La Vie privée, libertine et scandaleuse*, 1793; Paris, Bibliothèque Nationale. Reproduced with permission.

ABSENT MOTHER IN OPERA SERIA 45

7

By the latter half of the century both France and Italy were awash with tales of renegade fathers, errant and absent mothers, and orphaned children conveyed in both sentimental literature and *opera semiseria*. Familar examples of the latter include Paisiello's *Nina, ossia la pazza per amore* (1789) and Paer's *Camilla* (1799), both based on libretti by Marsollier des Vivetières and both objects of frenzied popularity on Italian soil.[46] Shifts in opera seria were slower to come. Since Metastasio had virtually expunged those few mothers who had been admitted to the genre by Zeno and others around 1700, opera seria later in the century tended at first to transform the family it depicted—first by lessening fathers morally or by killing them off. King Mitridate is a case in point: in Cigna-Santi's *Mitridate* of 1767 (set by Mozart for the Regio-Ducal Teatro of Milan three years later), the king is a tyrant who manages to redeem himself and (magically) his kingdom too; in Sografi's libretto (1796; rev. 1797), on the other hand, Mitridate is a monstrous enemy of justice who dies by his own sword to the relief of the populace—a revolutionary revision, if ever there was.[47]

In opera seria mothers came in for a only small share of parental demonization, since even late in the century the genre rarely resuscitated them. The striking countercase of Semiramide widely restored to the stage one mother whose motherhood Metastasio had all but suppressed in his *Semiramide riconosciuta*. By the mid-1780s, Semiramide had been changed into the notorious virago, familiar from Voltaire's play, in which she murders her husband, plots an incestuous marriage, and is stabbed to death by her son. A Milan version of 1784 by Moretti with music by Mortellari was content to have her lover assassinated. But the infamous Giovannino libretto *La vendetta di Nino, ossia La morte di Semiramide*, staged at Florence two years later in a dramatic setting by Alessio Prati, culminated in matricide onstage.[48]

The absent mother, banished by Metastasio, had thus returned as a twin to those representations of Marie Antoinette emerging around the same time across the Alps. Not that Moretti/Martellari or (even) Giovannini/Prati tried to demonize Semiramide through a prism of sexuality—not explicitly, to be sure. If anything, theirs was a chamber of horrors, with roots in the *ombra* scenes crafted by Mattia Verazi in earlier years. Yet it was a chamber designed to make viewers quiver with abomination, to be no less repulsive to the viewing subject—and no less undermining of his or her subjective order—than the spectacle of the queen's alleged atrocities in bed. Exit the *cicisbeo*, enter the bourgeois family, the panacea of the new social order and the order in which the new-made person was to emerge.

That it became possible to conjure up fathers and mothers as irredeemably guilty, and thus recast the plights of sons and daughters, was one token of a new subjectivity in later eighteenth-century Europe, a subjectivity that valorized the capacities of the individual for moral reflection, judgment, and self-improvement. As the individual's world became ever more scrutable, the happy ending of the familial history was demystified. With it, too, the old schismatics of representation, staged and not—which displaced singers from sets, characters from singers' genders, husbands from wives, and mothers from children—began to ease. Where once the theater reached past the worldly, with sets so abstruse and limitless that no singer could inhabit them, with sopranos resounding unaccountably from male bodies and ballets tucked radiantly but extraneously between operatic acts, now a new logic of representation imposed itself. The earlier ways had come to signal the perilous feints of the old order. And the scrutinies that reviewed them and forced them out were so many signs that the crisis of absolutism had been eclipsed by the coming crises of modernity. But that is another story.

The Absent Mother in Opera Seria

1. A useful sketch of the modernist paradigm of spectatorship is given in Kenneth Little, "Masochism, Spectacle, and the 'Broken Mirror' Clown Entrée: A Note on the Anthropology of Performance in Postmodern Culture," *Cultural Anthropology* 8 (1993): 117–29. Little's account is partly based on models of modernist visuality generally, on which see Martin Jay, "Scopic Regimes of Modernity," in *Vision and Visuality*, ed. Hal Foster (Seattle: Bay Press, 1988), 3–23.

2. See "Magic Mirrors and the *Seria* Stage: Thoughts toward a Ritual View," *Journal of the American Musicological Society* 48 (1995): 423–84, parts of which have been adapted for sections 2 through 4 below.

3. I use "king" and "monarch" generically here as structural equivalents for "sovereign," a category that may (in a given situation) pertain to a prince, a duke, and so forth. Indeed, for some analytic purposes, an absolutist ruling body in an oligarchy such as Venice may function in a manner equivalent to the monarch. Elsewhere I develop the notion that such abstract equivalencies, as part of the mythical power of sovereignty in the absolutist imaginary, account in part for the capacity of opera seria to resonate beyond the confines of the absolutist polity *sensu stricto*.

With respect to the relationship between the physical locations of boxes and the social positions of their occupants, I should also note that what I describe here is the most widespread model, on which there were numerous variations. The most common of these was the relegation of the first tier of boxes to a somewhat lower social station so that nobles could keep their distance from *hoi polloi* on the parterre. Also, the monarchical box was sometimes located nearer to the proscenium, on an inner

NOTES 255

side of the horseshoe curve that characterized the architecture of a typical eighteenth-century theater, in order to provide better viewing of the stage. For instance, the Regio-Ducal Teatro of Parma had a ducal box in such a location during the eighteenth century, while in Naples King Ferdinand IV often sat in the proscenium boxes at the San Carlo (although without ever altering the royal box architecturally).

4. Jürgen Habermas, *The Structural Transformation of the Public Sphere: An Inquiry into a Category of Bourgeois Society,* trans. Thomas Burger with Frederick Lawrence (Cambridge, Mass.: MIT Press, 1989); see especially the introduction and 43–51.

5. A rare exception is Dircea in Metastasio's *Demofoonte,* a woman thought to be a nobleman's daughter who has a son through a secret marriage to the king's heir; but through strange twists of fate she instead turns out to be the king's daughter, and her secret spouse in his turn is revealed to be the nobleman's son. Thus Dircea is put in the lowly place proper to a Metastasian mother by having to yield the throne to another (unmarried and childless) woman who then marries Dircea's brother, the king's real son. More typical of Metastasio is his *Semiramide,* who was evidently a mother everywhere throughout the long literary tradition she inhabited, *except* in Metastasio's 1748 libretto, composed in honor of the empress Maria Teresia, where the fact of her motherhood is suppressed.

6. The foundational text on this concept is Ernst H. Kantorowicz, *The King's Two Bodies: A Study in Medieval Political Thought* (Princeton: Princeton University Press, 1957)—though, as Kantorowicz shows, medieval Europe conceived the king's two bodies as having separate temporalities. On cross-cultural features of kingship and secondary literature thereon, see also Gillian Feeley-Harnik, "Issues in Divine Kingship," *Annual Review of Anthropology* 14 (1984): 273–313, and the introduction to *Rituals of Royalty: Power and Ceremonial in Traditional Societies,* ed. David Cannadine and Simon Price (Cambridge: Cambridge University Press, 1987). For an historical ethnography with strong resonances of the kingship of absolutist Naples see Clifford Geertz, *Negara: The Theatre State in Nineteenth-Century Bali* (Princeton: Princeton University Press, 1980), especially the conclusion.

7. The scene is dense with signs of the king as a divine father surrogate—and designed to be spectacular enough to win the audience's attention. Metastasio's stage directions place Artaserse before the populace for a magnificent coronation scene in which a throne is laid with crown and scepter and a burning altar is adorned with a simulacrum of the sun. Artaserse proclaims: "A voi, popoli, io m'offro / Non men padre, che Re. Siatemi voi / Più figli, che vassalli" [To you people, I offer myself, no less a father than a King. May you be more sons to me than vassals.] After the speech of which this forms a part, an attendant brings him the sacred cup.

8. See Norbert Elias, *The Court Society,* trans. Edmund Jephcott (Oxford: Basil Blackwell, 1983).

9. On this process in cross-cultural perspective see Valerio Valeri, *Enciclopedia Einaudi,* vol. 11, *Prodotti—Ricchezza;* s.v. "Regalità," (Turin: Einaudi, 1980), 764 and passim; forthcoming in translation by Lynn Westwater as s.v. "kingship," in Valerio Valeri, *Rituals and Annals: Between Anthropology and History,* ed. Janet Hoskins (Oxford: Berg). See also Georges Bataille's argument about the relationship between sovereignty and subjectivity in *Sovereignty,* vol. 3 of *The Accursed Share,* trans. Robert Hurley (New York: Zone Books, 1993).

10. Indeed one could say that opera seria in this sense was more necessary to affirming sovereignty when a monarch was absent than when present. For a comparative case see Ward Keeler, *Javanese Shadow Plays, Javanese Selves* (Princeton: Princeton University Press, 1987), chap. 8; see also Clifford Geertz, "Centers, Kings, and Charisma: Reflections on the Symbolics of Power," in his *Local Knowledge: Further Essays in Interpretive Anthropology* (New York: Basic Books, 1983), 121–46.

11. This resembles what Jonathan Z. Smith calls "signal[ing] significance without contributing signification"; *To Take Place: Toward Theory in Ritual* (Chicago and London: University of Chicago Press, 1987), 108.

12. I take the terms from Franco Piperno, who schematizes the actors in eighteenth-century opera as promoters, producers, and addressees; see "Il sistema produttivo fino al 1780," in *Storia dell'opera italiana*, vol. 4, ed. Lorenzo Bianconi and Giorgio Pestelli (Turin: E. D. T., 1987), 1–75.

13. This is a point I develop further in "Magic Mirrors and the *Seria* Stage."

14. The best general account of the institutions of the Italian family in the eighteenth century is that of Marzio Barbagli, *Sotto lo stesso tetto: mutamenti della famiglia in Italia del XV al XX secolo* (Bologna: Il Mulino, 1984).

15. Elisja Schulte van Kessel, "Virgins and Mothers between Heaven and Earth," trans. Clarissa Botsford, in *Renaissance and Enlightenment Paradoxes*, vol. 3 of *A History of Women in the West*, ed. Natalie Zemon Davis and Arlette Farge (Cambridge, Mass. and London: Belknap Press of Harvard University Press, 1993), 132–66, esp. 150.

16. For what follows I have relied (in the near absence of other writings) mostly on a variety of late-nineteenth-century and early-twentieth-century Italian chroniclers who rely in turn on extensive anecdotal accounts in travel literature, diaries, letters, treatises, and fictional sources, including plays, poems, and satires. See Achille Neri, *Costumanze e sollazzi* (Genoa: R. Istituto, 1883), 117–216; Antonio Marenduzzo, "I cicisbei nel Settecento," *Rivista d'Italia* 8 (1905): 271–82; Abd-el-Kader Salza, "I cicisbei nella vita e nella letteratura del Settecento," *Rivista d'Italia* 13 (1910): 184–251; Giulio Natali, *Idee, costumi, uomini del Settecento* (Turin: Società Tipografico-editrice Nazionale, 1916), 133–44; and most especially Luigi Valmaggi, *I cicisbei: contributo alla storia del costume italiano nel secolo XVIII*, post. ed. Luigi Piccioni (Turin: G. Chiantore, 1927). More recent treatments include Barbagli, *Sotto lo stesso tetto*, 360–65, and Luciano Guerci, *La discussione sulla donna nell'Italia del Settecento: aspetti e problemi* (Turin: Tirrenia, 1987), chap. 3, "Le conversazioni e il cicisbeismo," 89–140; and, most recently and provocatively, Roberto Bizzocchi, "Cicisbei: la morale italiana," *Storica* 9 (1997): 63–90, to whom I am grateful for promptly sending me a copy of his article. All in all, very little has been written on *cicisbeismo* in modern times, nor to my knowledge has serious archival work pertinent to it been carried out—work that may be quite onerous if, as Bizzocchi argues convincingly, the phenomenon was more part of informal social arrangements and unwritten practices than it was a juridical "institution" formalized in contracts, as has commonly been claimed (seemingly without evidence) in the past. My conversations with social historians Giulia Calvi and Ottavia Niccoli have persuaded me that such archival evidence as may exist (whether in family letters, court trials, etc.) could turn out to be quite difficult to cull.

NOTES 257

17. The verses of the Milanese poet Giuseppe Parini are filled with ironic commentary on the moral relation of the aristocracy to the *cicisbeo*. See especially his famous poem *Il giorno,* part two, "Il meriggio," vv. 39–49, and part 3, "Il vespro," vv. 270–83.

18. Information on Longhi's paintings is given in *L'opera completa di Pietro Longhi,* introduced and coordinated by Terisio Pignatti (Milan: Rizzoli, 1974). For "La dichiarazione" (plate 2) see nos. 281–84. According to Pignatti, the image provided here as plate 2 is most likely a copy of a lost original from 1750, corresponding to catalogue entry no. 284.

19. Barbagli, *Sotto lo stesso tetto,* 363.

20. Cited in Barbagli, 364.

21. The question of how many wives actually slept with their *cicisbei,* on the other hand, can only be—and has nevertheless copiously been—the subject of speculation (see the historical critique of Bizzocchi, "Cicisbei," 65); likewise the question (probably anachronistic in any case) of how many may have been homosexual or bisexual. De Brosses reports having been told by the Venetian ambassador that only about fifty of those he knew of slept with their "wives," but this doubtless says more about what the ambassador believed, or what he wanted de Brosses to think or write, than it does about what actually happened; see Salza, "I cicisbei nella vita e nella letteratura," 189.

22. See Valmaggi, *I cicisbei,* chap. 1, "Letteratura," 1–44. Happily, Roberto Bizzocchi has recently undertaken a large-scale study of *cicisbeismo* within a broader set of questions concerning the Italian character and social practices in the years 1700–1800.

23. The essay is the eleventh of his *Trattenimenti,* added to the *Ritiramenti per le dame* by the French Jesuit François Guilloré, which Maggi translated into Italian and published in Milan in 1687 (see Valmaggi, *I cicisbei,* 7–8). Similar views were held by the anonymous author of *Alcune conversazioni e loro difese esaminate coi principi della Teologia, dai quali facilmente si può dedurre quando sia illecito l'amore tra la gioventù* (Ferrara, 1711), an extremist in the Madre di Dio order who bristled that the world pretended the *cicisbeo* was a "noble servant."

24. Barile, *Alcune conversazioni,* 80; cited in Valmaggi, *I cicisbei,* 10–11.

25. See, for example, Valmaggi's discussion (11) of Costantino Roncaglia's *Moderne conversazioni volgarmente dette dei cicisbei* (1720; reprint, Lucca: Venturini, 1736).

26. *Dialogo nel quale esaminandosi la cagione per la quale le donne danzando non si stancano mai, si fa il ritratto d'un Petit Maître italiano affettato laudatore delle massime, e dei costumi dei Petits Maîtres oltramontani e cicisbei,* in vol. 2, pt. 1 of *Lettere e ragionamenti vari* (Perugia, 1741), 331 ff.; as cited in Valmaggi, *I cicisbei,* 11.

27. Valmaggi, *I cicisbei,* 11–12. Still more progressive was the Venetian lawyer Antonio Costantini, who published letters on the subject between 1751 and 1756 (see Valmaggi, 12–13).

28. Cited in Valmaggi, *I cicisbei,* 45–46 and 46 n.1.

29. From Baretti's "Gli Italiani," 234 ff.; cited in Valmaggi, *I cicisbei,* 69.

30. The woman in Goldoni's *La dama prudente,* for example, had several *cicisbei* "per prudenza," so that she wouldn't be left high and dry whenever her "cav-

alier di fiducia" could not be at her side. On taboos against husbands performing services for their wives, see Valmaggi, *I cicisbei,* 65.

31. Namely monsignor Nicolò Forteguerri; cited in Valmaggi, *I cicisbei,* 21 (emphasis mine).

32. My notion of a spectacle of normativity was inspired by my colleague Martin Stokes's analysis of Turkish pop stars in the context of the Turkish nation-state, as presented in a paper entitled "Mediterraneanism, Hypergender, and Realism," read to the study group on "The Anthropology of Music in Mediterranean Cultures" (meeting on Music as Representation of Gender in Mediterranean Cultures, Venice, Fondazione Levi, 9–11 June 1998).

33. Note here the linguistic continuity of *palco* and *palcoscenico:* the former refers to a box, the latter to the stage, but literally to a stage-box. It thus underscores the way in which the proscenium framed and boxed the stage, much as decorative architectural motifs in the hall did for the boxes of individual groups of spectators.

34. Amid the abundant literature cited by Salza are numerous treatises on the vanities of women ("I cicisbei nella vita e nella letteratura," 235 ff.). For one foreigner's explanation of how the practice of *cicisbeismo* related to masking see John Moore, *A View of Society and Manners in Italy,* 4th ed., 2 vols. (London, 1781), 1:240–48.

35. See Marenduzzo, "I cicisbei nel Settecento," 282, who cites Alfieri's play *La famiglia antiquariato,* 3.6.

36. I borrow the term from Lynn Hunt, *The Family Romance of the French Revolution* (Berkeley and Los Angeles: University of California Press, 1992), xiv. On the corruption of the nation by *cicisbeismo* from an eighteenth-century Italian perspective, see *Amore disarmato:* "The Nation in vain defends itself . . . yet still languishes with its sons" (cited by Salza, "I cisisbei nella vita e nella letteratura," 224). As pointed out by Bizzocchi ("Cicisbei," 63), the anxieties that linked the phenomenon with the decay of the nation were rearticulated in the early nineteenth century by Jean-Charles-Léonard Simonde de Sismondi, who viewed it as a form of decadence inseparable from Italy's loss of political and religious freedoms and dating from the sixteenth century (i.e., the foreign invasions and the Counter-Reformation).

37. See Salza, "I cicisbei nella vita e nella letteratura," 234 ff., esp. the views of Roncaglia, *Moderne conversazioni,* 239. As Salza points out, this impulse is part of an emergent work ethic voiced by noble literati who reject the premise that aristocrats should be people of leisure while the plebians are those who work. Of course many nobles had long since, of necessity, joined the work force, husbands included—a fact of life that was relevant both to the advent of *cicisbeismo* and the rejection of the nobility as a leisure class.

38. The language of father-son relations was pervasive in French parliamentary discourse, as shown by Jeffrey Merrick, "Patriarchalism and Constitutionalism in Eighteenth-Century Parliamentary Discourse," *Studies in Eighteenth-Century Culture* 20 (1990): 317–30. The family metaphor of course presupposes a body metaphor, applicable to the state as well as its individual members. See Antoine de Baecque, *The Body Politic: Corporeal Metaphor in Revolutionary France, 1770–1800,* trans. Charlotte Mandell (Stanford: Stanford University Press, 1997), esp. chaps. 1 and 4.

NOTES 259

39. See also Marthe Robert, *Origins of the Novel,* trans. Sacha Rabinovitch (Bloomington: Indiana University Press, 1980).

40. Hunt, *The Family Romance of the French Revolution,* 53.

41. *Moniteur universel,* no. 266, 22 September 1792 (cited in Hunt, 53 n. 1).

42. Quoted in Hunt, 10. Hunt reads the specific form of ritual sacrifice enacted in revolutionary France through the sacrificial theories of René Girard, *Violence and the Sacred,* trans. Patrick Gregory (Baltimore: University of Maryland Press, 1977).

43. Quoted in David P. Jordan, *The King's Trial: Louis XVI versus the French Revolution* (Berkeley and Los Angeles: University of California Press, 1979), 222.

44. Hunt, 93.

45. A sobering comparison of eighteenth-century representations of Marie Antoinette with twentieth-century representations of Hillary Clinton in leather magazines is offered by Pierre Saint-Amand in "Terrorizing Marie Antoinette," trans. Jennifer Curtis-Gage, *Critical Inquiry* 20 (1994): 379–400.

46. On *opera semiseria* and sentimental literature in Italy and France, see Stefano Castelvecchi, "Sentimental Opera: The Emergence of a Genre, 1760–1790" (Ph.D. diss., University of Chicago, 1996); and his "From *Nina* to *Nina*: Pyschodrama, Absorption and Sentiment in the 1780s," *Cambridge Opera Journal* 8 (1996): 91–112.

47. Indeed the production given at Venice on 21 May 1797, nine days after the Republic fell to Napoleon's forces, added liberty choruses at the end as the chorus rejoices at Mitridate's demise. See my "Opera, Festivity, and Spectacle in 'Revolutionary' Venice: Phantasms of Time and History," in V*enice Reconsidered: Venetian History and Civilization, 1297–1797,* ed. John Martin and Dennis Romano (Baltimore: John Hopkins University Press, in press).

48. For a history of these versions see Marita P. McClymonds, "'La morte di Semiramide ossia La vendetta di Nino' and the Restoration of Death and Tragedy to the Italian Operatic Stage in the 1780s and 90s," in Angelo Pompilio et al., eds., *Report of the 14th Congress of the International Musicological Society,* Bologna 1987 (Bologna: International Musicological Society, 1990), 285–92.

Insofar as neoclassical opera seria survived into the nineteenth century, this was no longer true by that time. As Philip Gossett has kindly pointed out to me, Rossini's neoclassical operas of 1818 to 1822 do have mothers and in some cases children too, including: *Mosè in Egitto* (1818; the character of Amaltea); *Ermione* (1819; Andromaca); and *Zelmira* (1822; the title character). More ambiguously, in *Maometto II* (1820) a mother's tomb is present onstage throughout the opera.

[26]

PRODUCING THE OPERATIC CHORUS AT PARMA'S TEATRO DUCALE, 1759–1769

MARGARET R. BUTLER

ABSTRACT

Italian opera is increasingly receiving well deserved attention. Yet the process by which the chorus in opera seria was created remains largely unexplored. Between 1759 and 1769 Tommaso Traetta and Christoph Gluck composed path-breaking, reform-inspired opere serie for Parma's Teatro Ducale which integrated chorus, dance and stage spectacle in the French manner. In an era when operatic choruses usually comprised amateurs and chapel singers, evidence from printed librettos and documents from Parma's Archivio di Stato reveal that many of the Teatro Ducale's choristers were professional singers hired from neighbouring Bologna. Perhaps in response to logistical and financial difficulties in engaging skilled personnel for Traetta's choruses, Parma established a singing school to provide choristers for theatre. Gluck's choruses employed a combination of students from this school and professionals. The evidence from Parma shows that the wide-ranging circuit within which Italy's opera theatres functioned embraced not only leading soloists and other personnel, but choral singers as well. It demonstrates the impact of practical circumstances surrounding the production of Parma's operatic choruses on the success of operatic reform in Parma.

The influence of production practices on the development of eighteenth-century opera is increasingly receiving well deserved attention.[1] Yet the process by which Italian operatic choruses were created remains largely unexplored. Although the genre of opera seria is known primarily for those structural features of its librettos that reinforced the supremacy of the solo singer, choruses occasionally appeared.[2] While in the

---

Research for this essay was conducted with the assistance of a grant from The University of Alabama's Research Advisory Committee. I am grateful to the Archivio di Stato di Parma for permission to reproduce the documents presented here. I am indebted to Dr Mariella Loiotile at the Archivio di Stato, and Drs Federica Riva, Raffaella Nardella and Sandra Martani at the Biblioteca del Conservatorio di Parma for their generous assistance during my research. I also thank Marita McClymonds, John Rice, Paul Corneilson and the anonymous readers of this essay for their helpful comments and suggestions.

1 Notable recent contributions to this area of scholarship include the chapters on operatic production by Franco Piperno and John Rosselli in *Storia dell'opera italiana 4: Il sistema produttivo e le sue competenze*, ed. Lorenzo Bianconi and Giorgio Pestelli (Turin: EDT, 1987; trans. Lydia G. Cochrane as *Operatic Production and Its Resources* (Chicago: University of Chicago Press, 1998), John Rosselli, *Singers of Italian Opera: The History of a Profession* (Cambridge: Cambridge University Press, 1992) and Anthony R. DelDonna, 'Production Practices at the Teatro di San Carlo, Naples, in the Late 18th Century', *Early Music* 30/3 (2002), 429–445, among others.

2 Marita Petzoldt McClymonds, 'Chorus. 1. Up to 1800', *The New Grove Dictionary of Opera*, ed. Stanley Sadie (London: Macmillan, 1992), volume 1, 850–851. While Metastasian *opere serie* usually concluded with a 'coro' – a chorus of soloists – this essay is concerned with the chorus as an ensemble of choristers. These appeared in Metastasian opera more often than is usually acknowledged, as noted in Marita Petzoldt McClymonds, 'The Myth of Metastasian Dramaturgy', paper read at 'Patrons, Music, and Art in Italy, 1738–1859', inaugural conference for the Ricasoli

traditional *dramma per musica* they essentially stood apart from and commented upon the action, in reform-inspired opera emerging around mid-century choruses participated more fully and were often integrated into the scenes, along with danced episodes. Francesco Algarotti advocated their use in his manifesto of operatic reform, the *Saggio sopra l'opera in musica* (1755), to heighten the spectacle and to create a continuous complex of various types of vocal music.[3] Algarotti and those echoing his sentiments in other mid-century writings desired the 'reform' of 'abuses' inflicted upon dramatic unity by the hegemony of solo singers. It was envisaged that the integration into the traditional Italian dramaturgical structure of chorus, dance and supernatural stage spectacle drawn from French opera might result in a greater emphasis on elements other than soloistic display.

Four operas by Tommaso Traetta exhibiting this stylistic mixture represent Parma's response to the calls for reform: *Ippolito ed Aricia*, *I Tindaridi*, *Le feste d'Imeneo* and *Enea e Lavinia*, composed between 1759 and 1761. Christoph Gluck's *Le feste d'Apollo*, written for Parma in 1769, has been seen as the conclusion of the Teatro Ducale's reform efforts.[4] The musical innovations of some of these operas have been acknowledged,[5] but the production practices that shaped them have remained unknown. Material from Parma's Archivio di Stato and evidence from printed librettos for the Parmesan performances present a fuller view of Parma's operatic choruses, leading to a more complete understanding of the circumstances behind their creation.

ITALIAN OPERATIC CHORUSES: PARMA AND ELSEWHERE

Choruses posed logistical problems for most eighteenth-century Italian opera theatres. Without standing bodies of choral singers at their disposal most theatres simply could not produce choruses on a regular basis. Consequently choral texts were often cut from librettos when they were adapted for Italian theatres.[6] When theatres decided to include choruses, choral singers were generally of three types: students from nearby conservatories, singers from the choirs of local churches or working-class amateurs.[7] Operatic choruses usually consisted of men only; when choruses were mixed, there were twice as many men as women.[8] The prominence of the solo voice in opera seria resulted in choruses maintaining a stylistically inferior role in the genre: according to John Rosselli, 'as long as audiences kept up the cult of the solo voice, they tolerated a

---

Collection, University of Louisville, 14–18 March 1989. I am grateful to Marita McClymonds for sharing her unpublished research with me.

3 Francesco Algarotti, *Saggio sopra l'opera in musica* (Venice: Giambatista Pasquale, 1755; reprint Livorno: Marco Coltellini, 1763). See the 1763 edition in *Francesco Algarotti: Saggi*, ed. Giovanni da Pozzo (Bari: Laterza, 1963): 'Il maraviglioso di essa [l'azione] darà campo al poeta d'intrecciarla di balli e di cori, d'introdurvi varie sorte di decorazione' (155); 'La bella modulazione trionferebbe del continuo nei recitativi, nelle arie, nei cori medesimamente di che vanno corredate le nostre opere' (166).

4 Paola Mecarelli, *Le feste di Apollo: Conclusione di un impegno riformistico a Parma* (Parma: Battei, 1991).

5 *Ippolito ed Aricia* is discussed by Daniel Heartz in 'Operatic Reform at Parma: *Ippolito ed Aricia*', in *Atti del convegno sul settecento parmense nel secondo centenario della morte di C. I. Frugoni. Parma 10–12 maggio 1968* (Parma: La Deputazione di storia patria per le province parmensi, 1969), 271–300. See also George W. Loomis, 'Tommaso Traetta's Operas for Parma' (PhD dissertation, Yale University, 1999); choral writing is examined in chapter 8. Loomis summarizes the composer's achievements in 'Traetta: Time to Rethink?', *Opera* 54 (March 2003), 284–290. Gluck's *Le feste d'Apollo* is discussed by Renate Ulm in *Glucks Orpheus-Opern*, European University Studies, Musicology 36/70 (Frankfurt am Main: Peter Lang, 1991).

6 McClymonds, 'Chorus. 1. Up to 1800', 851.

7 The following discussion is drawn from Rosselli, *Singers of Italian Opera*, 203–204.

8 In Turin in 1750, however, an operatic chorus consisting of six men and six women performed in Baldassarre Galuppi's *La vittoria d'Imeneo*. See Marie-Thérèse Bouquet, *Il teatro di corte dalle origini al 1788*, Storia del Teatro Regio di Torino 1, ed. Alberto Basso (Turin: Cassa di Risparmio di Torino, 1976), 235.

chorus fit only for simple music'.⁹ With respect to opera seria's central components – star singers, dancers in the entr'acte ballets and lavish stage spectacle – choruses were a mere afterthought. More is known about operatic choruses in the nineteenth century, and anecdotes report that later choral singers were second-rate singers, badly behaved and ill-prepared; choruses represented 'the disreputable end of the [singing] profession'.¹⁰

In Naples boys from the conservatories made up eighteenth-century opera choruses until this practice was abandoned during the 1780s; the long hours at the theatre in the evenings resulted in poor performance in their studies.¹¹ In Florence operatic choral singers were shopkeepers, presumably with little musical training.¹² Turin's Teatro Regio employed male and female choristers.¹³ Turinese musicians associated with the theatre and chapel hired and directed them; presumably therefore Turin's male operatic choristers also sang in the chapel's musical ensemble. The number of singers varied from opera to opera, and they received minimal payments. Turin seems to have produced choruses more often than most Italian theatres during the century, however, and operas with choruses enjoyed the greatest success there. Cities where opera seria was given outside Italy dealt with choruses in different ways depending on local circumstances.¹⁴

Even less is known about how choral singers were recruited and directed. The chorus master as an official associated with a particular theatre apparently did not develop until the nineteenth century.¹⁵ In Turin, however, the musician charged with procuring choral singers during the eighteenth century received a contract, similar to other personnel hired there, which clarified his duties: he was to engage a certain number of singers (with the number of women and men specified), teach them their music, assist at all the rehearsals and ensure that they were present for each performance. Apart from his payment he received a sum of money to distribute to the singers, which would be reduced if they missed any performances.¹⁶ Other eighteenth-century theatres must have employed someone who carried out similar duties.¹⁷

---

9 Rosselli, *Singers of Italian Opera*, 204.
10 Rosselli, *Singers of Italian Opera*, 203. While Rosselli makes this comment in reference to the nineteenth century, he implies that it was true earlier as well.
11 Francesco Degrada, 'L'opera napoletana', in *Storia dell'opera*, ed. Alberto Basso and Guglielmo Barblan (Turin: UTET, 1977), volume 1, part 1, 257, note 1.
12 Anecdotal evidence confirms that shopkeepers sang as choristers for Salieri's *La fiera di Venezia* (Florence, 1779). See Alexander Wheelock Thayer, *Salieri: Rival of Mozart*, ed. Theodore Albrecht (Kansas City, MO: The Philharmonia of Greater Kansas City, 1989), 67. See also Marita Petzoldt McClymonds, 'The Role of Innovation and Reform in the Florentine Opera Seria Repertory, 1760 to 1800', in *Music Observed: Studies in Memory of William C. Holmes*, ed. Colleen Reardon and Susan Parisi (Warren, MI: Harmonie Park Press, 2004), 281–299.
13 Choruses appeared in Turinese productions of *La vittoria d'Imeneo* as mentioned above (Galuppi, 1750) and in *Ifigenia in Aulide* (Bertoni, 1762), *Sofonisba* (Galuppi, 1764), *L'Olimpiade* (Hasse, 1764) and other operas in the 1770s and 80s. See Margaret Ruth Butler, *Operatic Reform at Turin's Teatro Regio: Aspects of Production and Stylistic Change in the 1760s* (Lucca: LIM, 2001), chapters 4 and 5 (on *Ifigenia in Aulide* and *Sofonisba*).
14 For example, St Petersburg used singers from the imperial chapel; see Daniel Heartz, *Music in European Capitals: The Galant Style, 1720–1780* (New York and London: Norton, 2003), 936–937.
15 John Rosselli, 'Chorus Master', in *The New Grove Dictionary of Opera*, volume 1, 852: 'There seems to be no evidence of a chorus master so called before 1800'.
16 Contracts and other payment documents for these individuals survive from 1750 through the 1780s in Turin, Archivio storico della città di Torino (hereafter ASCT); one such contract setting out these guidelines is found in *Carte sciolte* 6249 (1762–1766), contract for [Tomaso] Vallino, January 1762.
17 For example, Anton Ignatz Ulbrich functioned as a freelance choral director for the Viennese court theatres. I am grateful to John Rice for bringing this to my attention and for pointing me towards the following sources providing information on Ulbrich: Bruce Alan Brown, *Gluck and the French Theatre in Vienna* (Oxford: Clarendon, 1991), 91 (Ulbrich prepared singers drawn primarily from the Hofkapelle when required for academies and French or Italian operas); Dexter Edge, 'Mozart's Viennese Orchestras', *Early Music* 20/1 (1992), 68–71; John A. Rice, *Antonio Salieri and Viennese Opera* (Chicago: The University of Chicago Press, 1998), 215–216.

In contrast to most Italian theatres, Parma's Teatro Ducale frequently produced operas featuring choruses during the second half of the century. The French-inspired reform of music and theatre undertaken by Parma's Guillaume du Tillot, administrator of the Bourbon household and general intendant of the theatres, is by now well known.[18] Under his influence several French operas were imported to Parma from Paris in the 1750s. Among these works, all of which featured choruses, were *Castor et Pollux*, *L'Acte Turc* and *Titone et l'Aurora*.[19] Tommaso Traetta became maestro di cappella at Parma in 1758 and received the commission to write four Italian operas that responded to du Tillot's desire for a fusion of French elements with Italian style. Carlo Frugoni, Parma's court poet, provided texts for the first three operas, which consisted of reworkings of French librettos: Rameau's *Hippolyte et Aricie* served as the basis for *Ippolito ed Aricia*, which had its premiere in May 1759; *I Tindaridi*, based on Rameau's *Castor et Pollux*, was performed in May and June of 1760; and *Le feste d'Imeneo*, an opéra-ballet loosely modelled on Rameau's *Les fêtes d'Hébé*, was given in September 1760 for the wedding of the Infanta Isabella of Bourbon to Archduke Joseph II of Austria.[20] *Enea e Lavinia*, a reworking of the libretto for *Enée e Lavinie* set by Antoine Dauvergne, had its premiere in spring 1761.[21] Gluck came to Parma in the summer of 1769 to compose and stage his *Le feste d'Apollo* in celebration of the royal marriage of Maria Amalia, daughter of Maria Theresa of Austria, to Ferdinand IV of Bourbon. This work included a shortened form of his *Orfeo ed Euridice*, lavish spectacle and choral participation. With the departure of du Tillot in 1771, the French-inspired operatic endeavours came to an end. However, Sarti's monumental *Alessandro e Timoteo* of 1782 demonstrated that Parma did not abandon completely its taste for lavish supernatural stage spectacle, chorus and ballet.[22]

CHORUSES IN TRAETTA'S OPERAS FOR PARMA

In contrast to traditional practice, the printed librettos for Traetta's four operas for Parma give choral singers' names. The choristers are designated either 'attori cantanti nei cori' or simply 'attori cantanti'[23] and

---

18 For the social and political context the seminal work is Henry Bédarida, *Parme et la France de 1748 à 1789* (Paris: Champion, 1927). See also Heartz, 'Operatic Reform at Parma'; and Gian Paolo Minardi, 'Parma', in *The New Grove Dictionary of Opera*, volume 3, 886–888, and '"Le projet est abandonné": Note sul tramonto della "riforma" parmigiana', in *Cantabilis harmonia: Studi in onore di Giuseppe Massera* (Milan: Franco Angeli, 1985), 24–49; Giuliana Ferrari, Paola Mecarelli and Paola Melloni, 'L'organizzazione teatrale parmense all'epoca del Du Tillot: I rapporti fra la corte e gli impresari', in *Civiltà teatrale e settecento emiliano*, ed. Susi Davoli (Bologna: Il Mulino, 1986), 357–380; Brown, *Gluck and the French Theatre in Vienna*, chapters 1 (especially page 11) and 7; and Claudio Gallico, 'Cori a Parma, 1759–60', *Rivista italiana di musicologia* 32/1 (1997), 81–97.

19 These works are mentioned in archival documents from the 1750s. *Castore e Polluce* (*Castor e Pollux* by Jean-Philippe Rameau) premiered in November 1758, *L'Atto Turco* (*L'Acte Turc* by an unnamed composer) in November 1758 and *Titone e l'Aurora* (*Titon et l'Aurore* by Jean-Joseph Cassanéa de Mondonville) in 1759. While an accurate chronology for eighteenth-century opera at Parma does not exist, two of these works are mentioned in Paolo-Emilio Ferrari, *Spettacoli drammatico-musicali e coreografici in Parma dall'anno 1628 all'anno 1883* (Parma, 1884; reprinted Bologna: Forni, 1969), 34.

20 Bruce Alan Brown discusses this work in relation to parallel celebrations in Vienna in *Gluck and the French Theatre in Vienna*, chapter 7 (especially 263–266); see also Klaus Hortschansky, 'Feste teatrali a Parma intorno al 1760: Le Feste d'Imeneo di Carlo Innocenzo Frugoni', in *Musica e spettacolo a Parma nel settecento: atti del convegno di studi indetto dall'Istituto di Musicologia, Parma, 18–20 ottobre 1979*, ed. Nino Albarosa and Renato di Benedetto (Parma: Università di Parma, 1984), 237–246.

21 Jacopo Antonio Sanvitale wrote the libretto for *Enea e Lavinia*. Its source was a libretto by Bernard le Bovier de Fontenelle set by Pascal Collasse in 1690 which was later revised and set by Dauvergne in 1758.

22 Friedrich Lippmann, 'Giuseppe Sarti: *Giulio Sabino e Alessandro e Timoteo*', in *Musica e spettacolo a Parma nel settecento*, 105–115.

23 They are called 'attori cantanti nei cori' in the librettos for *Ippolito e Aricia* and *Le feste d'Imeneo* and 'attori cantanti' in those for *I Tindaridi* and *Enea e Lavinia*.

PRODUCING THE OPERATIC CHORUS AT PARMA'S TEATRO DUCALE

Table 1 Choristers as listed in Parma libretto for *Ippolito ed Aricia* (Parma: Stamperia Monti, 1759)

Signore	Signori
Domenica Lambertini	Francesco Cavalli
Antonia Fascitelli	Ludovico Felloni
Veronica Rainieri	Petronio Manelli
Girolima Maj	Domenico Tibaldi
Anna Boselli	Carlo Barbieri
Margherita Gianelli	Girolamo Landini
Barbara Girelli	Antonio Goldoni
Anna Lolli	Gaspero Tornielli
Isabella Beni	Matteo Sabattini

Table 2 Choristers as listed in Parma libretto for *I Tindaridi* (Parma: Stamperia Monti, 1760)

Signore	Signori
Girolama Maj	Ludovico Felloni
Anna Boselli	Girolamo Landi
Anna Lolli	Antonio Goldoni
Angela Majre	Nicola Agostino Bertelli
Lucia Bonetti	Carlo Barbieri
Anna Fascitelli	Giuseppe Ferri
Margherita Brandi	Gaspero Tornielli
Elisabetta Goradi	Filippo Sucarelli
Antonia Fioroni	Pietro Pizzimiglia
Geltruda Santi	Giuseppe Costa
Angela Foresti	Tommaso Caminati

listed together with the leading singers. The choristers as listed in the libretto for each opera appear in Tables 1–4.[24] According to the librettos, the number of choral singers varied: eighteen for *Ippolito ed Aricia*, twenty-two for *I Tindaridi*, twenty-eight for *Le feste d'Imeneo* and twenty-two for *Enea e Lavinia*. The presence of the choristers in the Parmesan librettos, and their designation as 'attori cantanti', suggest that these singers had a higher than usual status in Parma. Table 5 gives the names of these singers in an alphabetical list. It is clear that only a few of them performed in all the operas; these names appear in bold. The remaining singers took part in one or occasionally two other operas. Thus a core of eight choral singers – four women and four men – sang in all four of Traetta's operas.[25] Others were added for each production, with some overlap from one opera to the next. As valuable as they are for providing the names of the choral singers, however, the Parma librettos cannot always be relied upon to present a complete picture. Archival material provides information that supplements and sometimes contradicts that of the librettos. Few documents referring to singers survive for *Ippolito ed Aricia* and *Le feste d'Imeneo*, and none for

---

24 Lists of names in Tables 1–4 are drawn from librettos in the manuscript I-PAc.
25 Brigida Lolli and Anna Lolli are almost certainly the same person. Although this person's name appears as Anna in the first three librettos, including that of *I Tindaridi*, and Brigida in the libretto for *Enea e Lavinia*, it appears as Brigida in the document listing payments to the choristers of *I Tindaridi* in Figure 1, where no payment to an Anna Lolli is recorded. As explained below, Brigida's middle name was Anelli; perhaps she adopted a shortened form as her first name prior to 1761. Brigida Lolli appears in librettos after 1761, but no Anna Lolli seems to have sung after this year.

Table 3 Choristers as listed in Parma libretto for *Le feste d'Imeneo* (Parma: Stamperia Monti, 1760)

Signore	Signori
Anna Beni	Antonio Tibaldi
Anna Boselli	Ludovico Felloni
Girolama Mai	Antonio Goldoni
Anna Lolli	Girolamo Landi
Anna Farcelli	Filippo Sudadelli
Angela Majre	Pietro Cieccatini
Angela Merusi	Carlo Barbieri
Giuseppa Bonetti	Alessandro Franchis
Lucia Forti	Luigi de Sales
Maria Sartori	Giuseppe Ferri
Faustina Mainardi	Angelo Passavia
Anna Roselli	Pompeo Costa
Ludovica Forzoni	Pietro Muratori
Agostina Caccia	Filippo Luigioni

Table 4 Choristers as listed in Parma libretto for *Enea e Lavinia* (Parma: Stamperia Monti, 1761)

Signore	Signori
Anna Boselli	Ludovico Felloni
Girolama Maj	Antonio Goldoni
Brigida Lolli	Girolamo Landini
Angela Majre	Gaetano Donini
Caterina Merusi	Carlo Barbieri
Rosa Vitalba	Gaetano Rizzardi
Margherita Borasca	Giuseppe Afferri
Anna Farscelli	Agostino Viparino
Giuseppa Morelli	Giambattista Rosi
Geltruda Santi	Gasparo Tornielli
Margherita Brandi	Agostino Foresti

Enea e Lavinia. But those for *I Tindaridi* and *Le feste d'Apollo* provide evidence that can be used to achieve a better understanding of the other operas.

A payment roster for *I Tindaridi*, shown in Figure 1, reports names of choral singers who received payment for having performed in the opera.[26] One of them, Filippo Sucarelli, replaced Tommaso Caminati, who became ill at some point. Two boys, Pietro Pizzimiglia and Giuseppe Costa, sang with the women. Included in the group of paid singers are several names that do not appear in the libretto: Lucia Frigeri, Barbara Girelli, Anastasio Massa and Alessandro La Roche. The payment roster indicates that *I Tindaridi* featured eighteen paid choral singers; the libretto gives a total of twenty-two choristers. The singers who appear in the librettos but not in the payment lists might not actually have sung, or might have sung but were not paid.

---

26 Archivio di Stato di Parma (hereafter ASP), Teatro, Computisteria Borbonica, fili correnti, busta 933 (1760–1766), 'Per l'Opera de i Tindaridi, Ricevute degli Onnorarij de Sig.ri Cantanti de' Cori'. This document gives payments first in *zecchini gigliati* (for example, thirty-five for Alessandro la Roche, the first name listed) and then their equivalent in lire (L. 1540; the equivalent is arrived at by multiplying by forty-four).

PRODUCING THE OPERATIC CHORUS AT PARMA'S TEATRO DUCALE

A list of costumes and stage props for *Ippolito ed Aricia* confirms the presence of all the female choral singers given in the libretto for that opera.²⁷ The singers, each designated *chanteuse de choeur* in the document, are Rainieri, Maj, Boselli, Gianelli, Girelli, Lolli and Beni. Although Domenica Lambertini and Antonia Fascitelli appear in the libretto as choral singers, they also sang small roles in the opera and are listed in the libretto and this document along with the principals. The male choristers are not listed; perhaps their costumes and props were not as elaborate as those for the female singers. For the women, at least, the libretto for *Ippolito ed Aricia* accurately reports all the choral singers present.

A housing list from October 1760 provides information for *Le feste d'Imeneo*, performed in autumn of that year.²⁸ Two female choristers not mentioned in the libretto received housing that month: Lucia Frigeri and 'Baglioni detta la Carnaccina'.²⁹ No other singers appear there, though presumably documents for earlier months, now lost, reported the presence of male and other female choristers. With at least two singers appearing in the documents but not the libretto for *Le feste d'Imeneo*, this libretto appears less reliable regarding the choruses than that of *Ippolito ed Aricia*.

Who were the Parmesan choristers? Parma had no conservatory in the eighteenth century, and since the choral singers were paid, they were certainly trained musicians. In fact two of them, Anastasio Massa and Lucia Frigeri, must have been more highly skilled than the others; as can be seen in the payments to the leading singers in Figure 1, they earned the same fee as the lowest ranking solo singers, Francesco Cavalli and Giambattista Ristorini.³⁰ One might assume that, as trained musicians, the choral singers came from the musical establishment of one or more of Parma's churches (the men and boys, that is).

However, other documents reveal that many of the choral singers were in fact not local: they required lodging when they were in Parma, as shown in housing lists for the out-of-town singers and dancers from April 1760 (for *I Tindaridi*) given in Figure 2.³¹ At least eight (and possibly nine) choral singers – half of the total number, according to the payment documents – received housing: Lucia Frigeri, Anastasio Massa, Carlo Barbieri, Giuseppe Afferri, Antonio Goldoni, Alessandro 'il francese,' Girolamo Landini, Nicola Agostino Bertelli and perhaps Brigida Lolli, if she was the 'altra sorella' listed with the dancer Elisabetta Lolli.³² The others were local: Anna Boselli, Antonia Fascitelli, Barbara Girelli, Girolama Maj and Ludovico Felloni.³³

---

27 ASP, Teatro, Computisteria Borbonica, fili correnti, busta 932 (1758–1759), 'Etat des fournitures que j'ay faites pour le Theatre de SAR par ordre de S.r E.x du Tillot premier ministre par a commencer le 1 May 1759 pour l'Opera d'Hippolite et D'Aricie'. The names are given here in French spellings: Rainieri, Mai, Bozelly, Gianelly, Girelly, Lolly, Beni.

28 ASP, Teatro, Computisteria Borbonica, fili correnti, busta 933 (1760–1766), 'Conto delle Piggioni di Case occupate dalli sotto espressi nel Mese di Ottobre', dated '31 8bre 1760'.

29 The housing list offers a bit more information on these two singers. It reads in part: 'Baglioni detta la Carnaccina che doveva cantare l'Amore nel prologo, e che ha cantato ne cori' (who was supposed to sing Amore in the Prologue and who sang in the chorus). 'Baglioni detta la Carnaccina' was undoubtedly one of the daughters of Francesco Baglioni (a well known comic singer of the era, nicknamed 'Carnaccio'), perhaps Giovanna or Clementina, both of whom sang in other operas at Parma around this time. On this family of singers see Barbara Dobbs Mackenzie and Colin Timms, 'Baglioni' (1–3), in *The New Grove Dictionary of Opera*, volume 1, 277–278; I thank John Rice for bringing this relationship to my attention. The documents offer no explanation as to why 'la Carnaccina' did not sing Amore as apparently planned; according to the libretto Lucia Friggeri sang this role. The housing list also reads: 'Lucia Frigeri essendo restata per l'opera del Carnevale' (having stayed for the carnival opera); this opera was *I Tindaridi*.

30 ASP, Teatro, Computisteria Borbonica, fili correnti, busta 933 (1760–1766), 'Per l'Opera de i Tindaridi, Ricevute degli Onnorarj de Sig.ri Virtuosi'.

31 ASP, Teatro, Computisteria Borbonica, fili correnti, busta 933 (1760–1766), 'Pigioni di Case in occasione dell'opera della Primavera', dated 30 April 1760. Although the document does not provide the name of the opera to which it refers, it is a housing list for *I Tindaridi*, performed in May and June of 1760. (Similar housing lists survive for these months.) The housing list shows that the choristers received lodging for the month of April, though, judging from Traetta's letter, to be discussed below, they apparently did not arrive until at least the end of that month.

32 Although it is not certain that Brigida and Elisabetta Lolli were sisters, Brigida Lolli was not from Parma, would have required housing and does not appear in a separate entry in the housing list.

33 Other local singers include the two boys and Veronica Rainieri, who sang in other operas.

Table 5 Alphabetical list of all choristers whose names appear in librettos for Traetta's Parma operas (in documents from ASP where noted; alternative spellings reflect variant spellings in documents)

x = present in libretto
* = might not have sung, or sang and were not paid; do not appear in documents

Women	Ippolito ed Aricia	I Tindaridi	Le feste d'Imeneo	Enea e Lavinia
'Baglioni detta la Carnaccina'			x (not in libretto; in documents)	
Isabella Beni (Anna)	x		x (Anna)	
Giuseppa Bonetti			x*	
Anna Boselli (local)	x	x	x	x
Margherita Borasca				x*
Margherita Brandi		x*		x*
Agostina Caccia			x*	
Antonia Fascitelli (local)	x	x	x (Farcelli)	x (Farscelli)
Antonia Fioroni		x*		
Angela Foresti		x*		
Lucia Forti			x*	
Ludovica Forzoni			x*	
Lucia Frigeri (not local)		x (not in libretto; in documents)	x (not in libretto; in documents)	
Margherita Gianelli	x*			
Barbara Girelli	x	x (not in libretto; in documents)		
Elisabetta Goradi		x*		
Domenica Lambertini	x			
Anna (Brigida) Lolli (not local)	x	x (Brigida)	x	x (Brigida)
Faustina Mainardi			x*	
Girolama Maj (local)	x (Girolima)	x	x	x
Angela Majre		x	x	x
Angela Merusi (Caterina?)			x*	? (Caterina)
Giuseppa Morelli				x*
Veronica Rainieri (local)	x			
Anna Roselli			x*	
Geltruda Santi		x*		x
Maria Sartori			x*	
Rosa Vitalba				x*

Men	Ippolito ed Aricia	I Tindaridi	Le feste d'Imeneo	Enea e Lavinia
Carlo Barbieri (not local)	x	x	x	x
Nicola Agostino Bertelli (not local)		x		
Francesco Cavalli	x			
Tommaso Caminati		x		
Pietro Cieccatini			x*	

PRODUCING THE OPERATIC CHORUS AT PARMA'S TEATRO DUCALE

Table 5 *continued*

Men	Ippolito ed Aricia	I Tindaridi	Le feste d'Imeneo	Enea e Lavinia
Giuseppe Costa (boy)		x	? (Pompeo Costa)	
Gaetano Donini				x
Ludovico Felloni (local)	x	x	x	x
Giuseppe Ferri (not local)		x (Afferri)	x (Ferri)	x (Afferri)
Agostino Foresti				x*
Antonio Goldoni (not local)	x	x	x	x
Girolamo Landini (not local)	x	x (Landi)	x (Landi)	x
Filippo Luigioni			x*	
Petronio Manelli	x*			
Anastasio Massa (not local)		x (not in libretto; in documents)		
Pietro Muratori			x*	
Angelo Passavia			x*	
Pietro Pizzimiglia (boy)		x		
Gaetano Rizzardi				x
Alessandro La Roche detto 'il francese' (not local)		x (not in libretto; in documents)	x (Alessandro Franchis)	
Giambattista Rosi				x
Matteo Sabattini	x*			
Luigi de Sales			x*	
Filippo Sucarelli		x	x (Sudadelli)	
Domenico Tibaldi	x*		? (Antonio)	
Gaspero Tornielli	x	x (in libretto but not in documents)		x (Gasparo)
Agostino Viparino				x*

A document detailing the copying of the music for *I Tindaridi* reveals that the out-of-town choral singers came to Parma from Bologna.[34] The copyists were paid extra for having sent the choral parts there, and some Bolognese copyists received payment 'for having assisted during the final days because of time constraints'. The choral singers were apparently late in arriving in Parma for *I Tindaridi*, and their delay caused Traetta some anxiety. A letter of 23 April from the impresario Pio Quazza to du Tillot confirms this.[35] Quazza reports

---

34 ASP, Teatro, Computisteria Borbonica, fili correnti, busta 933 (1760–1766), 'Conto della Copiatura di Musica per l'Opera Intitolata i Tindaridi per il Reggio ducal Teatro', dated 30 June 1760. The last two entries in the document read: 'Piu per aver spedito le parti dei Cori a Bologna' and 'Piu per ricognizione di copiatura alli SS.ri Bolognesi che anno agiutato nelli ultimi giorni per la ristrezza del tempo'.

35 ASP, Carteggio du Tillot, Teatri, busta 88-T, letter from Pio Quazza dated 23 April 1760. The first section of the letter refers to the Bolognese singers: 'J'ai crù d'ecrire hier au soir, a Bologne, Monsieur, pour que le S.r Carmanini fisse partir incessemment tous les Choeurs, ainsi que M.r Traetta m'en avait fait baucoup d'istance; Lorsqu'a mon arrive à Parme j'ai trouvé une Lettre du susd.e Carmanini qui me demmande tout dabord cent Zequins pour les leur distribuer avant qu'ils partent ayant a arranger leurs affaires, et ils les attendent par le Courier de Vendredi pour pouvoir partir aussitot, n'etant pas trop bien aise M.r Traetta de ce delai a cause que le tems s'abrege, et qu'il voudroit faire commencer a repeter les Choeurs; mais ce n'est pas de notre faute' (I intended to write last night to Bologna, Sir, so that Mr

that his Bolognese contact Carmanini 'is preparing the choristers for their immediate departure', on which Traetta was insisting; he explains that Traetta would be 'displeased with the delay because time is growing short and he wishes to begin rehearsing them'. Quazza conveys Carmanini's request for an advance for the choral singers in the amount of one hundred zecchini so that they could 'get their affairs in order' before their departure.[36] Evidence of the eighteenth-century operatic rehearsal process is extremely rare, especially concerning choruses; this valuable letter demonstrates Traetta's concern for the choral singers' preparation and its importance to a successful production. It also shows that not only highly paid solo singers could make financial demands on a theatre and expect them to be met, but that sometimes the chorus could do so as well. Although it is not known when the singers arrived in Parma, the opera opened on 14 May, ran for thirty-one performances and closed 30 June.

Being from out of town apparently carried with it a certain cachet and usually resulted in higher payment. With only one exception, all of the non-local singers hired for *I Tindaridi* were paid more than those from Parma, as seen in Figure 1.[37] In addition, almost all of the men were consistently paid more than the women, with two exceptions: one of the men who replaced a singer who had become ill at some point (these two men earned less together than what the other men were paid) and Lucia Frigeri (Friggeri), a successful soloist from out of town, who earned more than most of the women. (Frigeri and Massa were the highest paid.) The preference given to choral singers from outside Parma continued to the end of the decade, as we shall see.

Not surprisingly, all choristers in *I Tindaridi* earned considerably less than the leading soloists in the opera. For example, the renowned prima donna Caterina Gabrielli earned a total of five hundred zecchini and Giuseppe Aprile, a leading soprano castrato, earned three hundred.[38] However, as mentioned above, the highest paid choristers, Anastasio Massa and Lucia Frigeri, both earned a total of forty zecchini. This sum is equal to the earnings of the lowest ranking solo singers, Francesco Cavalli and Giambattista Ristorini. While little evidence survives regarding choristers' payments elsewhere, in Turin each chorister in *Sofonisba* (1764) earned two lire per night for each of the opera's twenty-eight performances, for a total of fifty-six lire.[39] The Turinese choristers' low payments do not even approach those earned by Giuseppe Vignati, the lowest ranking solo singer in Turin's *Sofonisba*, who earned 250 lire for this opera (half of his five hundred lire payment for the two operas in Carnival 1764). In comparison with choristers in Turin, those in Parma were clearly more highly valued.

Carmanini would prepare all the choristers to depart right away, since Mr Traetta has insisted upon it; when I arrived in Parma I found a letter from the aforementioned Carmanini, who requests one hundred zecchini immediately to distribute to the choristers before they leave, so that they can put their affairs in order; they [the choristers] are waiting for it to arrive with Friday's mail, so that they can leave directly; Mr Traetta will be displeased with this delay as he wants to begin rehearsing the choristers and time is growing short, but this is not our fault.)

36 A payment document for various expenses incurred during April confirms that this was sent to the choristers; ASP, Teatro, Computisteria Borbonica, fili correnti, busta 933 (1760–1766), 'Conto di Spese che riguardano il Teatro occasionate nel mese di Aprile 1760'.

37 Brigida Lolli was paid less than some of the local singers.

38 ASP, Teatro, Computisteria Borbonica, fili correnti, busta 933 (1760–1766), 'Per L'Opera de i Tindaridi. Ricevute degli Onnorarj de Sig.ri Virtuosi'. This document reports earnings for all solo singers in zecchini and lire equivalents. Caterina Gabrielli earned four hundred zecchini and an extra payment of one hundred as a gift ('più per Regallo alla Sig.ra Gabrielli, zech. 100').

39 Payment information for singers in Turin is compiled from several documents in Turin, ASCT, cited in Butler, *Operatic Reform at Turin's Teatro Regio*, 163 and 292. Many currencies existed in this period, and no contemporary exchange rate is available. (On this topic see Rosselli, *Singers of Italian Opera*, 131–134.) Zecchini might be converted to lire in both Turin and Parma, but the lira was probably not equivalent in the two cities. Payment information from Turin, then, is not meant for purposes of comparison with singers' earnings in other places. It is presented only to provide comparisons of choristers' and soloists' earnings in Parma and in Turin, thus demonstrating the respective value of choristers in each city.

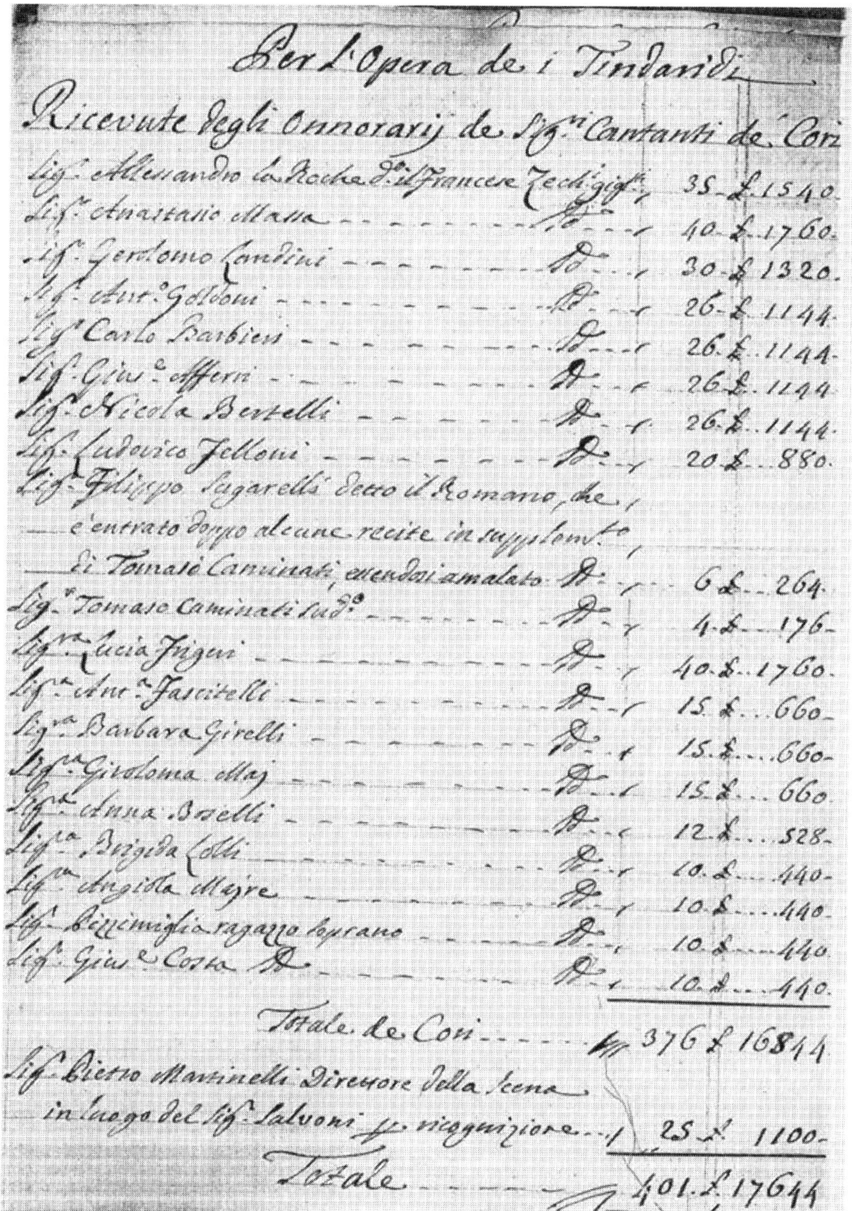

Per l'Opera de i Tindaridi

Ricevute degli Onnorarij de Sig.ri Cantanti de' Cori

Sig. Allessandro la Rocha d.o il Francese Zecchini		35	£ 1540
Sig. Anastasio Massa	d.o	40	£ 1760
Sig. Gerolomo Candini	d.o	30	£ 1320
Sig. Ant.o Goldoni	d.o	26	£ 1144
Sig. Carlo Barbieri	d.o	26	£ 1144
Sig. Giu.e Afferri	d.o	26	£ 1144
Sig. Nicola Bertelli	d.o	26	£ 1144
Sig. Ludovico Felloni	d.o	20	£ 880
Sig. Filippo Sugarelli detto il Romano, che è entrato dopo alcune recite in supplem.to di Tomasò Caminati, essendosi amalato	d.o	6	£ 264
Sig. Tomaso Caminati sud.o	d.o	4	£ 176
Sig.ra Lucia Frigeri	d.o	40	£ 1760
Sig.a Ant.a Fascitelli	d.o	15	£ 660
Sig.ra Barbara Girelli	d.o	15	£ 660
Sig.ra Girolama Maj	d.o	15	£ 660
Sig.a Anna Boselli	d.o	12	£ 528
Sig.ra Brigida Colli	d.o	10	£ 440
Sig.ra Angiola Magre	d.o	10	£ 440
Sig. Bizzimiglia ragazzo soprano	d.o	10	£ 440
Sig. Giu.e Costa d.o	d.o	10	£ 440
Totale de Cori		376	£ 16844
Sig. Pietro Martinelli Direttore della Scena in luogo del Sig. Salvoni per ricognizione		25	£ 1100
Totale		401	£ 17644

Figure 1 ASP, Teatro, Computisteria Borbonica, fili correnti, busta 933 (1760–1766), 'Per l'Opera de i Tindaridi, Ricevute degli Onnorarij de Sig.ri Cantanti de' Cori'. Reproduced with permission

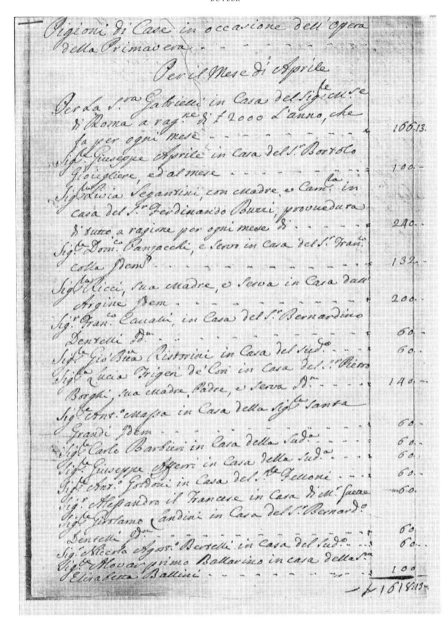

Figure 2   ASP, Teatro, Computisteria Borbonica, fili correnti, busta 933 (1760–1766), 'Pigioni di Case in occasione dell'opera della Primavera', dated 30 April 1760. Reproduced with permission

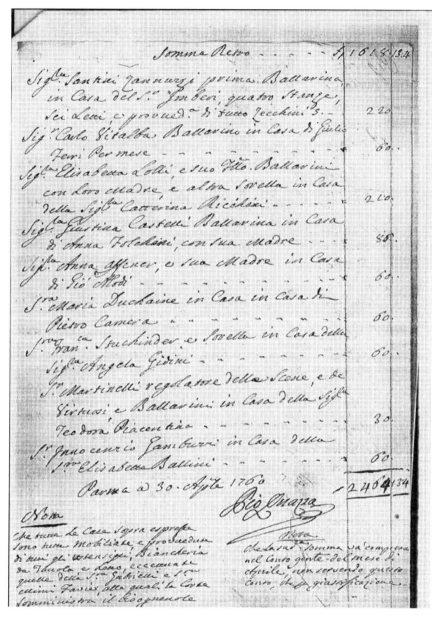

Figure 2 continued

It will be recalled that there were eight singers – four men and four women – who sang in all of the four reform operas. Contracts for Traetta's choral singers do not survive, and without them it is impossible to know when the choristers were hired or whether they were engaged for more than one opera at a time. The presence of a core of singers may have been a coincidence, but it is also possible that these singers were intentionally hired for the four operas all together as a group. A strong core would have provided stability in an otherwise flexible choral ensemble, the additional members of which changed from opera to opera. It may also have resulted in a degree of stylistic unity; with a standing body of the same eight singers at his disposal, Traetta would have known in advance, within certain parameters, the level of musical demands he could make on the choruses for all of the operas. Composers of eighteenth-century opera were known for constructing arias that showcased the particular abilities of their singers; perhaps this approach was taken with regard to choral music as well, at least in Parma.

Nothing is known about most of the choristers in the Parma librettos, other than their names, as shown in Table 5.[40] But the majority of those who appear in both the librettos and the payment documents sang in other theatres as well, almost all of them performing as soloists in smaller roles. This is true for all of the out-of-town singers and for some of the local singers as well.[41] Of the female choristers, three were from other cities. Both Isabella Beni 'di Bologna' and Lucia Frigeri 'di Milano' sang comic roles in Bologna before performing in Parma and went on to successful solo careers that lasted until the late 1770s. Frigeri also sang seria roles elsewhere before and after Parma. Brigida Anelli Lolli 'di Bergamo' sang in two *opere buffe* at Parma in 1771 and in others in various Italian cities in the 1760s and 1770s.[42]

The remaining five – Anna Boselli, Antonia Fascitelli, Barbara Girelli, Girolama Maj and Veronica Rainieri – were from Parma. Boselli came from a Parmesan noble family. She got her start as a chorus member in the French operas that were imported to Parma from Paris and later went on to sing in seria productions elsewhere through the 1770s.[43] Fascitelli had small roles in *Ippolito ed Aricia* and *Enea e Lavinia* and performed widely in most of the major Italian cities from the 1740s to the mid-1760s. Barbara Girelli, 'detta la Parmigiana', had small roles in two *opere serie* at Parma in 1758 and sang occasionally in other cities until 1771. Girolama Maj and Veronica Rainieri 'di Parma' were choristers in one of the French operas, along with Boselli;[44] Maj apparently did not sing elsewhere, but Rainieri had a small role in *I Tindaridi* and sang in other cities until 1763.

While most of the women were local, most of the men were not. Their careers vary widely. Carlo Barbieri 'di Bologna' debuted as a soloist in Bologna in 1751 and had roles in five other cities.[45] He is the only chorister from Traetta's operas who also sang in Gluck's *Le feste d'Apollo* in 1769. Nicola Agostino Bertelli sang a small role in Bologna before coming to Parma, then seems not to have sung elsewhere, while Giuseppe Ferri (Afferri) enjoyed a very successful career which brought him to most of the major Italian theatres. Domenico Tibaldi sang roles mostly in Bologna and Venice but had a prosperous career as well (he also sang a small role in *Ippolito ed Aricia*). Antonio Goldoni sang solo roles in Sassuolo before coming to Parma, then seems not to have sung elsewhere, and Girolamo Landini (Landi) and Petronio Manelli (along with Tibaldi) performed

---

40 The following discussion therefore omits them and focuses on the singers about which information is available.

41 The following sketches of the singers' careers are drawn from the singer index of Claudio Sartori, *I libretti italiani a stampa dalle origini al 1800: catalogo analitico con 16 indici*, volume 6, part 2 (Cuneo: Bertola & Locatelli, 1994). When not indicated in the Parma documents, origins of the singers are given as they appear in Sartori.

42 As mentioned above, Brigida Lolli and Anna Lolli are probably one and the same. Brigida Lolli appears in librettos after 1761, but after this year the name Anna Lolli does not appear. Sartori, *I libretti italiani*, volume 6, part 2, 370.

43 Numerous payment receipts to Anna Boselli for having sung in the chorus of the French operas survive, one for each month from December 1757 to March 1759 (ASP, Teatro, Computisteria Borbonica, fili correnti, busta 932 (1758–1759)). Boselli is the only singer for whom this is true, however. No evidence suggests that other Parmesan choristers participated in this many of the French operas.

44 Receipts for Maj and Rainieri 'per aver cantato nei Cori delle opere francese nel Carnovale prossimo scorso' dated 2 April 1759 survive in ASP, Teatro, Computisteria Borbonica, fili correnti, busta 932 (1758–1759).

45 'Di Bologna' in this case comes not from Sartori but from the list of choral singers for *Le feste d'Apollo* to be cited below.

as choristers in Reggio Emilia. Anastasio Massa 'di Bologna' performed mostly comic roles from the 1750s to the late 1770s in Venice, Bologna, Dresden and many other cities. Alessandro La Roche 'detto il francese' was presumably a member of the troupe that came from Paris; although he does not appear in the librettos for *I Tindaridi* and *Le feste d'Imeneo*, he received lodging in Parma for these operas. (In the housing list for the latter work he is called Alessandro Franchis, perhaps a variant of 'francese'.) Allexandre Reynaud sang in both *Titone et l'Aurora* and one of the earlier French operas.[46] Alessandro is perhaps a variant of Allexandre, and Reynaud, La Roche and Franchis may have been one and the same. If so, this French singer came to Parma in 1757, 1759 and 1760. Gaspero (Gasparo) Tornielli seems not to have performed at all beyond his role as a chorister in *I Tindaridi*, while Ludovico Felloni 'di Parma' led the choral ensemble for the French operas.[47] Together with the three Parmesan female choristers who sang in these operas and the male singer from France, Felloni serves as an important point of contact between the French repertory imported to Parma and Traetta's reform operas. Parma seems to have launched Felloni, as he went on to a successful career singing roles in Florence, Rome, Venice and other cities from 1766 until 1781.

The French operas imported to Parma from Paris clearly provided additional opportunities for some of the local singers and introduced them to French music. As mentioned above, four Parmesan choristers sang in them, supplementing the performing forces brought from Paris. These four choristers' introduction to the French style would have prepared them for the reform opera choruses, with their Italianate music integrated into the drama in the French manner. Perhaps the interaction of these groups of singers helped to unify the ensemble of the reform opera choruses – particularly because the chorus leader in the French operas, Ludovico Felloni, was not a French singer, but was from Parma and a member of the core chorus. Moreover, the presence in Traetta's choruses of one French choral singer, La Roche, reinforces the link between the French and Italian operatic styles and the overlap in personnel between the French and Italian opera choruses.

A few of the men were already familiar with Traetta's choral writing. Girolamo Landini, Petronio Manelli and Domenico Tibaldi, all of whom sang in *Ippolito ed Aricia*, had performed in the chorus of Traetta's *Nitteti* for Reggio Emilia's Teatro del Pubblico just two years earlier.[48] Landini was one of the core singers at Parma engaged in Bologna; this suggests that Reggio, like Parma, hired its choral singers from Bologna – Reggio's close proximity to both Bologna and Parma would have facilitated this situation. As mentioned above, the major Italian theatres sometimes produced choruses and therefore were at times able to overcome the financial and logistical obstacles they posed; apparently regional theatres such as Reggio Emilia were occasionally able to do so as well – even at times hiring professional choristers, as in Parma.

A group of singers this large undoubtedly required a stage director. Very little is known about stage directors in Italian theatres; it is generally assumed that the local librettist fulfilled this role.[49] This was not the case in Parma, where Pietro Martinelli (Martelli) and Luigi Salvoni, both from Bologna, served as stage directors. Quazza mentions a 'Sigr. Martelli di Bologna mio corrispondente teatrale' in a document from 1769. Martinelli (presumably the same person) appears as 'direttore della scena' in the personnel list for *I*

---

46 Reynaud performed as soloist and chorister in *Titone et l'Aurora* in 1759; Sartori, *I libretti italiani*, volume 5 (1992), 340. He also sang in the chorus of *Gl'Incà del Peru*, presented in Parma in 1757; Sartori, *I libretti italiani*, volume 6, part 2, 552.

47 ASP, Teatro, Computisteria Borbonica, fili correnti, busta 932 (1758–1759), 'Conto di Sig.ri Suonatori intervenuti all'Orchestra per le recite Francesi . . .': 'Al Sig.r Felloni cantore de cori delle opere francesi per nove recite', dated November 1758. Felloni also housed one of the visiting choristers: ASP, Teatro, Computisteria Borbonica, fili correnti, busta 933 (1760–1766), 'Pigioni di Case in occasione dell'opera della Primavera', dated 30 April 1760: 'Sig.re Ant.o Goldoni in Casa del S.r Felloni'.

48 Eight men are listed by name in the libretto for Reggio Emilia's production of *Nitteti*. Sartori, *I libretti italiani*, volume 4 (1991), 235. The opera included a single chorus, which is discussed in Loomis, 'Tommaso Traetta's Operas for Parma', 304–305.

49 Daniel Heartz, 'The Poet as Stage Director: Metastasio, Goldoni, and Da Ponte', in *Mozart's Operas*, ed. Thomas Bauman (Berkeley: University of California Press, 1990), 89–105.

Tindaridi; in the housing list he is named as 'regolatore delle scene, e de Virtuosi, e Ballarini'. He is also listed as having substituted for 'Sig. Salvoni' in the *Tindaridi* documents. Luigi Bernardo Salvoni (Salvonio) served as stage director for other operas at Parma during the 1750s, in 1769 for *Le feste d'Apollo* and in 1770.[50]

Martinelli and Salvoni received both lodging and payment equal to twice what some of the singers earned – they were obviously highly valued in Parma. And the stage directors already had some contact with the choristers, having come from Bologna with them; perhaps it was Martinelli who received the choral parts for *Tindaridi* sent to Bologna in advance and helped the choral singers prepare their music before their arrival. As already noted, the role of the chorus master is not thought not to have developed until much later; the evidence from Parma suggests that one of the duties of the stage director was to assist with the chorus as well.

Returning to the assumption that eighteenth-century choruses were all male, possibly amateurs or at best second-rate singers and generally treated as an afterthought, this evidence paints a very different picture of Parma's choruses. For Traetta's operas, they comprised men and women in roughly equal numbers, combined local and out-of-town singers, and were directed by a professional stage director. Many of the singers were professionals and active as soloists, which suggests that they possessed a certain level of ability, and two of them earned fees on a par with third- or fourth-ranking solo singers of *I Tindaridi*. Traetta considered the Bologna choristers a central component of the operatic ensemble, worthy of thorough musical preparation with his personal assistance. These important singers even received payment in advance of their trip to Parma for *I Tindaridi* beyond what they earned for that opera.

Bologna was the musical centre to which young singers flocked in order to begin their careers before the centre of activity shifted to Milan later in the century.[51] The fact that Traetta's choristers were hired by the Bolognese contact of Parma's impresario demonstrates the importance of Bologna as a source for Parma's personnel. It suggests that the performing circuit through which solo singers found work functioned in a similar manner for choral singers, too – at least when the choral singers were professionals, as in Parma.[52]

CONSEQUENCES OF TRAETTA'S OPERAS: THE *SCUOLA DI CANTO* AND GLUCK'S *LE FESTE D'APOLLO*

Traetta's operas for Parma were massive productions, extremely expensive and complex to put together. The lavish supernatural spectacle, with aerial appearances of numerous deities, complex ballets integrated within the scenes, ornate costumes, magnificent sets (with more scene changes than usual) and many other special effects 'imposed a financial burden more appropriate to a kingdom than to a tiny duchy'.[53] An army of carpenters, painters and other technical staff was employed. While few documents pertaining to the singers for the operas survive, many report the details involved in the operas' technical components. In 1768 a *scuola di canto* was established in order to supply singers for the theatre. The school was directed by the Parmesan musician Francesco Poncini and trained local singers until its closure in 1792.[54] The difficult logistics of Traetta's operas may have given rise to the establishment of this institution, which would have alleviated the need for (and expense of) hiring outside choristers in the future.

---

50 According to the 1769 payment documents, to be cited below, Salvoni 'ha dirretto, e messo in scena tutti gli atti d'opere'. He is also mentioned in documents from the 1750s and 1770.
51 Rosselli, *Singers of Italian Opera*, 152–153.
52 The contact between Parma and Bologna probably began much earlier, though very few administrative documents for Parma's Teatro Ducale prior to the 1750s survive. Salvoni appears in documents from the 1750s, and Quazza himself travelled to Bologna in the 1760s to hire singers. Singers of opera buffa at Parma were often hired in Bologna. The connection between these two cities and its implications for Parma's repertory as a whole merit further exploration.
53 Heartz, 'Operatic Reform at Parma', 296–297.
54 Parma's *scuola di canto* is discussed by Raffaella Nardella in 'Musica e musicisti alla corte di Don Ferdinando', essay forthcoming in a collection to be published by the Deputazione di Storia Patria per le Province Parmensi. I am grateful to Raffaella Nardella for sharing her unpublished research with me.

PRODUCING THE OPERATIC CHORUS AT PARMA'S TEATRO DUCALE

The singing school began functioning on 1 December 1768,[55] and in less than a year it produced singers who performed in Gluck's *Le feste d'Apollo*, which opened on 24 August 1769. Compared with Traetta's Parmesan operas, this work has received relatively little attention. Falling between *Alceste* of 1767, with its famous preface outlining the tenets of operatic reform, and *Paride ed Elena* of 1770, *Le feste d'Apollo* represents an extension of the composer's ideals and a continuation of the reform efforts begun in Parma ten years earlier.

The archival record is much more complete for *Le feste d'Apollo* than for the earlier reform operas and reveals more about the choristers. While the libretto does not list individual choral singers by name, a detailed personnel list with payments survives.[56] With only two exceptions, none of the choristers is the same as those who performed in Traetta's operas. One might presume that this is because the choral forces were now drawn from the singing school. However, choristers from the school apparently did not completely supplant the use of professionals. The choruses for *Le feste d'Apollo* comprised three types of singers: students from the singing school, locals who were not from the school (presumably adults) and other out-of-town singers, all but one from Bologna. The adult singers (those not from the school) appear in the document with their city of origin: 'di Bologna', 'di Parma' (or 'Parmegiano') and 'Reggiano'. The Bolognese singers are Anna Lazzari, Carlo Barbieri, Carlo Gentilucci and Pietro Vacchi. Those from Parma are America Biggi, Antonia Fascitelli, Francesco Crespi, Angelo Delbò and Gabriele Bonzani.[57] Giovanni Bedogni is listed as 'Reggiano'. *Le feste d'Apollo* thus employed ten professional adult singers.

The list continues with 'six young Parmesan boys from the singing school' and, in a separate group, 'ten Parmesan girls from the aforementioned school'.[58] The sixteen children were taught their music by Francesco Poncini, who also played harpsichord in the opera orchestra. A separate list gives the names of the students.[59] There were thus twenty-six choristers, two more than the total number given in the libretto. Luiggi Salvoni served as stage director of this large ensemble. The work received fifteen performances.

Contracts for the choral singers of *Le feste d'Apollo* survive and provide additional information as to the terms of their engagement. Although it is not known when the out-of-town singers arrived in Parma, the four Bolognese singers all signed their contracts on 9 July 1769 and received housing for August and September.[60] The Parmesan choral singers signed their contracts much earlier than the Bolognese singers; the contracts for the singers from Parma are all dated early to mid-March of the same year. Perhaps some rehearsal of the Parmesan singers, possibly together with the children from the school, occurred before the Bolognese singers arrived.

The choristers for *Le feste d'Apollo* did double duty in other Parmesan productions as well. The contracts end with a statement of receipt for payment (confirming the amount in the contract) and an additional phrase and separate amount 'for having sung in the Arcadia'.[61] This refers to a musical entertainment given in the royal gardens during the wedding festivities.[62] These include all but one of the adult singers (Angelo

---

55 ASP, Teatro, Computisteria Borbonica, fili correnti, busta 934a (1768–1769), 'Conto degli onorari dei musici . . .': 'Al sigr. Francesco Poncini come maestro della nuova scuola di canto . . . con l'assegno al sud.o di due mille lire all'anno, ed incominciata il primo giorno del sud.o mese', dated 31 December 1768.

56 The choristers in *Le feste d'Apollo* are referred to as '24 attori e attrici cantanti' in the libretto (Parma: Stamperia Reale, 1769). ASP, Teatro, Computisteria Borbonica, fili correnti, busta 934a (1768–1769), 'Conto generale di spese occorse per i Spettacoli Musicali di questo Reale Teatro in occasione delle Allegrezze per le Reali Nozze; nell'Estate 1769' (a portion of which appears in Figure 3), names them.

57 Antonia Fascitelli and Carlo Barbieri are the two who sang in both this work and Traetta's operas.

58 'Sei Giovani Parmegiani della Scuola del Canto' and 'dieci Ragazze Parmegiane della sud.a Scuola'.

59 One might speculate that these were the choristers who appeared in the librettos but not in the payment documents for Traetta's operas, but this is not the case.

60 Contracts for these singers and housing lists naming them are in ASP, Teatro, Computisteria Borbonica, fili correnti, busta 934a (1768–1769).

61 A separate document lists female and male choristers who received payment for 'the Arcadia in the Royal Garden'.

62 This work was composed by Antonio Rugarli, presumably from Parma but about whom nothing more seems to be known. His name does not appear in any other documents consulted for this study.

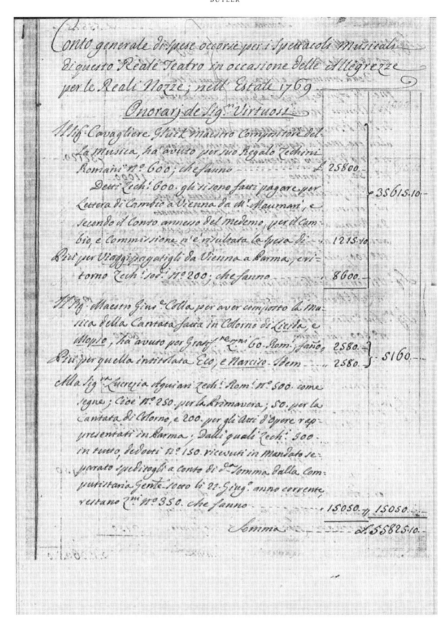

Figure 3   ASP, Teatro, Computisteria Borbonica, fili correnti, busta 934a (1768–1769), 'Conto generale di spese occorse per i Spettacoli Musicali di questo Reale Teatro in occasione delle Allegrezze per le Reali Nozze; nell'Estate 1769', unnumbered pages listing 'cori cantanti'

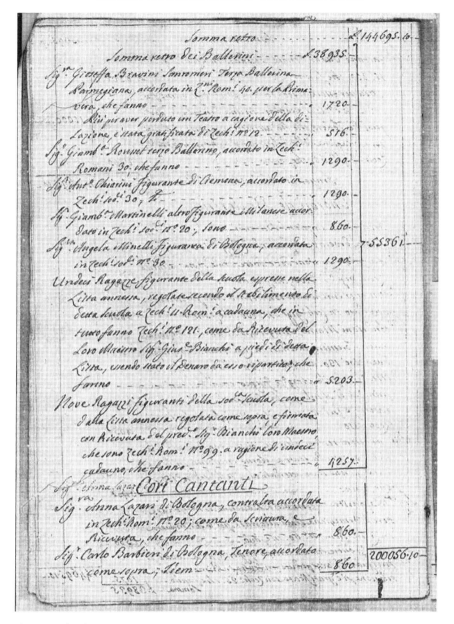

Figure 3 continued

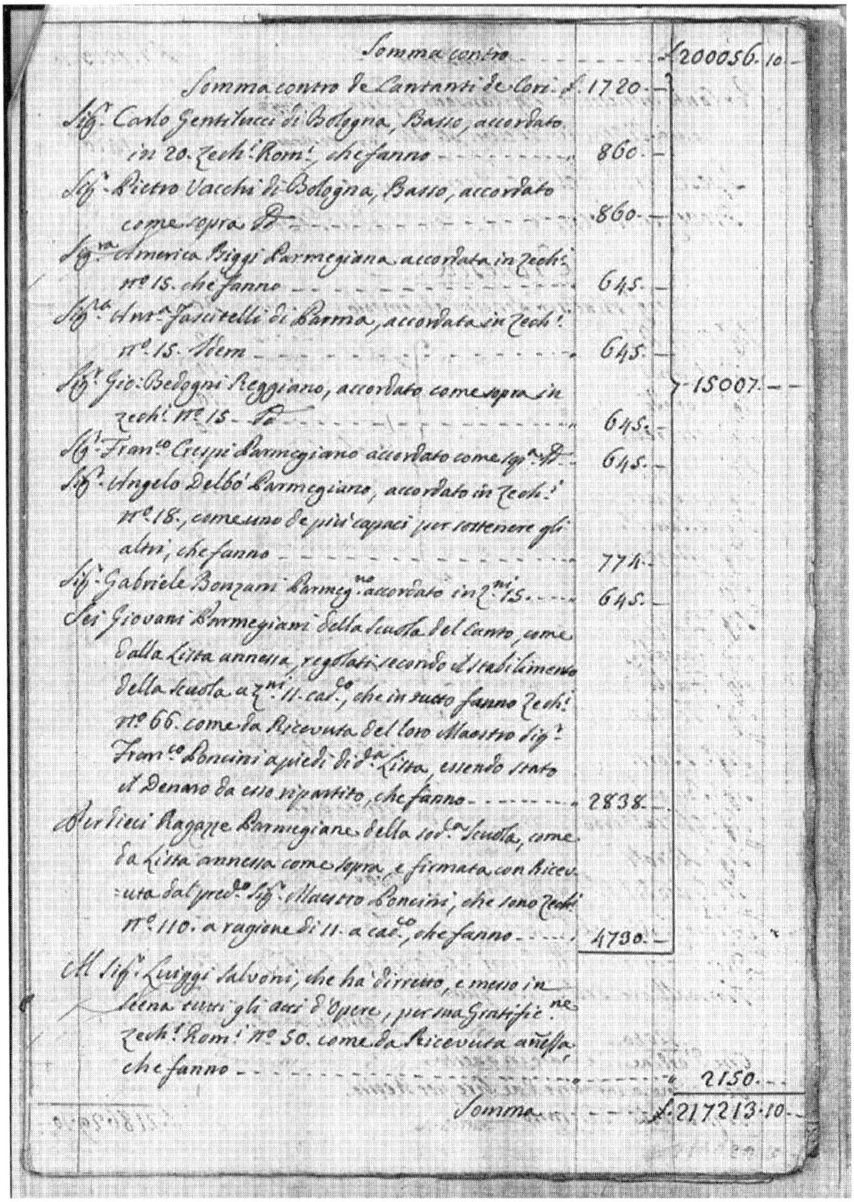

Somma contro ---- £ 200056.10

Somma contro de Cantanti de Cori £ 1720

Sig.r Carlo Gentilucci di Bologna, Basso, accordato in 20. Zech.i Rom.i, che fanno ---- 860

Sig.r Pietro Vacchi di Bologna, Basso, accordato come sopra d.o ---- 860

Sig.ra America Biggi Parmegiana accordata in Zech.i n.o 15. che fanno ---- 645

Sig.ra Ant.a Fascitelli di Parma, accordata in Zech.i n.o 15. Item ---- 645

Sig.r Gio: Bedogni Reggiano, accordato come sopra in Zech.i n.o 15. d.o ---- 645 } 15007

Sig.r Fran.co Crespi Parmegiano accordato come sop.a d.o ---- 645

Sig.r Angelo Delbò Parmegiano, accordato in Zech.i n.o 18., come uno de più capaci per sostenere gli altri, che fanno ---- 774

Sig.r Gabriele Bonzani Parmeg.no accordato in Z.ni 15. ---- 645

Sei Giovani Parmegiani della Scuola del Canto, come dalla Lista annessa, regolati secondo lo stabilimento della Scuola a Z.ni 11. cad.o, che in tutto fanno Zech.i n.o 66. come da Ricevuta del loro Maestro Sig.r Fran.co Bonzini a piedi di d.a Lista, essendo stato il Denaro da esso ripartito, che fanno ---- 2838

Per Dieci Ragazze Parmegiane della sud.a Scuola, come da Lista annessa come sopra, e firmata con Ricevuta dal pred.o Sig.r Maestro Bonzini, che sono Zech.i n.o 110. a ragione di 11. a cad.o, che fanno ---- 4730

Al Sig.r Luiggi Salvoni, che ha diretto, e messo in Scena tutti gli atti d'Opere, per sua Gratific.ne Zech.i Rom.i n.o 50. come da Ricevuta annessa che fanno ---- 2150

Somma ---- £ 217213.10

Figure 3 *continued*

Delbò does not appear), nine of the ten girls and the six boys, all of whom were paid extra for the event. The choristers' engagement at Parma for *Le feste d'Apollo* thus presented additional opportunities for the singers to increase their earnings.[63]

Without exception the out-of-town singers for *Le feste d'Apollo* commanded higher payments than the local singers, as seen in Figure 3. While the Bolognese singers earned a total of twenty zecchini each, most of the singers from Parma (and the one from Reggio) earned a total of fifteen.[64] Angelo Delbò earned eighteen; he was Poncini's assistant in the singing school and was rewarded with a slightly higher fee 'as one of the most capable of supporting the others'.[65] Each of the boys and girls received a total of eleven zecchini. It will be recalled that the highest paid choristers in *I Tindaridi* earned the same fee as the lowest-ranking solo singers. However, payments to choristers in *Le feste d'Apollo* are all very low compared to that of the lowest-ranking solo singer: Felicita Suardi, who sang the role of the seconda donna, received one hundred zecchini. The wide discrepancy might be due in part to the fact that *Le feste d'Apollo* includes no third-ranking role (as in *I Tindaridi*), and because there were significantly fewer performances of *Le feste d'Apollo*: fifteen to *I Tindaridi*'s thirty-one.

Although the French-inspired reform of opera at Parma is considered to have ended with *Le feste d'Apollo*, Parma continued producing choruses in later works. *Uranio ed Erasitea*, a cantata from 1771 by Parma's maestro di cappella Giuseppe Colla, employed choruses, as did Sarti's elaborate and complex opera *Alessandro e Timoteo* of 1782.[66] The Bolognese choristers do not appear in any documents after 1769; the singing school apparently eventually fulfilled its purpose and became the sole institution furnishing choral singers for Parma's theatrical productions.

Scholars have long known that eighteenth-century Italian opera functioned in the context of a wide-ranging circuit, with leading singers, dancers, choreographers and designers moving among Italy's many opera theatres. The evidence from Parma reveals that this circuit was broader than we have assumed, embracing choral singers as well. Most importantly, Parma's experience demonstrates the logistical and financial problems choruses presented for operatic reform, the solution to which was a long-standing commitment of resources. As Bruce Alan Brown has observed regarding the calls for reform by Algarotti and others, 'only with the right combination of artistic talent, material circumstances, and effective management could any theatre afford to listen to such basic criticism'.[67] For a short time Parma achieved the 'right combination', an important element of which was its expensive and talented chorus of professionals. The subsequent establishment of the singing school, which provided able choristers at a more manageable cost, was part of the attempt to sustain the combination, an attempt thwarted by du Tillot's departure from Parma shortly thereafter. The evidence given here sheds light on the complex logistics involved in producing operatic choruses, and understanding the Teatro Ducale's experience in managing these logistics broadens the context for the study of operatic production in the eighteenth century.

---

63 Giuseppe Colla, maestro di cappella at Parma, composed two cantatas for the festivities, *Licida e Mopso* and *Eco e Narciso*. It is not certain whether these works employed choruses, but documents mentioning both these and others for the festivities list choristers.

64 These singers earned a total of twenty or fifteen zecchini romani for the entire run of *Le feste d'Apollo*, not per performance; the document in Figure 3 summarizes all expenses incurred over the course of summer 1769. The singers' individual contracts confirm these total amounts.

65 'come uno de più capaci per sostenere gli altri'.

66 ASP, Teatro, Computisteria Borbonica, fili correnti, busta 935a (1772–1773), a booklet entitled '1773-Cantata-Uranio ed Erasitea-settembre 1773', contains a list of choristers. The libretto for Sarti's opera reports that twenty-six choristers participated, but no documents providing information about this work survive.

67 Brown, *Gluck and the French Theatre in Vienna*, 9.

Name Index

Abbate, Carolyn 71
Abert, Hermann 20, 63, 65, 66, 266, 376
Abraham, Gerald 17
Adamberger, Valentin xv
Adams, Samuel 284
Adelaide 478, 479
Adelung, Johann Christoph 345
Admet 57
Adrien 316
Afferri (Ferri), Giuseppe 527, 534
Agatina 141
Alamir 434
Alberti, Domenico 88
Alberti, Ignaz 422, 423
Alceste 8
Alcindor, King 437
Alessandro 23
Alfieri, Vittorio 510
Alfonso, Don 220, 223, 225, 226, 229, 255–9, 260, 261, 377, 399, 400, 406, 407, 411–413
Algarotti, Francesco 129, 522, 541
Aline 435
Allanbrook, Wye Jamison xvi, xx, 61, 63, 66, 68, 69, 70, 73, 76, 77, 185–96, 270, 376
Almovars 437
Amadis 436
Amande 438
Amélite 436
Aminta 23, 223
Amiti 287, 289, 294, 295, 297, 299, 302
Amore (Cupid) 220, 224, 227–8, 229, 230
Anderson, Benedict 344
Andreozzi, Gaetano 457, 487
Andromeda 155
Anfossi, Pasquale 119, 128, 129, 140, 176, 392, 450, 487, 491
Angélique 10, 13
Angermüller, Rudolph 393
Anglani, Bartolo 233–4
Anna 151
Anna, Donna 77, 80, 269, 273, 275, 278, 376
Annio 489

Aprile, Giuseppe 530
Arbace 27, 28, 29, 31–2, 33–4, 37–9, 41, 103, 154, 500–503, 505
Ariosto, Ludovica187, 224, 259 390, 398, 402
Arlequin 433
Armidero, Cavalier 170, 173
Arnaud, Baculard d' 199, 206, 208
Arnault, Antoine Vincent 322
Arne, Thomas 59
Arsace 455
Arsène 435
Artabano 27, 28, 33, 37–9, 41
Artaserse 27, 34–7, 39, 500, 501, 502
Artemesia, Donna 141
Artemis 154
Artois, Comte de 315
Asioli, Bonifazio 468, 469
Aspasia 151
Astaritta, Gennaro 487
Asteria 154
Asterio, King of Crete 154
Astolph 340–42
Astromonte 432
Atys 9
Auenbrugger, Joseph Leopold 400
Auenbrugger, Leopold von 363
Augustine, Saint 285
Aurora 342
Ayrenhoff, Cornelius von 363
Azor 204

Bach, Johann Christian 3, 15, 57, 119, 436
Bacon, Francis 285–6
Bajazet 456
Balthazar, Scott L. 465–86
Bandello, Matteo 47
Banti, Brigida 369
Barbarina 188
Barbieri, Carlo 527, 534, 537
Baretti, Joseph 508
Barile, Giandomenico 507–8
Barry, Spranger 44
Bartha, Joseph 357

Bartlet, Elizabeth C. xiii, xvi, xviii, 313–28
Bartolo, Dr 73, 74, 376–7
Basevi, Abramo 468
Basilio 66, 400
Bassa Selim 279, 280
Bastiano 297, 299, 301, 307–8
Balthazar, Scott xv
Batzko, Ludwig von 425, 442
Bauman, Thomas xiii, xiv, xv, xvi, xvii, xviii, xxi, 61, 62, 63, 65, 67, 73, 78, 278, 331
Beaumarchais, Pierre 185, 186, 187, 313–14, 407, 454
Bedogni, Giovanni 537
Beethoven, Ludwig van 62, 72, 111, 273, 346
Belfiore 251
Bellerophon 154
Bellini, Vincenzo 469, 473
Bellman, xvi
Benda, Jiří 43–4 *passim*, 50–52, 54, 55–7, 59, 60
Beni, Isabella 527, 534
Benincasa, Bartolomea 244, 253
Benvoglio 48
Berlicco, Don 303, 308
Berlioz, Hector 17
Bernardone 383
Bertelli, Nicola Agostino 527, 534
Bertoldino (Berto) 177
Bertoni, Ferdinando Giuseppe 449, 450, 452, 453, 487
Betzwieser xvii, xviii, xix
Bianca 456
Bianchi, Francesco 244, 450, 451, 452, 454, 457
Biggi, America 537
Binni, Walter 25, 27, 29, 31, 41
Blasio 399
Blom, Eric 16
Blümml, Emil Karl 424
Blumrosen, Alfred 291, 292, 298
Blumrosen, Ruth 291, 292, 298
Boccaccio 390, 411
Boccherini, Giovanni Gastone 398
Boer, Bertil van xvii
Bonaparte, Napoleon 323
Bonfil, Milord 237, 242, 258
Bonno, Giuseppe 407
Bonzani, Gabriele 537
Borghi, Giovanni Battista 450, 454
Born, Ignaz von 419, 422, 424, 442
Boselli, Anna 527, 534
Botturini, Mattia 454, 455, 456

Bourlin, Antoine-Jean (Duminiant) 436
Boyce, William 59
Brandimarte 402
Braunbehrens, Volkmar 424
Brauner, Charles 473
Bretzner, Christoph Friedrich 363, 430, 437
Britanni, 452
Britomarte 224, 227
Brophy, Brigid 428
Brosses, Charles de 25, 506
Brown, Bruce Alan xiii, xiv, xvii, xx, xxi, 389–415, 541
Brown, John 37, 41
Brünnhilde 74
Buch, David J. xix, xxi, 417–43
Budden, Julian 467
Buonafede 288
Burney, Charles 5, xix, 88
Butler, Margaret xvii, xviii, xix, xx, 521–41

Cadmus 24
Caesar, Julius 453
Caffarelli (Gaetano Majorano) 120
Cahusac, Louis de 428, 435
Callas, Maria 151
Calvesi, Vincenzo 220
Calvi, 456
Calzabigi, Ranieri de' 287–91 *passim*, 294, 295, 296, 298, 301, 302, 449, 452, 456, 457
Caminati, Tommaso 526
Campana, Alessandra xiv
Campobasso, Vincenzo 449
Candeille, Amélie-Julie 15
Candeille, Pierre 322
Cannabich, Christian 153
Capulet 48, 51–2, 56–7
Capulet, Lady 45, 48, 51
Carl Theodor, Elector of Bavaria 151, 153
Carlani, Carlo 123
Carlo III, King 498
Carmanini, 530
Carpani, Giuseppe 178, 197
Carter, Tim 61, 62, 65, 70, 72, 74, 75, 76, 78
Caruso, Luigi 487
Cassandre 17
Castelvecchi, Stefano xiv, xx, 97–218
Casti, Giovanni Battista (Giambattista) 370, 379, 398
Cato 398
Catone 149, 151

Cavalieri, Caterina xv, 136, 138–44 *passim*, 408
Cavalli, Francesco 527, 530
Ceccarelli, Francesco 157
Cecchina 170–75 *passim*, 180, 183
Cecilio 472
Cephalus 219
Ceracchini, Francesco 487
Cerlone, Francesco 284
Chabannes, Marc-Antoine-Jacques Rochon de 437
Chailley, Jacques 418, 419, 423, 432, 433, 438
Charlton, David xiii, xv, xix, xxi
Chamfort, Nicolas 306
Chapelier, Isaac Le 314–15
Charnois, Levacher de 320
Chaucer, Geoffrey 154
Chénier, André 313
Chénier, Marie-Joseph 313–14, 322
Cherinto 123
Cherubini, Luigi 15, 17, 487
Cherubino 66, 67, 68, 73, 74, 187, 192, 228, 279, 383, 385, 400
Cheyne, George 200
Chorèbe 17
Choron, Alexandre 467
Cibber, Theophilus 44
Cigna-Santi, Vittorio Amedeo 128, 129, 513
Cimarosa, Domenico 357, 383, 440, 472–3, 480, 482, 487, 488
Circe 455
Cirene 151, 152
Clark, Caryl xiii, xvii, xx
Clementi, Muzio 441
Clorinda 140
Cloris 251
Clubb, L.G. 227
Colbran, Isabella 218
Colla, Giuseppe 541
Coltelli, Michel Procope (Procope-Coutaux) 435
Coltellini, Marco 254, 398, 449, 452, 453
Columbus, Christopher 283, 309
Combe, François La 298
Cone, Edward T. 80
Cook, Elisabeth xv
Corebo 154
Corimba 453
Corneille, Pierre 363
Corneilson, Paul xv, xviii, xix, 149–65
Corrado 383
Corte, Andrea della 179

Cortez, Fernando (Hernán or Hernando) 128, 129–30
Costa, Giuseppe 526
Costelvecchi, Stefano xvi
Count, The (Almaviva) (from *Marriage of Figaro*) 186, 188, 189, 191–2, 193, 194–5, 278, 380–83, 385–6, 400
Count, The (from *Nina*) 204, 210, 211
Countess, the (from *Marriage of Figaro*) 186, 188–91 *passim*, 193–4, 195, 383, 385–6
Cour, Mathon de la 203, 206
Cramer, Carl Friedrich 19
Crespi, Francesco 537

Da Ponte, Lorenzo xv, 63, 64, 65, 67, 68, 78, 186–8, 219, 220, 221, 223, 225–6, 228, 244, 245, 247, 254, 255, 260–61, 277, 301, 351, 363, 364, 376, 377, 380, 381, 385, 390, 392, 397–9, 400, 401, 402, 403, 407–10, 411, 414–15
Dalayrac, Nicolas xvi, 178, 197–8, 201
Danchet, Antoine 153
Daniel, Norman 278
Dante 187
Danzi, Anton Ludwig 151
Danzi-Lebrun, Franziska 152
Dario 34, 35
Dauvergne, Antoine 11, 524
Davers, Mrs 238
De Liroux, 9
Dean, Winton 52, 56
Delbò, Angelo 537, 541
DelDonna, Anthony xx
Dent, Edward J. 63, 111, 197, 199, 376
Despina 225, 226, 227–8, 229, 230
Dezède, Nicolas 437
Diana 220, 222, 224, 226, 227–8, 229, 230
Diane 10
Diderot, Denis xvi, 44, 203, 206, 240, 241, 428, 489
Dido 449, 452
Didon 17
Dircea 469–70
Dittersdorf, Carl Ditters von xiii, 69, 301, 330, 357
Dolar, Mladen 294
Don Giovanni 76, 77, 258, 267, 268, 269, 270, 272, 273, 275, 276–81 *passim*, 411
Don Juan 65, 260

Dorabella 79, 220, 222, 226, 228, 377, 402–3, 408
Doralice 402
Doria, Paolo Mattia 506, 508
Doristella 181
Doristo 224, 227–8
Downes, E.O. 20
Dull, Mr 287–9, 293–6, 297, 298–9, 301, 302, 303, 308
Dunstan, Elizabeth 402
Duntalmo 453
Dupré, Monsieur 436
Durante, Sergio xiv, xviii, xx, xxi, 487–95
Dussek, Josephine (Josepha Duschek) 157

Echo 342
Edge, Dexter xix, xx, 349–73
Einsiedel, Friedrich Hildebrand von 431
Einstein, Alfred 3, 5, 17, 157
Electra 102
Elektra 7
Elettra 149, 152, 154, 156, 157
Elias, Norbert 503
Elisa 23–4
Elisabeth Auguste, Electress of Hanover 156
Elise 204
Elizabeth of Württemberg 407
Elvira, Donna 77, 258, 278, 280
Emery, Ted 234
Emile 340
Endimione 220, 226, 227
Endymion 10
Épinay, Madame d' 286
Epp, Friedrich 151
Erifile 456
Ermione 150
Ernestina 139, 399
Eros 188
Eschenburg, J.J. 47, 55
Europa, Princess of Tyre 154
Eutifronte 434
Eybler, Joseph 391
Ezio 21, 501

Farinelli 400
Farnace 456
Fascitelli, Antonia 527, 534, 537
Faur, L.F. 306
Favart, Charles-Simon 435
Federico, G.A. 170, 288

Feldman, Martha xviii, xxi, 497–519
Felloni, Ludovico 527, 535
Fénelon (Francois de Salignac de La Mothe-Fenelon) 153
Ferdinand IV of Bourbon 524
Ferrando 68, 79, 220, 222, 226, 230, 377, 401, 403, 412
Ferrarese del Bene, Adriana xv, 220, 390, 397
Fichte, Johann Gottlieb 345
Fielding, Henry 239
Figaro 67, 69, 73–4, 76, 79, 80,186–9, 192, 193–5, 277–8
Finfinette 434
Fiordiligi 79, 220, 222, 223, 226, 228, 258, 377, 390, 402, 410
Fischietti, Domenico 118
Florimo, Francesco 179
Foppa, Giuseppe 451, 452, 453, 454, 455, 456, 457
Forman, Edward 65
Fortis, Alberto 287
Framery, Nicolas-Étienne 6, 7–8, 10, 12
Franchis, Alessandro 535
Francis II, Holy Roman Emperor 316
Francis, Archduke 407
Franklin, Benjamin 290, 309
Frederik the Great 129
Fried, Michael 203, 204
Frigeri, Lucia (Friggeri) 526, 527, 530, 534
Frisi, Paolo 290, 291
Frugoni, Carlo 524
Frye, Northrop 236
Fuzelier, Louis 434

Gabrielli, Caterina 123, 126, 530
Gaius Marius 151
Galliani, Abbé Ferdinando 286
Galuppi, Baldassare 57, 113–14, 118, 122–3, 125–7, 128, 129, 130, 132, 134, 150
Gamerra, Giovanni de 452, 453, 454, 457, 488, 492
Garrick, David 44–5, 46, 49, 59, 206
Gassmann, Florian 397
Gazzaniga, Giuseppe 141, 440, 453
Gelinda 296–7, 299, 301–3, 307
Gellert, Christian Fürchtegott 346
Gentilucci, Carlo 537
Gerber, Ernst Ludwig 139
Gerl, Franz Xaver 432
Gervasoni, Carlo 467, 477

Ghita 247, 380
Gibson, Elizabeth xx
Gianelli, Margherita 527
Gianetta 176, 180
Giannina 383, 385
Giazotto, Remo 118
Gidwitz, Patricia Lewy xv, 135–47
Giesecke, Karl Ludwig 441
Gilliers, Jean-Claude 433
Ginguené, Pierre-Louis 7, 8, 9, 15
Giordani, Giuseppe 450
Giotti, Cosimo 454, 457
Giovannini, Pietro 451, 454, 455, 513
Girelli, Barbara 526, 527, 534
Giulietta 456
Giunia 151, 472
Gizziello (Gioacchino Conti) 120
Gleim, Johann Wilhelm Ludwig 49
Gluck, Christoph Willibald xiv, xvi, 3–7, 8, 9, 10, 11–17, 20, 21, 57, 59,118, 120, 127, 173, 289, 316, 410, 439, 440, 441, 448, 522, 524, 534, 537
Goehring, Edmund J. xvi, 231–61
Goethe, Johann Wolfgang von 47, 239, 363
Goldoni, Antonio 527, 534
Goldoni, Carlo 41, 118, 169–73 *passim*, 175, 177, 183, 206, Goldoni, Carlo 231–5 *passim*, 241–4, 247, 253, 254, 260–61, 288, 399, 403, 407, 409, 426
Gorsas, Antoine Joseph 316, 317, 319
Gossec, François-Joseph 4, 14, 15, 16, 322
Gossett, Philip 466, 467
Gotter, F.W. 43, 44, 48, 50–52, 54, 55–6, 59, 60
Gottlieb, Anna 438
Gottsched, Johann Christoph 345
Gozzi, Carlo 426, 428, 429
Gozzi, Gasparo 426
Grandval, Nicolas Ragot de 435
Graun, Carl Heinrich 21, 129
Grétry, André xvi, 12, 204, 316, 322
Greuze, Jean-Baptiste 203, 206, 207
Grimm, F.M. von 4, 9, 10, 15, 428
Griselda 180–83
Grua, Paul 153
Grynaeus, Simon 45
Guacozinga (Erismena) 129–30
Guarini, Giovanni Battista 221, 398
Guglielmi, Pietro 244, 259, 449, 452, 457
Guglielmo 79, 220, 222, 223, 226, 230, 377, 401, 402, 403, 412

Günther 109
Gürke 340
Gurnemanz 67

Habermas, Jürgen 329, 335
Hännschen 333
Hansell, Kathleen xiii, xiv, xvii, xix
Hanslick, Eduard 5
Harmonesus 422
Harpe, Jean-François de La 6
Harris, Ellen 223
Hartig, Franz 154
Hase, Hermann 334
Hasse, Johann Adolph xvii, 20, 21, 23, 24-5, 31, 39, 40, 41, 98, 103–4, 109, 111, 427
Haydn, Joseph xiii, xv, xvi, xvii, 20, 71, 73, 113, 129, 244, 266
Heartz, Daniel xiii, xv, xvii, xviii, xix, xx, xxi, 61, 63, 65, 67, 72, 74, 75, 79, 85–111, 228
Heinse, Friedrich 389, 390
Heinse, Wilhelm 150
Hensler, Karl Friedrich 430
Herder, Johann Gottfried 46, 345
Herz, Madame 143
Hill, Cecil 419
Hiller, Johann Adam xviii, 43, 44, 47, 329–35 *passim*, 337–9, 342, 343–6
Hoffman, François Benoît 315, 316–17, 319–20, 322
Holzbauer, Ignaz Jakob 86, 109, 150, 153
Homer 149, 398
Horace 285, 322
Horsley, Paul xiii
Horosius 285
Horus 421, 422
Hume, Robert D. xx, 175
Hunt, Lynn 510, 511
Hunter, Mary xiii, vi, xv, xvi, xvii, xx, xxi, 67, 169–84, 251, 298, 299, 306
Hüon 438
Hythloday, Raphael 285

Idalide 474–7 *passim*
Idamante 102, 154, 156
Idomeneo 86, 88 93, 95, 154, 156
Idomeneus 149
Ilia 149, 151, 154, 156
Insanguine, Giacomo Antonio Francesco Paolo Michele 128

Iphigenia 156
Isabella 402
Isabella of Bourbon, Infanta 524
Isis 421
Isménie 10

Jantz, Harold 285
Jerocades, Father 290
Jewkes, Mrs 240
Johnson, Samuel 218, 236
Jommelli, Niccolò xiv, 20, 87–8, 125–7, 134
Jordan, David P. 511
Joseph II, Holy Roman Emperor 139, 275, 349, 350, 351, 353, 363, 369, 370, 371–2, 399, 401, 407, 409, 410, 427, 524
Joubert, Estelle xviii, 329–46
Juliet 46, 48–52 passim, 54, 55, 56

Kantorowicz, Ernst 502
Kerman, Joseph 64, 277
Kierkegaard, Søren 279
Kimbell, David R.B. 467
Kinkead-Weekes, Mark 171
Knowles, Captain 291
Koch, Heinrich Gottfried 334
Konstanze 279
Kotzebue, August von 438
Krämer, Jörg 330, 331
Kunze, Stefan 61, 63, 65–7, 69, 70, 72, 74, 76, 77, 260

Laborde, Jean B. 338
Lajarte, T.J. 18
Lambertini, Domenica 527
Landini (Landi), Girolamo 527, 534, 535
Landon, H.C. Robbins 423, 488
Lange, Aloysia Weber xv, 136, 138–41, 143
Lanval 436
Laodamia (daughter of Bellerophon) 154
Laodamia (wife of Protesilaus) 154
Laodamia, Queen of Crete 154, 155, 156
Laura (nurse in *Romeo and Juliet*) 48, 51, 52, 57
Laurence, Friar 48, 51, 54
Lavinia 449
Lawton, David 467
Laya, Jean-Louis 321
Lazzari, Anna 537
Leeson, xx
Lemoyne, Jean Baptiste 15
Leopardi, Giacomo 31

Leopold II, Holy Roman Emperor 315, 317 363, 371, 414,488
Leporello 77, 258, 275, 277, 281, 383, 385
Lesage, Alain René 433
Lessing, Gotthold Ephraim 47
Levarie, Siegmund 75
Lévis, Anne-Claude-Philippe de Tubieres Grimoard de Pestels de , Comte de Caylus 435
Libby, Denis xv, xxi
Liebeskind, Jakob August 431
Lieschen 333
Lilla 245, 247, 255, 377, 383
Lindoro (Germeuil) 179, 180, 202, 210
Link, Dorothea xv, xvi, xxi, 219–30
Lippmann, Friedrich 472
Lisimaco 125
Livigni, Filippo 383
Loesser, Arthur 334
Lolli, Anna 527
Lolli, Brigida 527, 534
Lolli, Elisabetta 527
Longhi, Pietro 506
Lorenz, Alfred 64, 69, 76
Lorenzi, Giambattista 178, 197, 244, 288
Lottchen 340–42
Louis XVI, King of France 315, 316, 320, 511
Lubano 438
Lucinda, Marchesa 170, 171
Lucio Silla149, 151
Lully, Jean-Baptiste 3, 4, 5, 11, 13, 439, 441

Mackenzie, Henry 236
Maggi, Carlo Maria 506–7
Maio, De Francesco xvii
Maj, Girolima 527, 534
Majo, Gian Francesco de 128, 150
Makon 437
Malsora, King 437
Mandane 27, 28, 29, 31–2, 38, 39, 500–503, 505
Mandolino 432
Mandricardo 402
Manelli, Petronio 534, 535
Mansfield, Lord 291
Manuel, Pierre 317, 319
Manzuoli, Giovanni 85, 118, 122, 125, 126
Marcellina 66, 70, 73–4, 186, 187, 380
Marchant, François 319
Maria Amalia, Princess 524
Maria Antonia, Infante of Spain 118

Maria Theresia, Holy Roman Empress 275, 425, 524
Marie-Antoinette, Queen of France 185, 316, 320, 511, 513
Marinelli, Gaetano 455
Marmontel, Jean François 4–5, 6, 8, 10, 11, 12, 14, 204, 428, 436, 451
Marpurg, Wilhelm 20–23
Mars 187
Marsollier, Benoît-Joseph 197–8, 199, 200, 201, 202, 207, 208, 210
Marsollier, Joseph 178
Martín y Soler, Vicente 219–20, 245, 247, 363, 364, 375, 377, 403, 412
Martinelli (Martelli), Pietro 535
Marvell, Andrew 185
Marzia 151
Masetto 77, 267
Massa, Anastasio 526, 527, 530, 535
Massinissa 152
Mayr, Simone 469, 473, 475–6, 47–80, 482
Mazzolà, Carlo 377–8
Mazzolà, Caterino 399, 487, 489–90, 491, 492
McClymonds, Marita P. xiii, xiv, xv, xviii, 447–64
McKillop, Alan D. 169
Megabise 27, 29, 34–35
Megacles 501
Méhul, Etienne Nicolas 14, 17, 315, 317, 322
Melamed, Daniel xix
Meneghelli, Pier Antonio 456
Mengone 173
Mengotta 170, 174
Mercier, Louis Sebastien 206
Mercutio 48
Méreaux, 15
Merlin 434
Mesmer, Dr 228
Metastasio (Pietro Antonio Domenico Trapassi) 19, 23, 24–5 passim, 27, 31, 39, 41, 44, 87–9 passim, 92, 98, 102, 122, 123, 316, 398, 399, 400, 401, 407, 427, 452, 453, 455, 469–70, 472, 482, 487, 489, 490, 500, 502, 513
Meyer, Leonard B. 80
Milhous, Judith xx
Milmi 438
Mislivecek, Josef 128
Mitridate 456, 513
Mortellari, Michael 513

Monelle, Raymond xiv, 19–41
Monostatos 265, 270, 279, 280, 423
Monsigny, Pierre-Alexandre 435
Monson, Dale E. xv, 113–34
Montague 48
Montezuma (Motezuma) 128, 129–30, 132, 134, 283
More, Thomas 285
Morelli, Cosimo 364
Moretti, Ferdinando 449, 450, 451, 452, 455, 456, 513
Morichelli, Anna xv
Mosel, Ignaz von 401
Mouret, Jean-Joseph 435
Mozart, Constance (Constance Nissen) 389, 391–392, 407, 415, 427
Mozart, Leopold 85, 88, 90, 92, 93, 109, 139, 157, 410
Mozart, Wolfgang Amadeus xiii, xiv, xv, xvi, xvii, xviii, xix, xx, xxi, 4, 7, 14, 16, 20, 61–82 passim, 85–93 passim, 95, 97–8, 101–4, 107, 109, 111, 113, 119, 135, 136, 140–45 passim, 149–50, 151, 153, 154, 155, 156–7, 185, 186, 187, 188, 195, 234, 244, 254, 255, 260, 265–74 passim, 276, 277, 278–9, 280–81, 294, 303, 309, 349–51, 352, 353, 356, 357, 363, 364, 369, 371–3, 375–9, 380, 382–3, 385–7, 389, 390, 391–2, 393, 397, 398, 400–401, 402, 406, 407, 411–15 passim, 417, 418, 419, 422, 423, 424, 425, 426, 427, 431, 432, 438, 439, 441–3, 471–2, 477, 482, 487, 488, 490, 491–2, 513
Mühle, Nikolaus 437
Müller, Wenzel 430
Mutius Scevola 322

Nadine 438
Nadir 438
Narcissus 342
Nasolini, Sabastiano 454
Němetschek (Niemetschek), Franz Xaver 149, 156, 349, 389
Nettl, Paul 418, 419, 433, 438
Neumann, Friedrich-Heinrich xvii, 19, 20, 21
Neville, Don xv
Nina 178–81, 183, 197–8, 199, 200, 201–202, 204, 206, 207, 208, 210–11, 213, 215, 217, 247, 254
Nino 453

Nissen, Georg Nikolaus von 389, 427
Noske, Frits 75
Novello, Mary 391–2, 407
Novello, Vincent 391–2, 407

Ontario 289, 294, 295, 297
Opfer, Rache 423
Orazia 456, 457
Oreste(s) 9, 12, 156
Orfeo 173
Oriane 436
Orlando 402
Orsini-Rosenberg, Count 370, 372, 410, 415
Osiris 421
Osmida 489
Osmin 270, 273, 277, 278, 279
d'Orneval, Jacques-Philippe 433
Ottavio, Don 77, 80, 269, 273
Ovid 154, 390

Paer, Ferdinando 513
Paisiello, Giovanni xvi, 65, 69, 128, 129, 130, 132, 134, 178, 179, 180, 183, 197–8 *passim*, 200, 201, 207, 209, 210, 215, 218, 244, 247, 254, 287, 287, 299, 301, 302, 303, 309, 350, 357, 364, 375, 379, 449, 452, 453, 457, 469, 487, 492, 513
Palombo, Antonio 287
Palombo, Giuseppe 296
Pamela 170–71, 174–5, 180, 183, 235, 236, 237–9, 240, 241, 242, 247, 258
Pamina 280, 438, 440
Paoluccia 170
Papageno 279, 432, 438
Papillone 434
Parker, Roger 71
Parsifal 67
Parthenia 57
Pedrillo 270, 278
Pendle, Karin xiii
Penn, William 285
Pepoli, Count Alessandro 455–6
Perez, David 127
Pergolesi, Giovanni Battista 20, 113, 170, 299, 301
Perinet, Joachim 230, 425
Perl, Benjamin xvii, 265–81
Perrault, Charles 429
Petrosellini, Giuseppe 244
Philidor, François-André 4, 11, 14, 15, 16

Philipart, C.-A.-J. 109
Philips, Edith 285
Piccinni, Niccolò xiv, 3–5, 7, 8–10, 12, 13, 14, 15, 16, 17, 18, 127, 169, 173, 178, 244, 284, 286, 454
Pinel, Philippe 200, 202–3, 204, 208
Piovene, Agostino 448
Pizzaro y González, Francisco 128
Pizzi, Giovaccino 448
Pizzimiglia, Pietro 526
Platoff, John xv, xx, xxi, xxi, 65, 68, 375–87
Plutarch 422
Poggioli, Renato 223
Polybius 285
Polzonetti, Pierpaolo xiii, xiv, xvii, 283–309
Poncini, Francesco 536, 537, 541
Porpora, Nicola 20
Porto, Luigi da 47, 49
Poussin, xvi
Powers, Harold 467
Prati, Alessio 152, 451, 513
Price, Curtis xix
Procris 219
Protesilaus 154
Provence, Comte de 315
Puchberg, Michael 349–50, 353, 371–2, 392
Pulcinella 290
Puttini, Francesco 244

Quaglio, Lorenzo 109
Quazza, Pio 529, 530, 535
Quinault, Philippe 4, 11, 439, 449

Raaff, Anton xv, 86–93 *passim*, 95, 97–8, 101–4 *passim*, 107, 109, 111, 123, 135, 149, 153, 156
Rabin, Ronald xiii
Racine, Jean 6, 363
Rainieri, Veronica 527, 534
Rameau, Jean-Philippe 3, 11, 435–6, 441, 524
Ratner, Leonard 63
Raynal, Abbé 286–7, 298
Reichardt, J.F. 54, 55, 59, 60, 335, 344
Reinhard, Kurt 272
Réti, Rudolph 64
Reynaud, Allexandre 535
Rice, John A. xiii, xiv, xv, xvi, xvii, xxi, 389–415
Richardson, Samuel xvi, 169–71, 173, 174, 175, 183, 206, 218, 235–8 *passim*, 240, 241–2, 245, 251

Righini, Vincenzo xv
Ripaverde, Count 140
Ristorini, Giambattista 527, 530
Ritorni, Carlo 465, 468, 469
Robespierre, Maximilien 315
Robinson, Michael xiii, xvii, xx, 65
Roccaforte, Gaetano 448
Roche, Alessandro La 526, 535
Rodomonte 402
Roger de Sicile 433
Roland 10–11
Romagnesi, Jean-Antoine 435
Romeo 45, 48–52, 54, 55, 56, 57, 456
Rosen, Charles 64, 65, 76, 80
Rosina 247
Rossane 456
Rosselli, John 522
Rossi, Gaetano 454, 455
Rossini, Gioachino Antonio 466, 469, 470, 471, 472, 473, 475–6, 478, 479, 483
Rothe, Klara 364
Rousseau, Jean-Jacques 7, 329, 339, 345, 428
Ruggiero (Rinaldo) 177
Rumph, Stephen xx
Ruprecht, Joseph Martin 434
Rushton, Julian xiii, xiv, xviii, 3–18, 61, 62, 65, 77–8, 273, 275, 376, 418, 419
Rust, Giacomo 409

Sacchini, Antonio 7, 14, 128, 177, 316
Saint-Foix, Germaine-Francois Poullain de 435
Salieri, Antonio xvi, xvii, xx, xxi, 14, 15, 139, 152, 154, 220, 244, 350, 353, 357, 369, 373, 375, 391, 392–4, 396–8, 399, 400–401, 403, 406–10 *passim*, 411–15 *passim*, 452
Salvi, Antonio 448
Salvioni, Abate 449
Salvoni (Salvonio), Luigi Bernardo 535, 536, 537
Sanctis, Luigi de 457
Sandrina 170, 177
Sannazaro, Jacopo 390
Sanseverino, Carlo 55
Sarastro 279, 280, 421, 422, 424, 432, 438, 440
Sarpedon 154
Sarselli, Carolina 151
Sarselli, Pietro 151
Sarti, Giuseppe xv, 139, 450, 524, 541
Sartori, Claudio xiv
Savage, Roger xix

Scarlatti, Giuseppe 287
Schachtner, Andreas 90
Schack, Benedikt 438
Schäfer, Maria Josepha 154
Scheibe, Johann Adolph 345
Schenker, Heinrich 64
Schikaneder, Eleonore 430
Schikaneder, Emanuel xxi, 418, 419, 421–3, 424, 425, 426, 429, 430, 431–2, 434, 438, 441–3
Schiller, Friedrich 344, 346
Schlegel, August Wilhelm 47
Schmidt, Johann Friedrich 429
Schoenberg, Arnold 64
Schröder, Friedrich Ludwig 56
Schubart, Christian Friedrich Daniel 59, 150–51, 152, 272, 343, 439
Schuster, Joseph 449
Schwab, Heinrich W. 338
Schwanberg, Johann Gottfried 55
Schwarzburg, Günther von 149
Schweitzer, Anton 44, 57
Sedaine, Michel-Jean 202
Semira 27, 28, 29, 35–7, 39, 500
Semiramide 513
Sernicola, Carlo 456–7
Serpetta 170
Serpina 299, 301
Serse 28, 34, 35, 125, 500
Sertor, Gaetano 449, 450, 453, 454, 455, 457
Sesto 489
Shakespeare, William 6, 44, 45, 47–8, 50, 51, 55, 57, 186, 187, 192, 195, 438
Silberklang, Mademoiselle 143
Silvani, Francesco 448
Silvia 223, 225
Silvio 227, 229
Smith, Adam 239
Smollett, Tobias 119
Sofonisba 152
Sofrano 438
Sografi, Antonio 453–5, 456, 457, 513
Soler, Vicente Martin y xv, xxi
Solis y Rivadeneyra, Antonio de 128, 129
Solomon, Nicholas xix
Somerset 291–2
Sonneck, O.G. 25
Sonnleithner, Leopold von 425
Spaur, Graf von 430, 437
Spengler, Friedrich 430

Spontini, Gaspare 17, 18
St Phar, Madame de 207
St Phar, Monsieur de 207–8
Stephanie, Johann Gottlieb (Stephanie the Younger) 363
Steptoe, Andrew 61, 62, 70, 73, 76, 77, 78, 79
Sterne, Laurence 236
Storace, Nancy 139, 140, 141, 301, 303
Suardi, Felicita 537
Sucarelli, Filippo 526
Sulzer, Johann Georg 232–3
Susanna 66, 67, 68, 70, 73–4, 79, 186–90 *passim*, 192–5 *passim*, 278, 380–83, 385–6, 400

Tacchinardi, Niccola 468, 469
Tagliaferro 170
Tamino 280, 422, 438
Tammaro, Don 288
Tarare 435
Tarchi, Angelo 449, 455, 487
Tasso, Torquato 187, 221, 223
Tassoni, Alessandro 398
Tedeschi, Giovanni (Giovanni Tadeschi Amadori) 123
Temistocle 149, 151
Tenducci, Giusto Ferdinando (Il Senesino) xv, 114–20 *passim*, 122–3, 125–32 *passim*, 134
Terrasson, Jean 419, 421, 442
Terry, C.S. 3
Theorirus 185
Thoas 152
Thyrsis 251
Tibaldi, Domenico 534, 535
Tillot, Guillaume du 524, 529
Timante 469–70
Tishkoff, Doris xx
Tita 380
Tito 489
Tomeoni, Irene 200
Tomiri, Princess of Taurus 152
Tornielli, Gaspero (Gasparo) 535
Tosi, Pier Francesco 120
Tovey, D.F. 15, 72, 80
Traetta, Tommaso 150, 440, 449, 522, 524, 525, 529, 530, 534, 535, 536–7
Treitschke, Georg Friedrich 229–30
Tybalt 48, 56
Tyson, Alan xix, xx, xxi, 141, 397, 403, 414

Uberto 288, 299, 301
Ulysse 8
Umlauf, Ignaz 357
Urbélise 436

Vacchi, Pietro 537
Valmaggi, Luigi 506
Vandomo 478, 479
Varesco, Abbé 87, 88, 90–93, 156
Varese, Claudio 27, 41
Venus 187
Verazi, Giovanni Battista 154, 155
Verazi, Mattia 154, 449–50, 451, 452, 454, 455, 513
Verdi, Guiseppe 62, 80, 466
Vespone 308
Vespucci, Amerigo 285
Vignati, Giuseppe 530
Villeneuve, Jérôme Petion de 317, 318
Villeneuve, Louise 408, 415
Vinci, Leonardo 20, 25, 39, 41
Violante 247, 251, 255
Virgil 185
Vittorio Amedeo, Duke of Saxony 118
Vivetières, Marsollier des 513
Vogel, J.C. 14
Vogelsang, Herr 143
Vogler, Georg Joseph 152
Voisenon, Claude-Henri Fusée de 435
Voltaire 283, 285, 363, 451, 513
Vulcan 187
Vulpius, Christian August 434, 437

Wagenseil, Georg Christoph 118
Wagner, Heinrich Leopold 50
Wagner, Richard 5, 17, 21, 62, 64, 74, 80, 330, 331
Waldoff, Jessica xiii, xvi, xx, xxi
Walter, Ignaz 438
Warrack, John 331
Wasserman, Earl 240
Weber-Lange, Aloysia 152, 157
Webster, James xiii, xiv, xv, xx, xxi, 61–82
Weigl, Joseph 379
Weiss, Pietro 173
Weisse, Christian Felix 47–52 *passim*, 55, 329, 331–9 *passim*, 342, 344–6
Wendling, Dorothea 149–53 *passim*, 154, 155, 156, 157
Wendling, Elisabeth 149–53 *passim*, 156, 157

Wendling, Elisabeth Augusta 151
Wendling, Franz Anton 151
Wendling, Johann Baptist 150, 151
Wiel, 449
Wieland, Christoph Martin 43, 44–8 *passim*, 55, 59, 430, 431, 441
Willis, Stephen C. xvii
Winter, Peter 487
Wise, Steven 291, 292
Wolf, Ernst Wilhelm xix, 437
Wood, Gordon 306
Woodfield, Ian xx
Wranitzky, Paul 430, 441

Zaira 456
Zais 435

Zamoro 473–7 *passim*
Zehnmark, Ludwig 433
Zélide 435
Zelmira 152
Zémire 204
Zeno, Apostolo 448, 500, 513
Zephyr 342
Zerlina 76, 77, 275, 278
Zeus 154
Zingarelli, Niccolò Antonio 15, 129, 454, 488
Zini, Francesco Saverio 244
Zinzendorf, Count 139, 301
Žižek, Slavoj 294
Zonca, Giovanni Battista 154
Zoroastre 435–6